Sgt. Piggy's Lonely Hearts Club Comic

Other *Pearls Before Swine* Collections

This Little Piggy Stayed Home

BLTs Taste So Darn Good

Sgt. Piggy's Lonely Hearts Club Comic

A Pearls Before Swine Treasury

by Stephan Pastis

Andrews McMeel
Publishing

Kansas City

Pearls Before Swine is distributed internationally by United Feature Syndicate.

Sgt. Piggy's Lonely Hearts Club Comic copyright © 2004 by Stephan Pastis. All rights reserved. Printed in China. No part of this book may be used or reproduced in any manner whatsoever without written permission except in the case of reprints in the context of reviews. For permission information, write Andrews McMeel Publishing, LLC, an Andrews McMeel Universal company, 4520 Main Street, Kansas City, Missouri 64111.

07 08 MPT 10 9 8 7 6 5

ISBN-13: 978-0-7407-4807-3
ISBN-10: 0-7407-4807-6

Library of Congress Control Number: 2004106614

Pearls Before Swine can be viewed on the Internet at
www.comics.com/comics/pearls.

These strips appeared in newspapers from December 31, 2001, through July 13, 2003.

——— **ATTENTION: SCHOOLS AND BUSINESSES** ———

Andrews McMeel books are available at quantity discounts with bulk purchase for educational, business, or sales promotional use. For information, please write to: Special Sales Department, Andrews McMeel Publishing, 4520 Main Street, Kansas City, Missouri 64111.

**For Rick Daniels, the best fisherman
I've ever seen and an even better person**

INTRODUCTION

It all started when I realized that I could no longer stand European Economic Community Law.

It was the spring semester of my second year in law school and I was bored silly in yet another one of my classes. So during some lecture on the European-something-or-other-Parliament, I decided I would create a comic strip while sitting in class.

The great part about drawing a comic strip while sitting in class is that the professor can't tell you're screwing around. Unlike reading the newspaper or sleeping, drawing in your notebook looks remarkably like note-taking . . . given this prolific "note-taking," I'm sure he thought I was one of his more attentive students.

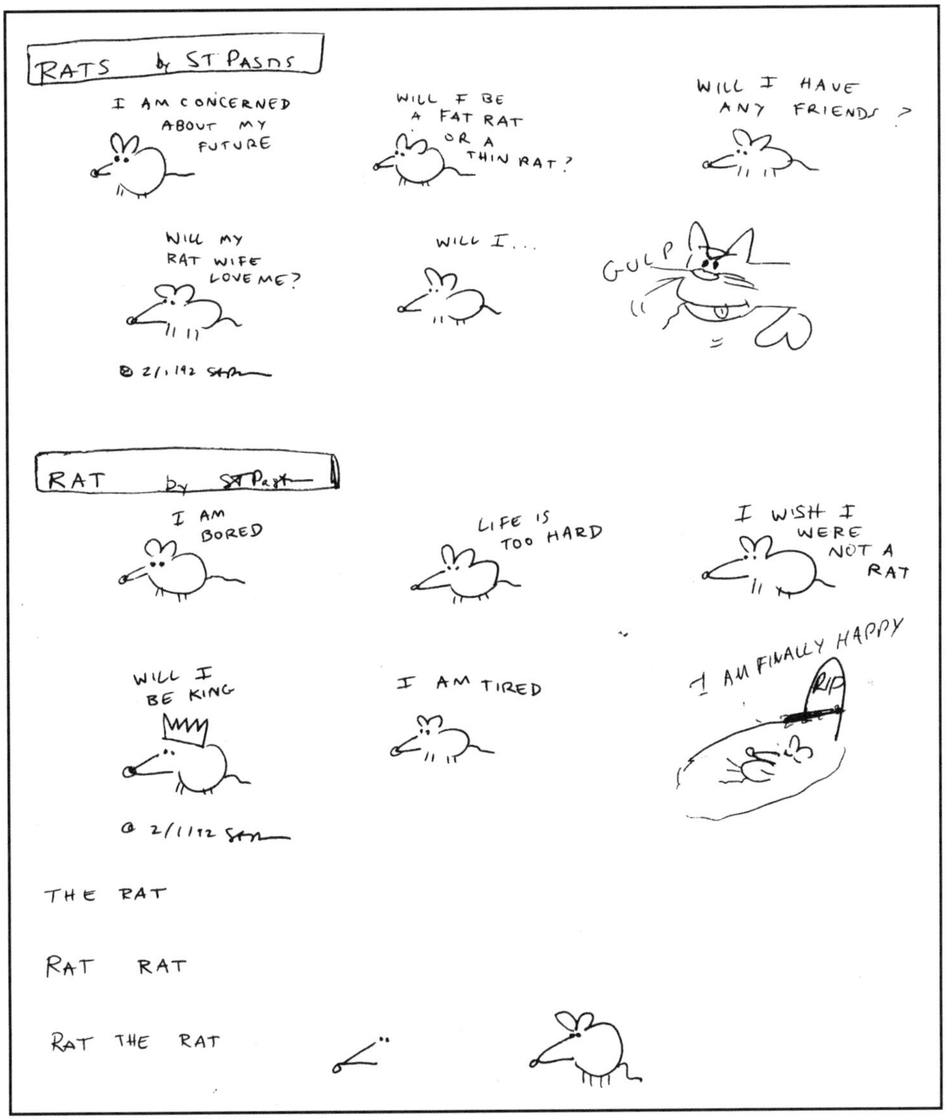

RATS
I AM CONCERNED ABOUT MY FUTURE
WILL I BE A FAT RAT OR A THIN RAT?
WILL I HAVE ANY FRIENDS?
WILL MY RAT WIFE LOVE ME?
WILL I...
GULP
© 2/1/92
RAT
I AM BORED
LIFE IS TOO HARD
I WISH I WERE NOT A RAT
WILL I BE KING
I AM TIRED
I AM FINALLY HAPPY
RIP
© 2/1/92
THE RAT
RAT RAT
RAT THE RAT

Drawing No. 1

What I drew that February, 1992, day was this strange, morbid little rat. He walked on four legs and was consumed by depressing, fatalistic thoughts. I didn't draw him with any real hope of becoming a syndicated cartoonist or ever getting him published. I drew him because I was bored.

But there was something interesting about him. Despite his crude, ballpoint-pen appearance, and the repetitive nature of the strip's "art," he seemed to have some life to him. I could draw him over and over and just give him all of my thoughts. I had found this little vehicle to illustrate what was going on in my head. Sure, this autobiographical vehicle was a rat, and sure, the thoughts were about death, but hey, I thought I was gonna have to be a lawyer for the rest of my life.

Drawing No. 1 is the piece of notebook paper upon which I first drew Rat that day. It contains the first two strips, and as you can see, Rat dies in both of them. The odd part is that he was only supposed to die in the *first* strip. In that second strip, I just had him falling asleep. That was before the guy sitting to the right of me (who I believe is now a prosecuting attorney) drew a grave around him and wrote the words, "I am finally happy." Apparently, law school students are a uniformly somber bunch.

I continued drawing Rat in all of my law school classes. One of those classes was called "Remedies," a class that apparently started at 10:00 a.m. and ended at 10:50 a.m. every morning. I don't actually remember what time the class was. I only know that from what I see in Drawing No. 2.

RAT by S.T. PASTIS
REMEDIES
10:00 AM
10:15 AM
ZZZ ZZ
10:30 AM
ZZZZ
10:45 AM
ZZZZ
10:50 AM
I AM FREE
11:00 AM

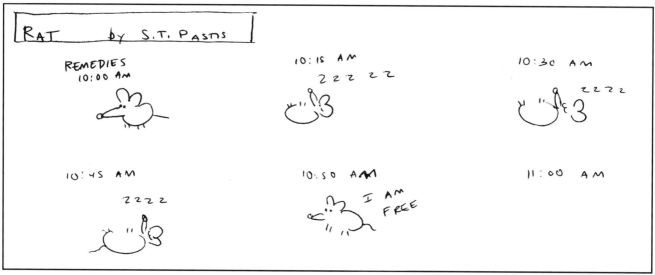

Drawing No. 2

In 1993, I graduated from law school and became a litigation attorney in San Francisco. Day after day, I put on my suit and carried my little black briefcase to and from my firm's downtown office, where I wrote motions, reviewed documents, and argued with plaintiffs' attorneys. But at nights and on weekends, I drew. At that point, I still drew just for the fun of it, with no plan to ever be syndicated. And mostly, I drew Rat, who now occasionally stood upright. The strip, still titled just "Rat," alternated

RAT
by Stephan T. Pastis
HOW FAR?
DO YOU KNOW ME?
WHEN I TRAVEL, I CARRY THIS: A DEEP DESIRE TO FIND SOMETHING MISSING IN MY LIFE.
AND WHEN I ARRIVE, THERE IT IS AGAIN — A LONGING TO RETURN HOME.
WHICH IS JUST A MEMORY WHEN I GET INSIDE MY SAD HOUSE.
WHICH IS WHY I TRY NOT TO THINK TOO MUCH.
©1995

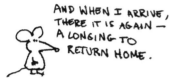

Drawing No. 3

between the philosophical (Drawing No. 3) and the uhhh . . . not so philosophical (Drawing No. 4).

At some point in 1996, I decided to try and get syndicated. Before submitting "Rat" to the syndicates, I "polished" the art a little, turned it into roughly a four-panel strip, and added a character named Poe. Poe was an overweight, pathetic guy whose species was a mystery. I believe Rat termed him the "the fat blob o' nothingness." Once I had around two dozen of these strips, I packaged them up and sent them to all the syndicates. Two of those strips I submitted are shown in Drawing No. 5, but be warned, because they're . . . well, dark. *Man*, are they dark.

Given the nature of the strips, it's a wonder the syndicates didn't burn them. As it was, most of the syndicates just sent form rejections. But two of the syndicate editors

RAT
by ST PASTIS
LOOK WHAT YOU'VE DONE.
YOU'VE GONE AND CONFUSED EVERYONE.
ISAAC NEWTON.
WAYNE NEWTON.
FIG NEWTON.

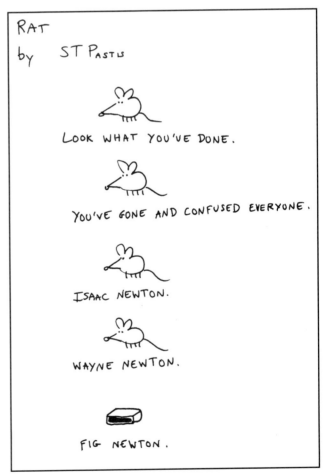

Drawing No. 4

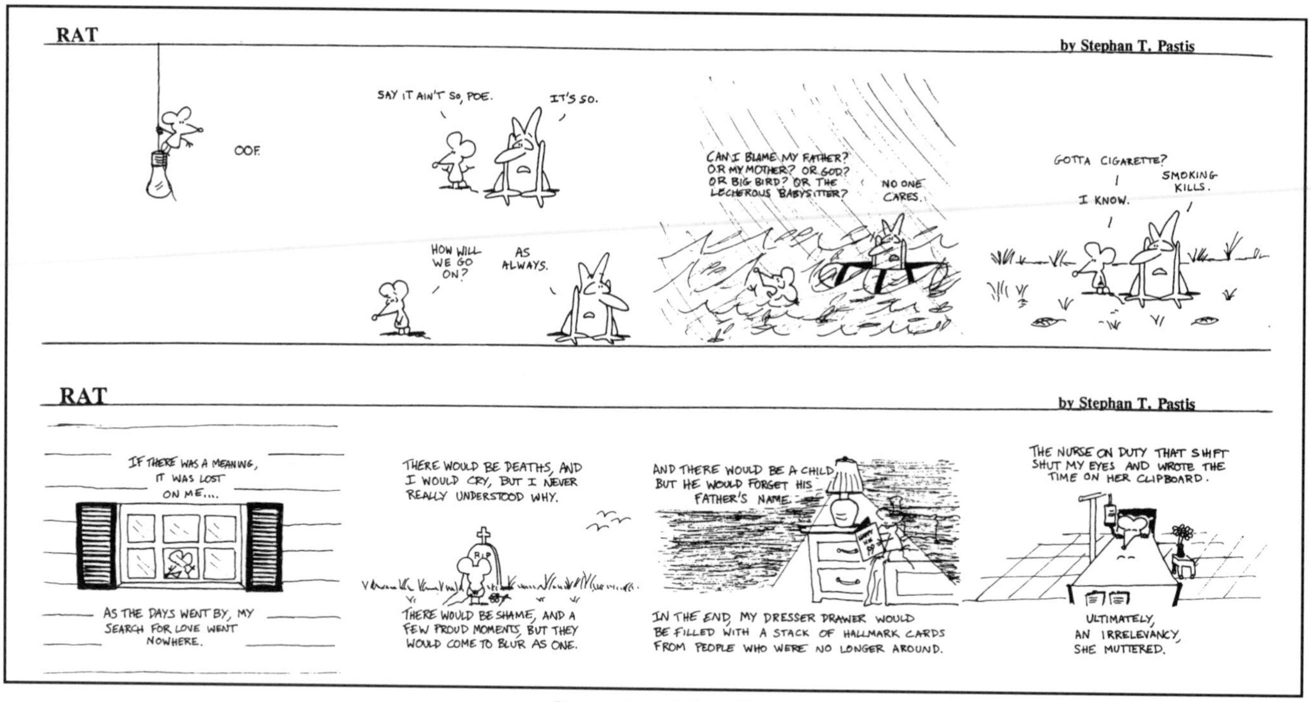
RAT
by Stephan T. Pastis
OOF.
SAY IT AIN'T SO, POE.
IT'S SO.
HOW WILL WE GO ON?
AS ALWAYS.
CAN I BLAME MY FATHER? OR MY MOTHER? OR GOD? OR BIG BIRD? OR THE LECHEROUS BABYSITTER?
NO ONE CARES.
GOTTA CIGARETTE?
I KNOW.
SMOKING KILLS.
RAT
by Stephan T. Pastis
IF THERE WAS A MEANING, IT WAS LOST ON ME....
AS THE DAYS WENT BY, MY SEARCH FOR LOVE WENT NOWHERE.
THERE WOULD BE DEATHS, AND I WOULD CRY, BUT I NEVER REALLY UNDERSTOOD WHY.
RIP
THERE WOULD BE SHAME, AND A FEW PROUD MOMENTS, BUT THEY WOULD COME TO BLUR AS ONE.
AND THERE WOULD BE A CHILD BUT HE WOULD FORGET HIS FATHER'S NAME.
IN THE END, MY DRESSER DRAWER WOULD BE FILLED WITH A STACK OF HALLMARK CARDS FROM PEOPLE WHO WERE NO LONGER AROUND.
THE NURSE ON DUTY THAT SHIFT SHUT MY EYES AND WROTE THE TIME ON HER CLIPBOARD.
ULTIMATELY, AN IRRELEVANCY, SHE MUTTERED.

Drawing No. 5

sent handwritten comments, which I understood to be a fairly rare and positive response. One of them said she liked the strip's "simplicity and poignancy," but warned, "(Don't) go too close to the edge of misery with this little guy . . . . (Readers) don't want to see him killed off." The other editor said, "There is something captivating about Rat's fatalism and smug superiority," but asked, "What is Poe?" Sadly, I didn't know.

Over the next couple years, I created three other comic strips and sent them to the syndicates, but they were all rejected. One of them was called *The Infirm*, and it was about a hapless law firm associate named "Bob Grossman." The only significance of *The Infirm* was that it was in that strip that I had Grossman mishandle a case brought against his client, Farmer Sal's Sausage, whose farm was filled with pigs (See Drawing No. 6). I liked the pigs so much that I decided I would take a simplified version of one of them and use him to replace the amorphous Poe in a new comic strip involving Rat.

But having been rejected so many times, I knew I needed to do something different. I needed to learn how to write.

So during my lunch hours at the law firm, I would go to a downtown bookstore, sit on the floor, and study what I thought was the funniest, most successful strip around: *Dilbert*. (Given that I was an attorney, I guess I could have afforded to *buy* these books and take them *home* to study, but I was too cheap, so I just read them there in the bookstore.) I knew *Dilbert* made people laugh, and I felt that if I was going to have a

THE INFIRM

Panel 1: GROSSMAN ARRIVES AT FARMER SAL'S SAUSAGE AND IS GREETED BY FARMER SAL.

BAD PIGGIE! BAD PIGGIE!

Panel 2: FARMER SAL HAS A BAD, BAD PIGGIE WHO COST FARMER SAL A DEFAULT JUDGMENT AND THOUSANDS OF DOLLARS.

Panel 3: BAD PIGGIE OWES FARMER SAL $900,000 AND WILL PAY IT BACK BY WORKING FOR MINIMUM WAGE ON FARMER SAL'S FARM.

Panel 4: GROSSMAN IS CONSOLED BY WELL-WISHERS.

I'M NO MISTER MATH, PAL, BUT AT THAT RATE, I THINK YOU'RE SCREWED.

©1997 Sdk

Drawing No. 6

chance, I, too, needed to make people laugh. So I studied everything . . . his timing, his economical writing, his setups, his tone. Everything.

I also decided that I wouldn't worry about anything other than being funny. I wouldn't worry about the setting or the backgrounds or the art or the strip's demographic or the characters' names (the rat would just be "rat" and the pig would just be "pig"). I wouldn't even pencil the strips first. I would just take a sheet of paper, draw a stick figure rat and pig, and write jokes. I would do 15 to 20 of these strips at a time, just learning how to write, in strip after strip after strip. Eventually, things seemed to click. The writing was more spontaneous and less contrived, more direct and less wordy. I decided to call the strip *Pearls Before Swine*, because so many of the strips seemed to involve Rat pontificating about something to this stupid pig.*

Some of the strips were terrible, as you can see in Drawing No. 7 (I'm still not sure what I had against Gloria Estefan. I think it was that %#$@ song where she counts, "One, Two, Three, Four . . ."). But some were okay. So when I had around two hundred that I liked, I took them to my law firm and showed them to around four or five associates, asking them to put little checkmarks by the ones they liked. Now the great part about this was that in a law firm, nobody likes each other. So the other

---

*The phrase "pearls before swine" comes from the New Testament, Matthew 7:6. ("Give not that which is holy unto the dogs, neither cast ye your pearls before swine, lest they trample them under their feet . . .") People often use the phrase to mean that you shouldn't waste your wisdom on those who aren't listening. In the strip, Rat feels that his "wisdom" is wasted on Pig.

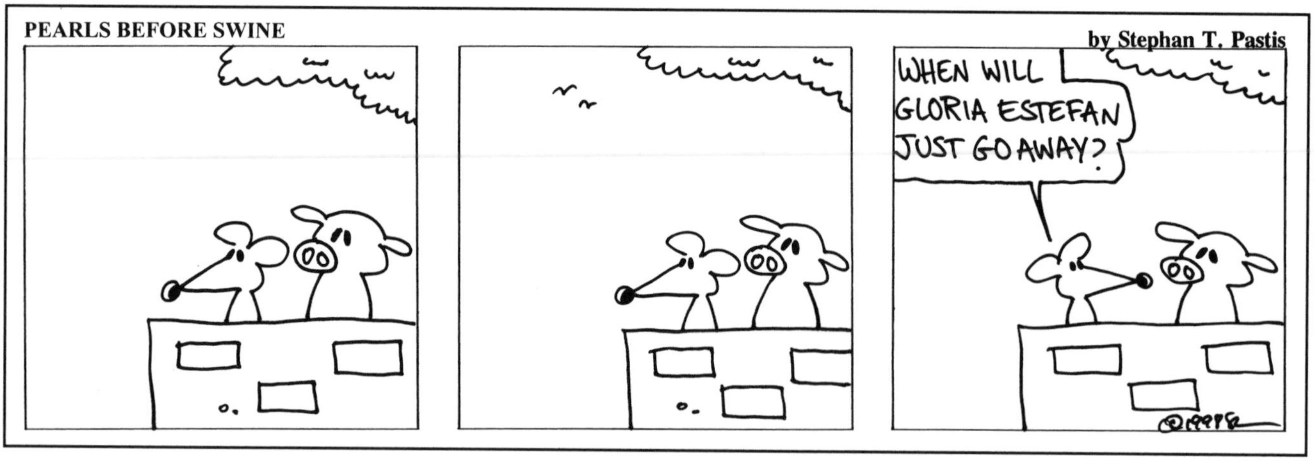
PEARLS BEFORE SWINE
by Stephan T. Pastis
WHEN WILL GLORIA ESTEFAN JUST GO AWAY?

Drawing No. 7

lawyers you show the strip to aren't going to do you any favors. If your strip sucks, they will *relish* telling you, "This sucks." But unbelievably, they actually liked some of them. So I took the forty strips that got the most votes, packaged them in an envelope . . .

And did nothing.

Absolutely nothing.

You see, I did nothing because I *liked* this comic strip. And I knew that if I sent the strip to all the syndicates again, it would be rejected. And I knew that that would be it for me and my cartooning dream, because this strip was the best I could do. In short, I would be stuck as an attorney for the rest of my life. So for eighteen months, the strips sat on a shelf in my basement and gathered dust, as I adhered to my new motto: "You can't fail if you don't try."

But in July 1999, I changed my mind.

I've always sort of nebulously said in interviews that I don't really know what made me change my mind and submit those strips to the syndicates, but the truth is, I do know.

It was in that month that I had flown to Los Angeles for a hearing on one of my cases. While I was there, I realized that the courthouse was near a cemetery where one of my college friends who had passed away was buried. Sadly, and very regrettably, I had lost touch with her after college, and I had never seen her grave. But when the hearing was done, I went to the cemetery and after a long search, I found it.

In college, we had been very close. She was so free-spirited and fun and brave and accepting. And for someone like me, who was leaving my conservative, sheltered little hometown for the first time to live in Berkeley, California, she meant everything. She made me see films I would never have seen, go to museums I never would have visited, try food I never would have tried, and go to protests I never would have gotten near. In short, she opened up my tiny, serious world and forced me to grow and be more free-spirited and more open to all of life's possibilities.

And yet there I stood on that hot July day.

There I stood in my black business suit with my black briefcase and a pocket filled with business cards that said, "Stephan Pastis, Insurance Defense Attorney."

And I felt terrible.

It wasn't because I had become an attorney that I felt terrible. There's nothing wrong or bad about being an attorney. It was because of what I *hadn't* become. Ever since I was a little kid, I had dreamed of one day becoming a cartoonist, and somehow I had given up. Somehow I had resigned myself to always being a lawyer. And as I stood there, I could just imagine her looking down at me, shaking her head, wondering how I had gone from the kid she knew in Berkeley to the serious, strait-laced person in that suit.

And so I flew home. And went straight to my basement. And grabbed the package. And I mailed it to the syndicates.

And two weeks later, while eating a rushed Chinese food lunch in my black suit behind my cluttered desk at my law firm, I got an e-mail from United Feature Syndicate.

They liked my strip.

Stephan Pastis,
September 2004

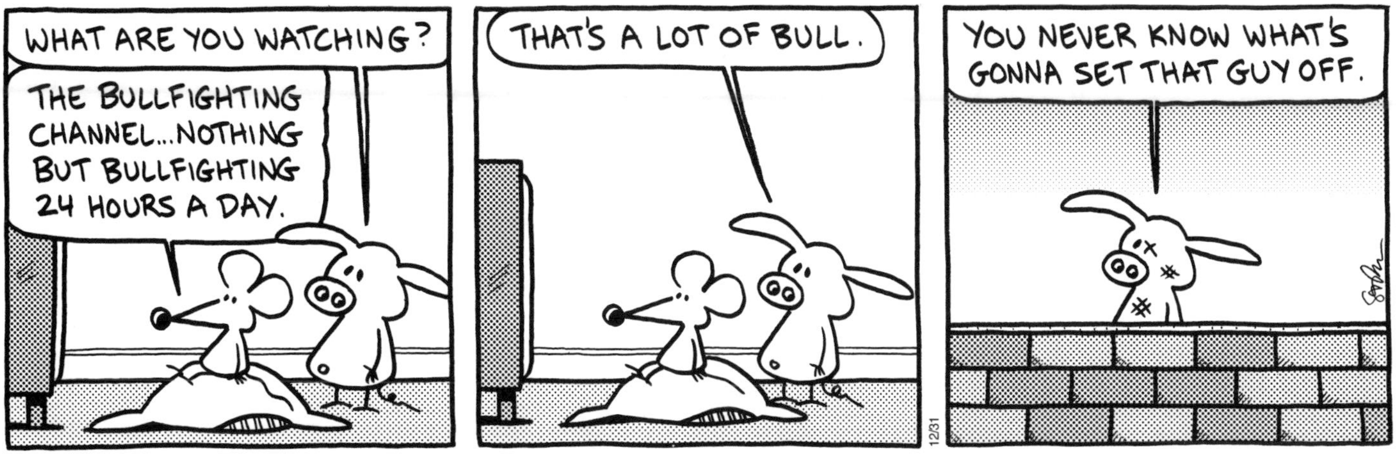
WHAT ARE YOU WATCHING?
THE BULLFIGHTING CHANNEL...NOTHING BUT BULLFIGHTING 24 HOURS A DAY.
THAT'S A LOT OF BULL.
YOU NEVER KNOW WHAT'S GONNA SET THAT GUY OFF.
12/31

Pearls was supposed to launch in newspapers on January 7, 2002. But just prior to the launch, the *Washington Post* bought the strip, and wanted to start running it a week early. Thus, this week of strips was quickly put together just for the *Post*, and this strip became the first *Pearls* strip, published in exactly one paper.

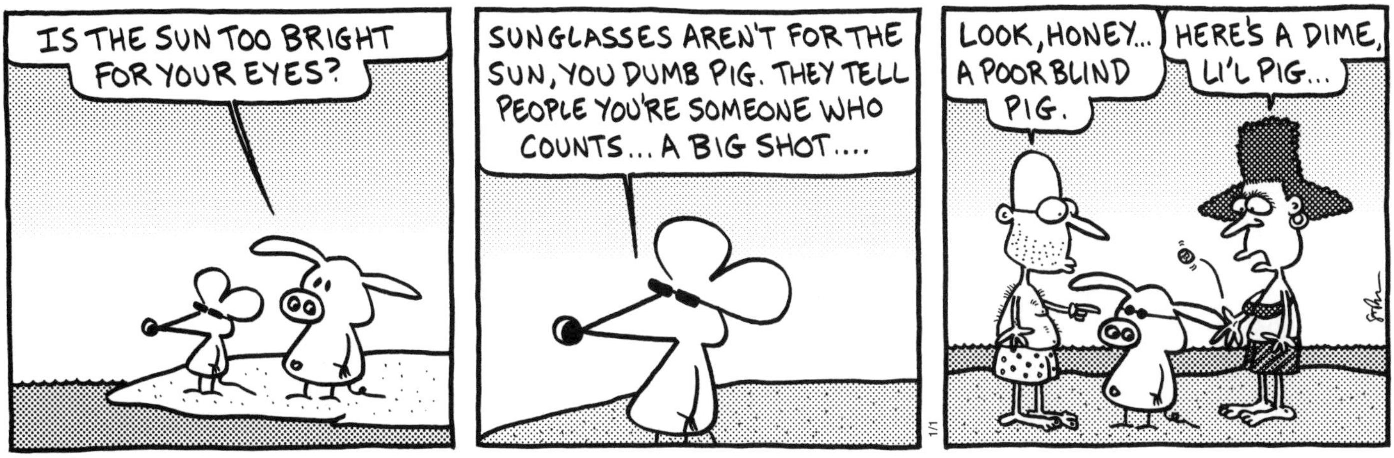
IS THE SUN TOO BRIGHT FOR YOUR EYES?
SUNGLASSES AREN'T FOR THE SUN, YOU DUMB PIG. THEY TELL PEOPLE YOU'RE SOMEONE WHO COUNTS... A BIG SHOT....
LOOK, HONEY... A POOR BLIND PIG.
HERE'S A DIME, LI'L PIG...
1/1

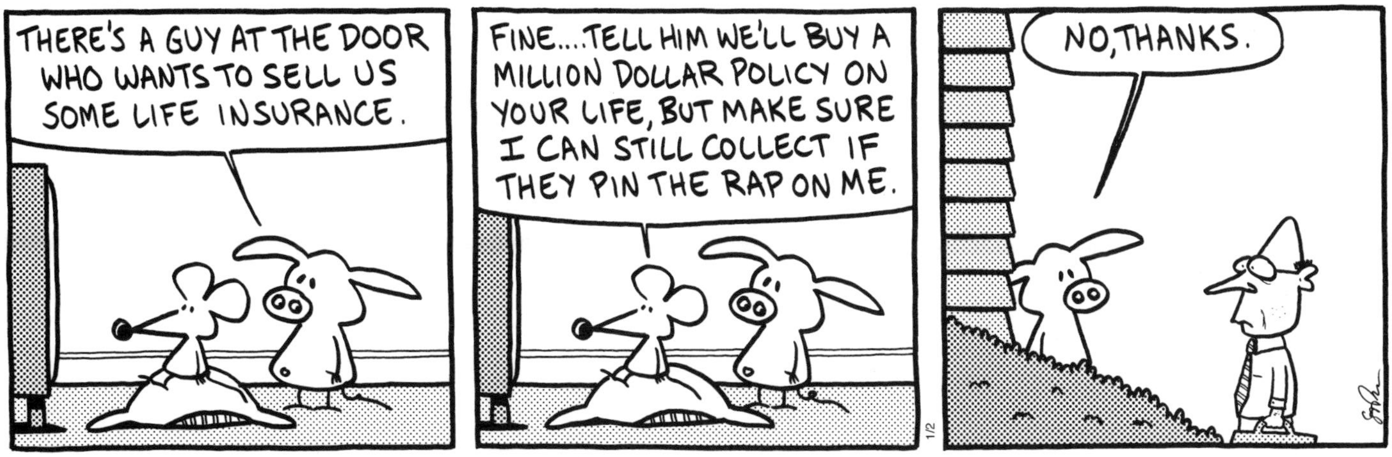
THERE'S A GUY AT THE DOOR WHO WANTS TO SELL US SOME LIFE INSURANCE.
FINE....TELL HIM WE'LL BUY A MILLION DOLLAR POLICY ON YOUR LIFE, BUT MAKE SURE I CAN STILL COLLECT IF THEY PIN THE RAP ON ME.
NO, THANKS.
1/2

This is the strip's first reference to death, a cherished *Pearls* theme.

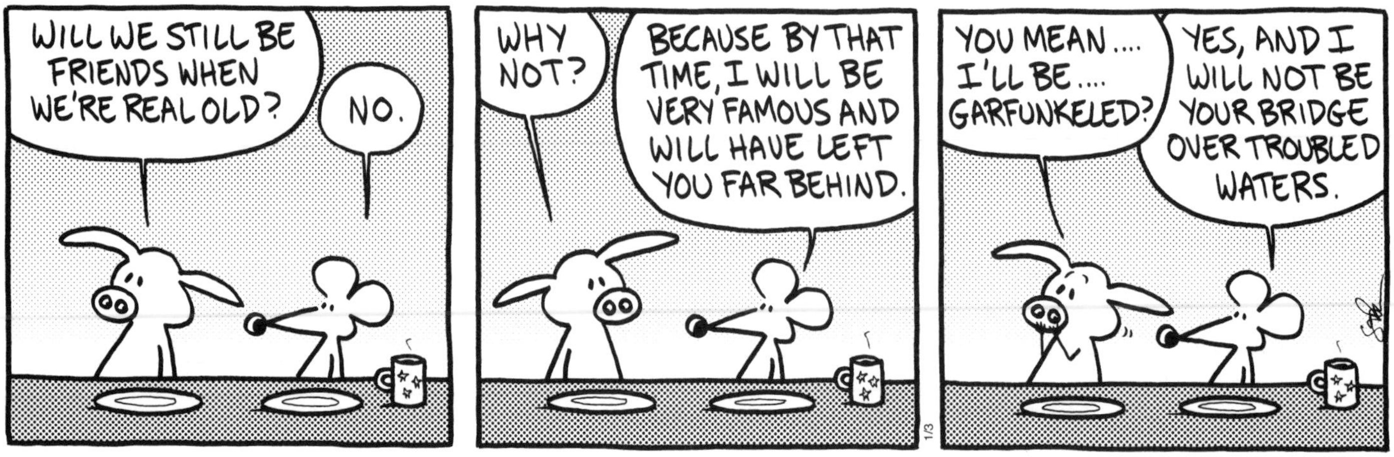
WILL WE STILL BE FRIENDS WHEN WE'RE REAL OLD?
NO.
WHY NOT?
BECAUSE BY THAT TIME, I WILL BE VERY FAMOUS AND WILL HAVE LEFT YOU FAR BEHIND.
YOU MEAN.... I'LL BE.... GARFUNKELED?
YES, AND I WILL NOT BE YOUR BRIDGE OVER TROUBLED WATERS.
1/3

I'm fairly certain that I'm the first person to turn "Garfunkel" into a verb.

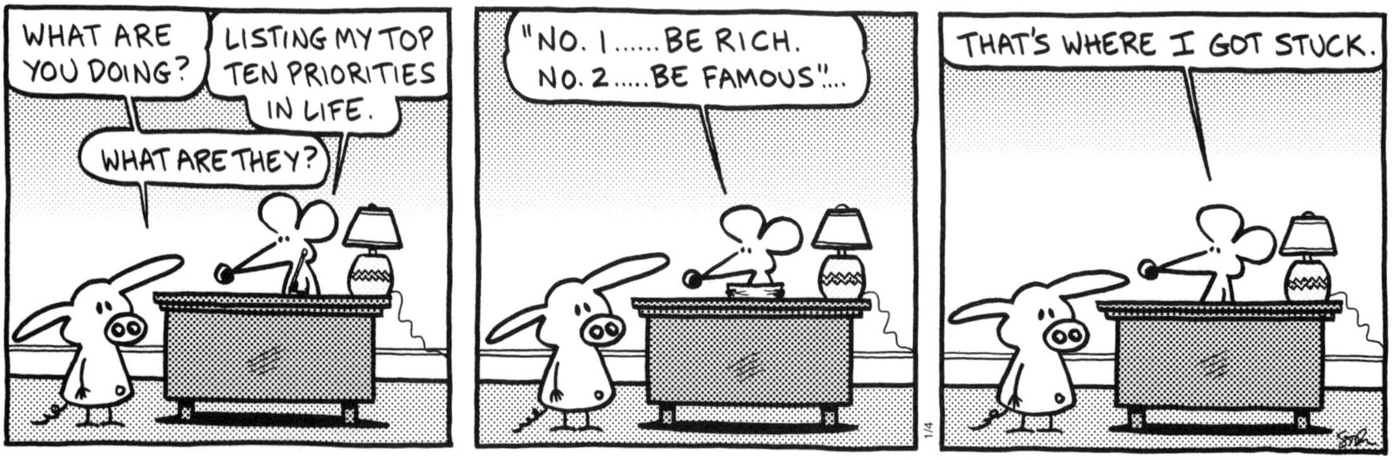
WHAT ARE YOU DOING?
LISTING MY TOP TEN PRIORITIES IN LIFE.
WHAT ARE THEY?
"NO. 1......BE RICH. NO. 2.....BE FAMOUS"....
THAT'S WHERE I GOT STUCK.
1/4

A number of lamps in *Pearls* contain the Charlie Brown shirt stripe. Charles Schulz was my biggest influence as a cartoonist, and this is just my small way of acknowledging him.

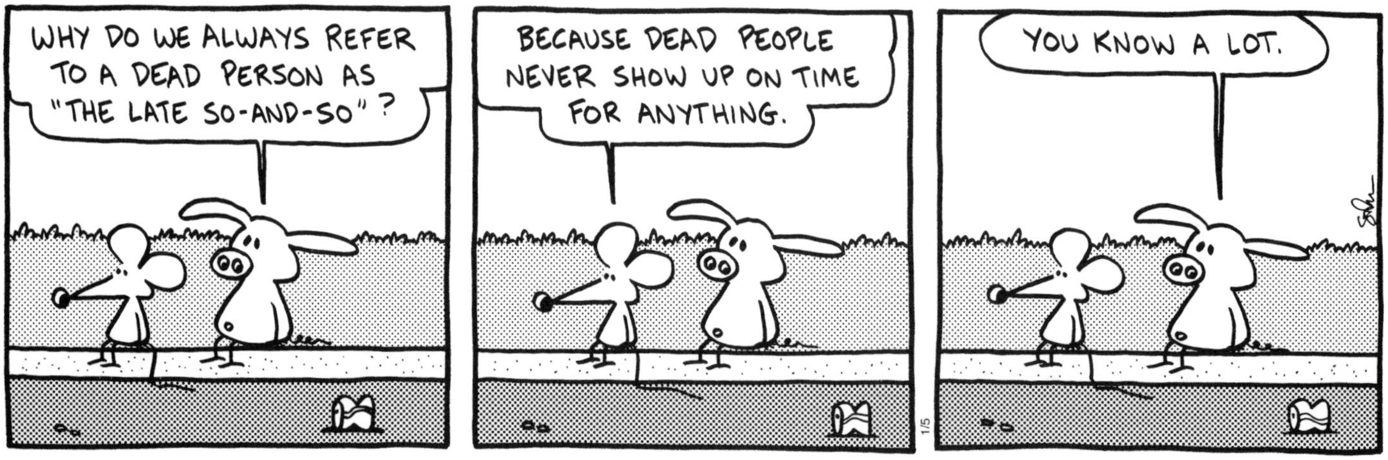
WHY DO WE ALWAYS REFER TO A DEAD PERSON AS "THE LATE SO-AND-SO"?
BECAUSE DEAD PEOPLE NEVER SHOW UP ON TIME FOR ANYTHING.
YOU KNOW A LOT.
1/5

Day 6 of the strip, and already I'm doing my second death joke. I see a trend developing.

I SPENT FIVE HOURS SEARCHING FOR MY CAR IN THE MALL PARKING LOT TODAY BECAUSE I FORGOT WHERE I PARKED IT.

AGAIN?.....DIDN'T I TELL YOU HOW TO AVOID THAT?

YEAH...I DID EVERYTHING YOU SAID. THE MOMENT I PARKED, I WROTE THE SECTION I WAS PARKED IN ON A LITTLE PIECE OF PAPER.

1/6/02

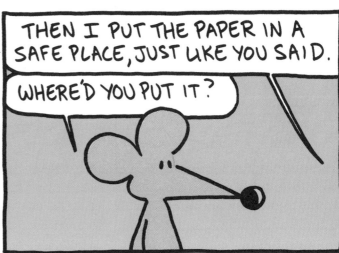

THEN I PUT THE PAPER IN A SAFE PLACE, JUST LIKE YOU SAID.

WHERE'D YOU PUT IT?

IN THE GLOVE COMPARTMENT.

NOTHING PERSONAL, BUT I DON'T THINK YOUR TIP SAVES A WHOLE LOT OF TIME.

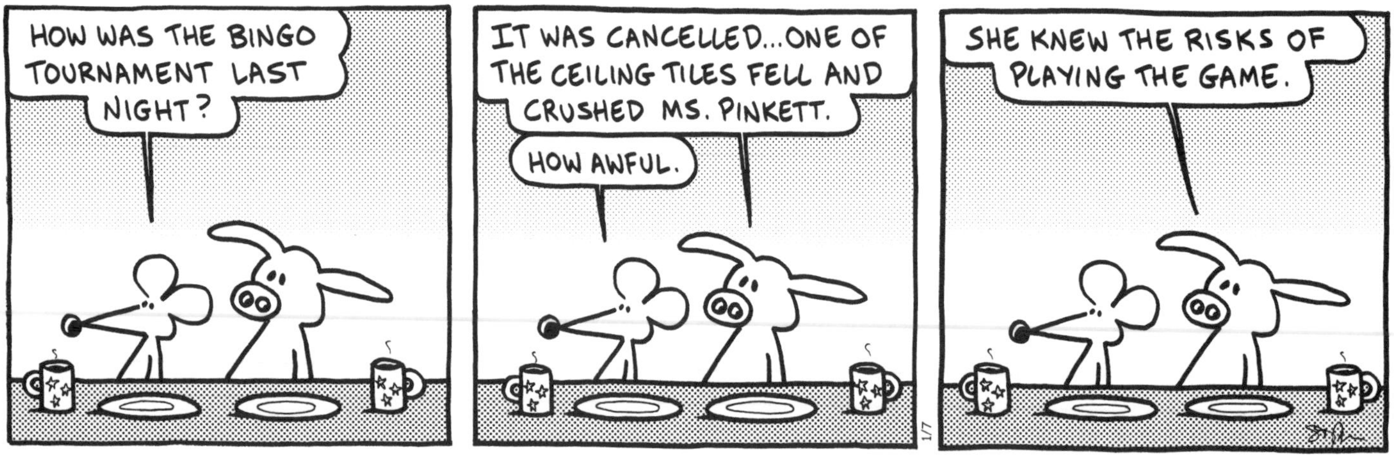
HOW WAS THE BINGO TOURNAMENT LAST NIGHT?
IT WAS CANCELLED...ONE OF THE CEILING TILES FELL AND CRUSHED MS. PINKETT.
HOW AWFUL.
SHE KNEW THE RISKS OF PLAYING THE GAME.
1/7

Pearls' real debut, in all newspapers but the *Washington Post,* was on this day. Thus, for the vast majority of readers, this was the first *Pearls* strip.

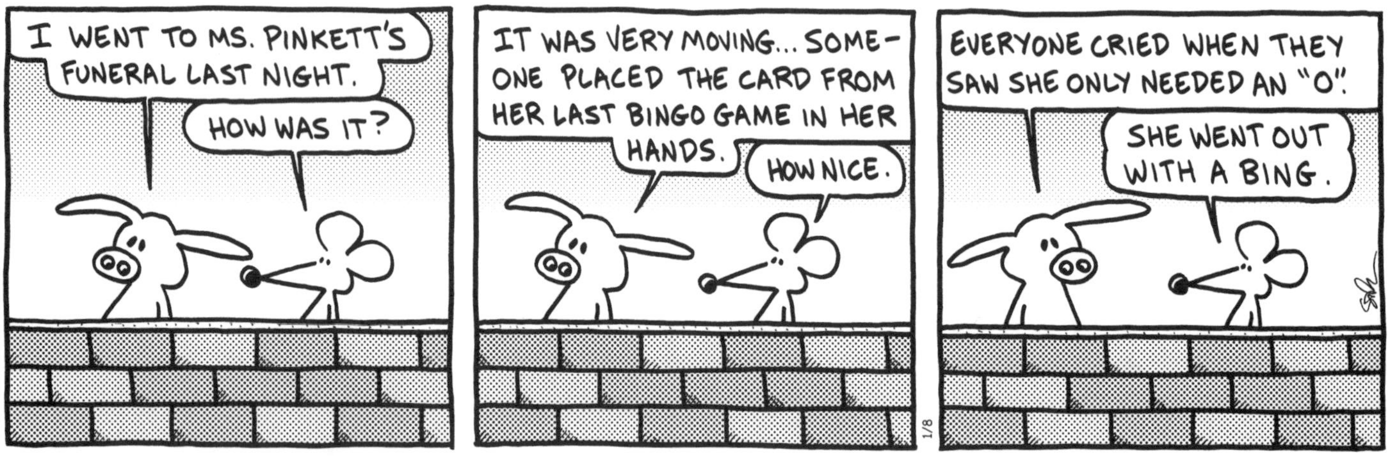
I WENT TO MS. PINKETT'S FUNERAL LAST NIGHT.
HOW WAS IT?
IT WAS VERY MOVING... SOMEONE PLACED THE CARD FROM HER LAST BINGO GAME IN HER HANDS.
HOW NICE.
EVERYONE CRIED WHEN THEY SAW SHE ONLY NEEDED AN "O".
SHE WENT OUT WITH A BING.
1/8

To get syndicated as a cartoonist, you send thirty to forty samples of your work to the syndicates. This strip and the previous one were on the top of my submission stack (meaning that I thought they were some of my better ones at the time). As they were successful in helping me get syndicated, I thought they'd be the best strips to start off *Pearls'* debut in papers.

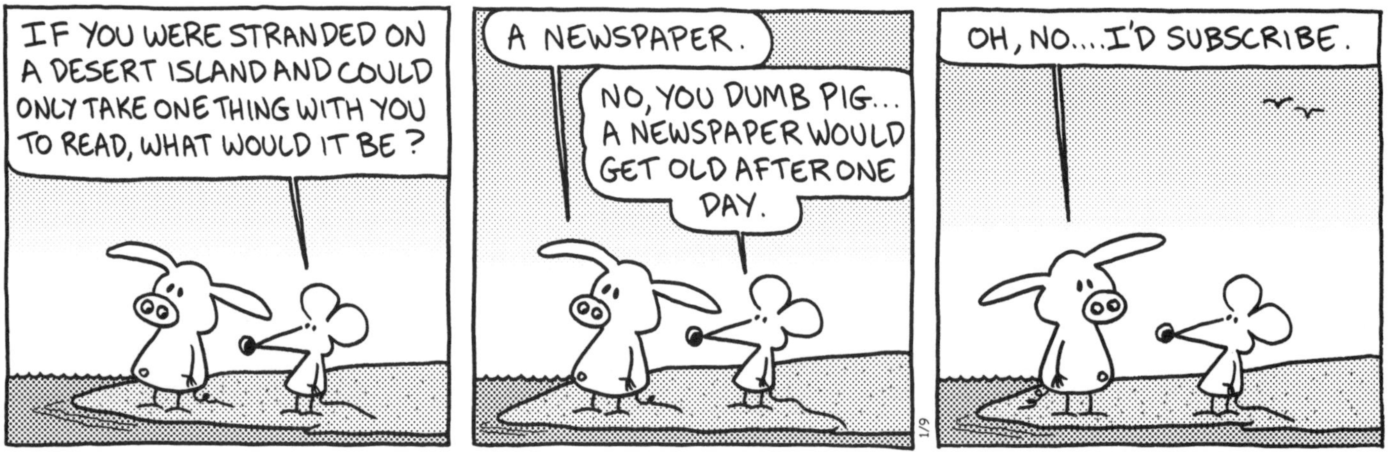
IF YOU WERE STRANDED ON A DESERT ISLAND AND COULD ONLY TAKE ONE THING WITH YOU TO READ, WHAT WOULD IT BE?
A NEWSPAPER.
NO, YOU DUMB PIG... A NEWSPAPER WOULD GET OLD AFTER ONE DAY.
OH, NO....I'D SUBSCRIBE.
1/9

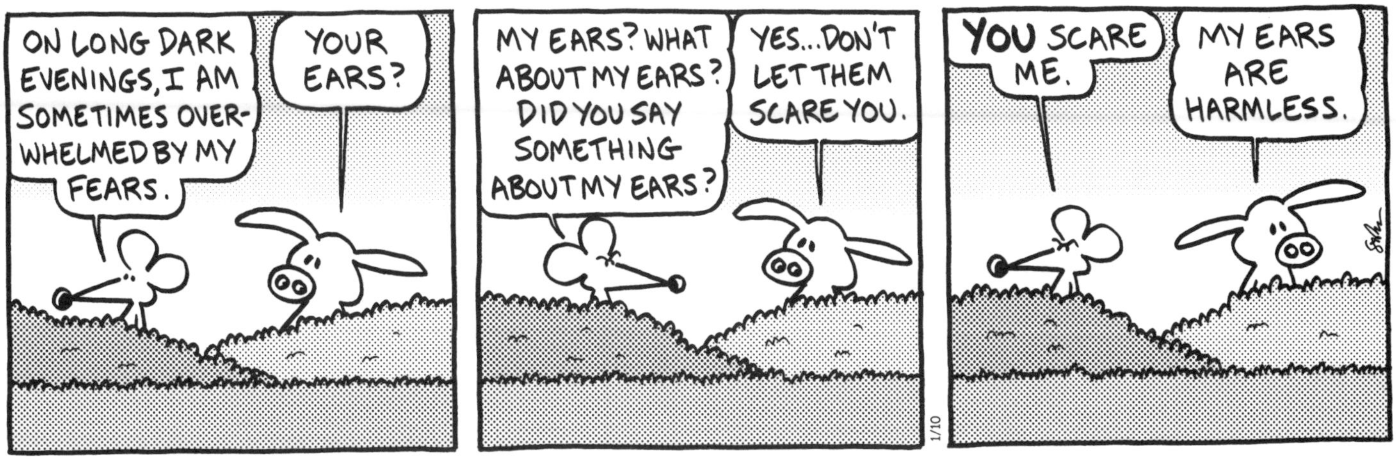
ON LONG DARK EVENINGS, I AM SOMETIMES OVERWHELMED BY MY FEARS.
YOUR EARS?
MY EARS? WHAT ABOUT MY EARS? DID YOU SAY SOMETHING ABOUT MY EARS?
YES...DON'T LET THEM SCARE YOU.
YOU SCARE ME.
MY EARS ARE HARMLESS.
1/10

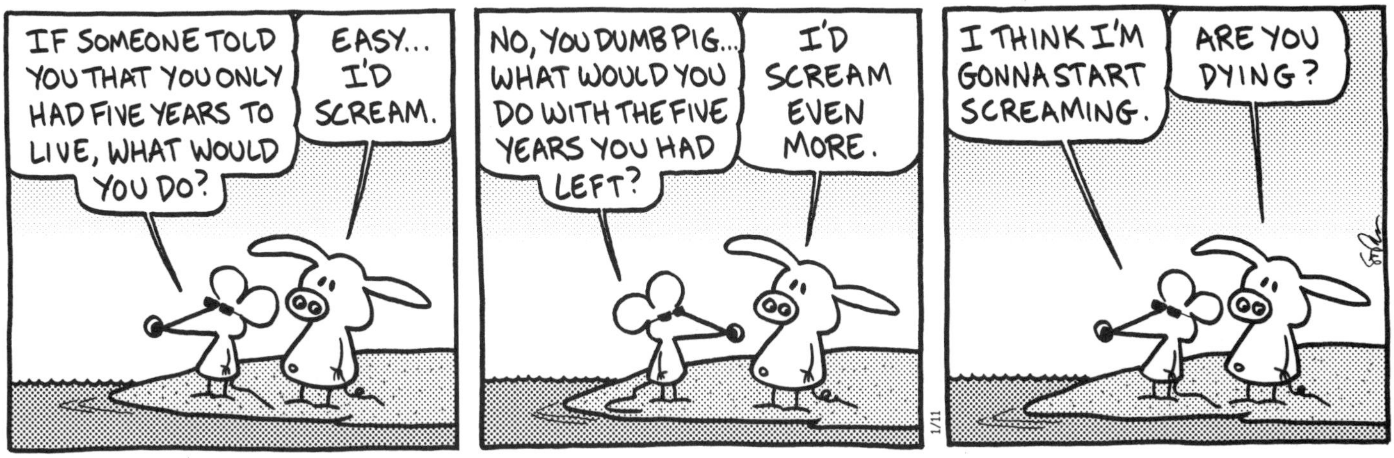
IF SOMEONE TOLD YOU THAT YOU ONLY HAD FIVE YEARS TO LIVE, WHAT WOULD YOU DO?
EASY... I'D SCREAM.
NO, YOU DUMB PIG... WHAT WOULD YOU DO WITH THE FIVE YEARS YOU HAD LEFT?
I'D SCREAM EVEN MORE.
I THINK I'M GONNA START SCREAMING.
ARE YOU DYING?
1/11

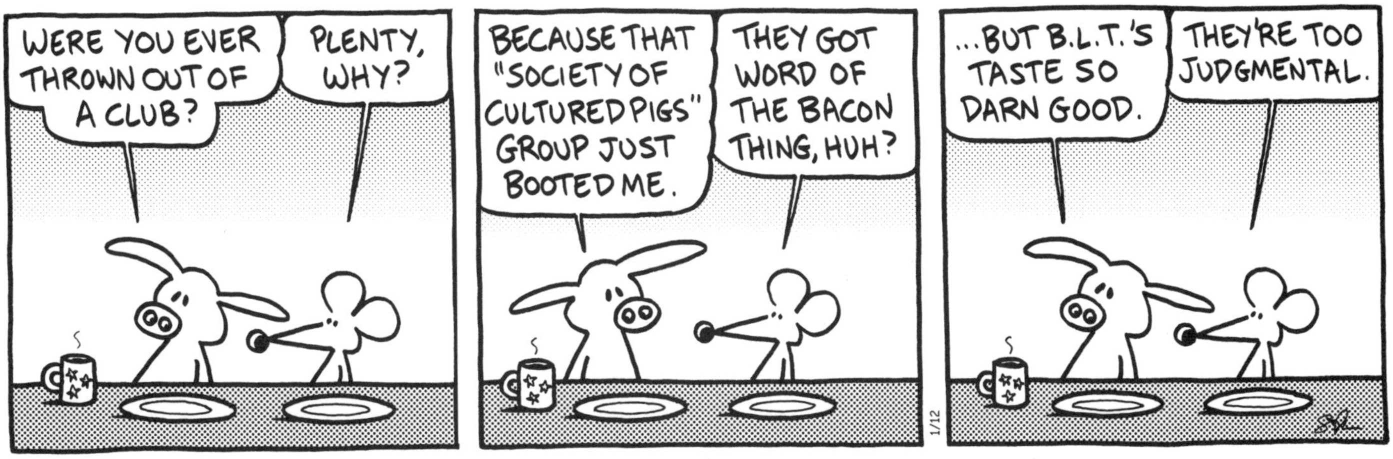
WERE YOU EVER THROWN OUT OF A CLUB?
PLENTY, WHY?
BECAUSE THAT "SOCIETY OF CULTURED PIGS" GROUP JUST BOOTED ME.
THEY GOT WORD OF THE BACON THING, HUH?
...BUT B.L.T.'s TASTE SO DARN GOOD.
THEY'RE TOO JUDGMENTAL.
1/12

Pig's line in the last panel became the title of the first *Pearls* book.

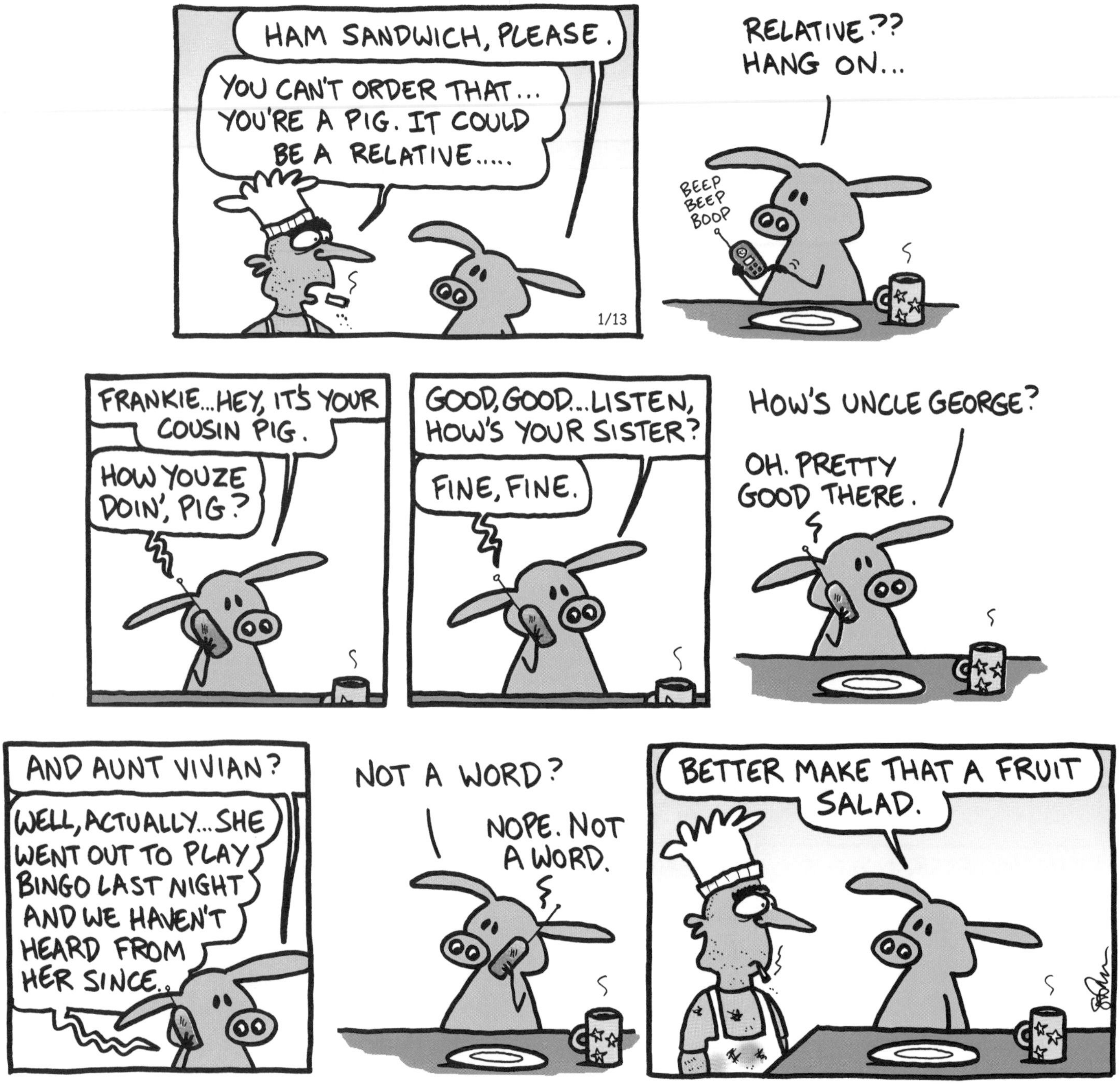
HAM SANDWICH, PLEASE.
YOU CAN'T ORDER THAT... YOU'RE A PIG. IT COULD BE A RELATIVE.....
1/13
RELATIVE?? HANG ON...
BEEP BEEP BOOP
FRANKIE...HEY, IT'S YOUR COUSIN PIG.
HOW YOUZE DOIN', PIG?
GOOD, GOOD...LISTEN, HOW'S YOUR SISTER?
FINE, FINE.
HOW'S UNCLE GEORGE?
OH. PRETTY GOOD THERE.
AND AUNT VIVIAN?
WELL, ACTUALLY...SHE WENT OUT TO PLAY BINGO LAST NIGHT AND WE HAVEN'T HEARD FROM HER SINCE.
NOT A WORD?
NOPE. NOT A WORD.
BETTER MAKE THAT A FRUIT SALAD.

I try to name all of the doomed animals in my strip after relatives. So yes, I have a real Aunt Vivian and Uncle George, and this strip is hanging in their kitchen.

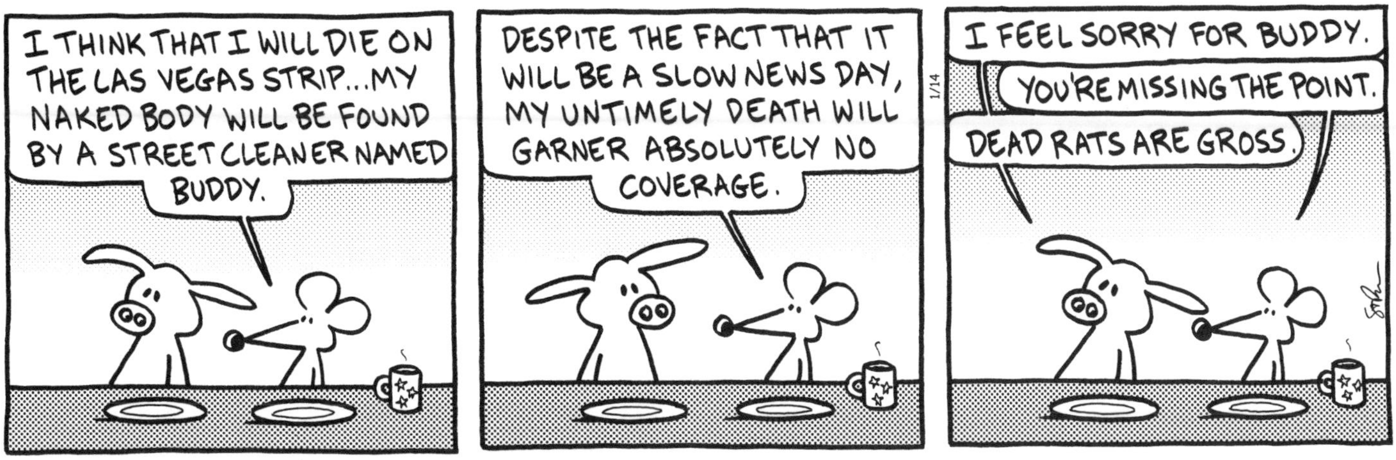
I THINK THAT I WILL DIE ON THE LAS VEGAS STRIP...MY NAKED BODY WILL BE FOUND BY A STREET CLEANER NAMED BUDDY.
DESPITE THE FACT THAT IT WILL BE A SLOW NEWS DAY, MY UNTIMELY DEATH WILL GARNER ABSOLUTELY NO COVERAGE.
1/14
I FEEL SORRY FOR BUDDY.
DEAD RATS ARE GROSS.
YOU'RE MISSING THE POINT.

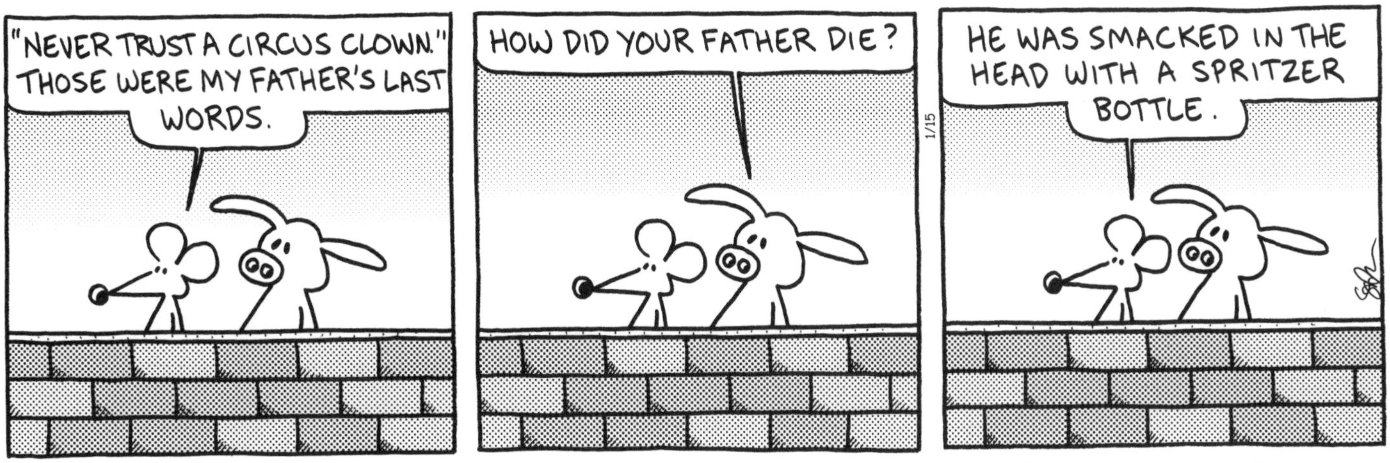
"NEVER TRUST A CIRCUS CLOWN." THOSE WERE MY FATHER'S LAST WORDS.
HOW DID YOUR FATHER DIE?
1/15
HE WAS SMACKED IN THE HEAD WITH A SPRITZER BOTTLE.

Whenever I want to write a strip involving Rat's dad, I have to remember that I killed him in this strip. Killing characters is a big limitation on using them in the future.

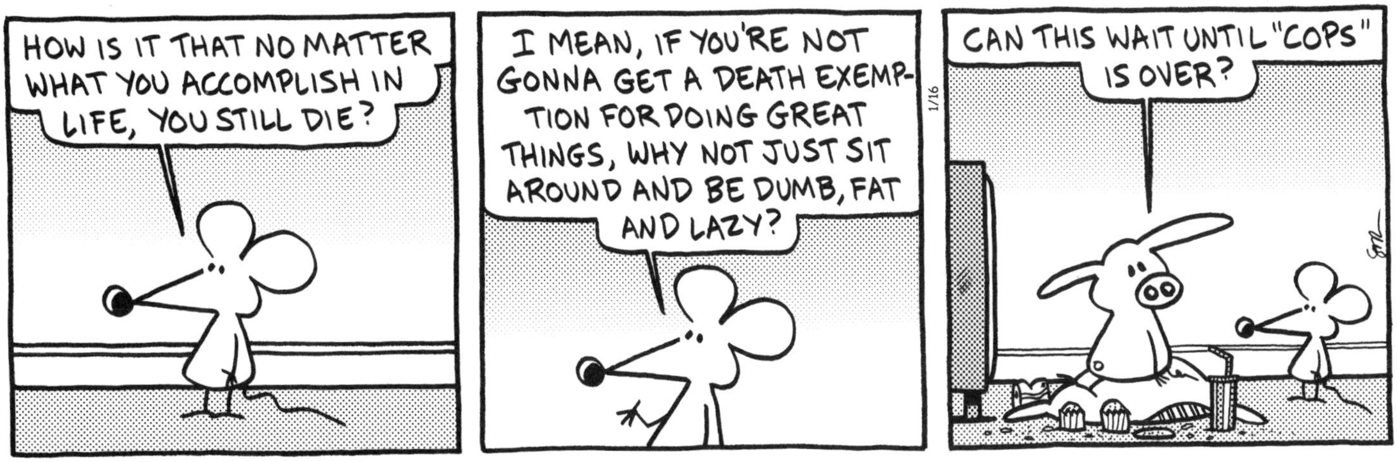
HOW IS IT THAT NO MATTER WHAT YOU ACCOMPLISH IN LIFE, YOU STILL DIE?
I MEAN, IF YOU'RE NOT GONNA GET A DEATH EXEMPTION FOR DOING GREAT THINGS, WHY NOT JUST SIT AROUND AND BE DUMB, FAT AND LAZY?
1/16
CAN THIS WAIT UNTIL "COPS" IS OVER?

"Bad boys, bad boys, whatcha gonna do . . ."

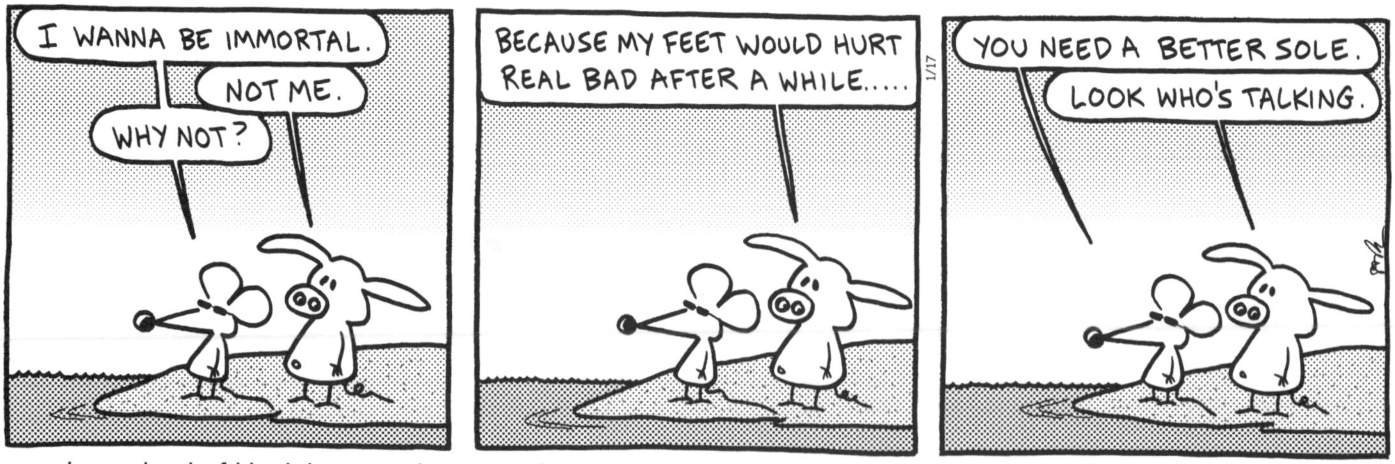
I WANNA BE IMMORTAL.
NOT ME.
WHY NOT?
BECAUSE MY FEET WOULD HURT REAL BAD AFTER A WHILE.....
YOU NEED A BETTER SOLE.
LOOK WHO'S TALKING.

I've always kind of liked this strip, because of the way each line builds on the one before. It's not easy to blend immortality and shoes into one joke.

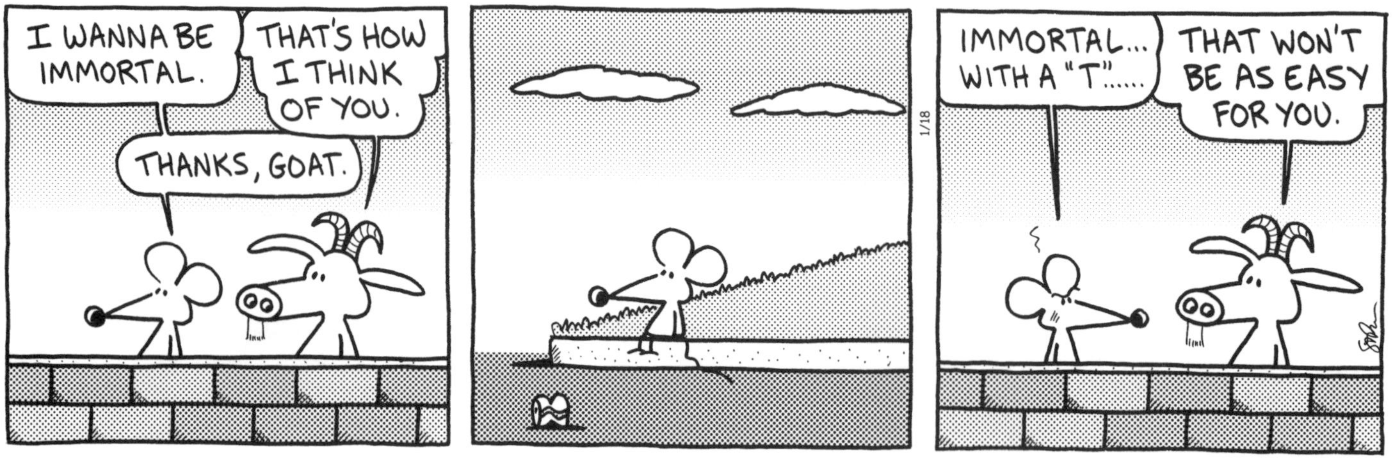
I WANNA BE IMMORTAL.
THAT'S HOW I THINK OF YOU.
THANKS, GOAT.
IMMORTAL... WITH A "T".....
THAT WON'T BE AS EASY FOR YOU.

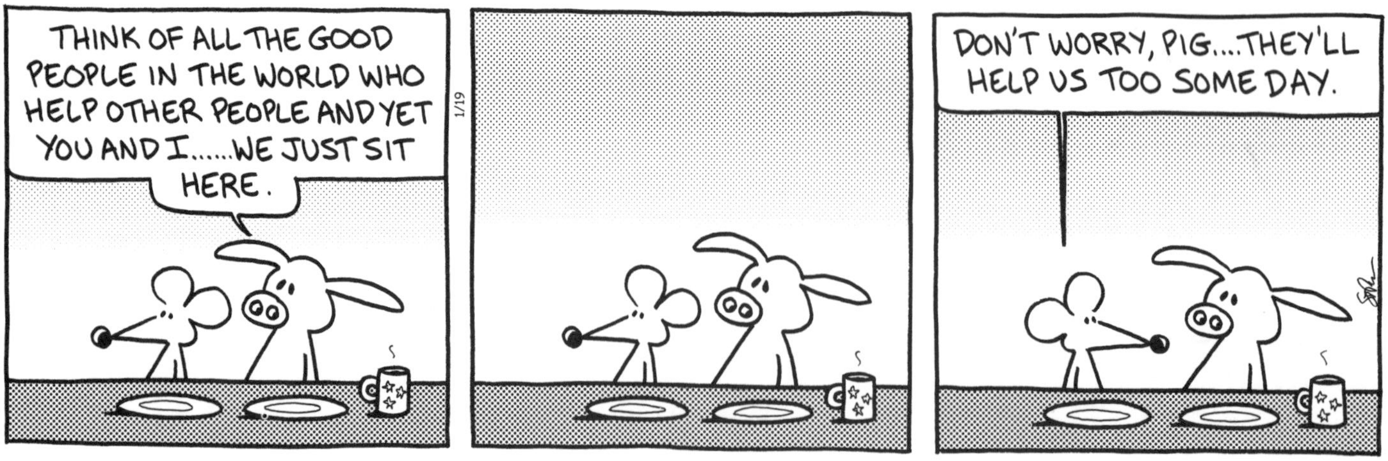
THINK OF ALL THE GOOD PEOPLE IN THE WORLD WHO HELP OTHER PEOPLE AND YET YOU AND I......WE JUST SIT HERE.
DON'T WORRY, PIG....THEY'LL HELP US TOO SOME DAY.

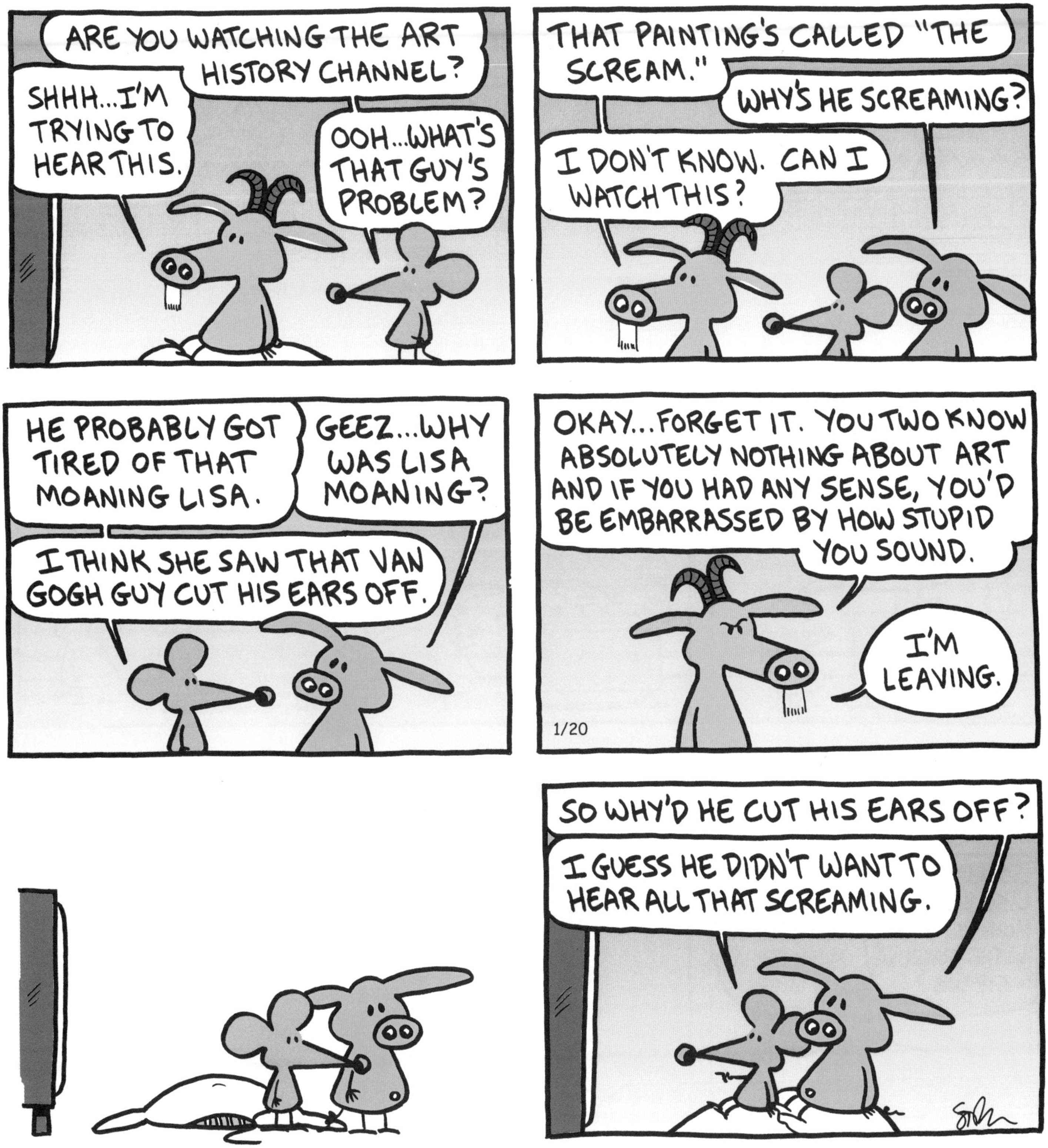
ARE YOU WATCHING THE ART HISTORY CHANNEL?
SHHH...I'M TRYING TO HEAR THIS.
OOH...WHAT'S THAT GUY'S PROBLEM?
THAT PAINTING'S CALLED "THE SCREAM."
WHY'S HE SCREAMING?
I DON'T KNOW. CAN I WATCH THIS?
HE PROBABLY GOT TIRED OF THAT MOANING LISA.
GEEZ...WHY WAS LISA MOANING?
I THINK SHE SAW THAT VAN GOGH GUY CUT HIS EARS OFF.
OKAY...FORGET IT. YOU TWO KNOW ABSOLUTELY NOTHING ABOUT ART AND IF YOU HAD ANY SENSE, YOU'D BE EMBARRASSED BY HOW STUPID YOU SOUND.
I'M LEAVING.
1/20
SO WHY'D HE CUT HIS EARS OFF?
I GUESS HE DIDN'T WANT TO HEAR ALL THAT SCREAMING.

This strip sort of defines Goat's personality. He's much smarter than the other characters and has to put up with their idocy.

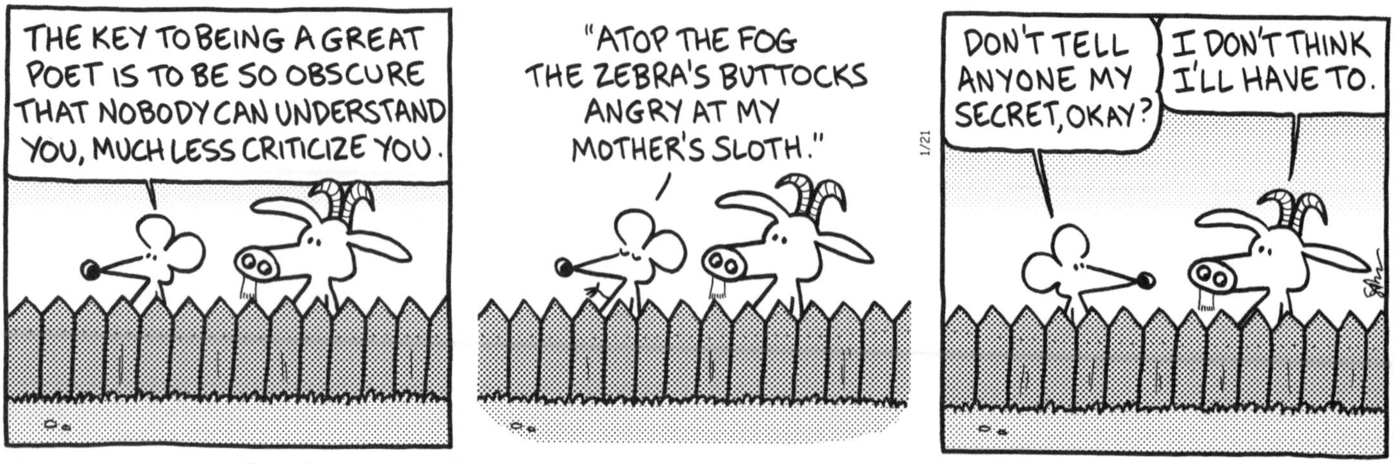
THE KEY TO BEING A GREAT POET IS TO BE SO OBSCURE THAT NOBODY CAN UNDERSTAND YOU, MUCH LESS CRITICIZE YOU.
"ATOP THE FOG THE ZEBRA'S BUTTOCKS ANGRY AT MY MOTHER'S SLOTH."
1/21
DON'T TELL ANYONE MY SECRET, OKAY?
I DON'T THINK I'LL HAVE TO.

Most poetry just confounds me. I really want to like it, but I can't help thinking it's a hoax.

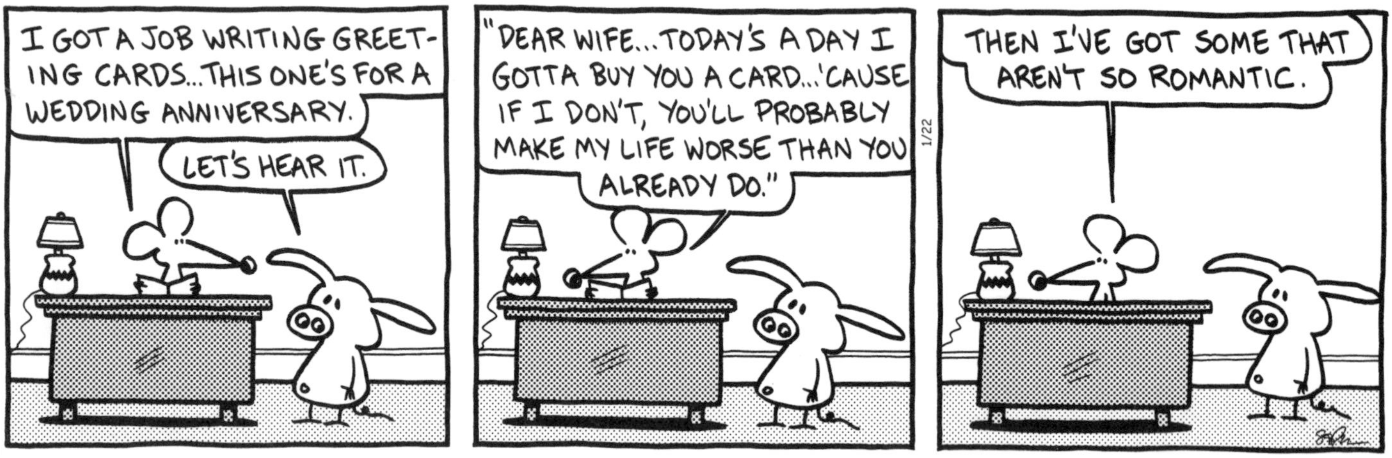
I GOT A JOB WRITING GREETING CARDS...THIS ONE'S FOR A WEDDING ANNIVERSARY.
LET'S HEAR IT.
"DEAR WIFE...TODAY'S A DAY I GOTTA BUY YOU A CARD...'CAUSE IF I DON'T, YOU'LL PROBABLY MAKE MY LIFE WORSE THAN YOU ALREADY DO."
1/22
THEN I'VE GOT SOME THAT AREN'T SO ROMANTIC.

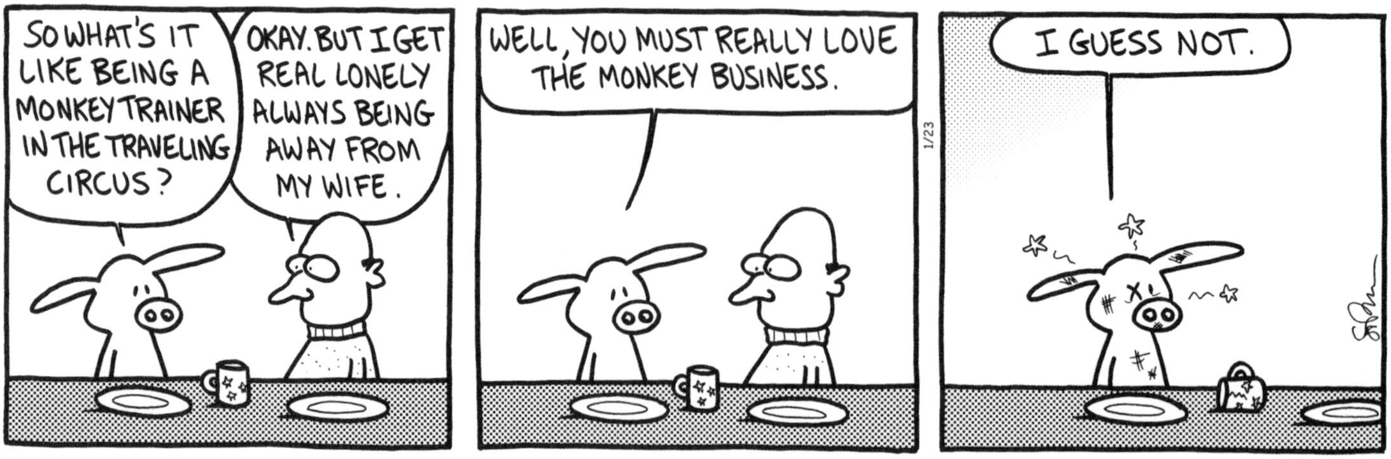
SO WHAT'S IT LIKE BEING A MONKEY TRAINER IN THE TRAVELING CIRCUS?
OKAY. BUT I GET REAL LONELY ALWAYS BEING AWAY FROM MY WIFE.
WELL, YOU MUST REALLY LOVE THE MONKEY BUSINESS.
1/23
I GUESS NOT.

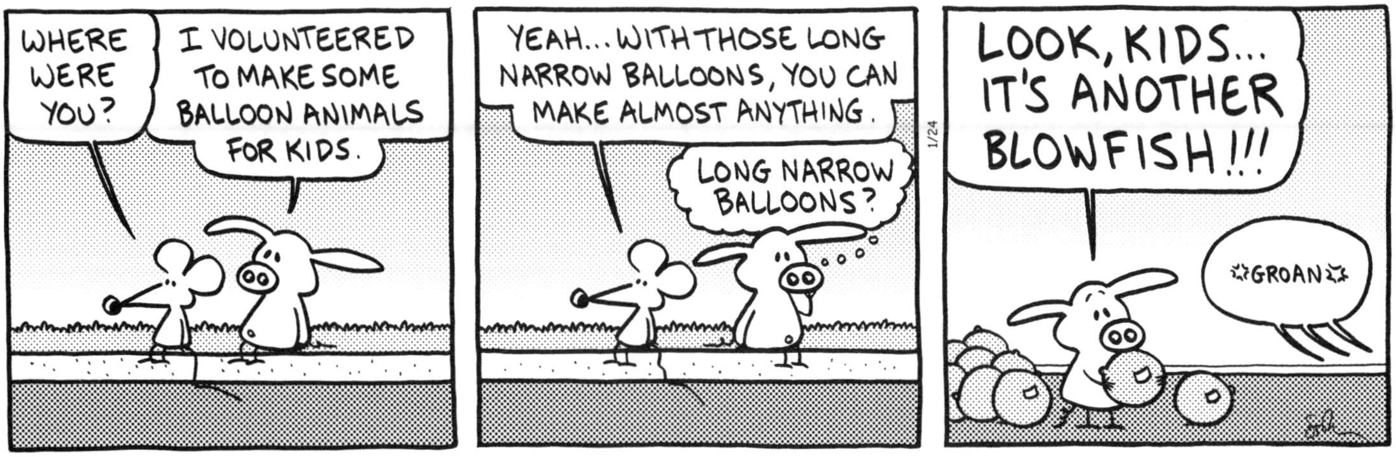
WHERE WERE YOU?
I VOLUNTEERED TO MAKE SOME BALLOON ANIMALS FOR KIDS.
YEAH... WITH THOSE LONG NARROW BALLOONS, YOU CAN MAKE ALMOST ANYTHING.
LONG NARROW BALLOONS?
1/24
LOOK, KIDS... IT'S ANOTHER BLOWFISH!!!
GROAN

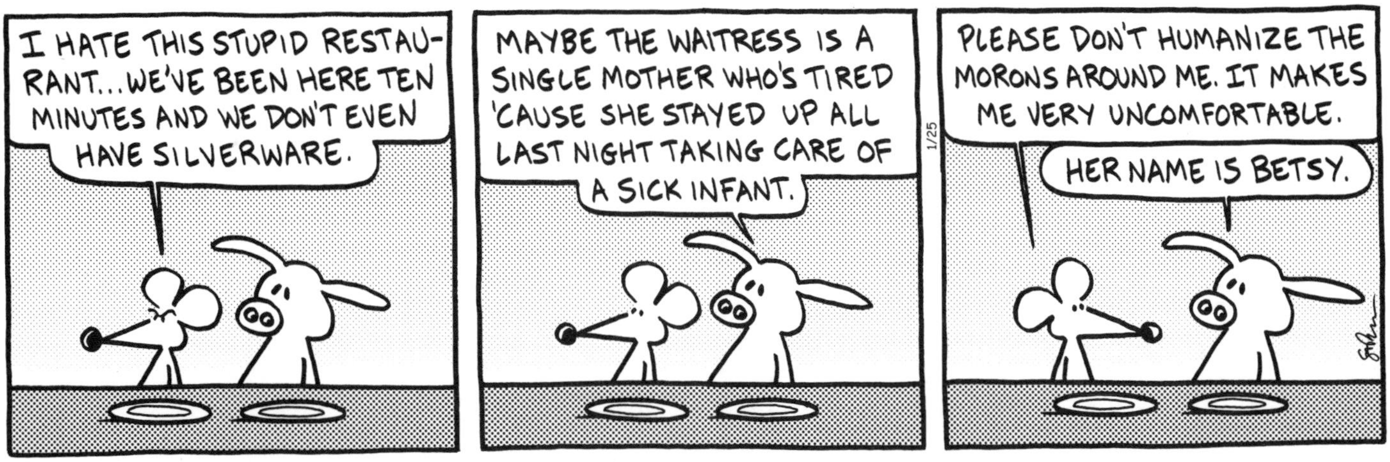
I HATE THIS STUPID RESTAURANT... WE'VE BEEN HERE TEN MINUTES AND WE DON'T EVEN HAVE SILVERWARE.
MAYBE THE WAITRESS IS A SINGLE MOTHER WHO'S TIRED 'CAUSE SHE STAYED UP ALL LAST NIGHT TAKING CARE OF A SICK INFANT.
1/25
PLEASE DON'T HUMANIZE THE MORONS AROUND ME. IT MAKES ME VERY UNCOMFORTABLE.
HER NAME IS BETSY.

When this strip ran, someone who knew me from my lawyer days wrote to me and said that Rat's line in the last panel sounded more like me than anything else I had ever written. I told him that he was wrong and was a moron for even suggesting that.

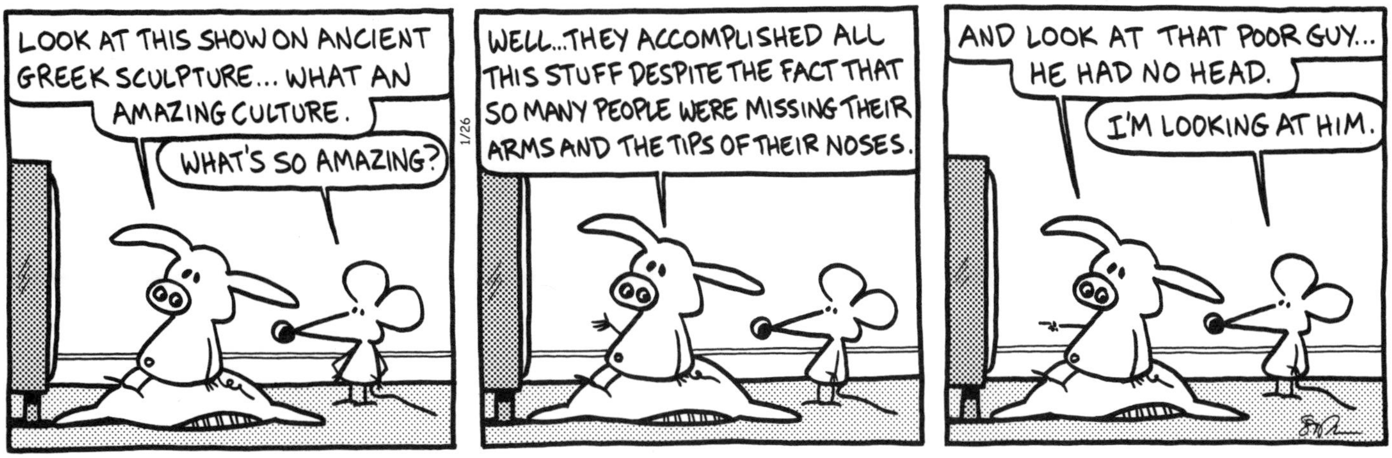
LOOK AT THIS SHOW ON ANCIENT GREEK SCULPTURE... WHAT AN AMAZING CULTURE.
WHAT'S SO AMAZING?
1/26
WELL...THEY ACCOMPLISHED ALL THIS STUFF DESPITE THE FACT THAT SO MANY PEOPLE WERE MISSING THEIR ARMS AND THE TIPS OF THEIR NOSES.
AND LOOK AT THAT POOR GUY... HE HAD NO HEAD.
I'M LOOKING AT HIM.

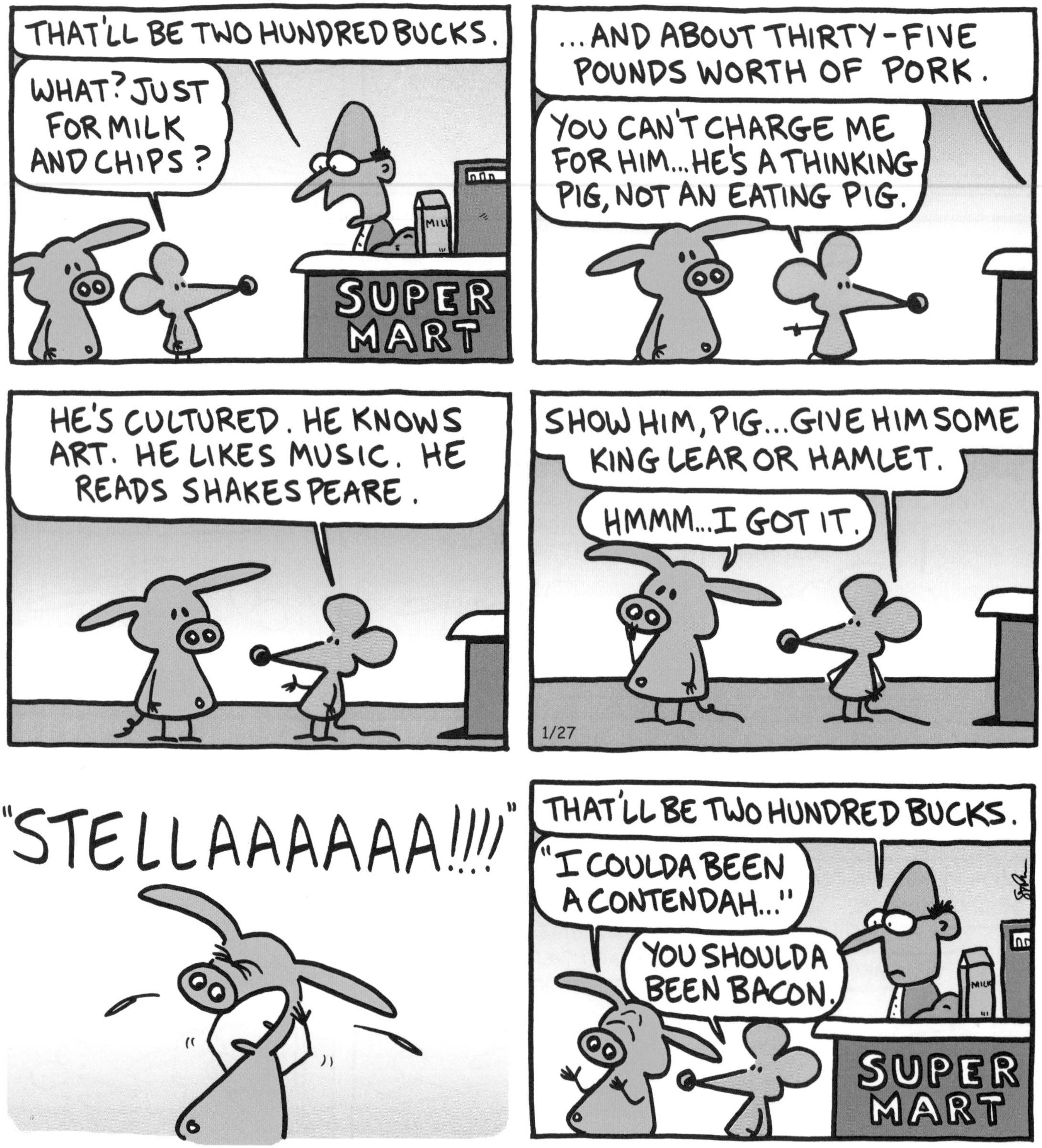
THAT'LL BE TWO HUNDRED BUCKS.
WHAT? JUST FOR MILK AND CHIPS?
SUPER MART
...AND ABOUT THIRTY-FIVE POUNDS WORTH OF PORK.
YOU CAN'T CHARGE ME FOR HIM...HE'S A THINKING PIG, NOT AN EATING PIG.
HE'S CULTURED. HE KNOWS ART. HE LIKES MUSIC. HE READS SHAKESPEARE.
SHOW HIM, PIG...GIVE HIM SOME KING LEAR OR HAMLET.
HMMM...I GOT IT.
1/27
"STELLAAAAAA!!!!"
THAT'LL BE TWO HUNDRED BUCKS.
"I COULDA BEEN A CONTENDAH..."
YOU SHOULDA BEEN BACON.
SUPER MART

I think Pig really does look like Marlon Brando in that last panel.

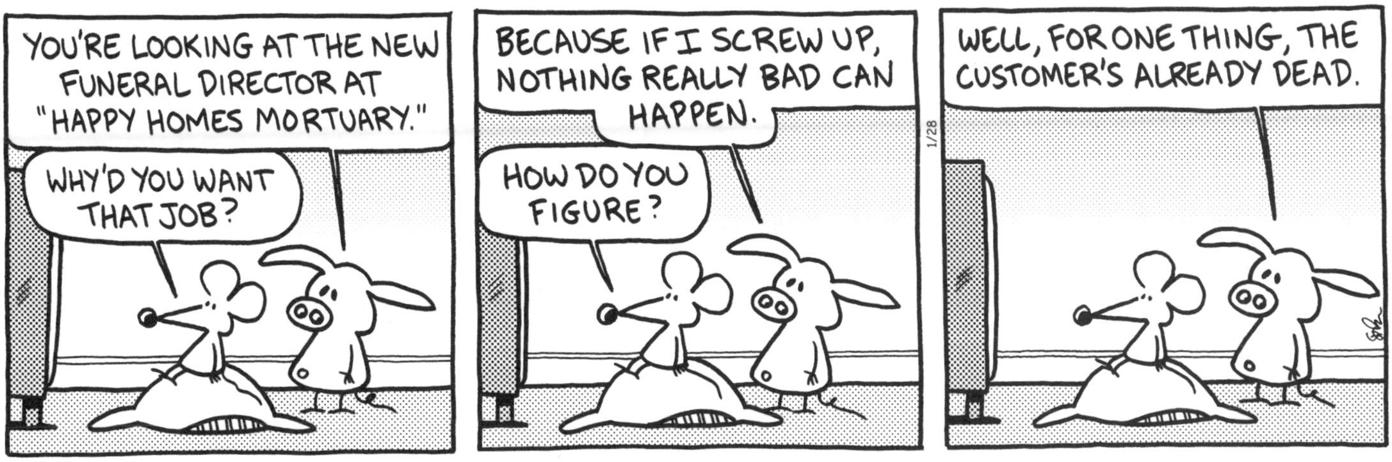
YOU'RE LOOKING AT THE NEW FUNERAL DIRECTOR AT "HAPPY HOMES MORTUARY."
WHY'D YOU WANT THAT JOB?
BECAUSE IF I SCREW UP, NOTHING REALLY BAD CAN HAPPEN.
HOW DO YOU FIGURE?
1/28
WELL, FOR ONE THING, THE CUSTOMER'S ALREADY DEAD.

The strip had gone a few days without any death jokes, so I thought I'd make up for it with three good death jokes in a row.

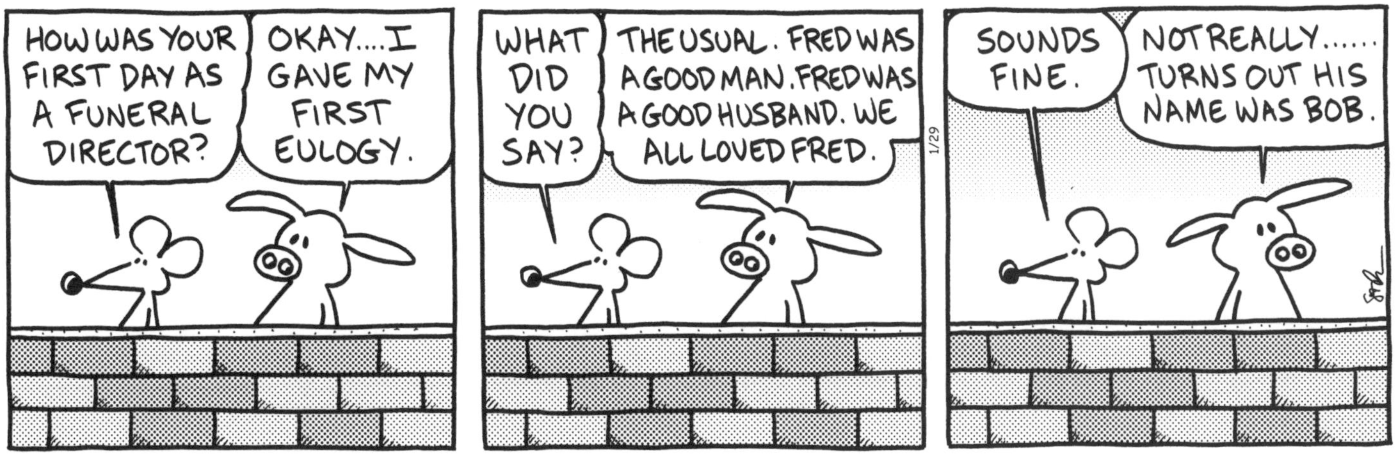
HOW WAS YOUR FIRST DAY AS A FUNERAL DIRECTOR?
OKAY....I GAVE MY FIRST EULOGY.
WHAT DID YOU SAY?
THE USUAL. FRED WAS A GOOD MAN. FRED WAS A GOOD HUSBAND. WE ALL LOVED FRED.
1/29
SOUNDS FINE.
NOT REALLY...... TURNS OUT HIS NAME WAS BOB.

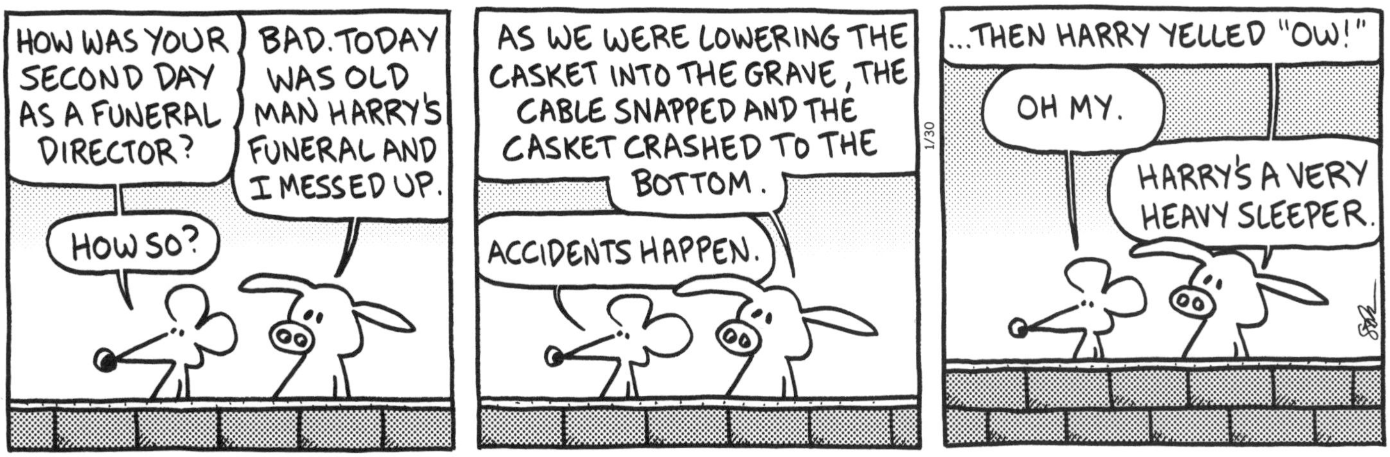
HOW WAS YOUR SECOND DAY AS A FUNERAL DIRECTOR?
BAD. TODAY WAS OLD MAN HARRY'S FUNERAL AND I MESSED UP.
HOW SO?
AS WE WERE LOWERING THE CASKET INTO THE GRAVE, THE CABLE SNAPPED AND THE CASKET CRASHED TO THE BOTTOM.
ACCIDENTS HAPPEN.
1/30
...THEN HARRY YELLED "OW!"
OH MY.
HARRY'S A VERY HEAVY SLEEPER.

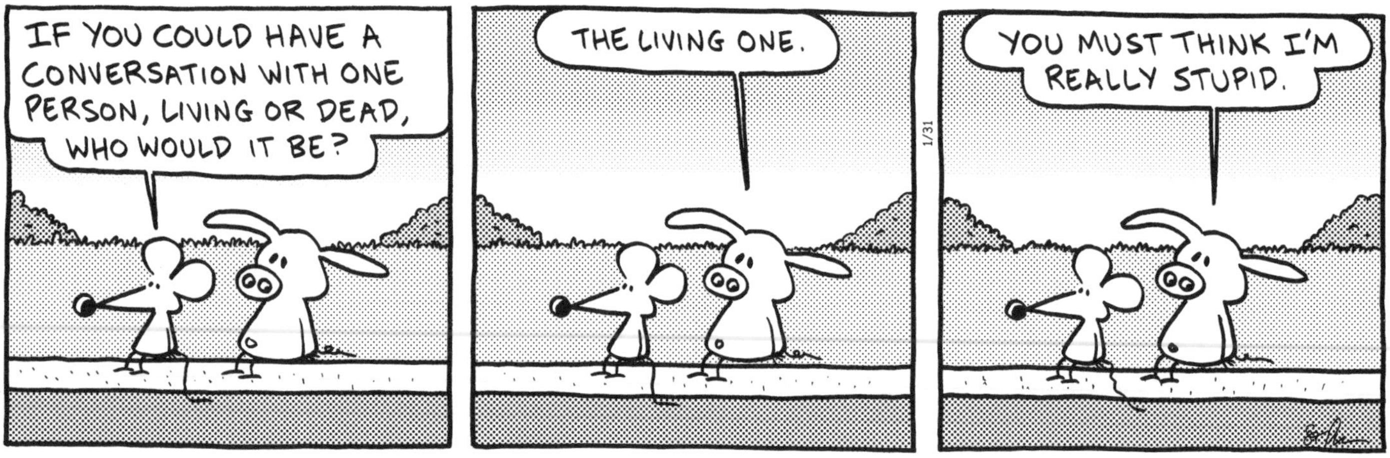
IF YOU COULD HAVE A CONVERSATION WITH ONE PERSON, LIVING OR DEAD, WHO WOULD IT BE?
THE LIVING ONE.
1/31
YOU MUST THINK I'M REALLY STUPID.

I think this is the single most popular daily strip.

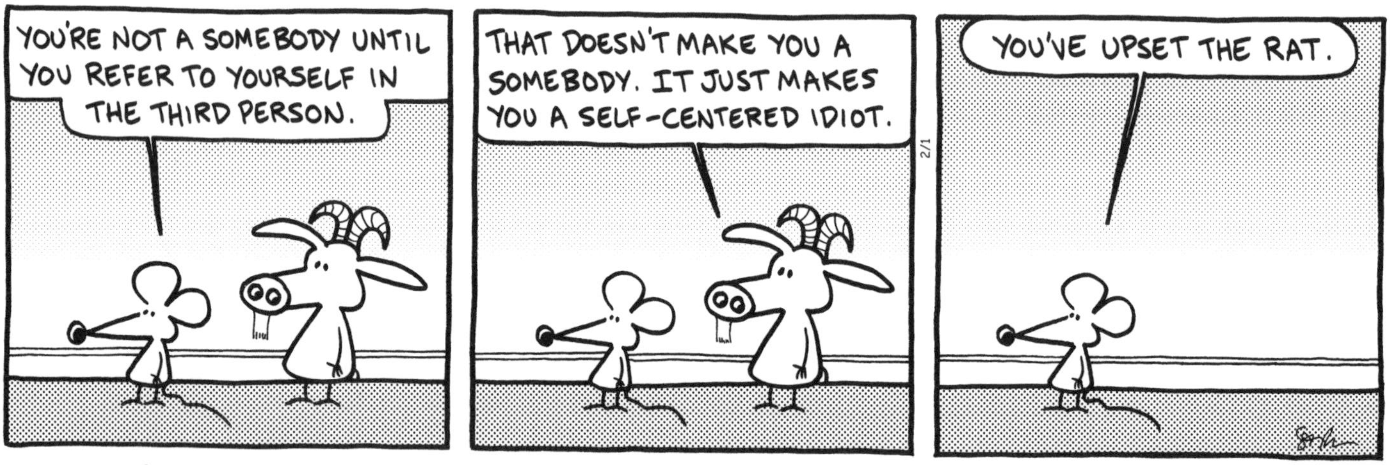
YOU'RE NOT A SOMEBODY UNTIL YOU REFER TO YOURSELF IN THE THIRD PERSON.
THAT DOESN'T MAKE YOU A SOMEBODY. IT JUST MAKES YOU A SELF-CENTERED IDIOT.
2/1
YOU'VE UPSET THE RAT.

You see professional athletes doing this all the time. I think it's a sign that your ego has grown completely out of check. Stephan hates that.

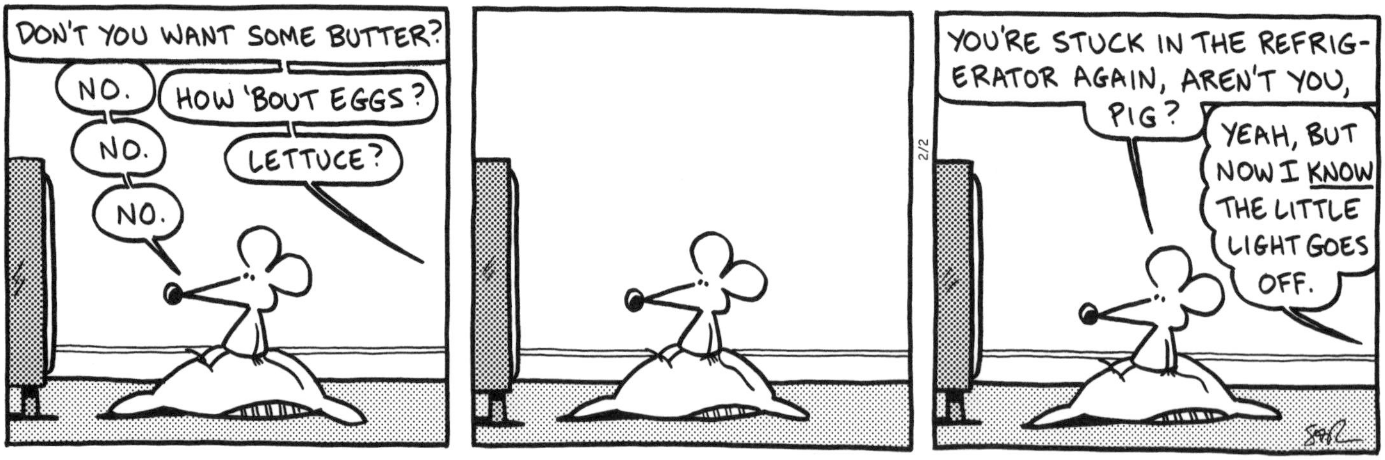
DON'T YOU WANT SOME BUTTER?
NO.
HOW 'BOUT EGGS?
NO.
LETTUCE?
NO.
2/2
YOU'RE STUCK IN THE REFRIGERATOR AGAIN, AREN'T YOU, PIG?
YEAH, BUT NOW I KNOW THE LITTLE LIGHT GOES OFF.

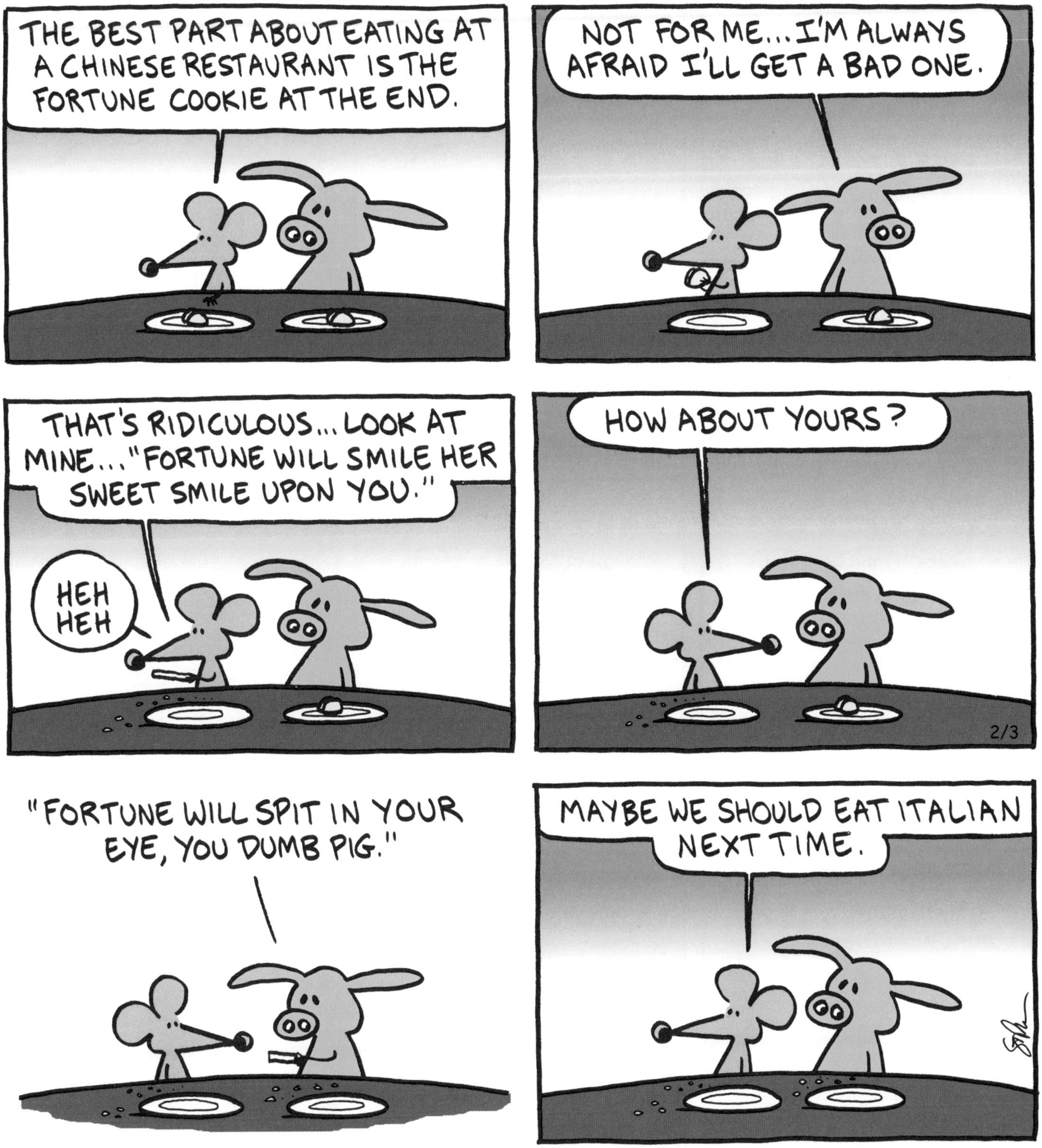
THE BEST PART ABOUT EATING AT A CHINESE RESTAURANT IS THE FORTUNE COOKIE AT THE END.
NOT FOR ME... I'M ALWAYS AFRAID I'LL GET A BAD ONE.
THAT'S RIDICULOUS... LOOK AT MINE... "FORTUNE WILL SMILE HER SWEET SMILE UPON YOU."
HEH HEH
HOW ABOUT YOURS?
2/3
"FORTUNE WILL SPIT IN YOUR EYE, YOU DUMB PIG."
MAYBE WE SHOULD EAT ITALIAN NEXT TIME.

Although this was not the first *Pearls* Sunday strip to appear in papers, it was the first one I ever drew. Due to their length (mine are typically at least six panels), Sunday strips are a whole different ballgame than the dailies. The timing of the joke is much different and it took me a little while to get used to that.

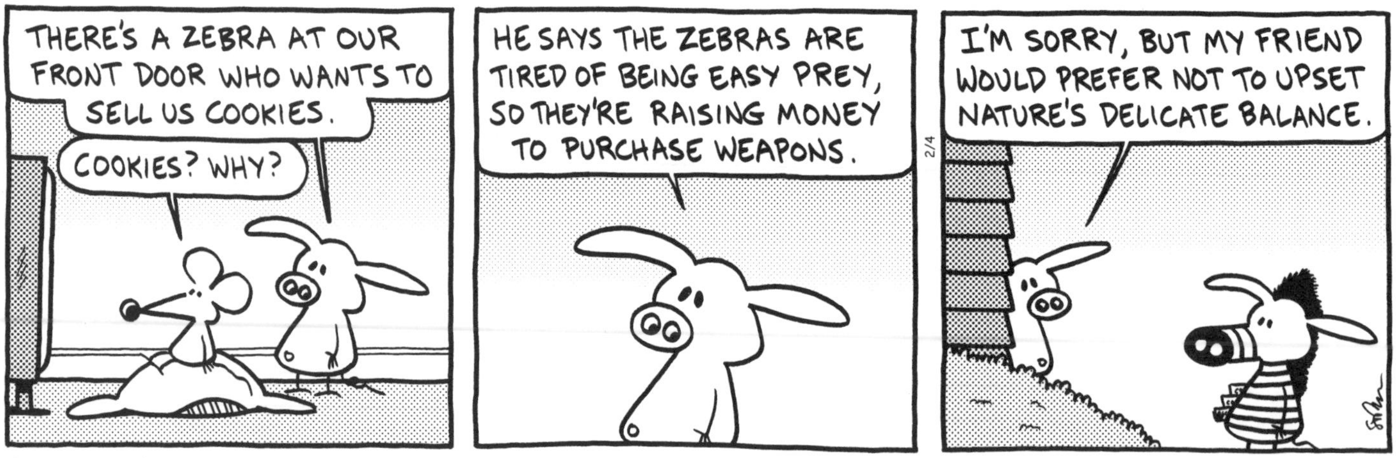
THERE'S A ZEBRA AT OUR FRONT DOOR WHO WANTS TO SELL US COOKIES.
COOKIES? WHY?
HE SAYS THE ZEBRAS ARE TIRED OF BEING EASY PREY, SO THEY'RE RAISING MONEY TO PURCHASE WEAPONS.
2/4
I'M SORRY, BUT MY FRIEND WOULD PREFER NOT TO UPSET NATURE'S DELICATE BALANCE.

This was Zebra's introduction into the strip. He was only meant to be a temporary character, but he turned out to be popular, so he became permanent.

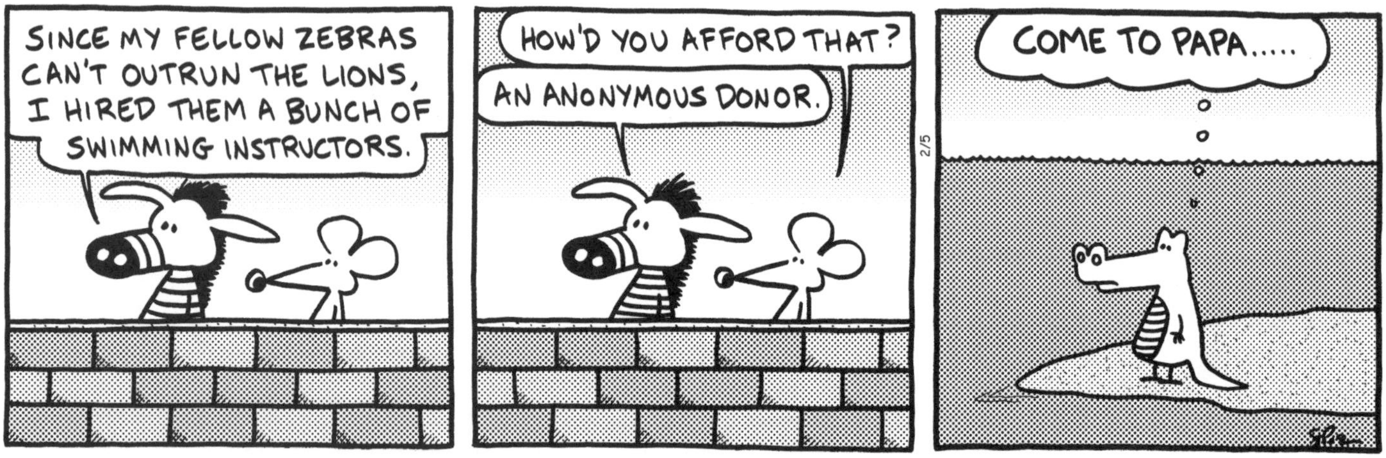
SINCE MY FELLOW ZEBRAS CAN'T OUTRUN THE LIONS, I HIRED THEM A BUNCH OF SWIMMING INSTRUCTORS.
HOW'D YOU AFFORD THAT?
AN ANONYMOUS DONOR.
2/5
COME TO PAPA.....

When I first got syndicated, Darby Conley, the creator of *Get Fuzzy*, was a tremendous help, teaching me a lot of the stuff I needed to know about syndication. To show him my appreciation, I offered him any *Pearls* strip he wanted, and he chose this one.

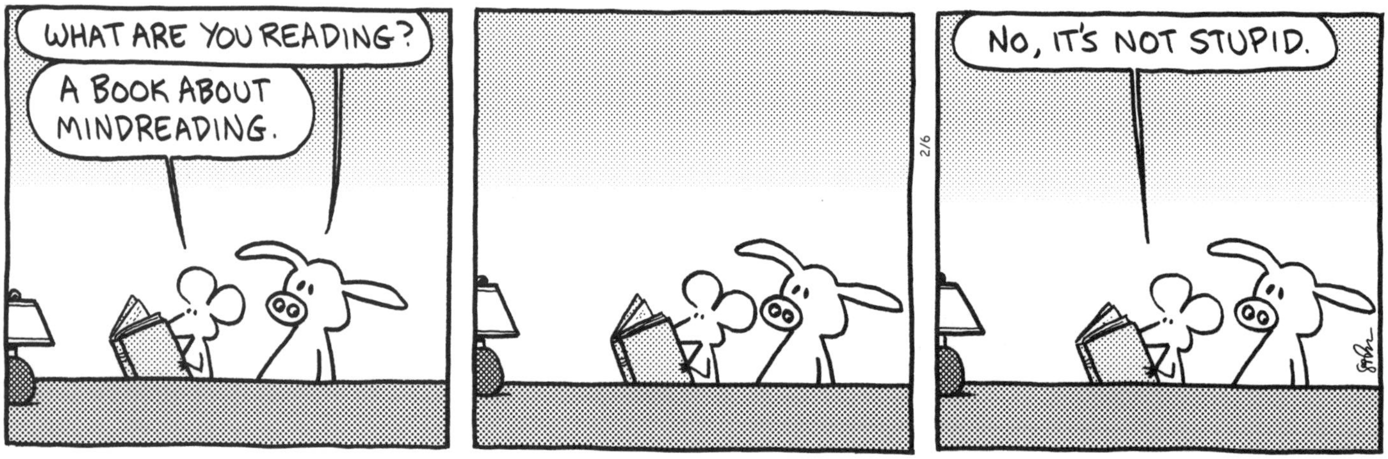
WHAT ARE YOU READING?
A BOOK ABOUT MINDREADING.
2/6
NO, IT'S NOT STUPID.

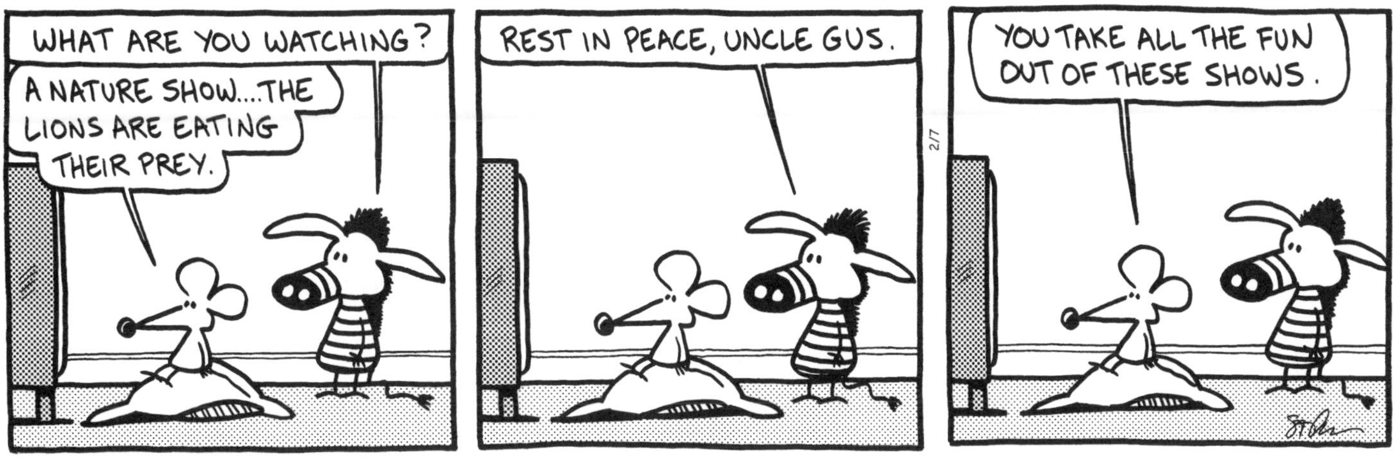
WHAT ARE YOU WATCHING?
A NATURE SHOW....THE LIONS ARE EATING THEIR PREY.
REST IN PEACE, UNCLE GUS.
YOU TAKE ALL THE FUN OUT OF THESE SHOWS.

Yes, I have a real Uncle Gus.

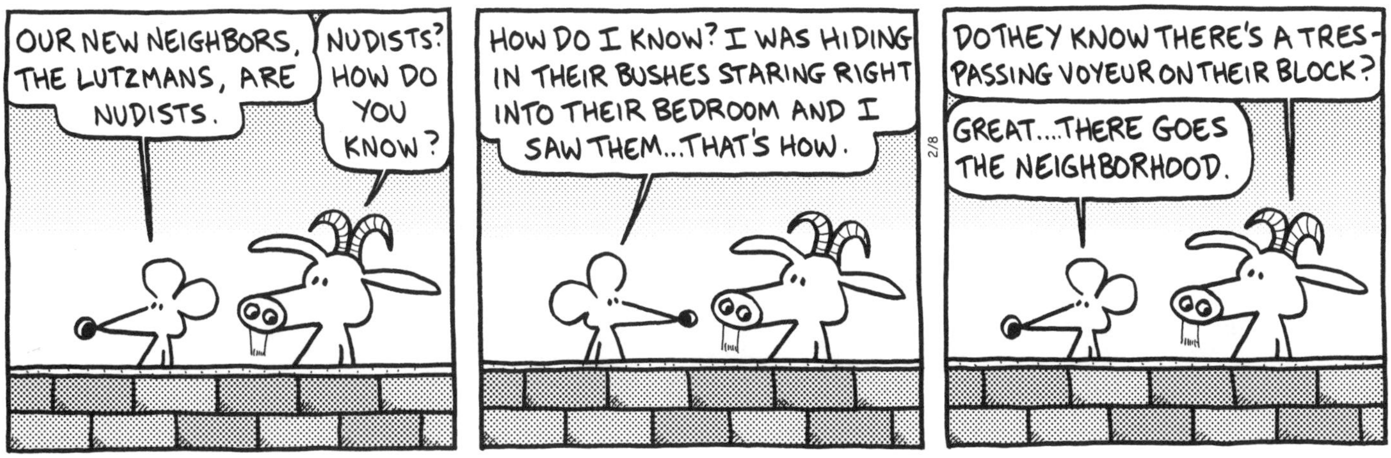
OUR NEW NEIGHBORS, THE LUTZMANS, ARE NUDISTS.
NUDISTS? HOW DO YOU KNOW?
HOW DO I KNOW? I WAS HIDING IN THEIR BUSHES STARING RIGHT INTO THEIR BEDROOM AND I SAW THEM...THAT'S HOW.
DO THEY KNOW THERE'S A TRES-PASSING VOYEUR ON THEIR BLOCK?
GREAT....THERE GOES THE NEIGHBORHOOD.

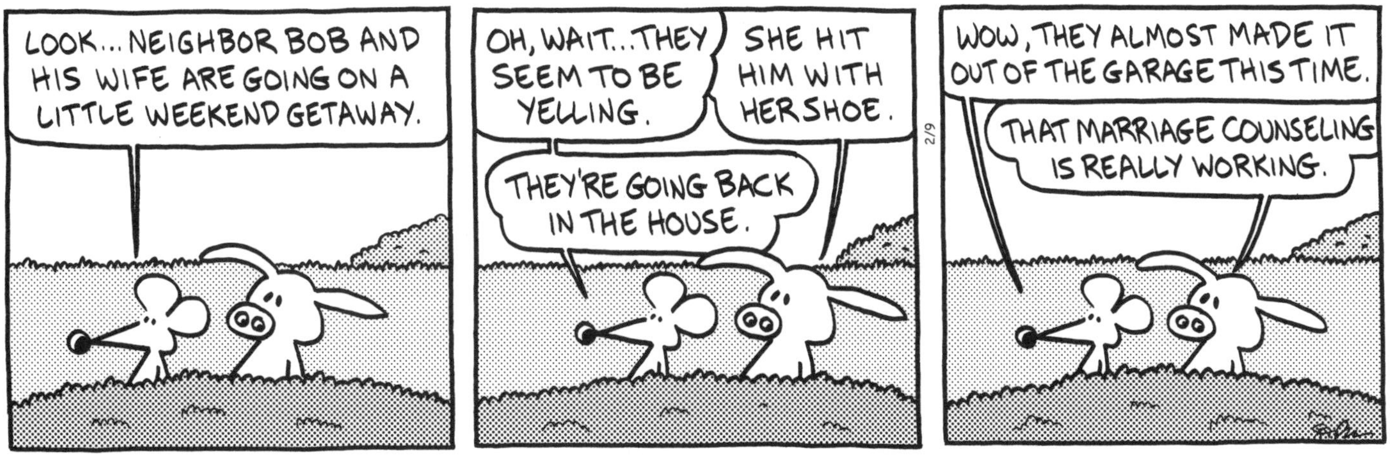
LOOK... NEIGHBOR BOB AND HIS WIFE ARE GOING ON A LITTLE WEEKEND GETAWAY.
OH, WAIT...THEY SEEM TO BE YELLING.
SHE HIT HIM WITH HER SHOE.
THEY'RE GOING BACK IN THE HOUSE.
WOW, THEY ALMOST MADE IT OUT OF THE GARAGE THIS TIME.
THAT MARRIAGE COUNSELING IS REALLY WORKING.

It's my theory that couples fight more on vacation than at any other time. Or so I've been told.

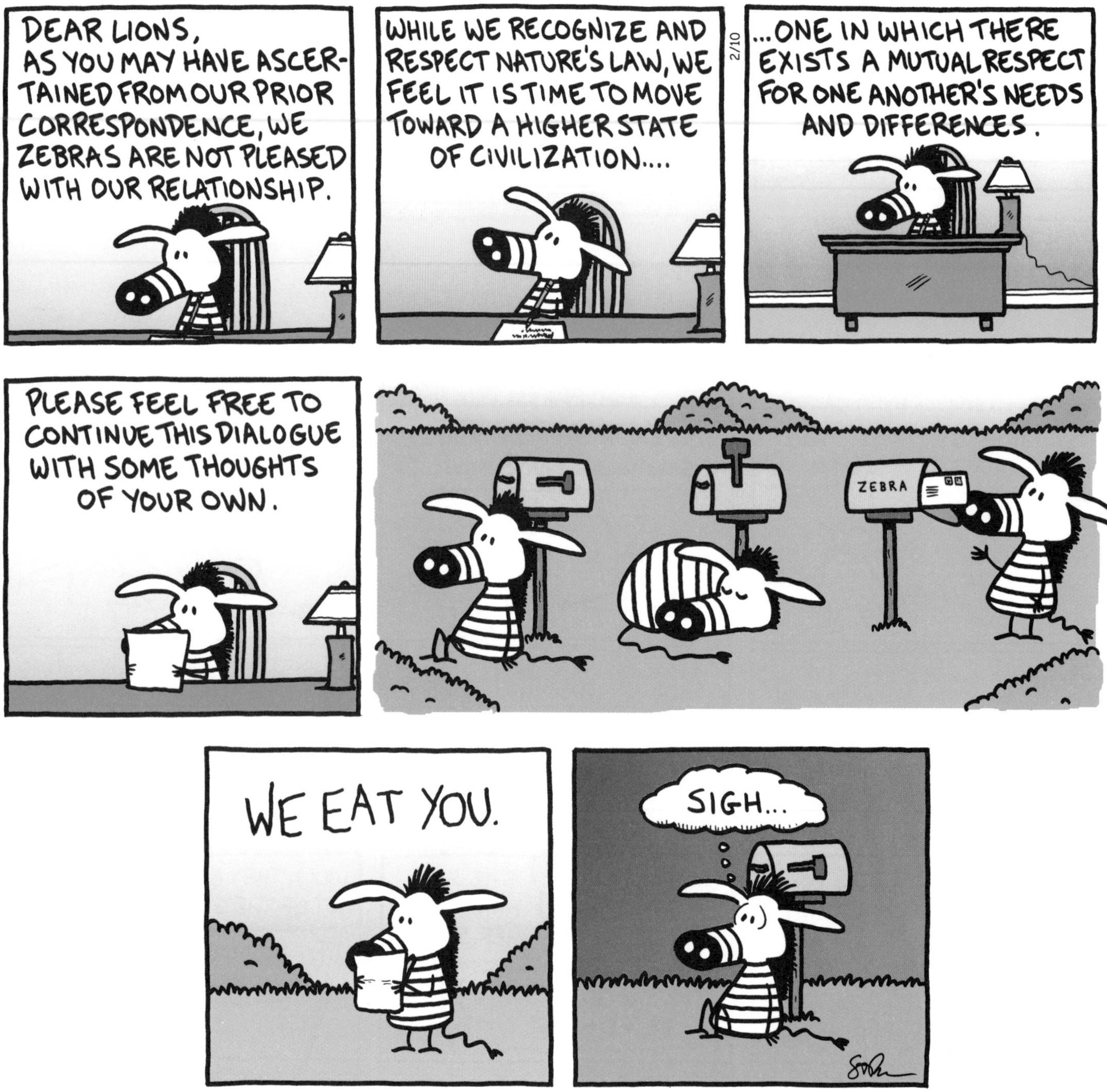
DEAR LIONS,
AS YOU MAY HAVE ASCERTAINED FROM OUR PRIOR CORRESPONDENCE, WE ZEBRAS ARE NOT PLEASED WITH OUR RELATIONSHIP.
WHILE WE RECOGNIZE AND RESPECT NATURE'S LAW, WE FEEL IT IS TIME TO MOVE TOWARD A HIGHER STATE OF CIVILIZATION....
2/10
...ONE IN WHICH THERE EXISTS A MUTUAL RESPECT FOR ONE ANOTHER'S NEEDS AND DIFFERENCES.
PLEASE FEEL FREE TO CONTINUE THIS DIALOGUE WITH SOME THOUGHTS OF YOUR OWN.
ZEBRA
WE EAT YOU.
SIGH...

This was one of the three or four most popular Sunday strips I've ever done, and it began the *Pearls* theme of having Zebra write letters to his tormentors.

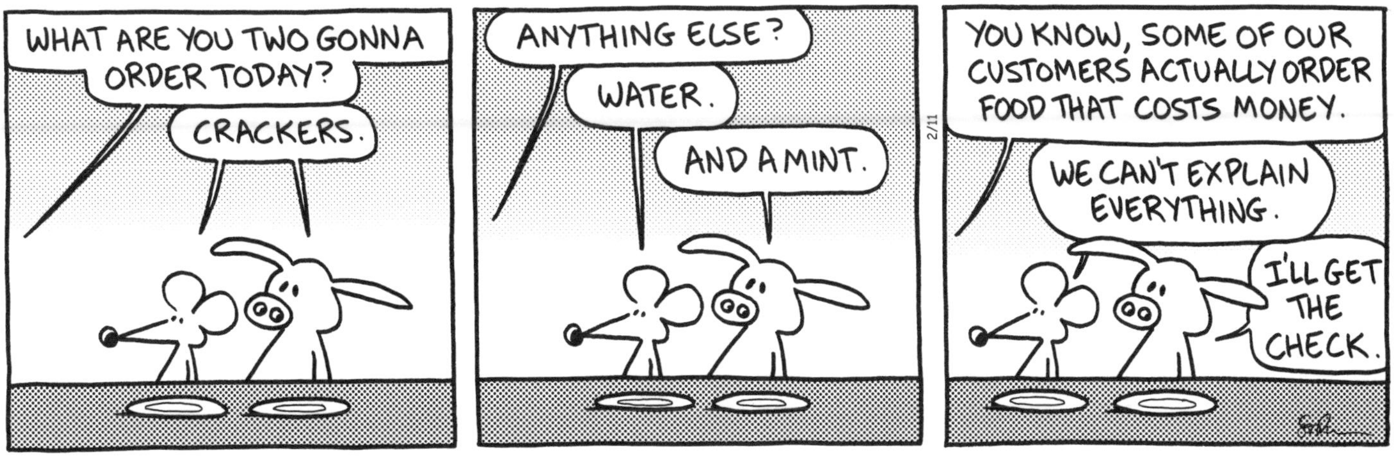
WHAT ARE YOU TWO GONNA ORDER TODAY?
CRACKERS.
ANYTHING ELSE?
WATER.
AND A MINT.
2/11
YOU KNOW, SOME OF OUR CUSTOMERS ACTUALLY ORDER FOOD THAT COSTS MONEY.
WE CAN'T EXPLAIN EVERYTHING.
I'LL GET THE CHECK.

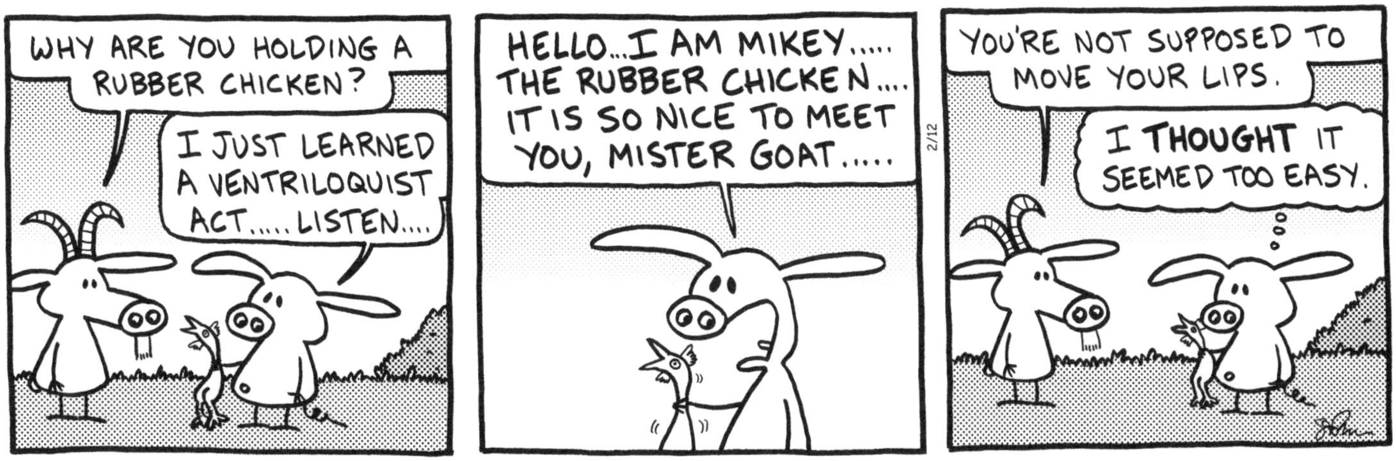
WHY ARE YOU HOLDING A RUBBER CHICKEN?
I JUST LEARNED A VENTRILOQUIST ACT..... LISTEN....
HELLO...I AM MIKEY..... THE RUBBER CHICKEN.... IT IS SO NICE TO MEET YOU, MISTER GOAT.....
2/12
YOU'RE NOT SUPPOSED TO MOVE YOUR LIPS.
I **THOUGHT** IT SEEMED TOO EASY.

This is one of the few instances where I've taken a suggestion from a reader. Someone wrote to say he was a member of some Rubber Chicken Club and would love to see a strip focusing on rubber chickens. It sounded like something that could be funny, and so I wrote the next four strips based on that theme. (Are there really Rubber Chicken Clubs?)

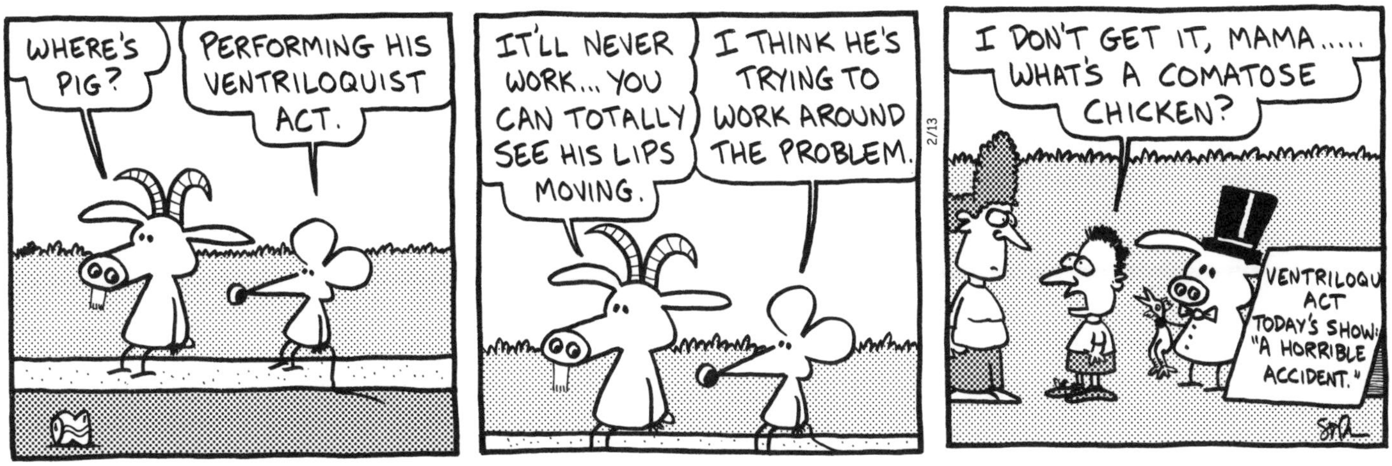
WHERE'S PIG?
PERFORMING HIS VENTRILOQUIST ACT.
IT'LL NEVER WORK... YOU CAN TOTALLY SEE HIS LIPS MOVING.
I THINK HE'S TRYING TO WORK AROUND THE PROBLEM.
2/13
I DON'T GET IT, MAMA..... WHAT'S A COMATOSE CHICKEN?
VENTRILOQU ACT TODAY'S SHOW: "A HORRIBLE ACCIDENT."

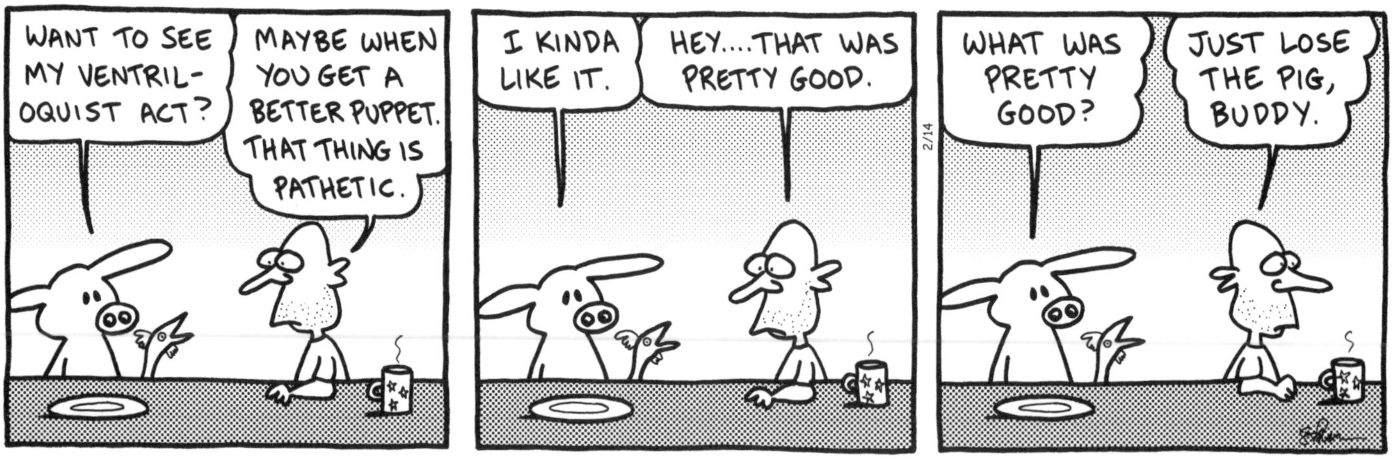
WANT TO SEE MY VENTRILOQUIST ACT?
MAYBE WHEN YOU GET A BETTER PUPPET. THAT THING IS PATHETIC.
I KINDA LIKE IT.
HEY....THAT WAS PRETTY GOOD.
2/14
WHAT WAS PRETTY GOOD?
JUST LOSE THE PIG, BUDDY.

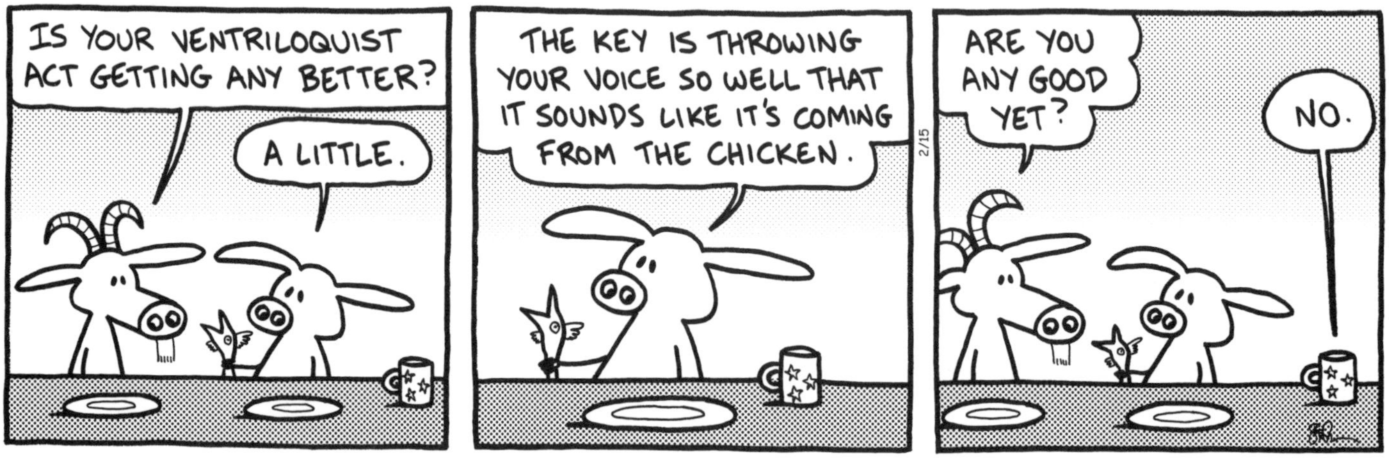
IS YOUR VENTRILOQUIST ACT GETTING ANY BETTER?
A LITTLE.
THE KEY IS THROWING YOUR VOICE SO WELL THAT IT SOUNDS LIKE IT'S COMING FROM THE CHICKEN.
2/15
ARE YOU ANY GOOD YET?
NO.

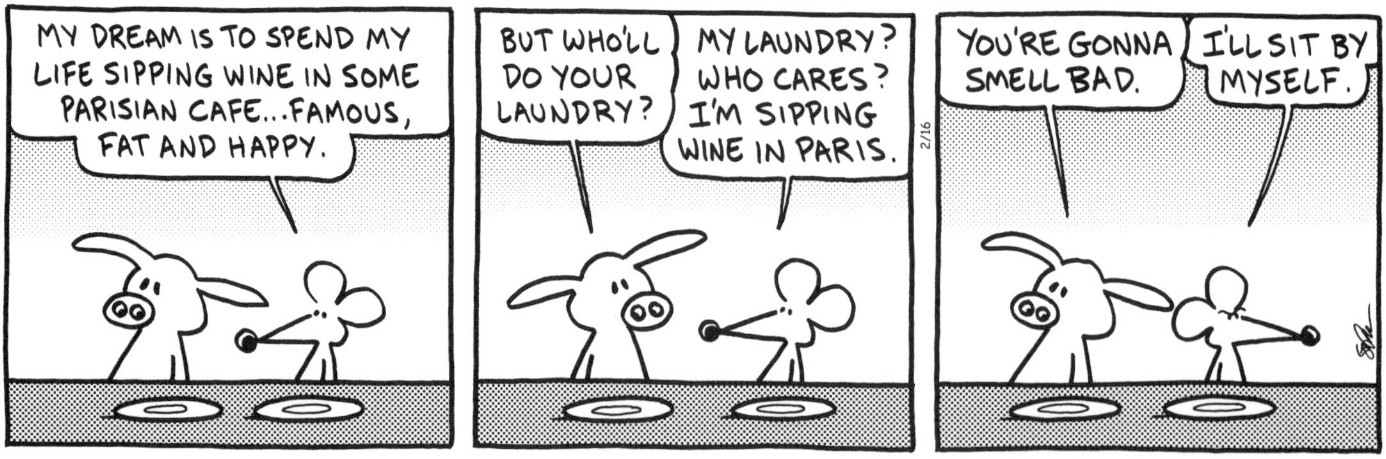
MY DREAM IS TO SPEND MY LIFE SIPPING WINE IN SOME PARISIAN CAFE...FAMOUS, FAT AND HAPPY.
BUT WHO'LL DO YOUR LAUNDRY?
MY LAUNDRY? WHO CARES? I'M SIPPING WINE IN PARIS.
2/16
YOU'RE GONNA SMELL BAD.
I'LL SIT BY MYSELF.

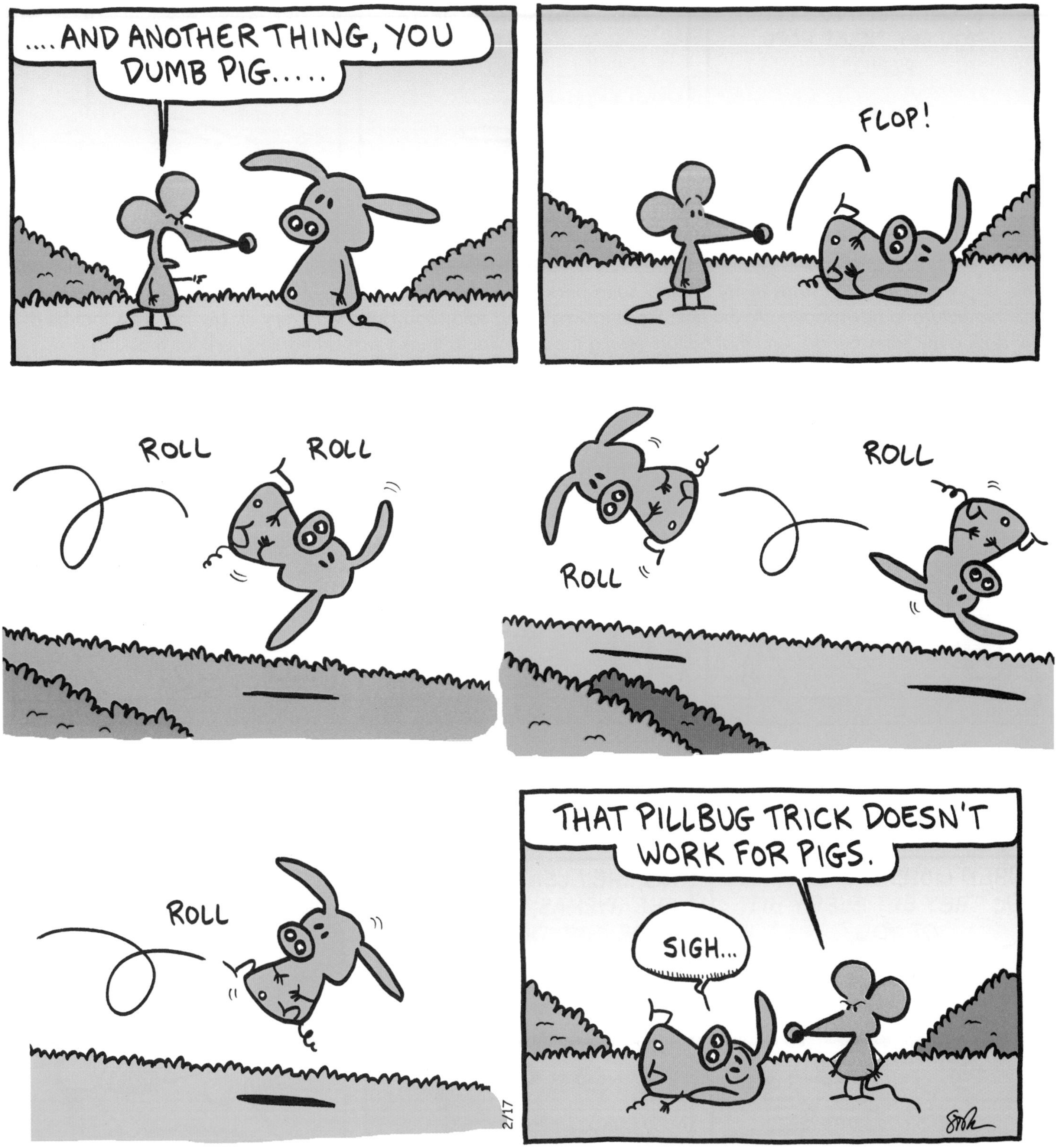
....AND ANOTHER THING, YOU DUMB PIG.....
FLOP!
ROLL
ROLL
ROLL
ROLL
ROLL
THAT PILLBUG TRICK DOESN'T WORK FOR PIGS.
SIGH...
2/17

This strip gave me my first experience with how regional some terms can be. Although I called these types of bugs "pill bugs," some people living in different parts of the country had never heard of "pill bugs." They use the term "roly poly" bugs. For clarity's sake, I suggest we all call them "pill bugs."

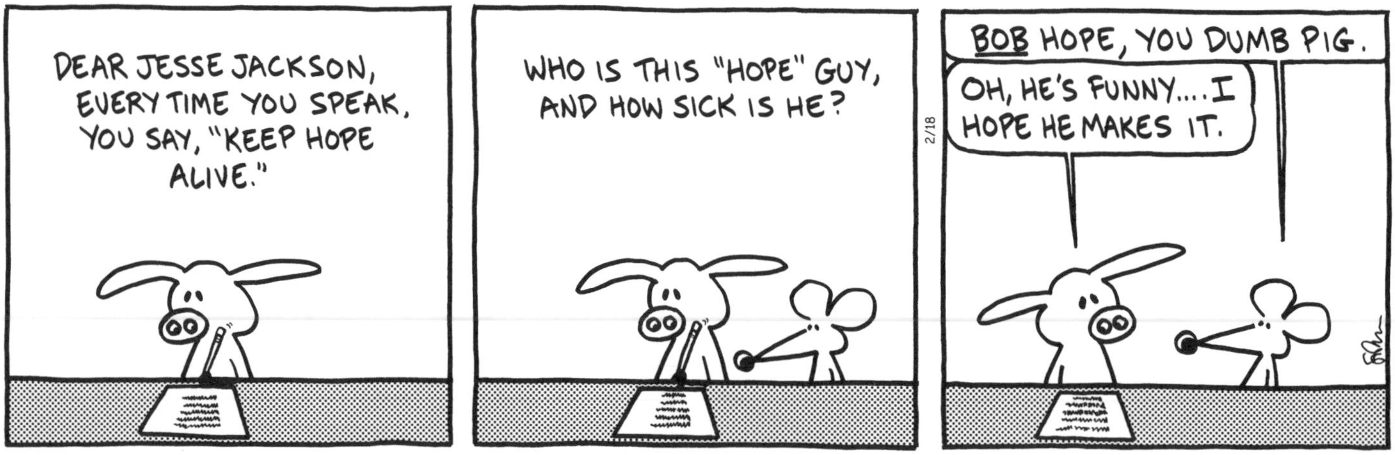
DEAR JESSE JACKSON, EVERY TIME YOU SPEAK, YOU SAY, "KEEP HOPE ALIVE."
WHO IS THIS "HOPE" GUY, AND HOW SICK IS HE?
2/18
BOB HOPE, YOU DUMB PIG.
OH, HE'S FUNNY.... I HOPE HE MAKES IT.

This strip was one of the strips in my original sales packet, which is an assembly of strips used by the syndicate to sell the feature to newspapers. At the time the strip was being sold, Bob Hope was very ill. My fear was that he'd die during my sales period, and that editors seeing the strip would think I was a heartless jerk for mocking a deceased man. Fortunately, he lived through the entire period of my sales launch, and for that, I owe him.

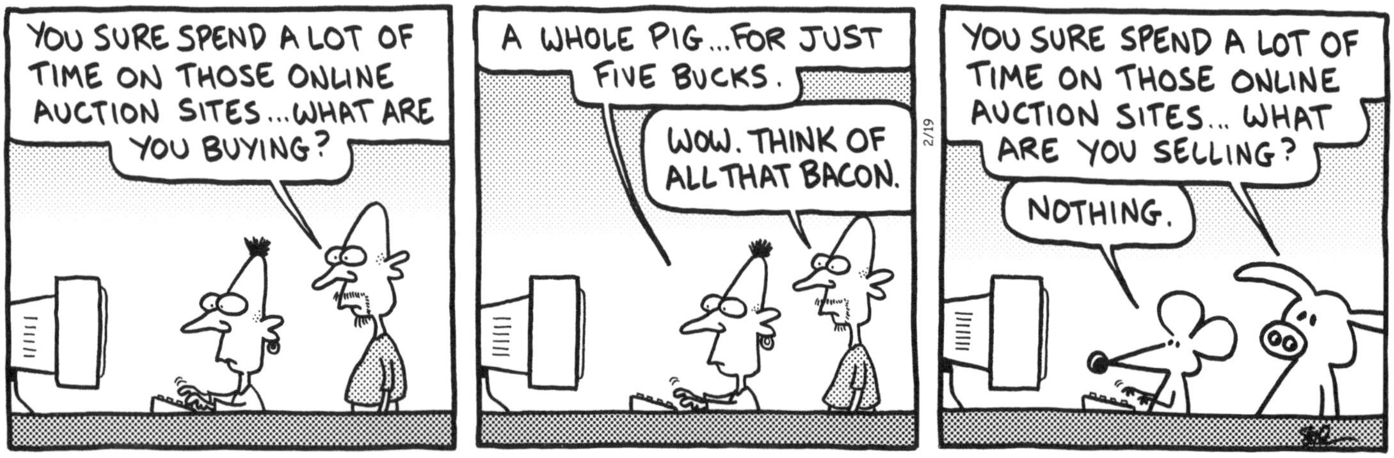
YOU SURE SPEND A LOT OF TIME ON THOSE ONLINE AUCTION SITES... WHAT ARE YOU BUYING?
A WHOLE PIG... FOR JUST FIVE BUCKS.
WOW. THINK OF ALL THAT BACON.
2/19
YOU SURE SPEND A LOT OF TIME ON THOSE ONLINE AUCTION SITES... WHAT ARE YOU SELLING?
NOTHING.

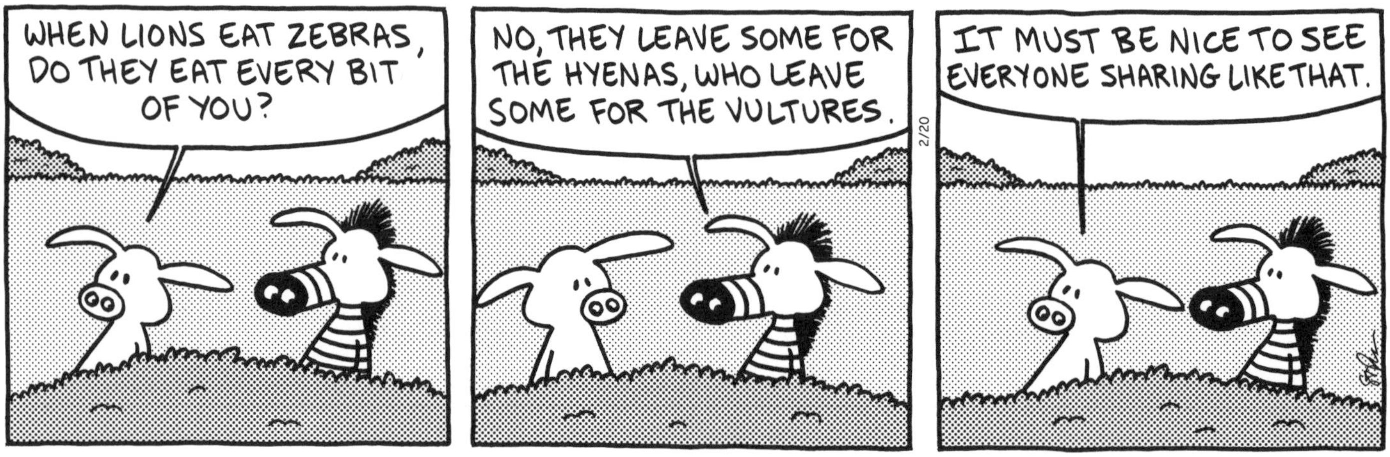
WHEN LIONS EAT ZEBRAS, DO THEY EAT EVERY BIT OF YOU?
NO, THEY LEAVE SOME FOR THE HYENAS, WHO LEAVE SOME FOR THE VULTURES.
2/20
IT MUST BE NICE TO SEE EVERYONE SHARING LIKE THAT.

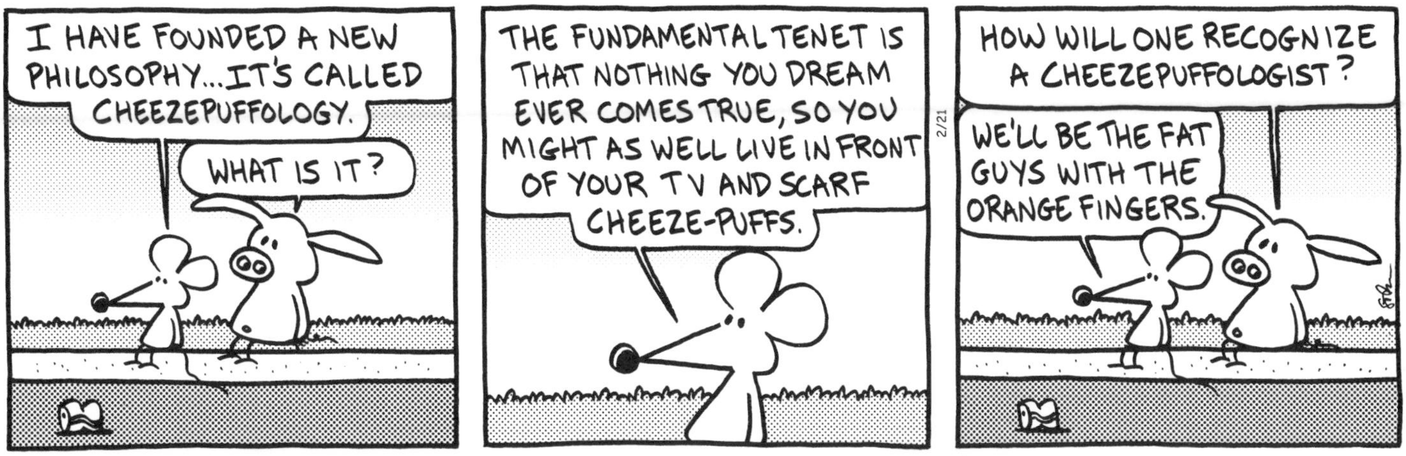
I HAVE FOUNDED A NEW PHILOSOPHY...IT'S CALLED CHEEZEPUFFOLOGY.
WHAT IS IT?
THE FUNDAMENTAL TENET IS THAT NOTHING YOU DREAM EVER COMES TRUE, SO YOU MIGHT AS WELL LIVE IN FRONT OF YOUR TV AND SCARF CHEEZE-PUFFS.
2/21
HOW WILL ONE RECOGNIZE A CHEEZEPUFFOLOGIST?
WE'LL BE THE FAT GUYS WITH THE ORANGE FINGERS.

I still have people writing to me from time to time saying that they're "cheesepuffologists."

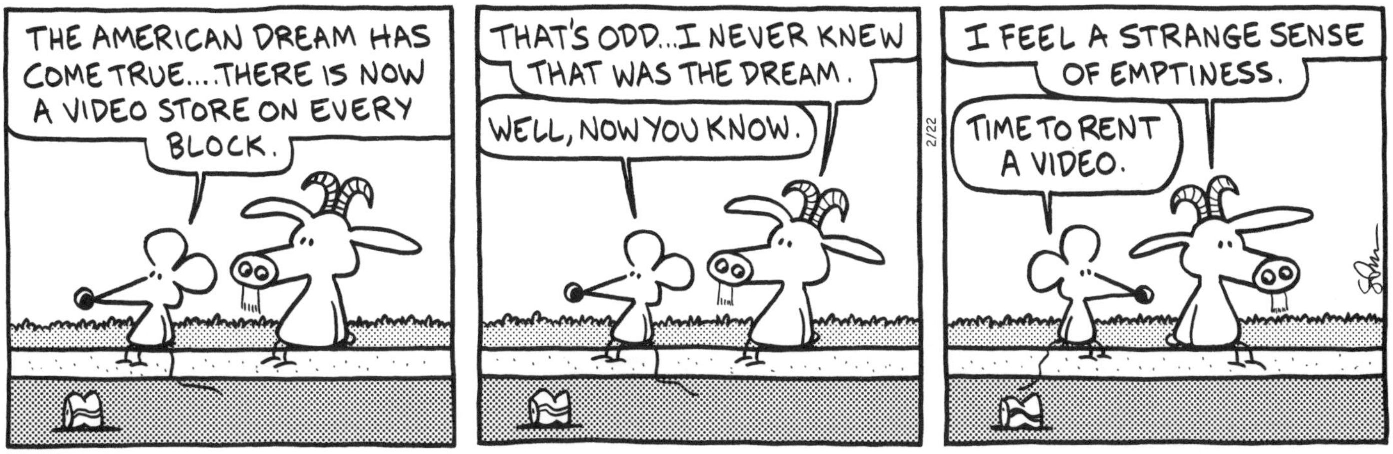
THE AMERICAN DREAM HAS COME TRUE....THERE IS NOW A VIDEO STORE ON EVERY BLOCK.
THAT'S ODD...I NEVER KNEW THAT WAS THE DREAM.
WELL, NOW YOU KNOW.
2/22
I FEEL A STRANGE SENSE OF EMPTINESS.
TIME TO RENT A VIDEO.

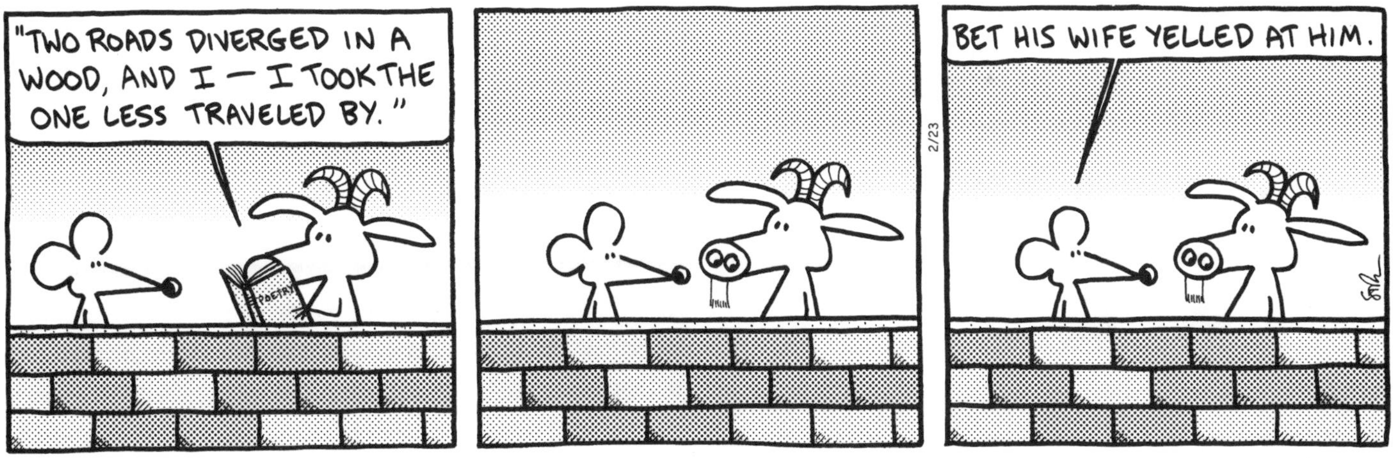
"TWO ROADS DIVERGED IN A WOOD, AND I — I TOOK THE ONE LESS TRAVELED BY."
2/23
BET HIS WIFE YELLED AT HIM.

Readers occasionally ask me why I'm so cynical about marriage. The odd part is that I don't think I'm cynical. I prefer the term "realistic."

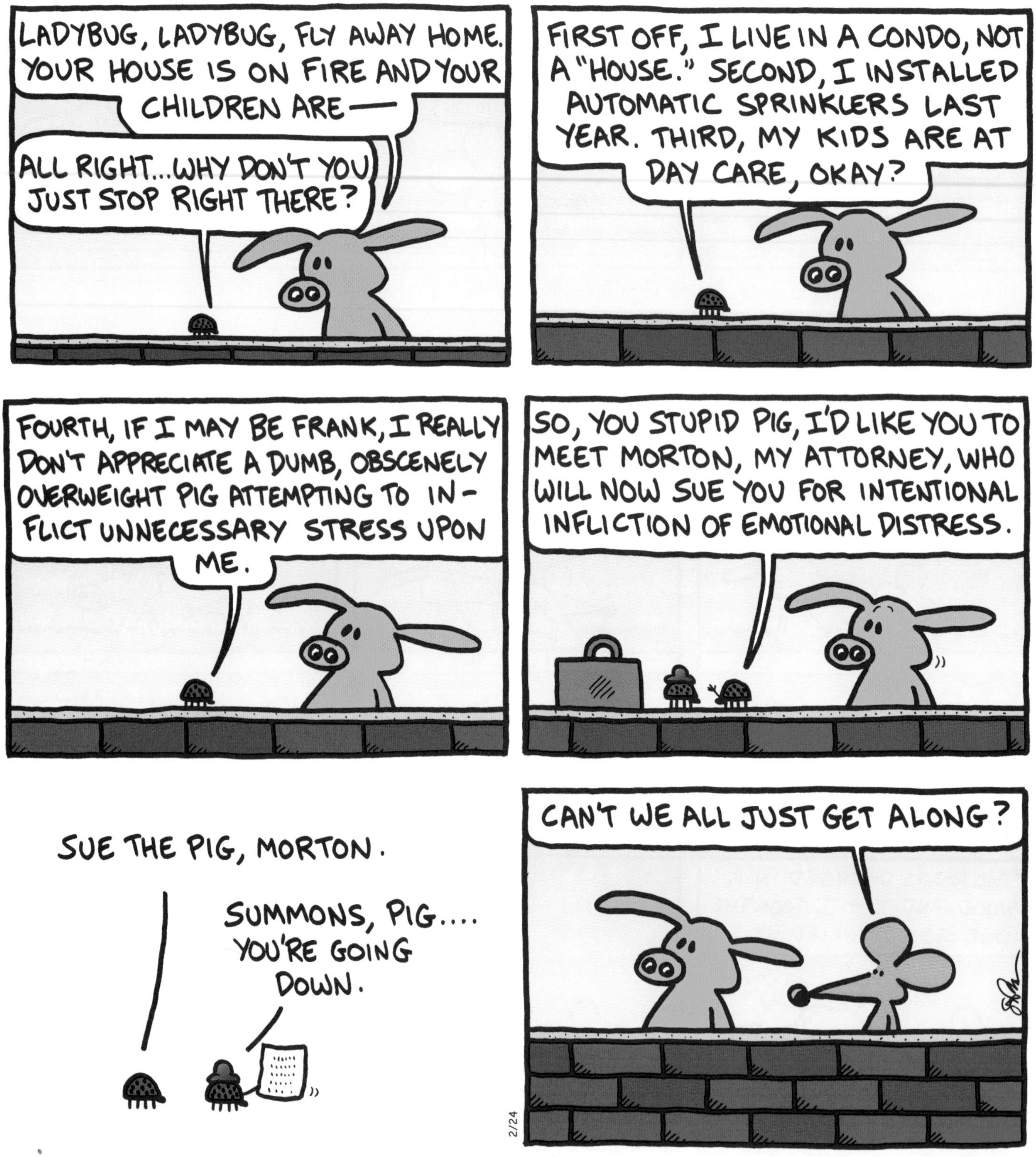
LADYBUG, LADYBUG, FLY AWAY HOME. YOUR HOUSE IS ON FIRE AND YOUR CHILDREN ARE—
ALL RIGHT...WHY DON'T YOU JUST STOP RIGHT THERE?
FIRST OFF, I LIVE IN A CONDO, NOT A "HOUSE." SECOND, I INSTALLED AUTOMATIC SPRINKLERS LAST YEAR. THIRD, MY KIDS ARE AT DAY CARE, OKAY?
FOURTH, IF I MAY BE FRANK, I REALLY DON'T APPRECIATE A DUMB, OBSCENELY OVERWEIGHT PIG ATTEMPTING TO IN-FLICT UNNECESSARY STRESS UPON ME.
SO, YOU STUPID PIG, I'D LIKE YOU TO MEET MORTON, MY ATTORNEY, WHO WILL NOW SUE YOU FOR INTENTIONAL INFLICTION OF EMOTIONAL DISTRESS.
SUE THE PIG, MORTON.
SUMMONS, PIG.... YOU'RE GOING DOWN.
CAN'T WE ALL JUST GET ALONG?
2/24

As most readers know, I was a lawyer for nine years before becoming a cartoonist. Although I don't do a lot of strips about it, it does come up occasionally.

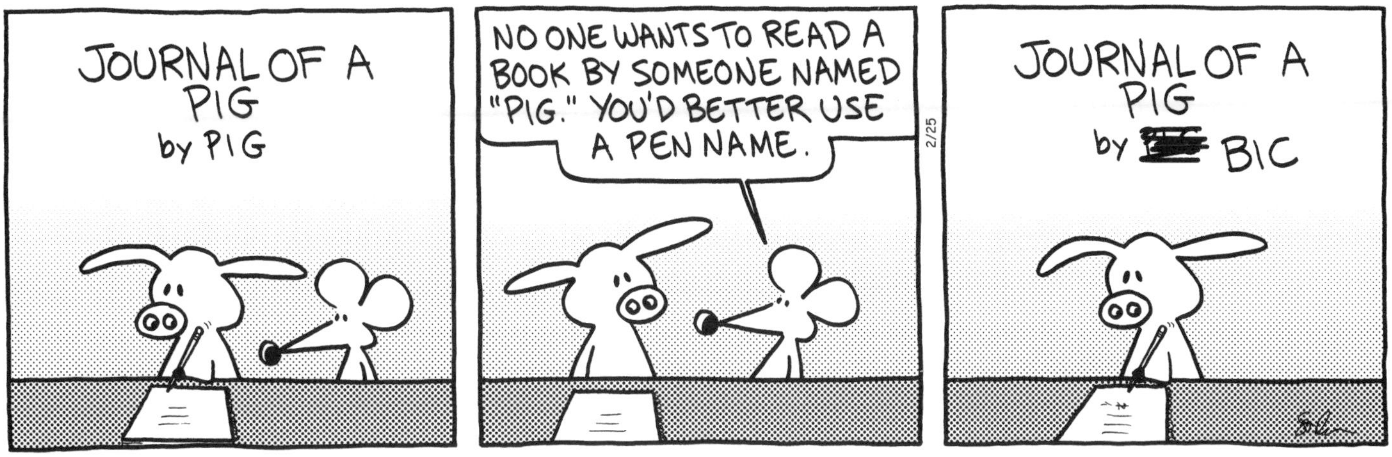
JOURNAL OF A PIG by PIG
NO ONE WANTS TO READ A BOOK BY SOMEONE NAMED "PIG." YOU'D BETTER USE A PEN NAME.
2/25
JOURNAL OF A PIG by BIC

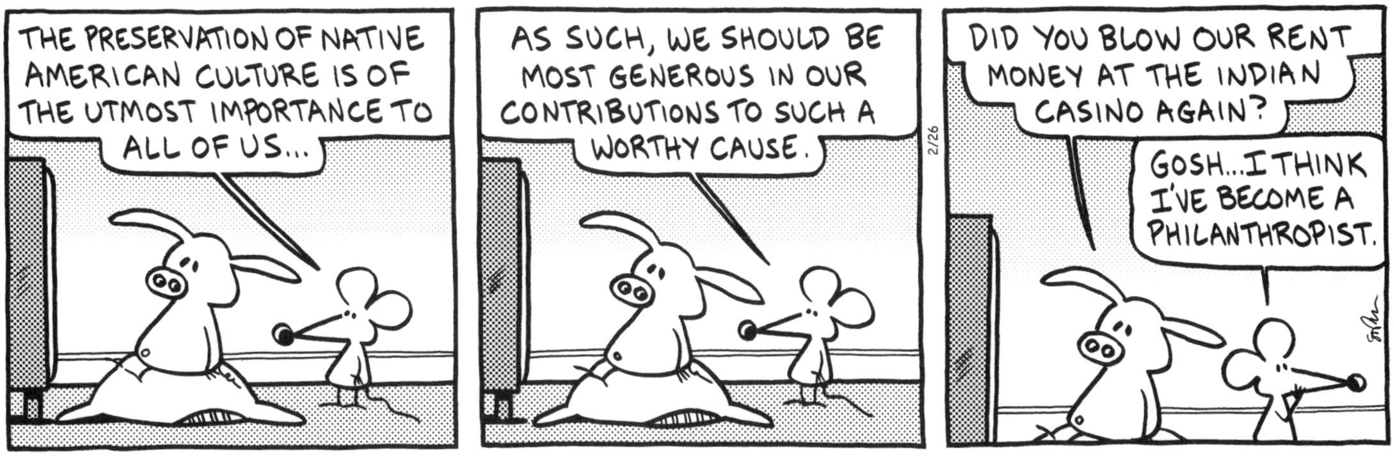
THE PRESERVATION OF NATIVE AMERICAN CULTURE IS OF THE UTMOST IMPORTANCE TO ALL OF US...
AS SUCH, WE SHOULD BE MOST GENEROUS IN OUR CONTRIBUTIONS TO SUCH A WORTHY CAUSE.
2/26
DID YOU BLOW OUR RENT MONEY AT THE INDIAN CASINO AGAIN?
GOSH...I THINK I'VE BECOME A PHILANTHROPIST.

All of my strips are reviewed by my editor at the syndicate. In this case, my editor and I went round and round on whether or not we should be saying “Native American” casino in that last panel. I just thought it sounded too stilted, and if a term is stilted, it can really break the rhythm of the joke, so we chose “Indian.”

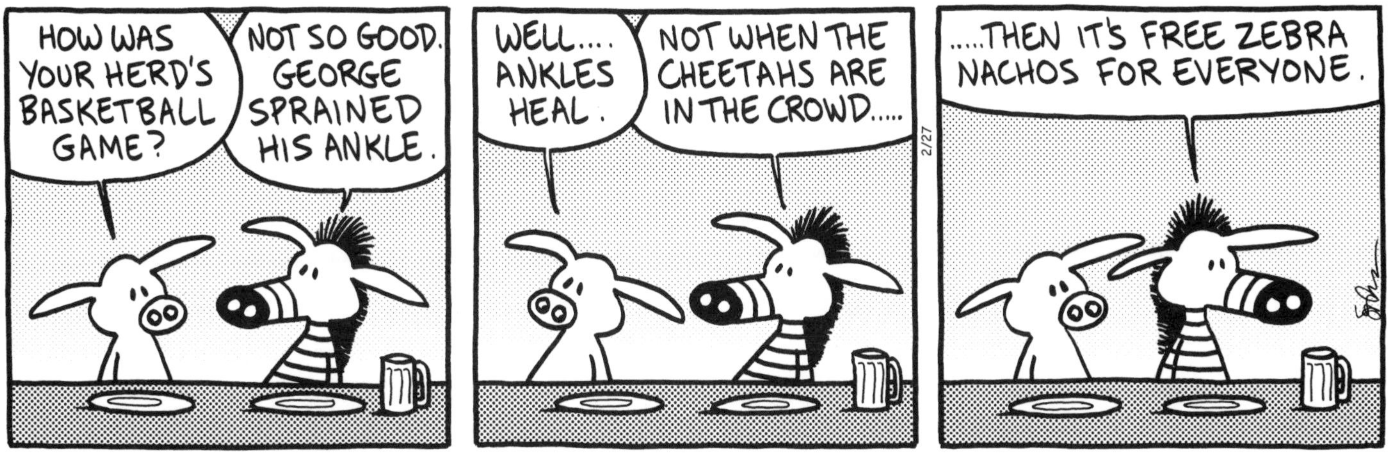
HOW WAS YOUR HERD'S BASKETBALL GAME?
NOT SO GOOD. GEORGE SPRAINED HIS ANKLE.
WELL.... ANKLES HEAL.
NOT WHEN THE CHEETAHS ARE IN THE CROWD.....
2/27
.....THEN IT'S FREE ZEBRA NACHOS FOR EVERYONE.

I’ve always wondered what Zebra nachos would taste like. They might not be that bad.

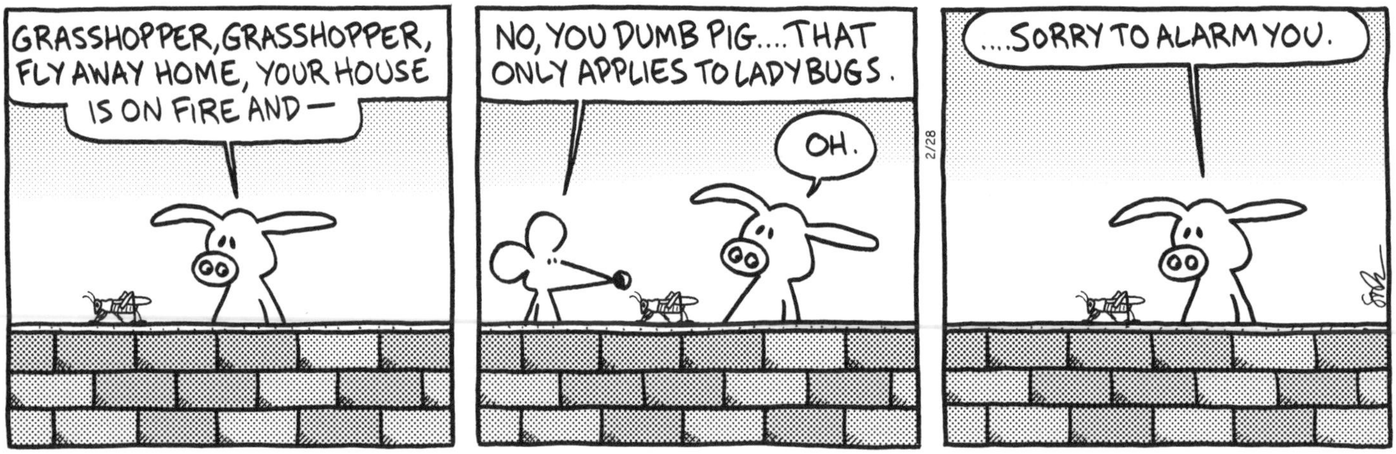
GRASSHOPPER, GRASSHOPPER, FLY AWAY HOME, YOUR HOUSE IS ON FIRE AND—
NO, YOU DUMB PIG....THAT ONLY APPLIES TO LADYBUGS.
OH.
2/28
....SORRY TO ALARM YOU.

I was so proud of how well I drew that grasshopper in the first panel that I cut and pasted it into the next five panels.

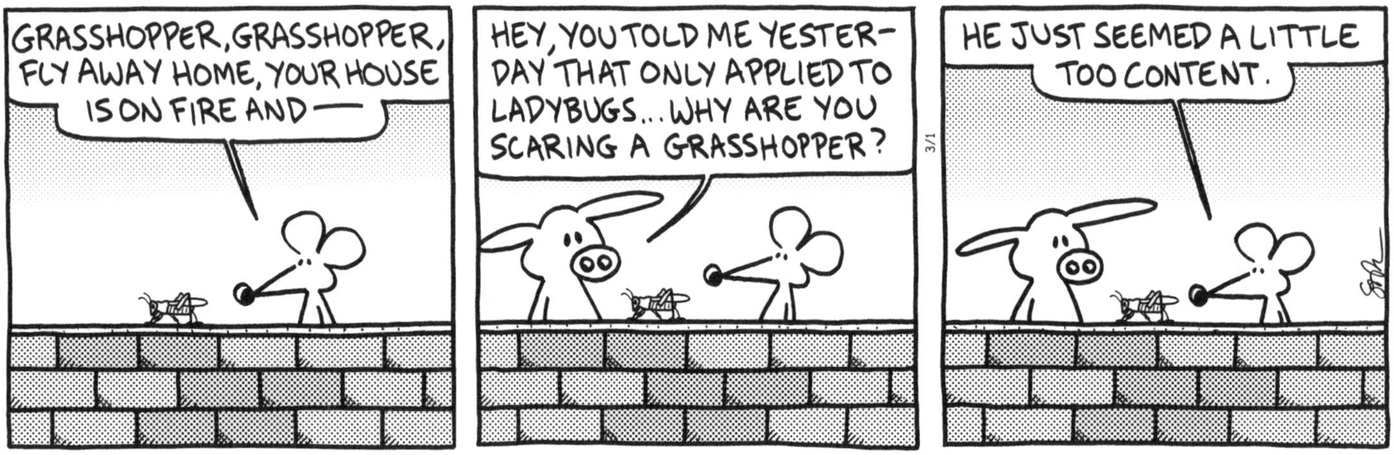
GRASSHOPPER, GRASSHOPPER, FLY AWAY HOME, YOUR HOUSE IS ON FIRE AND—
HEY, YOU TOLD ME YESTERDAY THAT ONLY APPLIED TO LADYBUGS... WHY ARE YOU SCARING A GRASSHOPPER?
3/1
HE JUST SEEMED A LITTLE TOO CONTENT.

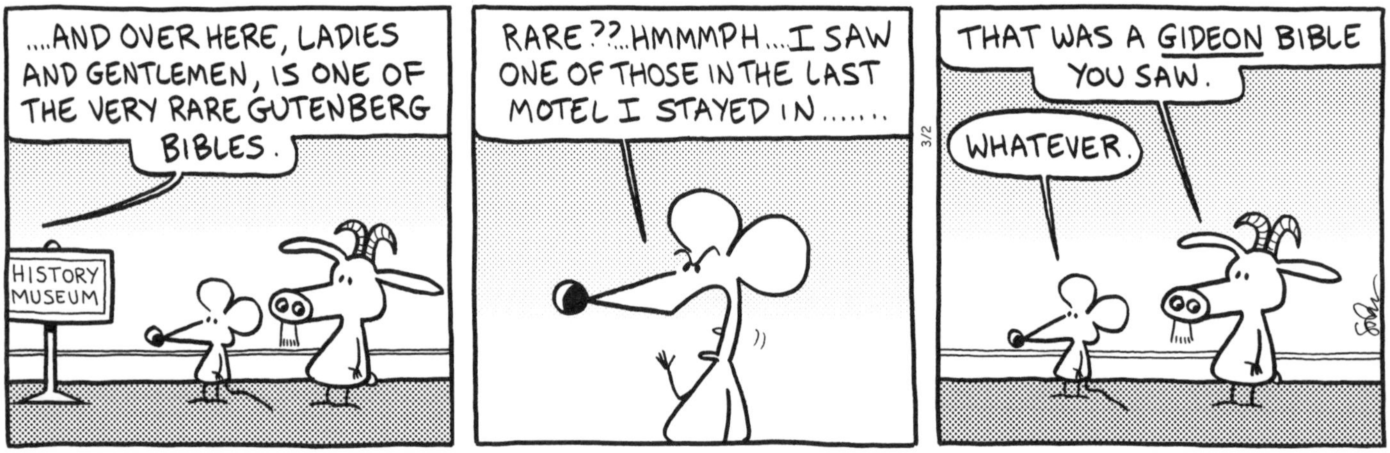
....AND OVER HERE, LADIES AND GENTLEMEN, IS ONE OF THE VERY RARE GUTENBERG BIBLES.
HISTORY MUSEUM
RARE??...HMMMPH....I SAW ONE OF THOSE IN THE LAST MOTEL I STAYED IN.......
3/2
THAT WAS A GIDEON BIBLE YOU SAW.
WHATEVER.

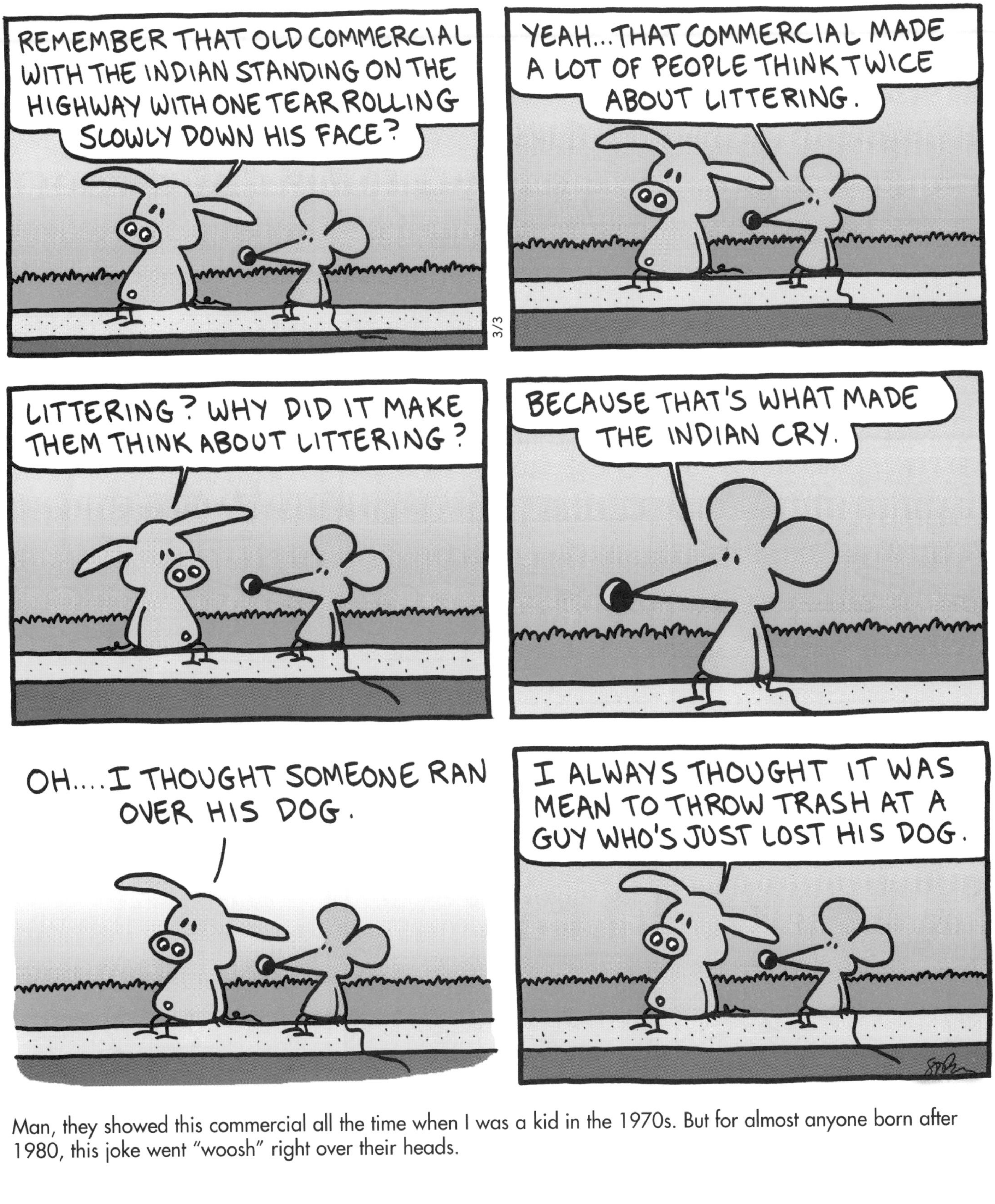
REMEMBER THAT OLD COMMERCIAL WITH THE INDIAN STANDING ON THE HIGHWAY WITH ONE TEAR ROLLING SLOWLY DOWN HIS FACE?
YEAH...THAT COMMERCIAL MADE A LOT OF PEOPLE THINK TWICE ABOUT LITTERING.
3/3
LITTERING? WHY DID IT MAKE THEM THINK ABOUT LITTERING?
BECAUSE THAT'S WHAT MADE THE INDIAN CRY.
OH....I THOUGHT SOMEONE RAN OVER HIS DOG.
I ALWAYS THOUGHT IT WAS MEAN TO THROW TRASH AT A GUY WHO'S JUST LOST HIS DOG.

Man, they showed this commercial all the time when I was a kid in the 1970s. But for almost anyone born after 1980, this joke went "woosh" right over their heads.

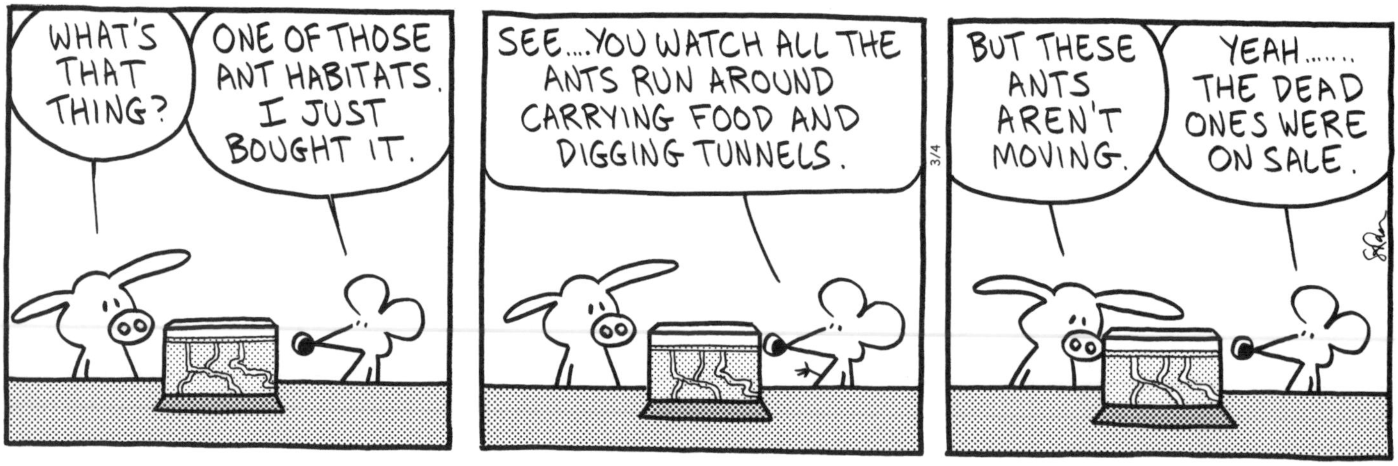
WHAT'S THAT THING?
ONE OF THOSE ANT HABITATS. I JUST BOUGHT IT.
SEE....YOU WATCH ALL THE ANTS RUN AROUND CARRYING FOOD AND DIGGING TUNNELS.
3/4
BUT THESE ANTS AREN'T MOVING.
YEAH...... THE DEAD ONES WERE ON SALE.

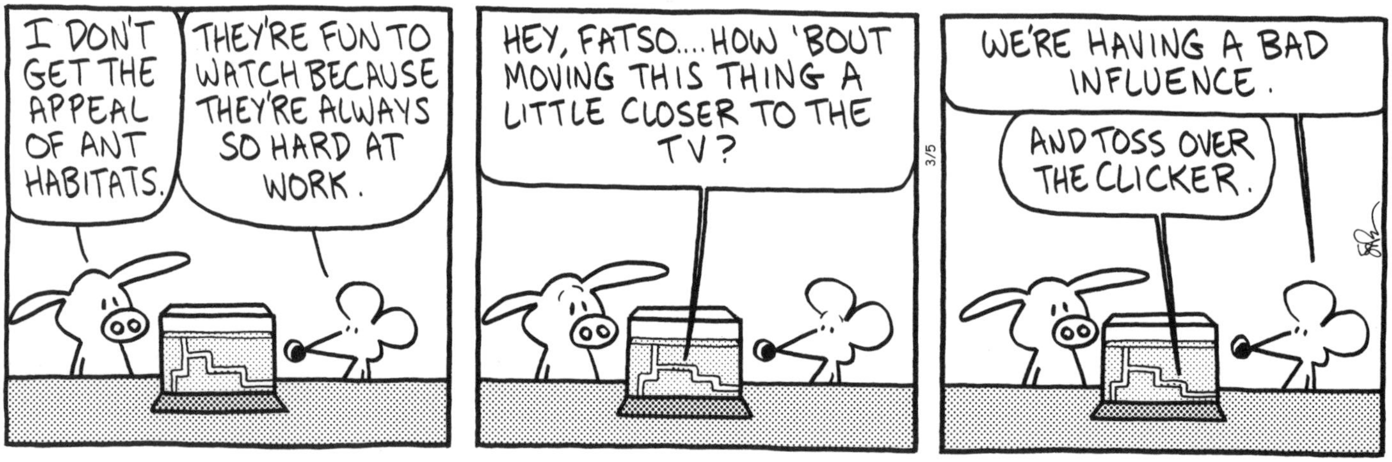
I DON'T GET THE APPEAL OF ANT HABITATS.
THEY'RE FUN TO WATCH BECAUSE THEY'RE ALWAYS SO HARD AT WORK.
HEY, FATSO.... HOW 'BOUT MOVING THIS THING A LITTLE CLOSER TO THE TV?
3/5
WE'RE HAVING A BAD INFLUENCE.
AND TOSS OVER THE CLICKER.

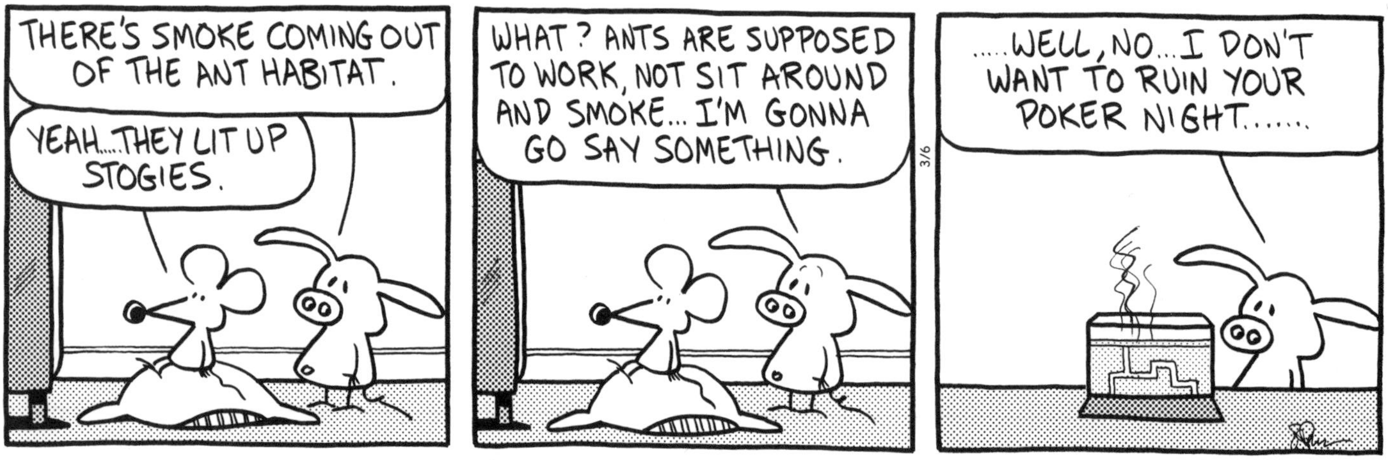
THERE'S SMOKE COMING OUT OF THE ANT HABITAT.
YEAH....THEY LIT UP STOGIES.
WHAT? ANTS ARE SUPPOSED TO WORK, NOT SIT AROUND AND SMOKE... I'M GONNA GO SAY SOMETHING.
3/6
.....WELL, NO... I DON'T WANT TO RUIN YOUR POKER NIGHT......

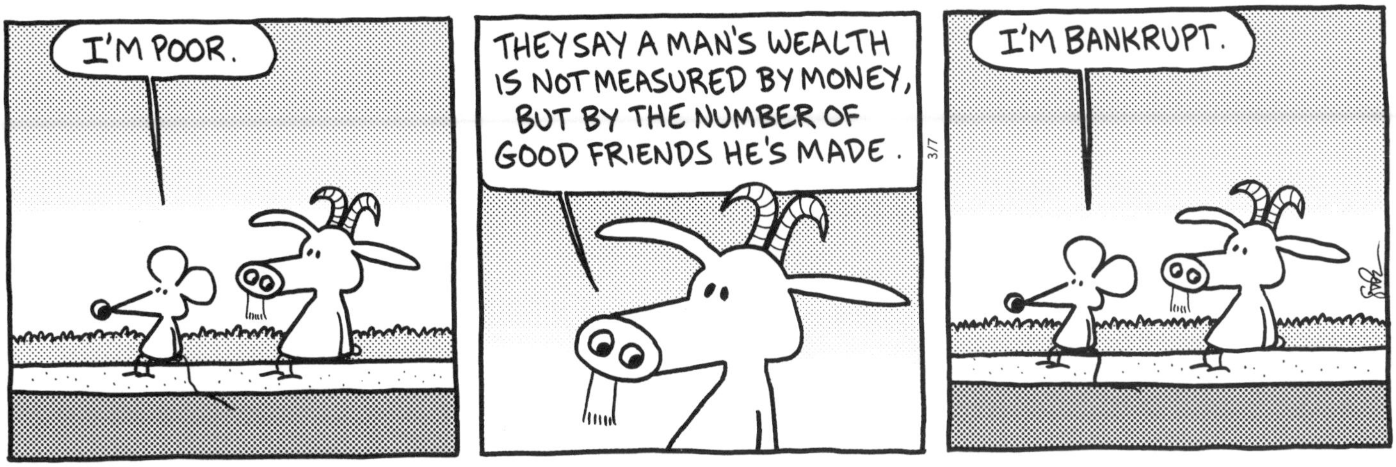
I'M POOR.
THEY SAY A MAN'S WEALTH IS NOT MEASURED BY MONEY, BUT BY THE NUMBER OF GOOD FRIENDS HE'S MADE.
3/7
I'M BANKRUPT.

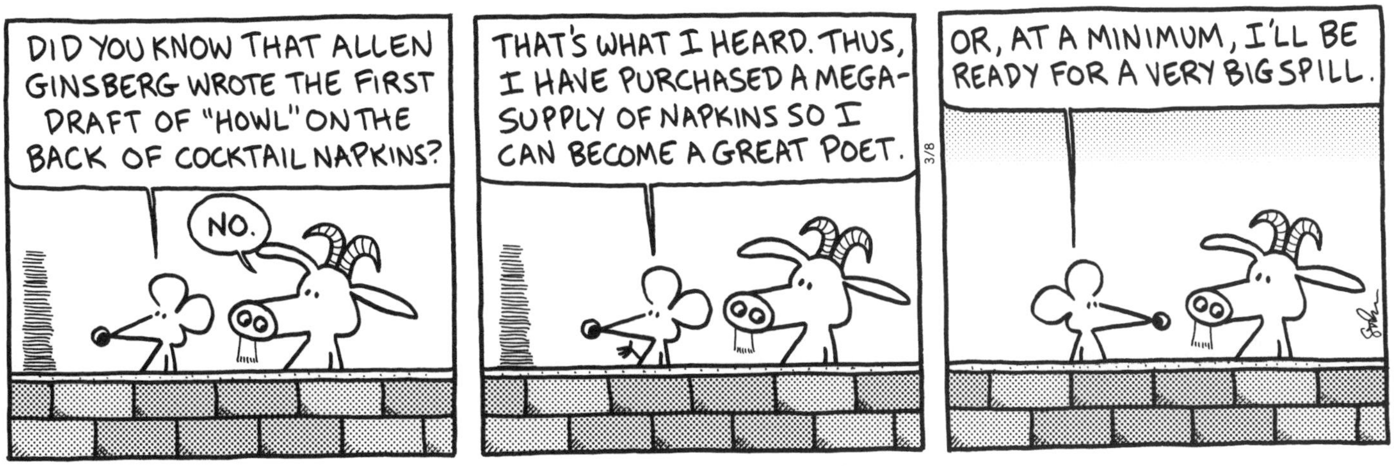
DID YOU KNOW THAT ALLEN GINSBERG WROTE THE FIRST DRAFT OF "HOWL" ON THE BACK OF COCKTAIL NAPKINS?
NO.
THAT'S WHAT I HEARD. THUS, I HAVE PURCHASED A MEGA-SUPPLY OF NAPKINS SO I CAN BECOME A GREAT POET.
3/8
OR, AT A MINIMUM, I'LL BE READY FOR A VERY BIG SPILL.

For a guy who's not too keen on poetry, I sure seem to reference it a lot.

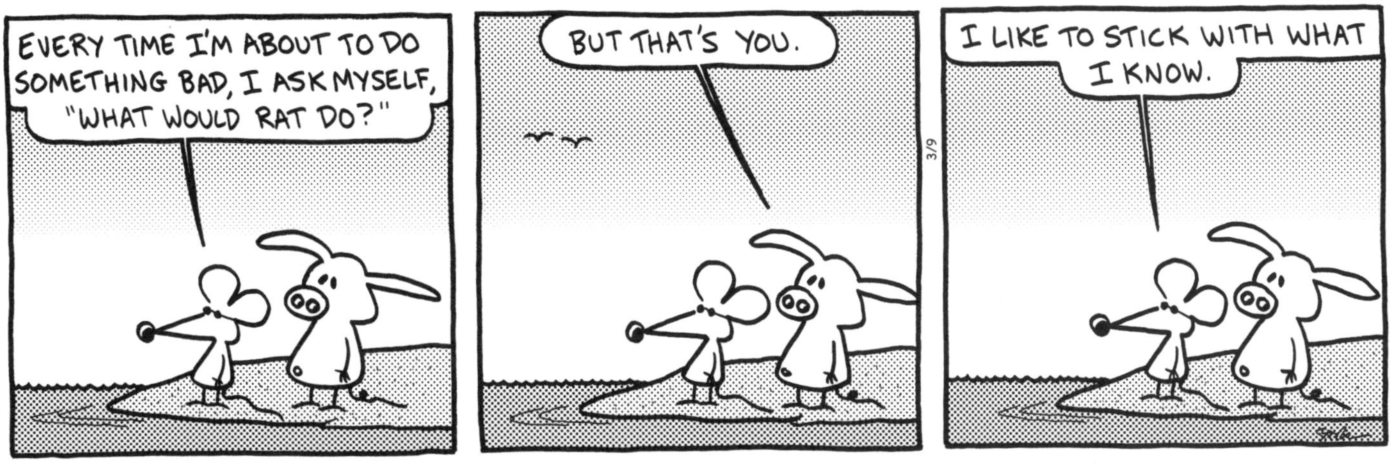
EVERY TIME I'M ABOUT TO DO SOMETHING BAD, I ASK MYSELF, "WHAT WOULD RAT DO?"
BUT THAT'S YOU.
3/9
I LIKE TO STICK WITH WHAT I KNOW.

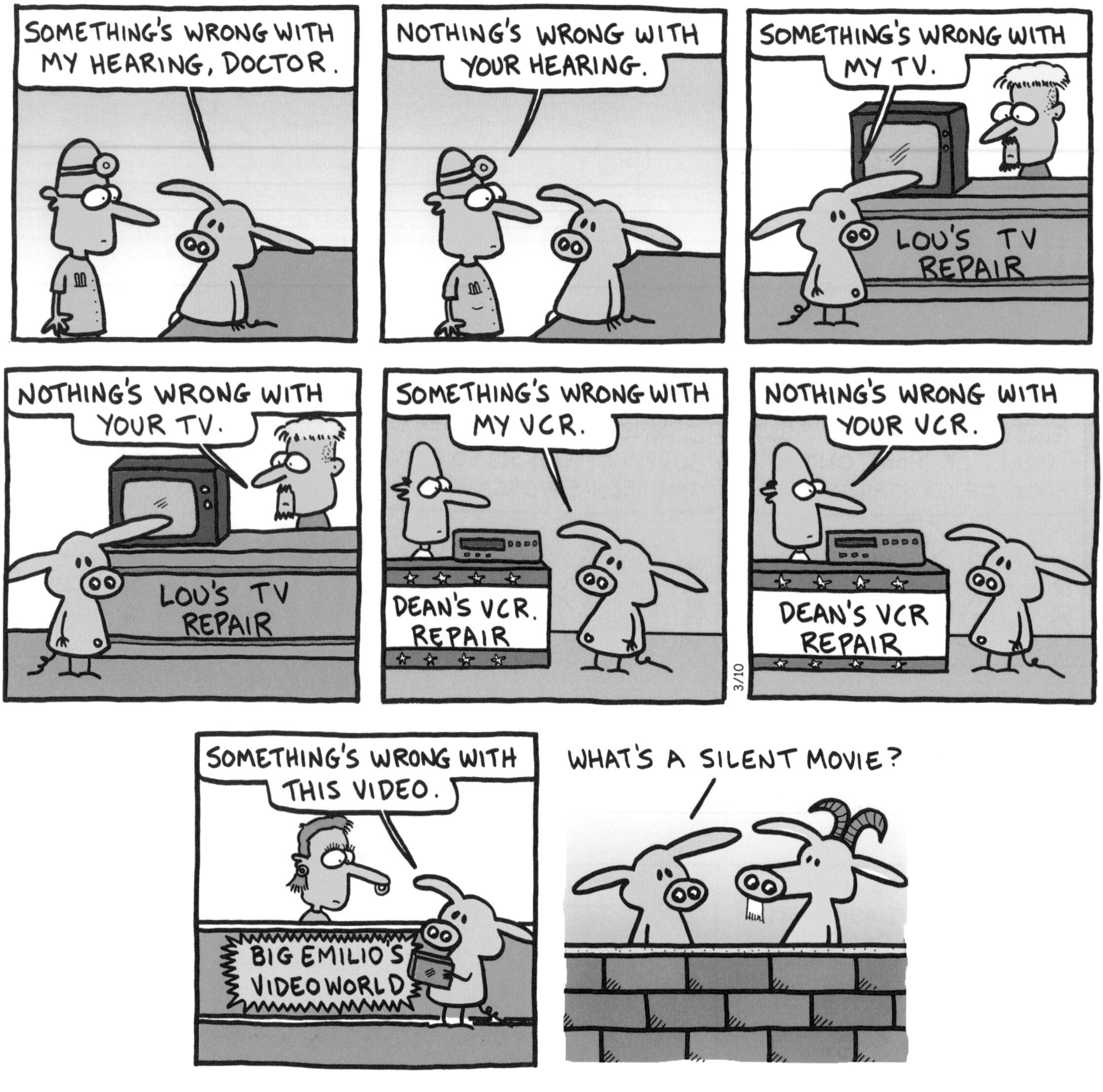
SOMETHING'S WRONG WITH MY HEARING, DOCTOR.
NOTHING'S WRONG WITH YOUR HEARING.
SOMETHING'S WRONG WITH MY TV.
LOU'S TV REPAIR
NOTHING'S WRONG WITH YOUR TV.
LOU'S TV REPAIR
SOMETHING'S WRONG WITH MY VCR.
DEAN'S VCR. REPAIR
NOTHING'S WRONG WITH YOUR VCR.
DEAN'S VCR REPAIR
3/10
SOMETHING'S WRONG WITH THIS VIDEO.
BIG EMILIO'S VIDEO WORLD
WHAT'S A SILENT MOVIE?

Dean and Louis are my cousins. Emilio is one of my closest friends. Hence, the names on the signs.

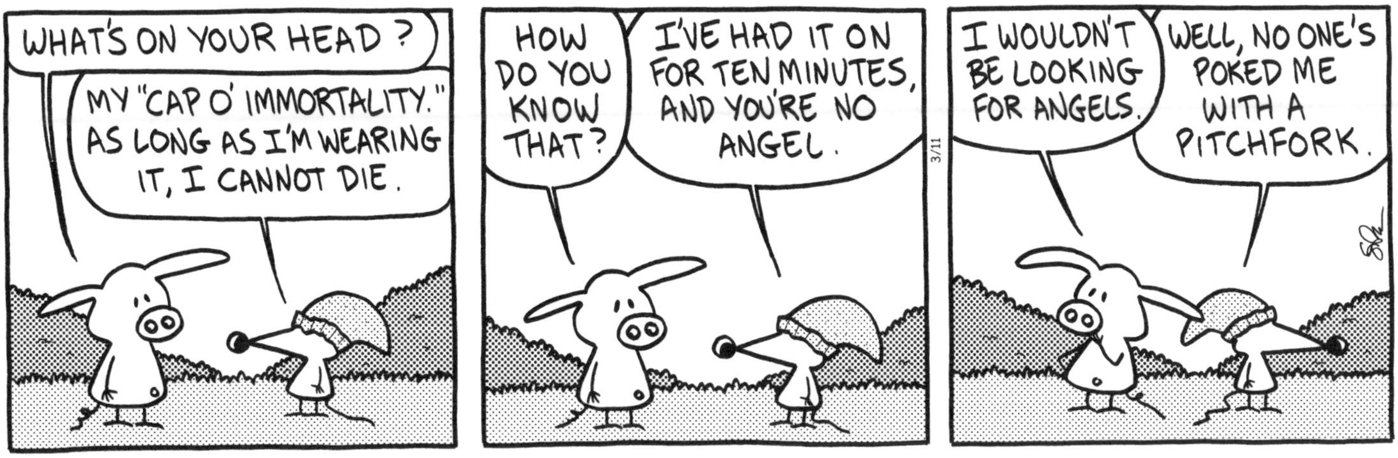
WHAT'S ON YOUR HEAD ?
MY "CAP O' IMMORTALITY." AS LONG AS I'M WEARING IT, I CANNOT DIE.
HOW DO YOU KNOW THAT ?
I'VE HAD IT ON FOR TEN MINUTES, AND YOU'RE NO ANGEL.
3/11
I WOULDN'T BE LOOKING FOR ANGELS.
WELL, NO ONE'S POKED ME WITH A PITCHFORK.

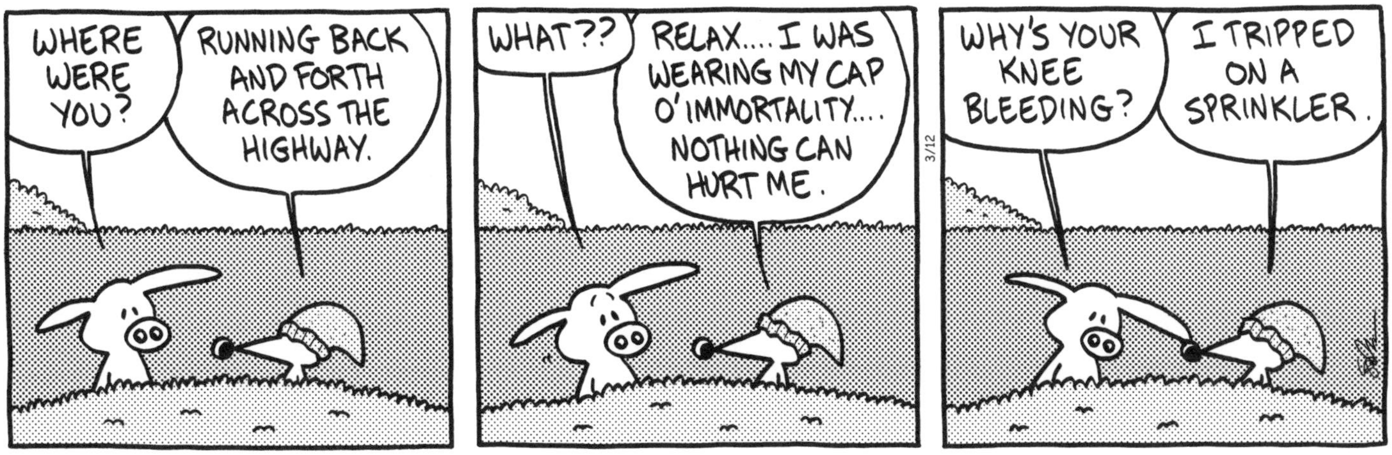
WHERE WERE YOU ?
RUNNING BACK AND FORTH ACROSS THE HIGHWAY.
WHAT??
RELAX.... I WAS WEARING MY CAP O' IMMORTALITY.... NOTHING CAN HURT ME.
3/12
WHY'S YOUR KNEE BLEEDING ?
I TRIPPED ON A SPRINKLER.

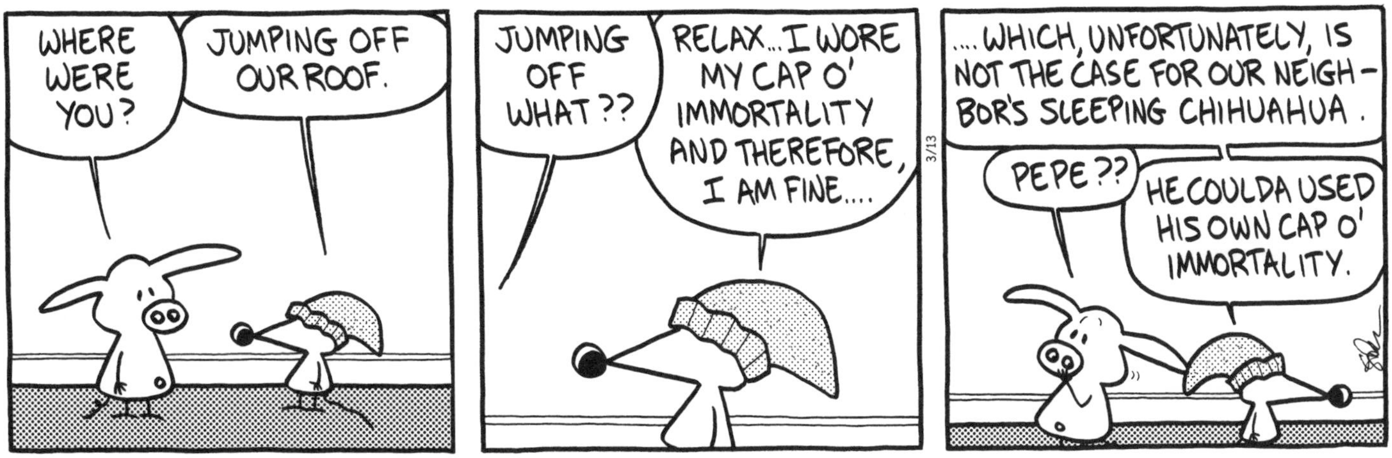
WHERE WERE YOU ?
JUMPING OFF OUR ROOF.
JUMPING OFF WHAT ??
RELAX... I WORE MY CAP O' IMMORTALITY AND THEREFORE, I AM FINE....
3/13
.... WHICH, UNFORTUNATELY, IS NOT THE CASE FOR OUR NEIGH-BOR'S SLEEPING CHIHUAHUA.
PEPE ??
HE COULDA USED HIS OWN CAP O' IMMORTALITY.

Squishing fictional Chihuahuas = instant comedy.

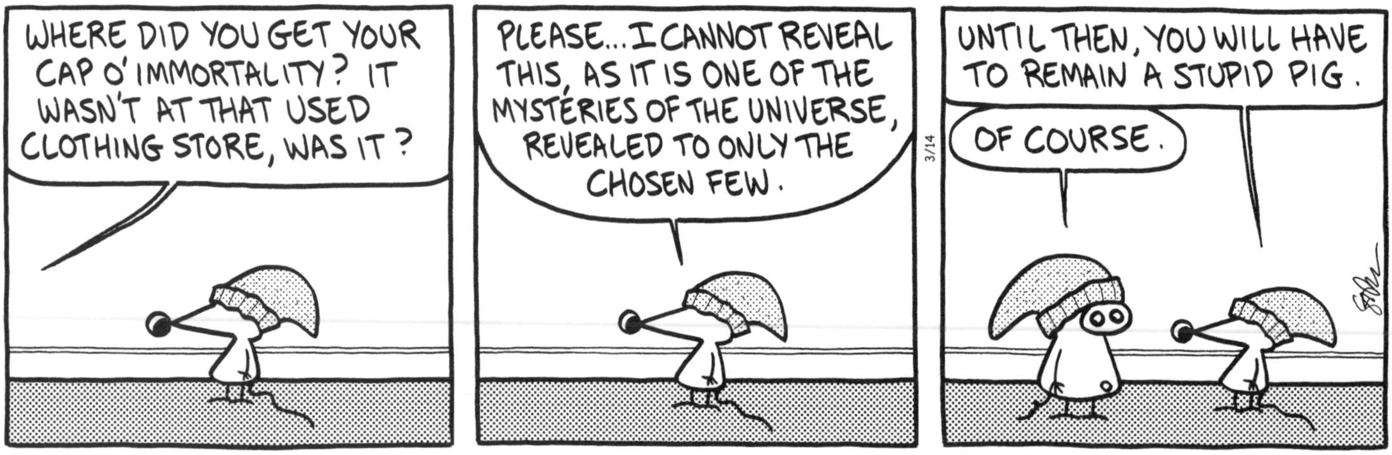
WHERE DID YOU GET YOUR CAP O' IMMORTALITY? IT WASN'T AT THAT USED CLOTHING STORE, WAS IT?
PLEASE... I CANNOT REVEAL THIS, AS IT IS ONE OF THE MYSTÉRIES OF THE UNIVERSE, REVEALED TO ONLY THE CHOSEN FEW.
3/14
UNTIL THEN, YOU WILL HAVE TO REMAIN A STUPID PIG.
OF COURSE.

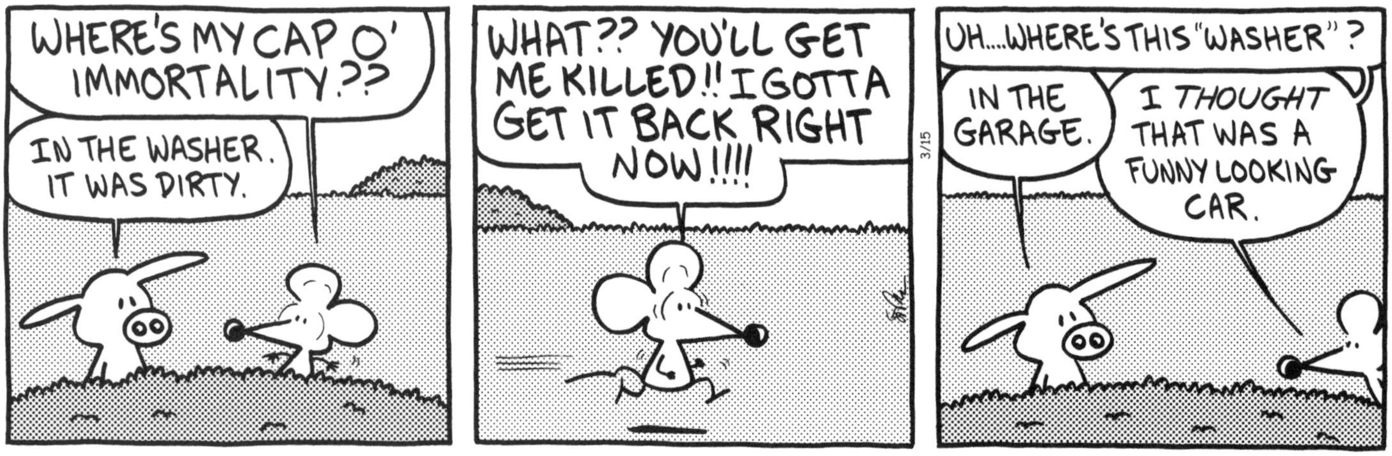
WHERE'S MY CAP O' IMMORTALITY??
IN THE WASHER. IT WAS DIRTY.
WHAT?? YOU'LL GET ME KILLED!! I GOTTA GET IT BACK RIGHT NOW!!!!
3/15
UH....WHERE'S THIS "WASHER"?
IN THE GARAGE.
I *THOUGHT* THAT WAS A FUNNY LOOKING CAR.

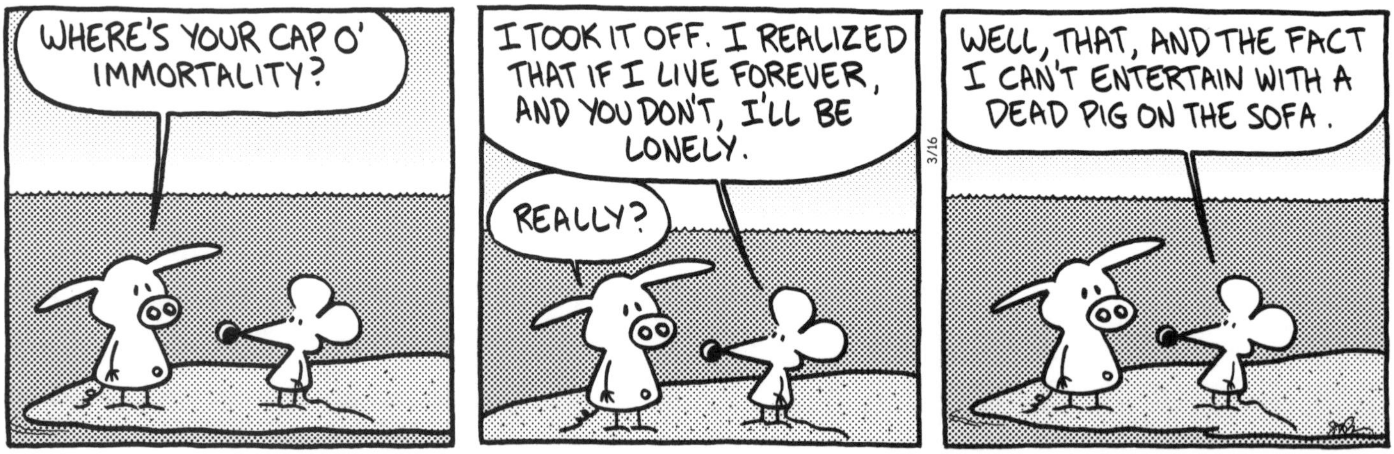
WHERE'S YOUR CAP O' IMMORTALITY?
I TOOK IT OFF. I REALIZED THAT IF I LIVE FOREVER, AND YOU DON'T, I'LL BE LONELY.
REALLY?
3/16
WELL, THAT, AND THE FACT I CAN'T ENTERTAIN WITH A DEAD PIG ON THE SOFA.

Rat's line in the second panel is one of the very few indications in the strip that he actually does have some sort of heart. Of course, he went back to being himself in the last panel. Can't get too sappy.

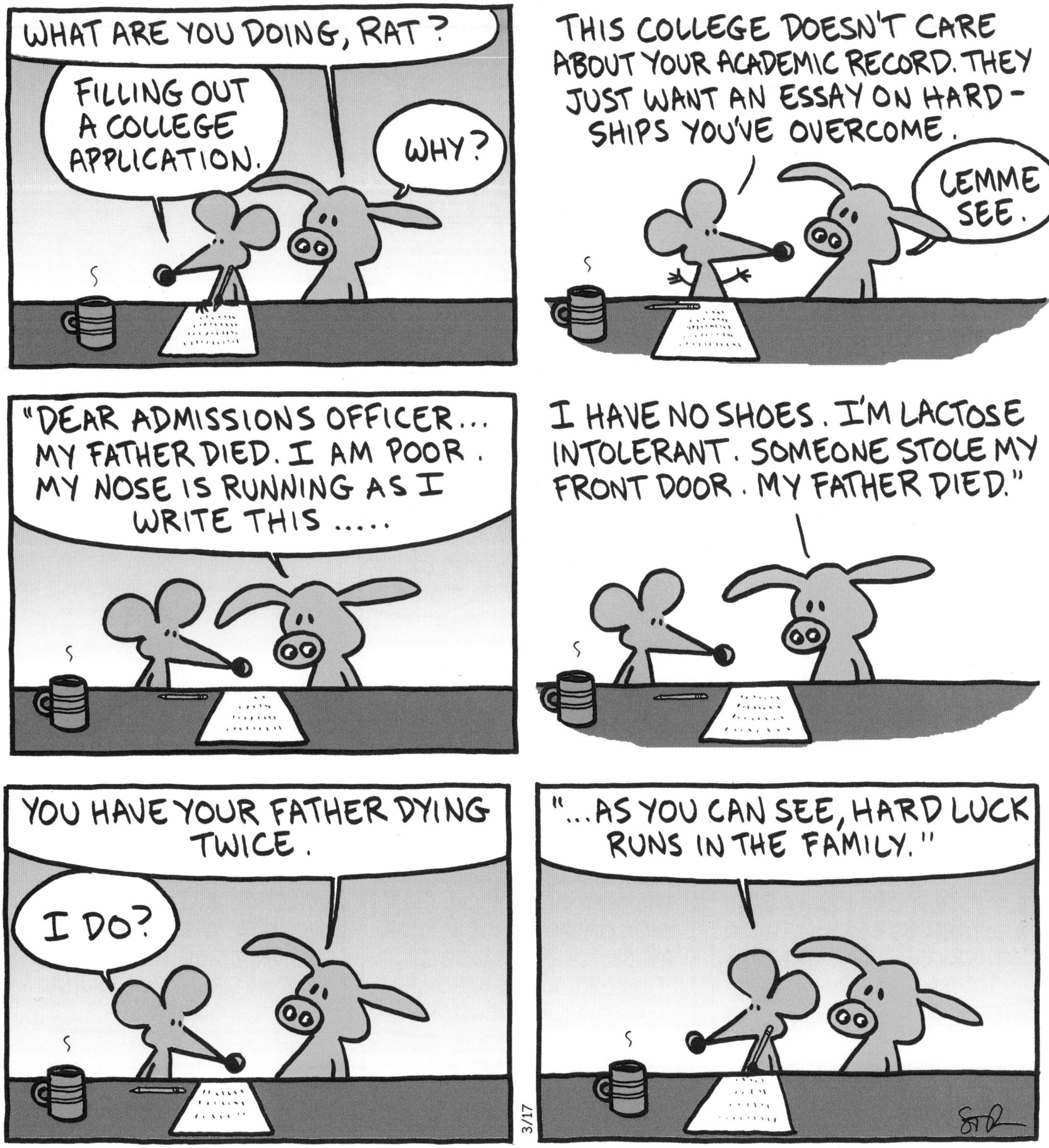
WHAT ARE YOU DOING, RAT?
FILLING OUT A COLLEGE APPLICATION.
WHY?
THIS COLLEGE DOESN'T CARE ABOUT YOUR ACADEMIC RECORD. THEY JUST WANT AN ESSAY ON HARD-SHIPS YOU'VE OVERCOME.
LEMME SEE.
"DEAR ADMISSIONS OFFICER... MY FATHER DIED. I AM POOR. MY NOSE IS RUNNING AS I WRITE THIS.....
I HAVE NO SHOES. I'M LACTOSE INTOLERANT. SOMEONE STOLE MY FRONT DOOR. MY FATHER DIED."
YOU HAVE YOUR FATHER DYING TWICE.
I DO?
"...AS YOU CAN SEE, HARD LUCK RUNS IN THE FAMILY."
3/17

This strip was based on something I had read in a newspaper about a university's admission policy. Part of the admission process was writing an essay on hardships you had overcome, and some admissions guy at the school commented in the article that he had never read about so many dead grandfathers in his life.

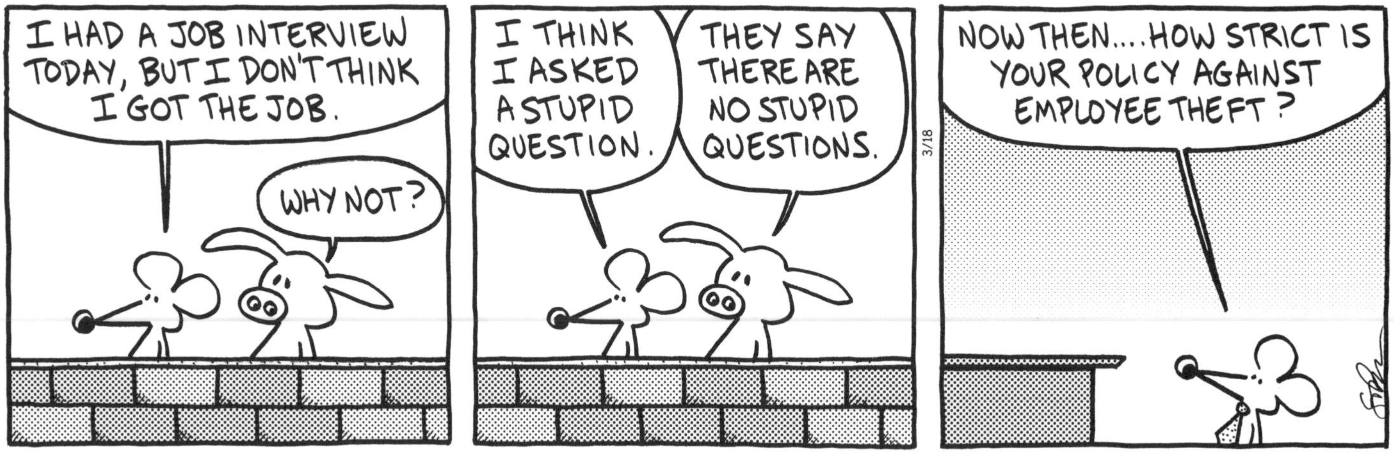
I HAD A JOB INTERVIEW TODAY, BUT I DON'T THINK I GOT THE JOB.
WHY NOT?
I THINK I ASKED A STUPID QUESTION.
THEY SAY THERE ARE NO STUPID QUESTIONS.
3/18
NOW THEN.... HOW STRICT IS YOUR POLICY AGAINST EMPLOYEE THEFT?

This was a pretty popular trio of strips. The 3/19 strip is one of two that I gave to *Dilbert* creator Scott Adams, who I credit for my career as a cartoonist. When *Pearls* started out on the Web, Scott endorsed it to his fans, which really made the strip take off. For that, I'll forever owe him.

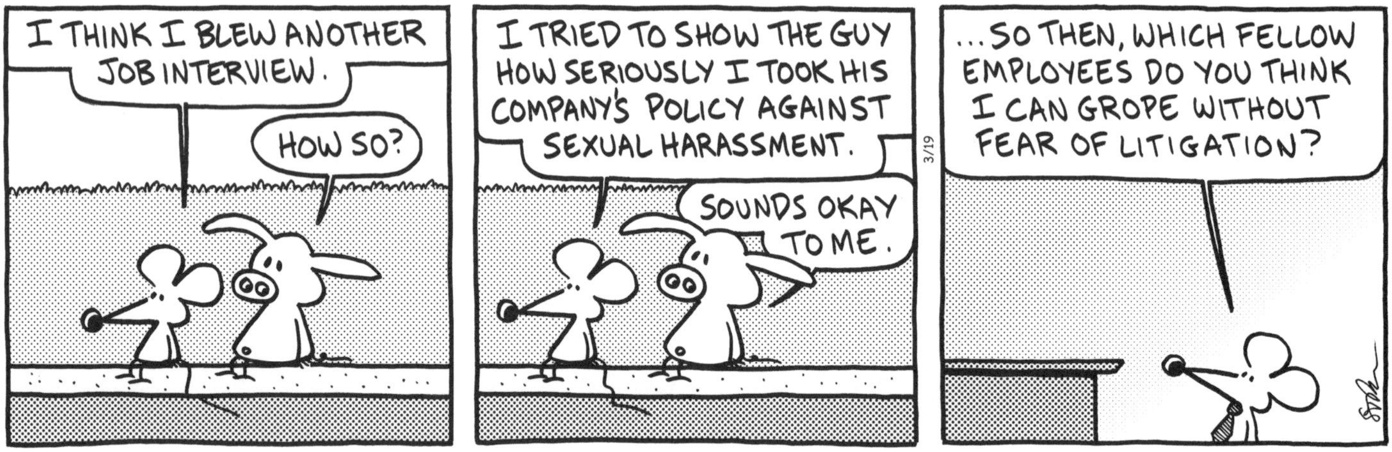
I THINK I BLEW ANOTHER JOB INTERVIEW.
HOW SO?
I TRIED TO SHOW THE GUY HOW SERIOUSLY I TOOK HIS COMPANY'S POLICY AGAINST SEXUAL HARASSMENT.
SOUNDS OKAY TO ME.
3/19
...SO THEN, WHICH FELLOW EMPLOYEES DO YOU THINK I CAN GROPE WITHOUT FEAR OF LITIGATION?

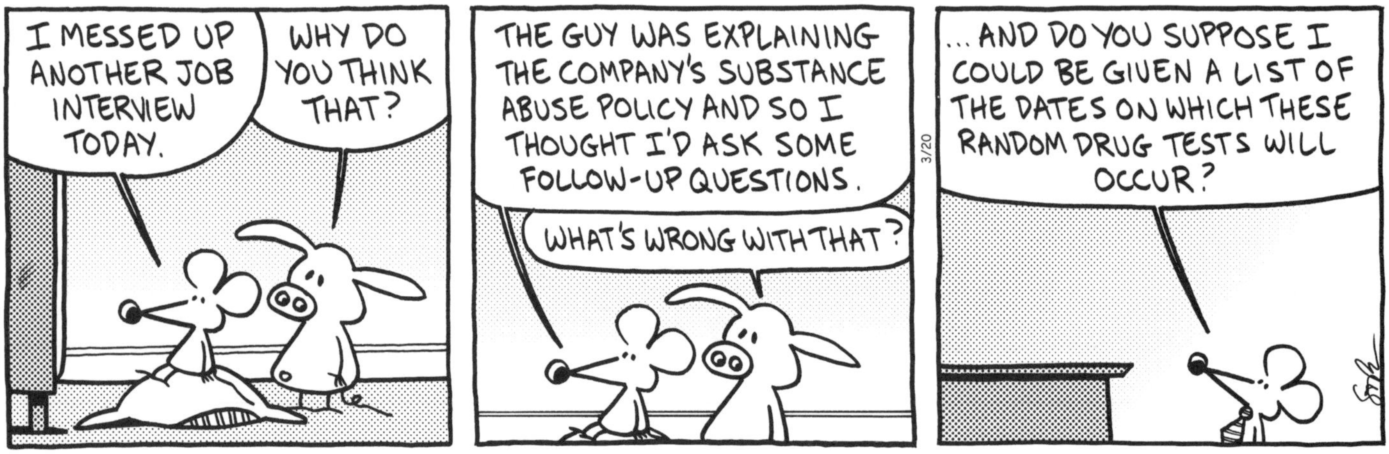
I MESSED UP ANOTHER JOB INTERVIEW TODAY.
WHY DO YOU THINK THAT?
THE GUY WAS EXPLAINING THE COMPANY'S SUBSTANCE ABUSE POLICY AND SO I THOUGHT I'D ASK SOME FOLLOW-UP QUESTIONS.
WHAT'S WRONG WITH THAT?
3/20
...AND DO YOU SUPPOSE I COULD BE GIVEN A LIST OF THE DATES ON WHICH THESE RANDOM DRUG TESTS WILL OCCUR?

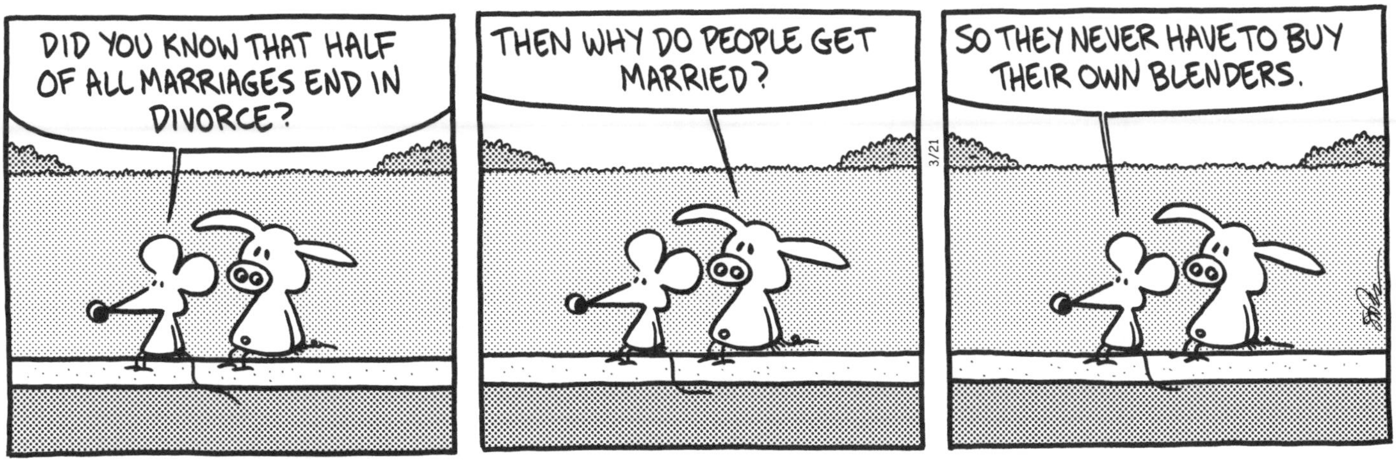
DID YOU KNOW THAT HALF OF ALL MARRIAGES END IN DIVORCE?
THEN WHY DO PEOPLE GET MARRIED?
3/21
SO THEY NEVER HAVE TO BUY THEIR OWN BLENDERS.

More marital "cynicism."

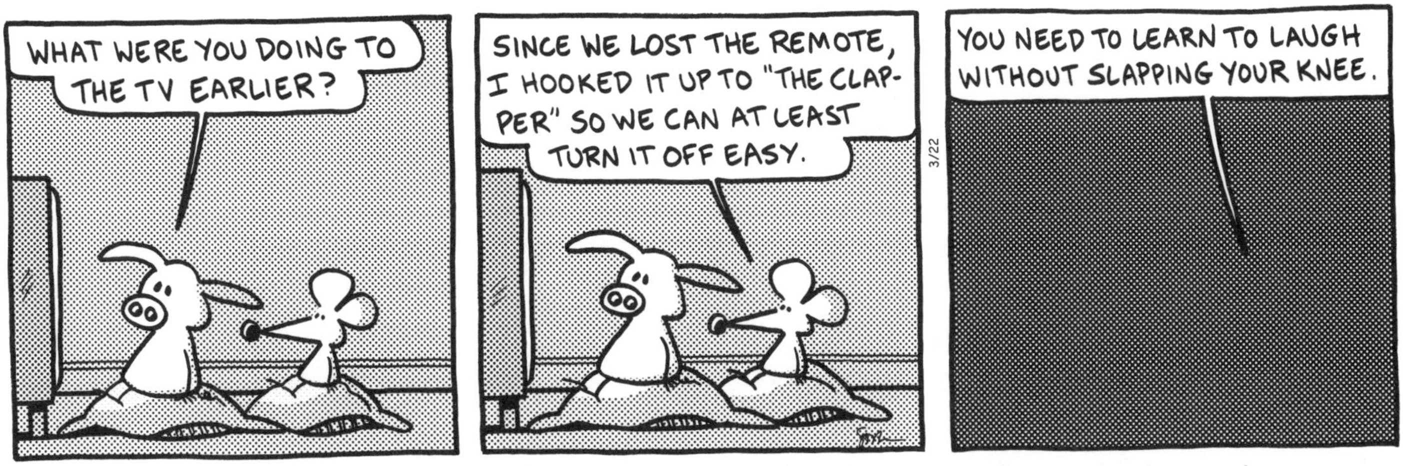
WHAT WERE YOU DOING TO THE TV EARLIER?
SINCE WE LOST THE REMOTE, I HOOKED IT UP TO "THE CLAPPER" SO WE CAN AT LEAST TURN IT OFF EASY.
3/22
YOU NEED TO LEARN TO LAUGH WITHOUT SLAPPING YOUR KNEE.

I'm proud of the way the shading on this strip actually makes it look like the TV is illuminating them. When you have as limited artistic abilities as me, you take pride in the little things.

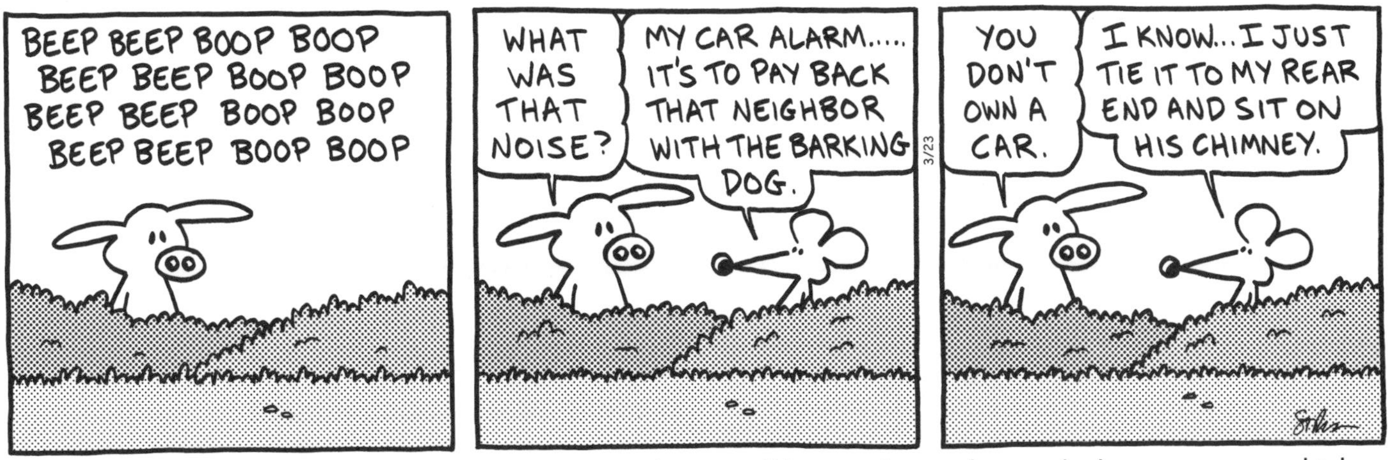
BEEP BEEP BOOP BOOP BEEP BEEP BOOP BOOP BEEP BEEP BOOP BOOP BEEP BEEP BOOP BOOP
WHAT WAS THAT NOISE?
MY CAR ALARM..... IT'S TO PAY BACK THAT NEIGHBOR WITH THE BARKING DOG.
3/23
YOU DON'T OWN A CAR.
I KNOW... I JUST TIE IT TO MY REAR END AND SIT ON HIS CHIMNEY.

I've never understood why we have car alarms. First, they go off by accident so frequently that no one ever thinks the car is being stolen when they hear the alarm. And for whatever reason, the owner is never around to turn it off. Which leads to my second point, which is that if the car really was being stolen, it would be a favor to all of us if the thief would just drive it away.

DEAR ANTELOPES,
GIVEN THE FACT THAT BOTH OF OUR HERDS ARE PURSUED BY THE DESPOTIC LIONS, WE HAVE AN OBVIOUS COMMONALITY OF INTEREST.
WE PROPOSE JOINTLY WRITING A BOOK FOR DISTRIBUTION AMONGST THE LIONS THAT WOULD PERSUADE THEM TO STOP PURSUING OUR RESPECTIVE HERDS.
ENCLOSED PLEASE FIND OUR PROPOSED CHAPTER ONE, TITLED, "WHY KILLING IS MORALLY WRONG."
3/24
WE WOULD GREATLY APPRECIATE IT IF YOU WOULD CONTRIBUTE A CHAPTER OF YOUR OWN.....
HO HUM.
OH, THANK YOU.
U.S.
DEAR ZEBRAS,
ENCLOSED PLEASE FIND CHAPTER TWO, "FIFTY WAYS TO BARBECUE A ZEBRA."
SIGH....

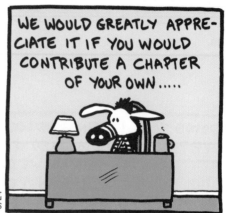

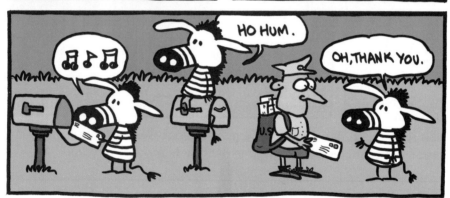

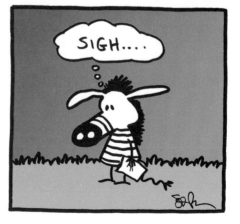

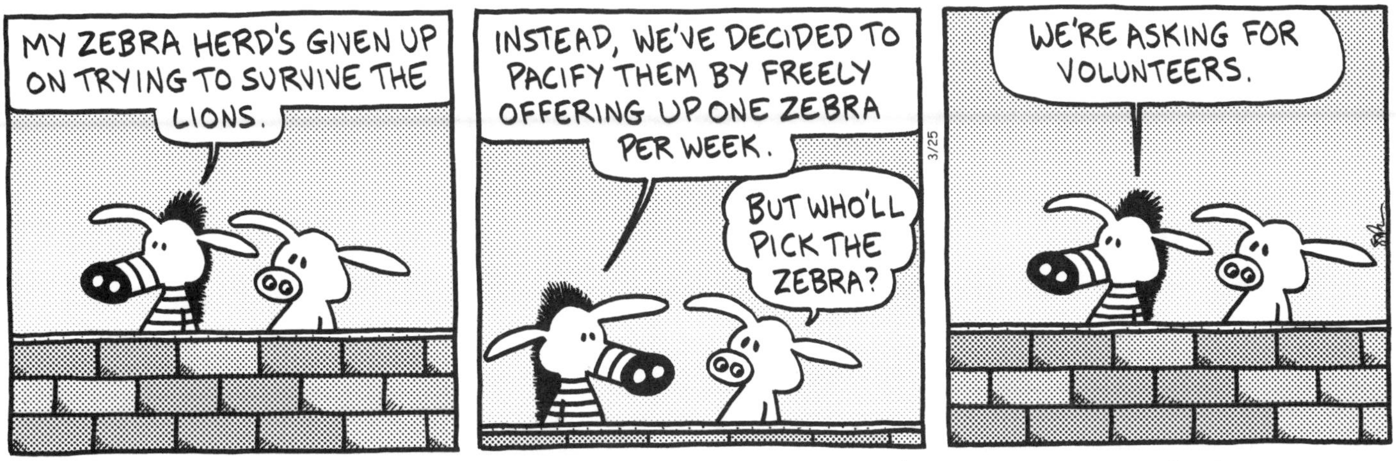
MY ZEBRA HERD'S GIVEN UP ON TRYING TO SURVIVE THE LIONS.
INSTEAD, WE'VE DECIDED TO PACIFY THEM BY FREELY OFFERING UP ONE ZEBRA PER WEEK.
BUT WHO'LL PICK THE ZEBRA?
3/25
WE'RE ASKING FOR VOLUNTEERS.

The zebras' doomed effort to overcome their various predators seems to be one of the most popular themes among *Pearls* readers. I think somehow everyone relates to the zebras.

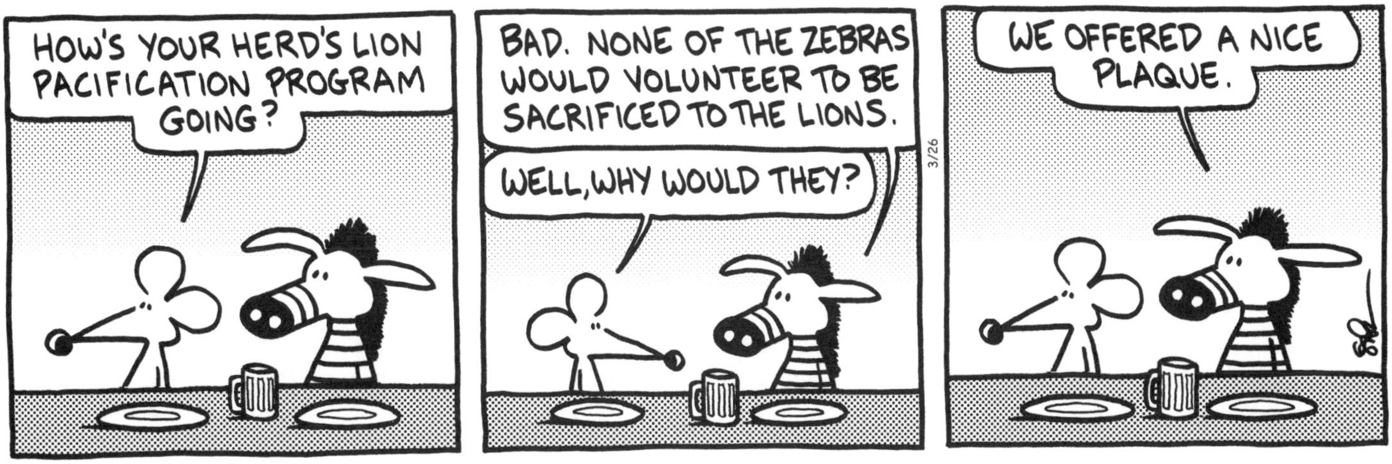
HOW'S YOUR HERD'S LION PACIFICATION PROGRAM GOING?
BAD. NONE OF THE ZEBRAS WOULD VOLUNTEER TO BE SACRIFICED TO THE LIONS.
WELL, WHY WOULD THEY?
3/26
WE OFFERED A NICE PLAQUE.

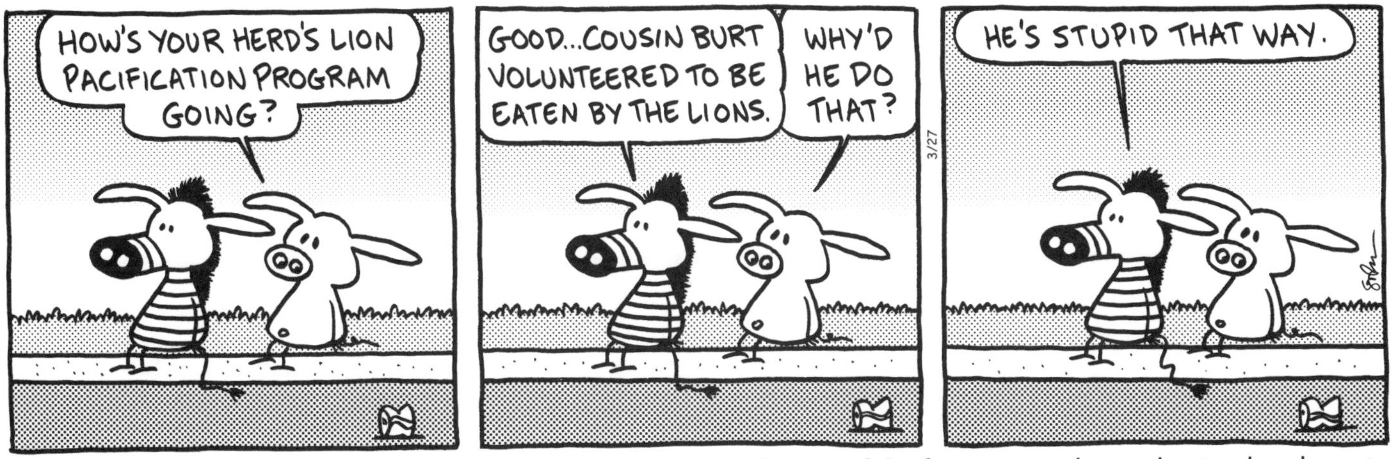
HOW'S YOUR HERD'S LION PACIFICATION PROGRAM GOING?
GOOD...COUSIN BURT VOLUNTEERED TO BE EATEN BY THE LIONS.
WHY'D HE DO THAT?
3/27
HE'S STUPID THAT WAY.

I do not have any family member named "Burt." Thus, this marks one of the few times a doomed animal in the strip is not named after one of my relatives.

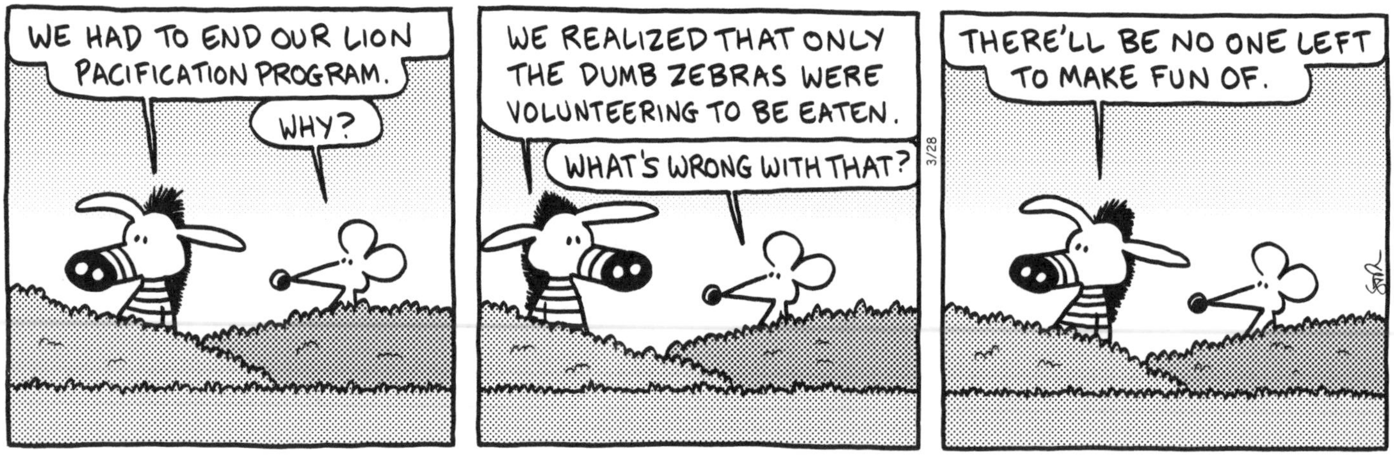
WE HAD TO END OUR LION PACIFICATION PROGRAM.
WHY?
WE REALIZED THAT ONLY THE DUMB ZEBRAS WERE VOLUNTEERING TO BE EATEN.
WHAT'S WRONG WITH THAT?
3/28
THERE'LL BE NO ONE LEFT TO MAKE FUN OF.

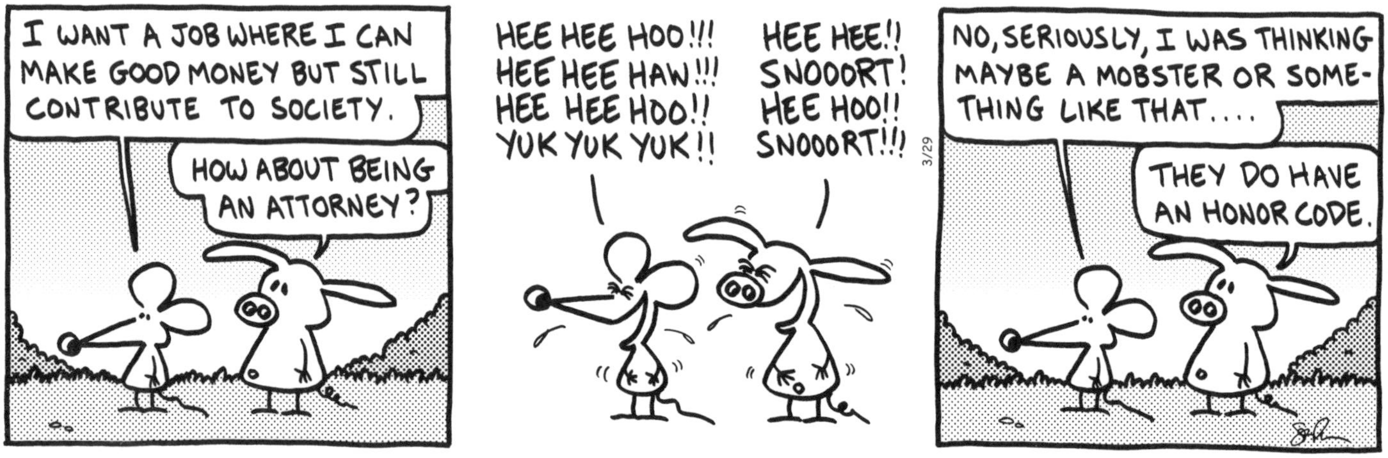
I WANT A JOB WHERE I CAN MAKE GOOD MONEY BUT STILL CONTRIBUTE TO SOCIETY.
HOW ABOUT BEING AN ATTORNEY?
HEE HEE HOO!!! HEE HEE HAW!!! HEE HEE HOO!! YUK YUK YUK!!
HEE HEE!! SNOOORT! HEE HOO!! SNOOORT!!!
3/29
NO, SERIOUSLY, I WAS THINKING MAYBE A MOBSTER OR SOMETHING LIKE THAT....
THEY DO HAVE AN HONOR CODE.

I couldn't resist.

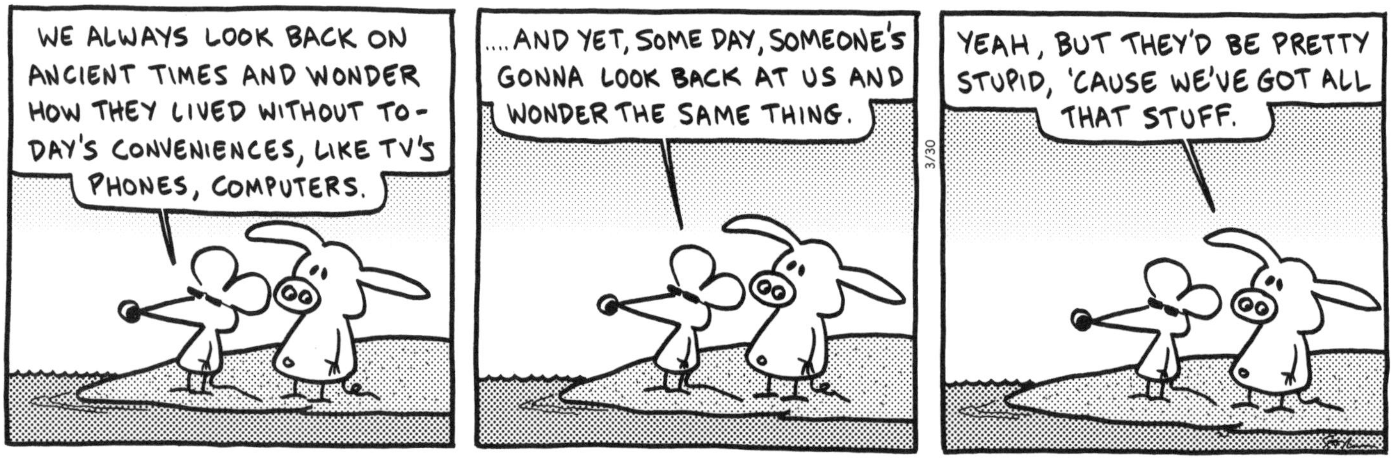
WE ALWAYS LOOK BACK ON ANCIENT TIMES AND WONDER HOW THEY LIVED WITHOUT TODAY'S CONVENIENCES, LIKE TV'S PHONES, COMPUTERS.
....AND YET, SOME DAY, SOMEONE'S GONNA LOOK BACK AT US AND WONDER THE SAME THING.
3/30
YEAH, BUT THEY'D BE PRETTY STUPID, 'CAUSE WE'VE GOT ALL THAT STUFF.

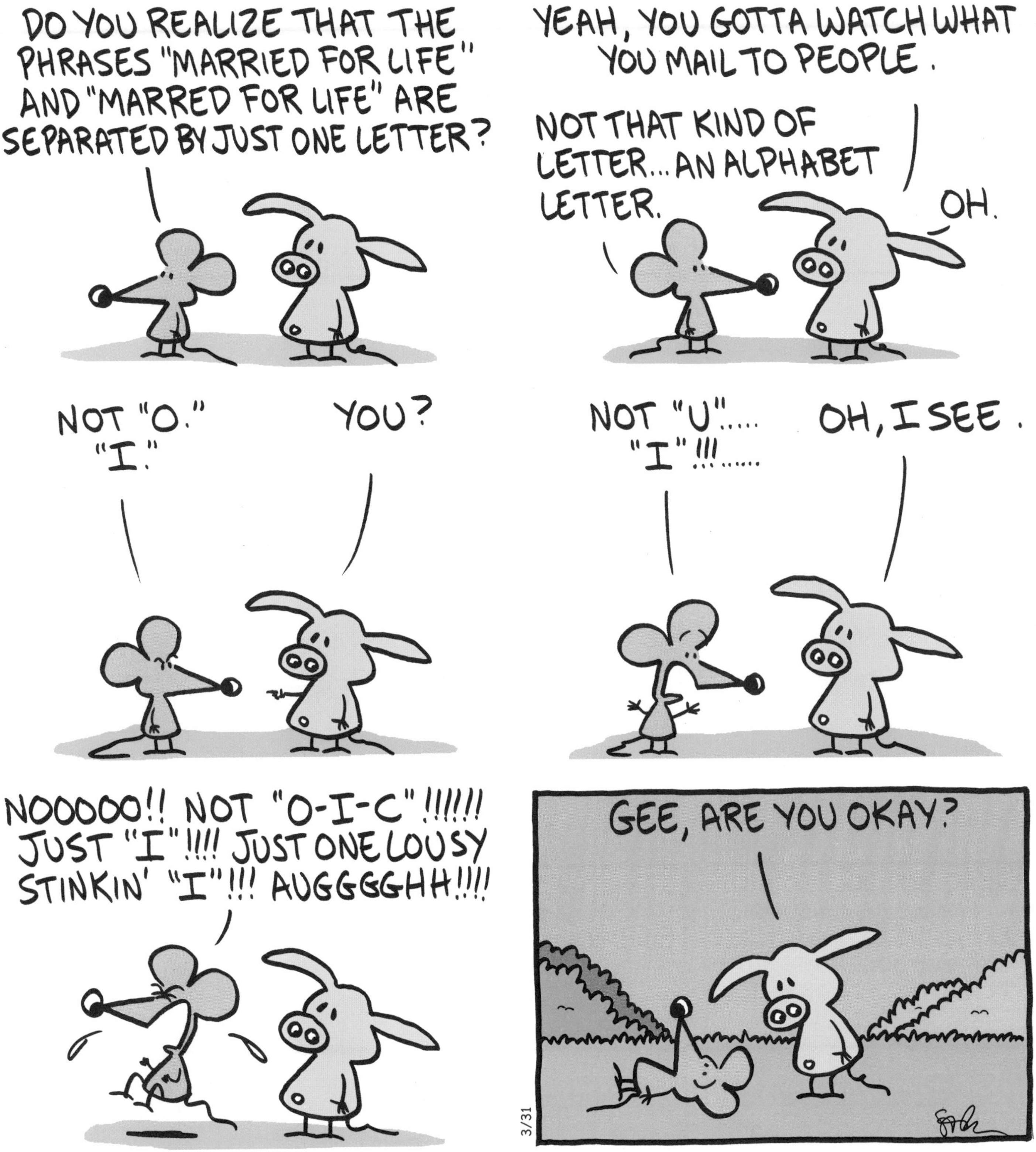
DO YOU REALIZE THAT THE PHRASES "MARRIED FOR LIFE" AND "MARRED FOR LIFE" ARE SEPARATED BY JUST ONE LETTER?
YEAH, YOU GOTTA WATCH WHAT YOU MAIL TO PEOPLE.
NOT THAT KIND OF LETTER... AN ALPHABET LETTER.
OH.
NOT "O." "I."
YOU?
NOT "U"..... "I"!!!......
OH, I SEE.
NOOOOO!! NOT "O-I-C"!!!!!! JUST "I"!!!! JUST ONE LOUSY STINKIN' "I"!!! AUGGGGHH!!!!
GEE, ARE YOU OKAY?
3/31

I usually start writing in the morning, right when I wake up. I find that I can't write much after about three in the afternoon. But this strip was an exception. I wrote it one night around midnight when I was lying in bed and couldn't sleep. Creativity can strike at odd times.

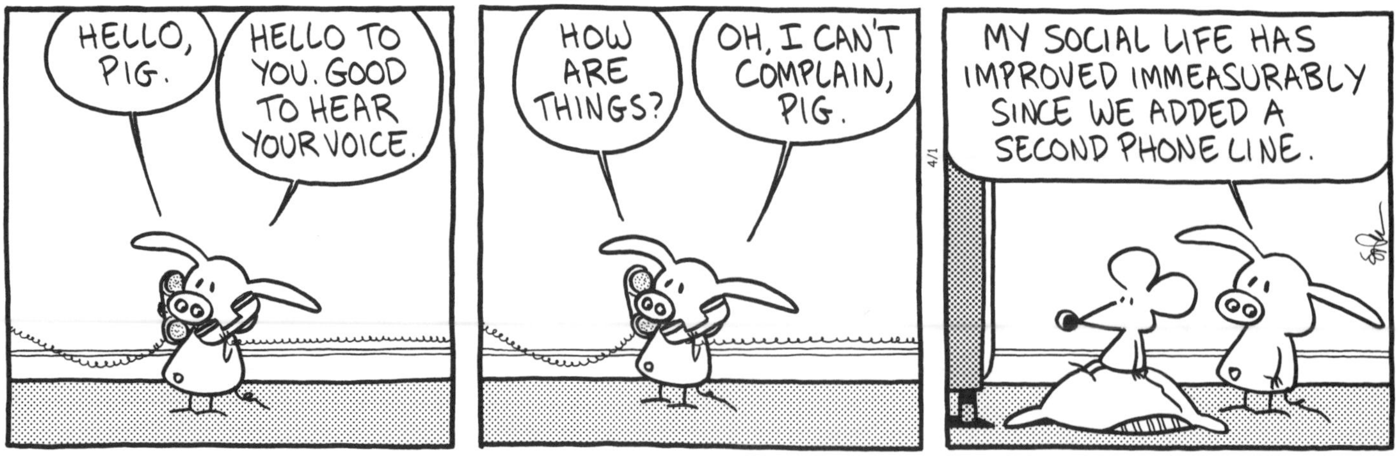
HELLO, PIG.
HELLO TO YOU. GOOD TO HEAR YOUR VOICE.
HOW ARE THINGS?
OH, I CAN'T COMPLAIN, PIG.
4/1
MY SOCIAL LIFE HAS IMPROVED IMMEASURABLY SINCE WE ADDED A SECOND PHONE LINE.

Man, I hate drawing phones. Lately, I've been drawing a lot of the cordless ones. I think they're easier.

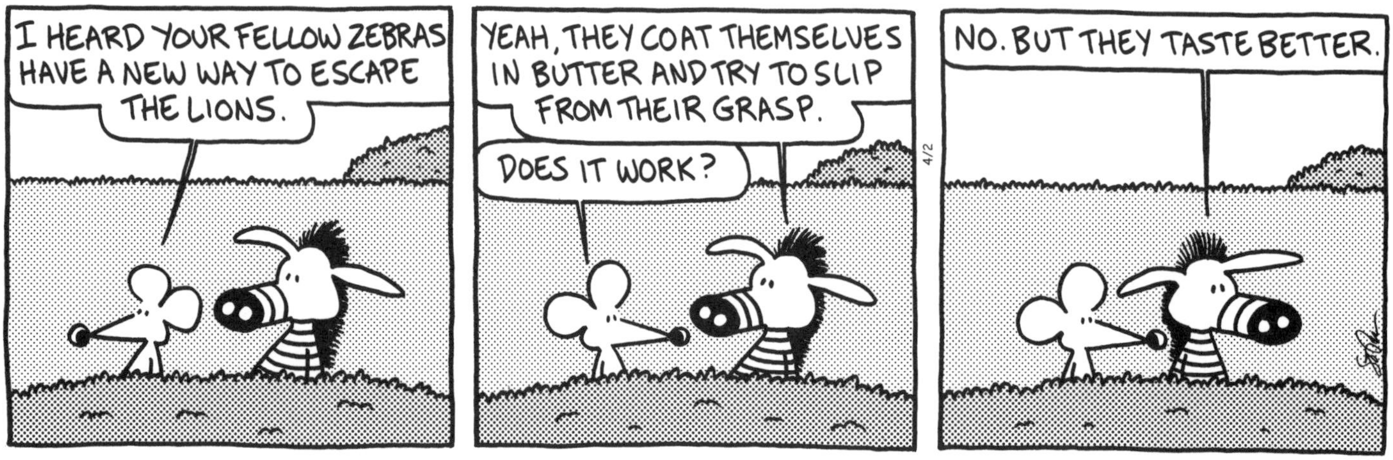
I HEARD YOUR FELLOW ZEBRAS HAVE A NEW WAY TO ESCAPE THE LIONS.
YEAH, THEY COAT THEMSELVES IN BUTTER AND TRY TO SLIP FROM THEIR GRASP.
DOES IT WORK?
4/2
NO. BUT THEY TASTE BETTER.

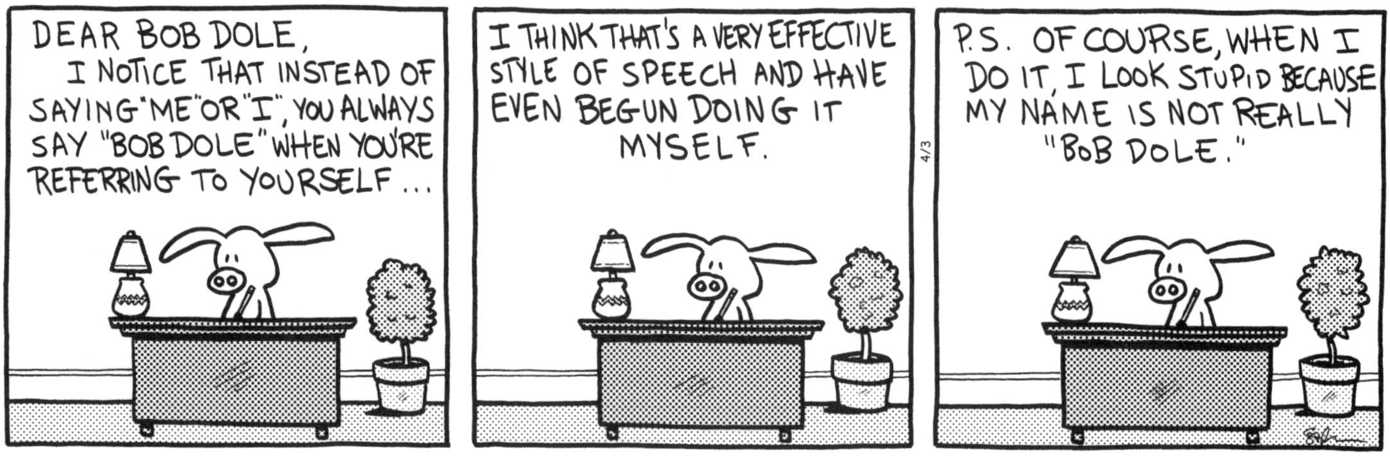
DEAR BOB DOLE,
I NOTICE THAT INSTEAD OF SAYING "ME" OR "I", YOU ALWAYS SAY "BOB DOLE" WHEN YOU'RE REFERRING TO YOURSELF...
I THINK THAT'S A VERY EFFECTIVE STYLE OF SPEECH AND HAVE EVEN BEGUN DOING IT MYSELF.
4/3
P.S. OF COURSE, WHEN I DO IT, I LOOK STUPID BECAUSE MY NAME IS NOT REALLY "BOB DOLE."

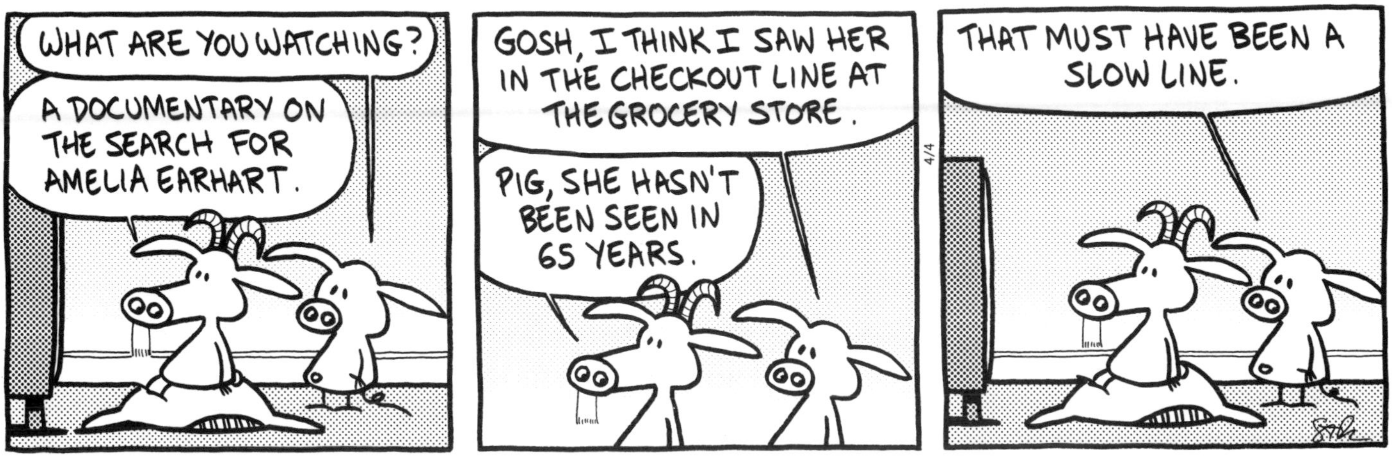
WHAT ARE YOU WATCHING?
A DOCUMENTARY ON THE SEARCH FOR AMELIA EARHART.
GOSH, I THINK I SAW HER IN THE CHECKOUT LINE AT THE GROCERY STORE.
PIG, SHE HASN'T BEEN SEEN IN 65 YEARS.
4/4
THAT MUST HAVE BEEN A SLOW LINE.

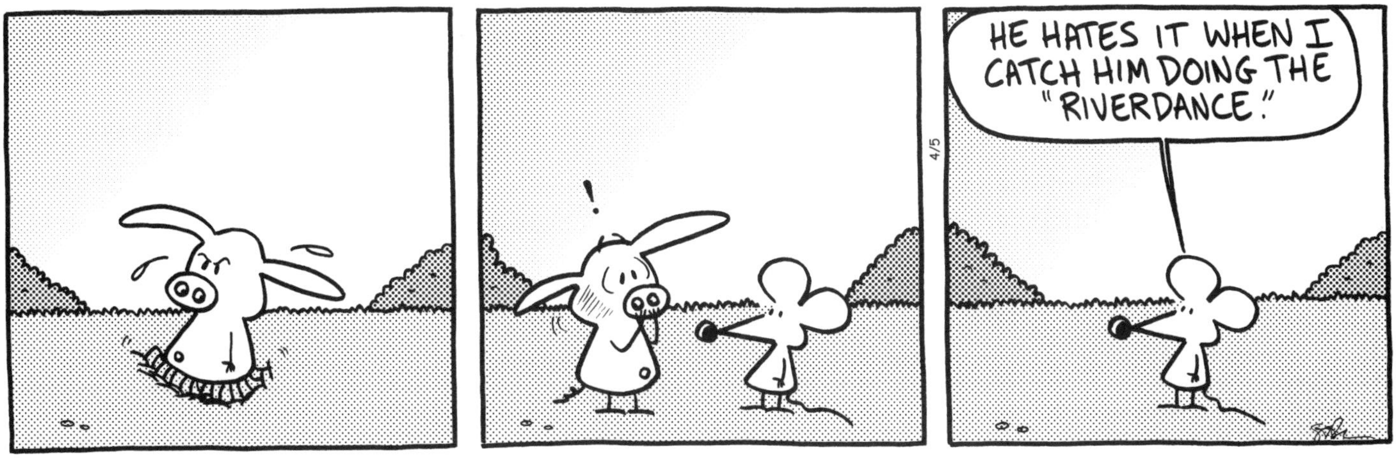
!
4/5
HE HATES IT WHEN I CATCH HIM DOING THE "RIVERDANCE."

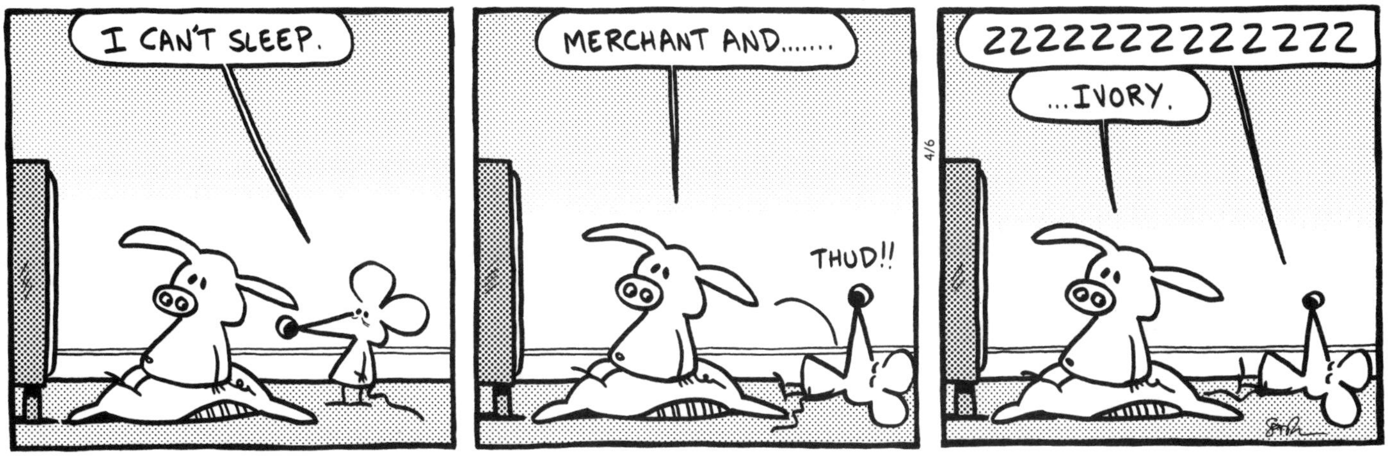
I CAN'T SLEEP.
MERCHANT AND.......
THUD!!
4/6
ZZZZZZZZZZZZZ
...IVORY.

A lot of readers didn't get this joke because they didn't know who "Merchant and Ivory" were. Merchant and Ivory are the makers of such films as *Howard's End* and *A Room with a View*. Whenever I see people with British accents picnicking in a meadow, I fall instantly to sleep.

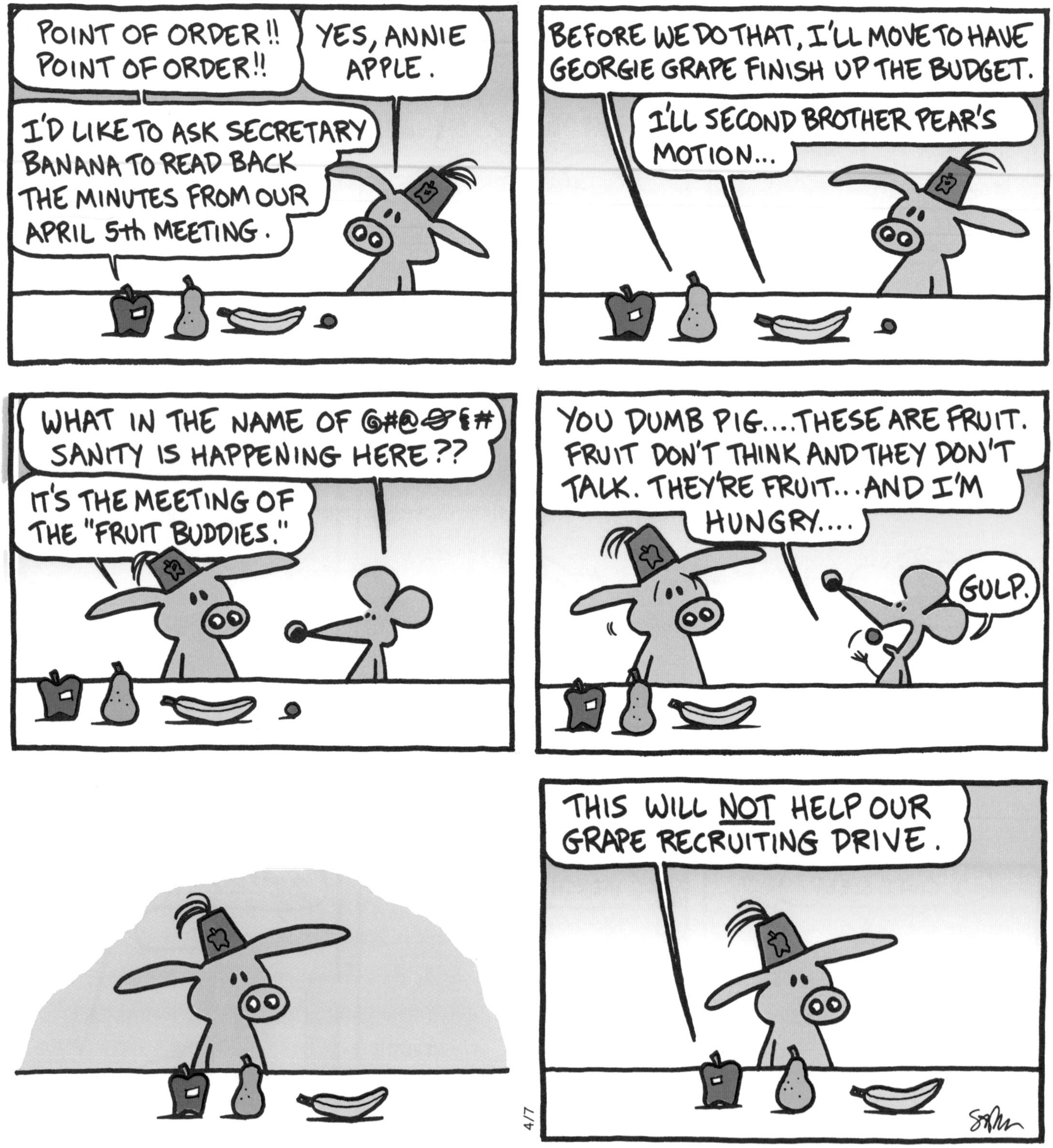
POINT OF ORDER!! POINT OF ORDER!!
YES, ANNIE APPLE.
I'D LIKE TO ASK SECRETARY BANANA TO READ BACK THE MINUTES FROM OUR APRIL 5th MEETING.
BEFORE WE DO THAT, I'LL MOVE TO HAVE GEORGIE GRAPE FINISH UP THE BUDGET.
I'LL SECOND BROTHER PEAR'S MOTION...
WHAT IN THE NAME OF @#@ SANITY IS HAPPENING HERE??
IT'S THE MEETING OF THE "FRUIT BUDDIES."
YOU DUMB PIG....THESE ARE FRUIT. FRUIT DON'T THINK AND THEY DON'T TALK. THEY'RE FRUIT...AND I'M HUNGRY....
GULP.
THIS WILL NOT HELP OUR GRAPE RECRUITING DRIVE.
4/7

My six-year old son really liked this strip. Sometimes when we eat, I'll swallow a grape and reenact the tragic death of Georgie Grape.

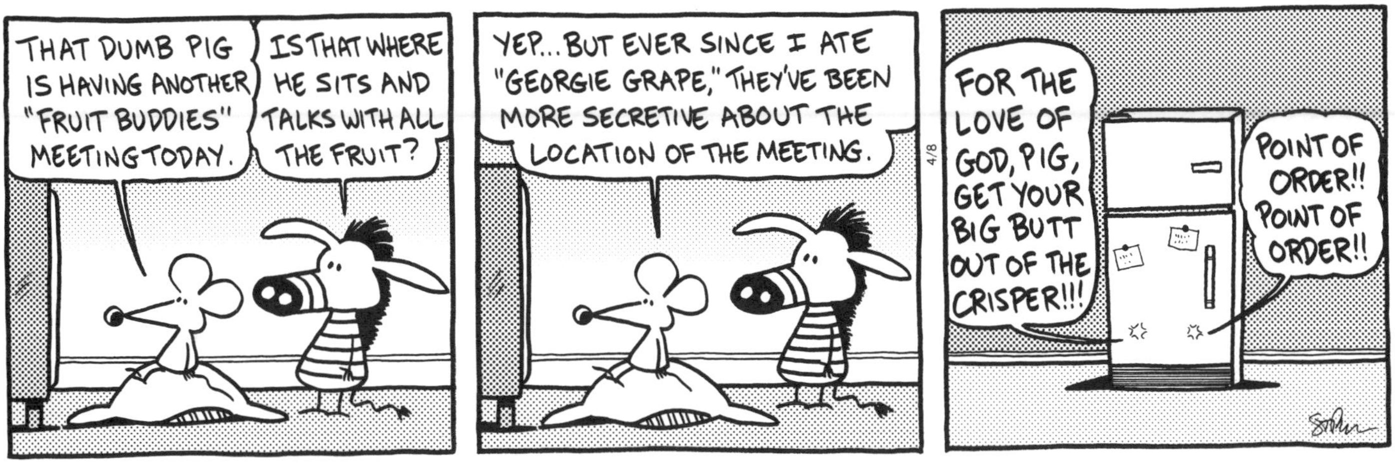
THAT DUMB PIG IS HAVING ANOTHER "FRUIT BUDDIES" MEETING TODAY.
IS THAT WHERE HE SITS AND TALKS WITH ALL THE FRUIT?
YEP... BUT EVER SINCE I ATE "GEORGIE GRAPE," THEY'VE BEEN MORE SECRETIVE ABOUT THE LOCATION OF THE MEETING.
4/8
FOR THE LOVE OF GOD, PIG, GET YOUR BIG BUTT OUT OF THE CRISPER!!!
POINT OF ORDER!! POINT OF ORDER!!

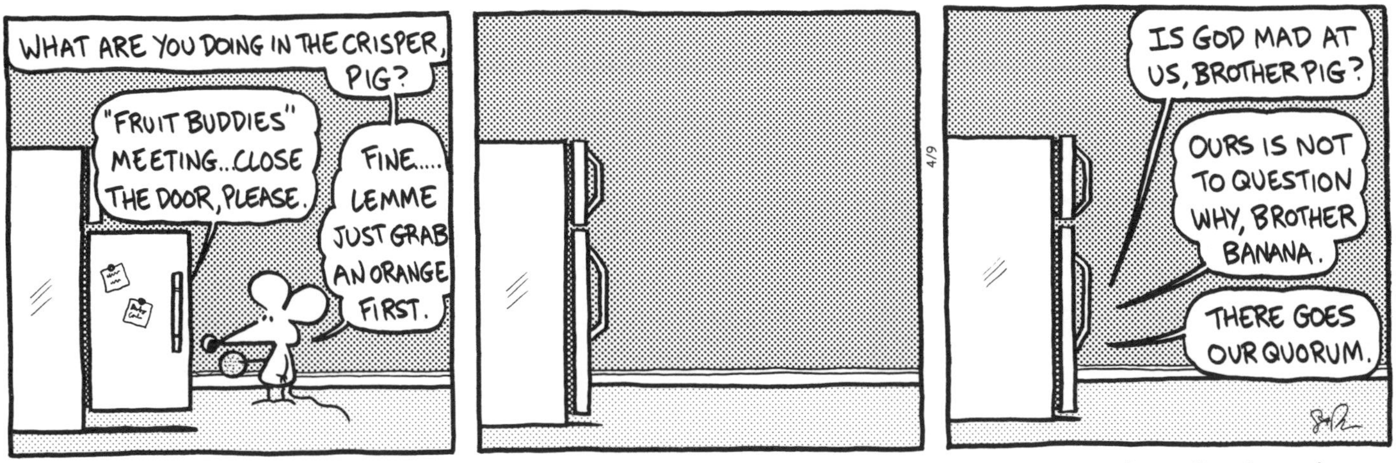
WHAT ARE YOU DOING IN THE CRISPER, PIG?
"FRUIT BUDDIES" MEETING...CLOSE THE DOOR, PLEASE.
FINE..... LEMME JUST GRAB AN ORANGE FIRST.
4/9
IS GOD MAD AT US, BROTHER PIG?
OURS IS NOT TO QUESTION WHY, BROTHER BANANA.
THERE GOES OUR QUORUM.

I had no idea how to draw a refrigerator from the side, so I stole it from a *Get Fuzzy* strip. If you flip through Darby's first book, *The Dog Is Not a Toy*, you'll probably find the source of my "inspiration."

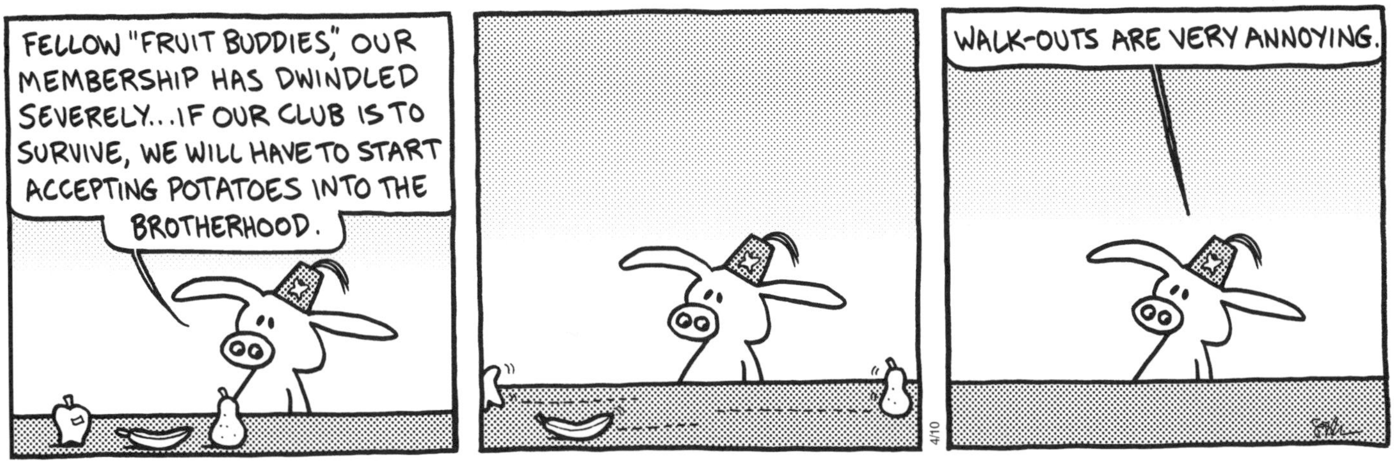
FELLOW "FRUIT BUDDIES," OUR MEMBERSHIP HAS DWINDLED SEVERELY...IF OUR CLUB IS TO SURVIVE, WE WILL HAVE TO START ACCEPTING POTATOES INTO THE BROTHERHOOD.
4/10
WALK-OUTS ARE VERY ANNOYING.

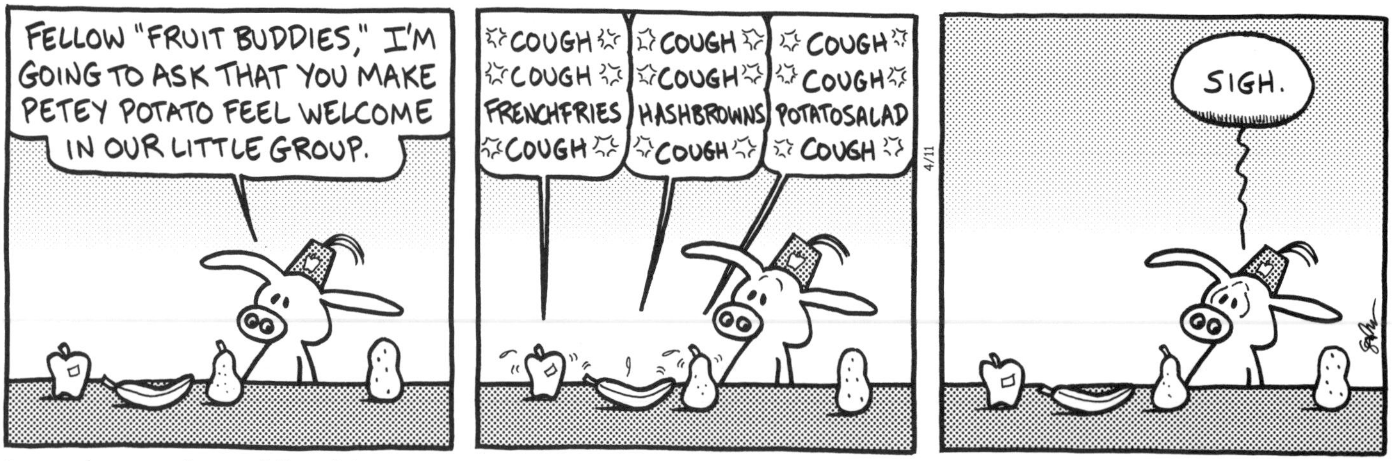
FELLOW "FRUIT BUDDIES," I'M GOING TO ASK THAT YOU MAKE PETEY POTATO FEEL WELCOME IN OUR LITTLE GROUP.
COUGH COUGH FRENCHFRIES COUGH
COUGH COUGH HASHBROWNS COUGH
COUGH COUGH POTATOSALAD COUGH
4/11
SIGH.

Somewhere in the middle of this series was the first strip that my syndicate ever nixed. In it, the potatoes and fruit mimicked the dialogue of the Arab/Israeli conflict, with the fruit proclaiming, "We are God's chosen fruit!" and the potatoes responding, "We will push you into the sea!" I suppose it's a good thing it never ran.

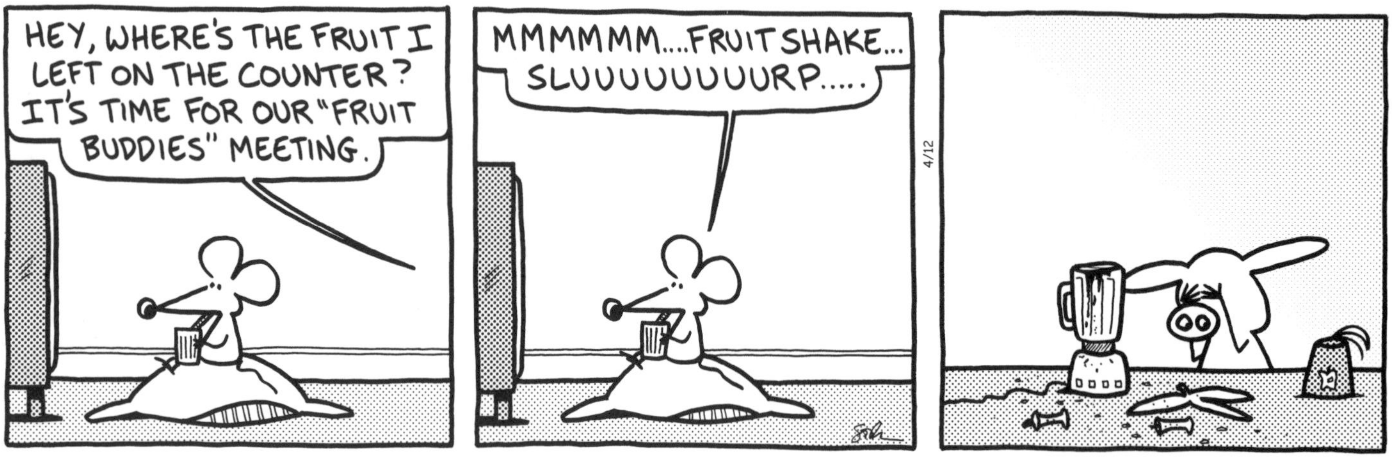
HEY, WHERE'S THE FRUIT I LEFT ON THE COUNTER? IT'S TIME FOR OUR "FRUIT BUDDIES" MEETING.
MMMMMM....FRUIT SHAKE... SLUUUUUUUURP.....
4/12

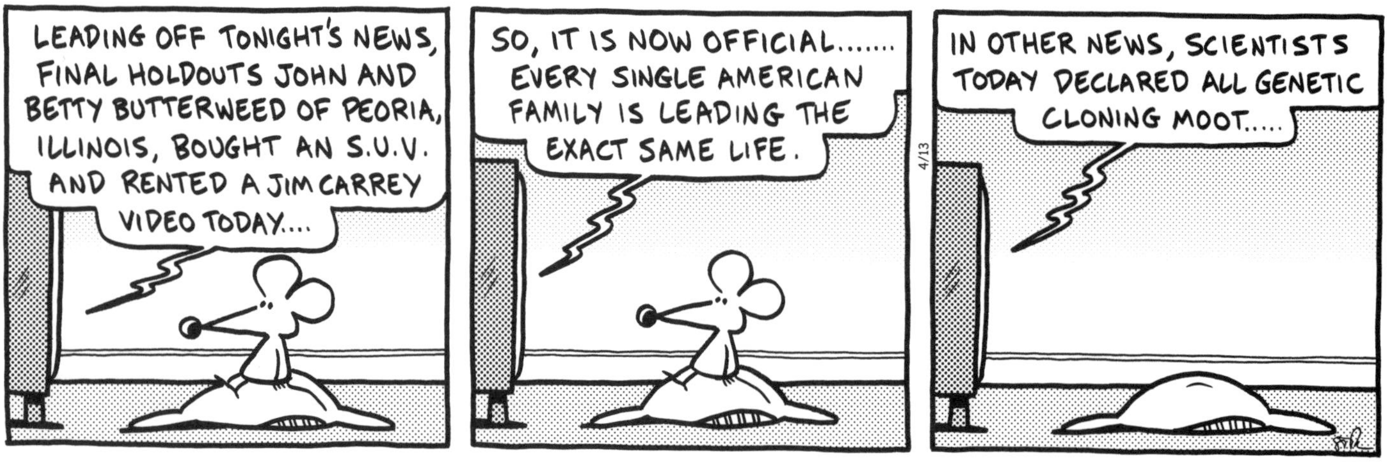
LEADING OFF TONIGHT'S NEWS, FINAL HOLDOUTS JOHN AND BETTY BUTTERWEED OF PEORIA, ILLINOIS, BOUGHT AN S.U.V. AND RENTED A JIM CARREY VIDEO TODAY....
SO, IT IS NOW OFFICIAL....... EVERY SINGLE AMERICAN FAMILY IS LEADING THE EXACT SAME LIFE.
4/13
IN OTHER NEWS, SCIENTISTS TODAY DECLARED ALL GENETIC CLONING MOOT.....

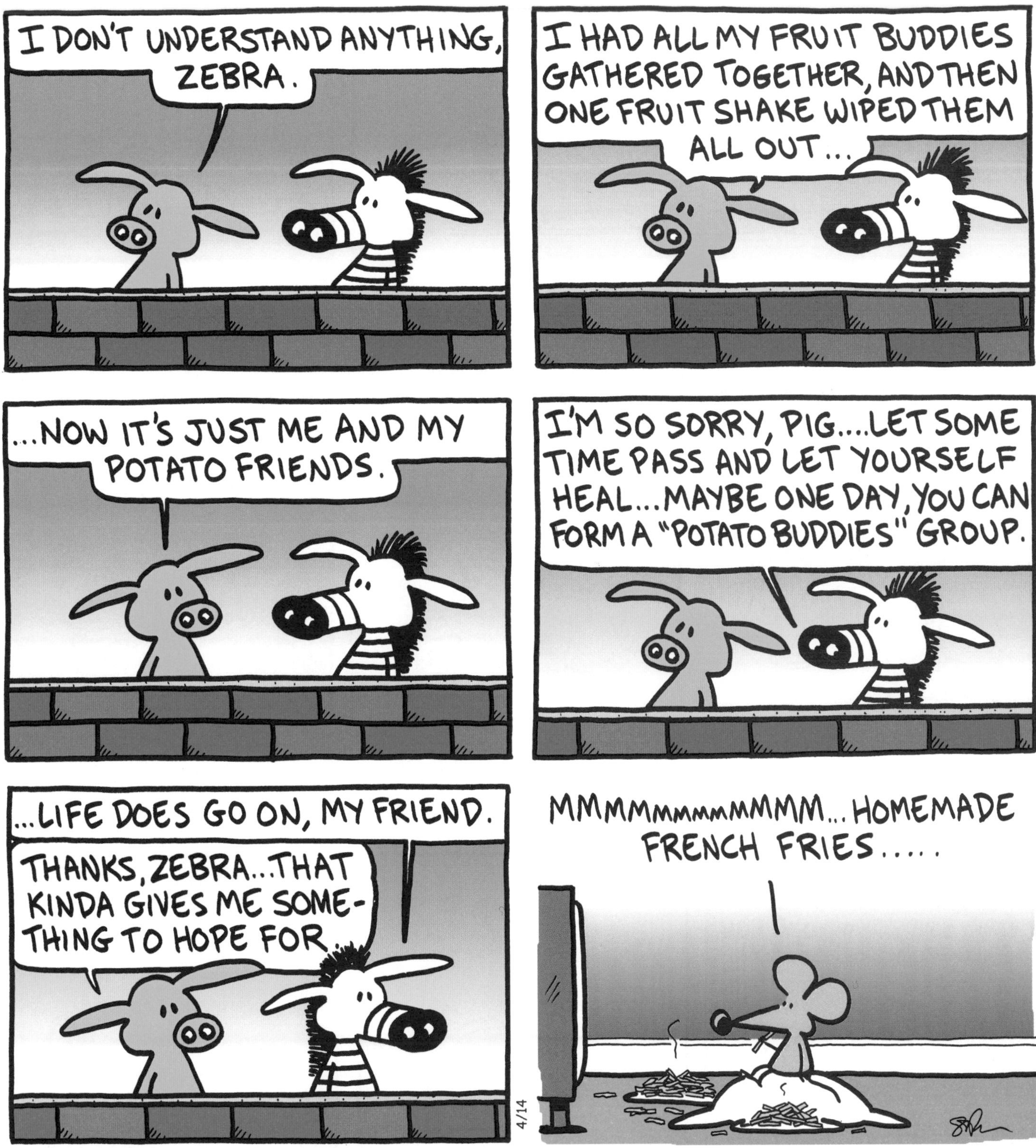
I DON'T UNDERSTAND ANYTHING, ZEBRA.
I HAD ALL MY FRUIT BUDDIES GATHERED TOGETHER, AND THEN ONE FRUIT SHAKE WIPED THEM ALL OUT...
...NOW IT'S JUST ME AND MY POTATO FRIENDS.
I'M SO SORRY, PIG....LET SOME TIME PASS AND LET YOURSELF HEAL...MAYBE ONE DAY, YOU CAN FORM A "POTATO BUDDIES" GROUP.
...LIFE DOES GO ON, MY FRIEND.
THANKS, ZEBRA...THAT KINDA GIVES ME SOME-THING TO HOPE FOR.
4/14
MMMMMMMMMMM... HOMEMADE FRENCH FRIES.....

I don't think anyone could ever call *Pearls* a "feel-good" strip.

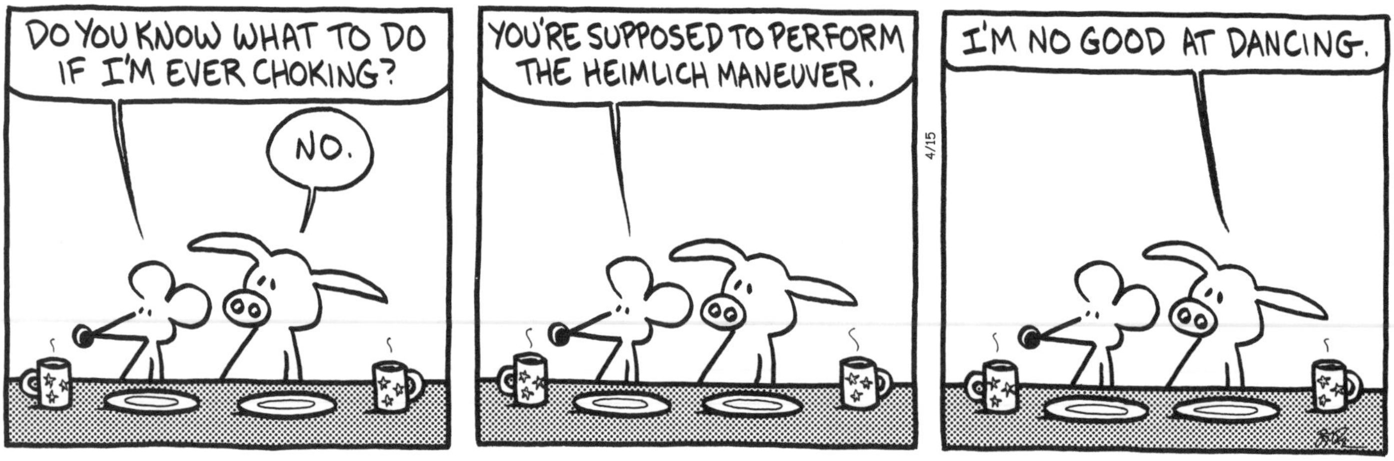
DO YOU KNOW WHAT TO DO IF I'M EVER CHOKING?
NO.
YOU'RE SUPPOSED TO PERFORM THE HEIMLICH MANEUVER.
4/15
I'M NO GOOD AT DANCING.

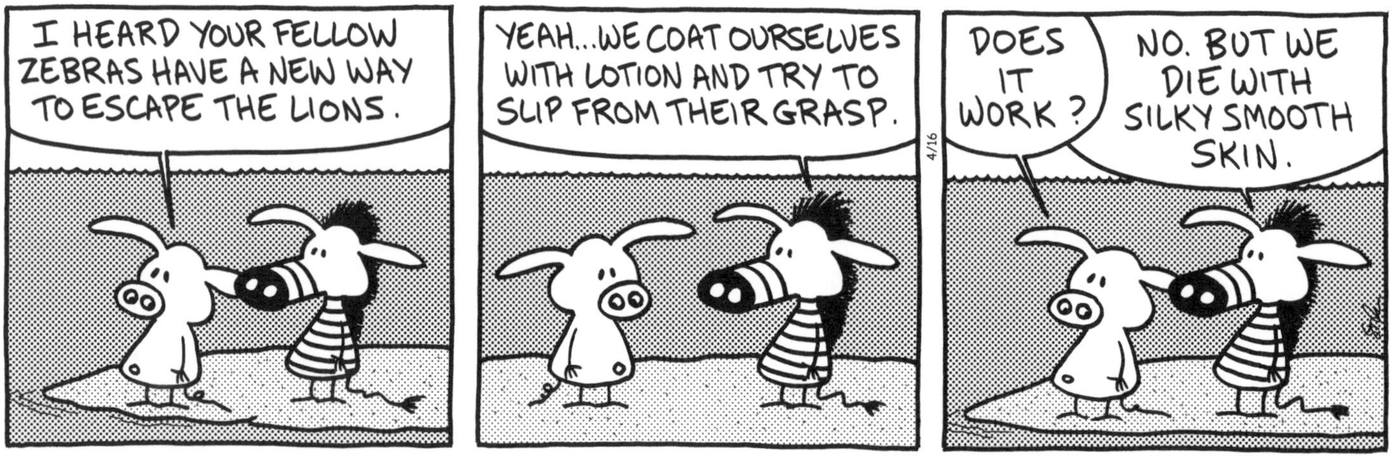
I HEARD YOUR FELLOW ZEBRAS HAVE A NEW WAY TO ESCAPE THE LIONS.
YEAH...WE COAT OURSELVES WITH LOTION AND TRY TO SLIP FROM THEIR GRASP.
4/16
DOES IT WORK?
NO. BUT WE DIE WITH SILKY SMOOTH SKIN.

My editor at United told me she wanted to nix this strip because she thought it was in poor taste. I didn't think it was in any poorer taste than any of the other strips, and so we ran it.

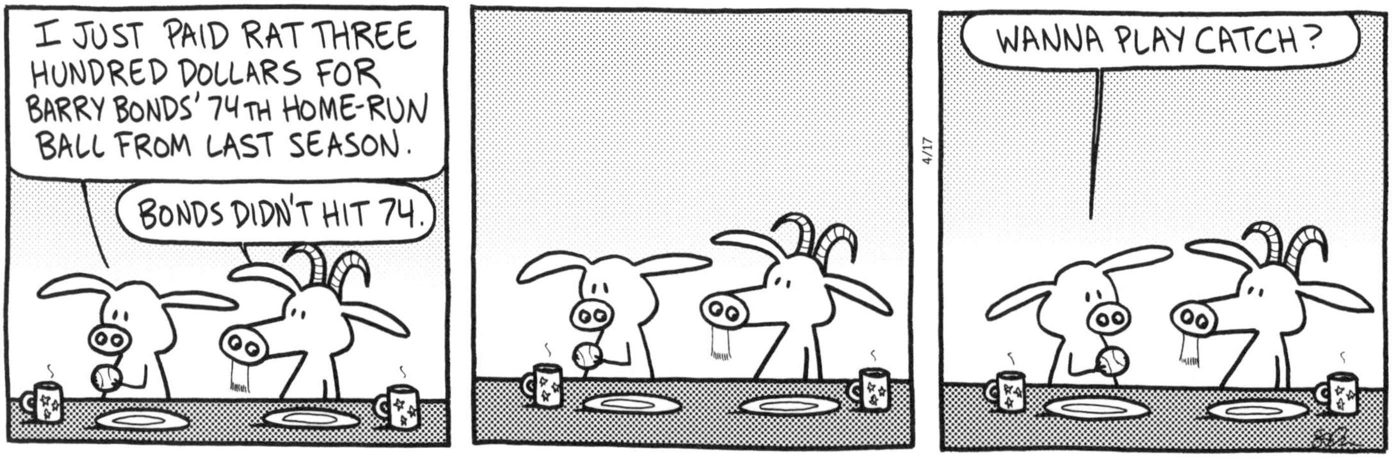
I JUST PAID RAT THREE HUNDRED DOLLARS FOR BARRY BONDS' 74TH HOME-RUN BALL FROM LAST SEASON.
BONDS DIDN'T HIT 74.
4/17
WANNA PLAY CATCH?

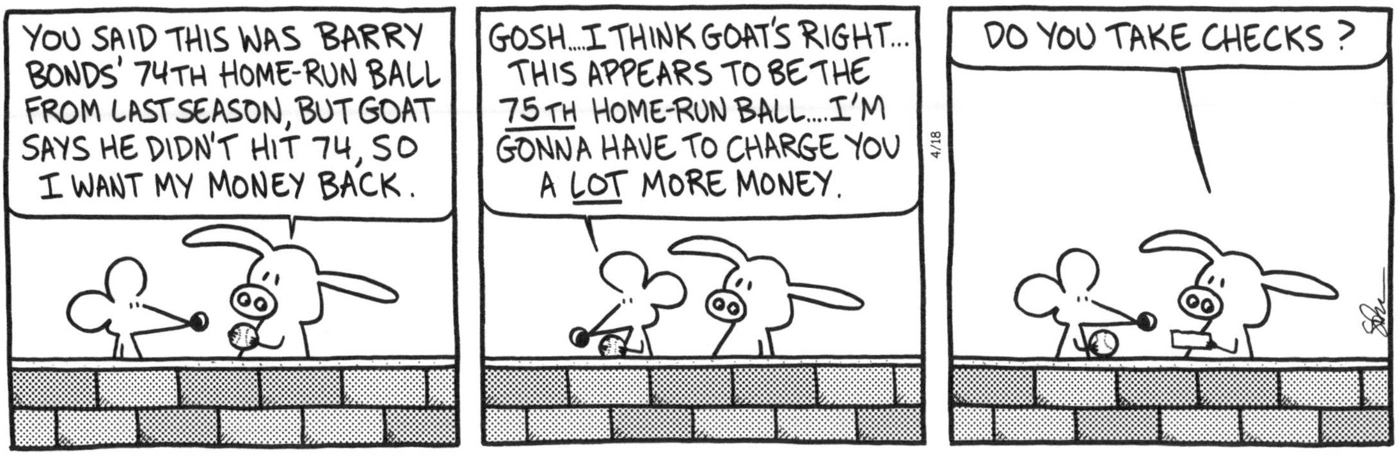
YOU SAID THIS WAS BARRY BONDS' 74TH HOME-RUN BALL FROM LAST SEASON, BUT GOAT SAYS HE DIDN'T HIT 74, SO I WANT MY MONEY BACK.
GOSH....I THINK GOAT'S RIGHT... THIS APPEARS TO BE THE 75TH HOME-RUN BALL....I'M GONNA HAVE TO CHARGE YOU A LOT MORE MONEY.
4/18
DO YOU TAKE CHECKS?

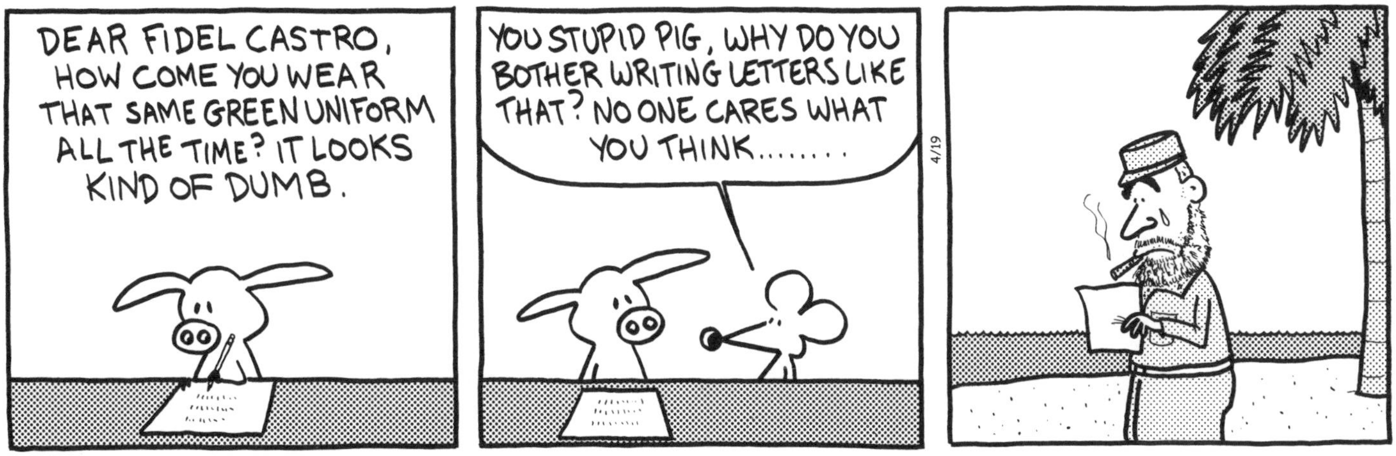
DEAR FIDEL CASTRO, HOW COME YOU WEAR THAT SAME GREEN UNIFORM ALL THE TIME? IT LOOKS KIND OF DUMB.
YOU STUPID PIG, WHY DO YOU BOTHER WRITING LETTERS LIKE THAT? NO ONE CARES WHAT YOU THINK........
4/19

I was so frustrated by my inability to draw Castro and a palm tree that I almost tore up this strip. I'm glad I didn't, because it became one of the most popular daily strips.

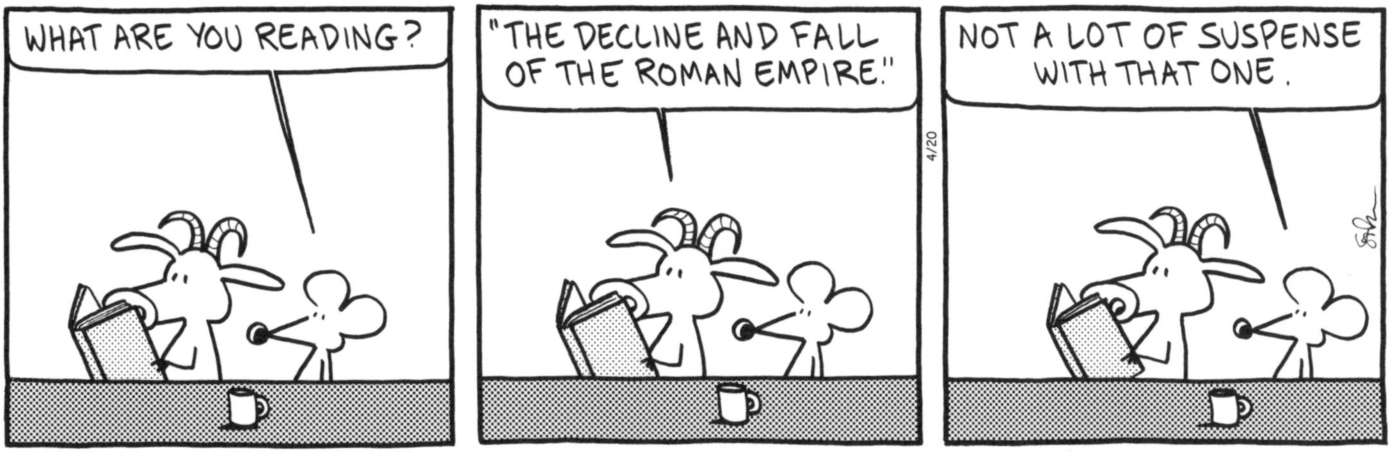
WHAT ARE YOU READING?
"THE DECLINE AND FALL OF THE ROMAN EMPIRE."
4/20
NOT A LOT OF SUSPENSE WITH THAT ONE.

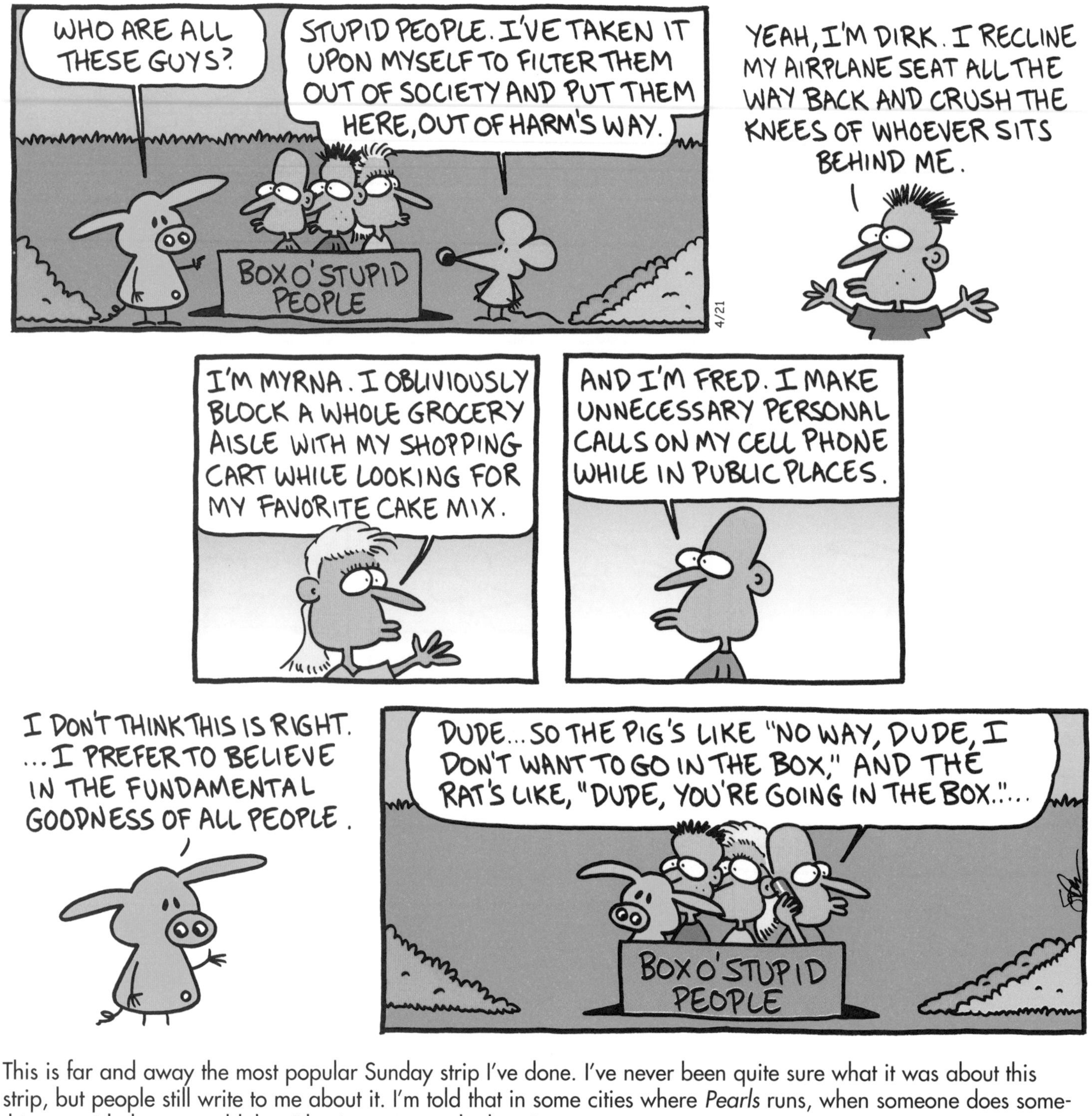
WHO ARE ALL THESE GUYS?
STUPID PEOPLE. I'VE TAKEN IT UPON MYSELF TO FILTER THEM OUT OF SOCIETY AND PUT THEM HERE, OUT OF HARM'S WAY.
BOX O' STUPID PEOPLE
4/21
YEAH, I'M DIRK. I RECLINE MY AIRPLANE SEAT ALL THE WAY BACK AND CRUSH THE KNEES OF WHOEVER SITS BEHIND ME.
I'M MYRNA. I OBLIVIOUSLY BLOCK A WHOLE GROCERY AISLE WITH MY SHOPPING CART WHILE LOOKING FOR MY FAVORITE CAKE MIX.
AND I'M FRED. I MAKE UNNECESSARY PERSONAL CALLS ON MY CELL PHONE WHILE IN PUBLIC PLACES.
I DON'T THINK THIS IS RIGHT. ...I PREFER TO BELIEVE IN THE FUNDAMENTAL GOODNESS OF ALL PEOPLE.
DUDE... SO THE PIG'S LIKE "NO WAY, DUDE, I DON'T WANT TO GO IN THE BOX," AND THE RAT'S LIKE, "DUDE, YOU'RE GOING IN THE BOX."...
BOX O' STUPID PEOPLE

This is far and away the most popular Sunday strip I've done. I've never been quite sure what it was about this strip, but people still write to me about it. I'm told that in some cities where *Pearls* runs, when someone does something stupid, they are told that "they're going in the box."

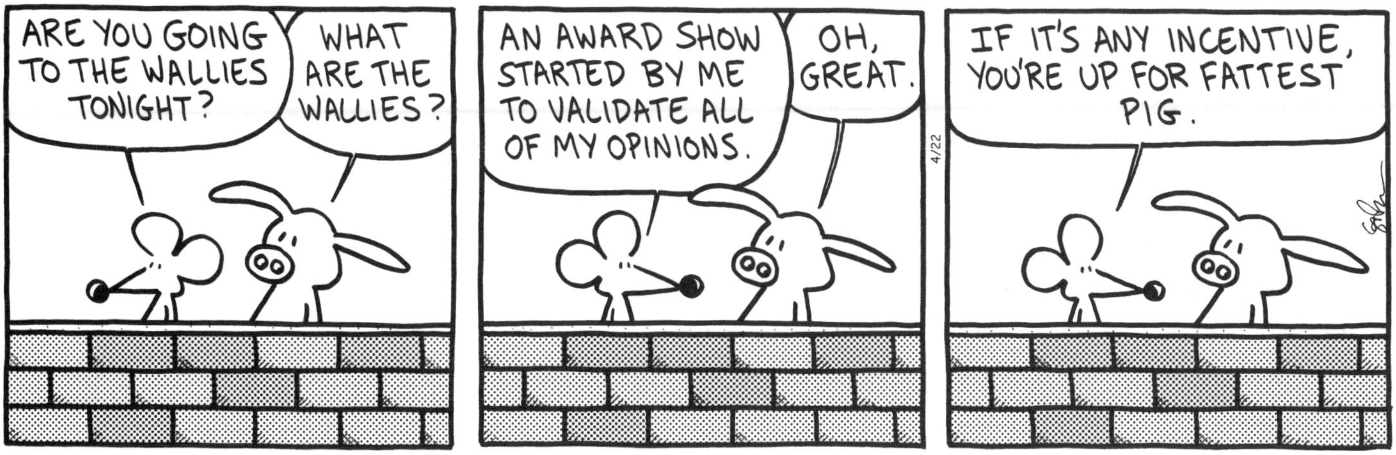
ARE YOU GOING TO THE WALLIES TONIGHT?
WHAT ARE THE WALLIES?
AN AWARD SHOW STARTED BY ME TO VALIDATE ALL OF MY OPINIONS.
OH, GREAT.
4/22
IF IT'S ANY INCENTIVE, YOU'RE UP FOR FATTEST PIG.

WALLIES stands for, "We All Love Little Intelligent Engaging ratS."

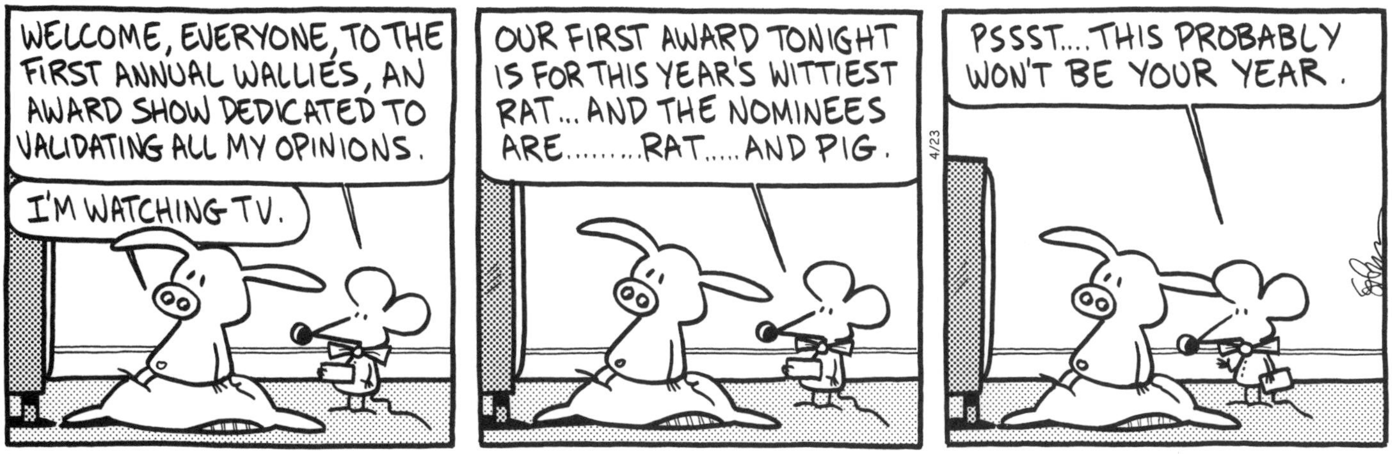
WELCOME, EVERYONE, TO THE FIRST ANNUAL WALLIES, AN AWARD SHOW DEDICATED TO VALIDATING ALL MY OPINIONS.
I'M WATCHING TV.
OUR FIRST AWARD TONIGHT IS FOR THIS YEAR'S WITTIEST RAT... AND THE NOMINEES ARE.........RAT.....AND PIG.
4/23
PSSST....THIS PROBABLY WON'T BE YOUR YEAR.

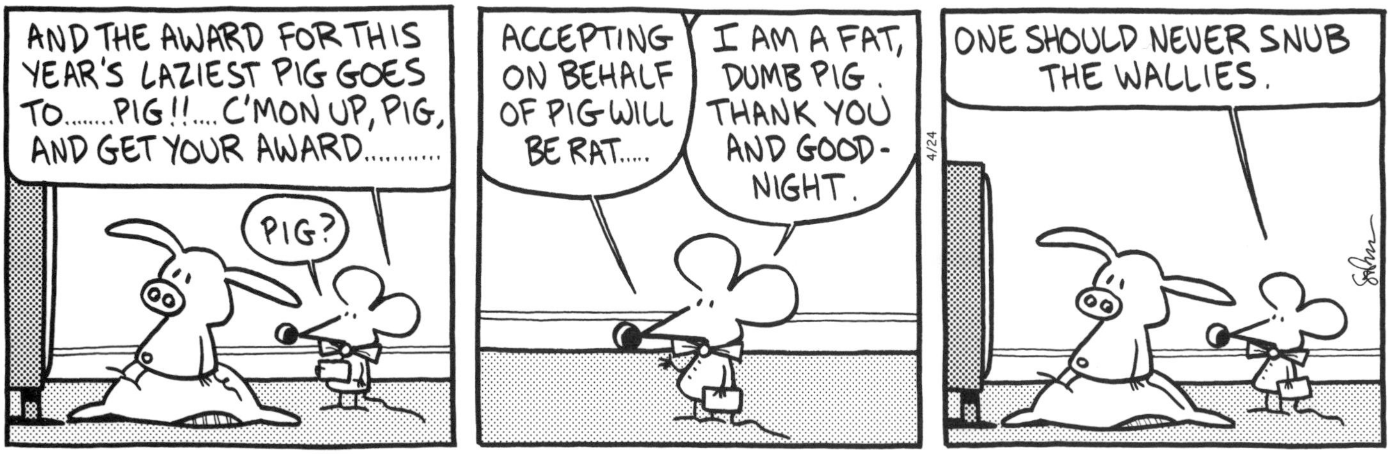
AND THE AWARD FOR THIS YEAR'S LAZIEST PIG GOES TO........PIG!!.... C'MON UP, PIG, AND GET YOUR AWARD..........
PIG?
ACCEPTING ON BEHALF OF PIG WILL BE RAT.....
I AM A FAT, DUMB PIG. THANK YOU AND GOOD-NIGHT.
4/24
ONE SHOULD NEVER SNUB THE WALLIES.

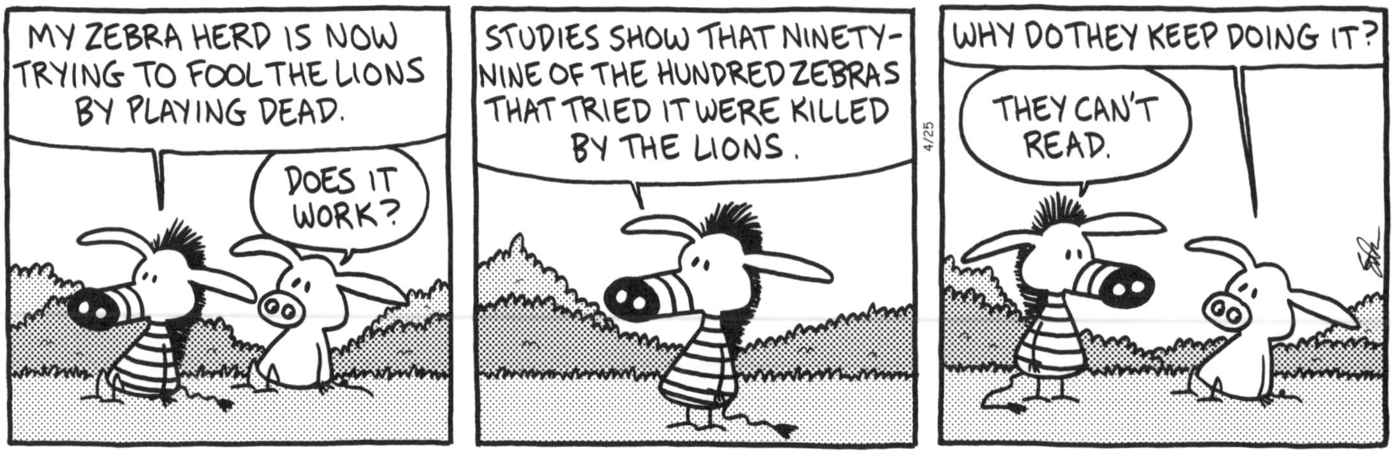
MY ZEBRA HERD IS NOW TRYING TO FOOL THE LIONS BY PLAYING DEAD.
DOES IT WORK?
STUDIES SHOW THAT NINETY-NINE OF THE HUNDRED ZEBRAS THAT TRIED IT WERE KILLED BY THE LIONS.
4/25
WHY DO THEY KEEP DOING IT?
THEY CAN'T READ.

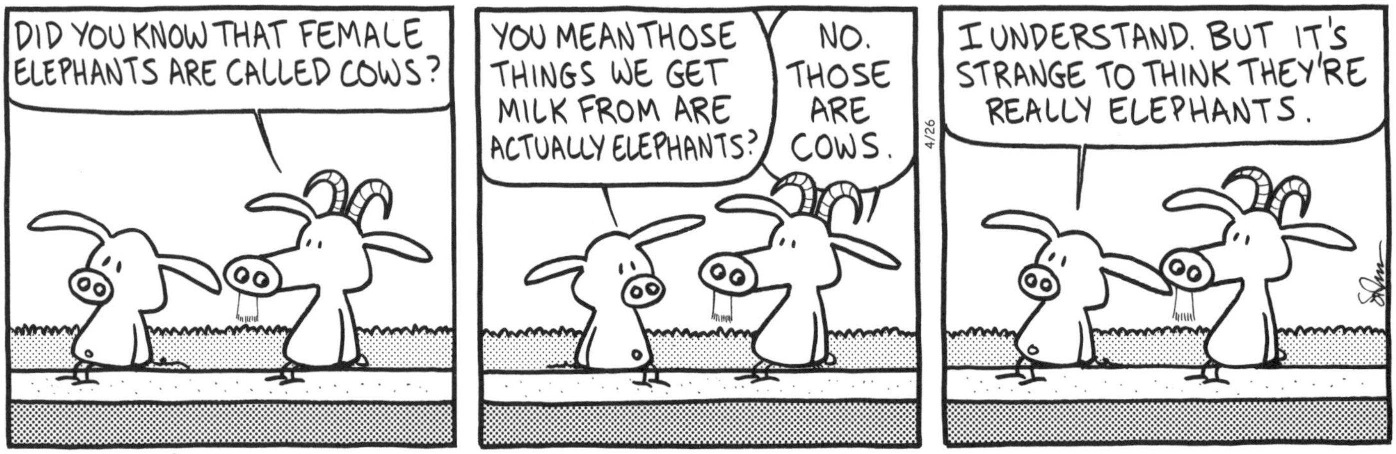
DID YOU KNOW THAT FEMALE ELEPHANTS ARE CALLED COWS?
YOU MEAN THOSE THINGS WE GET MILK FROM ARE ACTUALLY ELEPHANTS?
NO. THOSE ARE COWS.
4/26
I UNDERSTAND. BUT IT'S STRANGE TO THINK THEY'RE REALLY ELEPHANTS.

This strip still confuses me. When one of your own strips confuses you, you've got a problem.

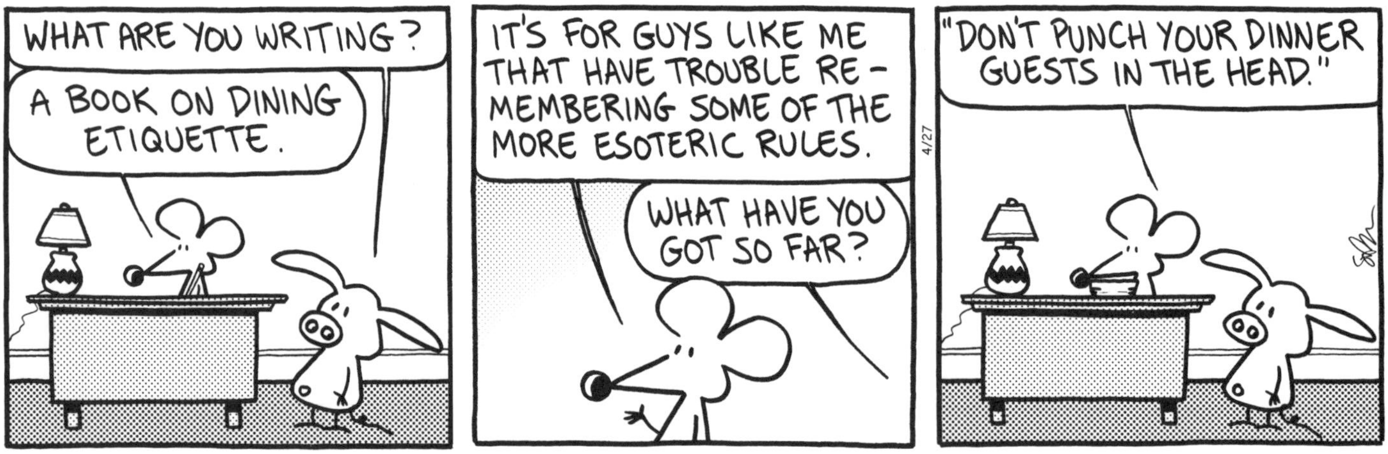
WHAT ARE YOU WRITING?
A BOOK ON DINING ETIQUETTE.
IT'S FOR GUYS LIKE ME THAT HAVE TROUBLE RE-MEMBERING SOME OF THE MORE ESOTERIC RULES.
WHAT HAVE YOU GOT SO FAR?
4/27
"DON'T PUNCH YOUR DINNER GUESTS IN THE HEAD."

I'm very big on those Charlie Brown lamps.

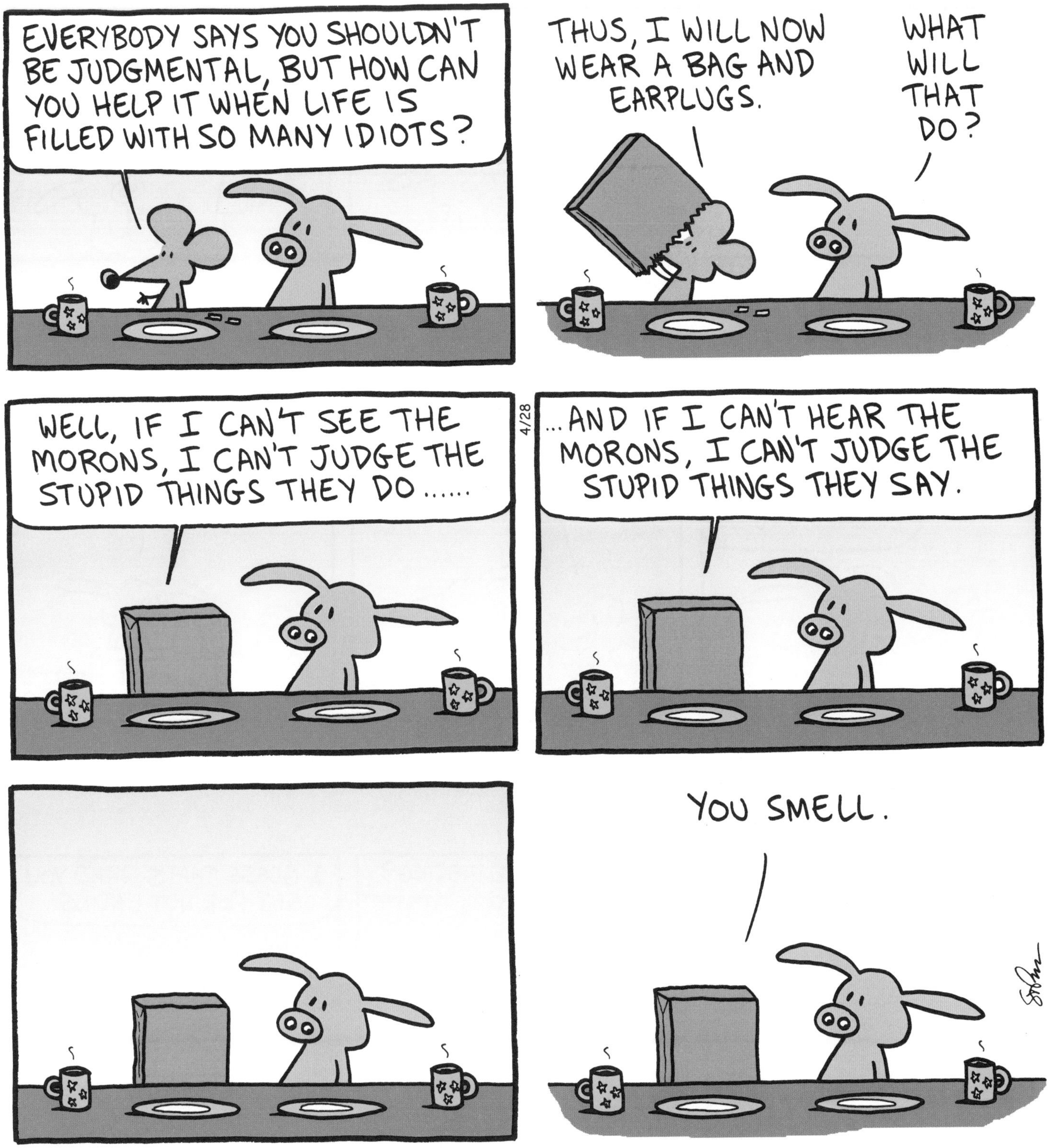
EVERYBODY SAYS YOU SHOULDN'T BE JUDGMENTAL, BUT HOW CAN YOU HELP IT WHEN LIFE IS FILLED WITH SO MANY IDIOTS?
THUS, I WILL NOW WEAR A BAG AND EARPLUGS.
WHAT WILL THAT DO?
4/28
WELL, IF I CAN'T SEE THE MORONS, I CAN'T JUDGE THE STUPID THINGS THEY DO......
...AND IF I CAN'T HEAR THE MORONS, I CAN'T JUDGE THE STUPID THINGS THEY SAY.
YOU SMELL.

This isn't such a bad idea.

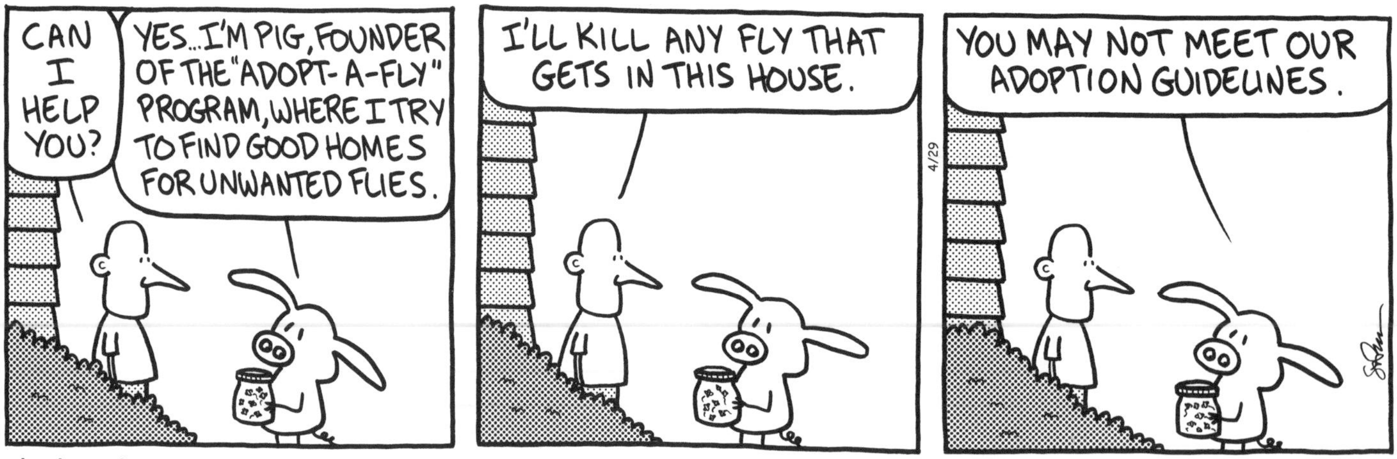
CAN I HELP YOU?
YES...I'M PIG, FOUNDER OF THE "ADOPT-A-FLY" PROGRAM, WHERE I TRY TO FIND GOOD HOMES FOR UNWANTED FLIES.
I'LL KILL ANY FLY THAT GETS IN THIS HOUSE.
4/29
YOU MAY NOT MEET OUR ADOPTION GUIDELINES.

I think understatement is a key to good comedy.

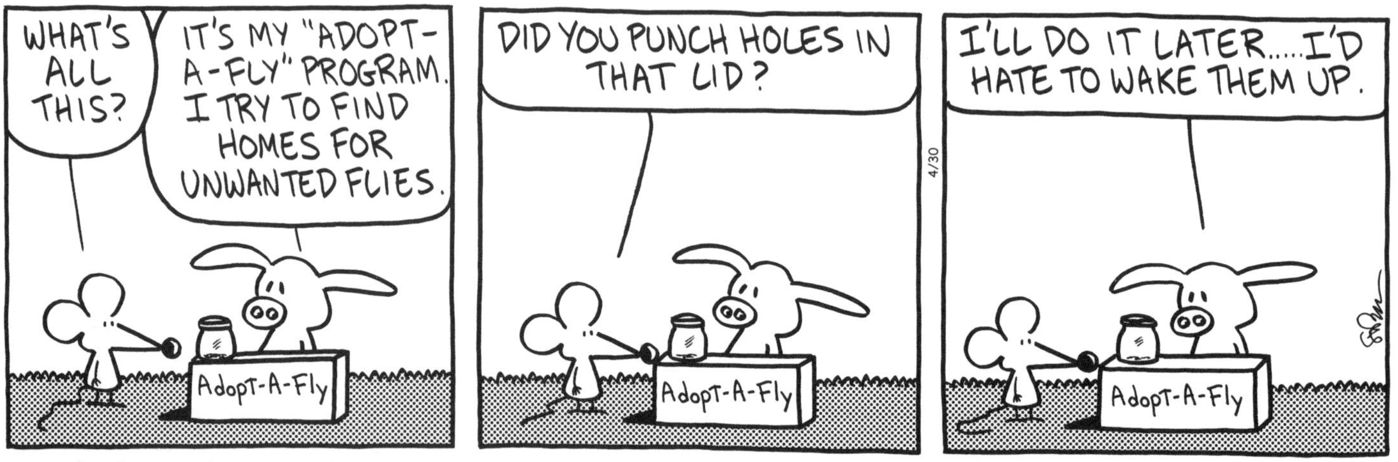
WHAT'S ALL THIS?
IT'S MY "ADOPT-A-FLY" PROGRAM. I TRY TO FIND HOMES FOR UNWANTED FLIES.
Adopt-A-Fly
DID YOU PUNCH HOLES IN THAT LID?
4/30
I'LL DO IT LATER.....I'D HATE TO WAKE THEM UP.

So is death. Death = comedy.

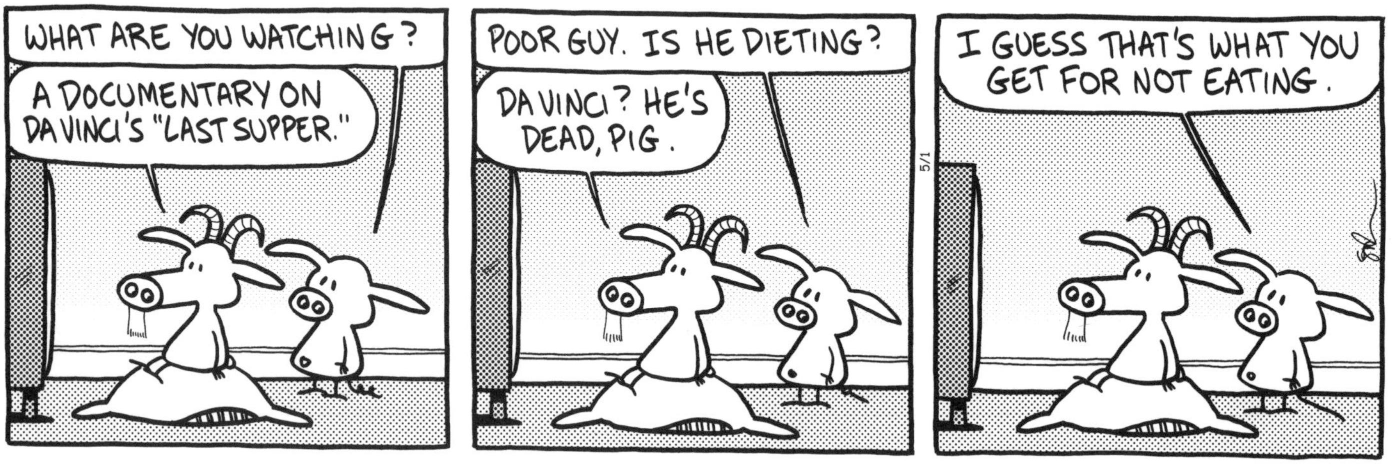
WHAT ARE YOU WATCHING?
A DOCUMENTARY ON DA VINCI'S "LAST SUPPER."
POOR GUY. IS HE DIETING?
DA VINCI? HE'S DEAD, PIG.
5/1
I GUESS THAT'S WHAT YOU GET FOR NOT EATING.

LOOK AT THAT GUY SMOKING...... HE THINKS HE'S A CHICK MAGNET 'CAUSE HE WEARS TURTLENECK SWEATERS AND LITTLE SUNGLASSES.

AND LOOK AT THOSE SUPERFICIAL BABES TALKING TO HIM......... LOOOOOOOOOSEEEEEEERS.

HYPOCRITE.

OUR STRIP IS BEST VIEWED IN LETTERBOX FORMAT.

This strip also confused a lot of people. When most movies are shown on TV, the movies have to be cropped on the sides to fit your TV screen. Directors complain about this because it eliminates important stuff on the edges of the scene, so they try to insist that their films be shown in this wide "letterbox" format.

IT'S IMPORTANT THAT WE ALWAYS KEEP THE LINES OF COMMUNICATION OPEN.

OH, YES! WHAT A BEYOOOOTIFUL IDEA...POMPOUS RAT.

HEE HEE. STUPID ZEBRA FOLLOWS ANYTHING I SAY.

OKAY.

GREAT.

67

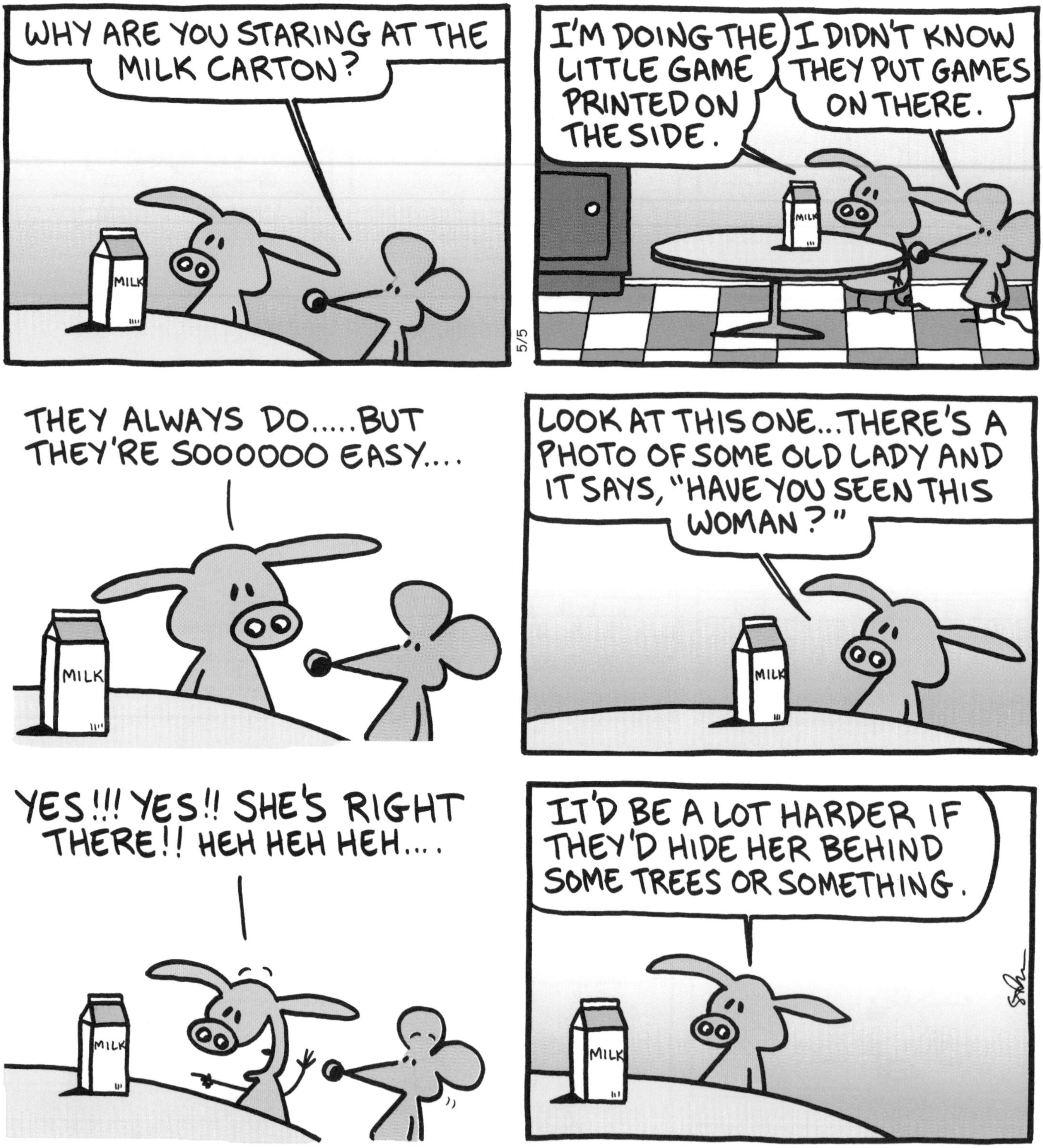
WHY ARE YOU STARING AT THE MILK CARTON?
I'M DOING THE LITTLE GAME PRINTED ON THE SIDE.
I DIDN'T KNOW THEY PUT GAMES ON THERE.
THEY ALWAYS DO.....BUT THEY'RE SOOOOOO EASY....
LOOK AT THIS ONE...THERE'S A PHOTO OF SOME OLD LADY AND IT SAYS, "HAVE YOU SEEN THIS WOMAN?"
YES!!! YES!! SHE'S RIGHT THERE!! HEH HEH HEH....
IT'D BE A LOT HARDER IF THEY'D HIDE HER BEHIND SOME TREES OR SOMETHING.
MILK
5/5

That kitchen scene in the second panel is one of the first times I tried to draw an actual room scene in *Pearls* (usually my backgrounds are very sparse or nonexistent). At the time, I knew absolutely nothing about perspective (and still don't know very much). Had this been an actual kitchen, Pig and Rat would have been sliding right toward you, due to my wonderful rendering of perspective on the floor tiles.

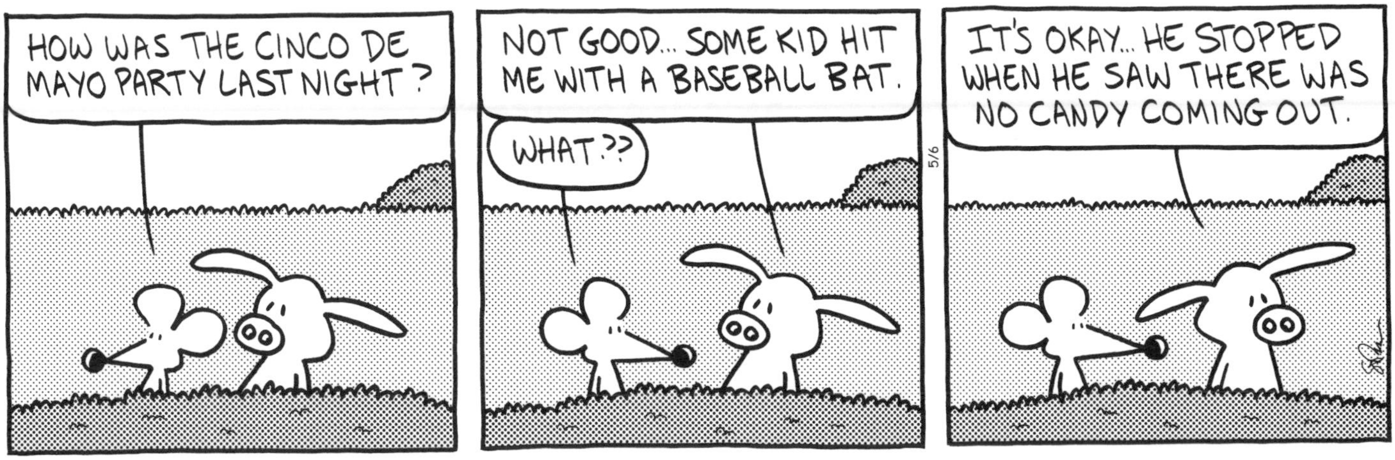
HOW WAS THE CINCO DE MAYO PARTY LAST NIGHT?
NOT GOOD... SOME KID HIT ME WITH A BASEBALL BAT.
WHAT??
5/6
IT'S OKAY... HE STOPPED WHEN HE SAW THERE WAS NO CANDY COMING OUT.

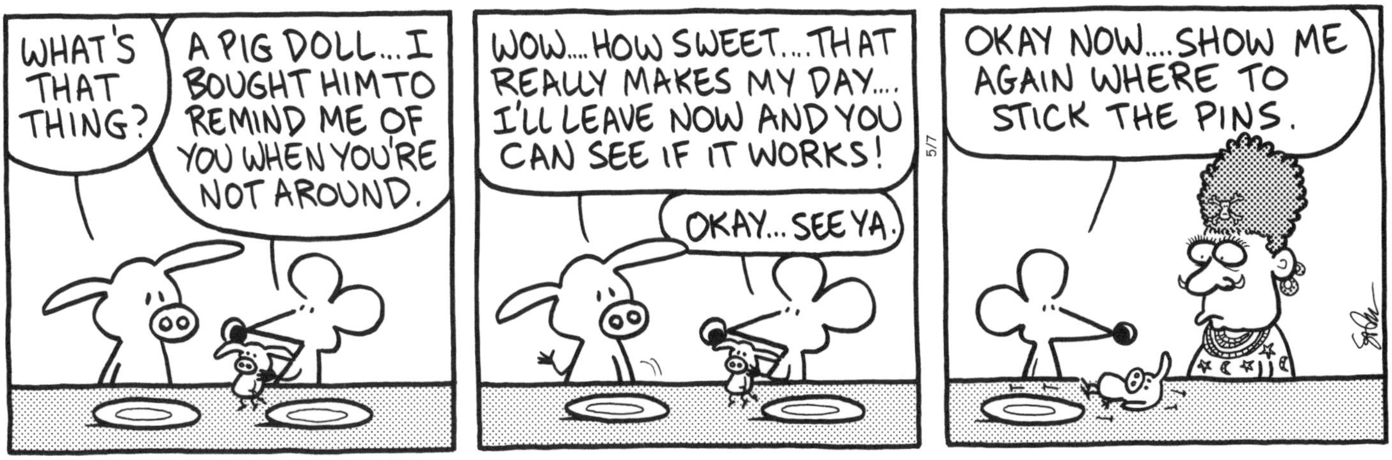
WHAT'S THAT THING?
A PIG DOLL... I BOUGHT HIM TO REMIND ME OF YOU WHEN YOU'RE NOT AROUND.
WOW.... HOW SWEET.... THAT REALLY MAKES MY DAY.... I'LL LEAVE NOW AND YOU CAN SEE IF IT WORKS!
OKAY... SEE YA.
5/7
OKAY NOW.... SHOW ME AGAIN WHERE TO STICK THE PINS.

Whenever someone feels happy and secure in *Pearls*, you can bet that they are headed for something bad.

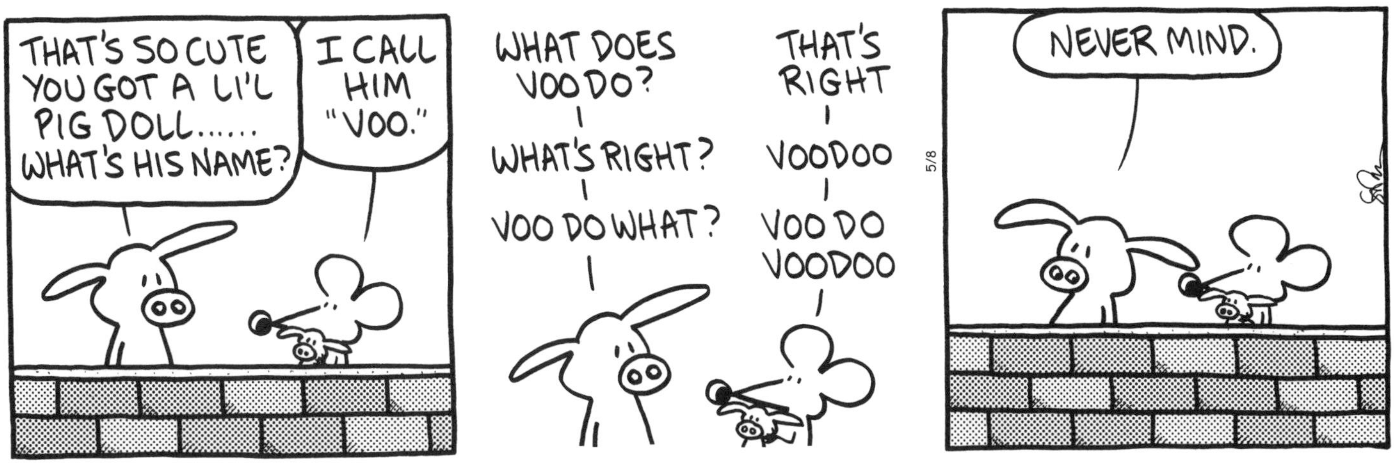
THAT'S SO CUTE YOU GOT A LI'L PIG DOLL...... WHAT'S HIS NAME?
I CALL HIM "VOO."
WHAT DOES VOO DO?
THAT'S RIGHT
WHAT'S RIGHT?
VOODOO
VOO DO WHAT?
VOO DO VOODOO
5/8
NEVER MIND.

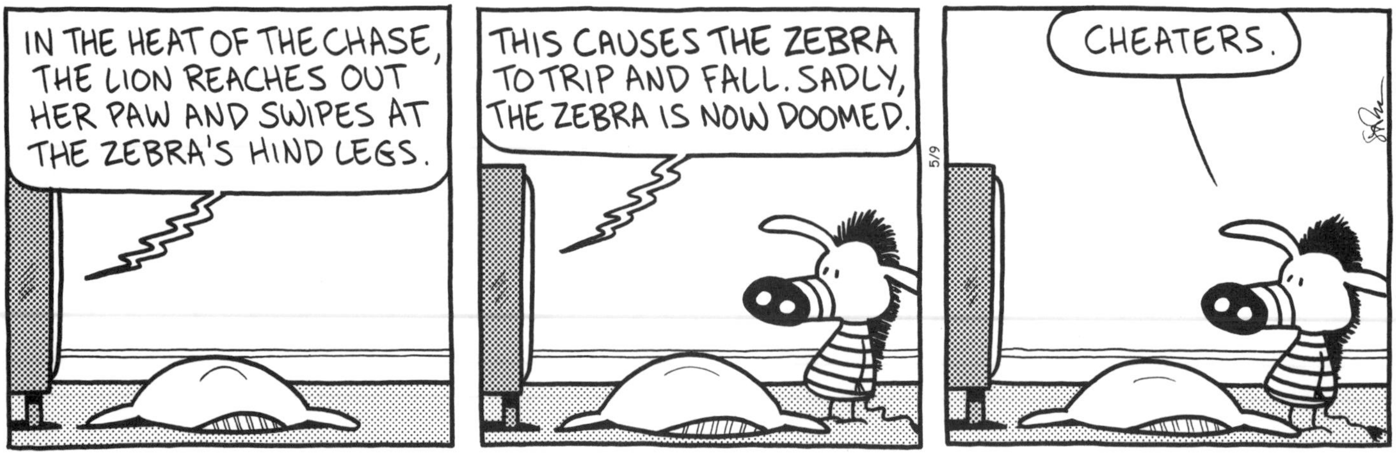
IN THE HEAT OF THE CHASE, THE LION REACHES OUT HER PAW AND SWIPES AT THE ZEBRA'S HIND LEGS.
THIS CAUSES THE ZEBRA TO TRIP AND FALL. SADLY, THE ZEBRA IS NOW DOOMED.
5/9
CHEATERS.

I love nature shows. This is where I learned of the lions' neat tripping trick.

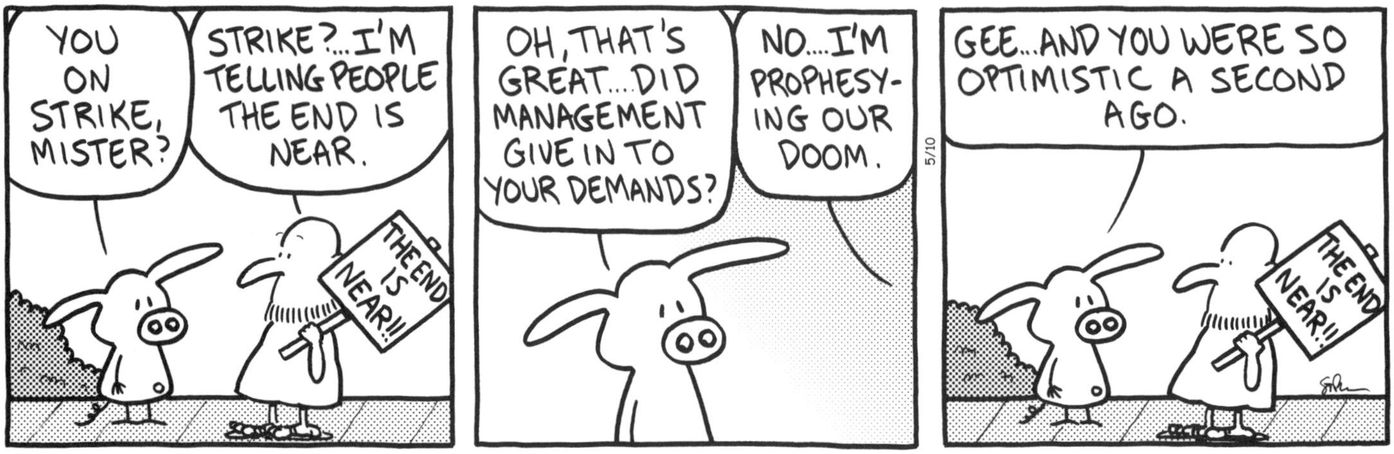
YOU ON STRIKE, MISTER?
STRIKE?... I'M TELLING PEOPLE THE END IS NEAR.
THE END IS NEAR!!
OH, THAT'S GREAT.... DID MANAGEMENT GIVE IN TO YOUR DEMANDS?
NO.... I'M PROPHESYING OUR DOOM.
5/10
GEE... AND YOU WERE SO OPTIMISTIC A SECOND AGO.
THE END IS NEAR!!

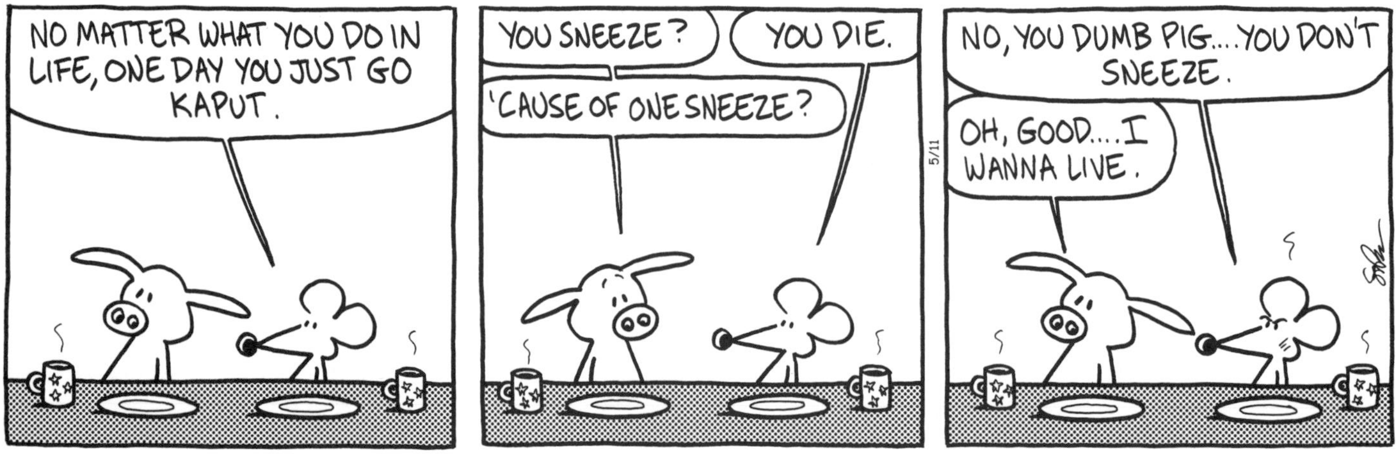
NO MATTER WHAT YOU DO IN LIFE, ONE DAY YOU JUST GO KAPUT.
YOU SNEEZE?
YOU DIE.
'CAUSE OF ONE SNEEZE?
5/11
NO, YOU DUMB PIG.... YOU DON'T SNEEZE.
OH, GOOD.... I WANNA LIVE.

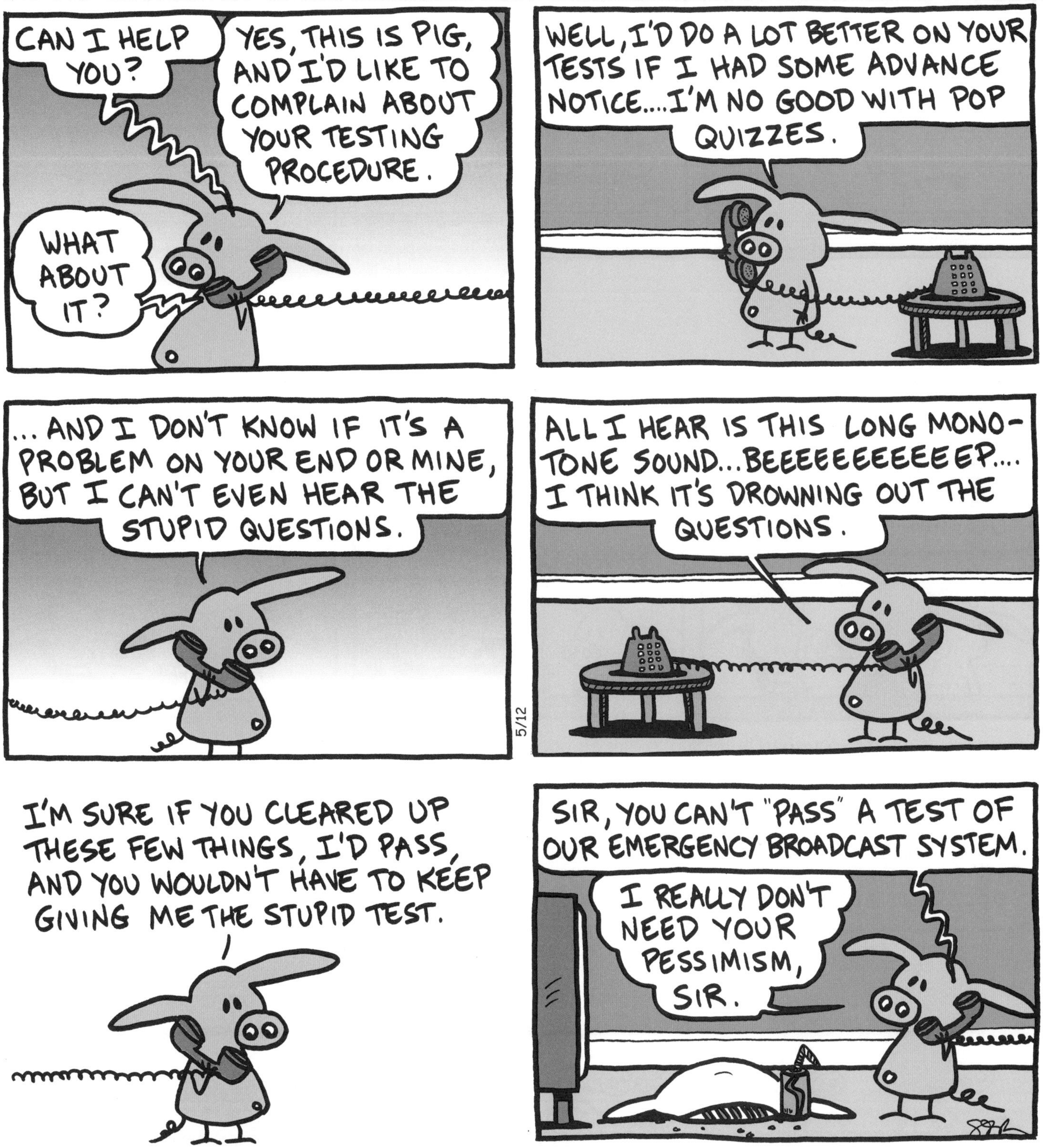
CAN I HELP YOU?
YES, THIS IS PIG, AND I'D LIKE TO COMPLAIN ABOUT YOUR TESTING PROCEDURE.
WHAT ABOUT IT?
WELL, I'D DO A LOT BETTER ON YOUR TESTS IF I HAD SOME ADVANCE NOTICE....I'M NO GOOD WITH POP QUIZZES.
...AND I DON'T KNOW IF IT'S A PROBLEM ON YOUR END OR MINE, BUT I CAN'T EVEN HEAR THE STUPID QUESTIONS.
5/12
ALL I HEAR IS THIS LONG MONO-TONE SOUND...BEEEEEEEEEEEP.... I THINK IT'S DROWNING OUT THE QUESTIONS.
I'M SURE IF YOU CLEARED UP THESE FEW THINGS, I'D PASS, AND YOU WOULDN'T HAVE TO KEEP GIVING ME THE STUPID TEST.
SIR, YOU CAN'T "PASS" A TEST OF OUR EMERGENCY BROADCAST SYSTEM.
I REALLY DON'T NEED YOUR PESSIMISM, SIR.

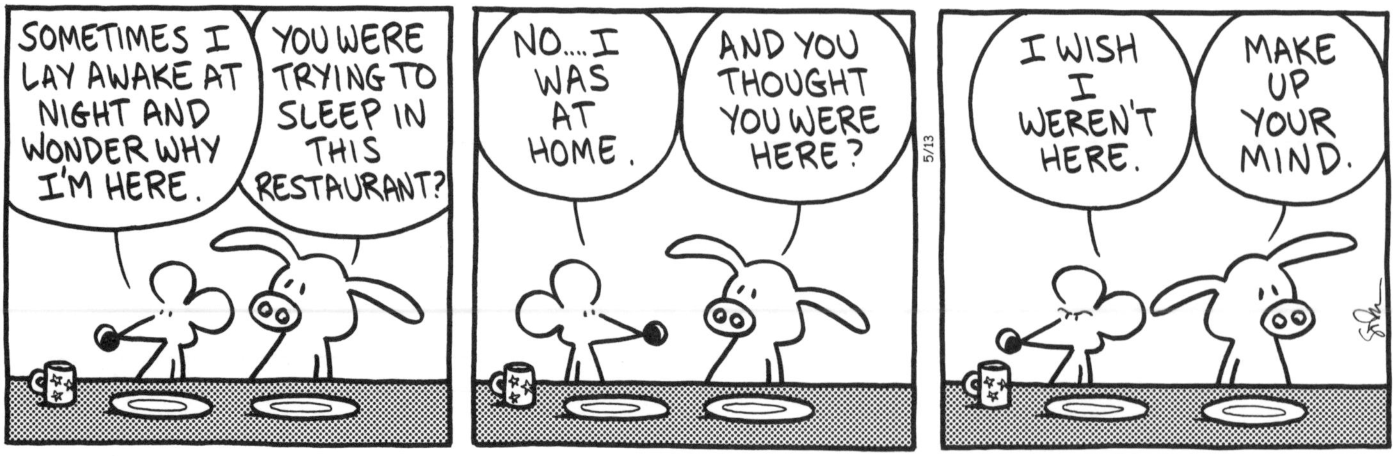
SOMETIMES I LAY AWAKE AT NIGHT AND WONDER WHY I'M HERE.
YOU WERE TRYING TO SLEEP IN THIS RESTAURANT?
NO.... I WAS AT HOME.
AND YOU THOUGHT YOU WERE HERE?
5/13
I WISH I WEREN'T HERE.
MAKE UP YOUR MIND.

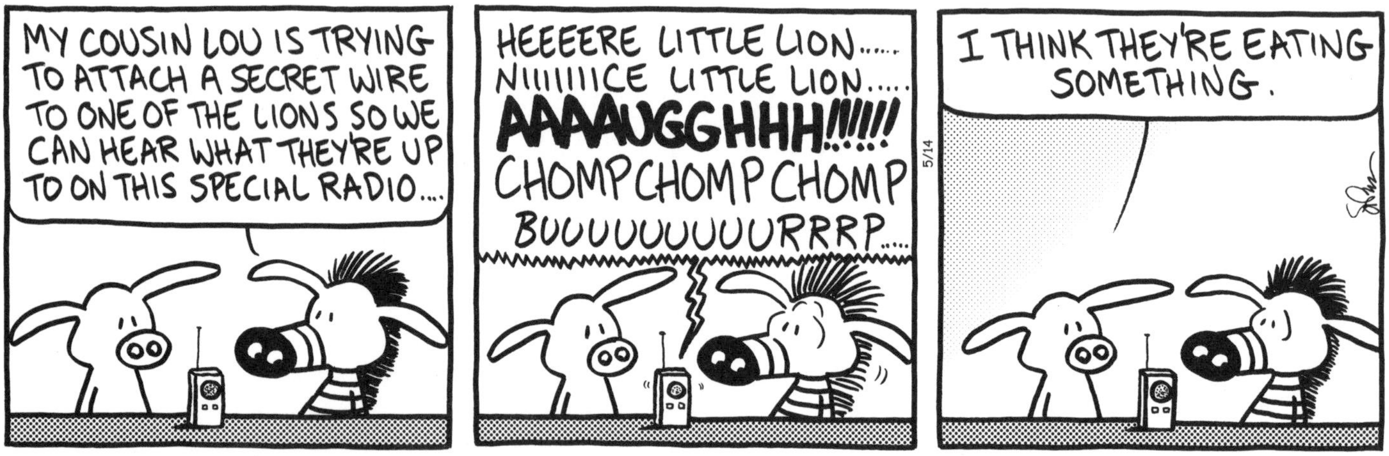
MY COUSIN LOU IS TRYING TO ATTACH A SECRET WIRE TO ONE OF THE LIONS SO WE CAN HEAR WHAT THEY'RE UP TO ON THIS SPECIAL RADIO....
HEEEERE LITTLE LION......
NIIIIIIICE LITTLE LION.....
AAAAUGGHHH!!!!!!
CHOMP CHOMP CHOMP
BUUUUUUUUURRRP.....
5/14
I THINK THEY'RE EATING SOMETHING.

Cousin Lou is my real cousin. I'm related to him on both my mother's and father's side of the family. With family relations like that, it's no wonder I'm messed up.

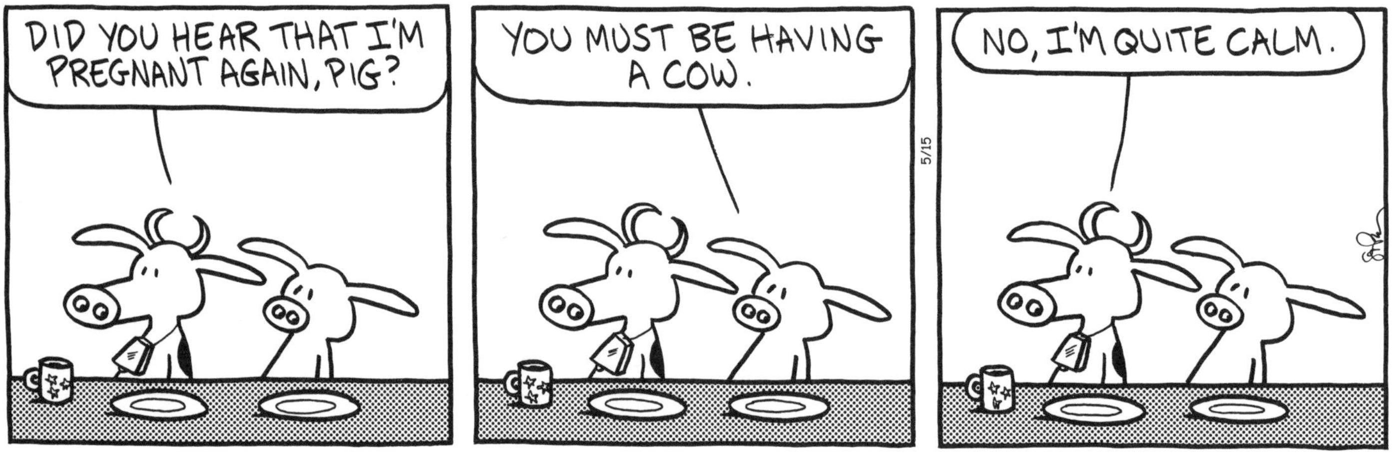
DID YOU HEAR THAT I'M PREGNANT AGAIN, PIG?
YOU MUST BE HAVING A COW.
5/15
NO, I'M QUITE CALM.

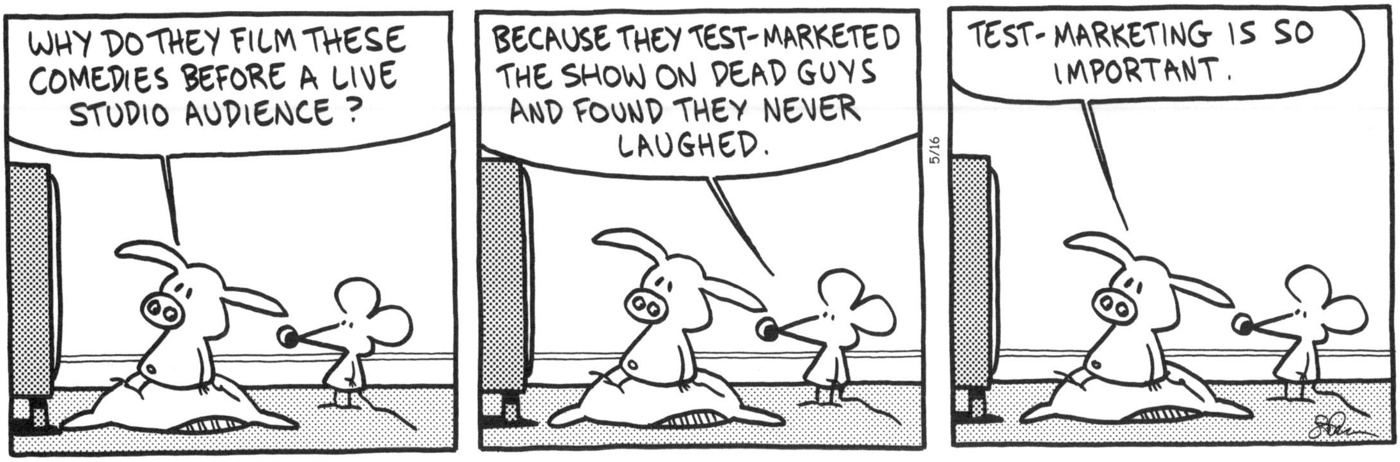
WHY DO THEY FILM THESE COMEDIES BEFORE A LIVE STUDIO AUDIENCE ?
BECAUSE THEY TEST-MARKETED THE SHOW ON DEAD GUYS AND FOUND THEY NEVER LAUGHED.
TEST- MARKETING IS SO IMPORTANT.

More death, more comedy.

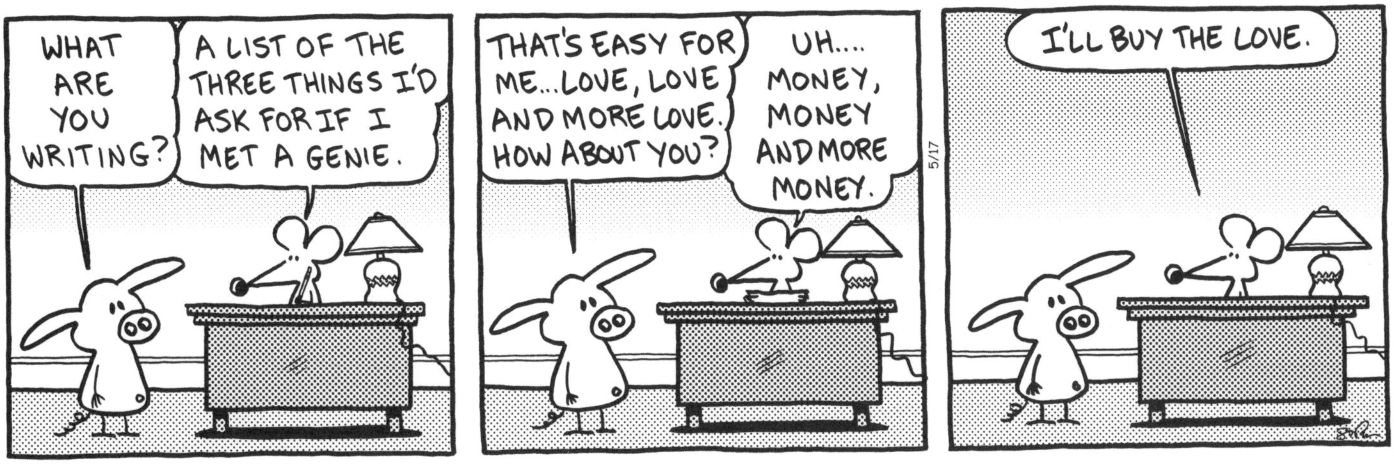
WHAT ARE YOU WRITING?
A LIST OF THE THREE THINGS I'D ASK FOR IF I MET A GENIE.
THAT'S EASY FOR ME...LOVE, LOVE AND MORE LOVE. HOW ABOUT YOU?
UH.... MONEY, MONEY AND MORE MONEY.
I'LL BUY THE LOVE.

And more Charlie Brown lamps.

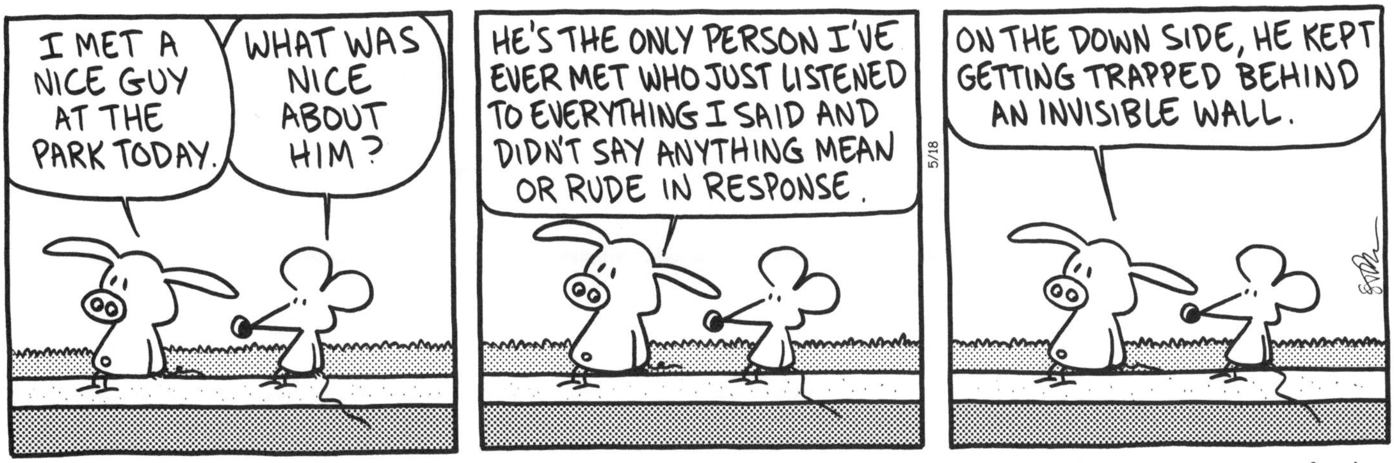
I MET A NICE GUY AT THE PARK TODAY.
WHAT WAS NICE ABOUT HIM?
HE'S THE ONLY PERSON I'VE EVER MET WHO JUST LISTENED TO EVERYTHING I SAID AND DIDN'T SAY ANYTHING MEAN OR RUDE IN RESPONSE.
ON THE DOWN SIDE, HE KEPT GETTING TRAPPED BEHIND AN INVISIBLE WALL.

A lot of people wrote to say they didn't get this. So for all of you who fall into that camp, let me say just one final time that Pig's friend was a MIME!! A MIME!!!

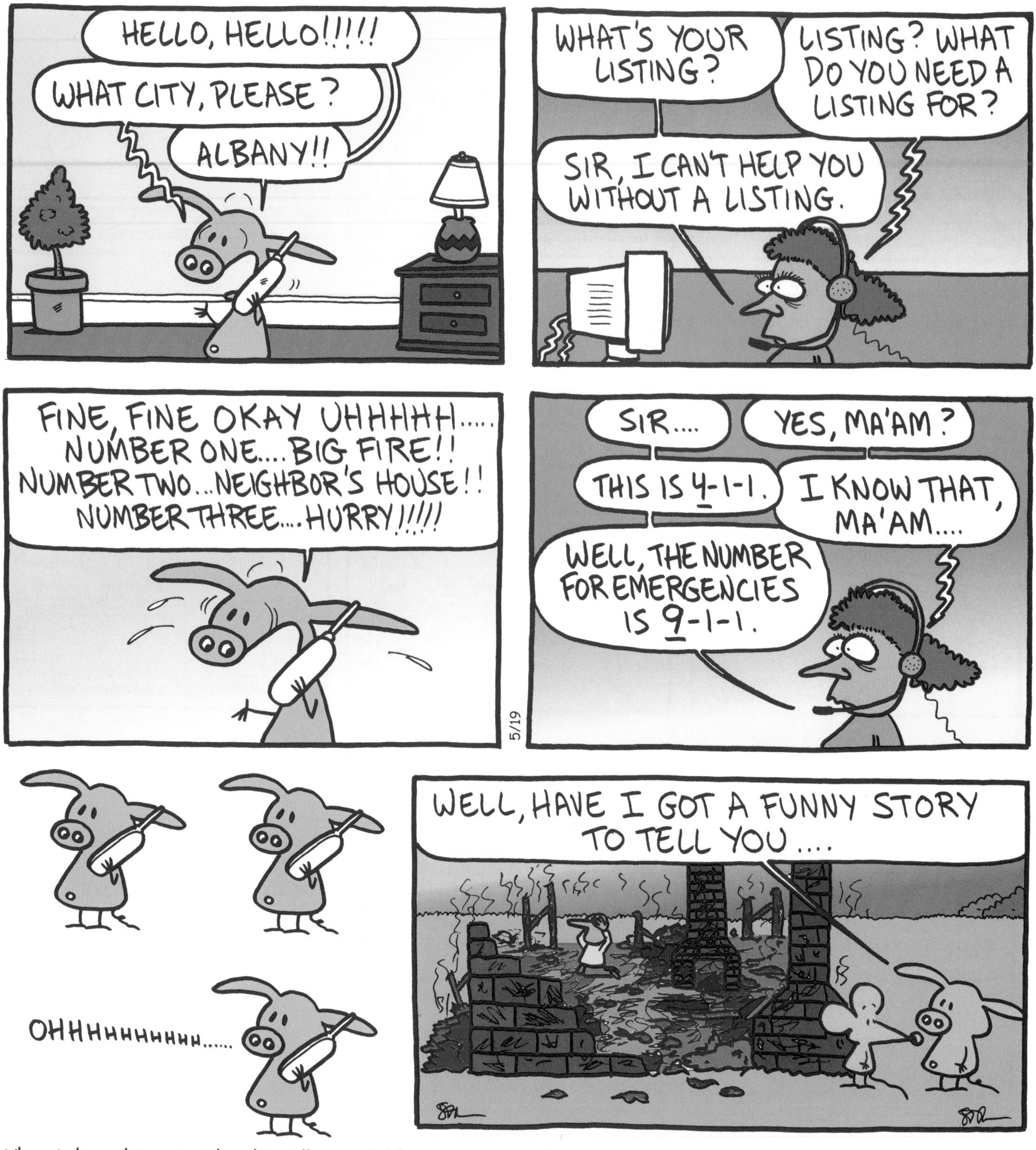
HELLO, HELLO!!!!!
WHAT CITY, PLEASE?
ALBANY!!
WHAT'S YOUR LISTING?
LISTING? WHAT DO YOU NEED A LISTING FOR?
SIR, I CAN'T HELP YOU WITHOUT A LISTING.
FINE, FINE OKAY UHHHHH..... NUMBER ONE.... BIG FIRE!! NUMBER TWO...NEIGHBOR'S HOUSE!! NUMBER THREE....HURRY!!!!!
5/19
SIR....
YES, MA'AM?
THIS IS 4-1-1.
I KNOW THAT, MA'AM....
WELL, THE NUMBER FOR EMERGENCIES IS 9-1-1.
OHHHHHHHHHH......
WELL, HAVE I GOT A FUNNY STORY TO TELL YOU ....

When I drew this strip, I lived in Albany, California. But I now know that there are many other Albanys around the country, and everyone who lives in one of those Albanys thinks the strip is in reference to their town.

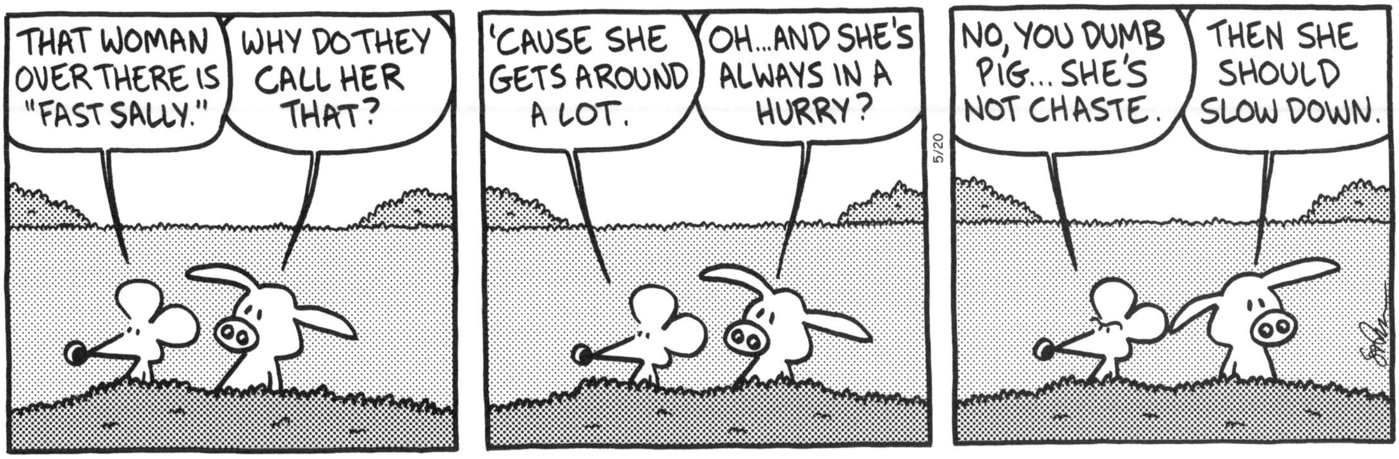
THAT WOMAN OVER THERE IS "FAST SALLY."
WHY DO THEY CALL HER THAT?
'CAUSE SHE GETS AROUND A LOT.
OH...AND SHE'S ALWAYS IN A HURRY?
NO, YOU DUMB PIG... SHE'S NOT CHASTE.
THEN SHE SHOULD SLOW DOWN.
5/20

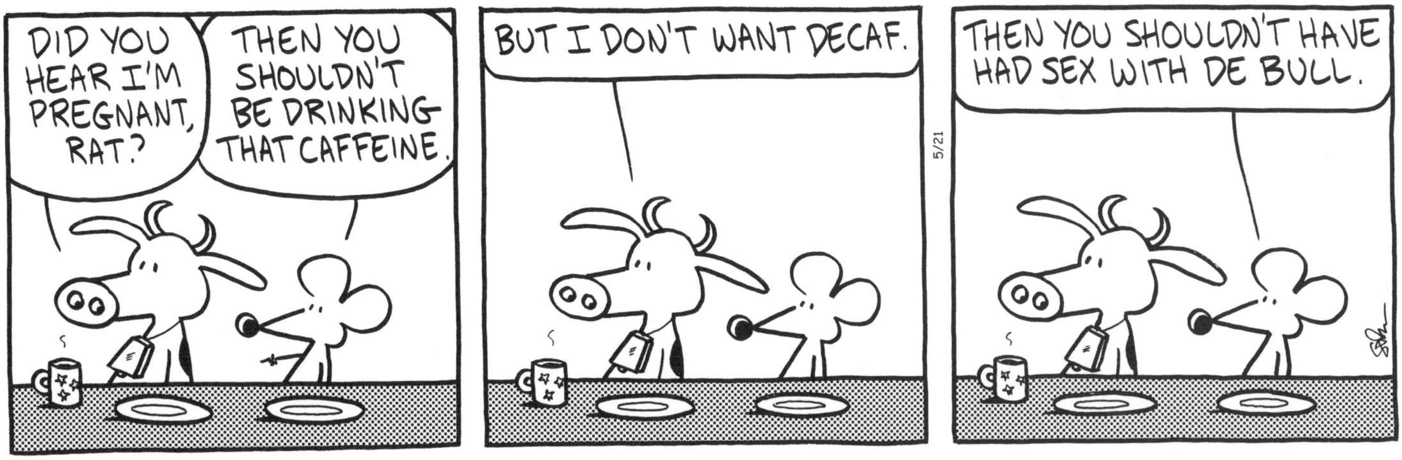
DID YOU HEAR I'M PREGNANT, RAT?
THEN YOU SHOULDN'T BE DRINKING THAT CAFFEINE.
BUT I DON'T WANT DECAF.
THEN YOU SHOULDN'T HAVE HAD SEX WITH DE BULL.
5/21

Another very popular daily strip. My editor at the syndicate wanted to change "had sex with" to "mated with," because the word "sex" was too "edgy." I stuck with "sex" because everything else sounded forced.

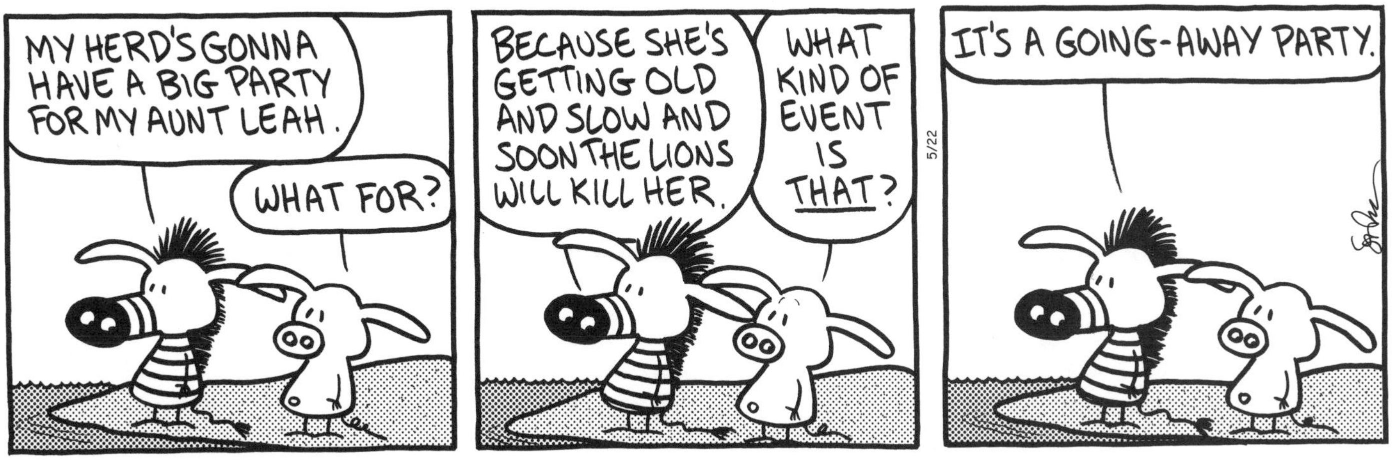
MY HERD'S GONNA HAVE A BIG PARTY FOR MY AUNT LEAH.
WHAT FOR?
BECAUSE SHE'S GETTING OLD AND SLOW AND SOON THE LIONS WILL KILL HER.
WHAT KIND OF EVENT IS THAT?
IT'S A GOING-AWAY PARTY.
5/22

My Aunt Leah is my Cousin Lou's mother. I'm telling you . . . it really pays to be related to me.

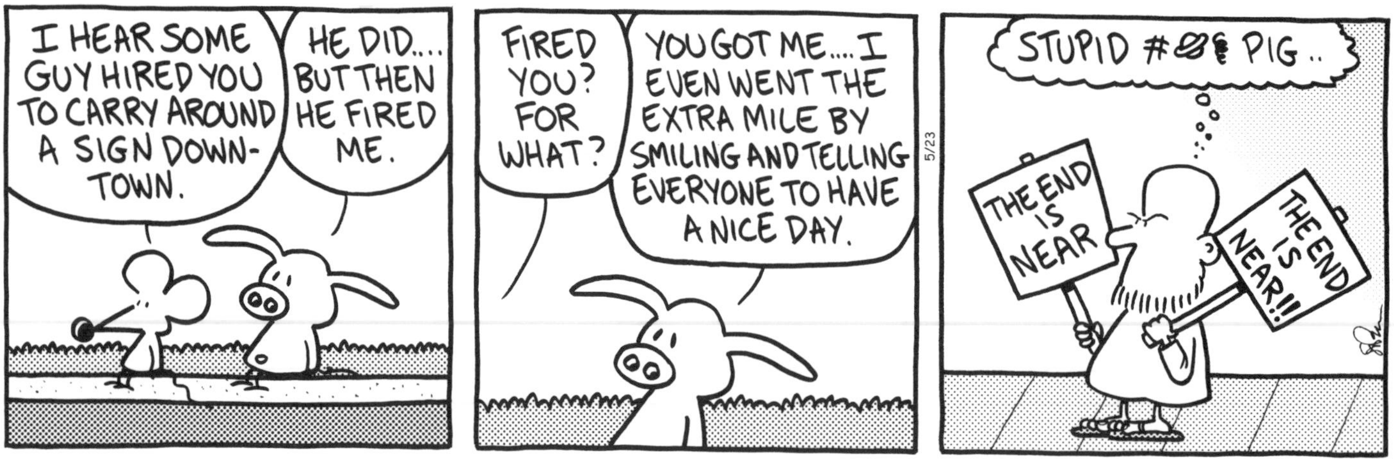

I HEAR SOME GUY HIRED YOU TO CARRY AROUND A SIGN DOWN-TOWN.
HE DID.... BUT THEN HE FIRED ME.
FIRED YOU? FOR WHAT?
YOU GOT ME.... I EVEN WENT THE EXTRA MILE BY SMILING AND TELLING EVERYONE TO HAVE A NICE DAY.
5/23
STUPID # PIG ..
THE END IS NEAR
THE END IS NEAR!!!

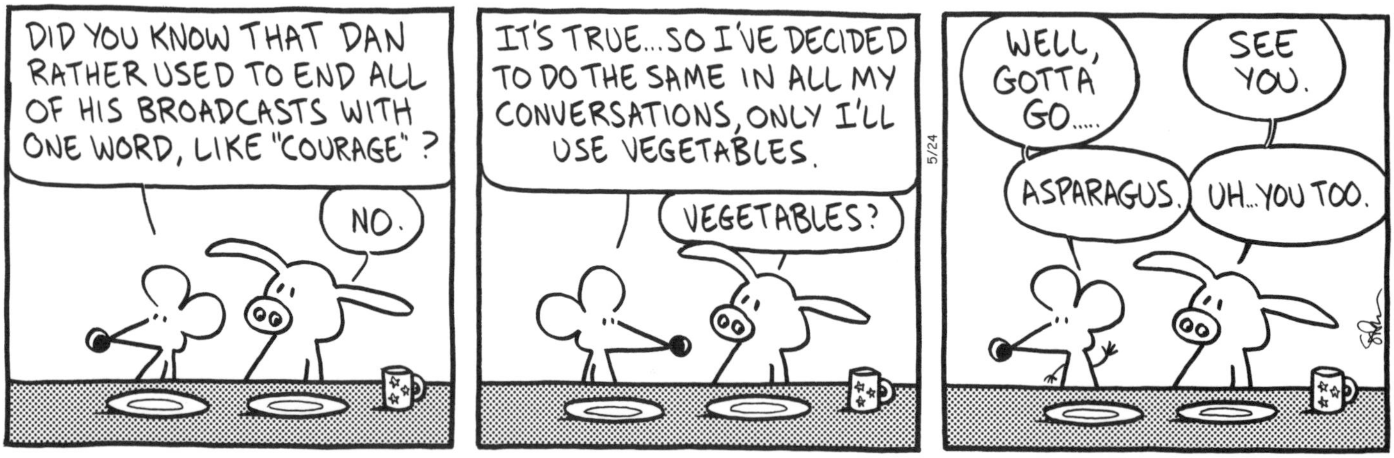

DID YOU KNOW THAT DAN RATHER USED TO END ALL OF HIS BROADCASTS WITH ONE WORD, LIKE "COURAGE"?
NO.
IT'S TRUE... SO I'VE DECIDED TO DO THE SAME IN ALL MY CONVERSATIONS, ONLY I'LL USE VEGETABLES.
VEGETABLES?
5/24
WELL, GOTTA GO.....
SEE YOU.
ASPARAGUS.
UH... YOU TOO.

Dan Rather really did this. Because Dan does some funny stuff, he's come up a few times in the strip.

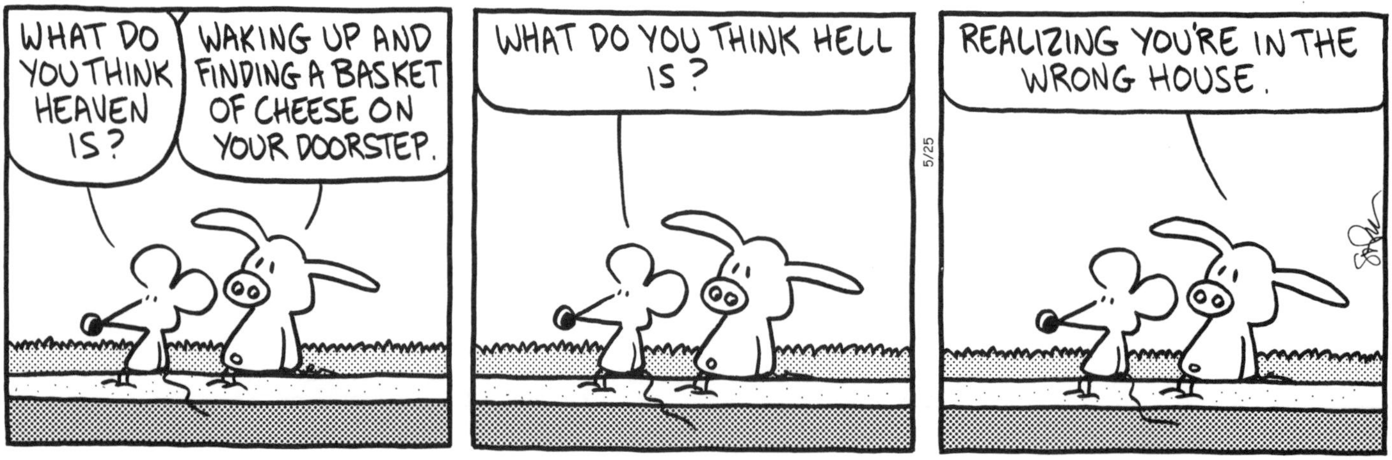

WHAT DO YOU THINK HEAVEN IS?
WAKING UP AND FINDING A BASKET OF CHEESE ON YOUR DOORSTEP.
WHAT DO YOU THINK HELL IS?
5/25
REALIZING YOU'RE IN THE WRONG HOUSE.

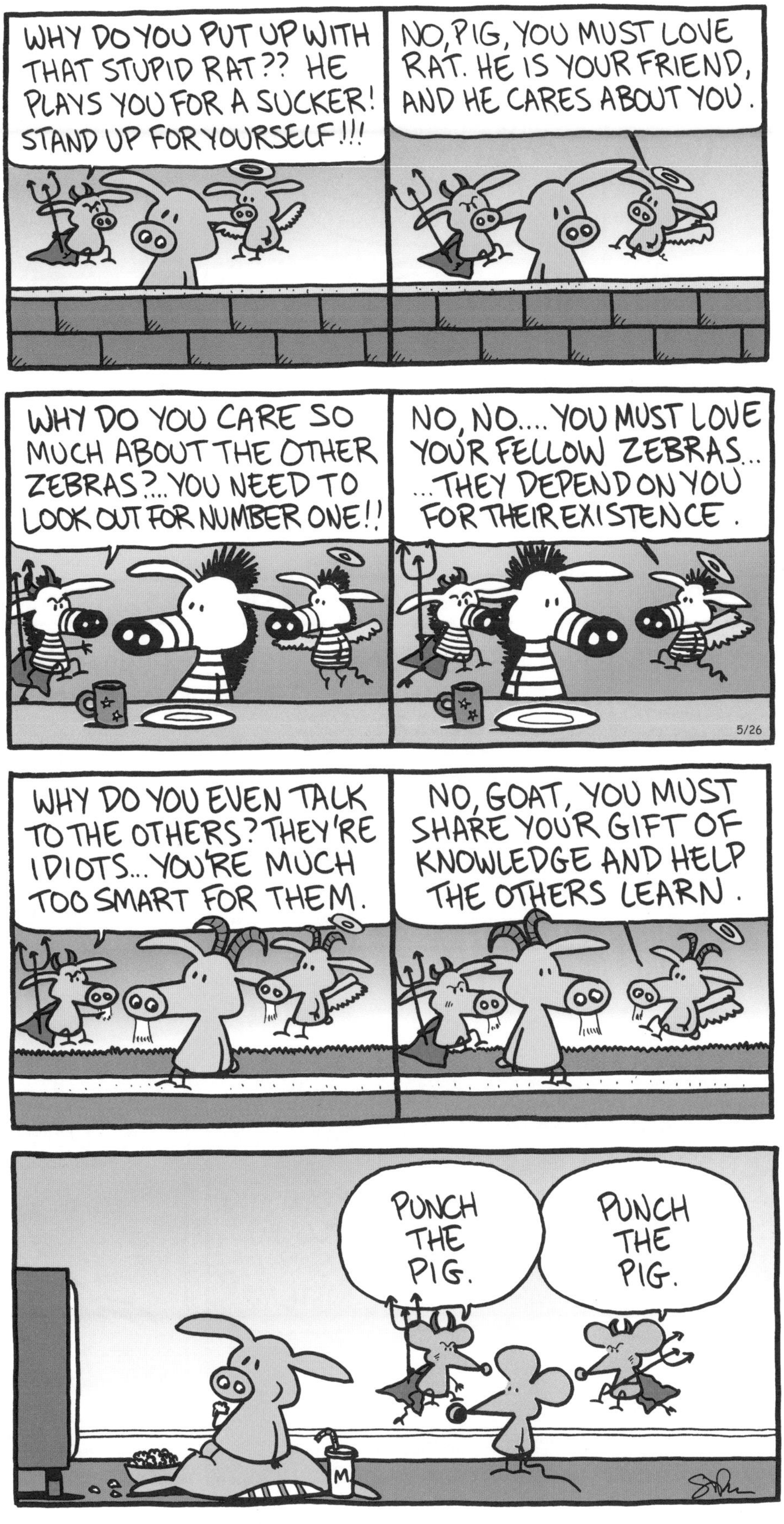
WHY DO YOU PUT UP WITH THAT STUPID RAT?? HE PLAYS YOU FOR A SUCKER! STAND UP FOR YOURSELF!!!
NO, PIG, YOU MUST LOVE RAT. HE IS YOUR FRIEND, AND HE CARES ABOUT YOU.
WHY DO YOU CARE SO MUCH ABOUT THE OTHER ZEBRAS?... YOU NEED TO LOOK OUT FOR NUMBER ONE!!
NO, NO.... YOU MUST LOVE YOUR FELLOW ZEBRAS... ...THEY DEPEND ON YOU FOR THEIR EXISTENCE.
5/26
WHY DO YOU EVEN TALK TO THE OTHERS? THEY'RE IDIOTS... YOU'RE MUCH TOO SMART FOR THEM.
NO, GOAT, YOU MUST SHARE YOUR GIFT OF KNOWLEDGE AND HELP THE OTHERS LEARN.
PUNCH THE PIG.
PUNCH THE PIG.
M

I think this strip defines the personalities of the four characters really well.

WHAT ARE YOU WATCHING?

SOME GUY THAT CLAIMS TO BE A SPIRITUAL MEDIUM.

WHAT'S THE GUY DO?

PEOPLE PAY HIM TONS OF CASH SO THEY CAN TALK TO THEIR DEAD RELATIVES.

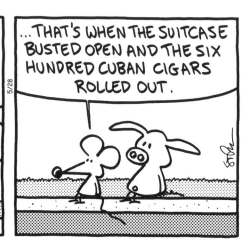
GOSH... I DON'T EVEN WANT TO TALK TO MY LIVING ONES.

I've had relatives ask if I really felt that way about them. I said no.

AND SO THE GUY SAYS, "SORRY, SIR, ALL PASSENGER CARRY-ON ITEMS MUST GO THROUGH THE X-RAY MACHINE..."

WHAT'D YOU DO?

I GRABBED MY SUITCASE WITH BOTH HANDS AND GAVE A BIG SPEECH ABOUT HOW SAD IT IS THAT NO ONE CAN TRUST ANYONE ANY MORE.

THEN WHAT?

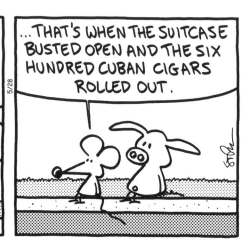
...THAT'S WHEN THE SUITCASE BUSTED OPEN AND THE SIX HUNDRED CUBAN CIGARS ROLLED OUT.

Hypocrisy = good comedy.

I'VE JUST JOINED THIS PIG GROUP DEDICATED TO ELIMINATING PIG-BASED INSULTS FROM OUR EVERYDAY LANGUAGE.

LIKE WHAT?

WE'RE GONNA START WITH "COMMIE PIG." IT'S VERY DEROGATORY TOWARD PIGS.

WHAT ARE YOU PROPOSING PEOPLE SAY INSTEAD?

"COMMIE COW."

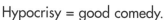

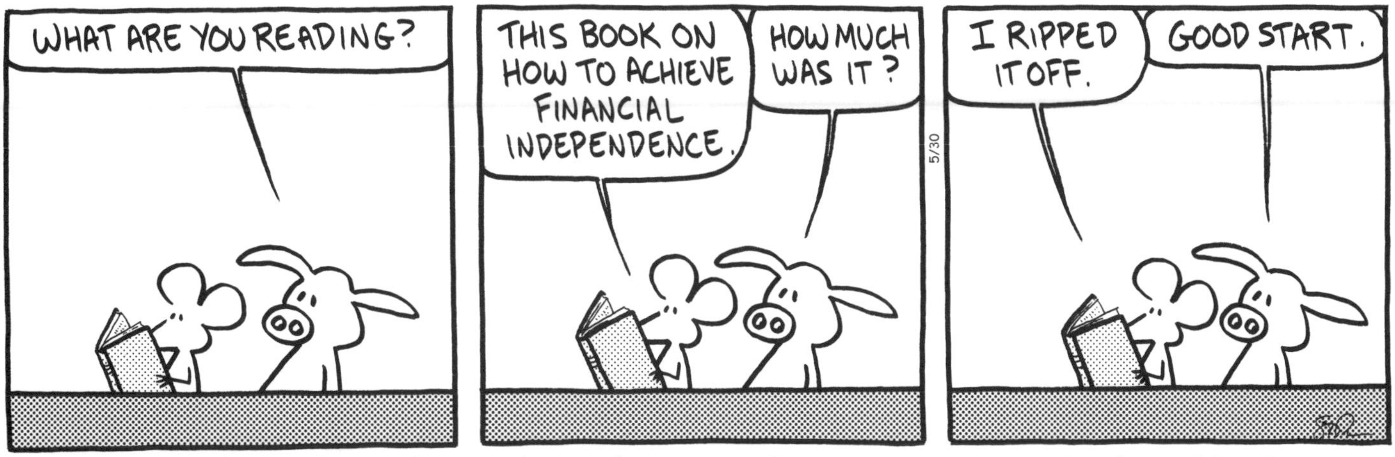
WHAT ARE YOU READING?
THIS BOOK ON HOW TO ACHIEVE FINANCIAL INDEPENDENCE.
HOW MUCH WAS IT?
5/30
I RIPPED IT OFF.
GOOD START.

This strip generated a handwritten letter to the *Washington Post* from an angry woman who claimed that the strip "advocates stealing as a proper way to begin financial management."

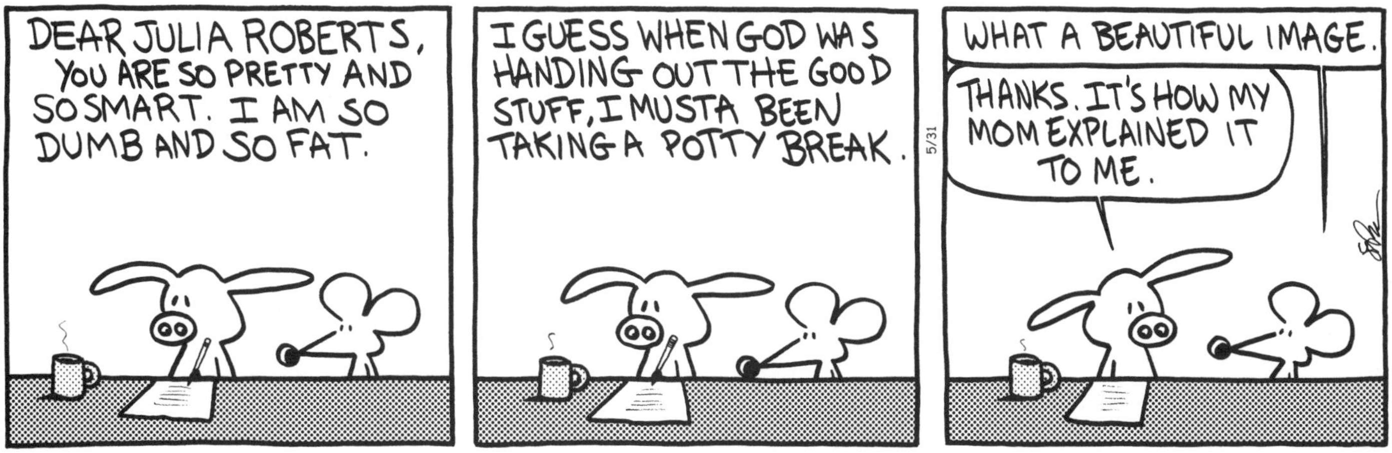
DEAR JULIA ROBERTS, YOU ARE SO PRETTY AND SO SMART. I AM SO DUMB AND SO FAT.
I GUESS WHEN GOD WAS HANDING OUT THE GOOD STUFF, I MUSTA BEEN TAKING A POTTY BREAK.
5/31
WHAT A BEAUTIFUL IMAGE.
THANKS. IT'S HOW MY MOM EXPLAINED IT TO ME.

I always hoped this strip would get the attention of Julia Roberts. But it didn't.

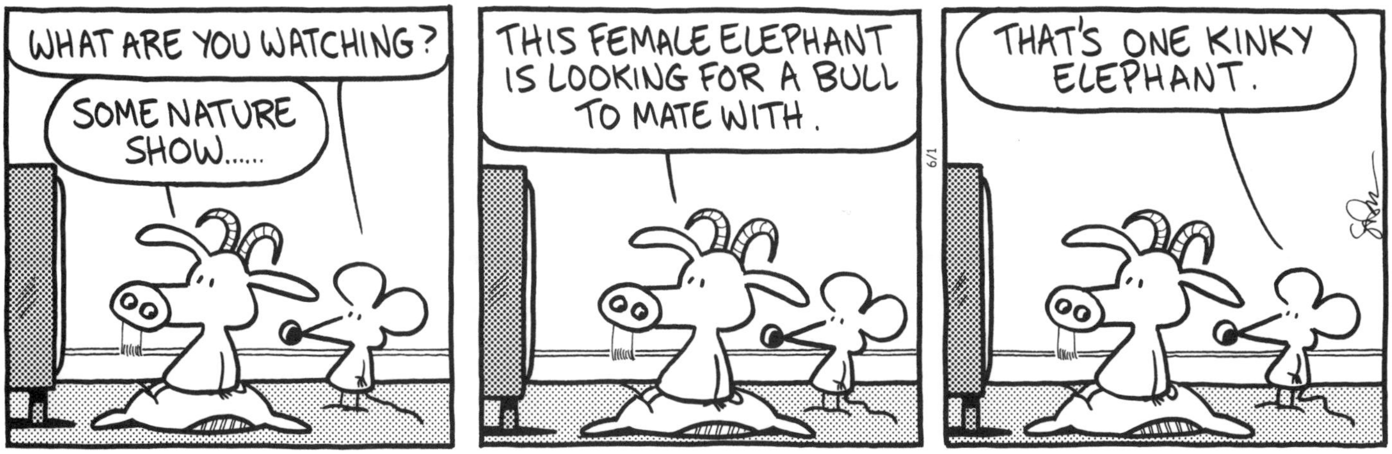
WHAT ARE YOU WATCHING?
SOME NATURE SHOW......
THIS FEMALE ELEPHANT IS LOOKING FOR A BULL TO MATE WITH.
6/1
THAT'S ONE KINKY ELEPHANT.

When this strip ran in papers, it had a different punch line, although I can't remember what it was. My editor felt that the reference to a "kinky elephant" was a bit too much for mainstream newspapers.

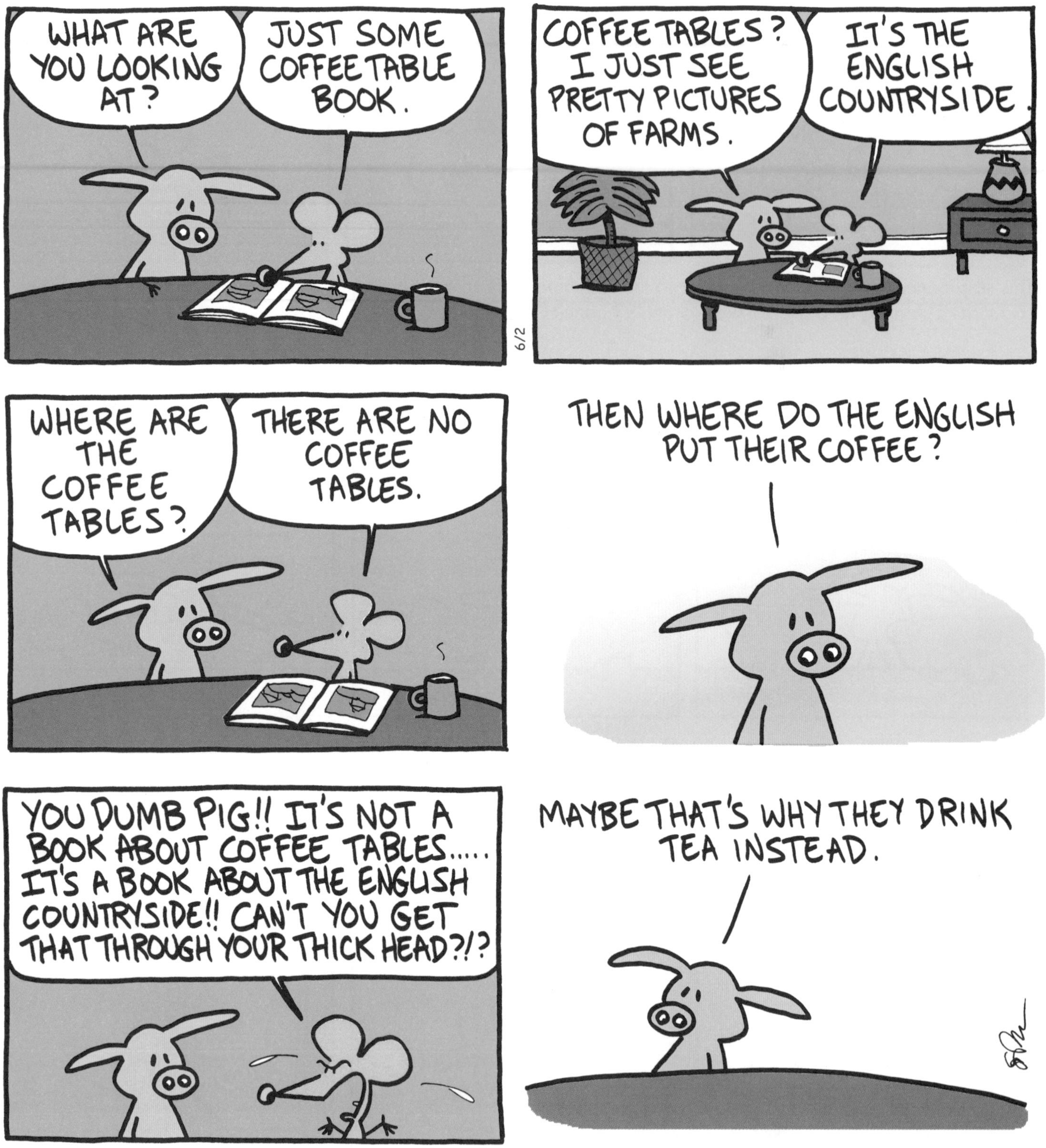
WHAT ARE YOU LOOKING AT?
JUST SOME COFFEE TABLE BOOK.
COFFEE TABLES? I JUST SEE PRETTY PICTURES OF FARMS.
IT'S THE ENGLISH COUNTRYSIDE.
6/2
WHERE ARE THE COFFEE TABLES?
THERE ARE NO COFFEE TABLES.
THEN WHERE DO THE ENGLISH PUT THEIR COFFEE?
YOU DUMB PIG!! IT'S NOT A BOOK ABOUT COFFEE TABLES..... IT'S A BOOK ABOUT THE ENGLISH COUNTRYSIDE!! CAN'T YOU GET THAT THROUGH YOUR THICK HEAD?!?
MAYBE THAT'S WHY THEY DRINK TEA INSTEAD.

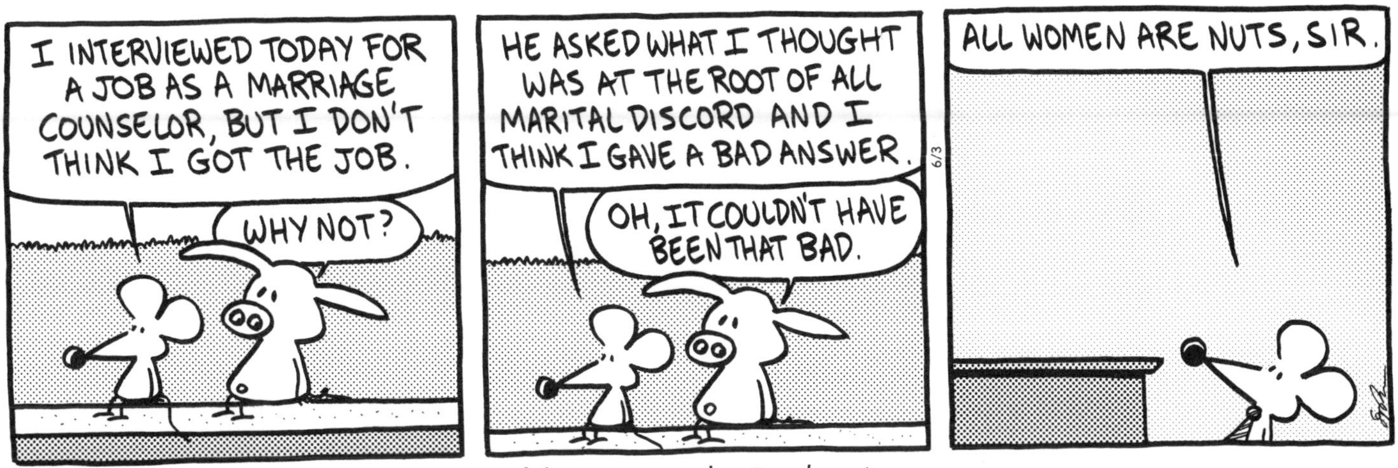
I INTERVIEWED TODAY FOR A JOB AS A MARRIAGE COUNSELOR, BUT I DON'T THINK I GOT THE JOB.
WHY NOT?
HE ASKED WHAT I THOUGHT WAS AT THE ROOT OF ALL MARITAL DISCORD AND I THINK I GAVE A BAD ANSWER.
OH, IT COULDN'T HAVE BEEN THAT BAD.
6/3
ALL WOMEN ARE NUTS, SIR.

The "marriage counselor" series was one of the most popular *Pearls* series.

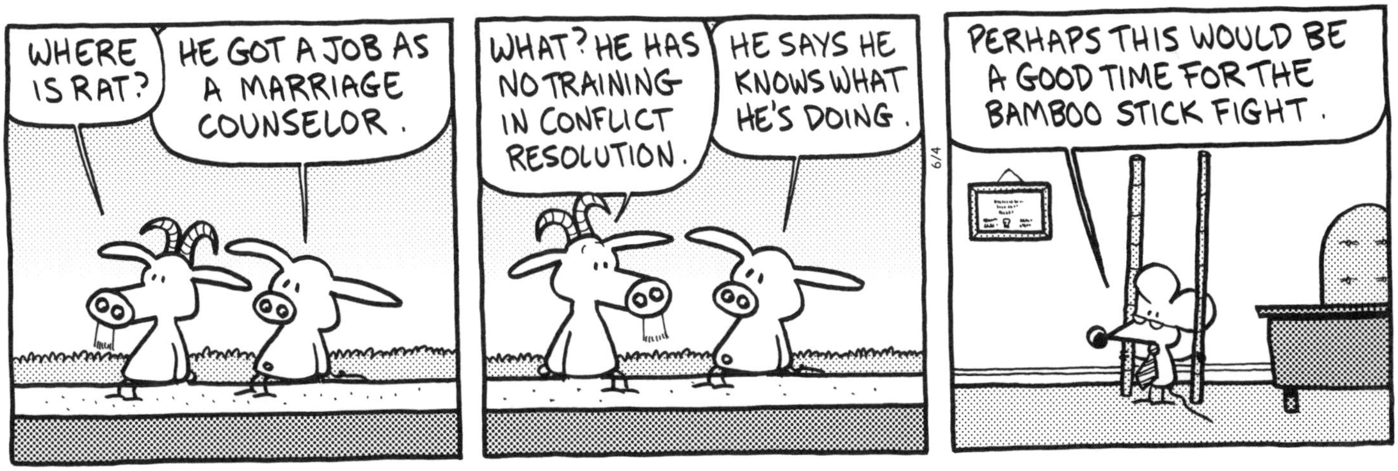
WHERE IS RAT?
HE GOT A JOB AS A MARRIAGE COUNSELOR.
WHAT? HE HAS NO TRAINING IN CONFLICT RESOLUTION.
HE SAYS HE KNOWS WHAT HE'S DOING.
6/4
PERHAPS THIS WOULD BE A GOOD TIME FOR THE BAMBOO STICK FIGHT.

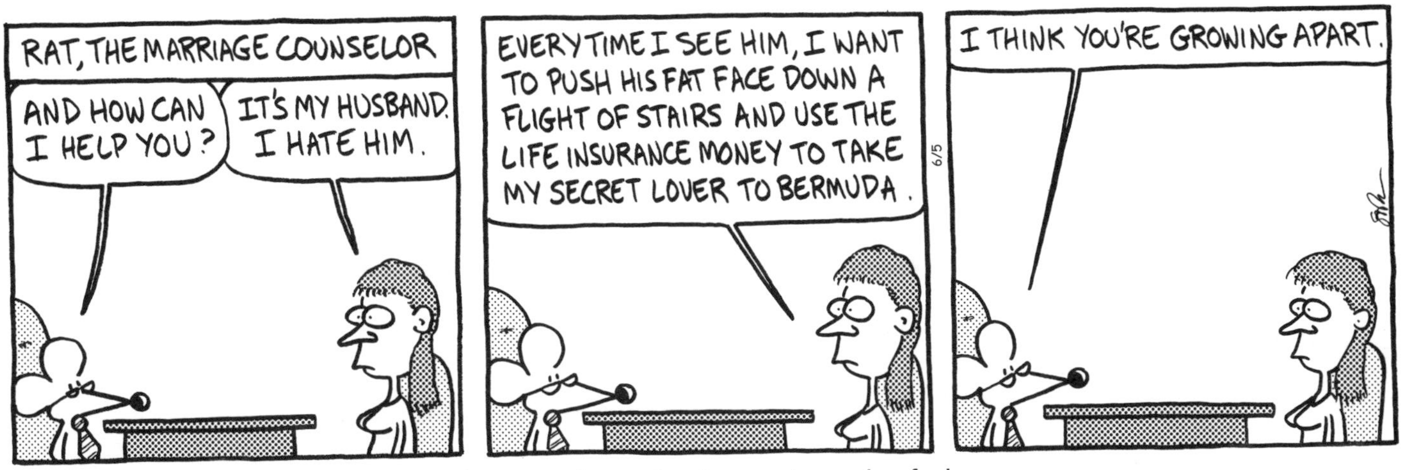
RAT, THE MARRIAGE COUNSELOR
AND HOW CAN I HELP YOU?
IT'S MY HUSBAND. I HATE HIM.
EVERY TIME I SEE HIM, I WANT TO PUSH HIS FAT FACE DOWN A FLIGHT OF STAIRS AND USE THE LIFE INSURANCE MONEY TO TAKE MY SECRET LOVER TO BERMUDA.
6/5
I THINK YOU'RE GROWING APART.

I've always liked the woman's line in the second panel. It has a nice, edgy feel.

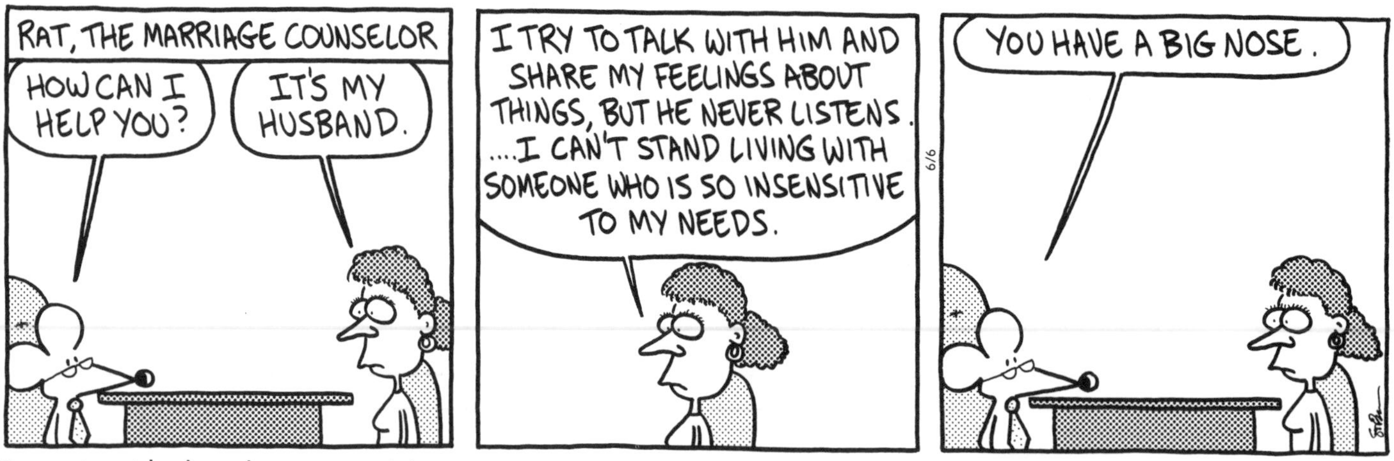
RAT, THE MARRIAGE COUNSELOR
HOW CAN I HELP YOU?
IT'S MY HUSBAND.
I TRY TO TALK WITH HIM AND SHARE MY FEELINGS ABOUT THINGS, BUT HE NEVER LISTENS. ....I CAN'T STAND LIVING WITH SOMEONE WHO IS SO INSENSITIVE TO MY NEEDS.
6/6
YOU HAVE A BIG NOSE.

Every time I look at this strip and the next one, I can't help noticing how badly I screwed up Rat's nose. It's way, way too long.

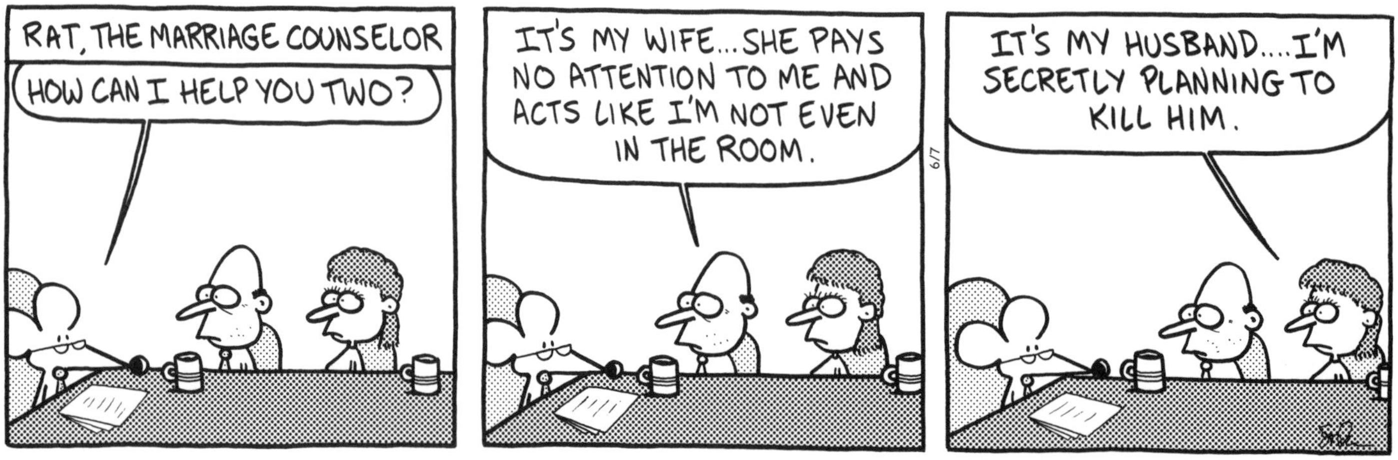
RAT, THE MARRIAGE COUNSELOR
HOW CAN I HELP YOU TWO?
IT'S MY WIFE...SHE PAYS NO ATTENTION TO ME AND ACTS LIKE I'M NOT EVEN IN THE ROOM.
6/7
IT'S MY HUSBAND....I'M SECRETLY PLANNING TO KILL HIM.

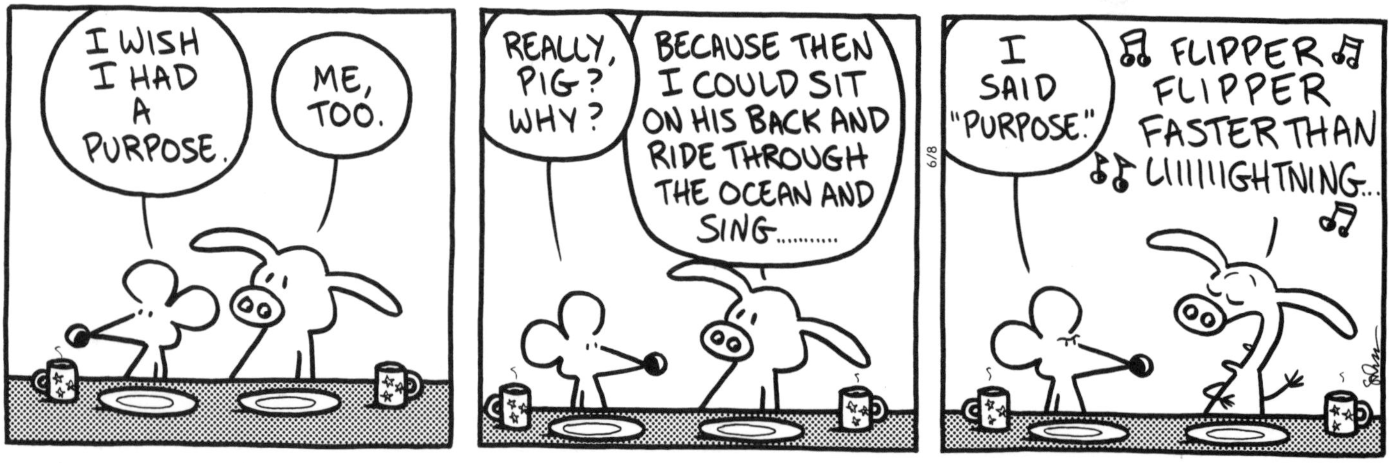
I WISH I HAD A PURPOSE.
ME, TOO.
REALLY, PIG? WHY?
BECAUSE THEN I COULD SIT ON HIS BACK AND RIDE THROUGH THE OCEAN AND SING..........
6/8
I SAID "PURPOSE."
FLIPPER FLIPPER FASTER THAN LIIIIIIGHTNING...

I tend to put my weaker strips on Saturday, because that's when I figure the fewest number of people are reading the paper. But the reaction to this one completely surprised me. People seemed to love it. I think people enjoyed the visual of Pig singing. Or maybe there are just a lot of "Flipper" fans out there.

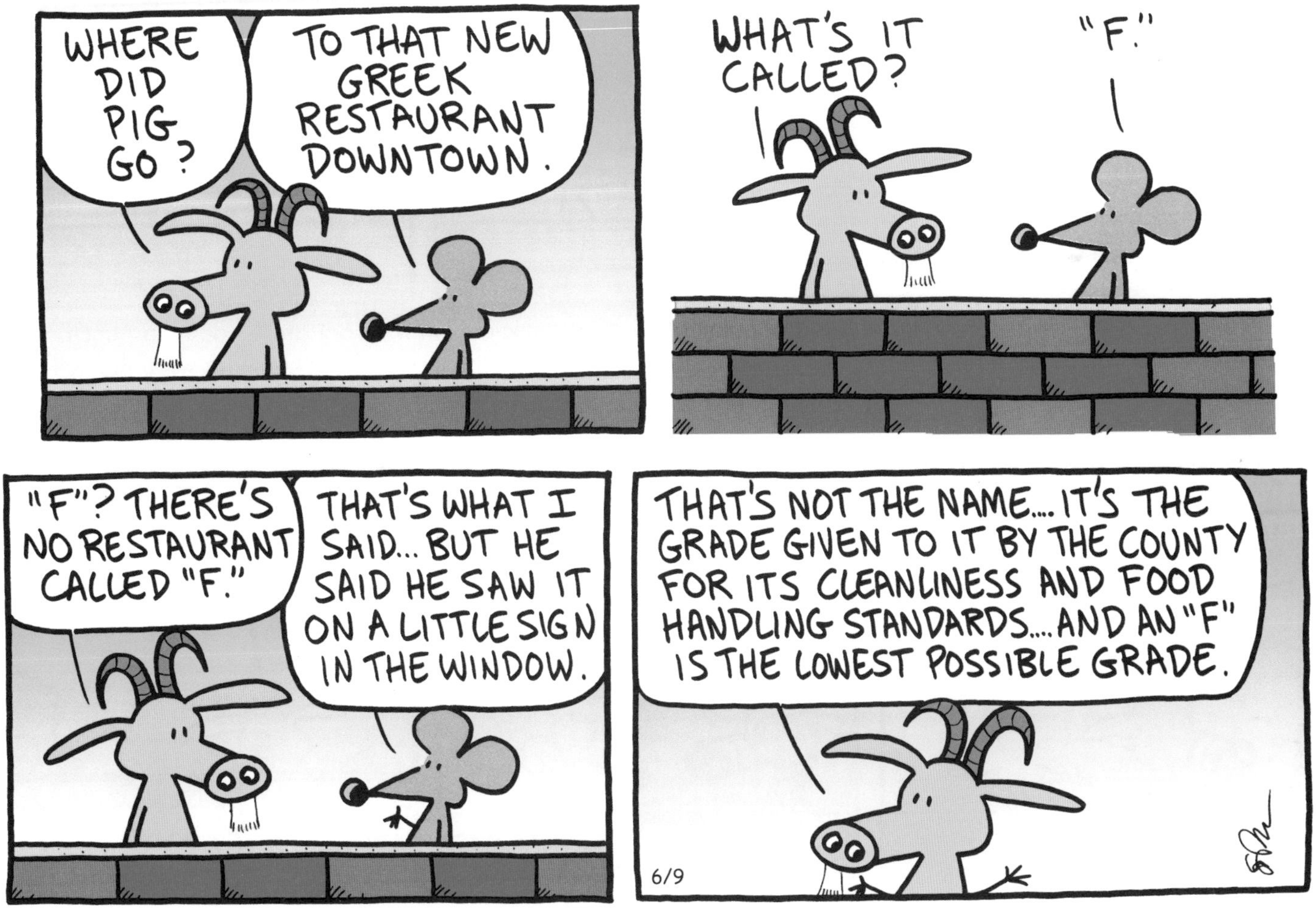
WHERE DID PIG GO?
TO THAT NEW GREEK RESTAURANT DOWNTOWN.
WHAT'S IT CALLED?
"F."
"F"? THERE'S NO RESTAURANT CALLED "F."
THAT'S WHAT I SAID... BUT HE SAID HE SAW IT ON A LITTLE SIGN IN THE WINDOW.
THAT'S NOT THE NAME.... IT'S THE GRADE GIVEN TO IT BY THE COUNTY FOR ITS CLEANLINESS AND FOOD HANDLING STANDARDS.... AND AN "F" IS THE LOWEST POSSIBLE GRADE.
6/9

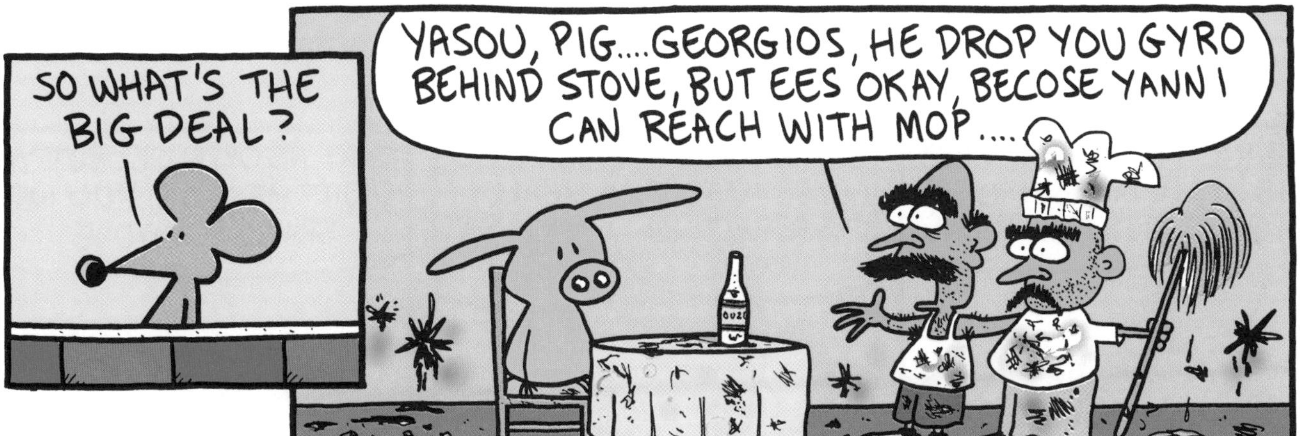
SO WHAT'S THE BIG DEAL?
YASOU, PIG....GEORGIOS, HE DROP YOU GYRO BEHIND STOVE, BUT EES OKAY, BECOSE YANN I CAN REACH WITH MOP....
OUZO

This June 9th strip was my first experience with reader outrage. I thought that I could get away with it because I was Greek. That was not the case. Greeks everywhere complained. While I wouldn't do it again, I still maintain that everyone is just a wee bit too sensitive these days.

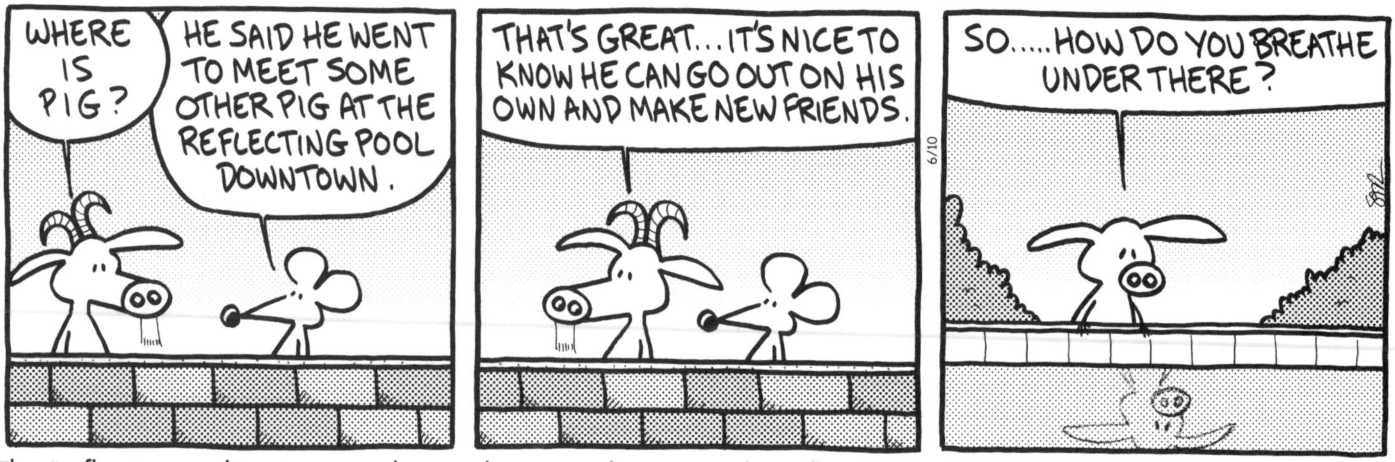
WHERE IS PIG?
HE SAID HE WENT TO MEET SOME OTHER PIG AT THE REFLECTING POOL DOWNTOWN.
THAT'S GREAT... IT'S NICE TO KNOW HE CAN GO OUT ON HIS OWN AND MAKE NEW FRIENDS.
6/10
SO.....HOW DO YOU BREATHE UNDER THERE?

The "reflecting pool" strips turned out to be a popular series. The reflections in the pool are all done in pencil, which, I should note, vary widely in line quality from strip to strip. Ahh, the perils of not knowing what the hell you are doing.

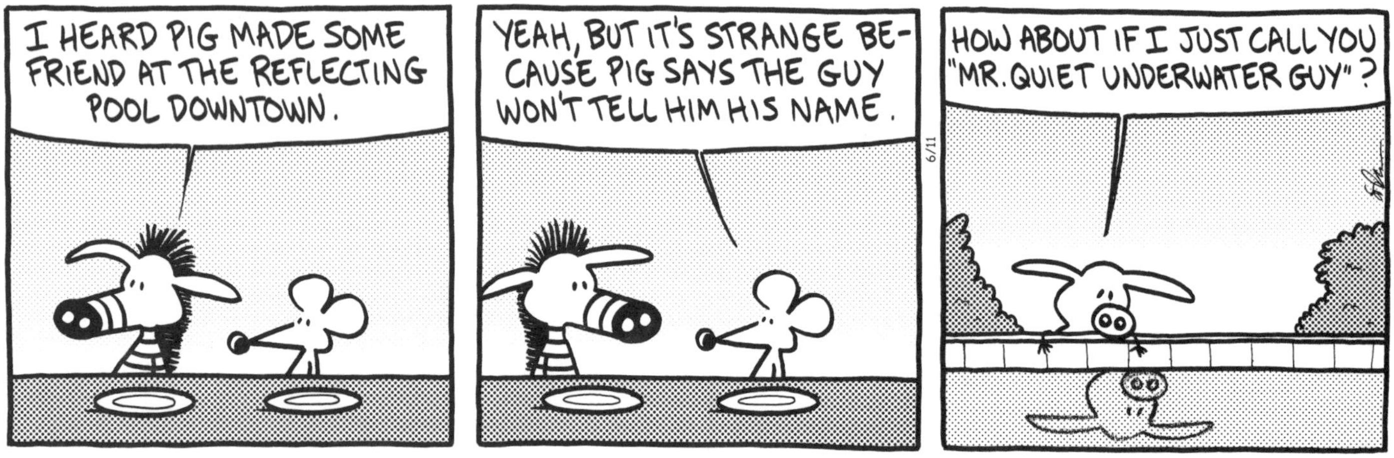
I HEARD PIG MADE SOME FRIEND AT THE REFLECTING POOL DOWNTOWN.
YEAH, BUT IT'S STRANGE BECAUSE PIG SAYS THE GUY WON'T TELL HIM HIS NAME.
6/11
HOW ABOUT IF I JUST CALL YOU "MR. QUIET UNDERWATER GUY"?

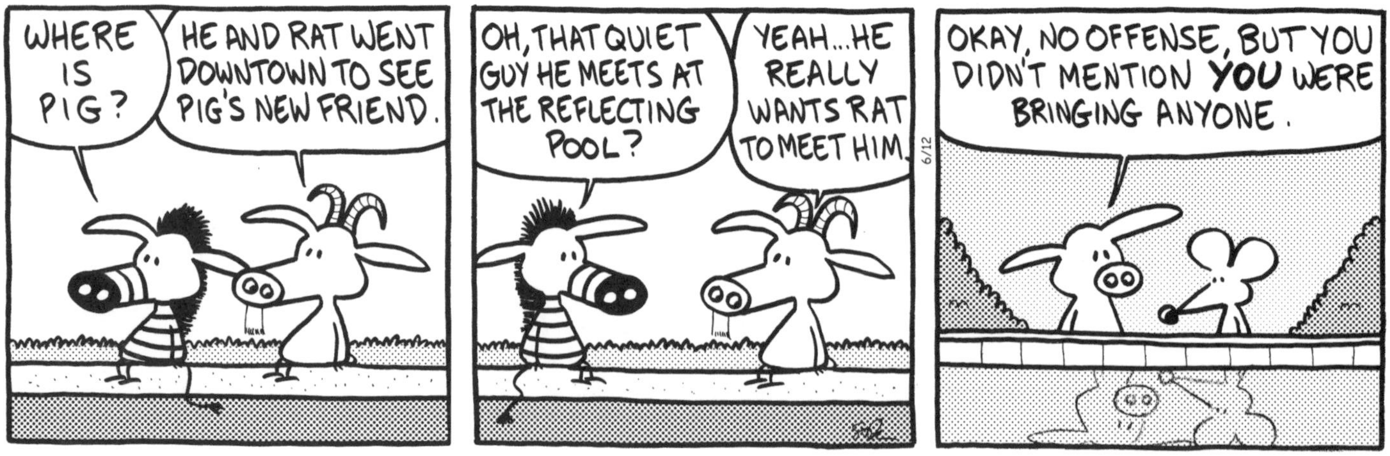
WHERE IS PIG?
HE AND RAT WENT DOWNTOWN TO SEE PIG'S NEW FRIEND.
OH, THAT QUIET GUY HE MEETS AT THE REFLECTING POOL?
YEAH...HE REALLY WANTS RAT TO MEET HIM.
6/12
OKAY, NO OFFENSE, BUT YOU DIDN'T MENTION **YOU** WERE BRINGING ANYONE.

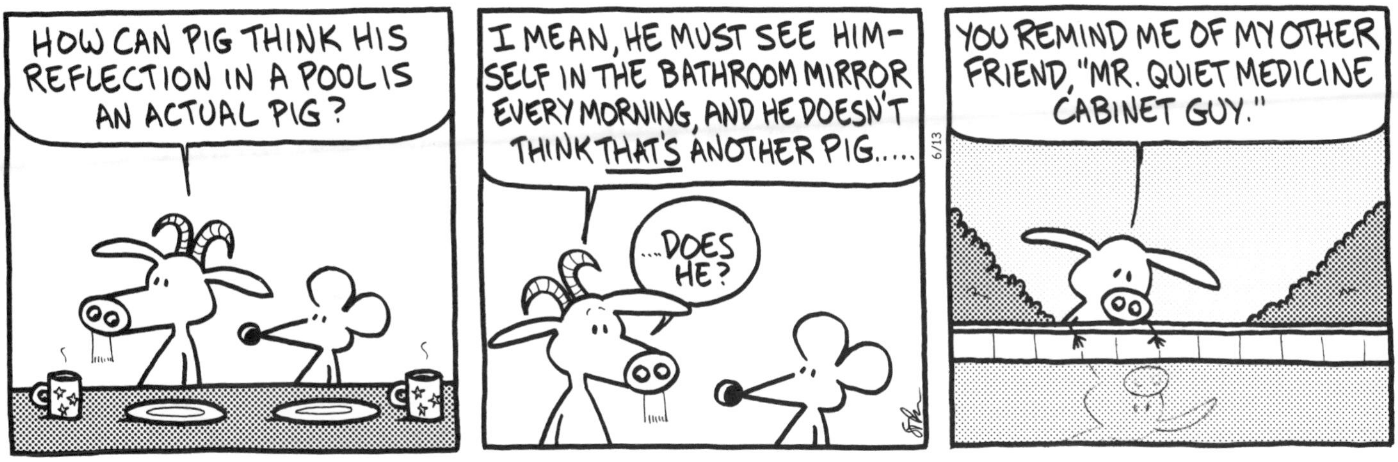
HOW CAN PIG THINK HIS REFLECTION IN A POOL IS AN ACTUAL PIG?
I MEAN, HE MUST SEE HIMSELF IN THE BATHROOM MIRROR EVERY MORNING, AND HE DOESN'T THINK THAT'S ANOTHER PIG.....
...DOES HE?
6/13
YOU REMIND ME OF MY OTHER FRIEND, "MR. QUIET MEDICINE CABINET GUY."

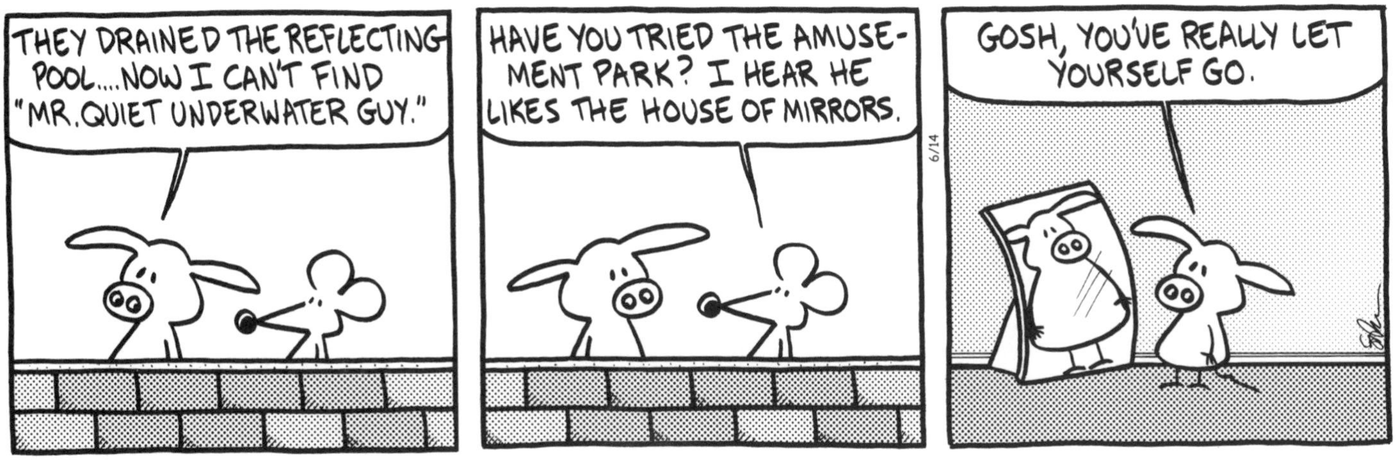
THEY DRAINED THE REFLECTING POOL....NOW I CAN'T FIND "MR. QUIET UNDERWATER GUY."
HAVE YOU TRIED THE AMUSEMENT PARK? I HEAR HE LIKES THE HOUSE OF MIRRORS.
6/14
GOSH, YOU'VE REALLY LET YOURSELF GO.

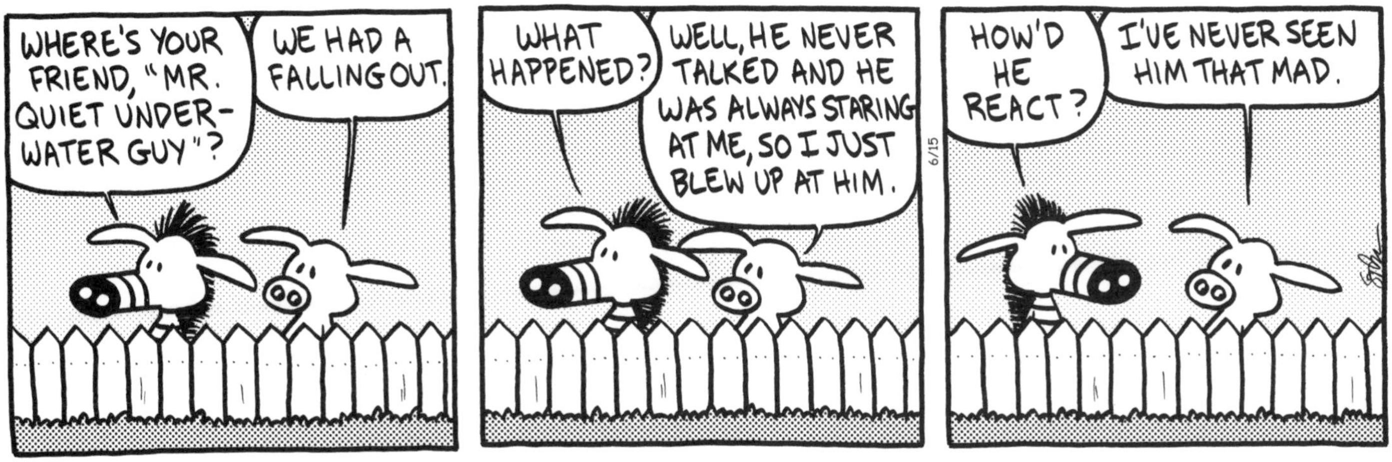
WHERE'S YOUR FRIEND, "MR. QUIET UNDERWATER GUY"?
WE HAD A FALLING OUT.
WHAT HAPPENED?
WELL, HE NEVER TALKED AND HE WAS ALWAYS STARING AT ME, SO I JUST BLEW UP AT HIM.
6/15
HOW'D HE REACT?
I'VE NEVER SEEN HIM THAT MAD.

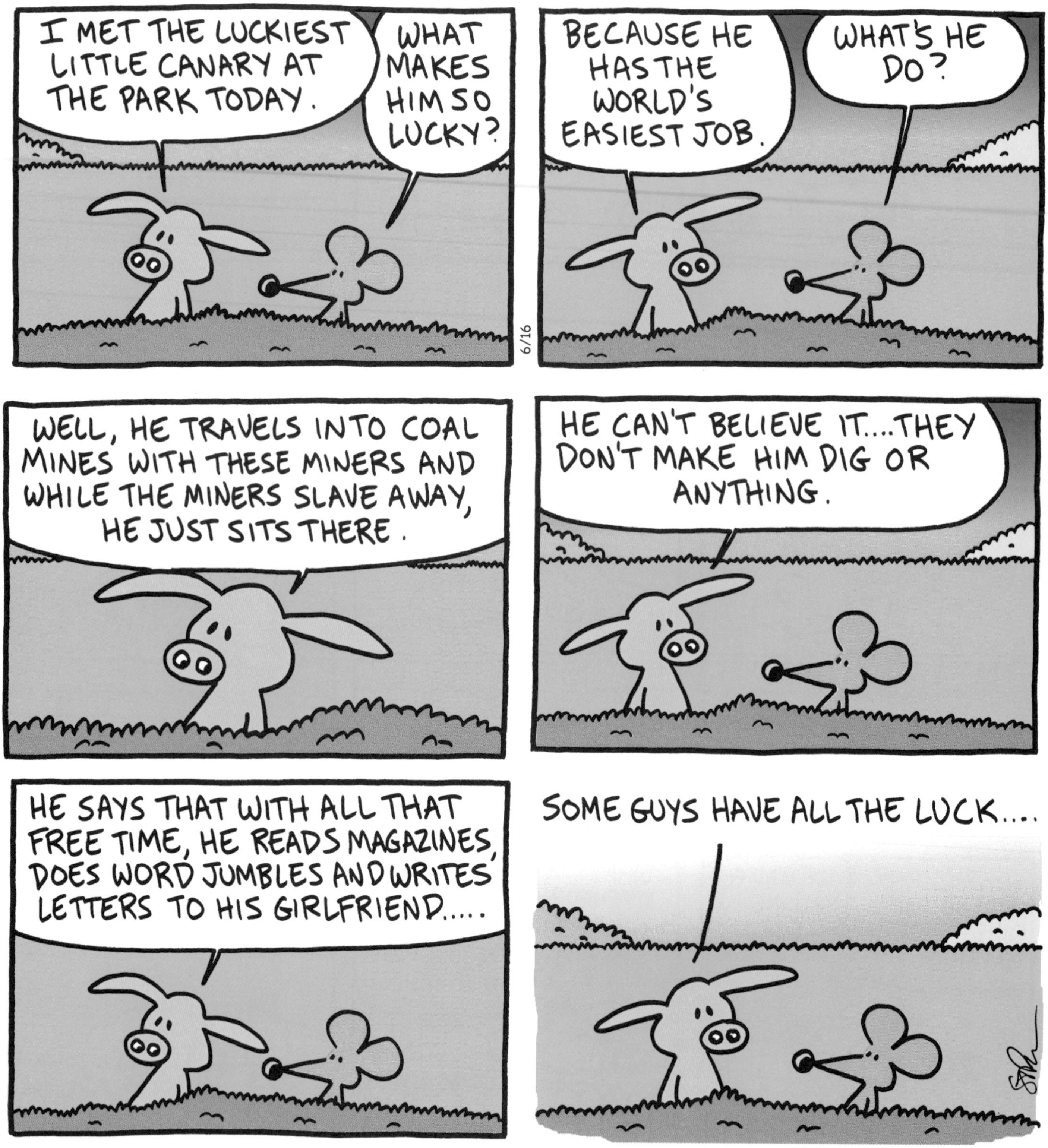
I MET THE LUCKIEST LITTLE CANARY AT THE PARK TODAY.
WHAT MAKES HIM SO LUCKY?
6/16
BECAUSE HE HAS THE WORLD'S EASIEST JOB.
WHAT'S HE DO?
WELL, HE TRAVELS INTO COAL MINES WITH THESE MINERS AND WHILE THE MINERS SLAVE AWAY, HE JUST SITS THERE.
HE CAN'T BELIEVE IT....THEY DON'T MAKE HIM DIG OR ANYTHING.
HE SAYS THAT WITH ALL THAT FREE TIME, HE READS MAGAZINES, DOES WORD JUMBLES AND WRITES LETTERS TO HIS GIRLFRIEND.....
SOME GUYS HAVE ALL THE LUCK....

Some people who wrote to me didn't know that canaries were once used in mines as a warning to miners that deadly gas was around. If the canary died, the miners knew it was time to leave.

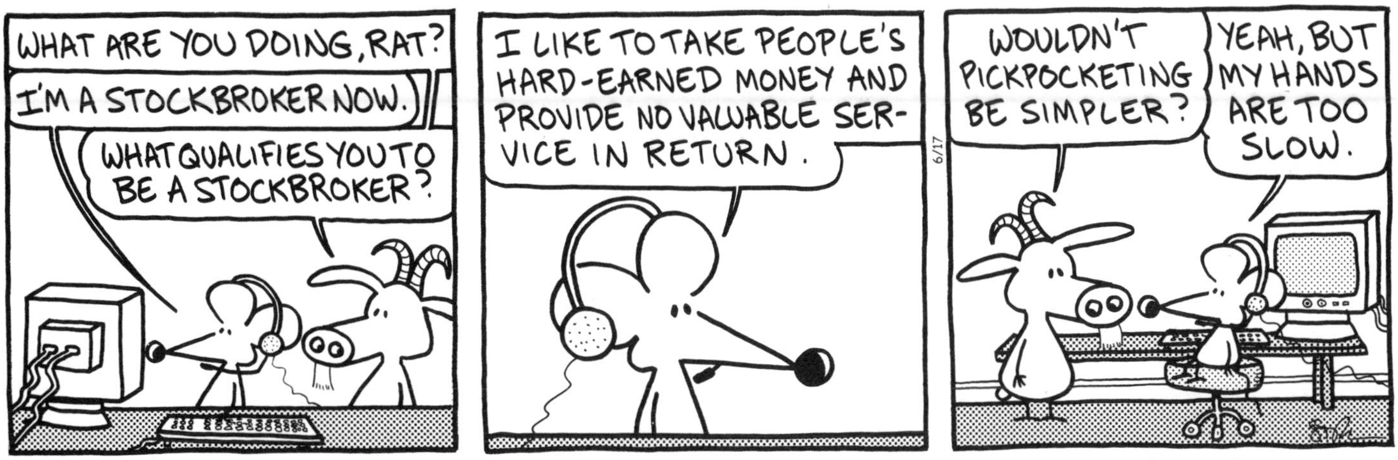
WHAT ARE YOU DOING, RAT?
I'M A STOCKBROKER NOW.
WHAT QUALIFIES YOU TO BE A STOCKBROKER?
I LIKE TO TAKE PEOPLE'S HARD-EARNED MONEY AND PROVIDE NO VALUABLE SERVICE IN RETURN.
6/17
WOULDN'T PICKPOCKETING BE SIMPLER?
YEAH, BUT MY HANDS ARE TOO SLOW.

This broker series was surprisingly popular with brokers. It was also popular with investors, as the market was tanking around the time this series ran.

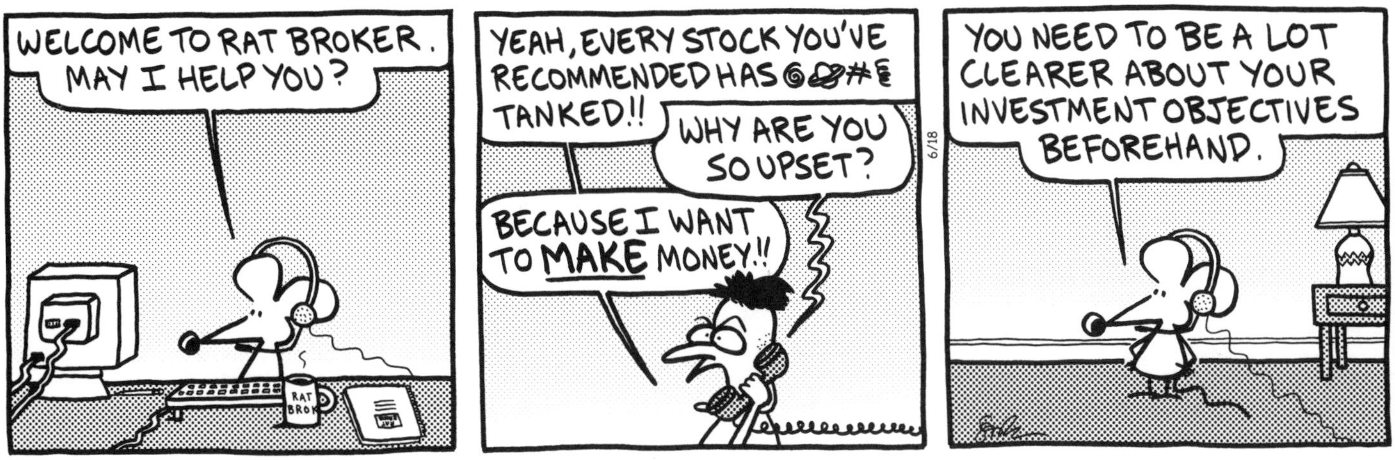
WELCOME TO RAT BROKER. MAY I HELP YOU?
YEAH, EVERY STOCK YOU'VE RECOMMENDED HAS
TANKED!!
WHY ARE YOU SO UPSET?
BECAUSE I WANT TO **MAKE** MONEY!!
6/18
YOU NEED TO BE A LOT CLEARER ABOUT YOUR INVESTMENT OBJECTIVES BEFOREHAND.

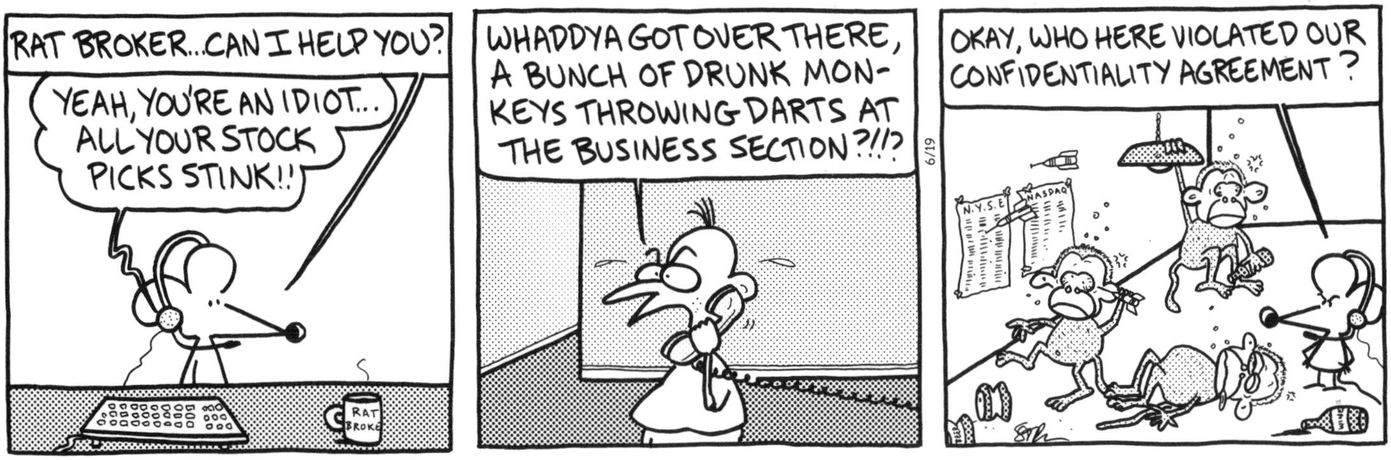
RAT BROKER...CAN I HELP YOU?
YEAH, YOU'RE AN IDIOT... ALL YOUR STOCK PICKS STINK!!
WHADDYA GOT OVER THERE, A BUNCH OF DRUNK MONKEYS THROWING DARTS AT THE BUSINESS SECTION?!!?
6/19
OKAY, WHO HERE VIOLATED OUR CONFIDENTIALITY AGREEMENT?
N.Y.S.E.
NASDAQ

Drunk monkeys = instant comedy.

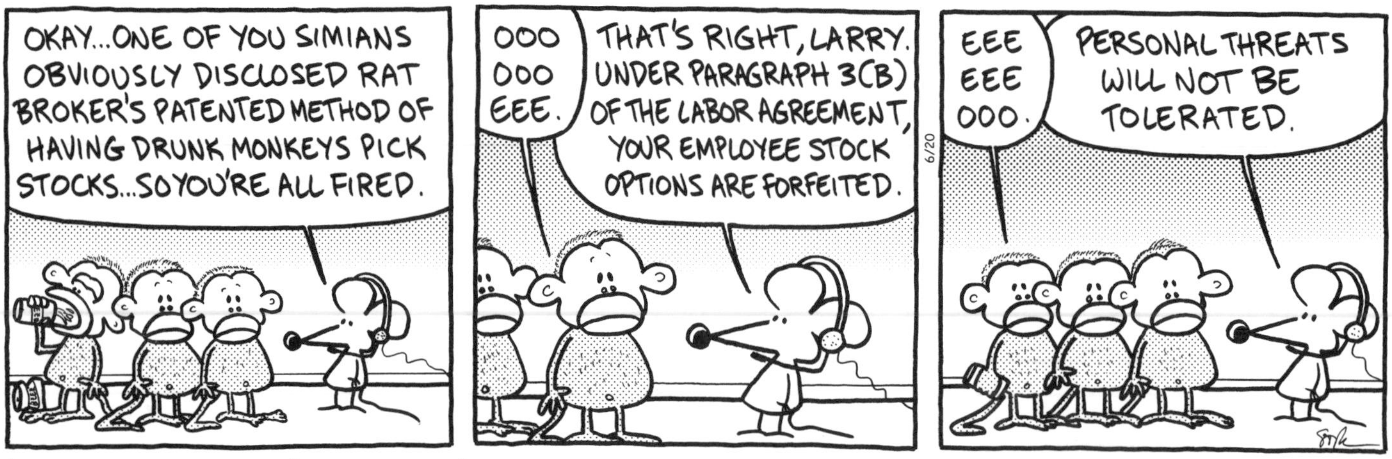
OKAY...ONE OF YOU SIMIANS OBVIOUSLY DISCLOSED RAT BROKER'S PATENTED METHOD OF HAVING DRUNK MONKEYS PICK STOCKS...SO YOU'RE ALL FIRED.
OOO OOO EEE.
THAT'S RIGHT, LARRY. UNDER PARAGRAPH 3(B) OF THE LABOR AGREEMENT, YOUR EMPLOYEE STOCK OPTIONS ARE FORFEITED.
6/20
EEE EEE OOO.
PERSONAL THREATS WILL NOT BE TOLERATED.

This strip goes to prove that no matter how poorly you draw monkeys, you can't ruin a "drunk monkey" joke.

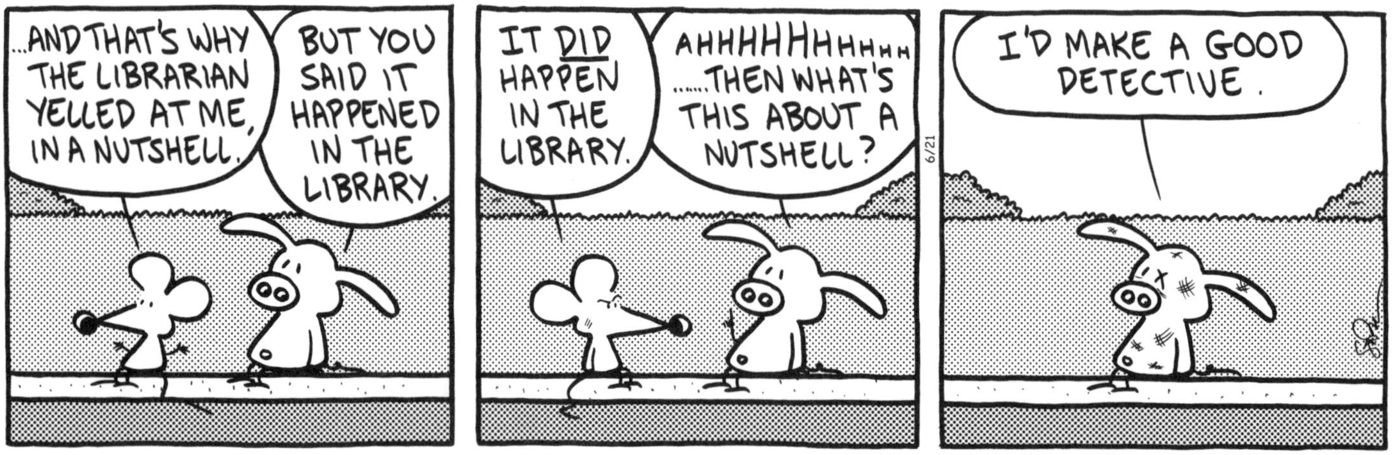
...AND THAT'S WHY THE LIBRARIAN YELLED AT ME, IN A NUTSHELL.
BUT YOU SAID IT HAPPENED IN THE LIBRARY.
IT DID HAPPEN IN THE LIBRARY.
AHHHHHHHHHH ......THEN WHAT'S THIS ABOUT A NUTSHELL?
6/21
I'D MAKE A GOOD DETECTIVE.

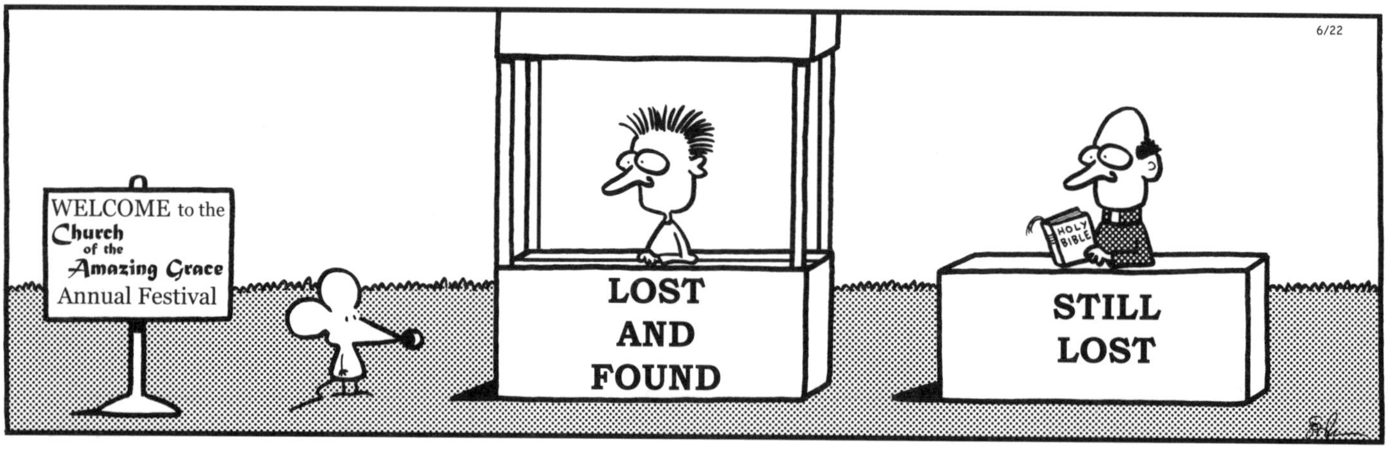
6/22
WELCOME to the Church of the Amazing Grace Annual Festival
LOST AND FOUND
HOLY BIBLE
STILL LOST

This had both non-religious and religious people complaining that I was making fun of them. Religion is dangerous ground in comic-land.

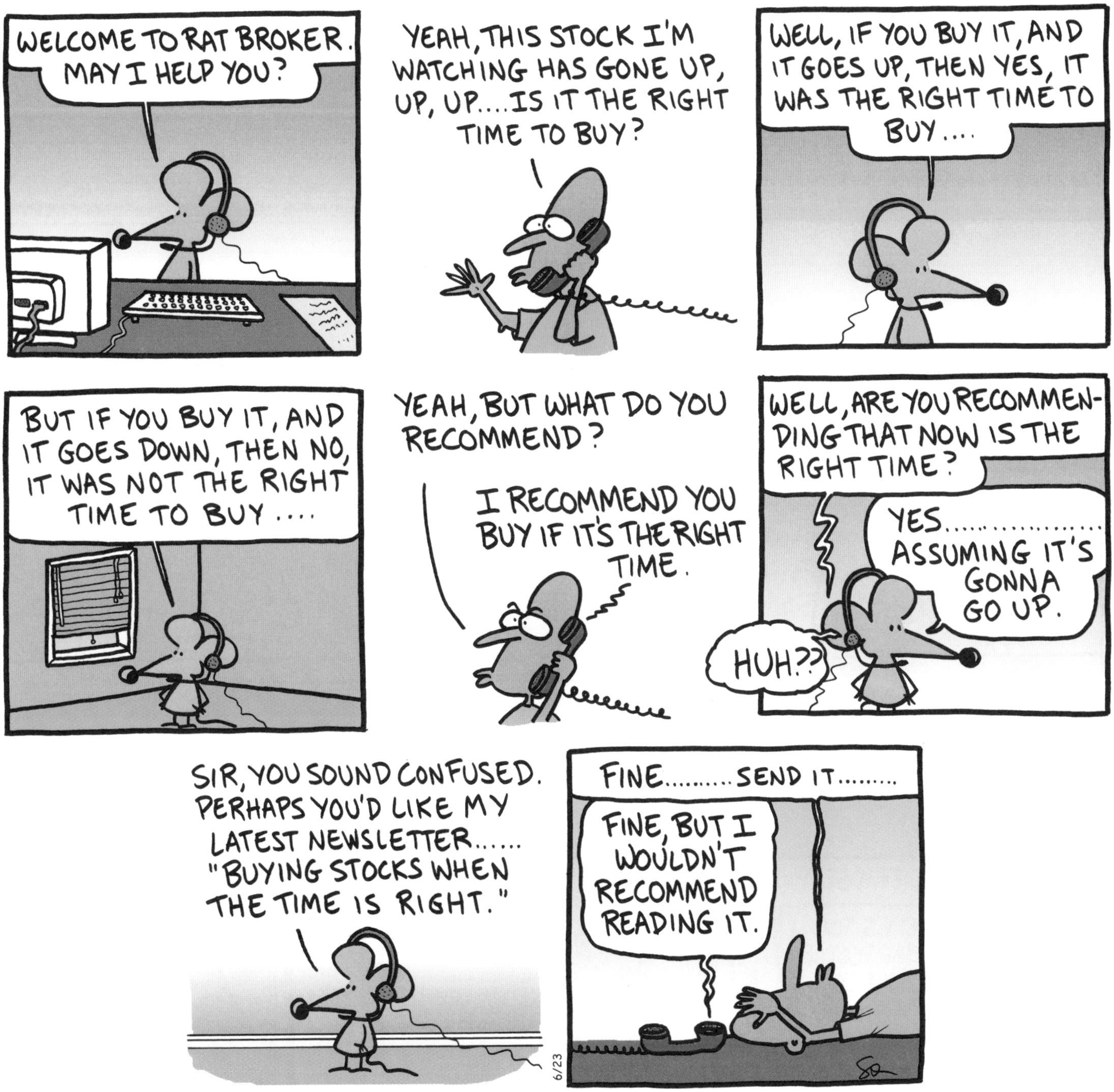
WELCOME TO RAT BROKER. MAY I HELP YOU?
YEAH, THIS STOCK I'M WATCHING HAS GONE UP, UP, UP.... IS IT THE RIGHT TIME TO BUY?
WELL, IF YOU BUY IT, AND IT GOES UP, THEN YES, IT WAS THE RIGHT TIME TO BUY....
BUT IF YOU BUY IT, AND IT GOES DOWN, THEN NO, IT WAS NOT THE RIGHT TIME TO BUY....
YEAH, BUT WHAT DO YOU RECOMMEND?
I RECOMMEND YOU BUY IF IT'S THE RIGHT TIME.
WELL, ARE YOU RECOMMENDING THAT NOW IS THE RIGHT TIME?
YES.................. ASSUMING IT'S GONNA GO UP.
HUH??
SIR, YOU SOUND CONFUSED. PERHAPS YOU'D LIKE MY LATEST NEWSLETTER...... "BUYING STOCKS WHEN THE TIME IS RIGHT."
FINE.......... SEND IT.........
FINE, BUT I WOULDN'T RECOMMEND READING IT.
6/23

That window in the fourth panel is just out of control. Shortly after drawing this, I learned what the word "perspective" meant.

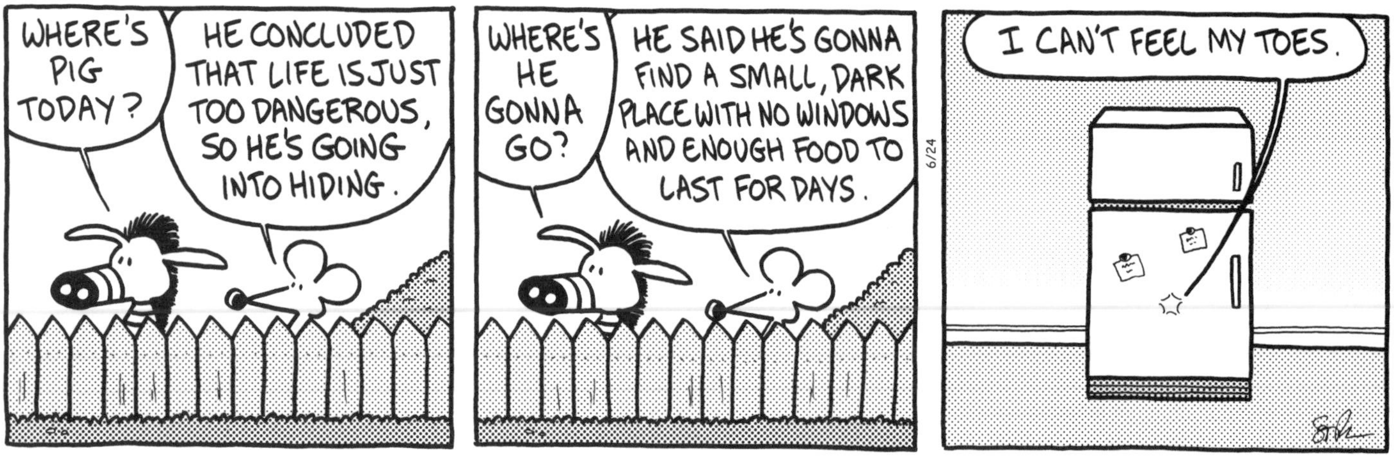
WHERE'S PIG TODAY?
HE CONCLUDED THAT LIFE IS JUST TOO DANGEROUS, SO HE'S GOING INTO HIDING.
WHERE'S HE GONNA GO?
HE SAID HE'S GONNA FIND A SMALL, DARK PLACE WITH NO WINDOWS AND ENOUGH FOOD TO LAST FOR DAYS.
6/24
I CAN'T FEEL MY TOES.

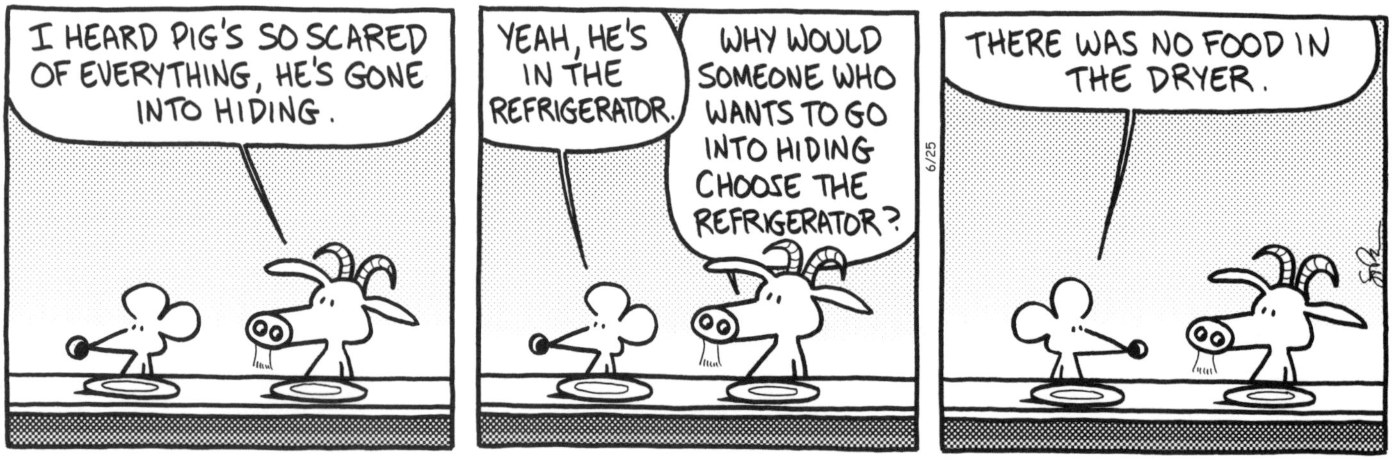
I HEARD PIG'S SO SCARED OF EVERYTHING, HE'S GONE INTO HIDING.
YEAH, HE'S IN THE REFRIGERATOR.
WHY WOULD SOMEONE WHO WANTS TO GO INTO HIDING CHOOSE THE REFRIGERATOR?
6/25
THERE WAS NO FOOD IN THE DRYER.

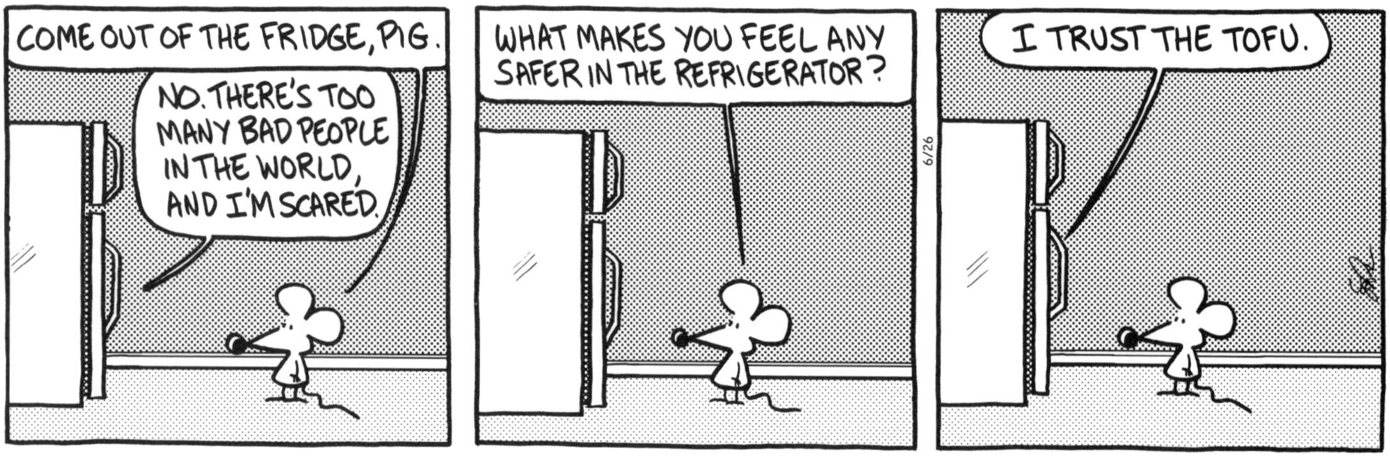
COME OUT OF THE FRIDGE, PIG.
NO. THERE'S TOO MANY BAD PEOPLE IN THE WORLD, AND I'M SCARED.
WHAT MAKES YOU FEEL ANY SAFER IN THE REFRIGERATOR?
6/26
I TRUST THE TOFU.

WHAT ARE YOU DOING OUT OF THE REFRIGERATOR?

I LEFT... IT WAS WAY TOO UNSAFE.

UNSAFE?

YEAH. GANGS RUN THE PLACE... IF YOU WANT PROTECTION, YOU GOTTA EITHER HANG WITH THE CONDIMENTS OR THE BEER....

WHO'D YOU PICK?

THE COTTAGE CHEESE. YOU FOOL!

YES... I CHEATED DEATH...

6/27

I like the notion of condiments forming gangs.

HEY, A HOPSCOTCH BOARD!

YIPPEEEEE!!

HOP HOP HOP

IS THERE A PROBLEM, OFFICER?

POLICE LINE DO NOT CROSS POLICE LINE DO NOT CROSS POLICE LINE DO NOT CRO

6/28

Hopscotch + murder scenes = instant comedy.

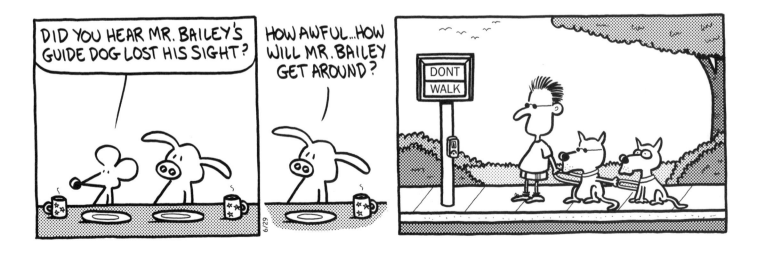

DID YOU HEAR MR. BAILEY'S GUIDE DOG LOST HIS SIGHT?

HOW AWFUL...HOW WILL MR. BAILEY GET AROUND?

6/29

DONT WALK

91

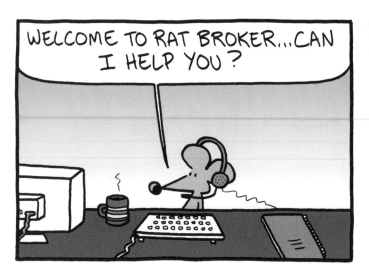

WELCOME TO RAT BROKER...CAN I HELP YOU?

YEAH....YESTERDAY YOU TOLD ME TO PUT MY KID'S ENTIRE COLLEGE SAVINGS INTO SOME INTERNET STOCK AND TODAY IT DROPPED 94%......

THAT'S BAD.....YOU SHOULD SELL THAT DOG.

WHAT?? JUST YESTERDAY YOU GAVE IT YOUR HIGHEST RECOMMENDATION.

GOOD POINT.....YOU SHOULD BUY MORE.

BUT YOU JUST SAID—

FORGET WHAT I SAID....

FORGET?? HOW AM I SUPPOSED TO PAY FOR MY KID'S COLLEGE?

6/30

HAVE YOU THOUGHT ABOUT BEING A STOCK BROKER?

Ahh, here I begin the transition to cordless phones. Much, much easier to draw than the old rotary type.

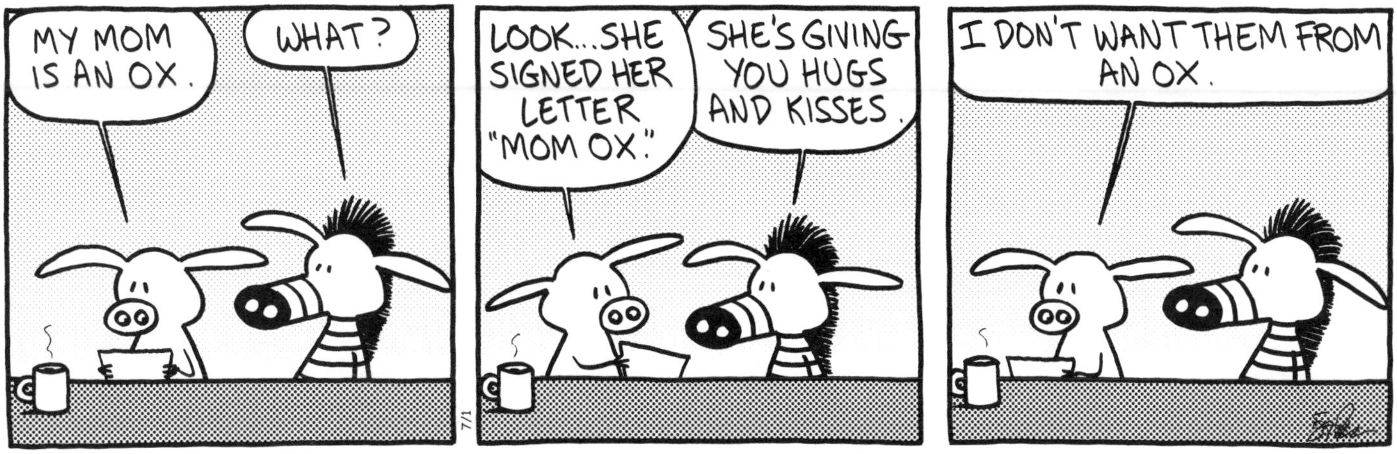
MY MOM IS AN OX.
WHAT?
LOOK...SHE SIGNED HER LETTER "MOM OX."
SHE'S GIVING YOU HUGS AND KISSES.
I DON'T WANT THEM FROM AN OX.
7/1

This was a very popular strip with readers, some of whom wrote to say that their mothers now signed their letters, "Mom Ox."

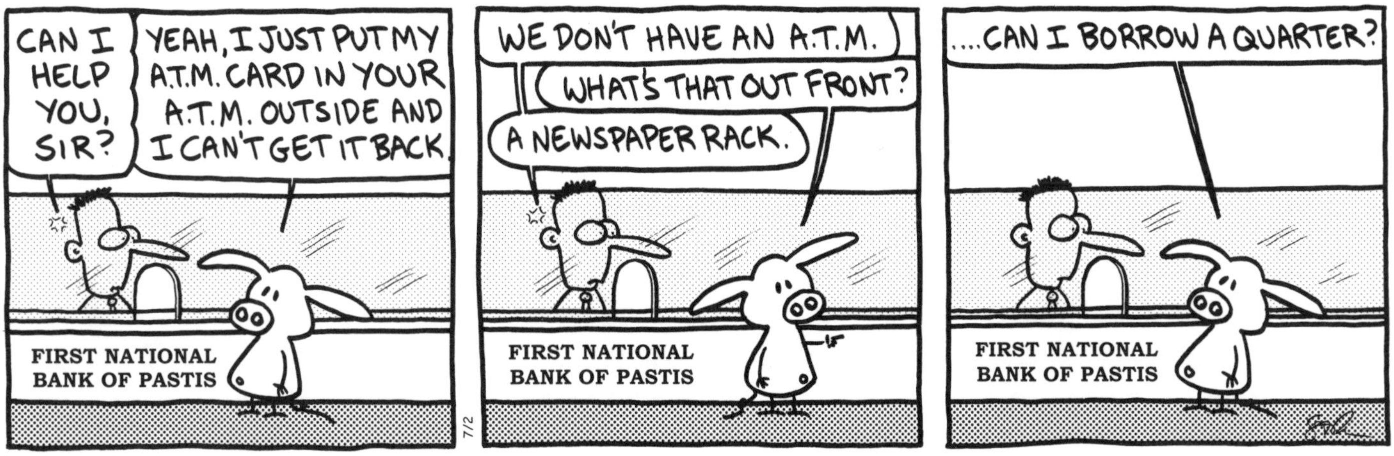
CAN I HELP YOU, SIR?
YEAH, I JUST PUT MY A.T.M. CARD IN YOUR A.T.M. OUTSIDE AND I CAN'T GET IT BACK.
FIRST NATIONAL BANK OF PASTIS
WE DON'T HAVE AN A.T.M.
WHAT'S THAT OUT FRONT?
A NEWSPAPER RACK.
FIRST NATIONAL BANK OF PASTIS
....CAN I BORROW A QUARTER?
FIRST NATIONAL BANK OF PASTIS
7/2

Nothing like putting your own last name in a comic strip. Who said cartoonists have big egos?

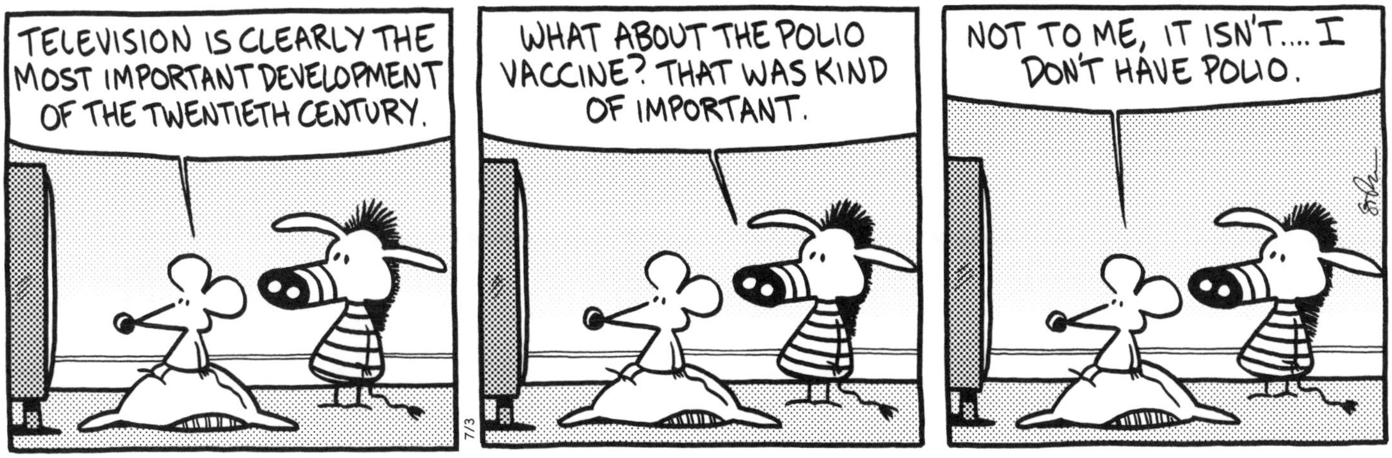
TELEVISION IS CLEARLY THE MOST IMPORTANT DEVELOPMENT OF THE TWENTIETH CENTURY.
WHAT ABOUT THE POLIO VACCINE? THAT WAS KIND OF IMPORTANT.
NOT TO ME, IT ISN'T.... I DON'T HAVE POLIO.
7/3

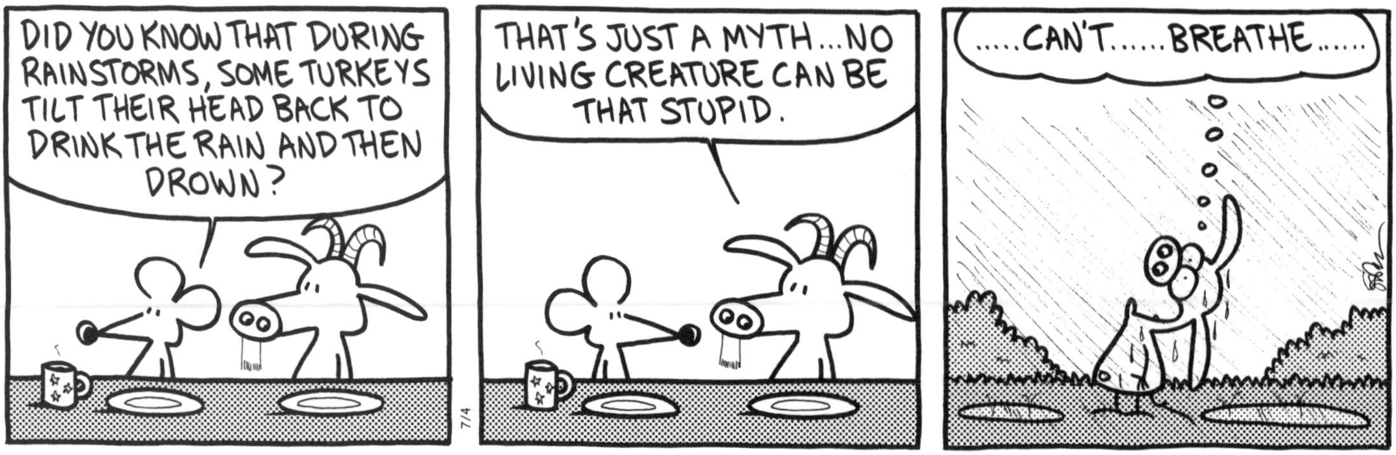
DID YOU KNOW THAT DURING RAINSTORMS, SOME TURKEYS TILT THEIR HEAD BACK TO DRINK THE RAIN AND THEN DROWN?
7/4
THAT'S JUST A MYTH...NO LIVING CREATURE CAN BE THAT STUPID.
.....CAN'T......BREATHE......

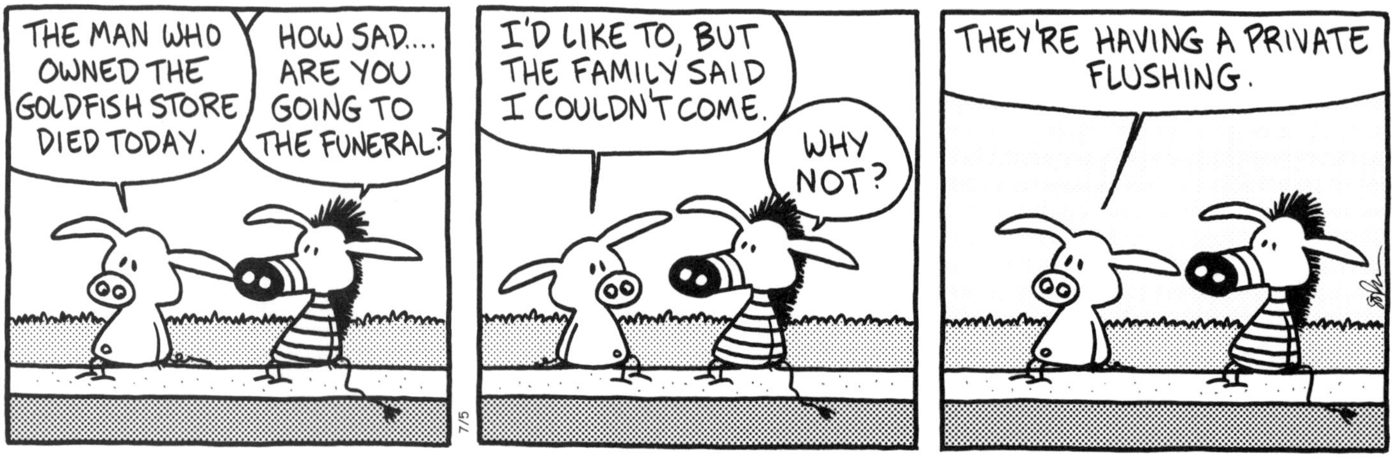
THE MAN WHO OWNED THE GOLDFISH STORE DIED TODAY.
HOW SAD.... ARE YOU GOING TO THE FUNERAL?
7/5
I'D LIKE TO, BUT THE FAMILY SAID I COULDN'T COME.
WHY NOT?
THEY'RE HAVING A PRIVATE FLUSHING.

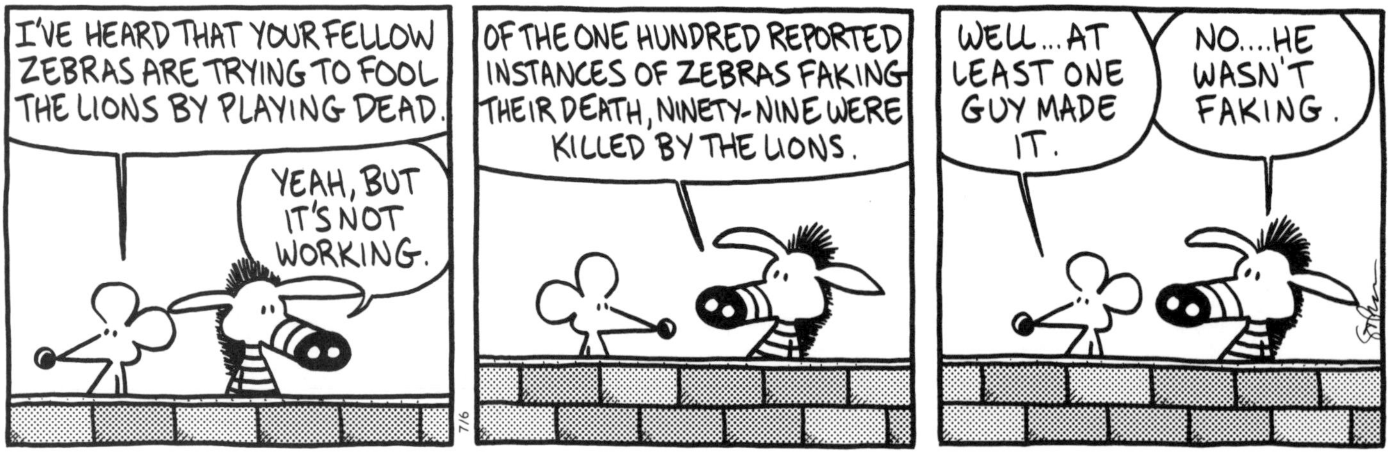
I'VE HEARD THAT YOUR FELLOW ZEBRAS ARE TRYING TO FOOL THE LIONS BY PLAYING DEAD.
YEAH, BUT IT'S NOT WORKING.
7/6
OF THE ONE HUNDRED REPORTED INSTANCES OF ZEBRAS FAKING THEIR DEATH, NINETY-NINE WERE KILLED BY THE LIONS.
WELL...AT LEAST ONE GUY MADE IT.
NO....HE WASN'T FAKING.

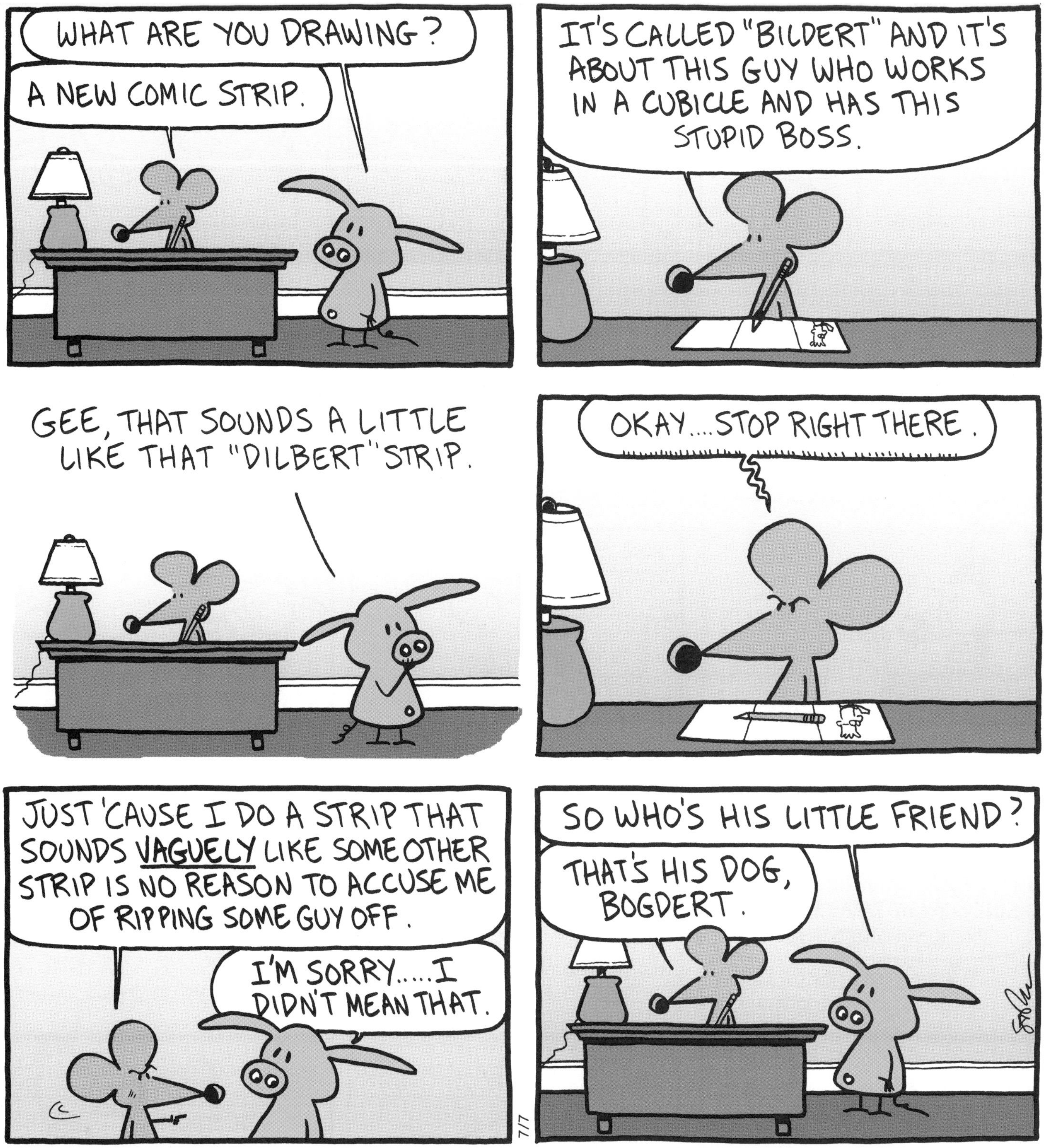
WHAT ARE YOU DRAWING?
A NEW COMIC STRIP.
IT'S CALLED "BILDERT" AND IT'S ABOUT THIS GUY WHO WORKS IN A CUBICLE AND HAS THIS STUPID BOSS.
GEE, THAT SOUNDS A LITTLE LIKE THAT "DILBERT" STRIP.
OKAY....STOP RIGHT THERE.
JUST 'CAUSE I DO A STRIP THAT SOUNDS VAGUELY LIKE SOME OTHER STRIP IS NO REASON TO ACCUSE ME OF RIPPING SOME GUY OFF.
I'M SORRY.....I DIDN'T MEAN THAT.
SO WHO'S HIS LITTLE FRIEND?
THAT'S HIS DOG, BOGDERT.

As stated elsewhere in this book, I pretty much owe my career to Scott Adams. What better way to thank him than by ripping him off.

Panel 1: I HEARD YOU'RE DRAWING A COMIC STRIP THAT IS A RIP-OFF OF "DILBERT."

Panel 2: OH, I SEE...JUST BECAUSE I DO A STRIP ABOUT AN OFFICE WORKER NAMED "BILDERT", I'M RIPPING SOMEONE OFF, HUH?

Panel 3: THE TIE THAT CURLS UPWARD IS ANOTHER HINT.

PLEASE...IT'S WINDY WHERE BILDERT LIVES.

Panel 4: WHAT'D YOU BUY?

A COLLECTION OF LAST YEAR'S "DILBERT" STRIPS.

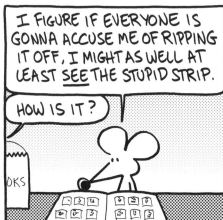

Panel 5: I FIGURE IF EVERYONE IS GONNA ACCUSE ME OF RIPPING IT OFF, I MIGHT AS WELL AT LEAST SEE THE STUPID STRIP.

HOW IS IT?

Panel 6: BORING......DID I MENTION I RECENTLY HAD ABOUT 365 NEW IDEAS FOR MY BILDERT STRIP?

Panel 7: MY BILDERT STRIP HAS IMPROVED SINCE MY INTRODUCTION OF THE PRICKLY-HAIRED BOSS.

THAT LOOKS EXACTLY LIKE DILBERT'S BOSS.

Panel 8: PLEASE. DILBERT'S BOSS'S HAIR STICKS UP AT A NINETY DEGREE ANGLE FROM THE TOP OF HIS HEAD...THE HAIR ON BILDERT'S BOSS IS AT AN OBVIOUS SEVENTY-EIGHT DEGREE ANGLE.

Panel 9: ....YOU NEED TO THINK BEFORE YOU TALK.

SORRY...I LEFT MY PROTRACTOR AT HOME.

Panel 1: GOAT SAYS YOUR BILDERT STRIP IS A BLATANT RIP-OFF OF "DILBERT."

Panel 2: HE DID, HUH? WELL, ASK HIM IF HE THINKS DA VINCI'S "LAST SUPPER" IS A RIP-OFF..... AFTER ALL, THE LAST SUPPER WASN'T HIS IDEA, NOW WAS IT?

7/11

Panel 3: YOU'RE A GOOD DEBATER.

Panel 1: SCOTT ADAMS IS SUING ME...... HE SAYS MY BILDERT STRIP IS A COMPLETE RIP-OFF OF HIS "DILBERT" STRIP.

Panel 2: WHAT ARE YOU GONNA DO?

FIND A LAWYER WHO'LL RECOGNIZE THE OBVIOUS DIFFERENCES AND DEFEND ME.

7/12

Panel 3: DILBERT: FIVE LUMPS OF HAIR.

BILDERT: NO MORE THAN FOUR.

The important thing to note here is that chair in the last panel. It is a well-drawn, solid chair. I am quite proud.

Panel 1: THIS BOOK I'M READING SAYS THAT WHEN A MAN GETS MARRIED, HIS LIFE IS OVER.... HOWEVER, MOST MEN WILL NOT ACKNOWLEDGE THAT FACT.

OH.

Panel 2: INSTEAD, THEY ENTER A STAGE OF DENIAL WHERE THEY TRY TO CONVINCE THEMSELVES AND OTHERS THAT THEY REMAIN FREE, VIRILE BEINGS.

WHEN DOES THAT END?

7/13

Panel 3: WHEN THEY BUY THEIR FIRST MINI-VAN.....THEN THE GIG IS UP.

There's nothing quite like opening your e-mail one quiet July morning to find twenty-five separate people telling you that the word is "jig," not "gig."

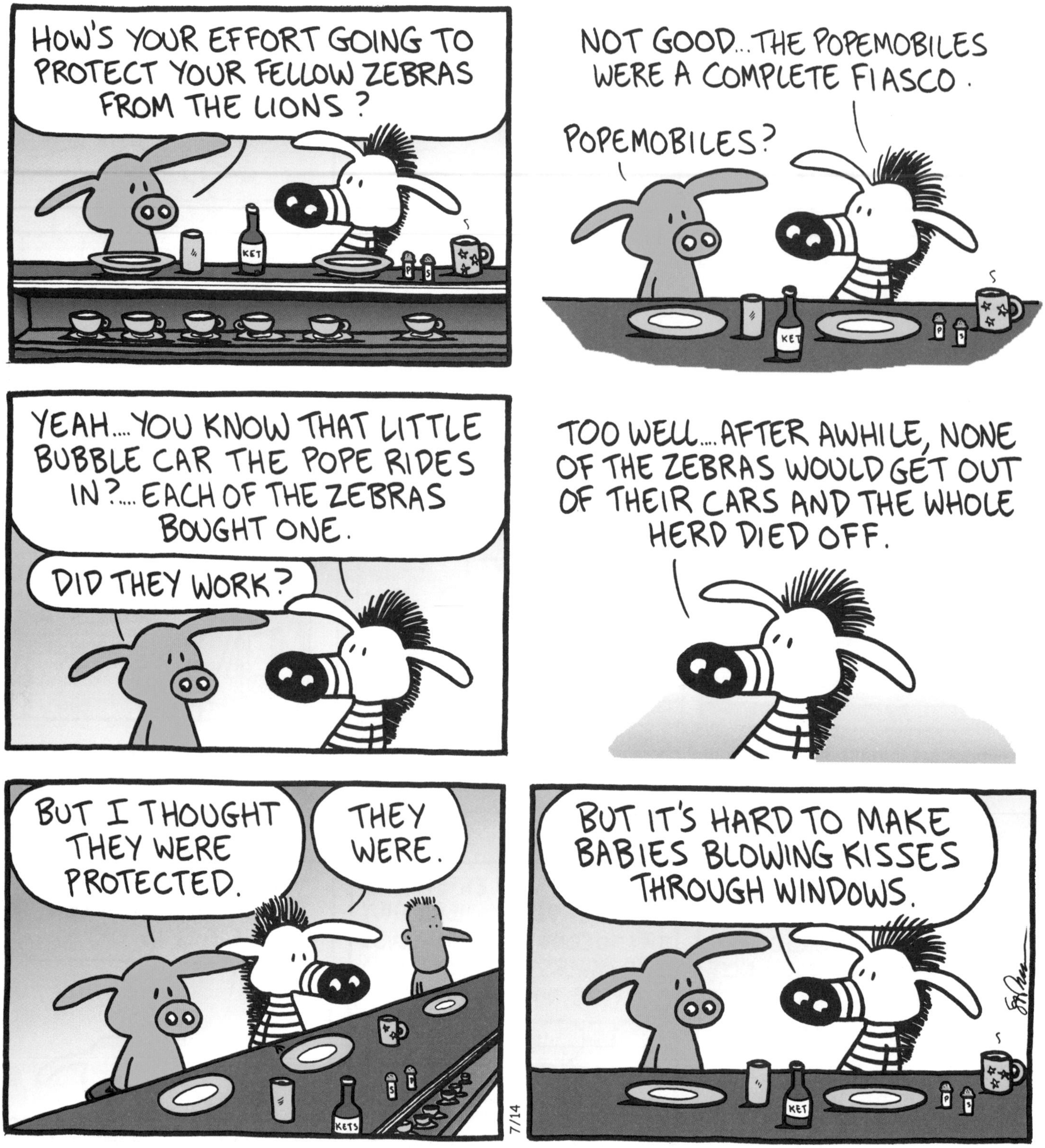
HOW'S YOUR EFFORT GOING TO PROTECT YOUR FELLOW ZEBRAS FROM THE LIONS?
KET
NOT GOOD...THE POPEMOBILES WERE A COMPLETE FIASCO.
POPEMOBILES?
KET
YEAH....YOU KNOW THAT LITTLE BUBBLE CAR THE POPE RIDES IN?....EACH OF THE ZEBRAS BOUGHT ONE.
DID THEY WORK?
TOO WELL....AFTER AWHILE, NONE OF THE ZEBRAS WOULD GET OUT OF THEIR CARS AND THE WHOLE HERD DIED OFF.
BUT I THOUGHT THEY WERE PROTECTED.
THEY WERE.
KETS
7/14
BUT IT'S HARD TO MAKE BABIES BLOWING KISSES THROUGH WINDOWS.
KET

I'm still not quite sure why I went to all that trouble drawing those cups, ketchup bottles, and salt and pepper shakers. I think the Popemobile joke would have survived without them.

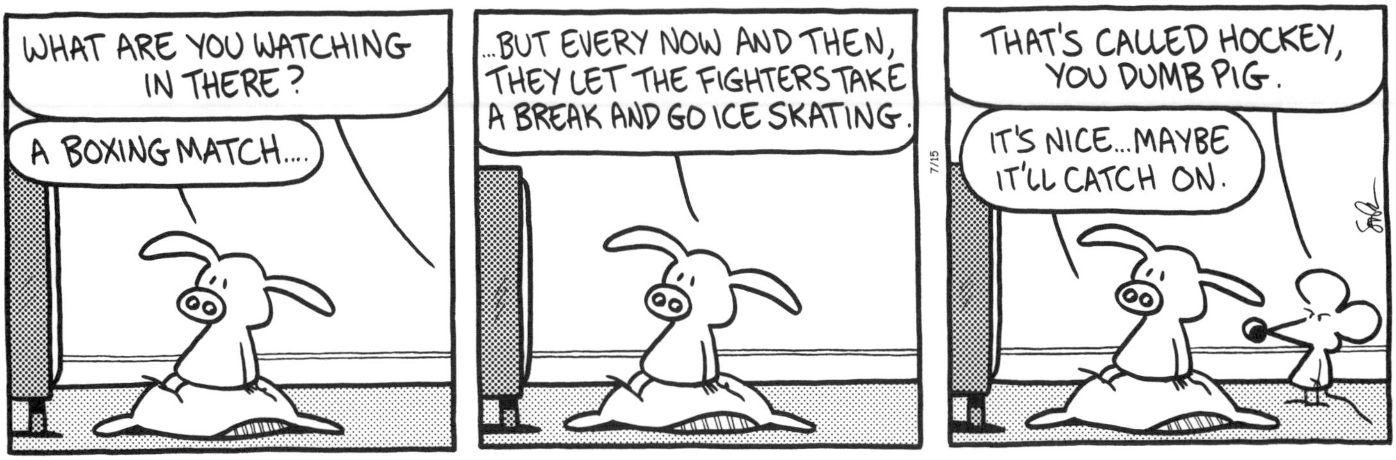
WHAT ARE YOU WATCHING IN THERE?
A BOXING MATCH....
...BUT EVERY NOW AND THEN, THEY LET THE FIGHTERS TAKE A BREAK AND GO ICE SKATING.
7/15
THAT'S CALLED HOCKEY, YOU DUMB PIG.
IT'S NICE...MAYBE IT'LL CATCH ON.

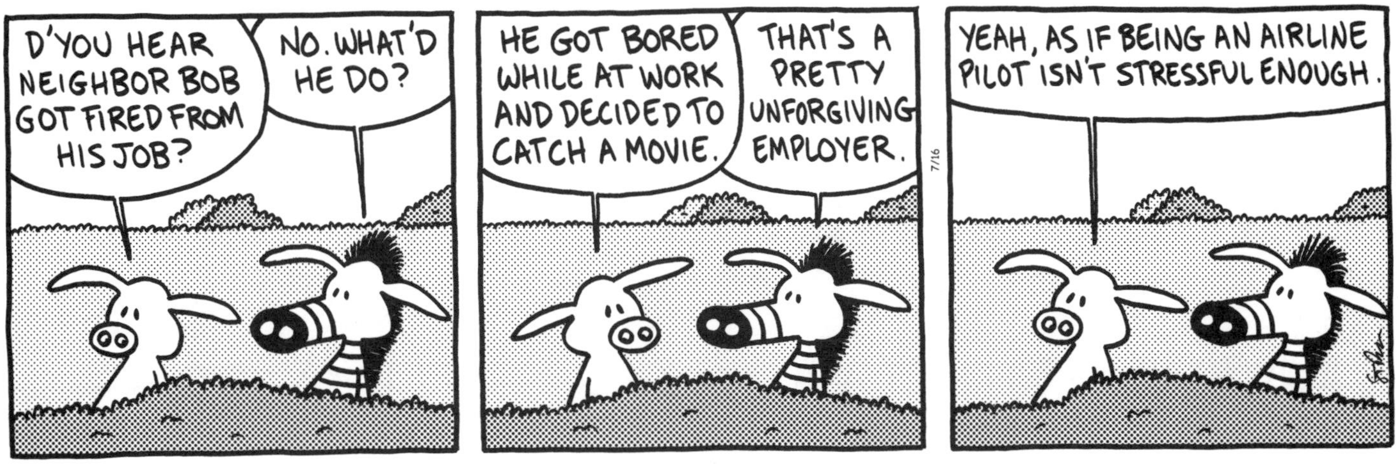
D'YOU HEAR NEIGHBOR BOB GOT FIRED FROM HIS JOB?
NO. WHAT'D HE DO?
HE GOT BORED WHILE AT WORK AND DECIDED TO CATCH A MOVIE.
THAT'S A PRETTY UNFORGIVING EMPLOYER.
7/16
YEAH, AS IF BEING AN AIRLINE PILOT ISN'T STRESSFUL ENOUGH.

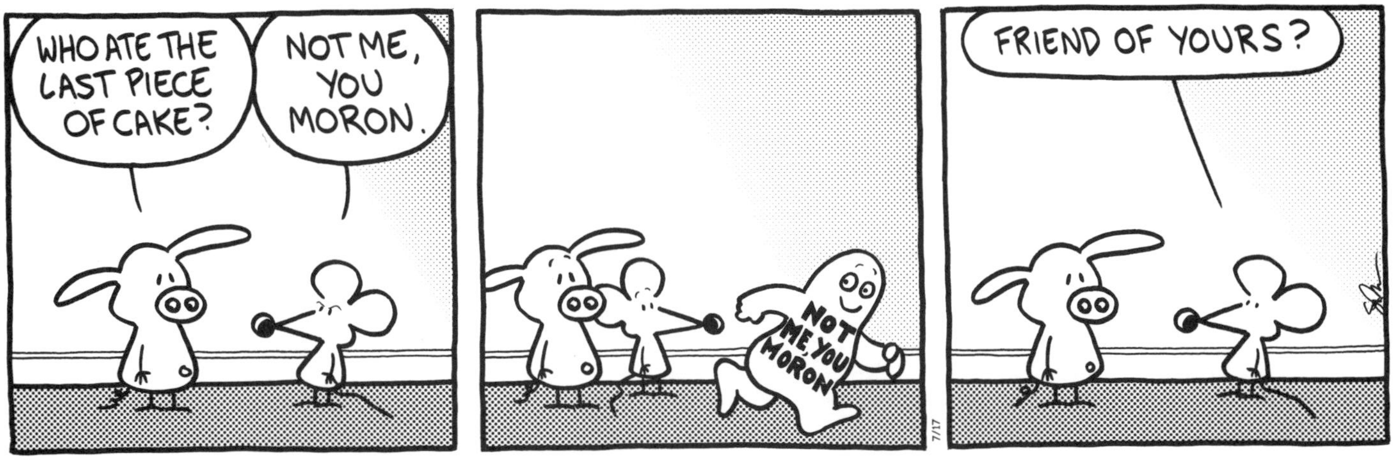
WHO ATE THE LAST PIECE OF CAKE?
NOT ME, YOU MORON.
NOT ME YOU MORON
7/17
FRIEND OF YOURS?

This ghost is from the comic, *The Family Circus*. But in *The Family Circus*, it only says "Not me" on the ghost's chest. The "you moron" part is my own thoughtful contribution.

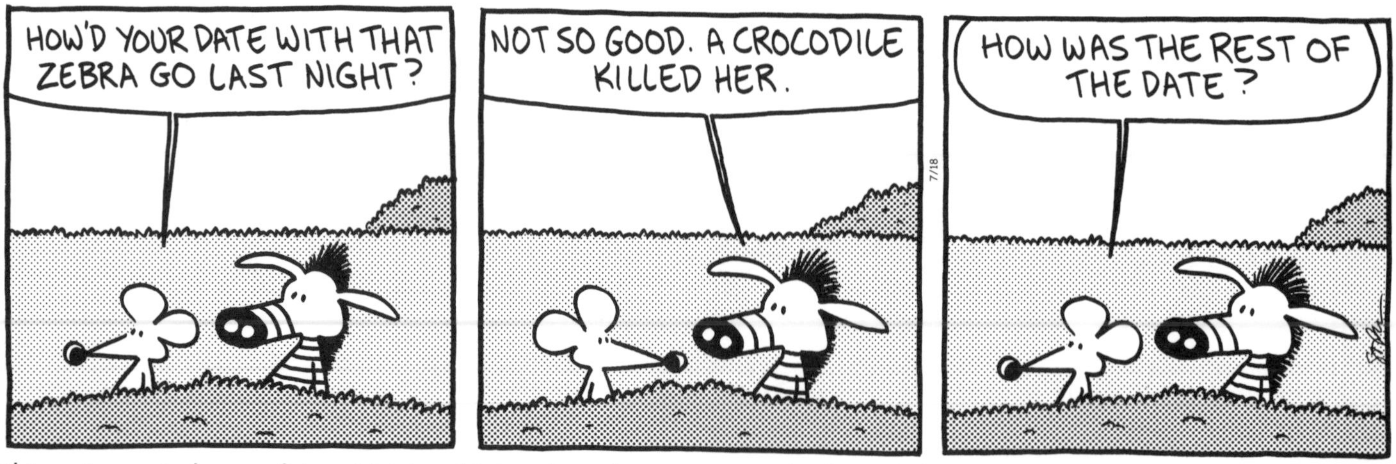
HOW'D YOUR DATE WITH THAT ZEBRA GO LAST NIGHT?
NOT SO GOOD. A CROCODILE KILLED HER.
7/18
HOW WAS THE REST OF THE DATE?

This strip reminds me of the old joke, "Other than that, Mrs. Lincoln, how did you like the play?"

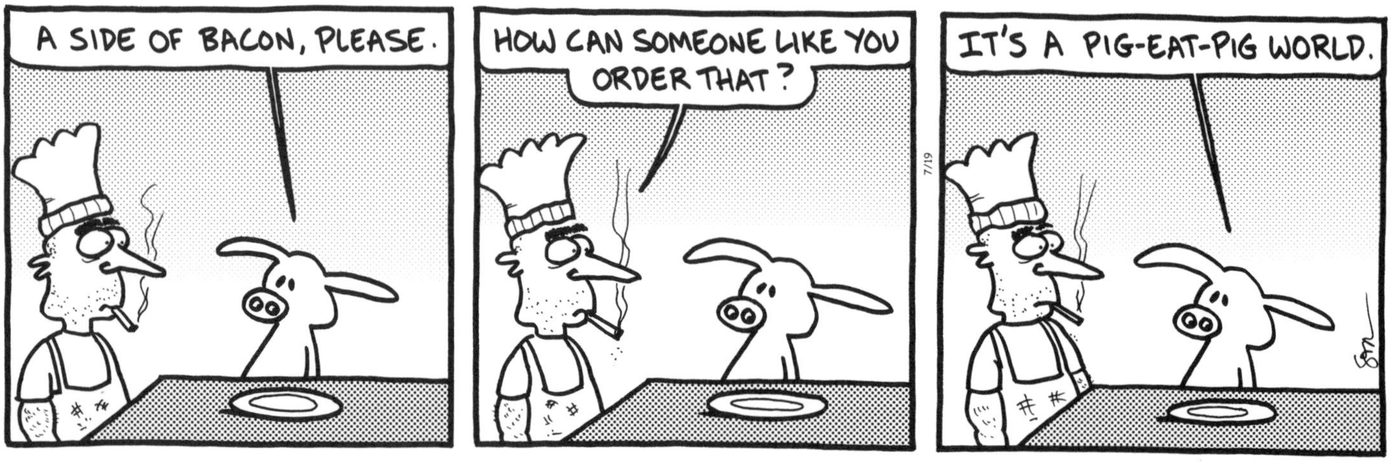
A SIDE OF BACON, PLEASE.
HOW CAN SOMEONE LIKE YOU ORDER THAT?
7/19
IT'S A PIG-EAT-PIG WORLD.

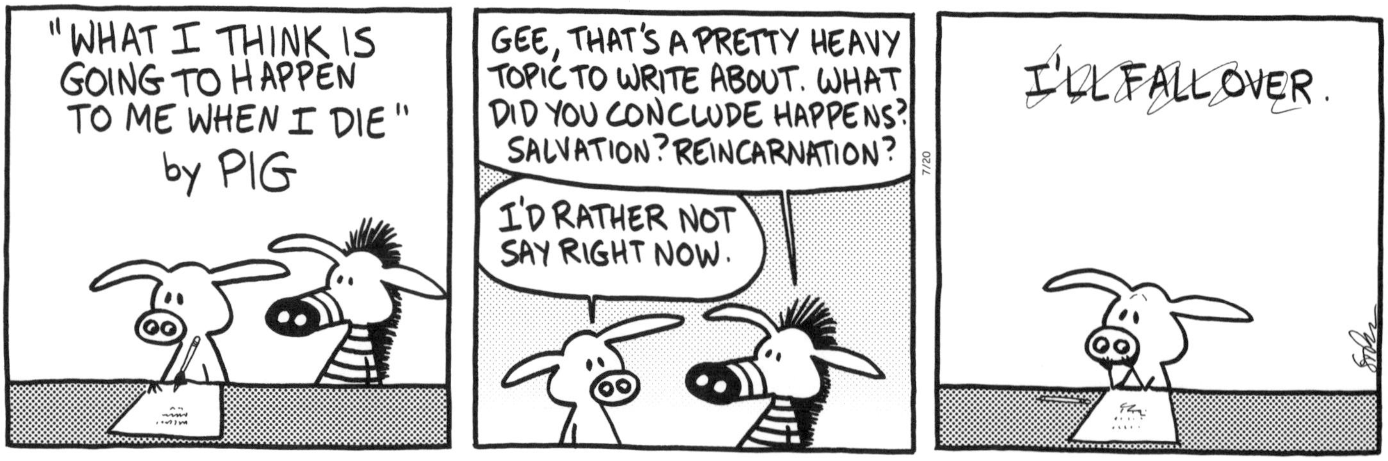
"WHAT I THINK IS GOING TO HAPPEN TO ME WHEN I DIE" by PIG
GEE, THAT'S A PRETTY HEAVY TOPIC TO WRITE ABOUT. WHAT DID YOU CONCLUDE HAPPENS? SALVATION? REINCARNATION?
I'D RATHER NOT SAY RIGHT NOW.
7/20
I'LL FALL OVER.

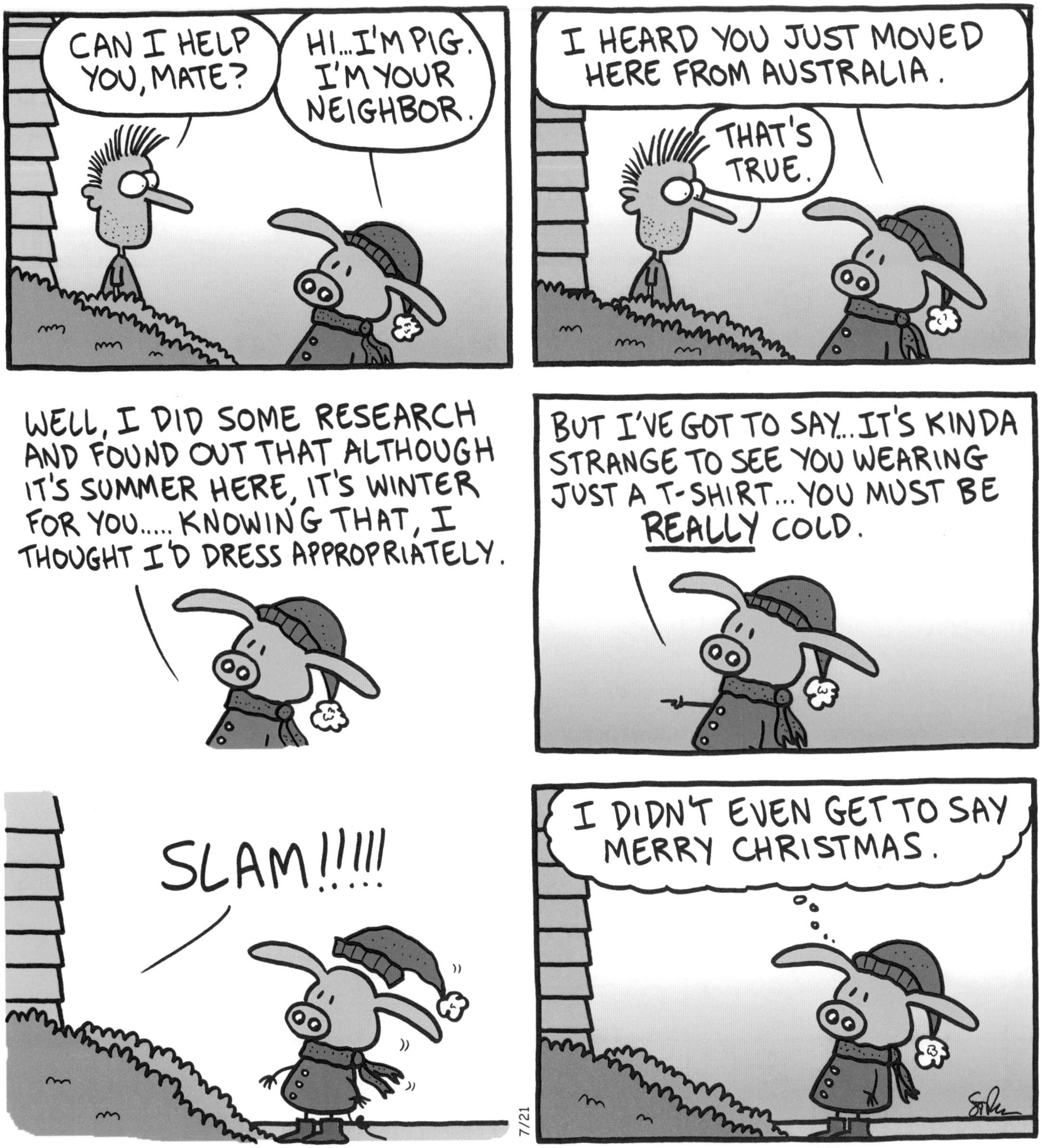
CAN I HELP YOU, MATE?
HI...I'M PIG. I'M YOUR NEIGHBOR.
I HEARD YOU JUST MOVED HERE FROM AUSTRALIA.
THAT'S TRUE.
WELL, I DID SOME RESEARCH AND FOUND OUT THAT ALTHOUGH IT'S SUMMER HERE, IT'S WINTER FOR YOU..... KNOWING THAT, I THOUGHT I'D DRESS APPROPRIATELY.
BUT I'VE GOT TO SAY...IT'S KINDA STRANGE TO SEE YOU WEARING JUST A T-SHIRT... YOU MUST BE REALLY COLD.
SLAM!!!!!
I DIDN'T EVEN GET TO SAY MERRY CHRISTMAS.
7/21

Pig looks cute in winter attire.

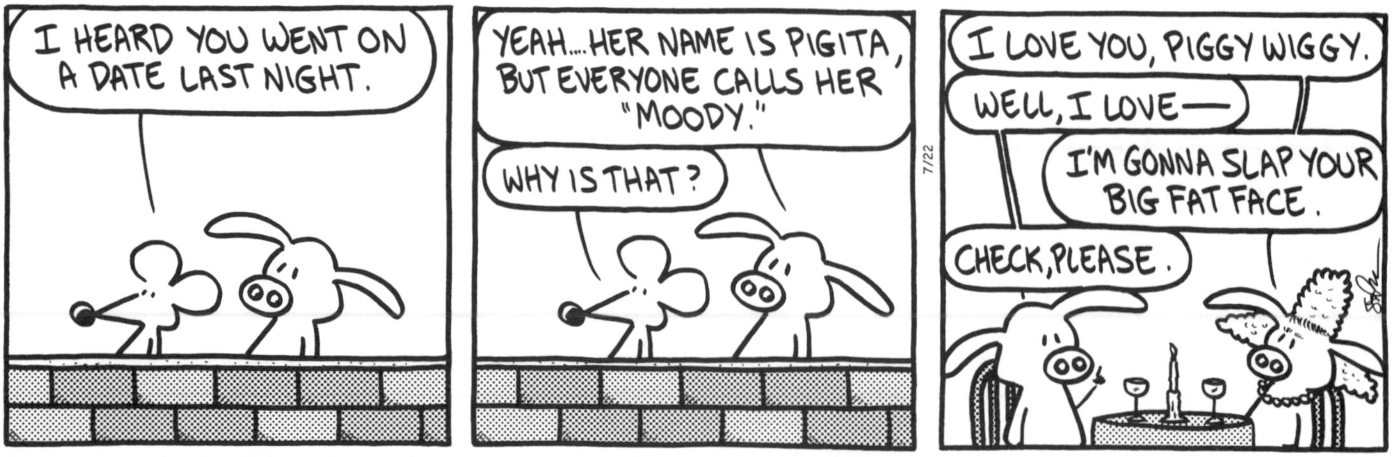
I HEARD YOU WENT ON A DATE LAST NIGHT.
YEAH....HER NAME IS PIGITA, BUT EVERYONE CALLS HER "MOODY."
WHY IS THAT?
7/22
I LOVE YOU, PIGGY WIGGY.
WELL, I LOVE—
I'M GONNA SLAP YOUR BIG FAT FACE.
CHECK, PLEASE.

This strip marks the debut of Moody Pigita, Pig's on-again, off-again girlfriend.

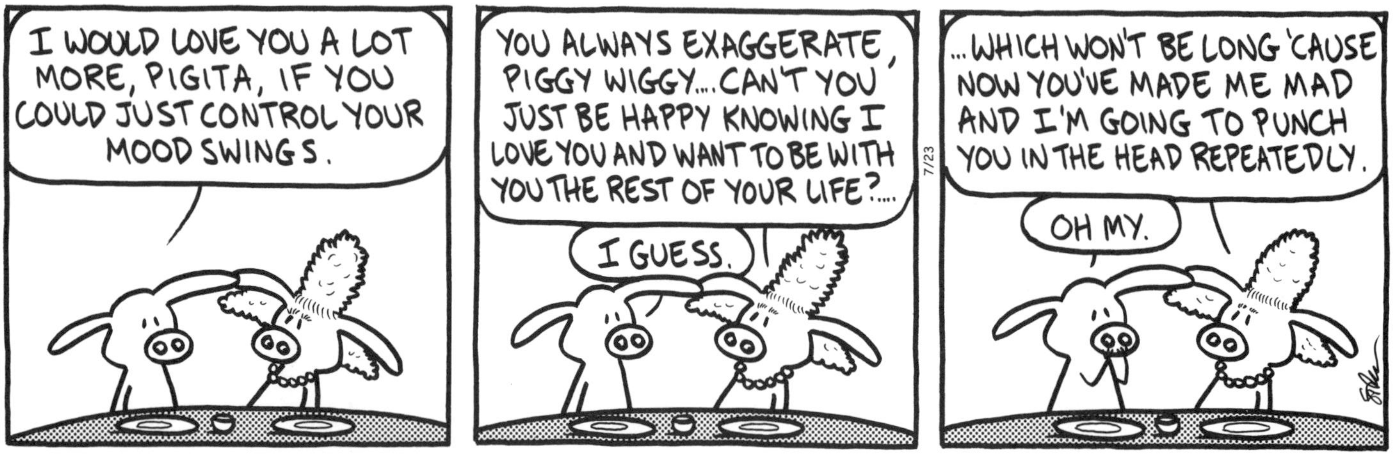
I WOULD LOVE YOU A LOT MORE, PIGITA, IF YOU COULD JUST CONTROL YOUR MOOD SWINGS.
YOU ALWAYS EXAGGERATE, PIGGY WIGGY....CAN'T YOU JUST BE HAPPY KNOWING I LOVE YOU AND WANT TO BE WITH YOU THE REST OF YOUR LIFE?....
I GUESS.
7/23
...WHICH WON'T BE LONG 'CAUSE NOW YOU'VE MADE ME MAD AND I'M GOING TO PUNCH YOU IN THE HEAD REPEATEDLY.
OH MY.

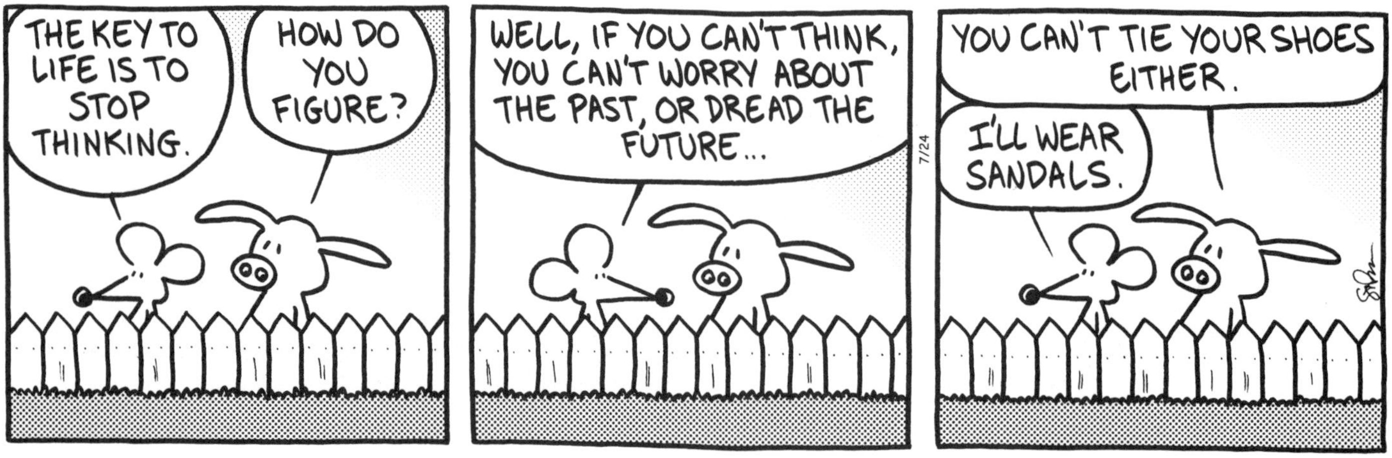
THE KEY TO LIFE IS TO STOP THINKING.
HOW DO YOU FIGURE?
WELL, IF YOU CAN'T THINK, YOU CAN'T WORRY ABOUT THE PAST, OR DREAD THE FUTURE...
7/24
YOU CAN'T TIE YOUR SHOES EITHER.
I'LL WEAR SANDALS.

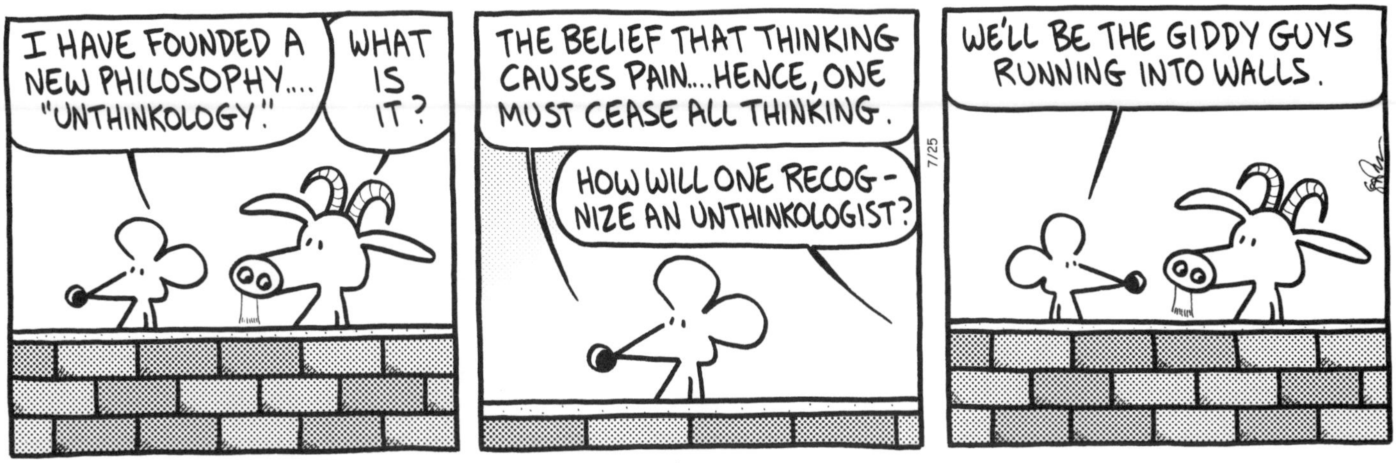
I HAVE FOUNDED A NEW PHILOSOPHY.... "UNTHINKOLOGY."
WHAT IS IT?
THE BELIEF THAT THINKING CAUSES PAIN....HENCE, ONE MUST CEASE ALL THINKING.
HOW WILL ONE RECOGNIZE AN UNTHINKOLOGIST?
7/25
WE'LL BE THE GIDDY GUYS RUNNING INTO WALLS.

I could never be an unthinkologist. I worry about *everything*.

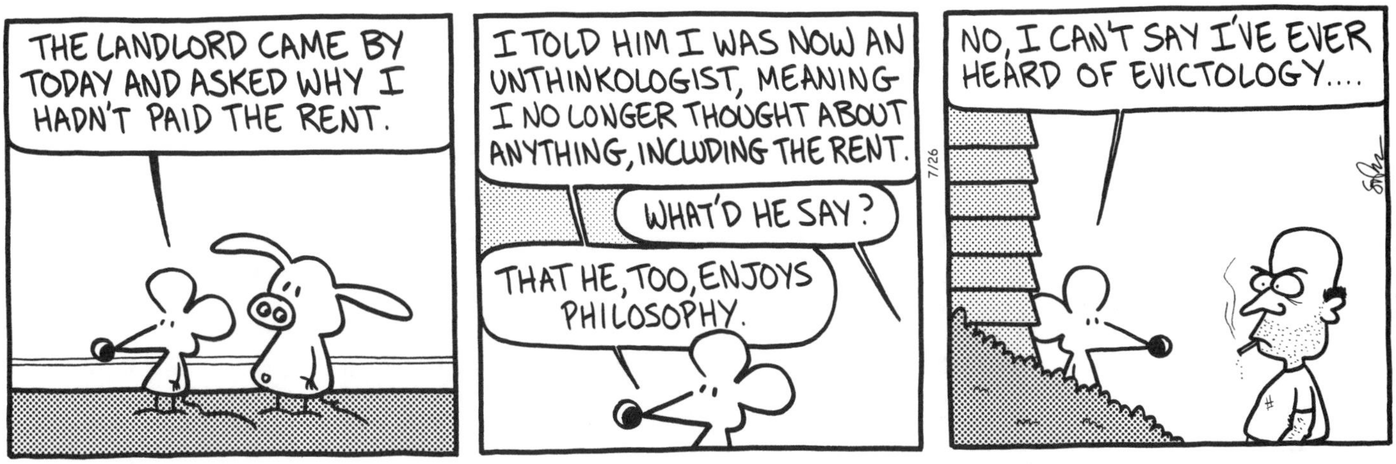
THE LANDLORD CAME BY TODAY AND ASKED WHY I HADN'T PAID THE RENT.
I TOLD HIM I WAS NOW AN UNTHINKOLOGIST, MEANING I NO LONGER THOUGHT ABOUT ANYTHING, INCLUDING THE RENT.
WHAT'D HE SAY?
THAT HE, TOO, ENJOYS PHILOSOPHY.
7/26
NO, I CAN'T SAY I'VE EVER HEARD OF EVICTOLOGY....

In comic strips, good landlord characters have to smoke and have a five-o'clock shadow. It's a rule.

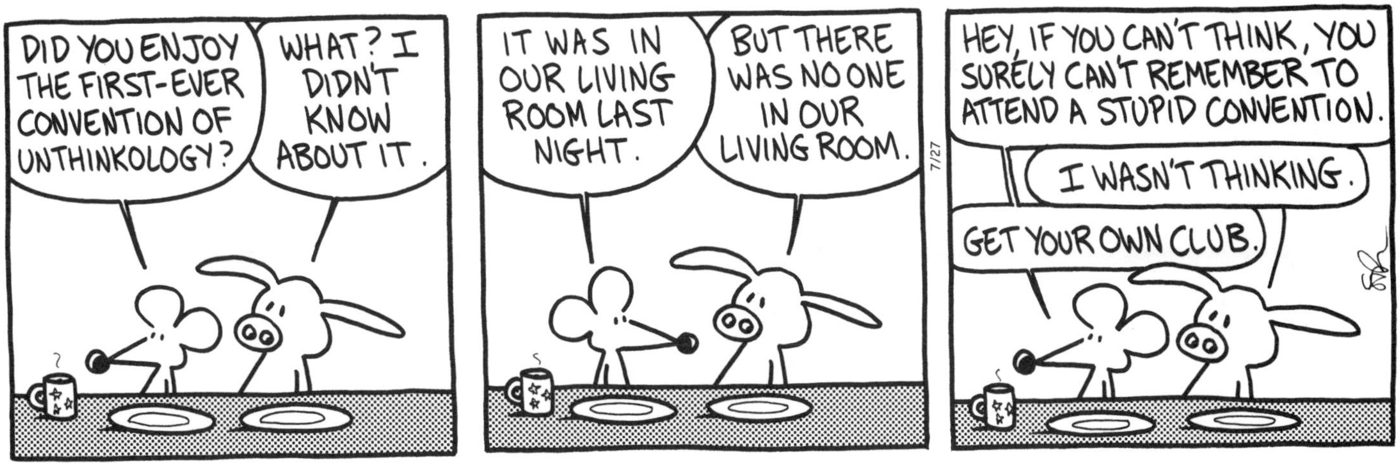
DID YOU ENJOY THE FIRST-EVER CONVENTION OF UNTHINKOLOGY?
WHAT? I DIDN'T KNOW ABOUT IT.
IT WAS IN OUR LIVING ROOM LAST NIGHT.
BUT THERE WAS NO ONE IN OUR LIVING ROOM.
7/27
HEY, IF YOU CAN'T THINK, YOU SURELY CAN'T REMEMBER TO ATTEND A STUPID CONVENTION.
I WASN'T THINKING.
GET YOUR OWN CLUB.

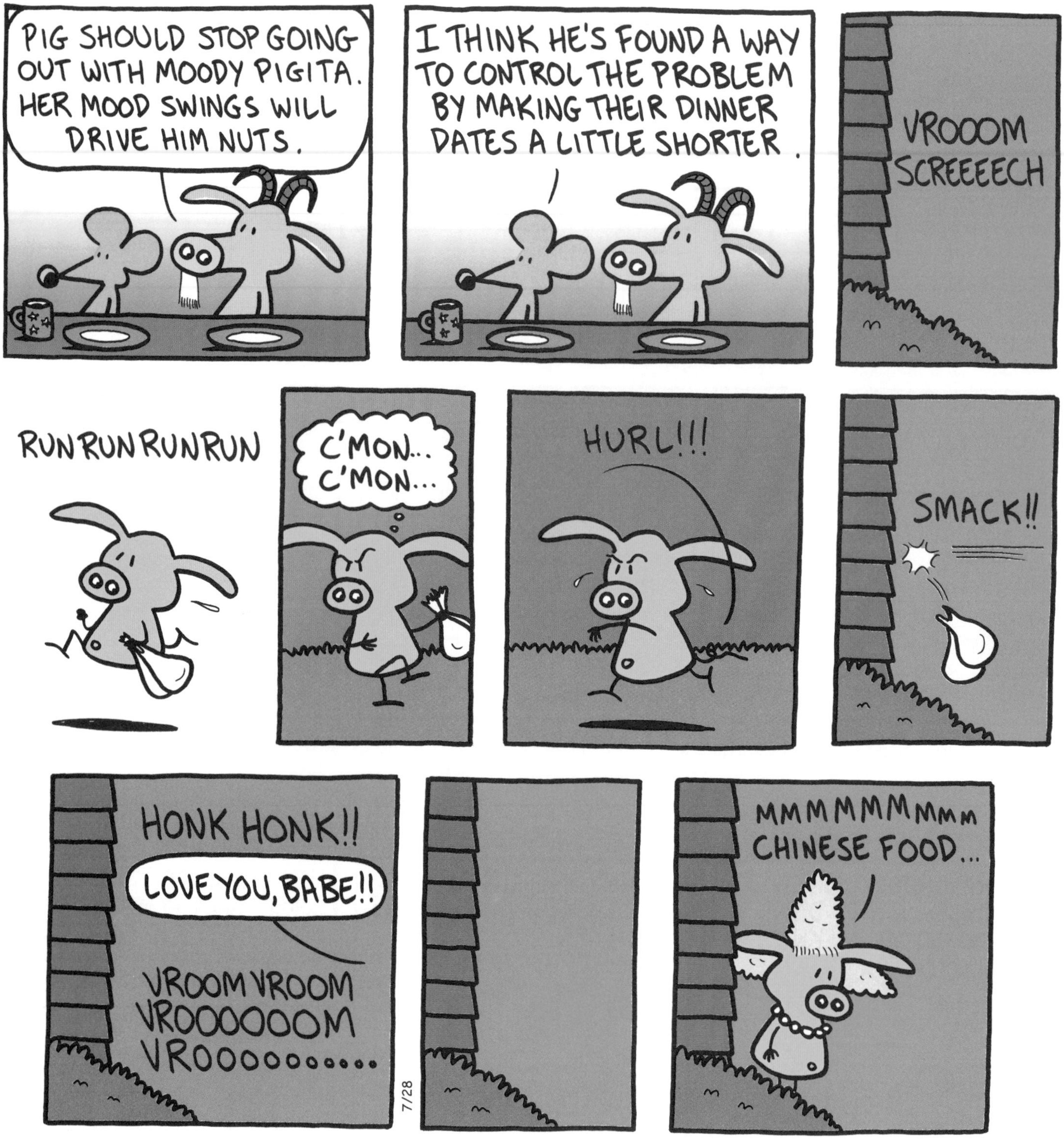
PIG SHOULD STOP GOING OUT WITH MOODY PIGITA. HER MOOD SWINGS WILL DRIVE HIM NUTS.
I THINK HE'S FOUND A WAY TO CONTROL THE PROBLEM BY MAKING THEIR DINNER DATES A LITTLE SHORTER.
VROOOM
SCREEEECH
RUNRUNRUNRUN
C'MON... C'MON...
HURL!!!
SMACK!!
HONK HONK!!
LOVE YOU, BABE!!
VROOM VROOM
VROOOOOOM
VROOOOOOOOO
7/28
MMMMMMMMM CHINESE FOOD...

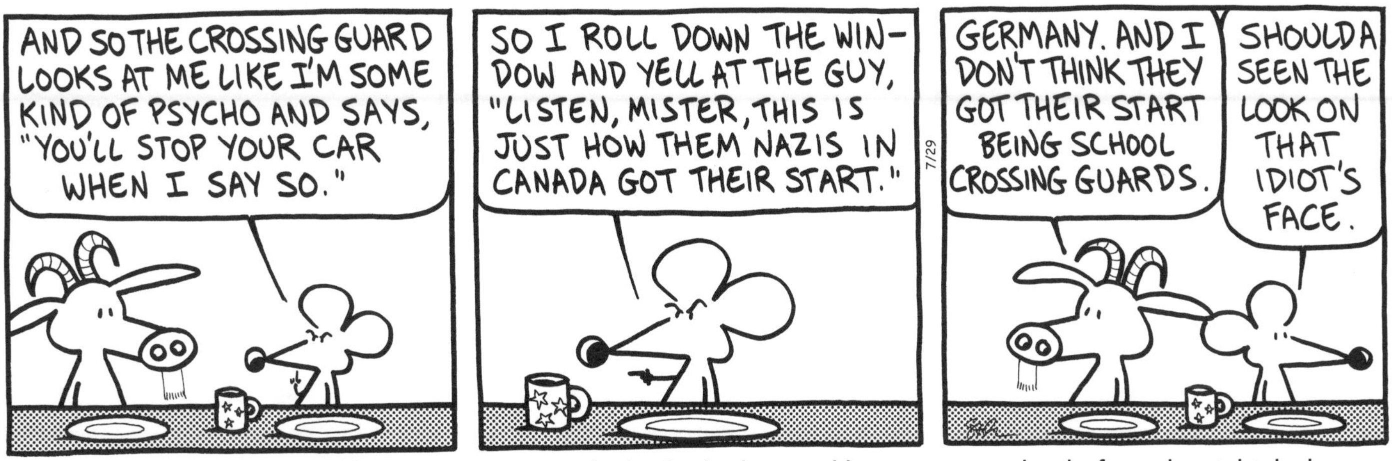
AND SO THE CROSSING GUARD LOOKS AT ME LIKE I'M SOME KIND OF PSYCHO AND SAYS, "YOU'LL STOP YOUR CAR WHEN I SAY SO."
SO I ROLL DOWN THE WIN-DOW AND YELL AT THE GUY, "LISTEN, MISTER, THIS IS JUST HOW THEM NAZIS IN CANADA GOT THEIR START."
7/29
GERMANY. AND I DON'T THINK THEY GOT THEIR START BEING SCHOOL CROSSING GUARDS.
SHOULDA SEEN THE LOOK ON THAT IDIOT'S FACE.

This comic strip was inspired by a crossing guard who looked at me like I was some kind of psycho. I think she thought I was coming down the hill a little fast, but I was fully in control of my vehicle.

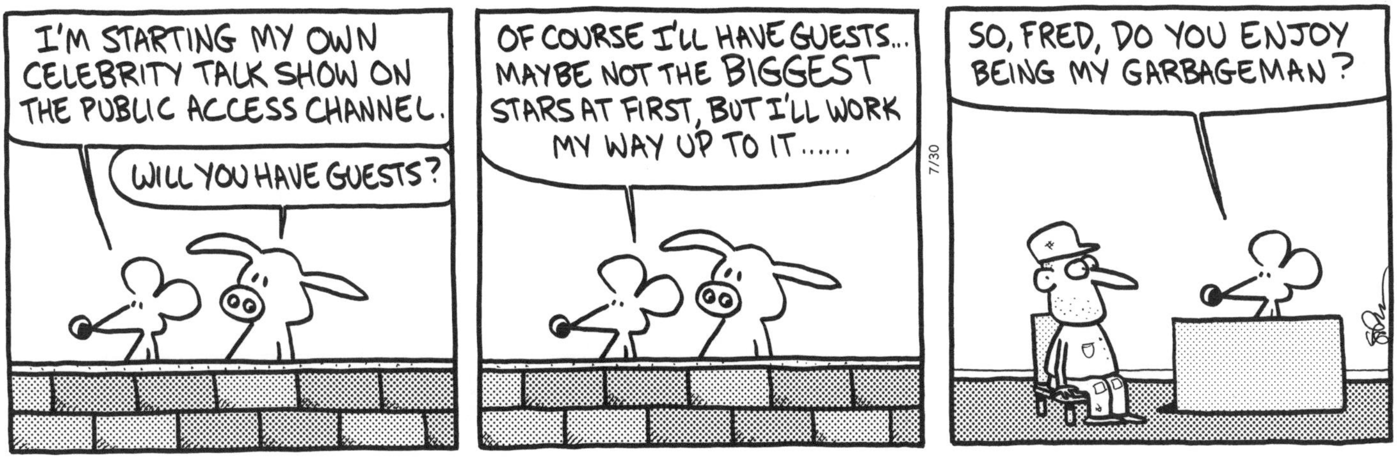
I'M STARTING MY OWN CELEBRITY TALK SHOW ON THE PUBLIC ACCESS CHANNEL.
WILL YOU HAVE GUESTS?
OF COURSE I'LL HAVE GUESTS... MAYBE NOT THE BIGGEST STARS AT FIRST, BUT I'LL WORK MY WAY UP TO IT......
7/30
SO, FRED, DO YOU ENJOY BEING MY GARBAGEMAN?

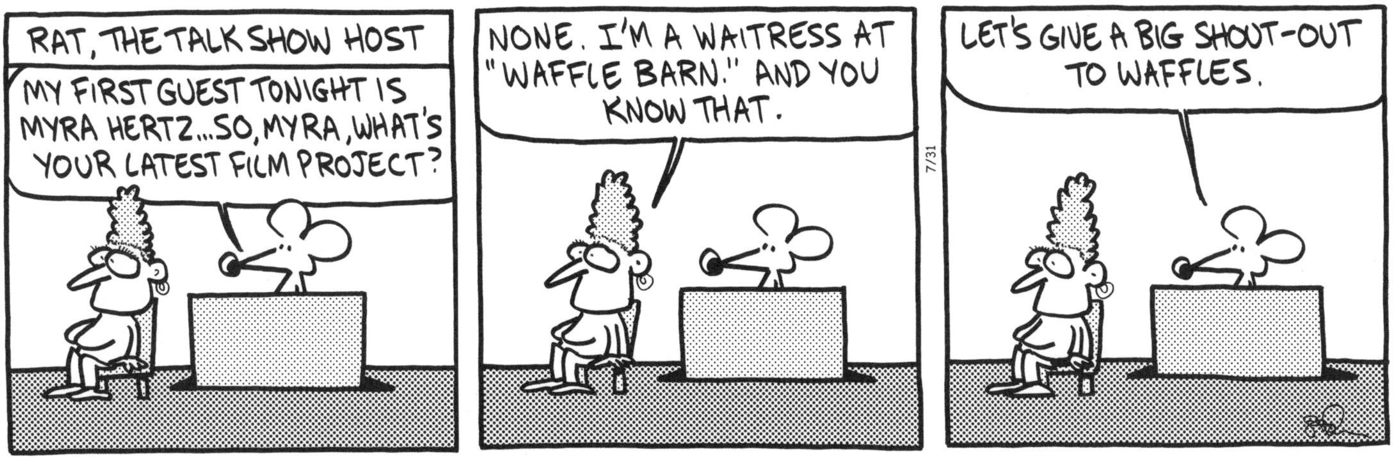
RAT, THE TALK SHOW HOST
MY FIRST GUEST TONIGHT IS MYRA HERTZ...SO, MYRA, WHAT'S YOUR LATEST FILM PROJECT?
NONE. I'M A WAITRESS AT "WAFFLE BARN." AND YOU KNOW THAT.
7/31
LET'S GIVE A BIG SHOUT-OUT TO WAFFLES.

The notion of giving a "shout-out" to a waffle makes me laugh. By the way, I'm quite proud of Rat's desk. It is a model of simplicity. Nothing like drawing a square and calling it a desk.

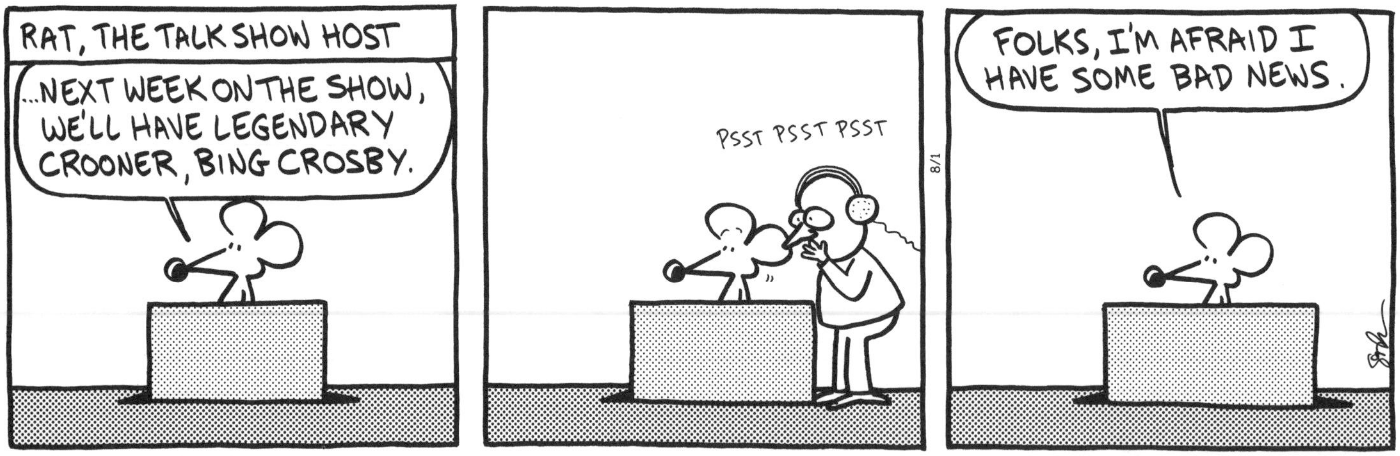
RAT, THE TALK SHOW HOST
...NEXT WEEK ON THE SHOW, WE'LL HAVE LEGENDARY CROONER, BING CROSBY.
PSST PSST PSST
8/1
FOLKS, I'M AFRAID I HAVE SOME BAD NEWS.

For those people who didn't get this one, Bing Crosby is dead. As such, he would have a hard time being a guest.

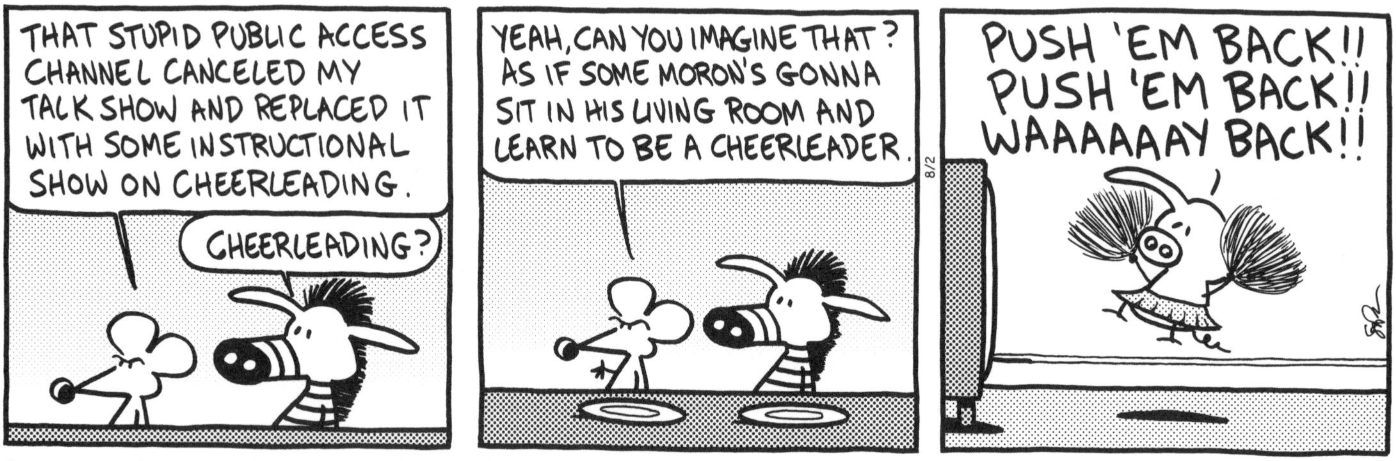
THAT STUPID PUBLIC ACCESS CHANNEL CANCELED MY TALK SHOW AND REPLACED IT WITH SOME INSTRUCTIONAL SHOW ON CHEERLEADING.
CHEERLEADING?
YEAH, CAN YOU IMAGINE THAT? AS IF SOME MORON'S GONNA SIT IN HIS LIVING ROOM AND LEARN TO BE A CHEERLEADER.
8/2
PUSH 'EM BACK!! PUSH 'EM BACK!! WAAAAAAY BACK!!

If I'm ever short on ideas, I can always draw Pig in some goofy costume.

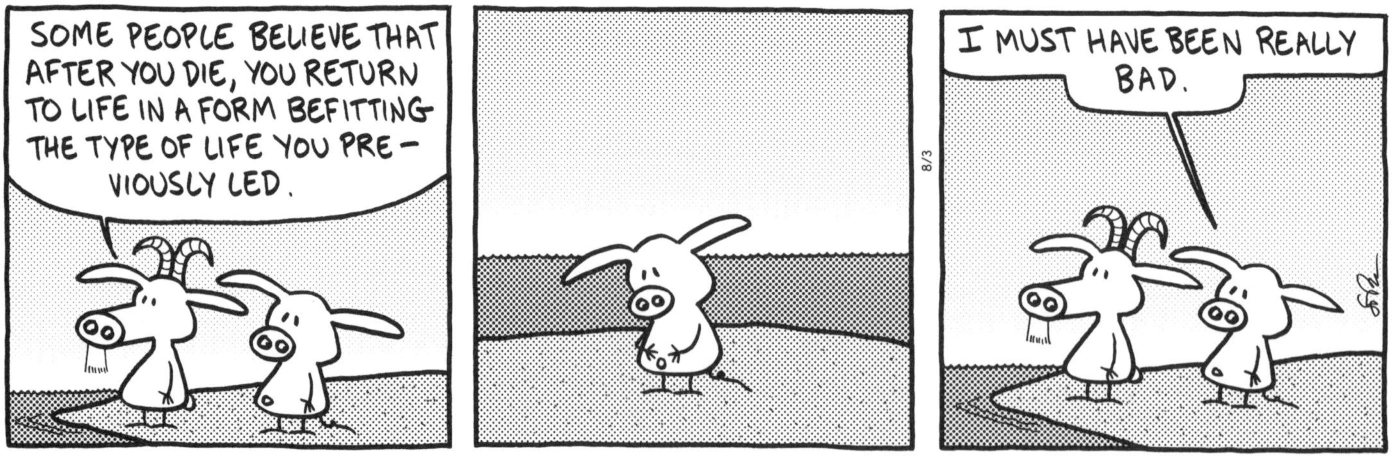
SOME PEOPLE BELIEVE THAT AFTER YOU DIE, YOU RETURN TO LIFE IN A FORM BEFITTING THE TYPE OF LIFE YOU PRE-VIOUSLY LED.
8/3
I MUST HAVE BEEN REALLY BAD.

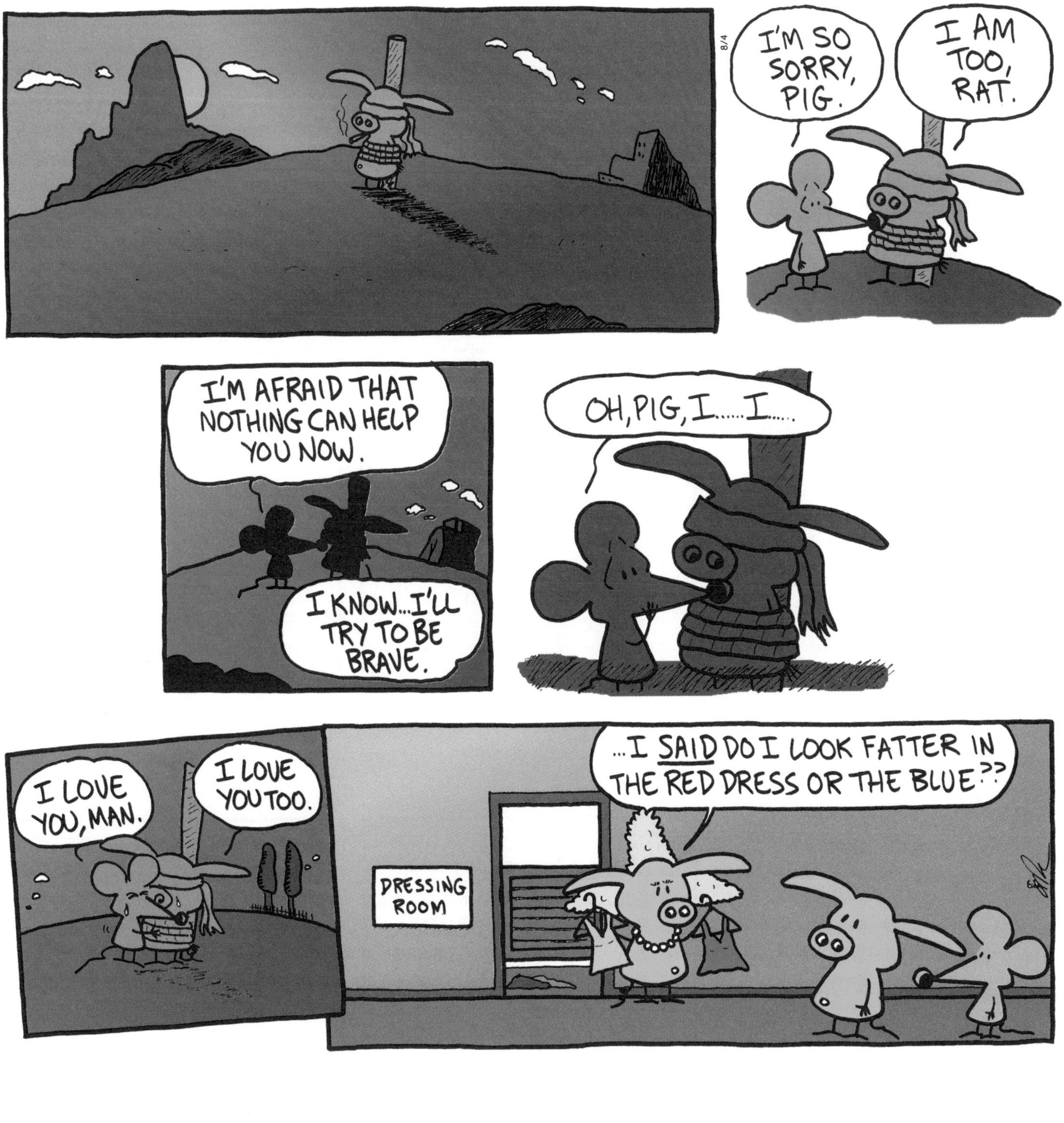
8/4
I'M SO SORRY, PIG.
I AM TOO, RAT.
I'M AFRAID THAT NOTHING CAN HELP YOU NOW.
I KNOW...I'LL TRY TO BE BRAVE.
OH, PIG, I...... I......
I LOVE YOU, MAN.
I LOVE YOU TOO.
DRESSING ROOM
...I SAID DO I LOOK FATTER IN THE RED DRESS OR THE BLUE??

The backgrounds in the first, third, and fifth panels are my tribute to the comic strip *Krazy Kat*, considered by many to be the greatest comic strip ever created. If you've never read it, you should.

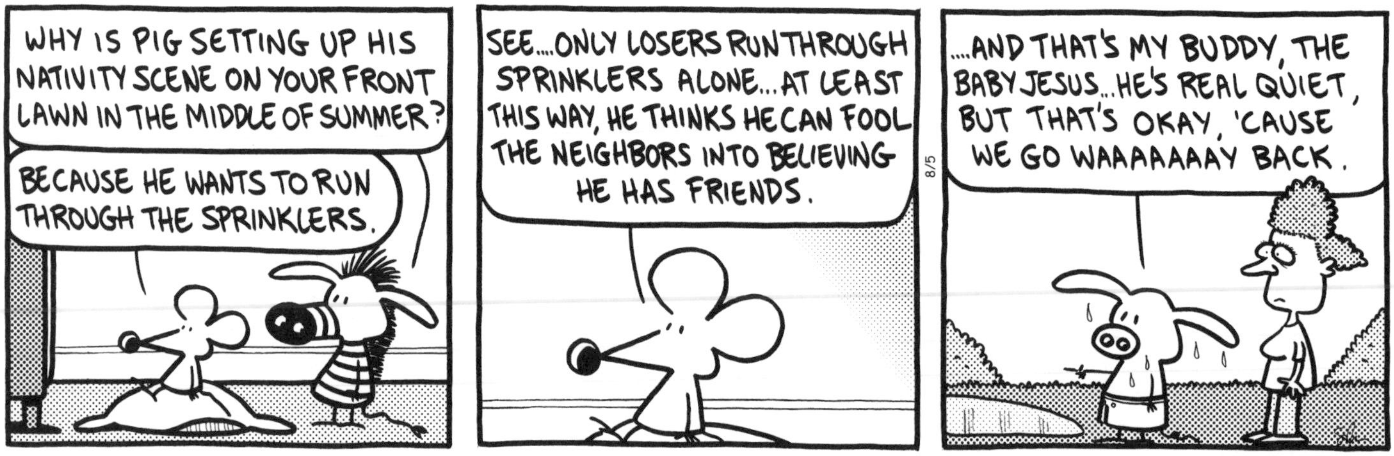
WHY IS PIG SETTING UP HIS NATIVITY SCENE ON YOUR FRONT LAWN IN THE MIDDLE OF SUMMER?
BECAUSE HE WANTS TO RUN THROUGH THE SPRINKLERS.
SEE....ONLY LOSERS RUN THROUGH SPRINKLERS ALONE... AT LEAST THIS WAY, HE THINKS HE CAN FOOL THE NEIGHBORS INTO BELIEVING HE HAS FRIENDS.
8/5
....AND THAT'S MY BUDDY, THE BABY JESUS...HE'S REAL QUIET, BUT THAT'S OKAY, 'CAUSE WE GO WAAAAAAAY BACK.

Because this series was set to run midsummer, I had to create a reason for the nativity scene to be on the lawn. Hey, whatever works.

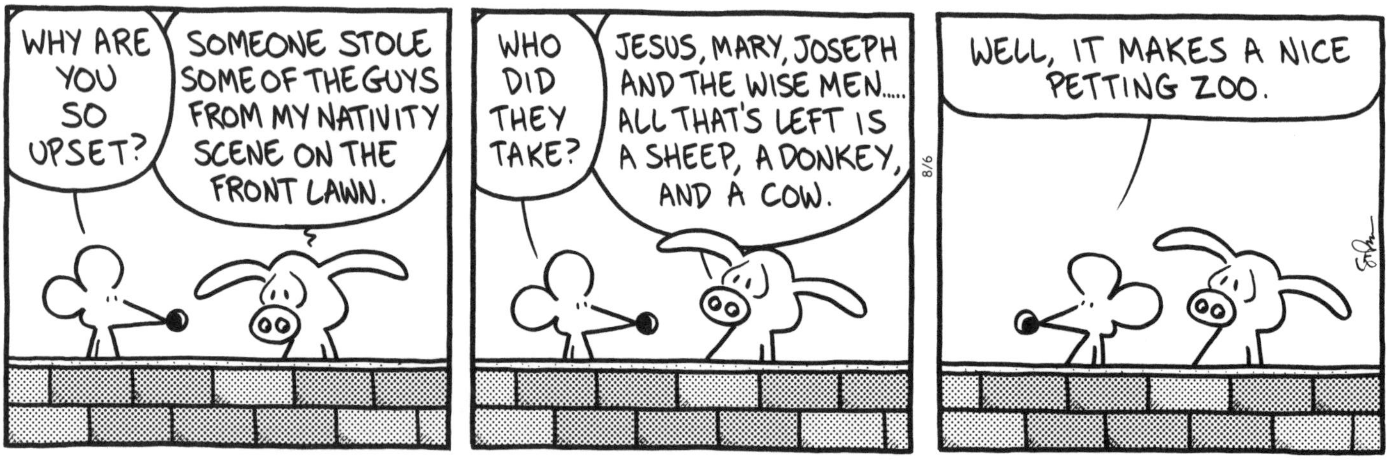
WHY ARE YOU SO UPSET?
SOMEONE STOLE SOME OF THE GUYS FROM MY NATIVITY SCENE ON THE FRONT LAWN.
WHO DID THEY TAKE?
JESUS, MARY, JOSEPH AND THE WISE MEN..... ALL THAT'S LEFT IS A SHEEP, A DONKEY, AND A COW.
8/6
WELL, IT MAKES A NICE PETTING ZOO.

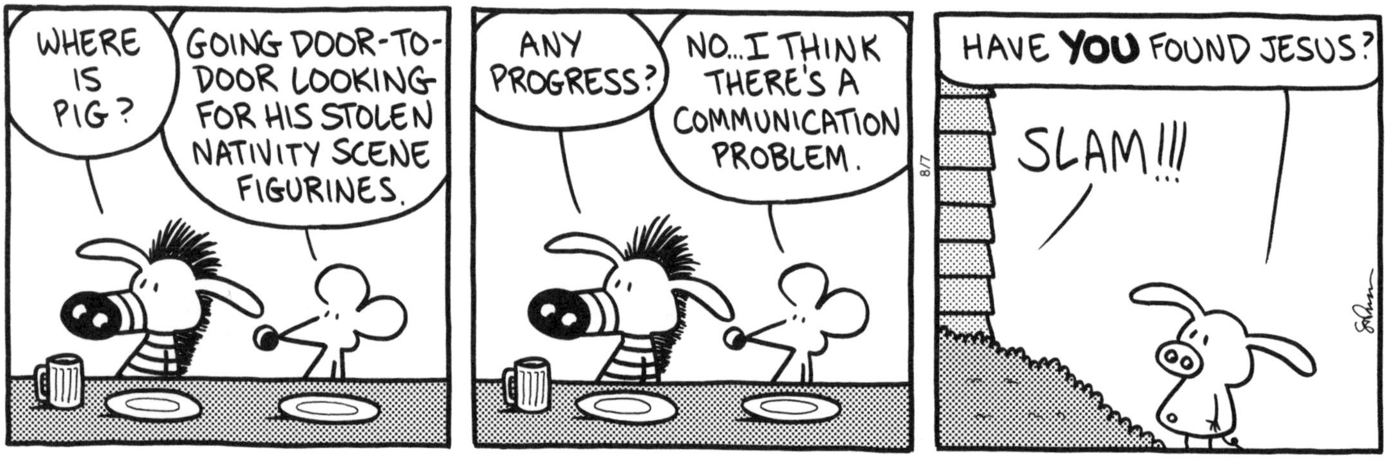
WHERE IS PIG?
GOING DOOR-TO-DOOR LOOKING FOR HIS STOLEN NATIVITY SCENE FIGURINES.
ANY PROGRESS?
NO...I THINK THERE'S A COMMUNICATION PROBLEM.
8/7
HAVE **YOU** FOUND JESUS?
SLAM!!!

This was one of the most popular dailies I've done. I expected to take some flak, due to the religious theme, but there were very few complaints.

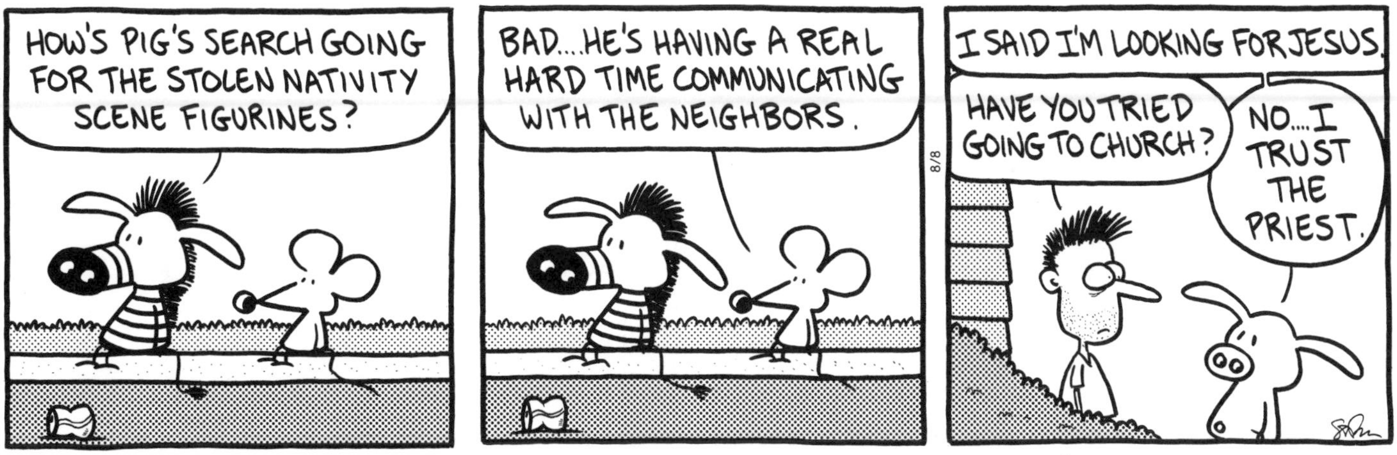
HOW'S PIG'S SEARCH GOING FOR THE STOLEN NATIVITY SCENE FIGURINES?
BAD....HE'S HAVING A REAL HARD TIME COMMUNICATING WITH THE NEIGHBORS.
8/8
I SAID I'M LOOKING FOR JESUS.
HAVE YOU TRIED GOING TO CHURCH?
NO....I TRUST THE PRIEST.

This comic illustrates the cartoonists' credo that if you have a good idea, repeat it day after day with minor variations and hope no one notices.

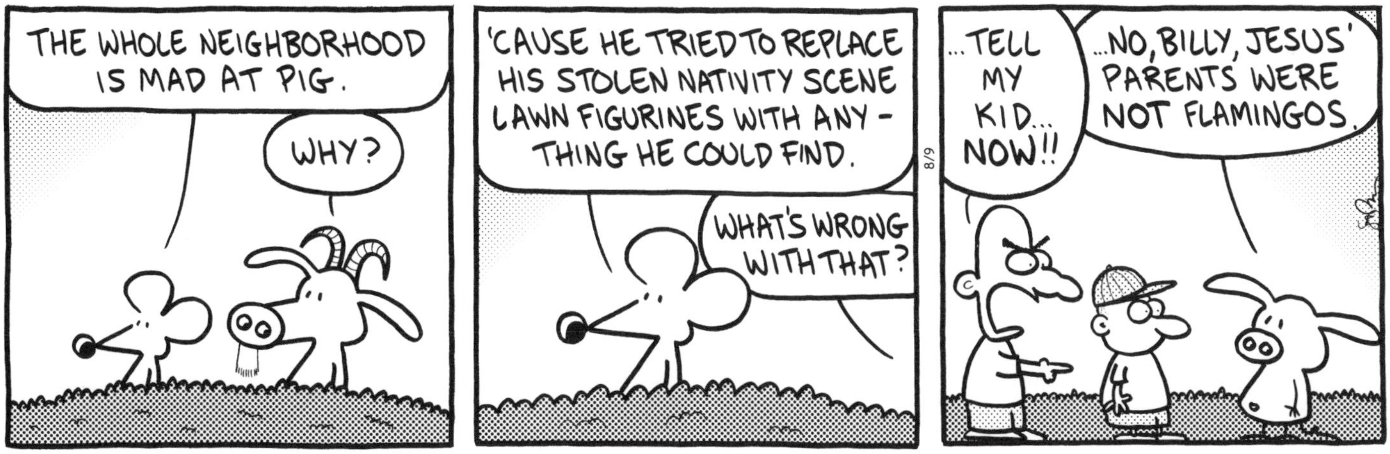
THE WHOLE NEIGHBORHOOD IS MAD AT PIG.
WHY?
'CAUSE HE TRIED TO REPLACE HIS STOLEN NATIVITY SCENE LAWN FIGURINES WITH ANY-THING HE COULD FIND.
WHAT'S WRONG WITH THAT?
8/9
...TELL MY KID... NOW!!
...NO, BILLY, JESUS' PARENTS WERE NOT FLAMINGOS.

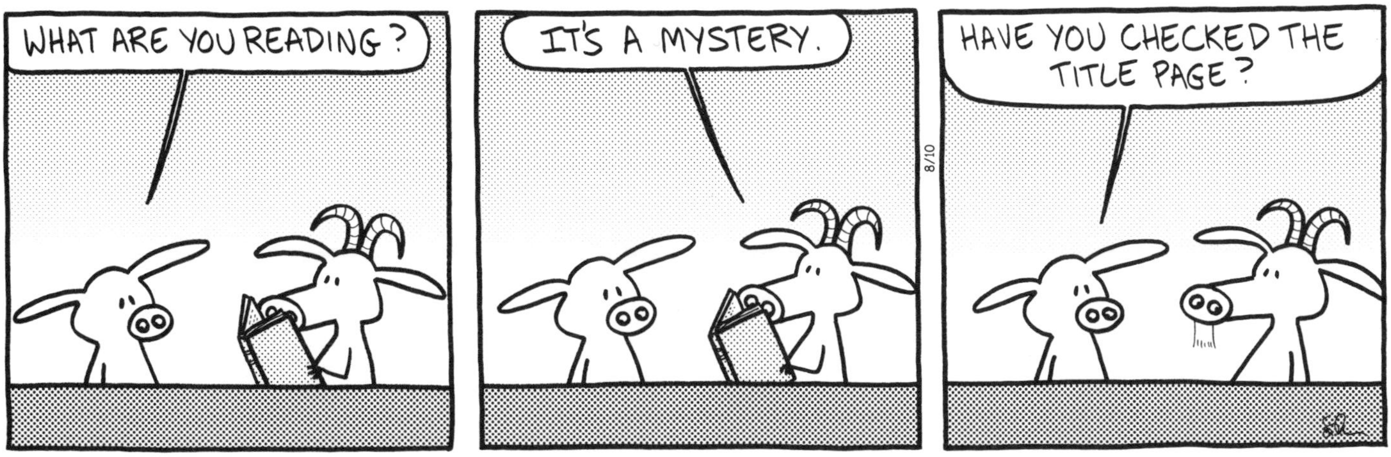
WHAT ARE YOU READING?
IT'S A MYSTERY.
8/10
HAVE YOU CHECKED THE TITLE PAGE?

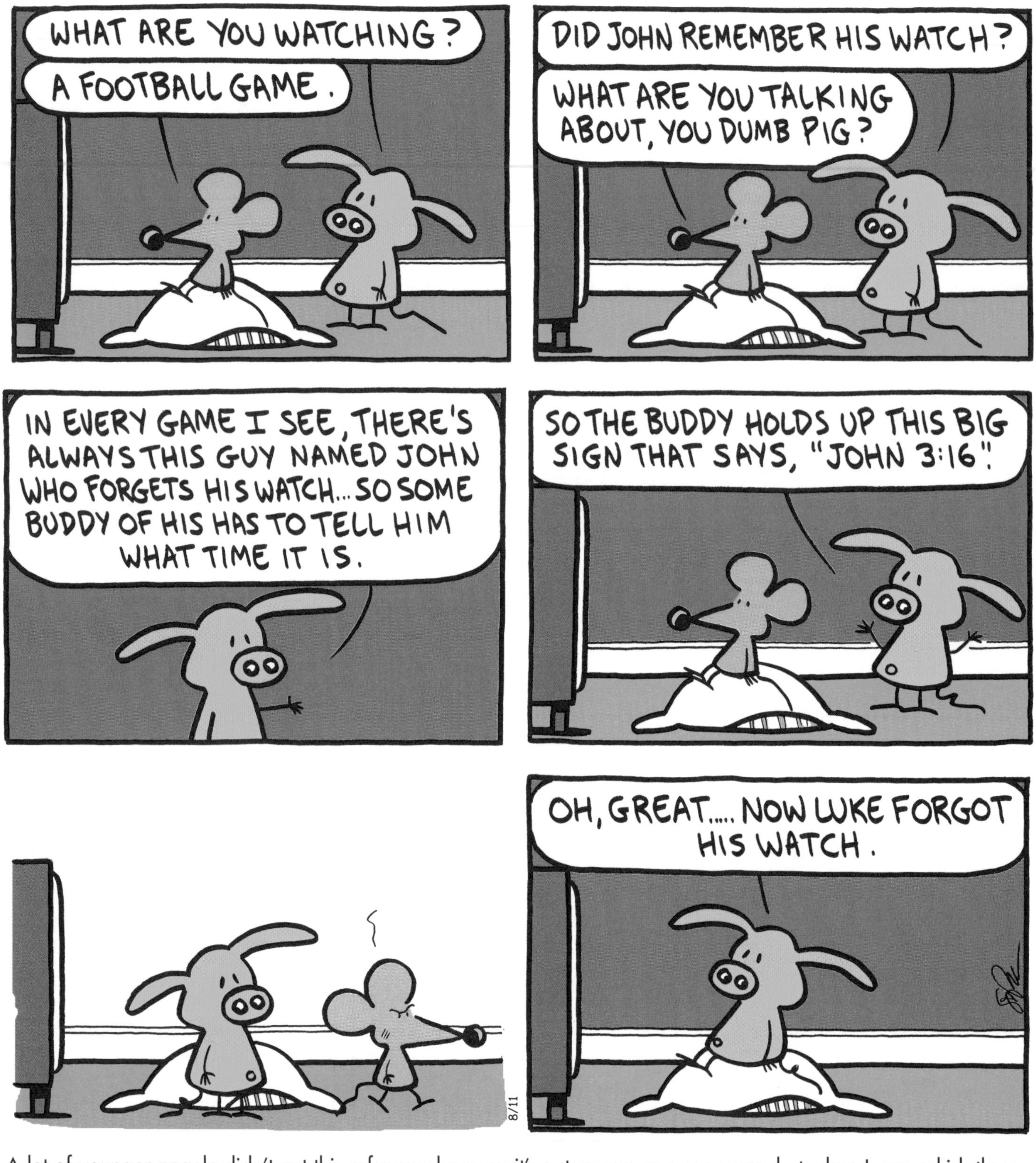
WHAT ARE YOU WATCHING?
A FOOTBALL GAME.
DID JOHN REMEMBER HIS WATCH?
WHAT ARE YOU TALKING ABOUT, YOU DUMB PIG?
IN EVERY GAME I SEE, THERE'S ALWAYS THIS GUY NAMED JOHN WHO FORGETS HIS WATCH... SO SOME BUDDY OF HIS HAS TO TELL HIM WHAT TIME IT IS.
SO THE BUDDY HOLDS UP THIS BIG SIGN THAT SAYS, "JOHN 3:16".
OH, GREAT..... NOW LUKE FORGOT HIS WATCH.
8/11

A lot of younger people didn't get this reference because it's not as common anymore, but when I was a kid, there was this one guy who held up that "John 3:16" sign at EVERY sporting event.

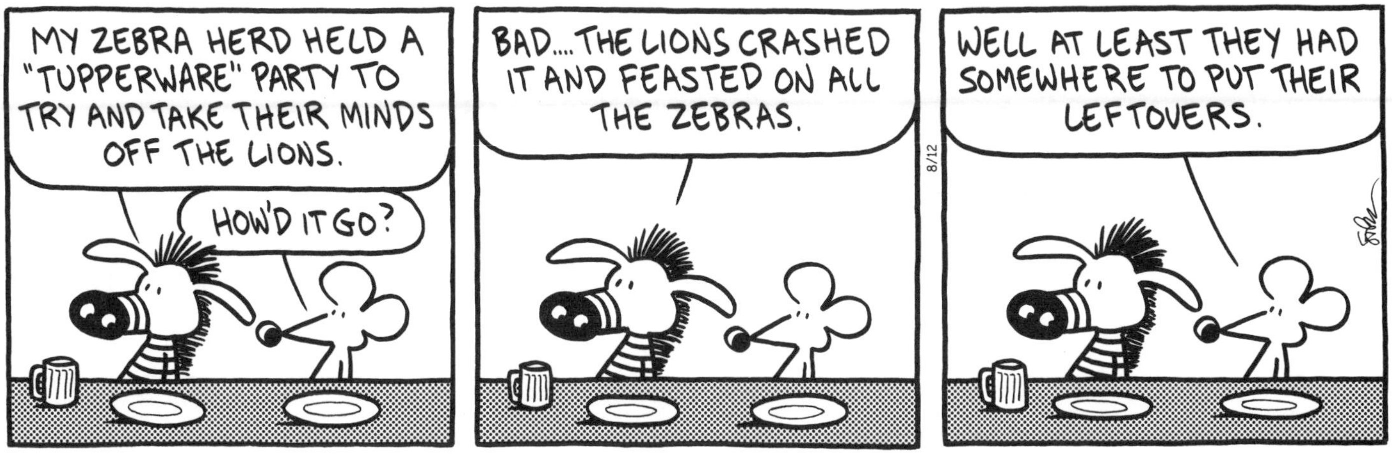
MY ZEBRA HERD HELD A "TUPPERWARE" PARTY TO TRY AND TAKE THEIR MINDS OFF THE LIONS.
HOW'D IT GO?
BAD.... THE LIONS CRASHED IT AND FEASTED ON ALL THE ZEBRAS.
8/12
WELL AT LEAST THEY HAD SOMEWHERE TO PUT THEIR LEFTOVERS.

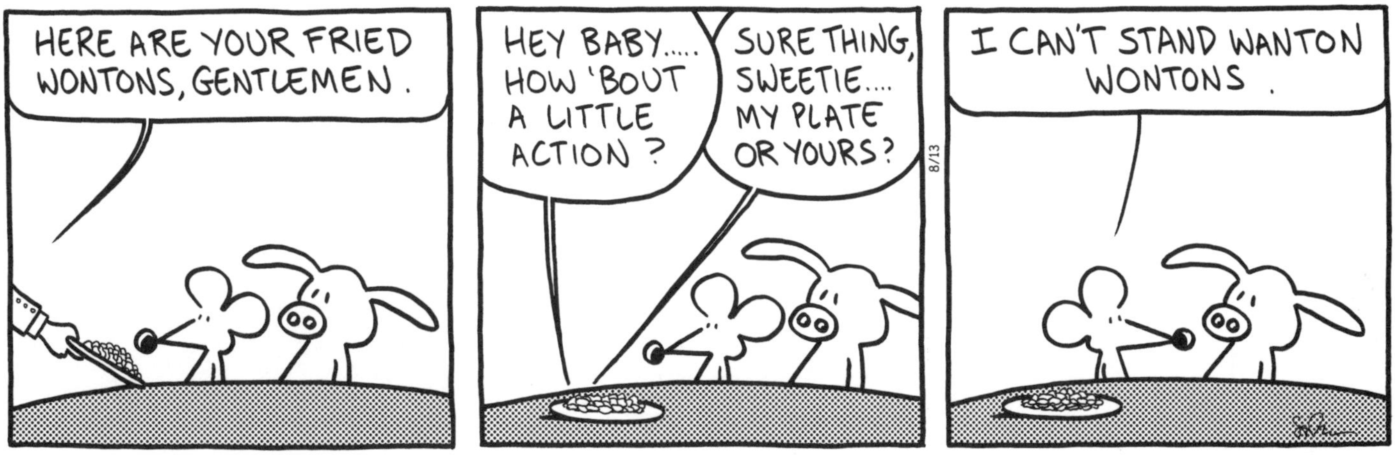
HERE ARE YOUR FRIED WONTONS, GENTLEMEN.
HEY BABY..... HOW 'BOUT A LITTLE ACTION?
SURE THING, SWEETIE.... MY PLATE OR YOURS?
8/13
I CAN'T STAND WANTON WONTONS.

This is one of the few comics that I've done that came straight out of my own life. One day at my law firm, I mispronounced the word "wanton," so that it sounded like the Chinese food "wonton." One of the attorneys at the firm corrected me. A better question is why I was yelling out "wanton" at my law firm.

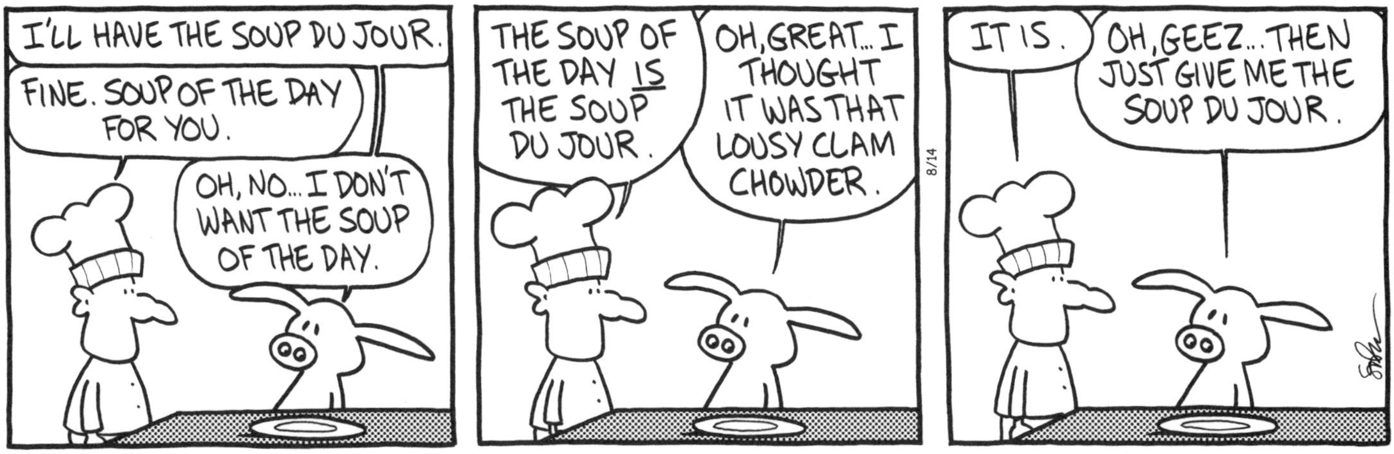
I'LL HAVE THE SOUP DU JOUR.
FINE. SOUP OF THE DAY FOR YOU.
OH, NO... I DON'T WANT THE SOUP OF THE DAY.
THE SOUP OF THE DAY IS THE SOUP DU JOUR.
OH, GREAT... I THOUGHT IT WAS THAT LOUSY CLAM CHOWDER.
8/14
IT IS.
OH, GEEZ... THEN JUST GIVE ME THE SOUP DU JOUR.

Man, this joke still confuses me.

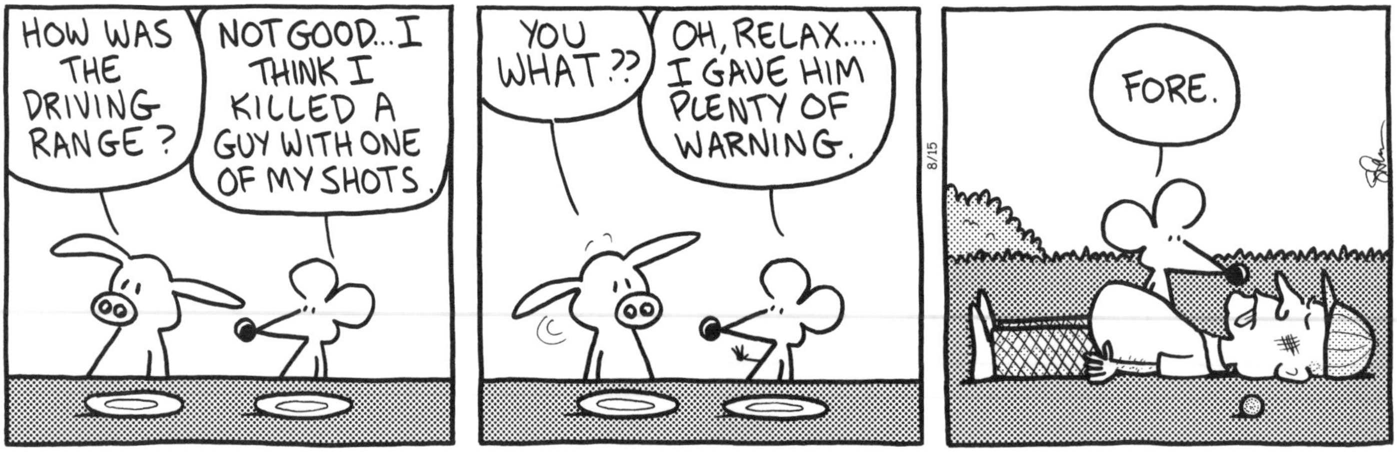
HOW WAS THE DRIVING RANGE?
NOT GOOD... I THINK I KILLED A GUY WITH ONE OF MY SHOTS.
YOU WHAT??
OH, RELAX.... I GAVE HIM PLENTY OF WARNING.
8/15
FORE.

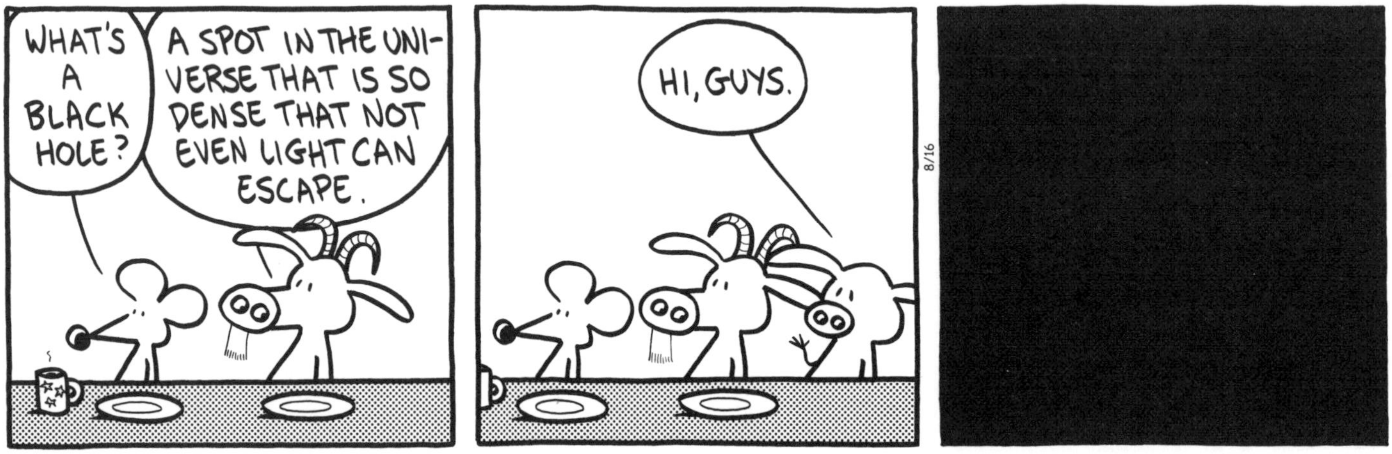
WHAT'S A BLACK HOLE?
A SPOT IN THE UNIVERSE THAT IS SO DENSE THAT NOT EVEN LIGHT CAN ESCAPE.
HI, GUYS.
8/16

Whenever I can do a completely black panel in one of my daily strips, it cuts down on my workload by 33%.

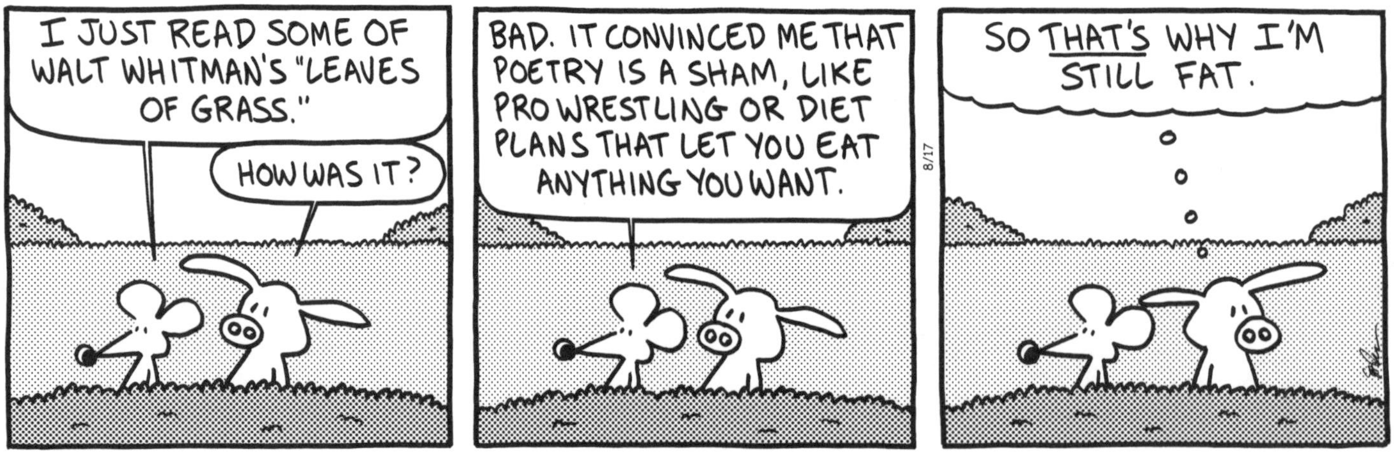
I JUST READ SOME OF WALT WHITMAN'S "LEAVES OF GRASS."
HOW WAS IT?
BAD. IT CONVINCED ME THAT POETRY IS A SHAM, LIKE PRO WRESTLING OR DIET PLANS THAT LET YOU EAT ANYTHING YOU WANT.
8/17
SO THAT'S WHY I'M STILL FAT.

I've tried to read *Leaves of Grass* twice now. I just can't get through it.

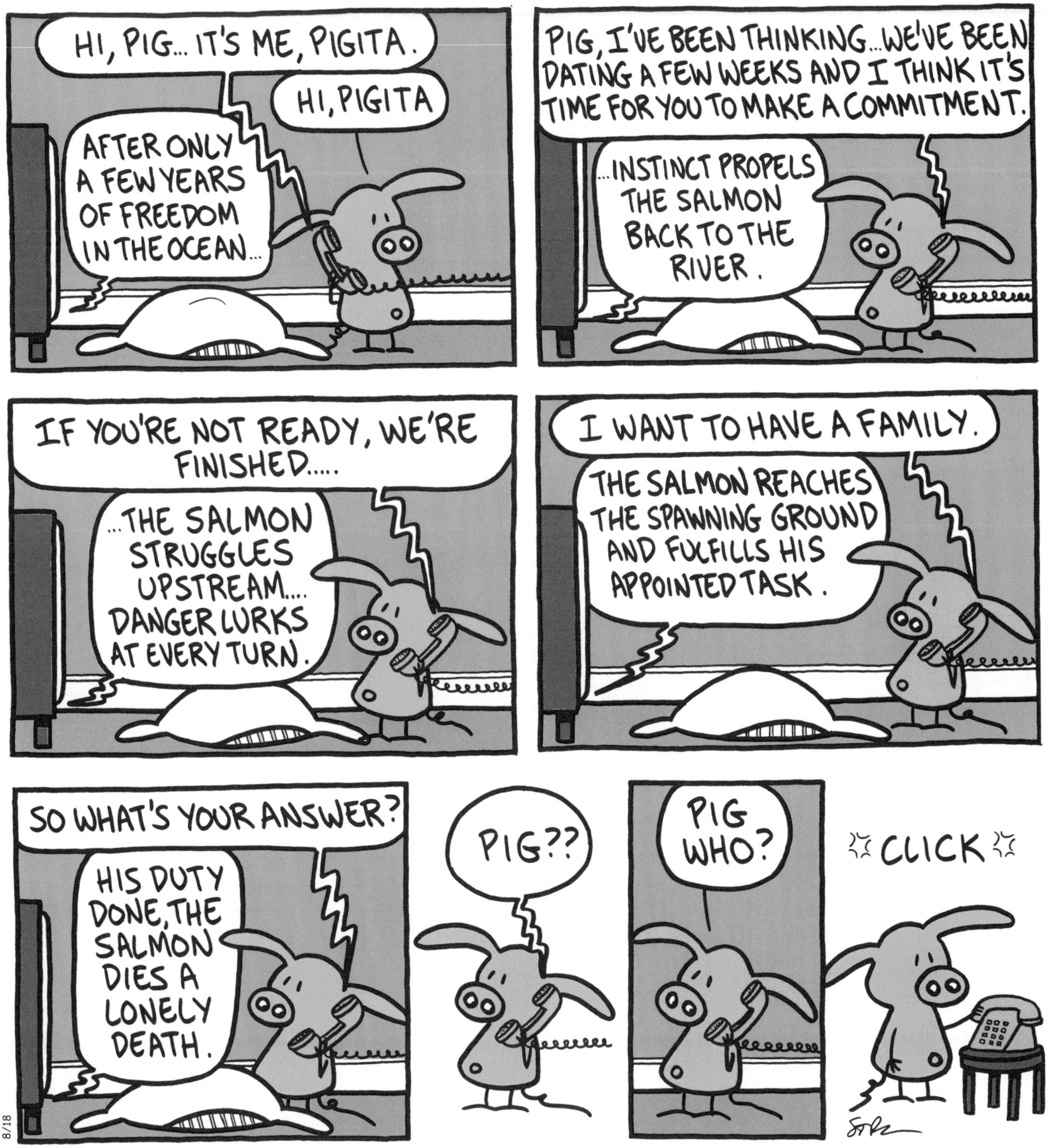
HI, PIG... IT'S ME, PIGITA.
HI, PIGITA
AFTER ONLY A FEW YEARS OF FREEDOM IN THE OCEAN...
PIG, I'VE BEEN THINKING...WE'VE BEEN DATING A FEW WEEKS AND I THINK IT'S TIME FOR YOU TO MAKE A COMMITMENT.
...INSTINCT PROPELS THE SALMON BACK TO THE RIVER.
IF YOU'RE NOT READY, WE'RE FINISHED.....
...THE SALMON STRUGGLES UPSTREAM.... DANGER LURKS AT EVERY TURN.
I WANT TO HAVE A FAMILY.
THE SALMON REACHES THE SPAWNING GROUND AND FULFILLS HIS APPOINTED TASK.
SO WHAT'S YOUR ANSWER?
HIS DUTY DONE, THE SALMON DIES A LONELY DEATH.
PIG??
PIG WHO?
CLICK
8/18

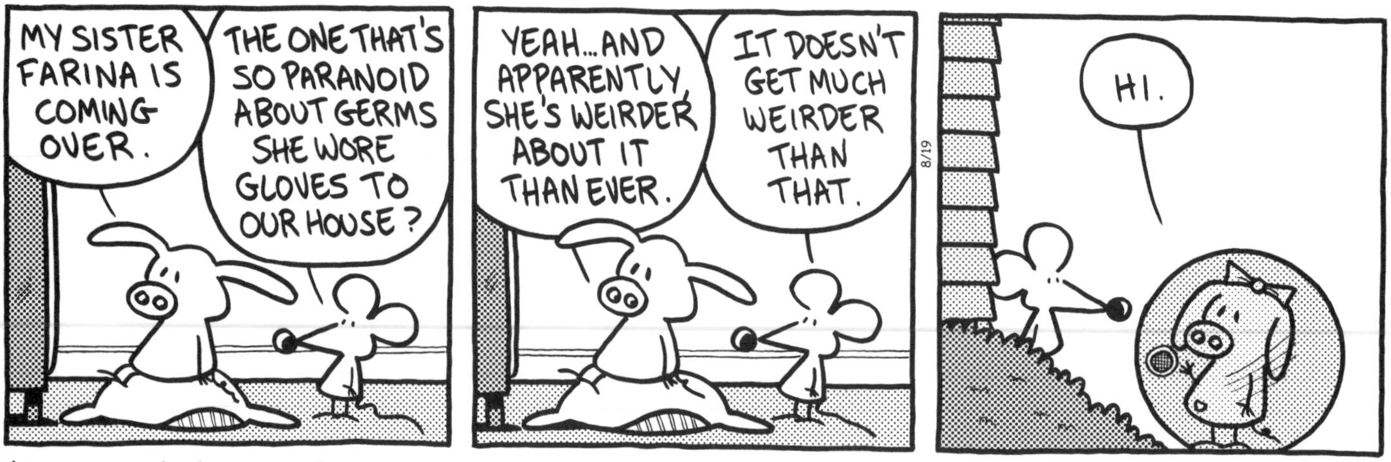
MY SISTER FARINA IS COMING OVER.
THE ONE THAT'S SO PARANOID ABOUT GERMS SHE WORE GLOVES TO OUR HOUSE?
YEAH...AND APPARENTLY, SHE'S WEIRDER ABOUT IT THAN EVER.
IT DOESN'T GET MUCH WEIRDER THAN THAT.
8/19
HI.

This strip marked Farina's first appearance in *Pearls*. I like Farina, but she is dangerous to draw because she requires a compass, and I invariably stab my own finger. Nothing ruins an original strip like blood.

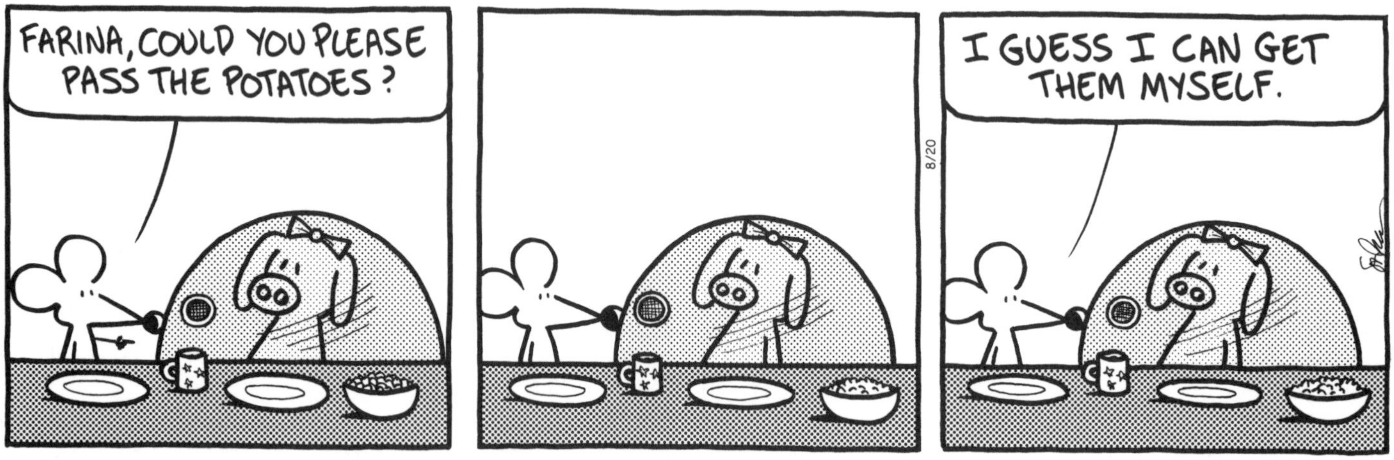
FARINA, COULD YOU PLEASE PASS THE POTATOES?
8/20
I GUESS I CAN GET THEM MYSELF.

Look how the appearance of the food changes between the first and second panels. Somehow the potatoes morphed from little round things to a more oatmeal-like consistency.

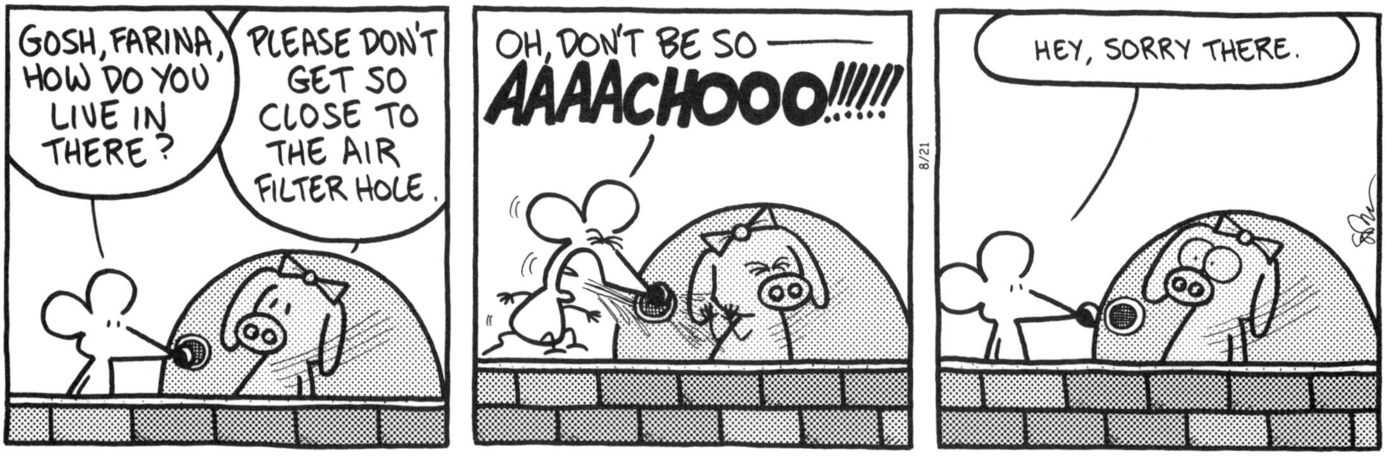
GOSH, FARINA, HOW DO YOU LIVE IN THERE?
PLEASE DON'T GET SO CLOSE TO THE AIR FILTER HOLE.
OH, DON'T BE SO —
AAAACHOOO!!!!!!
8/21
HEY, SORRY THERE.

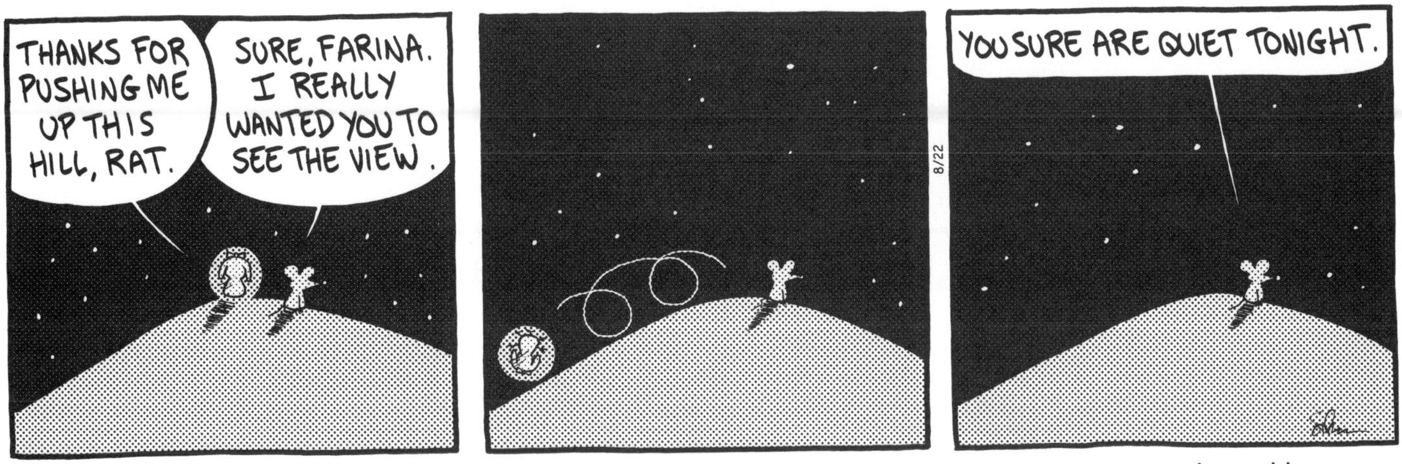
THANKS FOR PUSHING ME UP THIS HILL, RAT.
SURE, FARINA. I REALLY WANTED YOU TO SEE THE VIEW.
8/22
YOU SURE ARE QUIET TONIGHT.

You slowly start to see Rat caring for her. I think this marked the first time in the strip that Rat ever showed he was capable of such feelings.

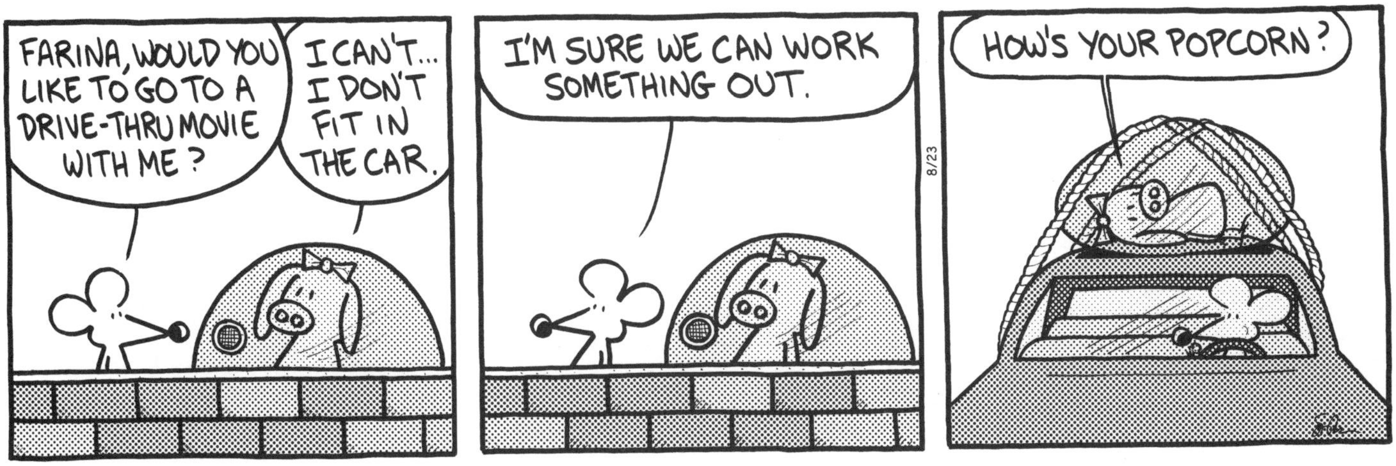
FARINA, WOULD YOU LIKE TO GO TO A DRIVE-THRU MOVIE WITH ME?
I CAN'T... I DON'T FIT IN THE CAR.
I'M SURE WE CAN WORK SOMETHING OUT.
8/23
HOW'S YOUR POPCORN?

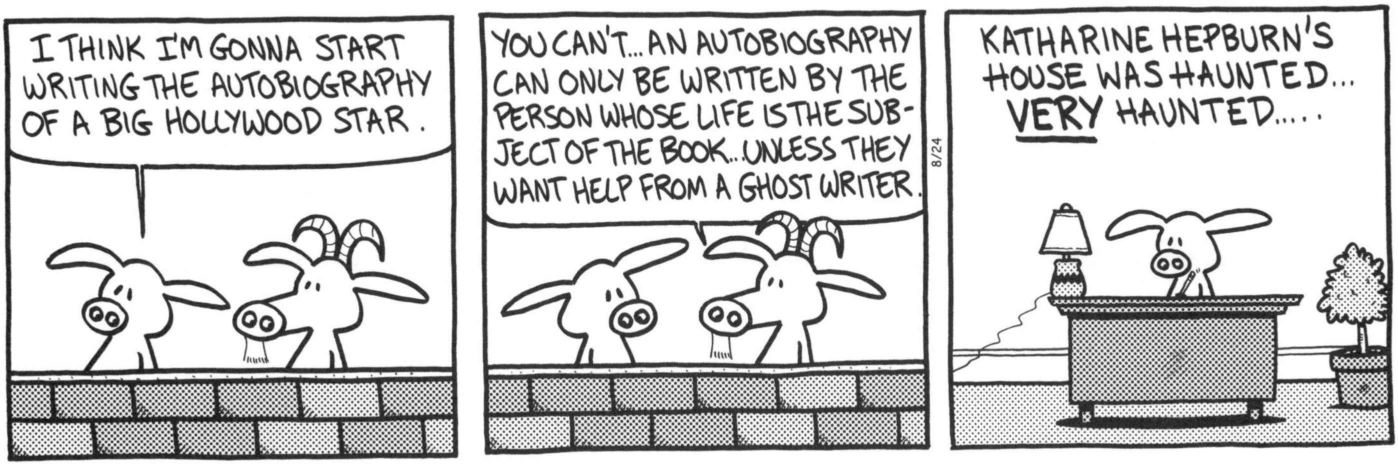
I THINK I'M GONNA START WRITING THE AUTOBIOGRAPHY OF A BIG HOLLYWOOD STAR.
YOU CAN'T... AN AUTOBIOGRAPHY CAN ONLY BE WRITTEN BY THE PERSON WHOSE LIFE IS THE SUBJECT OF THE BOOK... UNLESS THEY WANT HELP FROM A GHOST WRITER.
8/24
KATHARINE HEPBURN'S HOUSE WAS HAUNTED... VERY HAUNTED.....

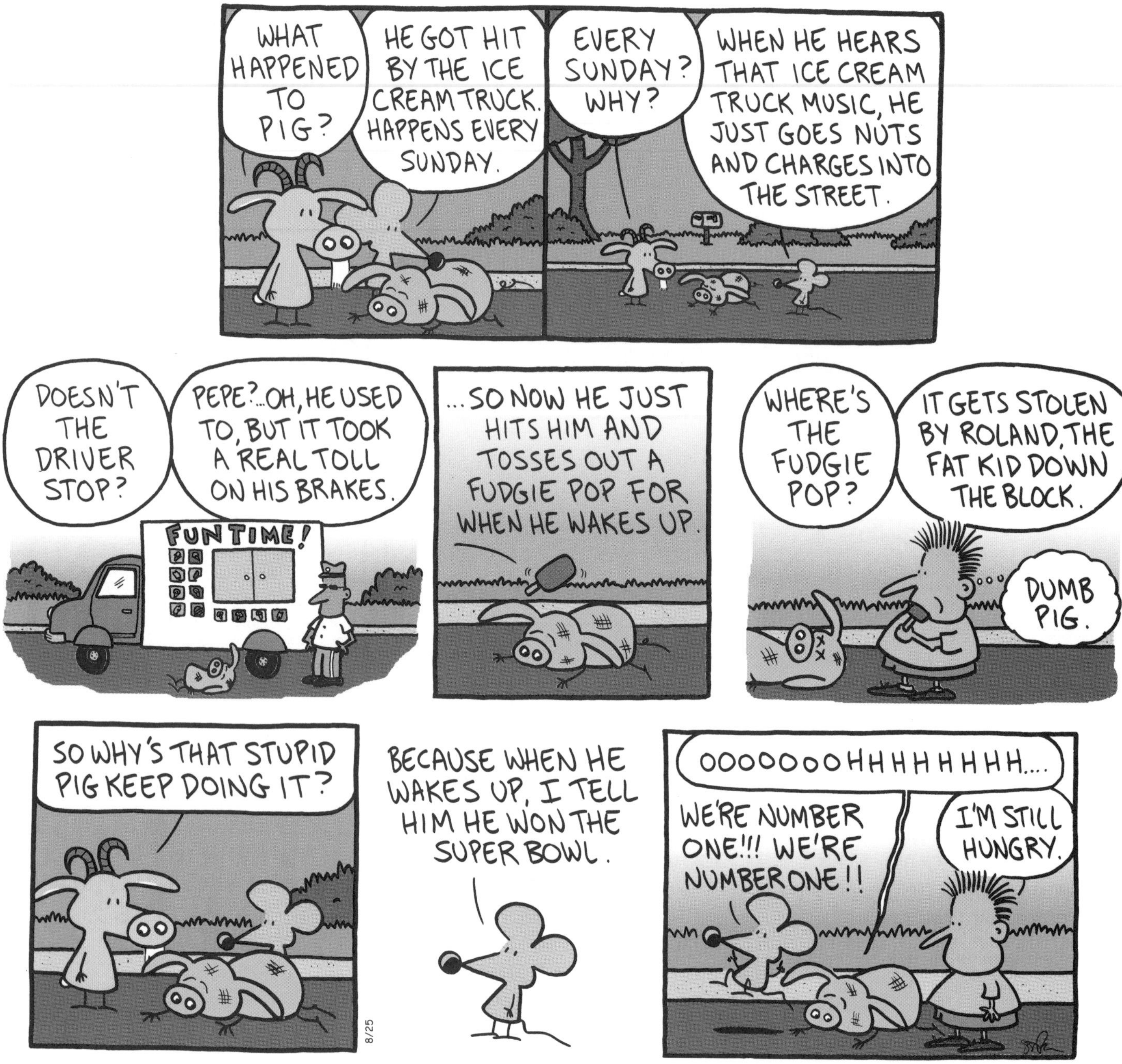
WHAT HAPPENED TO PIG?
HE GOT HIT BY THE ICE CREAM TRUCK. HAPPENS EVERY SUNDAY.
EVERY SUNDAY? WHY?
WHEN HE HEARS THAT ICE CREAM TRUCK MUSIC, HE JUST GOES NUTS AND CHARGES INTO THE STREET.
DOESN'T THE DRIVER STOP?
PEPE?...OH, HE USED TO, BUT IT TOOK A REAL TOLL ON HIS BRAKES.
FUN TIME!
...SO NOW HE JUST HITS HIM AND TOSSES OUT A FUDGIE POP FOR WHEN HE WAKES UP.
WHERE'S THE FUDGIE POP?
IT GETS STOLEN BY ROLAND, THE FAT KID DOWN THE BLOCK.
DUMB PIG.
SO WHY'S THAT STUPID PIG KEEP DOING IT?
8/25
BECAUSE WHEN HE WAKES UP, I TELL HIM HE WON THE SUPER BOWL.
OOOOOOOHHHHHHHH....
WE'RE NUMBER ONE!!! WE'RE NUMBER ONE!!
I'M STILL HUNGRY.

After drawing that ice cream truck in the third panel, I decided I would never try to draw an ice cream truck again.

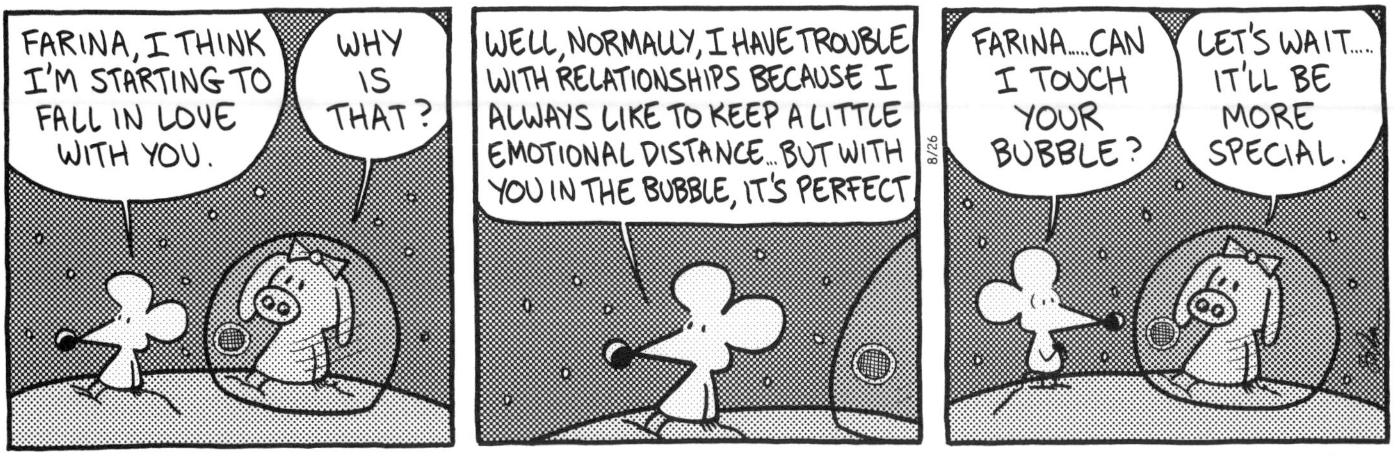
FARINA, I THINK I'M STARTING TO FALL IN LOVE WITH YOU.
WHY IS THAT?
WELL, NORMALLY, I HAVE TROUBLE WITH RELATIONSHIPS BECAUSE I ALWAYS LIKE TO KEEP A LITTLE EMOTIONAL DISTANCE... BUT WITH YOU IN THE BUBBLE, IT'S PERFECT.
8/26
FARINA.....CAN I TOUCH YOUR BUBBLE?
LET'S WAIT..... IT'LL BE MORE SPECIAL.

In newspaper comic strips, the topic of sex is totally taboo. So, you need to create little euphemisms, like "touching one's bubble."

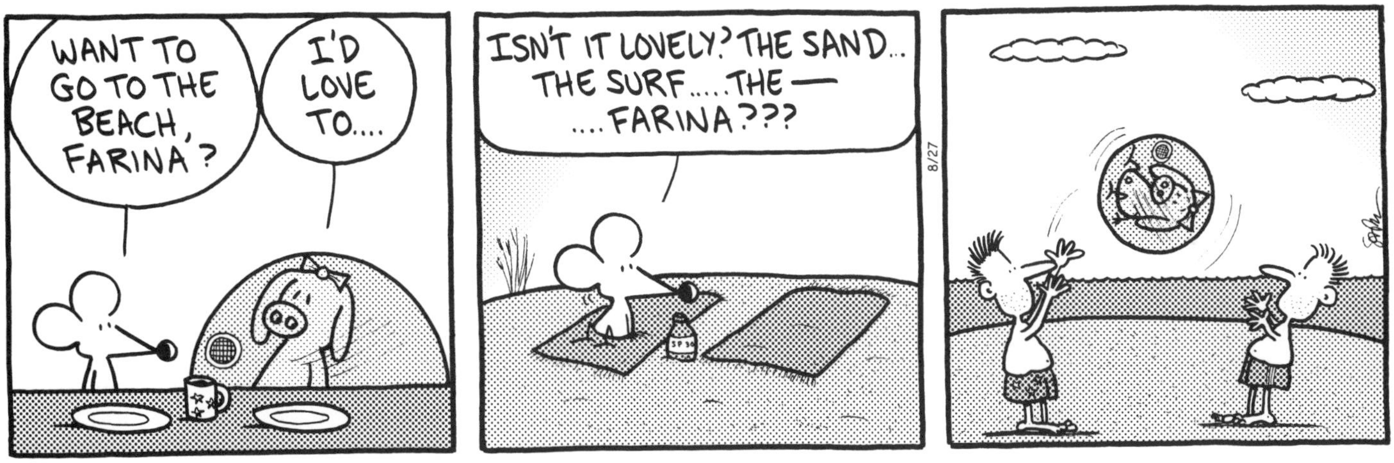
WANT TO GO TO THE BEACH, FARINA?
I'D LOVE TO....
ISN'T IT LOVELY? THE SAND... THE SURF.....THE— ....FARINA???
8/27

Farina's being in a round ball makes for some easy jokes.

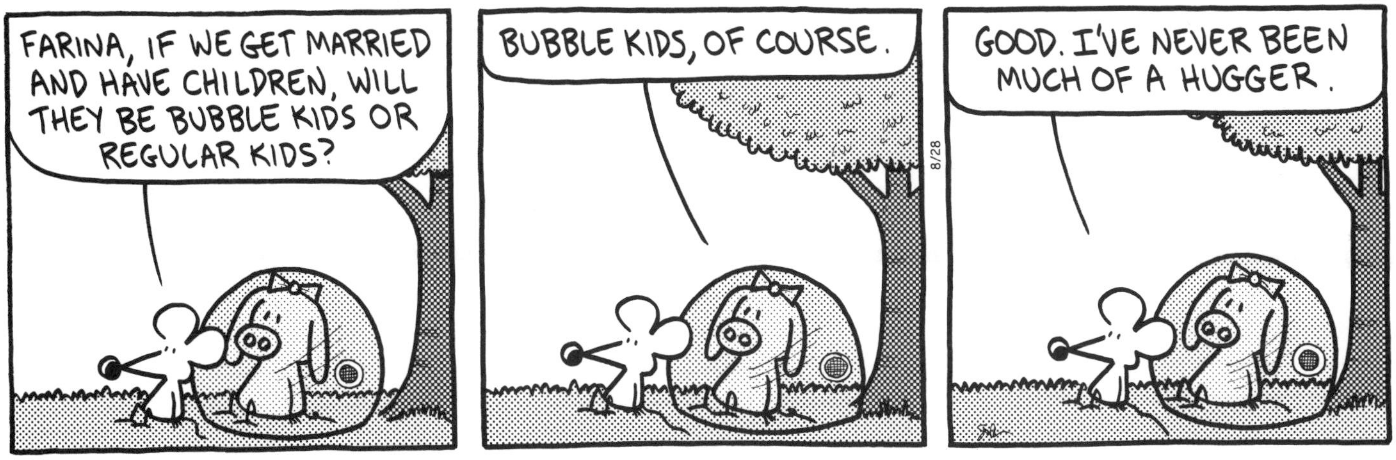
FARINA, IF WE GET MARRIED AND HAVE CHILDREN, WILL THEY BE BUBBLE KIDS OR REGULAR KIDS?
BUBBLE KIDS, OF COURSE.
8/28
GOOD. I'VE NEVER BEEN MUCH OF A HUGGER.

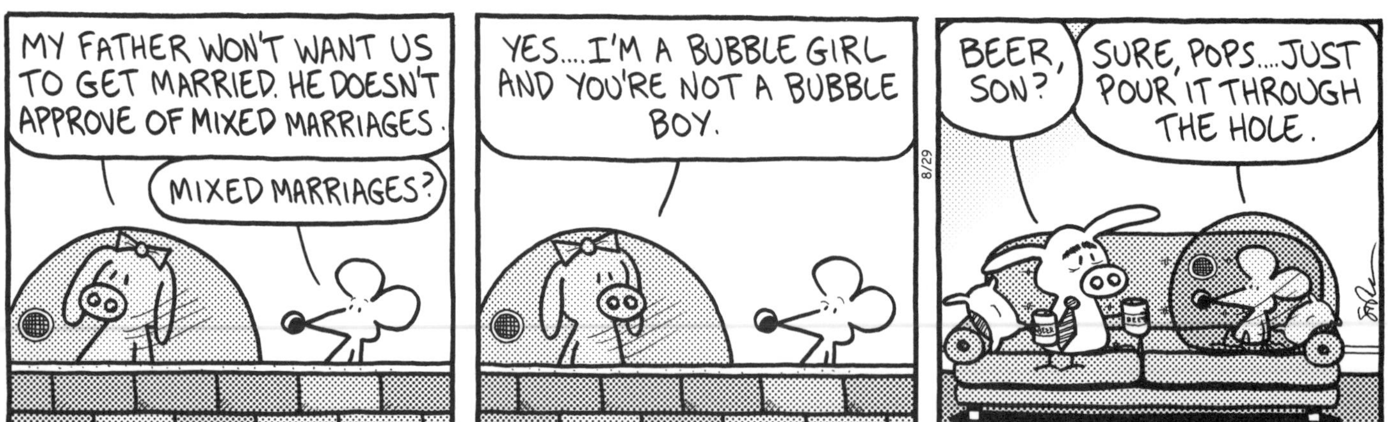
MY FATHER WON'T WANT US TO GET MARRIED. HE DOESN'T APPROVE OF MIXED MARRIAGES.
MIXED MARRIAGES?
YES.... I'M A BUBBLE GIRL AND YOU'RE NOT A BUBBLE BOY.
8/29
BEER, SON?
SURE, POPS.... JUST POUR IT THROUGH THE HOLE.

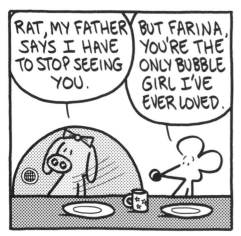

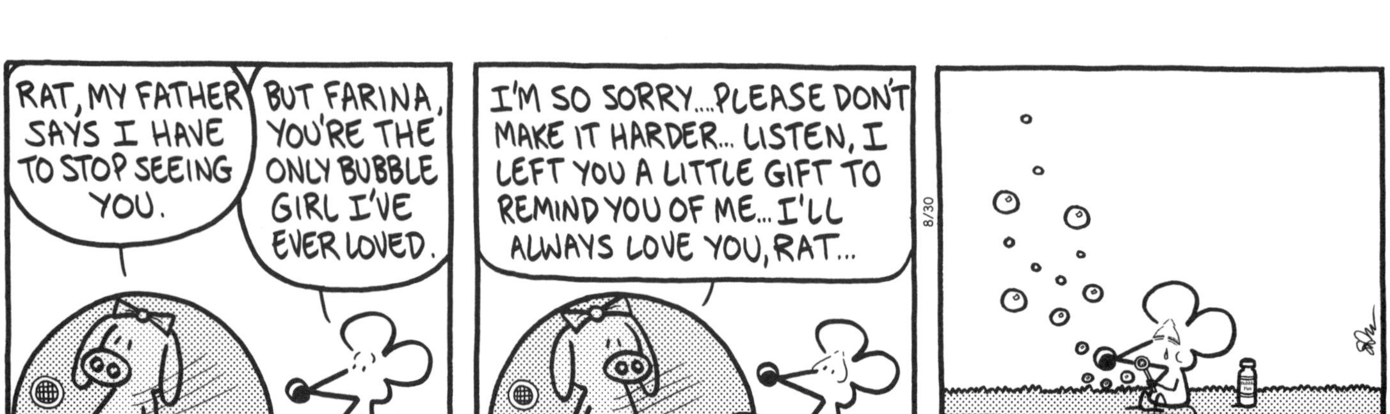
RAT, MY FATHER SAYS I HAVE TO STOP SEEING YOU.
BUT FARINA, YOU'RE THE ONLY BUBBLE GIRL I'VE EVER LOVED.
I'M SO SORRY.... PLEASE DON'T MAKE IT HARDER... LISTEN, I LEFT YOU A LITTLE GIFT TO REMIND YOU OF ME... I'LL ALWAYS LOVE YOU, RAT...
8/30

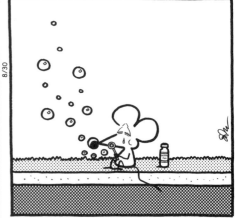

I think this is the first time Rat is ever shown being hurt by someone else. I like it, because it sort of rounds out his personality.

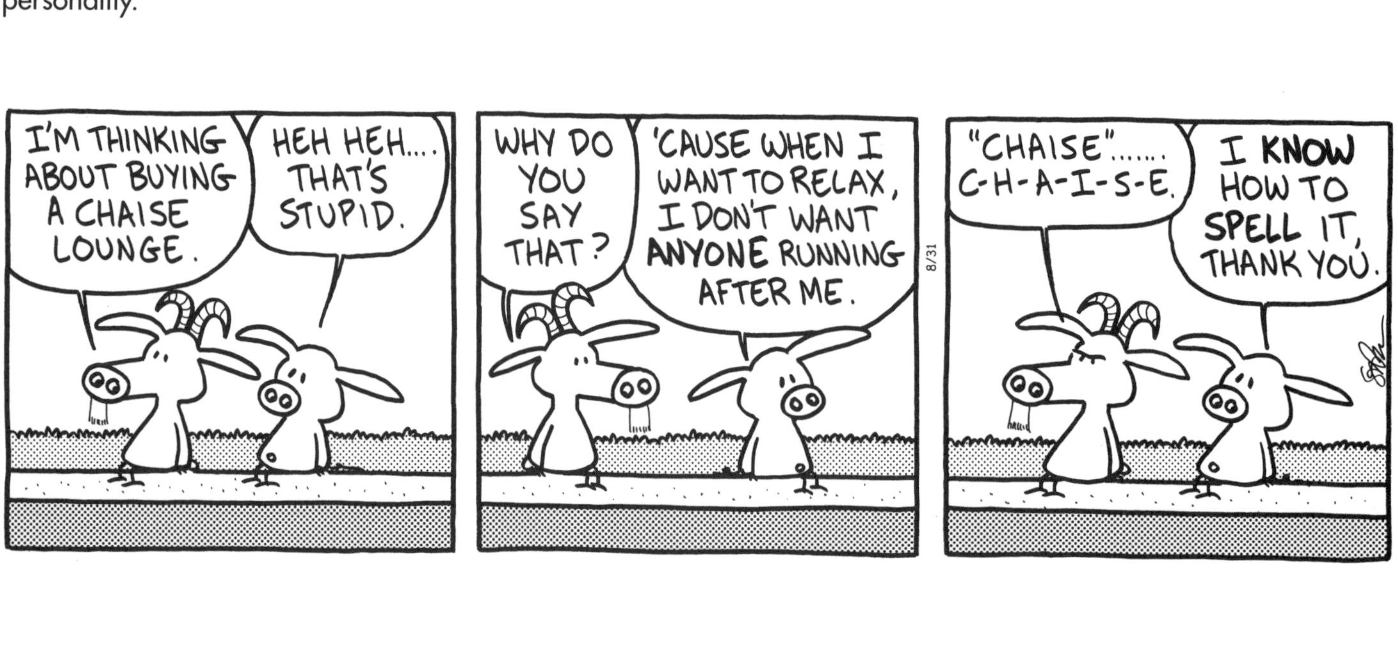
I'M THINKING ABOUT BUYING A CHAISE LOUNGE.
HEH HEH.... THAT'S STUPID.
WHY DO YOU SAY THAT?
'CAUSE WHEN I WANT TO RELAX, I DON'T WANT ANYONE RUNNING AFTER ME.
8/31
"CHAISE"...... C-H-A-I-S-E.
I KNOW HOW TO SPELL IT, THANK YOU.

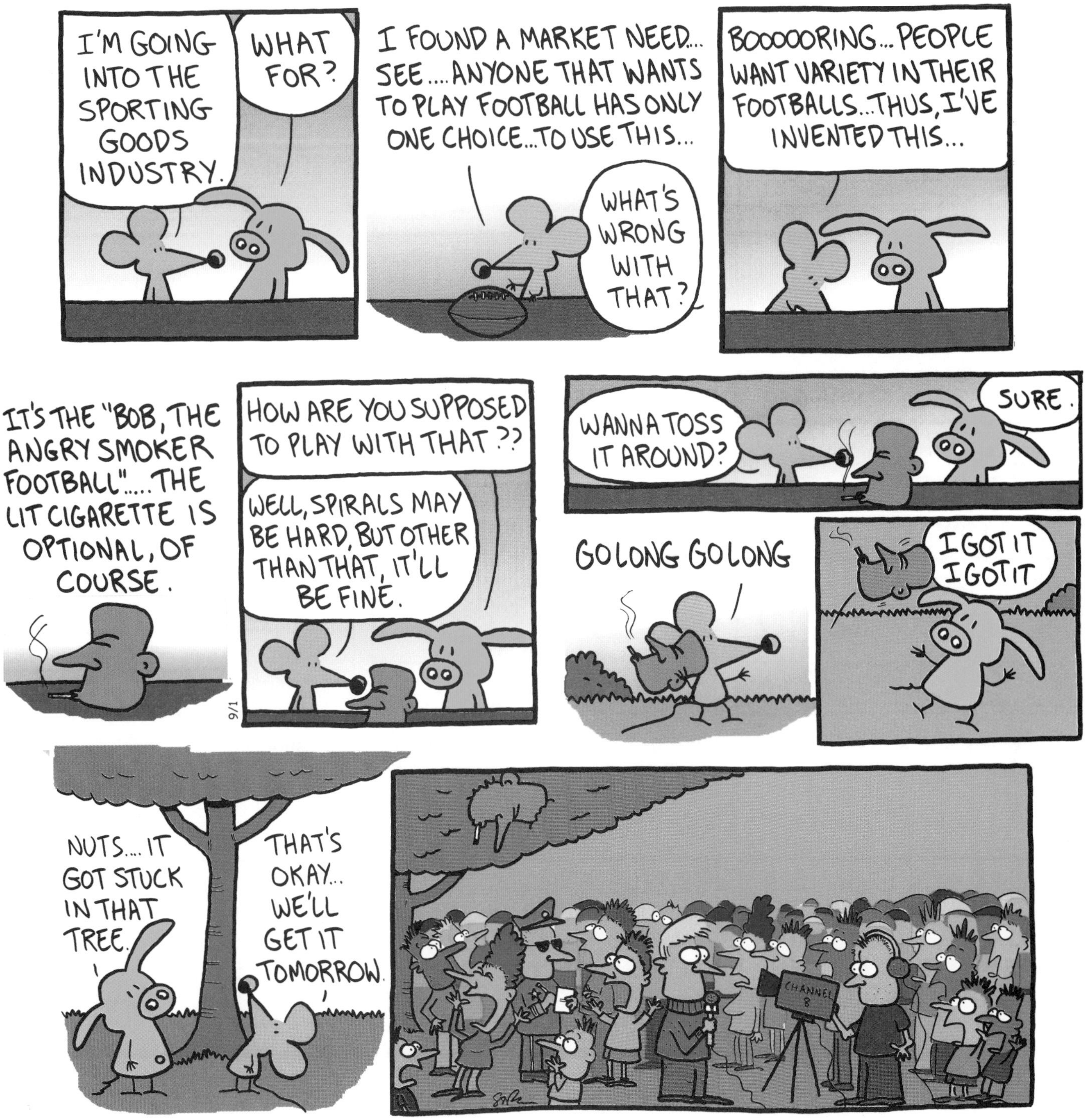
I'M GOING INTO THE SPORTING GOODS INDUSTRY.
WHAT FOR?
I FOUND A MARKET NEED.... SEE.... ANYONE THAT WANTS TO PLAY FOOTBALL HAS ONLY ONE CHOICE...TO USE THIS...
WHAT'S WRONG WITH THAT?
BOOOOORING... PEOPLE WANT VARIETY IN THEIR FOOTBALLS...THUS, I'VE INVENTED THIS...
IT'S THE "BOB, THE ANGRY SMOKER FOOTBALL"..... THE LIT CIGARETTE IS OPTIONAL, OF COURSE.
HOW ARE YOU SUPPOSED TO PLAY WITH THAT??
WELL, SPIRALS MAY BE HARD, BUT OTHER THAN THAT, IT'LL BE FINE.
9/1
WANNA TOSS IT AROUND?
SURE.
GO LONG GO LONG
I GOT IT I GOT IT
NUTS.... IT GOT STUCK IN THAT TREE.
THAT'S OKAY... WE'LL GET IT TOMORROW.
CHANNEL 8

Sometimes when I look at certain *Pearls* strips, I think that something may actually be wrong with me. This would qualify as one of those strips.

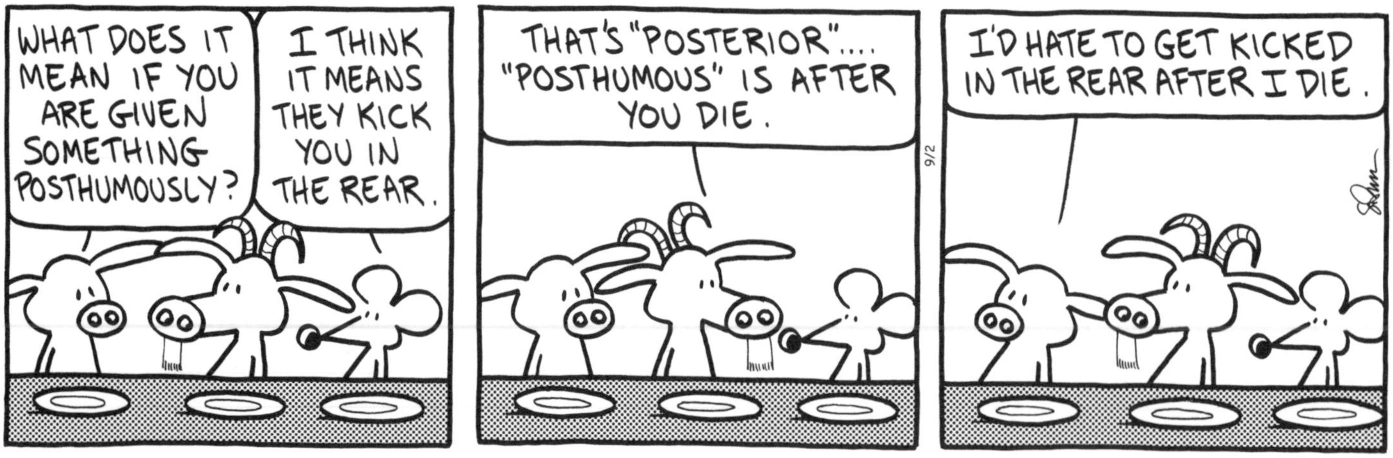
WHAT DOES IT MEAN IF YOU ARE GIVEN SOMETHING POSTHUMOUSLY?
I THINK IT MEANS THEY KICK YOU IN THE REAR.
THAT'S "POSTERIOR".... "POSTHUMOUS" IS AFTER YOU DIE.
9/2
I'D HATE TO GET KICKED IN THE REAR AFTER I DIE.

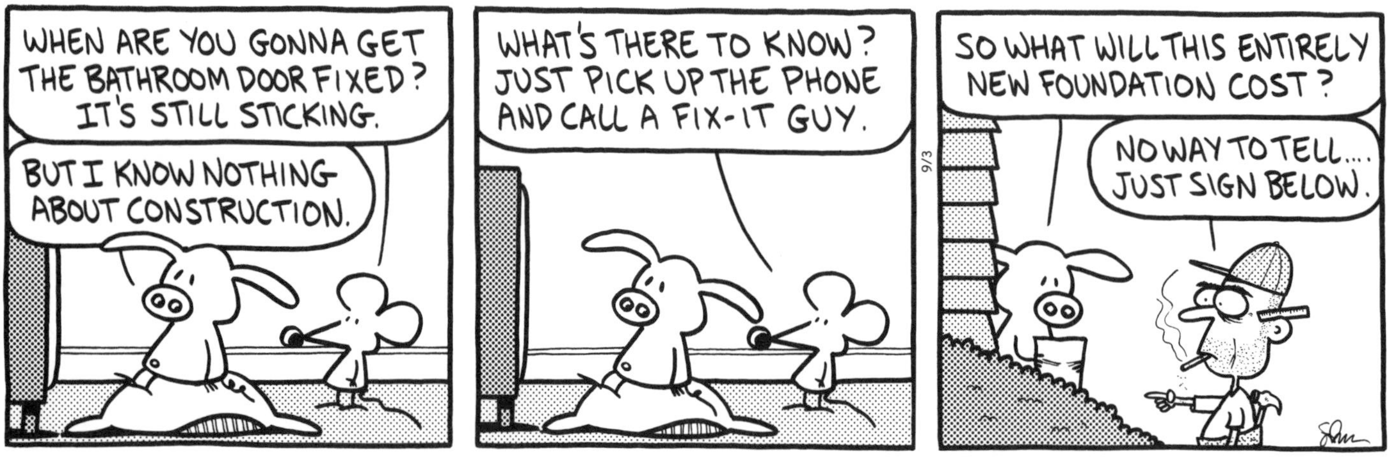
WHEN ARE YOU GONNA GET THE BATHROOM DOOR FIXED? IT'S STILL STICKING.
BUT I KNOW NOTHING ABOUT CONSTRUCTION.
WHAT'S THERE TO KNOW? JUST PICK UP THE PHONE AND CALL A FIX-IT GUY.
9/3
SO WHAT WILL THIS ENTIRELY NEW FOUNDATION COST?
NO WAY TO TELL.... JUST SIGN BELOW.

In comic strips, shady contractor characters have to smoke and have a five-o'clock shadow. It's a rule.

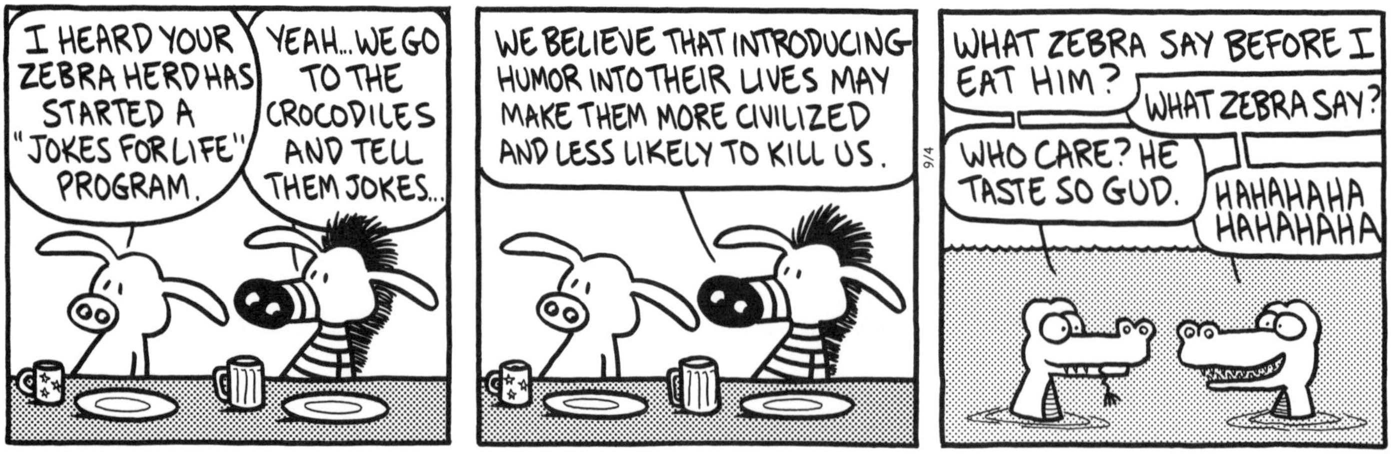
I HEARD YOUR ZEBRA HERD HAS STARTED A "JOKES FOR LIFE" PROGRAM.
YEAH... WE GO TO THE CROCODILES AND TELL THEM JOKES...
WE BELIEVE THAT INTRODUCING HUMOR INTO THEIR LIVES MAY MAKE THEM MORE CIVILIZED AND LESS LIKELY TO KILL US.
9/4
WHAT ZEBRA SAY BEFORE I EAT HIM?
WHAT ZEBRA SAY?
WHO CARE? HE TASTE SO GUD.
HAHAHAHA HAHAHAHA

For some reason, my crocodiles appear to be speaking with a Russian accent. This is odd, as one would not expect to find a lot of crocodiles in Russia.

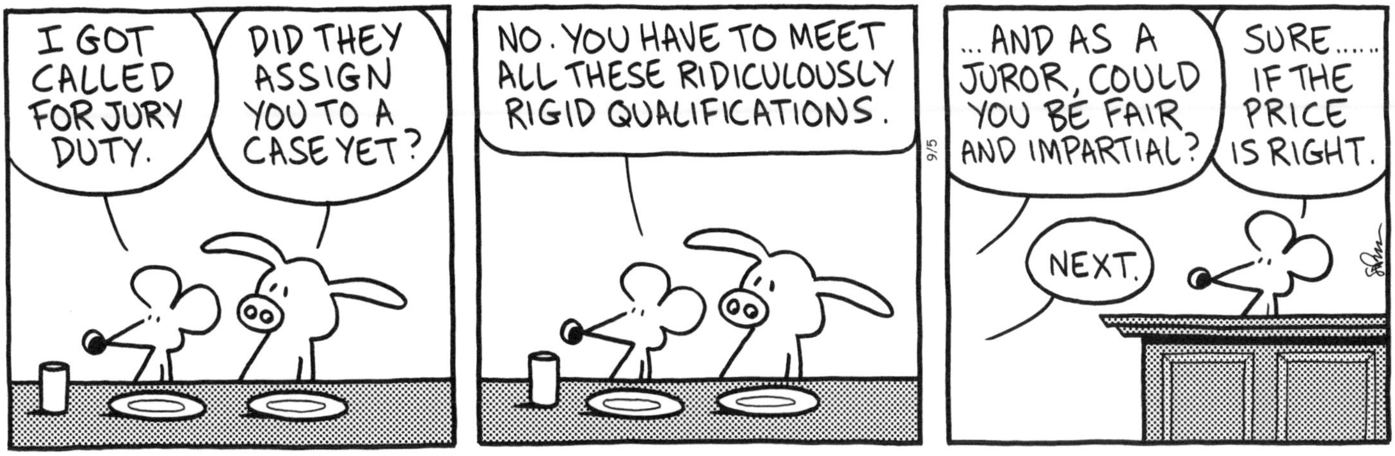
I GOT CALLED FOR JURY DUTY.
DID THEY ASSIGN YOU TO A CASE YET?
NO. YOU HAVE TO MEET ALL THESE RIDICULOUSLY RIGID QUALIFICATIONS.
9/5
...AND AS A JUROR, COULD YOU BE FAIR AND IMPARTIAL?
SURE...... IF THE PRICE IS RIGHT.
NEXT.

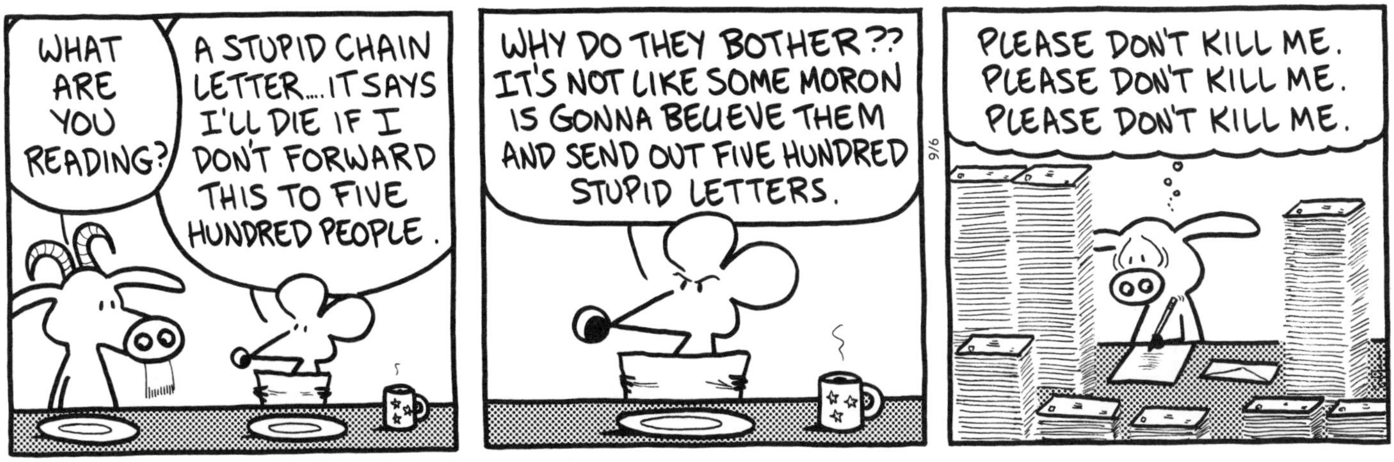
WHAT ARE YOU READING?
A STUPID CHAIN LETTER.... IT SAYS I'LL DIE IF I DON'T FORWARD THIS TO FIVE HUNDRED PEOPLE.
WHY DO THEY BOTHER?? IT'S NOT LIKE SOME MORON IS GONNA BELIEVE THEM AND SEND OUT FIVE HUNDRED STUPID LETTERS.
9/6
PLEASE DON'T KILL ME. PLEASE DON'T KILL ME. PLEASE DON'T KILL ME.

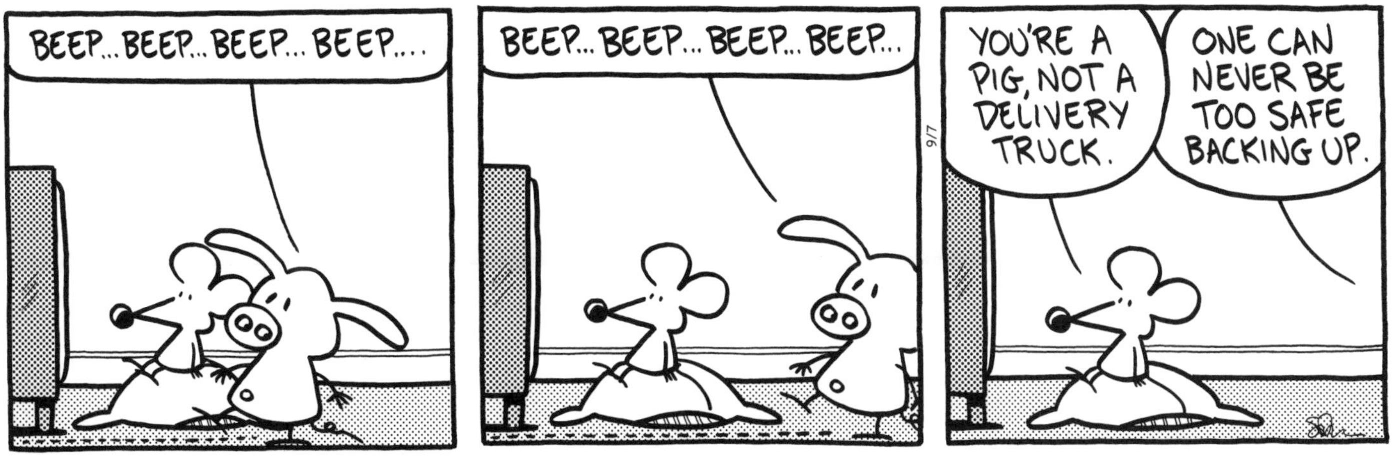
BEEP... BEEP... BEEP... BEEP....
BEEP... BEEP... BEEP... BEEP...
9/7
YOU'RE A PIG, NOT A DELIVERY TRUCK.
ONE CAN NEVER BE TOO SAFE BACKING UP.

I still don't get why trucks make this sound when they're backing up. Do people have trouble seeing trucks when they're moving in reverse? If so, wouldn't that same problem apply to trucks moving forward?

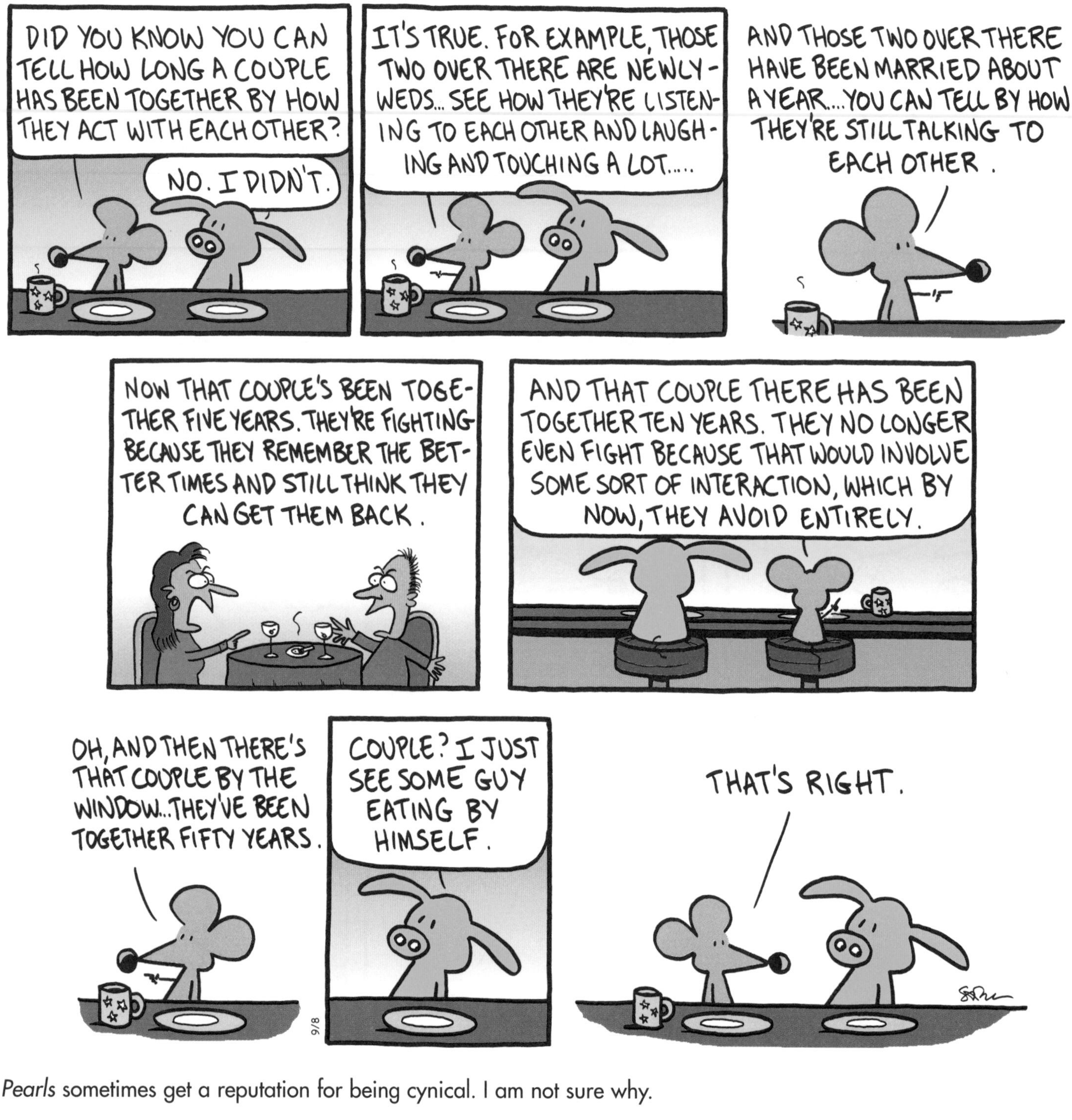
DID YOU KNOW YOU CAN TELL HOW LONG A COUPLE HAS BEEN TOGETHER BY HOW THEY ACT WITH EACH OTHER?
NO. I DIDN'T.
IT'S TRUE. FOR EXAMPLE, THOSE TWO OVER THERE ARE NEWLY-WEDS... SEE HOW THEY'RE LISTENING TO EACH OTHER AND LAUGHING AND TOUCHING A LOT.....
AND THOSE TWO OVER THERE HAVE BEEN MARRIED ABOUT A YEAR.... YOU CAN TELL BY HOW THEY'RE STILL TALKING TO EACH OTHER.
NOW THAT COUPLE'S BEEN TOGETHER FIVE YEARS. THEY'RE FIGHTING BECAUSE THEY REMEMBER THE BETTER TIMES AND STILL THINK THEY CAN GET THEM BACK.
AND THAT COUPLE THERE HAS BEEN TOGETHER TEN YEARS. THEY NO LONGER EVEN FIGHT BECAUSE THAT WOULD INVOLVE SOME SORT OF INTERACTION, WHICH BY NOW, THEY AVOID ENTIRELY.
OH, AND THEN THERE'S THAT COUPLE BY THE WINDOW... THEY'VE BEEN TOGETHER FIFTY YEARS.
COUPLE? I JUST SEE SOME GUY EATING BY HIMSELF.
THAT'S RIGHT.
9/8

Pearls sometimes get a reputation for being cynical. I am not sure why.

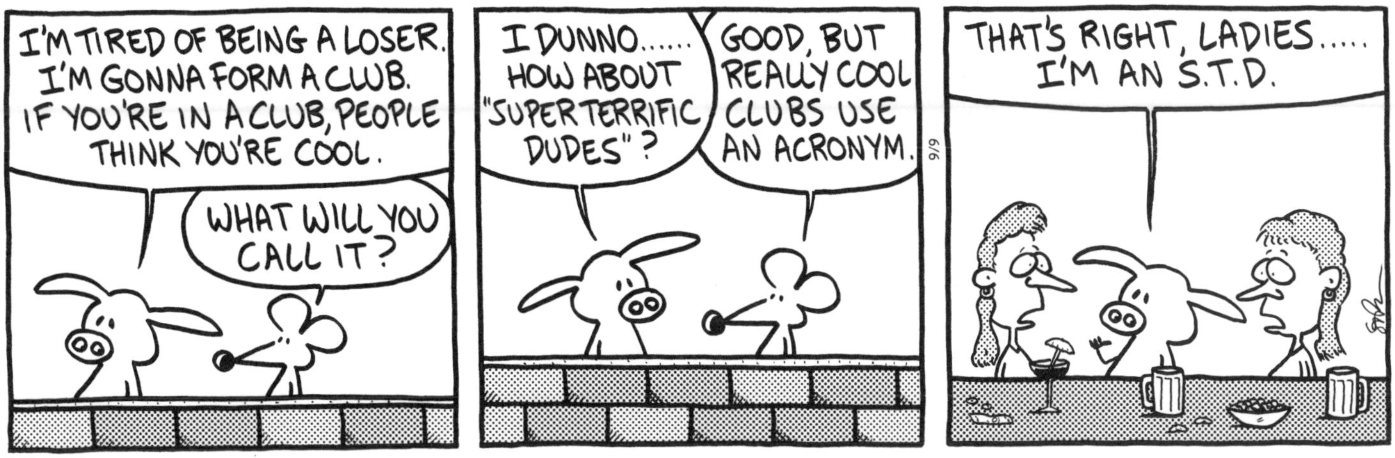
I'M TIRED OF BEING A LOSER. I'M GONNA FORM A CLUB. IF YOU'RE IN A CLUB, PEOPLE THINK YOU'RE COOL.
WHAT WILL YOU CALL IT?
I DUNNO...... HOW ABOUT "SUPER TERRIFIC DUDES"?
GOOD, BUT REALLY COOL CLUBS USE AN ACRONYM.
9/9
THAT'S RIGHT, LADIES..... I'M AN S.T.D.

It's not every day you hear STDs mentioned in the comics pages.

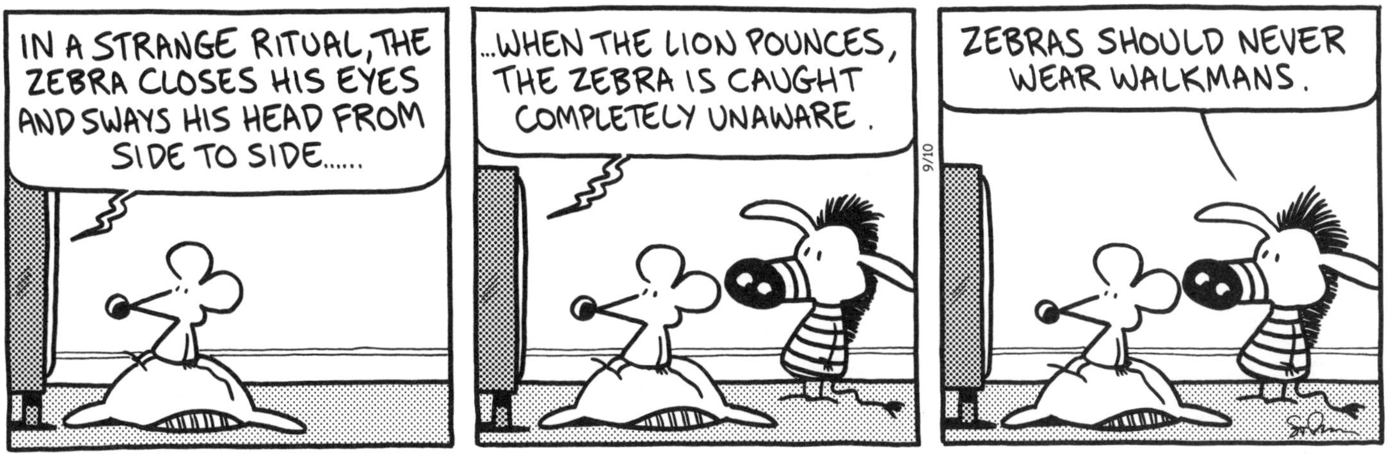
IN A STRANGE RITUAL, THE ZEBRA CLOSES HIS EYES AND SWAYS HIS HEAD FROM SIDE TO SIDE......
...WHEN THE LION POUNCES, THE ZEBRA IS CAUGHT COMPLETELY UNAWARE.
9/10
ZEBRAS SHOULD NEVER WEAR WALKMANS.

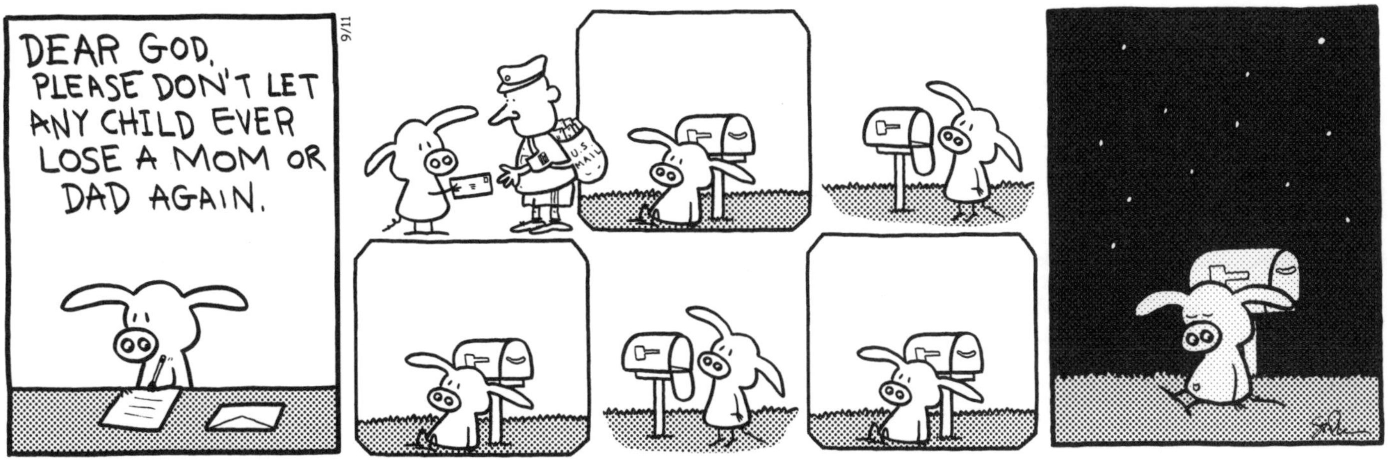
DEAR GOD, PLEASE DON'T LET ANY CHILD EVER LOSE A MOM OR DAD AGAIN.
9/11
U.S. MAIL

This was the strip I wrote to commemorate the one-year anniversary of 9/11.

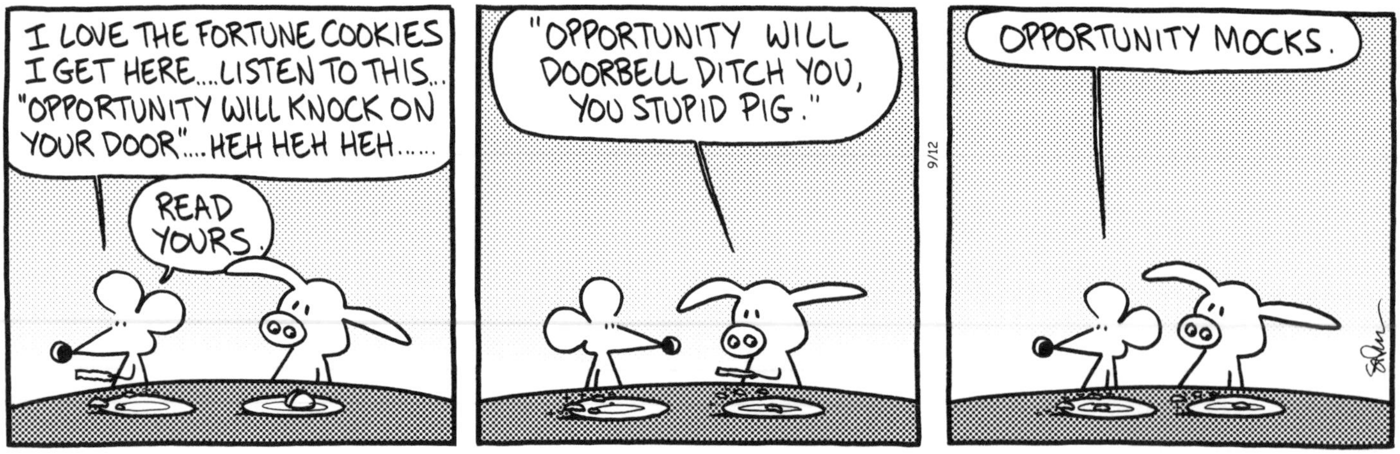
I LOVE THE FORTUNE COOKIES I GET HERE....LISTEN TO THIS... "OPPORTUNITY WILL KNOCK ON YOUR DOOR"....HEH HEH HEH......
READ YOURS.
"OPPORTUNITY WILL DOORBELL DITCH YOU, YOU STUPID PIG."
9/12
OPPORTUNITY MOCKS.

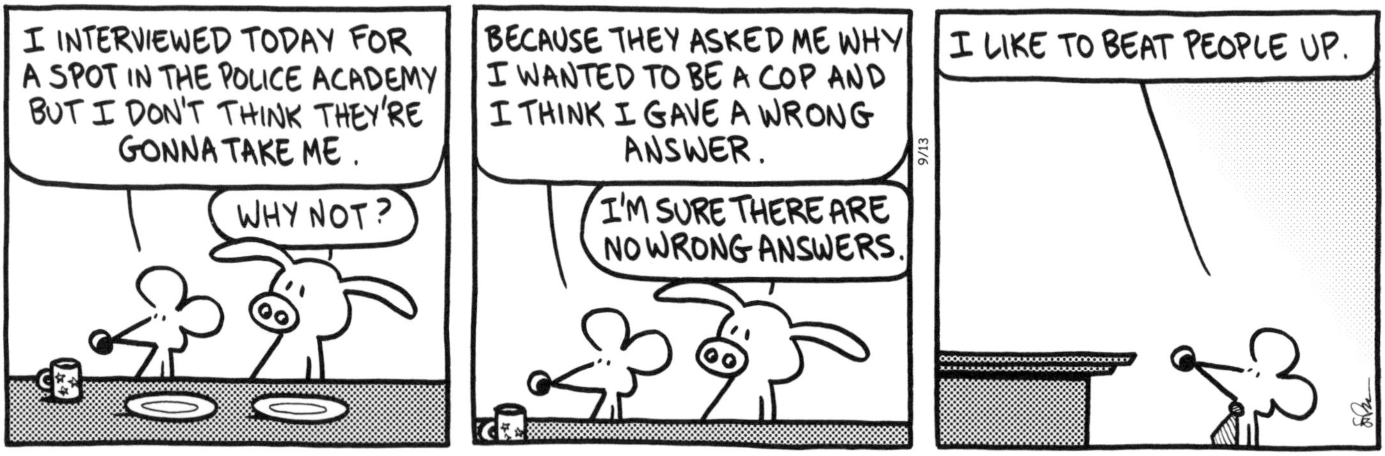
I INTERVIEWED TODAY FOR A SPOT IN THE POLICE ACADEMY BUT I DON'T THINK THEY'RE GONNA TAKE ME.
WHY NOT?
BECAUSE THEY ASKED ME WHY I WANTED TO BE A COP AND I THINK I GAVE A WRONG ANSWER.
I'M SURE THERE ARE NO WRONG ANSWERS.
9/13
I LIKE TO BEAT PEOPLE UP.

This drew a complaint from a female reader in Texas, who was outraged at my perceived lack of respect for policemen. The complaint was filled with so much anger that I thought for sure it was one of my friends faking an e-mail to me. As it turned out, it was a real reader. Oh, my.

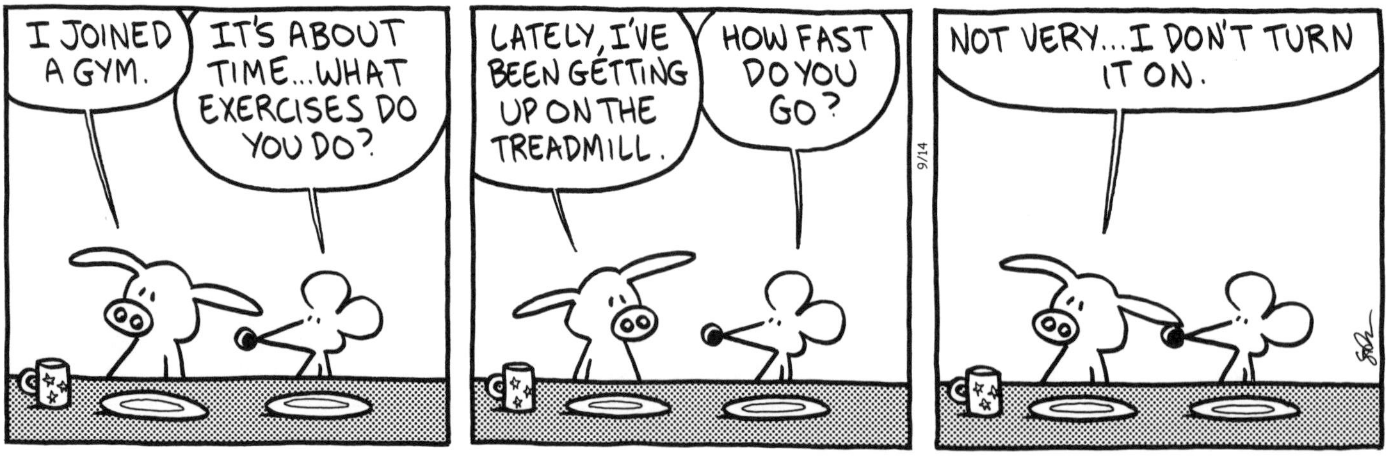
I JOINED A GYM.
IT'S ABOUT TIME...WHAT EXERCISES DO YOU DO?
LATELY, I'VE BEEN GETTING UP ON THE TREADMILL.
HOW FAST DO YOU GO?
9/14
NOT VERY...I DON'T TURN IT ON.

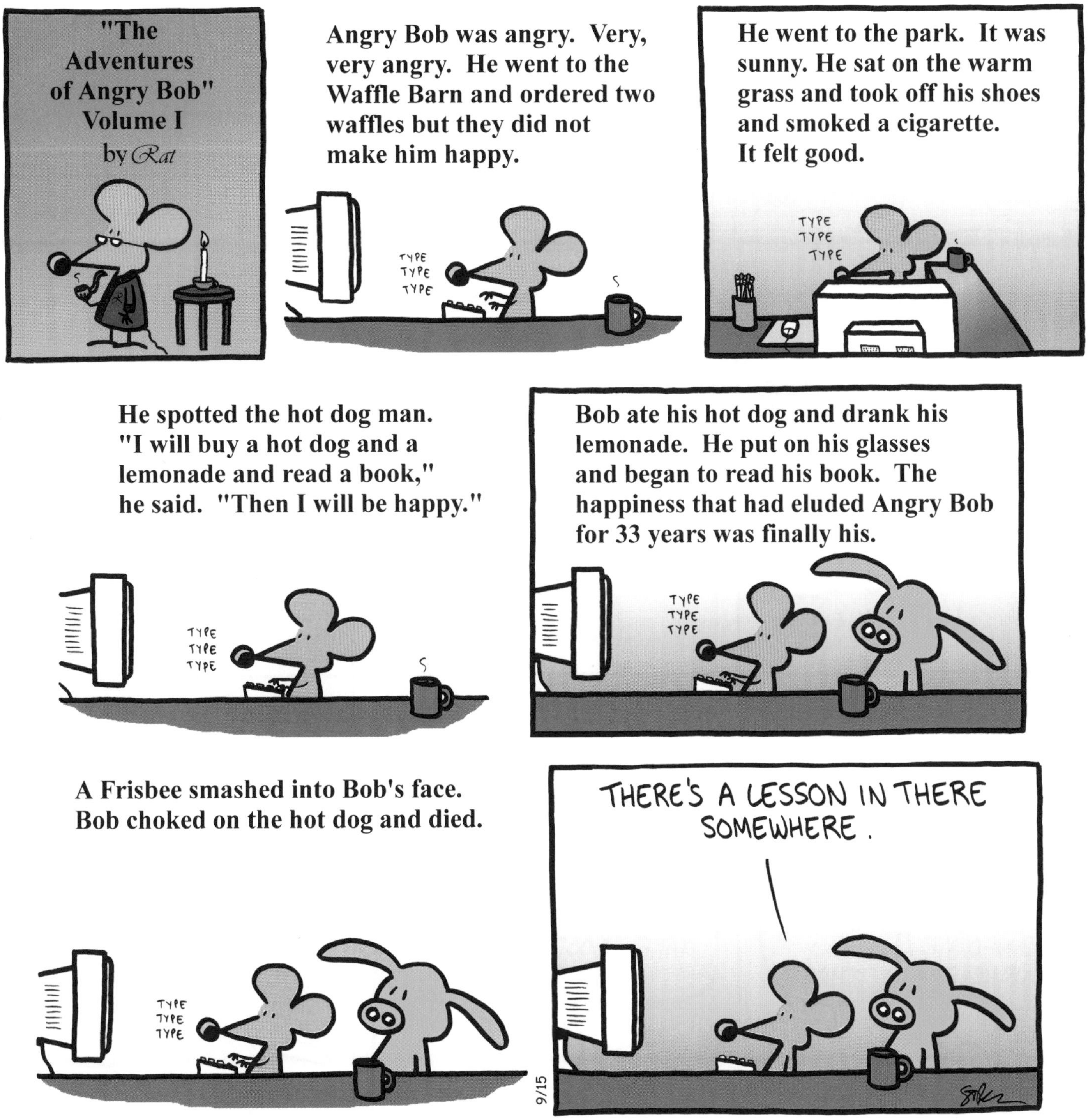
"The Adventures of Angry Bob" Volume I
by Rat
Angry Bob was angry. Very, very angry. He went to the Waffle Barn and ordered two waffles but they did not make him happy.
TYPE TYPE TYPE
He went to the park. It was sunny. He sat on the warm grass and took off his shoes and smoked a cigarette. It felt good.
TYPE TYPE TYPE
He spotted the hot dog man. "I will buy a hot dog and a lemonade and read a book," he said. "Then I will be happy."
TYPE TYPE TYPE
Bob ate his hot dog and drank his lemonade. He put on his glasses and began to read his book. The happiness that had eluded Angry Bob for 33 years was finally his.
TYPE TYPE TYPE
A Frisbee smashed into Bob's face. Bob choked on the hot dog and died.
TYPE TYPE TYPE
9/15
THERE'S A LESSON IN THERE SOMEWHERE.

This strip marked the debut of Angry Bob. When I wrote it, I was hesitant to publish it, mostly because it was so different. There's almost no character dialogue and no change in the art, and the theme is very dark. As it turned out, it became one of the most popular recurring gags in the strip.

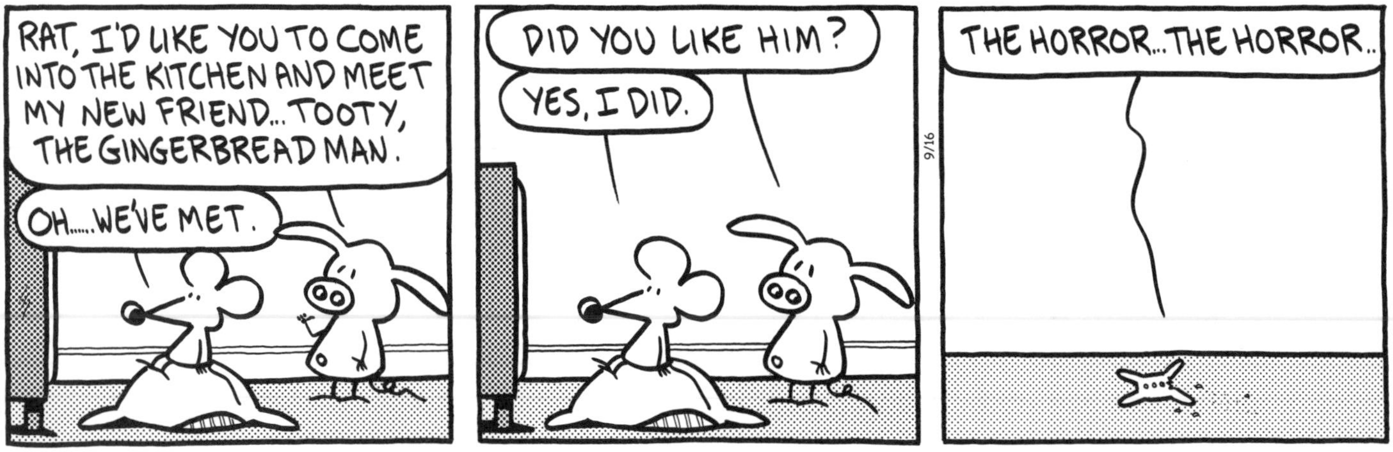

RAT, I'D LIKE YOU TO COME INTO THE KITCHEN AND MEET MY NEW FRIEND... TOOTY, THE GINGERBREAD MAN.
OH..... WE'VE MET.
DID YOU LIKE HIM?
YES, I DID.
9/16
THE HORROR... THE HORROR...

Tooty's line in the last panel is a quote from the novel *Heart of Darkness*, by Joseph Conrad. But I only know that because I looked it up on the Internet. *I* used it because it was something cool that Marlon Brando mumbled in *Apocalypse Now*.

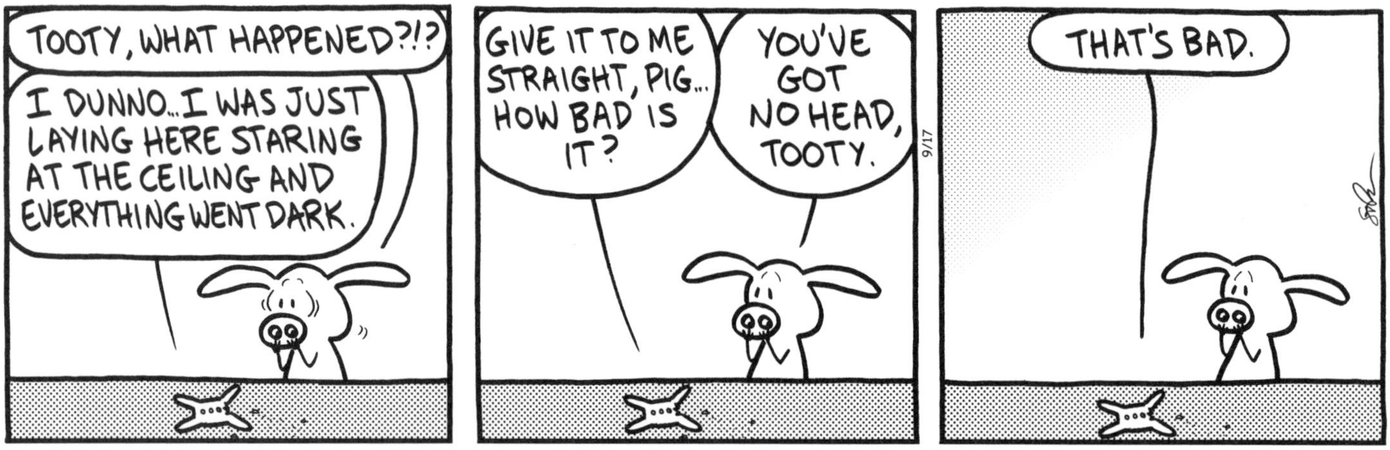

TOOTY, WHAT HAPPENED?!?
I DUNNO... I WAS JUST LAYING HERE STARING AT THE CEILING AND EVERYTHING WENT DARK.
GIVE IT TO ME STRAIGHT, PIG... HOW BAD IS IT?
YOU'VE GOT NO HEAD, TOOTY.
9/17
THAT'S BAD.

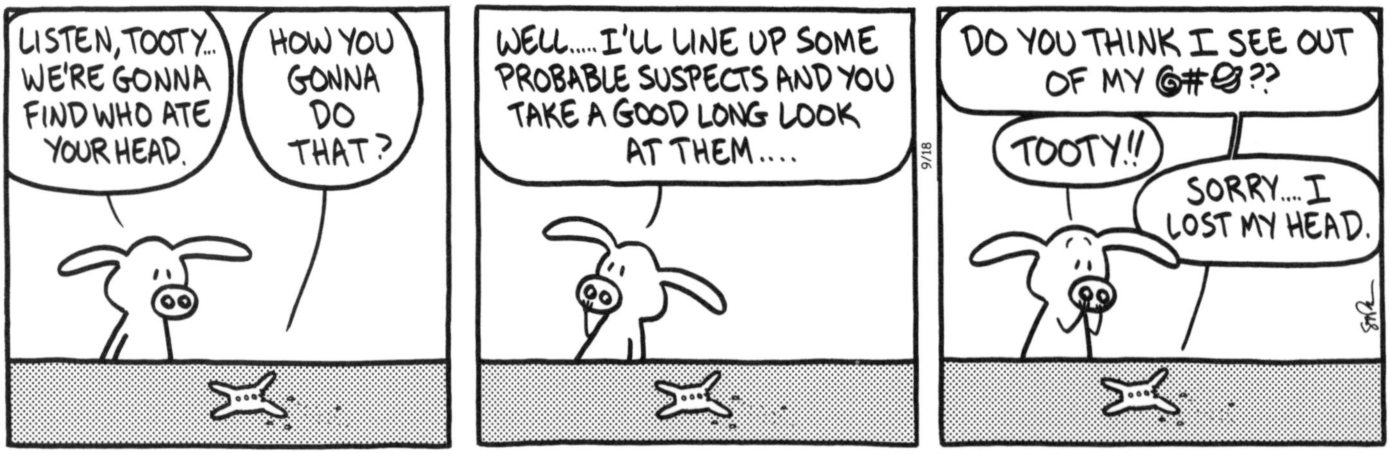

LISTEN, TOOTY... WE'RE GONNA FIND WHO ATE YOUR HEAD.
HOW YOU GONNA DO THAT?
WELL..... I'LL LINE UP SOME PROBABLE SUSPECTS AND YOU TAKE A GOOD LONG LOOK AT THEM....
9/18
DO YOU THINK I SEE OUT OF MY @#$??
TOOTY!!
SORRY.... I LOST MY HEAD.

This one pretty closely telegraphed the word "ass," something you can't say on the comics page. When trying to say the word "ass" on the comics page, it's very tempting to use the swear squiggles, "@$$," because they look just like the word. But alas, I wimped out.

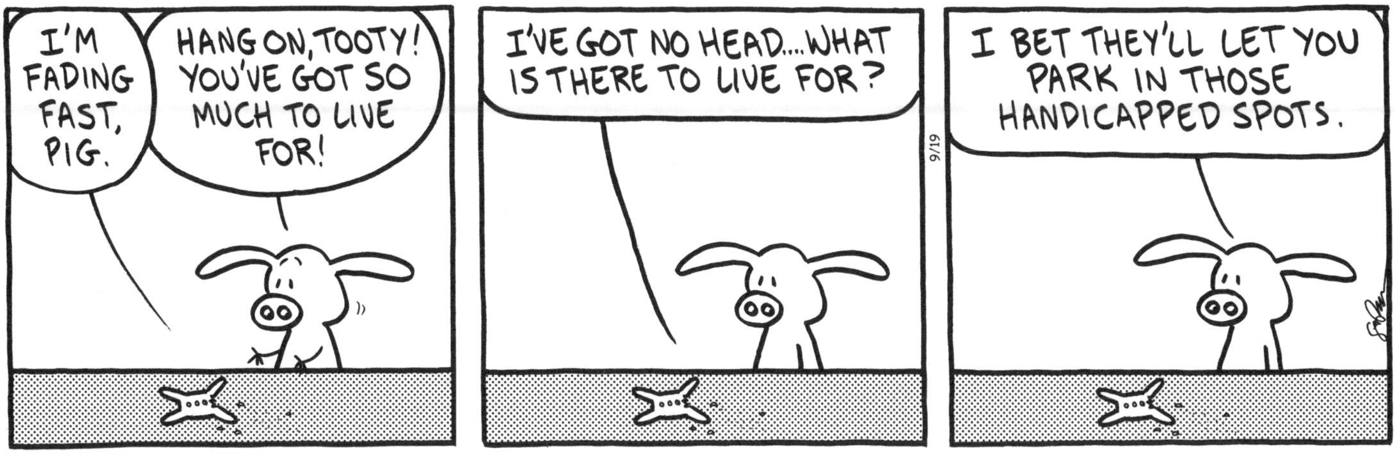

I'M FADING FAST, PIG.
HANG ON, TOOTY! YOU'VE GOT SO MUCH TO LIVE FOR!
I'VE GOT NO HEAD....WHAT IS THERE TO LIVE FOR?
9/19
I BET THEY'LL LET YOU PARK IN THOSE HANDICAPPED SPOTS.

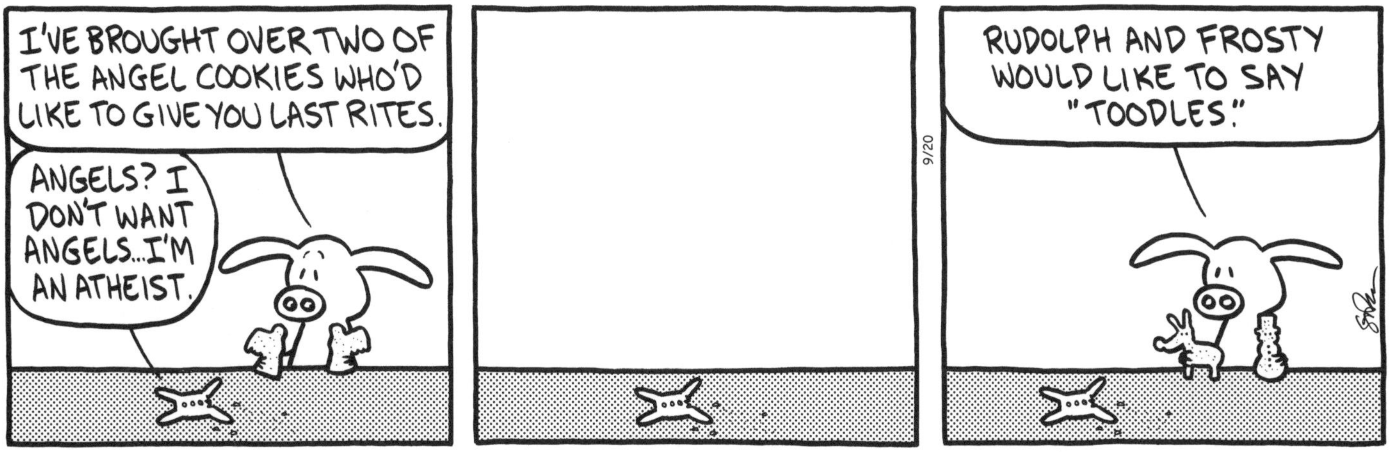

I'VE BROUGHT OVER TWO OF THE ANGEL COOKIES WHO'D LIKE TO GIVE YOU LAST RITES.
ANGELS? I DON'T WANT ANGELS...I'M AN ATHEIST.
9/20
RUDOLPH AND FROSTY WOULD LIKE TO SAY "TOODLES."

Atheist gingerbread men. Religious angels. Secular reindeer. This has it all.

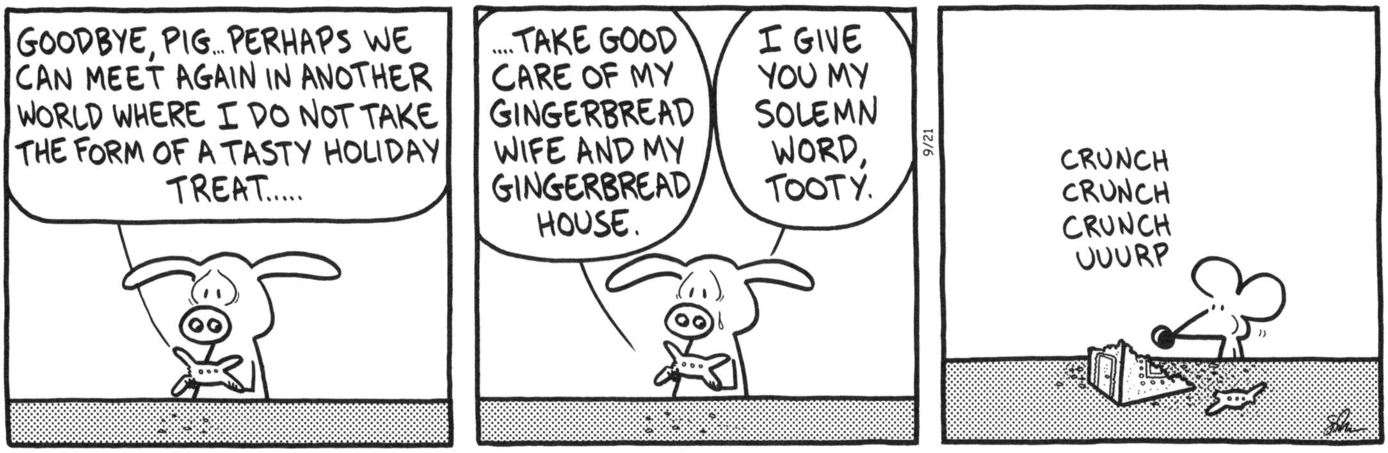

GOODBYE, PIG...PERHAPS WE CAN MEET AGAIN IN ANOTHER WORLD WHERE I DO NOT TAKE THE FORM OF A TASTY HOLIDAY TREAT.....
....TAKE GOOD CARE OF MY GINGERBREAD WIFE AND MY GINGERBREAD HOUSE.
I GIVE YOU MY SOLEMN WORD, TOOTY.
9/21
CRUNCH CRUNCH CRUNCH UUURP

I like setting up dramatic, hopeful scenes, only to cut away to Rat's indifference.

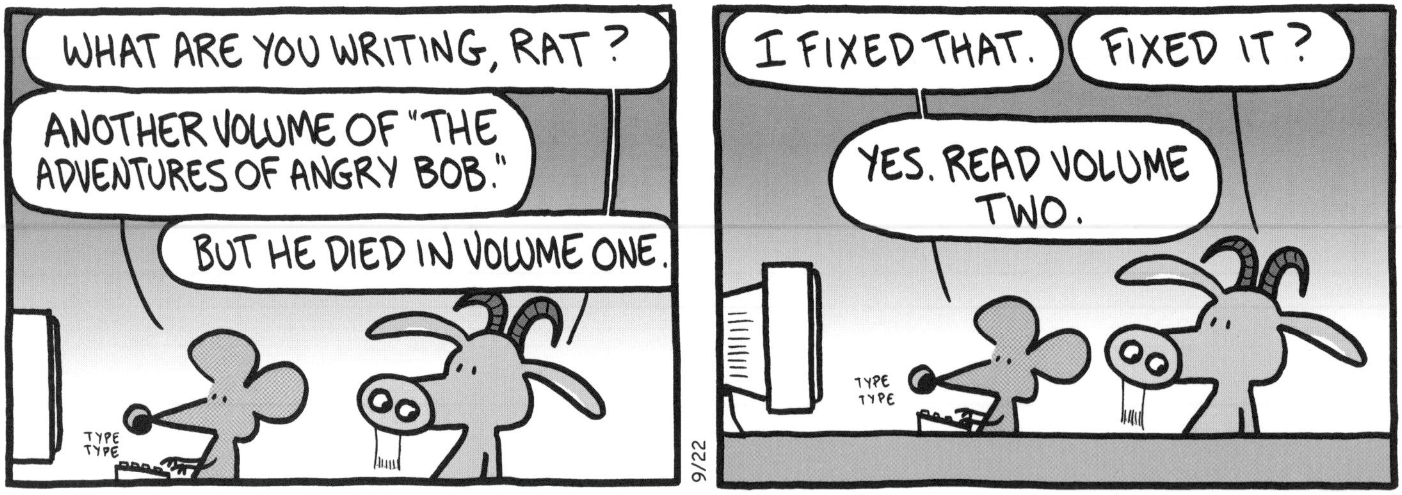
WHAT ARE YOU WRITING, RAT?
ANOTHER VOLUME OF "THE ADVENTURES OF ANGRY BOB."
BUT HE DIED IN VOLUME ONE.
TYPE TYPE
9/22
I FIXED THAT.
FIXED IT?
YES. READ VOLUME TWO.
TYPE TYPE

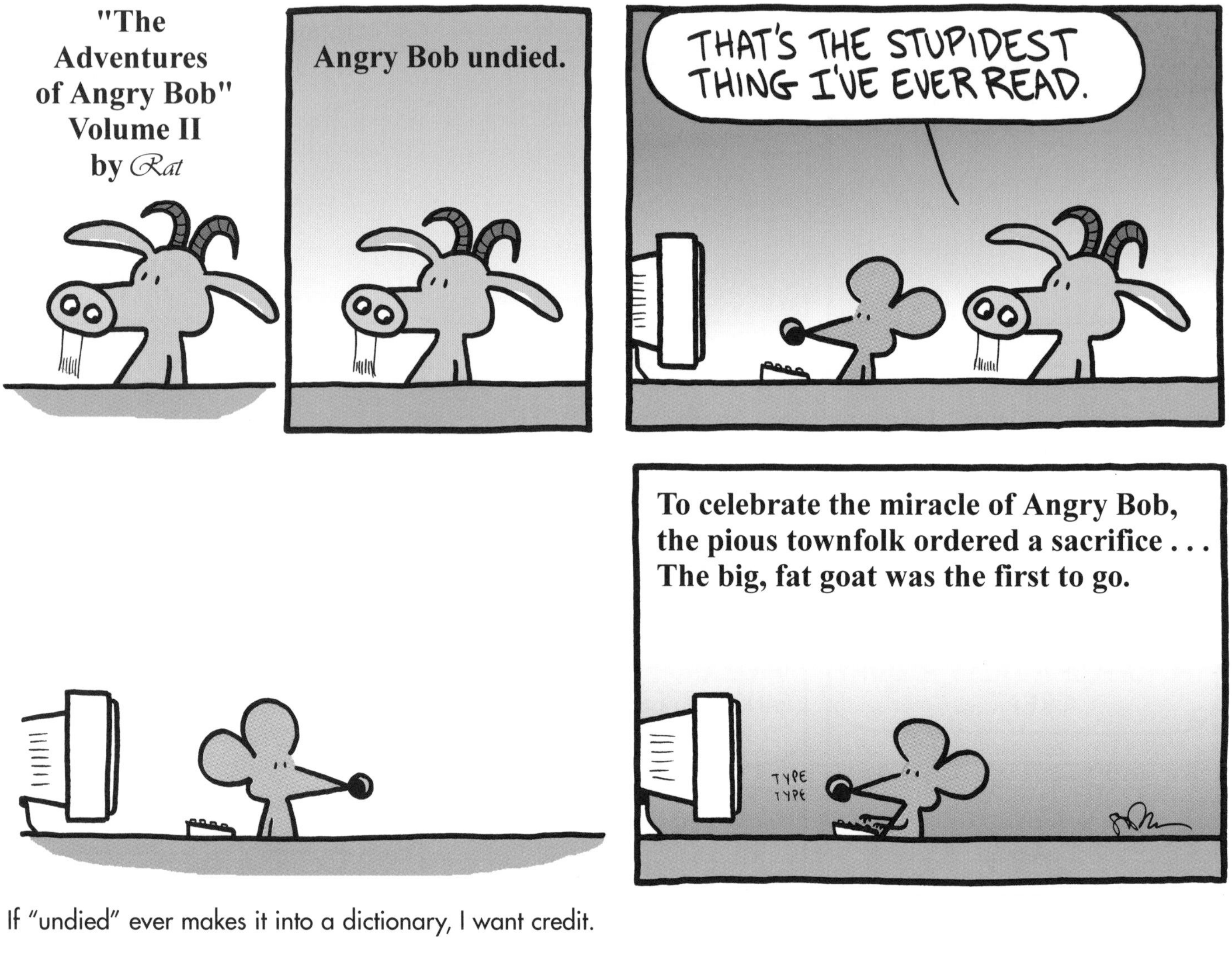
"The Adventures of Angry Bob" Volume II by Rat
Angry Bob undied.
THAT'S THE STUPIDEST THING I'VE EVER READ.
To celebrate the miracle of Angry Bob, the pious townfolk ordered a sacrifice . . . The big, fat goat was the first to go.
TYPE TYPE

If "undied" ever makes it into a dictionary, I want credit.

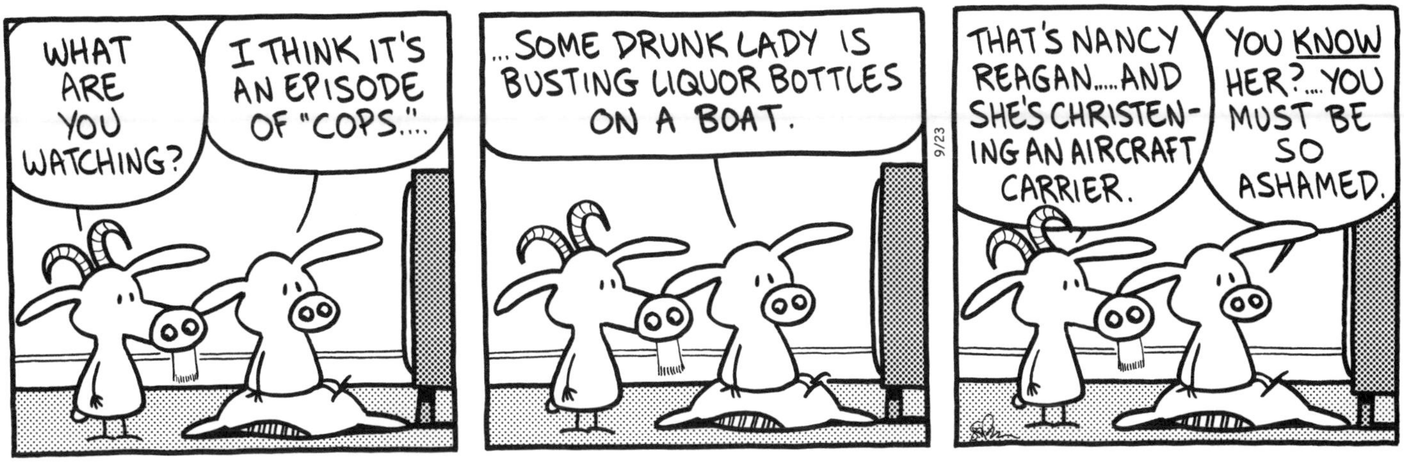
WHAT ARE YOU WATCHING?
I THINK IT'S AN EPISODE OF "COPS."...
...SOME DRUNK LADY IS BUSTING LIQUOR BOTTLES ON A BOAT.
9/23
THAT'S NANCY REAGAN.....AND SHE'S CHRISTEN-ING AN AIRCRAFT CARRIER.
YOU KNOW HER?....YOU MUST BE SO ASHAMED.

Context is everything.

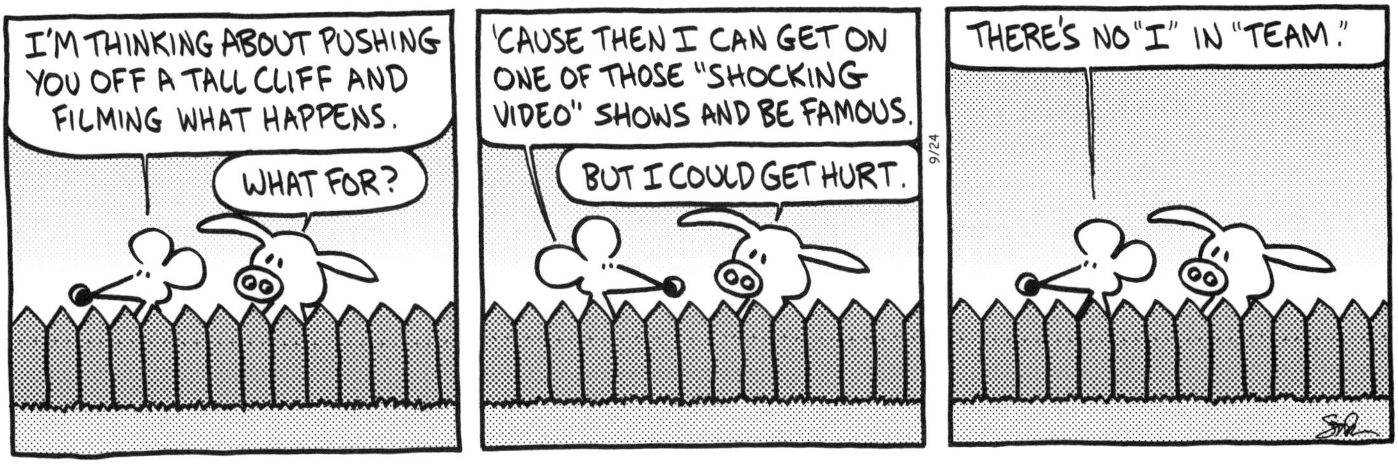
I'M THINKING ABOUT PUSHING YOU OFF A TALL CLIFF AND FILMING WHAT HAPPENS.
WHAT FOR?
'CAUSE THEN I CAN GET ON ONE OF THOSE "SHOCKING VIDEO" SHOWS AND BE FAMOUS.
BUT I COULD GET HURT.
9/24
THERE'S NO "I" IN "TEAM."

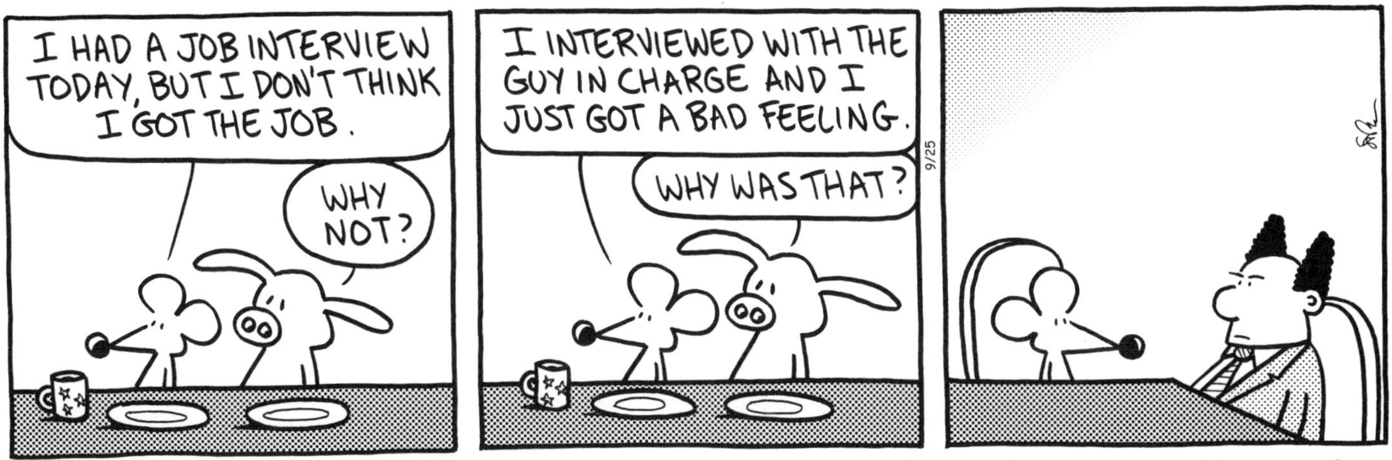
I HAD A JOB INTERVIEW TODAY, BUT I DON'T THINK I GOT THE JOB.
WHY NOT?
I INTERVIEWED WITH THE GUY IN CHARGE AND I JUST GOT A BAD FEELING.
WHY WAS THAT?
9/25

I like drawing Scott's characters for two reasons: 1) They're fairly easy to draw; and 2) I'm reasonably certain he won't sue me.

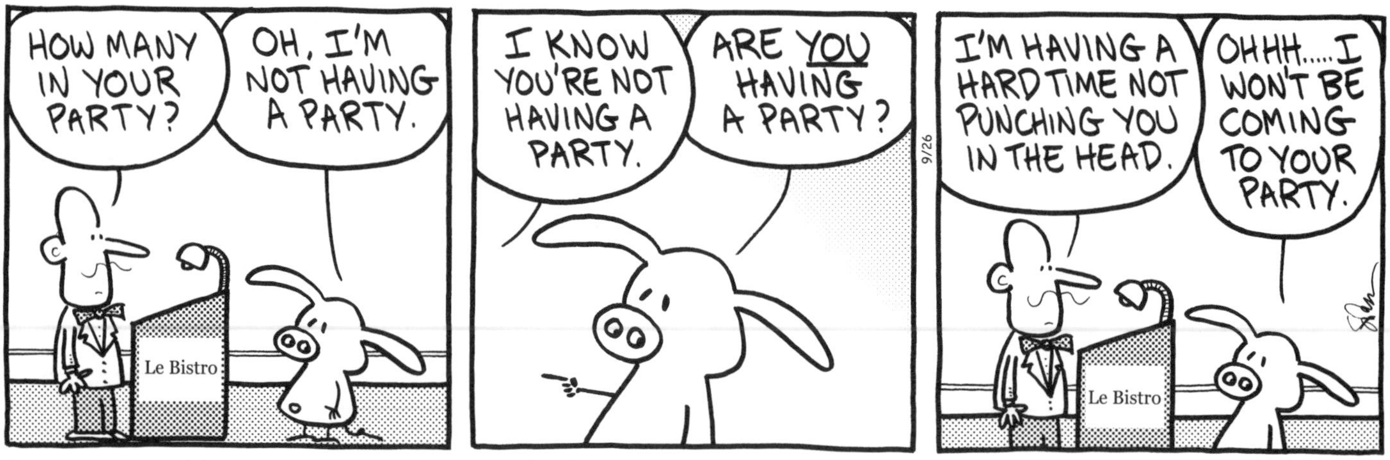
HOW MANY IN YOUR PARTY?
OH, I'M NOT HAVING A PARTY.
Le Bistro
I KNOW YOU'RE NOT HAVING A PARTY.
ARE YOU HAVING A PARTY?
9/26
I'M HAVING A HARD TIME NOT PUNCHING YOU IN THE HEAD.
OHHH.....I WON'T BE COMING TO YOUR PARTY.
Le Bistro

This was one of the more popular dailies. I think it's interesting that every time I draw a host at a restaurant, I give him a handlebar mustache and a bow tie.

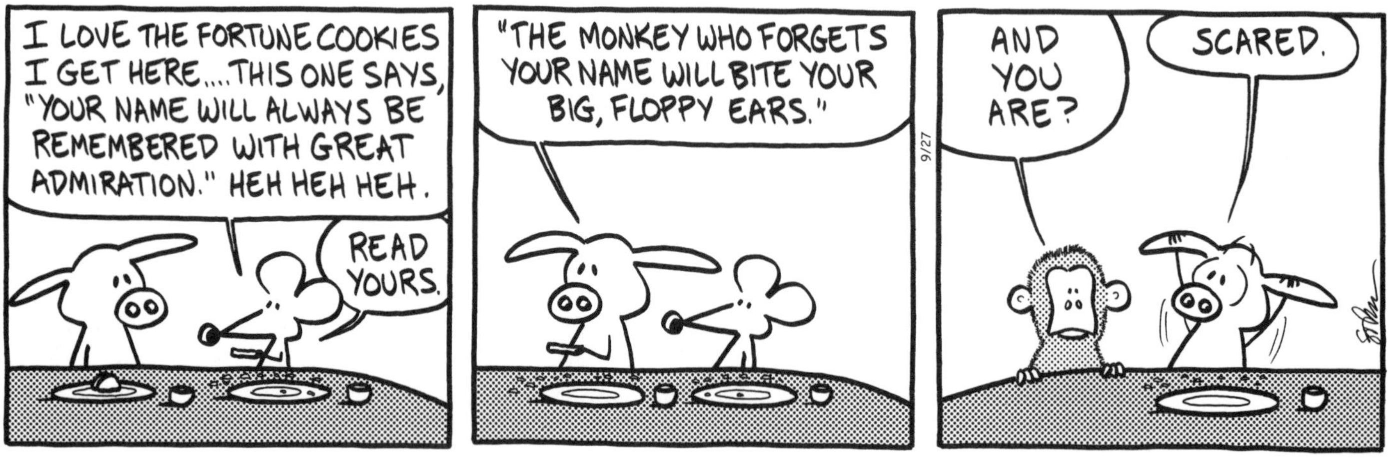
I LOVE THE FORTUNE COOKIES I GET HERE....THIS ONE SAYS, "YOUR NAME WILL ALWAYS BE REMEMBERED WITH GREAT ADMIRATION." HEH HEH HEH.
READ YOURS.
"THE MONKEY WHO FORGETS YOUR NAME WILL BITE YOUR BIG, FLOPPY EARS."
9/27
AND YOU ARE?
SCARED.

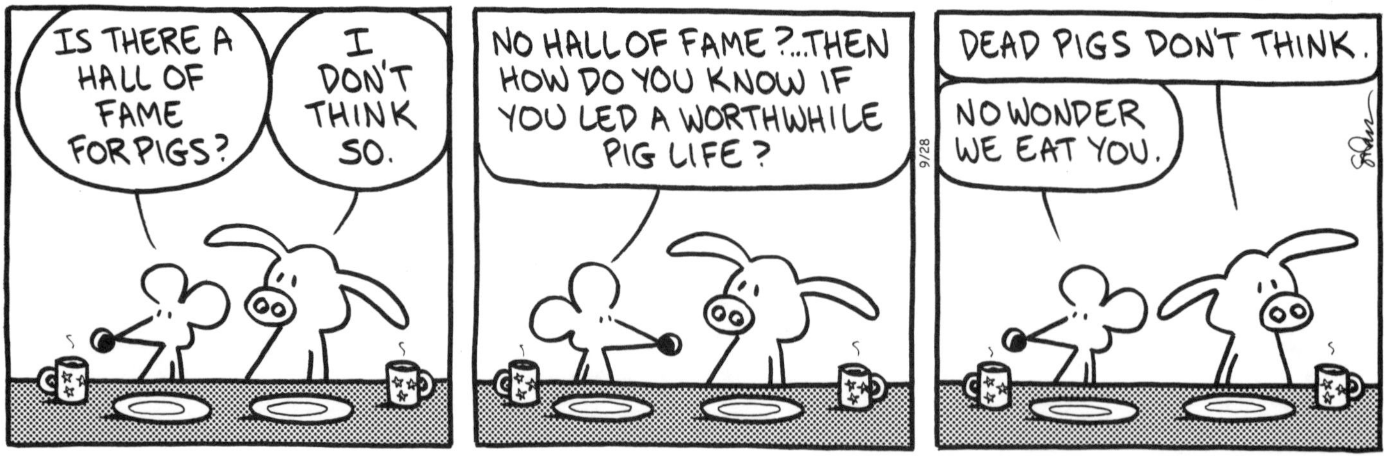
IS THERE A HALL OF FAME FOR PIGS?
I DON'T THINK SO.
NO HALL OF FAME?...THEN HOW DO YOU KNOW IF YOU LED A WORTHWHILE PIG LIFE?
9/28
DEAD PIGS DON'T THINK.
NO WONDER WE EAT YOU.

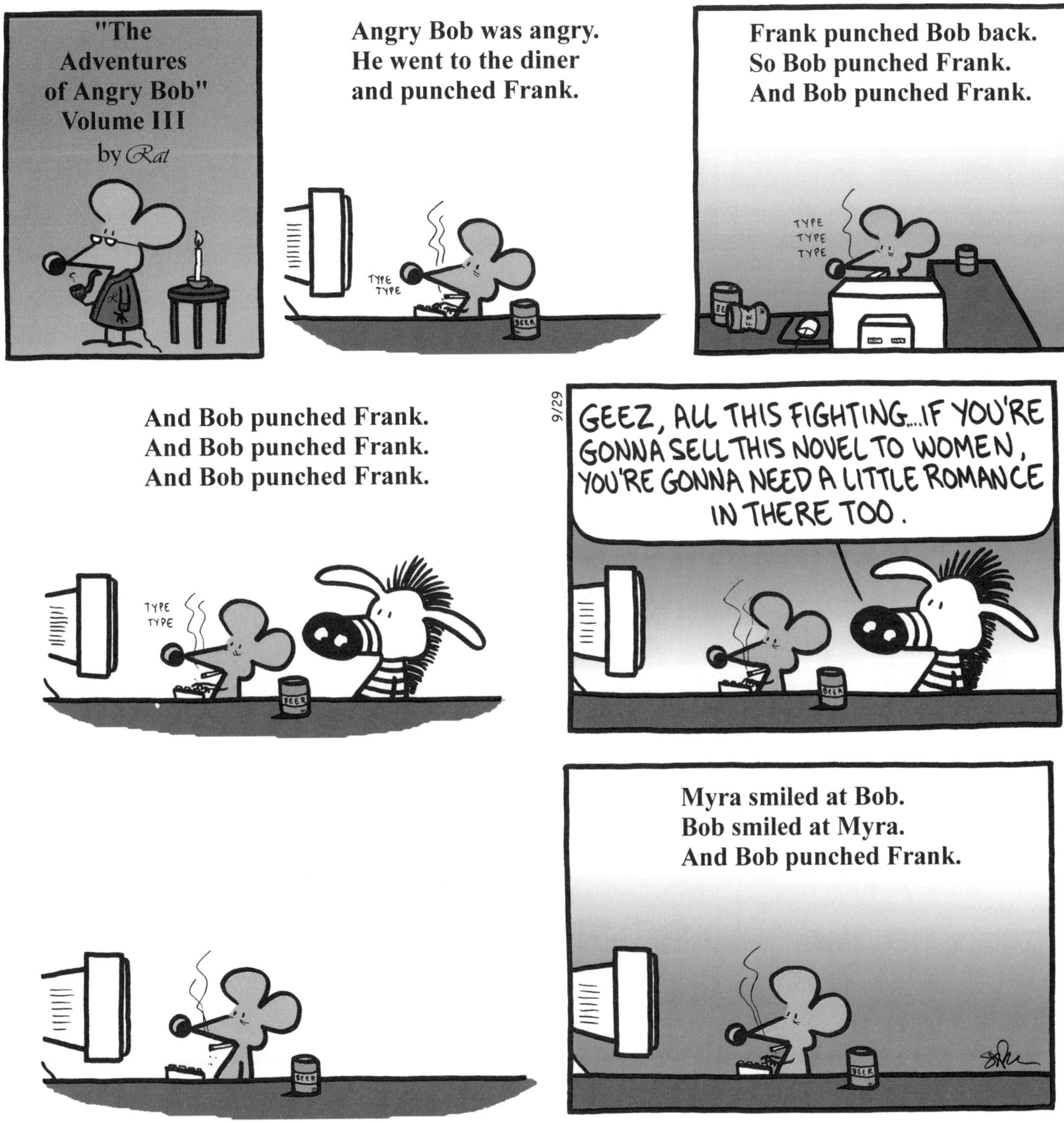
"The Adventures of Angry Bob" Volume III
by Rat
Angry Bob was angry.
He went to the diner
and punched Frank.
Frank punched Bob back.
So Bob punched Frank.
And Bob punched Frank.
TYPE TYPE TYPE
BEER
And Bob punched Frank.
And Bob punched Frank.
And Bob punched Frank.
TYPE TYPE
9/29
GEEZ, ALL THIS FIGHTING....IF YOU'RE GONNA SELL THIS NOVEL TO WOMEN, YOU'RE GONNA NEED A LITTLE ROMANCE IN THERE TOO.
Myra smiled at Bob.
Bob smiled at Myra.
And Bob punched Frank.

I occasionally receive criticism for drawing Rat with a cigarette in the Angry Bob strips. I do it because I think it's in keeping with his tough-guy Norman Mailer/Ernest Hemingway writing persona. Oddly, no one's ever complained about the beer.

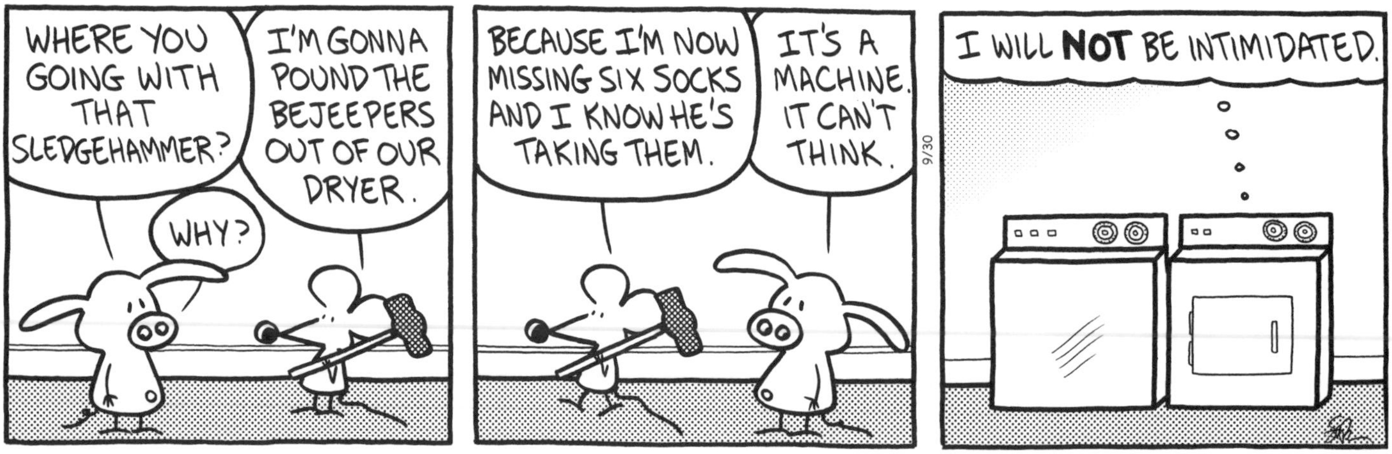
WHERE YOU GOING WITH THAT SLEDGEHAMMER?
I'M GONNA POUND THE BEJEEPERS OUT OF OUR DRYER.
WHY?
BECAUSE I'M NOW MISSING SIX SOCKS AND I KNOW HE'S TAKING THEM.
IT'S A MACHINE. IT CAN'T THINK.
9/30
I WILL **NOT** BE INTIMIDATED.

Rat's anger at inanimate objects comes from my own sad life. Once, when a pen failed to work right, I broke it in two and showed the broken pieces to my other pens. This effort at intimidation apparently worked, as I experienced no problems with the other pens.

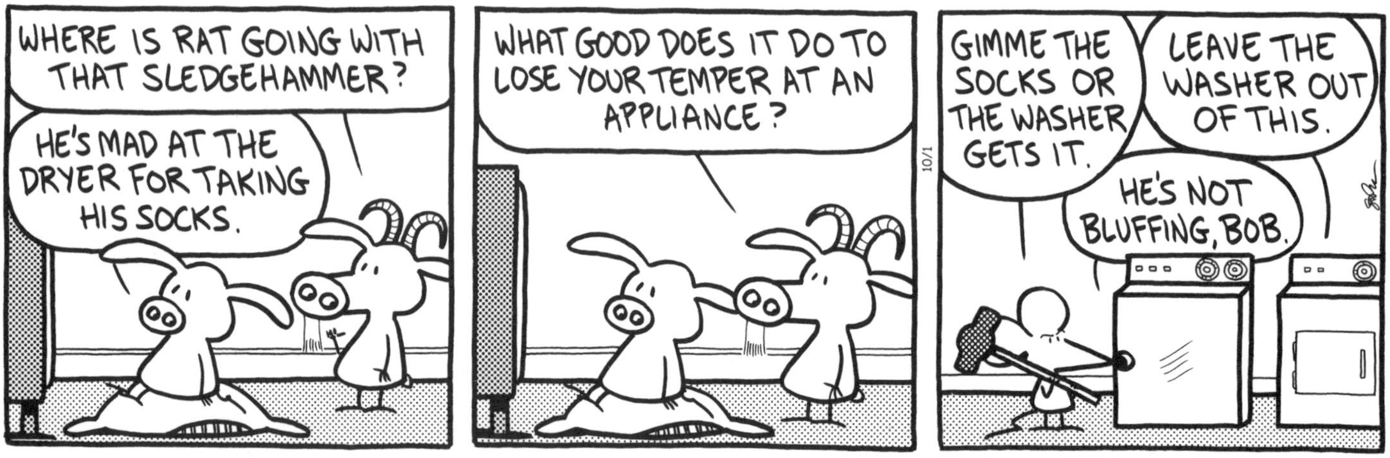
WHERE IS RAT GOING WITH THAT SLEDGEHAMMER?
HE'S MAD AT THE DRYER FOR TAKING HIS SOCKS.
WHAT GOOD DOES IT DO TO LOSE YOUR TEMPER AT AN APPLIANCE?
10/1
GIMME THE SOCKS OR THE WASHER GETS IT.
LEAVE THE WASHER OUT OF THIS.
HE'S NOT BLUFFING, BOB.

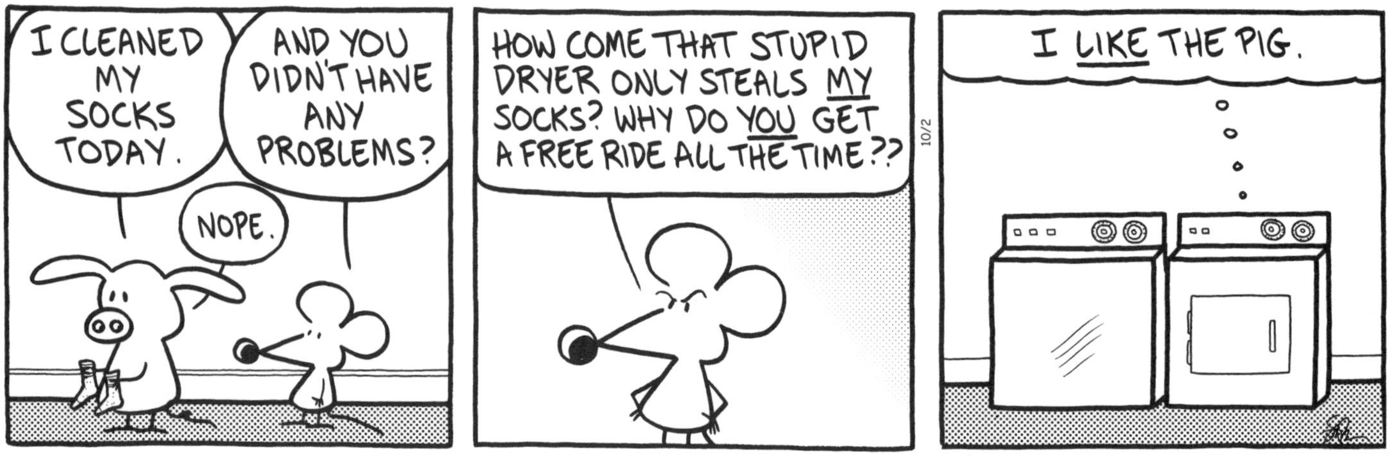
I CLEANED MY SOCKS TODAY.
AND YOU DIDN'T HAVE ANY PROBLEMS?
NOPE.
HOW COME THAT STUPID DRYER ONLY STEALS MY SOCKS? WHY DO YOU GET A FREE RIDE ALL THE TIME??
10/2
I LIKE THE PIG.

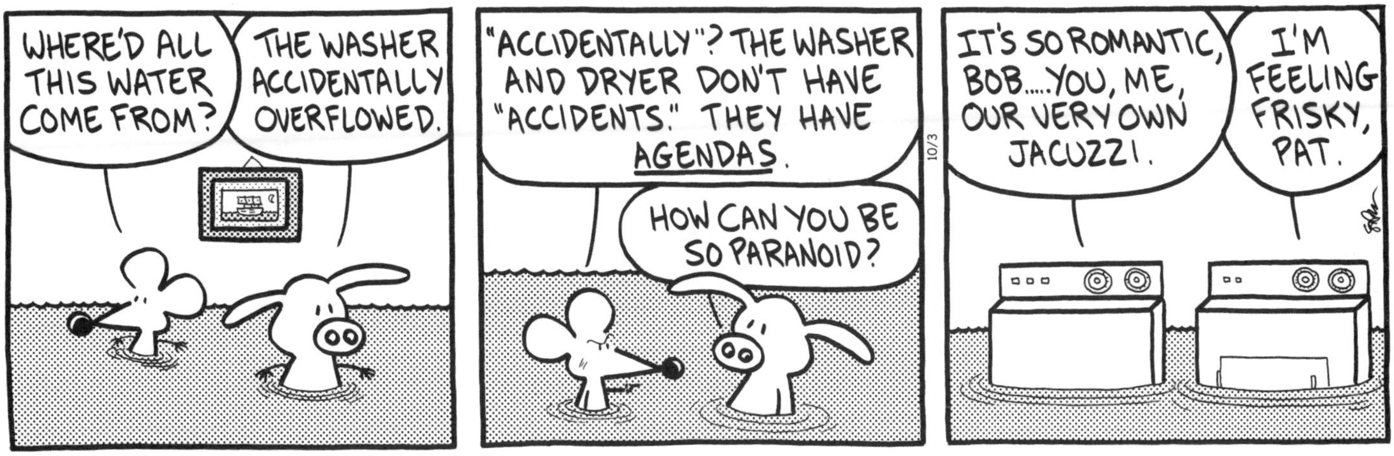
WHERE'D ALL THIS WATER COME FROM?
THE WASHER ACCIDENTALLY OVERFLOWED.
"ACCIDENTALLY"? THE WASHER AND DRYER DON'T HAVE "ACCIDENTS." THEY HAVE AGENDAS.
HOW CAN YOU BE SO PARANOID?
10/3
IT'S SO ROMANTIC, BOB.....YOU, ME, OUR VERY OWN JACUZZI.
I'M FEELING FRISKY, PAT.

When this strip originally ran on the Internet, the washer's name in the last panel was "Dave," meaning that the washer and dryer were gay. This, however, was considered too risqué for mainstream newspapers, so when it came time for publication in those papers, I had to tone it down to the more ambiguous "Pat." I thus became the first syndicated cartoonist to be censored for having homosexual appliances.

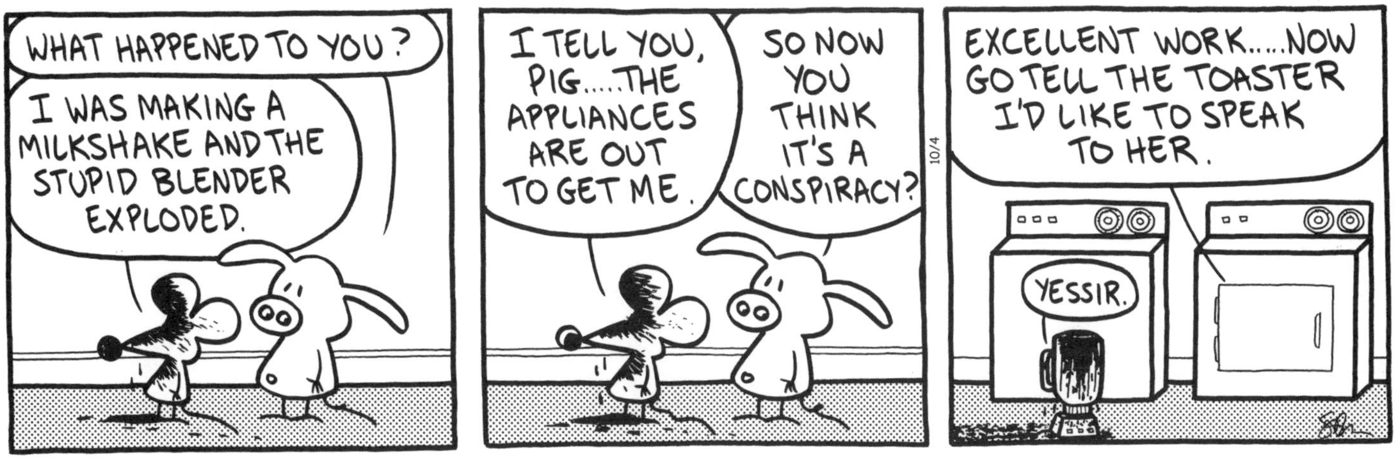
WHAT HAPPENED TO YOU?
I WAS MAKING A MILKSHAKE AND THE STUPID BLENDER EXPLODED.
I TELL YOU, PIG.....THE APPLIANCES ARE OUT TO GET ME.
SO NOW YOU THINK IT'S A CONSPIRACY?
10/4
EXCELLENT WORK.....NOW GO TELL THE TOASTER I'D LIKE TO SPEAK TO HER.
YESSIR.

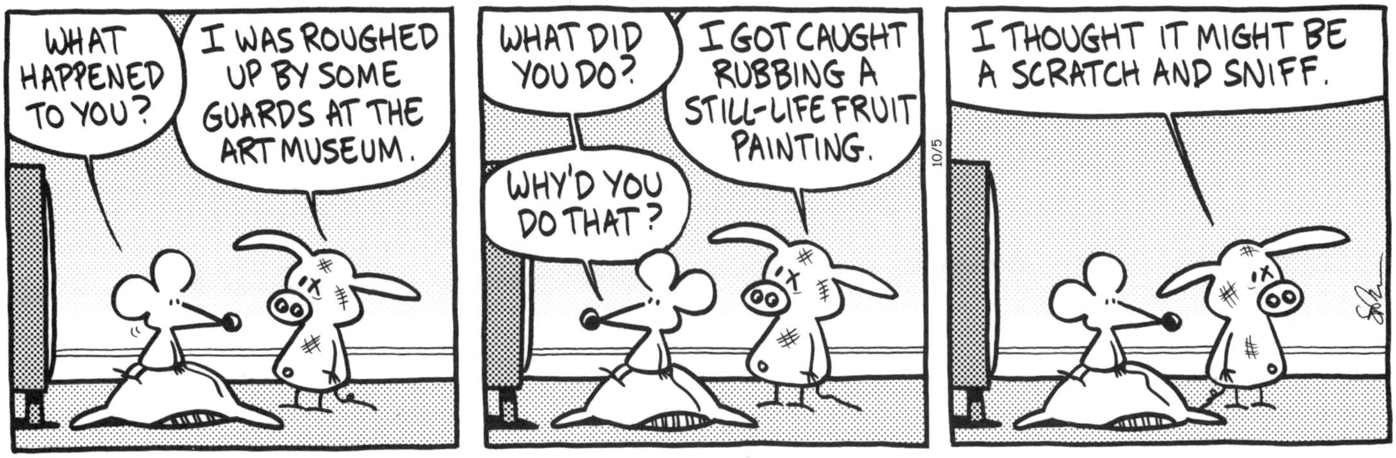
WHAT HAPPENED TO YOU?
I WAS ROUGHED UP BY SOME GUARDS AT THE ART MUSEUM.
WHAT DID YOU DO?
I GOT CAUGHT RUBBING A STILL-LIFE FRUIT PAINTING.
WHY'D YOU DO THAT?
10/5
I THOUGHT IT MIGHT BE A SCRATCH AND SNIFF.

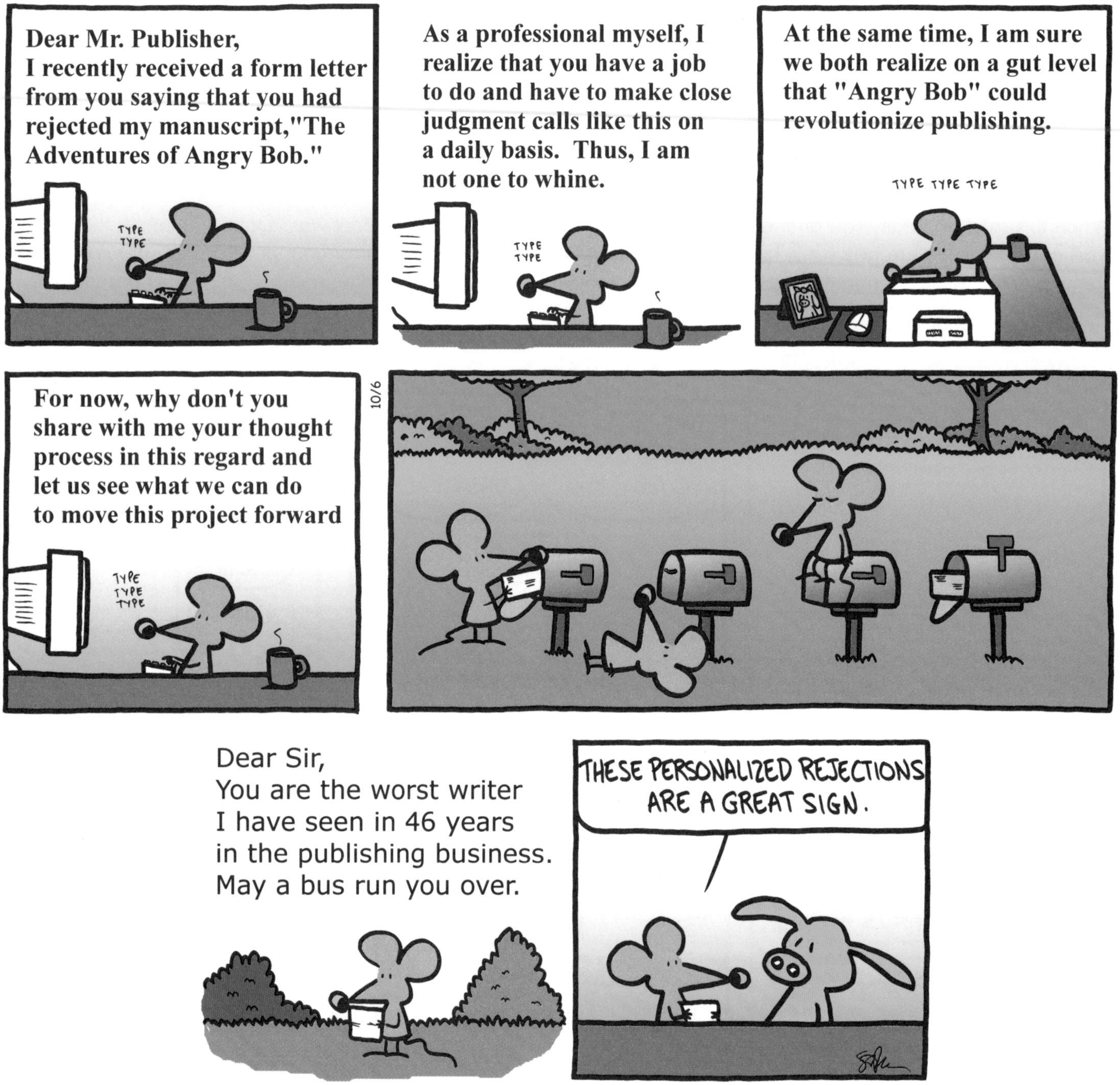
Dear Mr. Publisher,
I recently received a form letter from you saying that you had rejected my manuscript,"The Adventures of Angry Bob."
TYPE TYPE
As a professional myself, I realize that you have a job to do and have to make close judgment calls like this on a daily basis. Thus, I am not one to whine.
TYPE TYPE
At the same time, I am sure we both realize on a gut level that "Angry Bob" could revolutionize publishing.
TYPE TYPE TYPE
For now, why don't you share with me your thought process in this regard and let us see what we can do to move this project forward
TYPE TYPE TYPE
10/6
Dear Sir,
You are the worst writer I have seen in 46 years in the publishing business.
May a bus run you over.
THESE PERSONALIZED REJECTIONS ARE A GREAT SIGN.

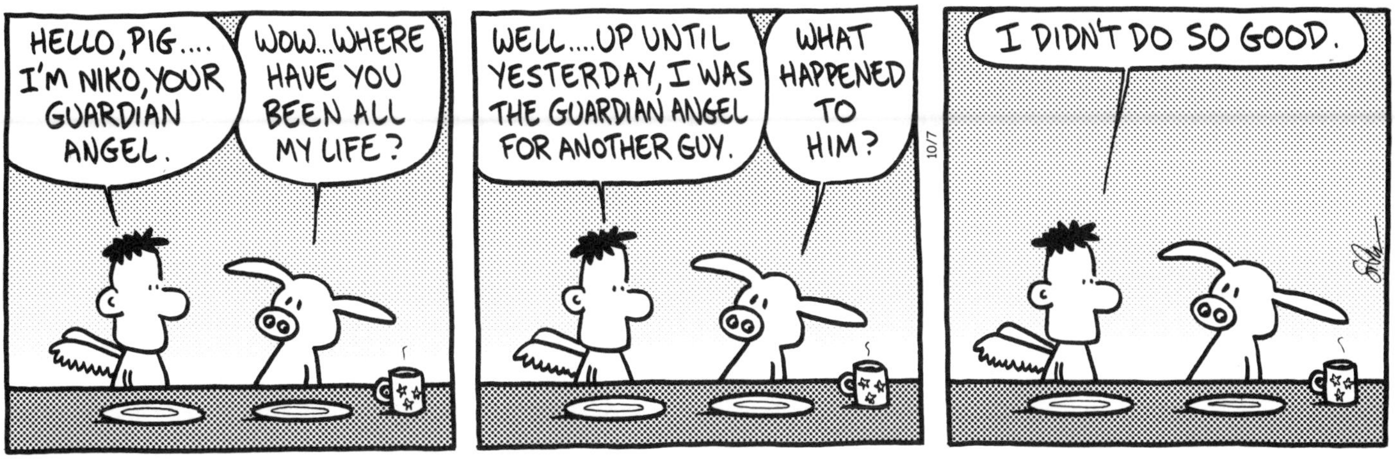
HELLO, PIG.... I'M NIKO, YOUR GUARDIAN ANGEL.
WOW...WHERE HAVE YOU BEEN ALL MY LIFE?
WELL....UP UNTIL YESTERDAY, I WAS THE GUARDIAN ANGEL FOR ANOTHER GUY.
WHAT HAPPENED TO HIM?
10/7
I DIDN'T DO SO GOOD.

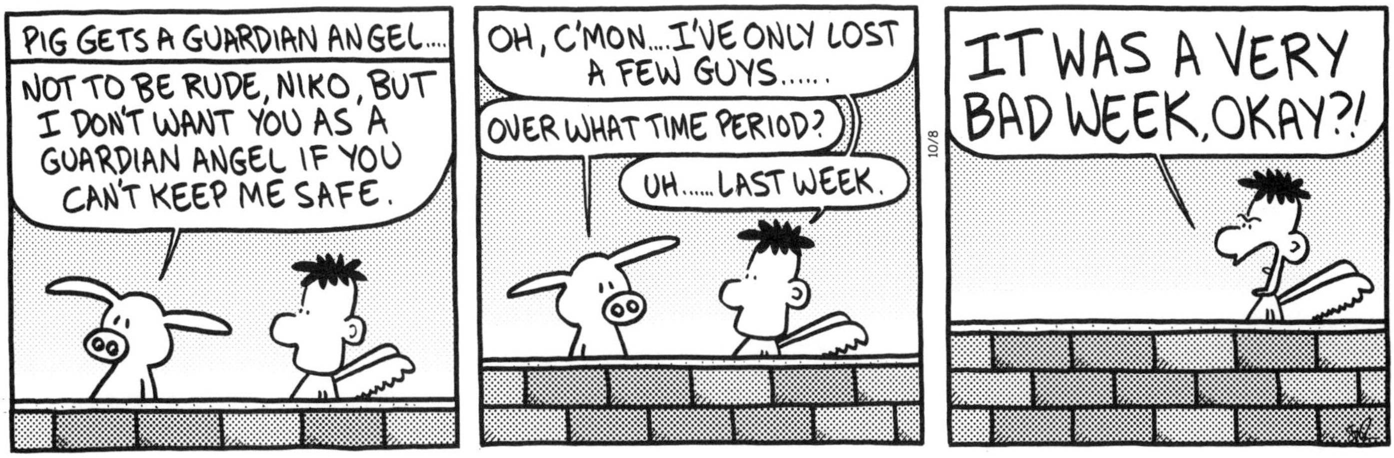
PIG GETS A GUARDIAN ANGEL....
NOT TO BE RUDE, NIKO, BUT I DON'T WANT YOU AS A GUARDIAN ANGEL IF YOU CAN'T KEEP ME SAFE.
OH, C'MON....I'VE ONLY LOST A FEW GUYS......
OVER WHAT TIME PERIOD?
UH......LAST WEEK.
10/8
IT WAS A VERY BAD WEEK, OKAY?!

When I look back at this strip, I can really see how much Charles Schulz influenced me, as many *Peanuts* strips used to close with one of the characters yelling at someone (often unseen) in the final panel.

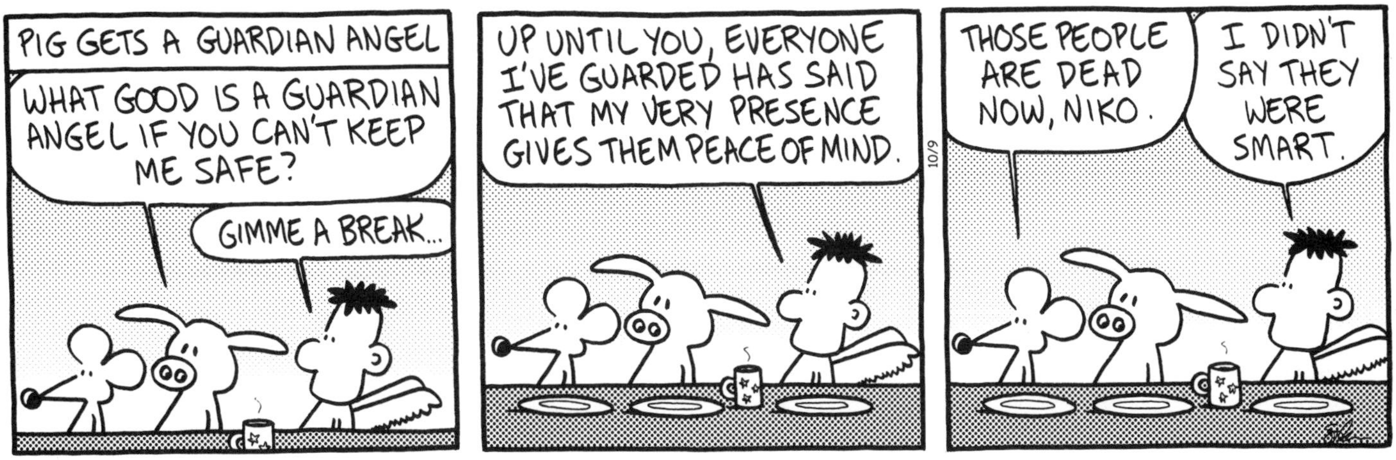
PIG GETS A GUARDIAN ANGEL
WHAT GOOD IS A GUARDIAN ANGEL IF YOU CAN'T KEEP ME SAFE?
GIMME A BREAK...
UP UNTIL YOU, EVERYONE I'VE GUARDED HAS SAID THAT MY VERY PRESENCE GIVES THEM PEACE OF MIND.
10/9
THOSE PEOPLE ARE DEAD NOW, NIKO.
I DIDN'T SAY THEY WERE SMART.

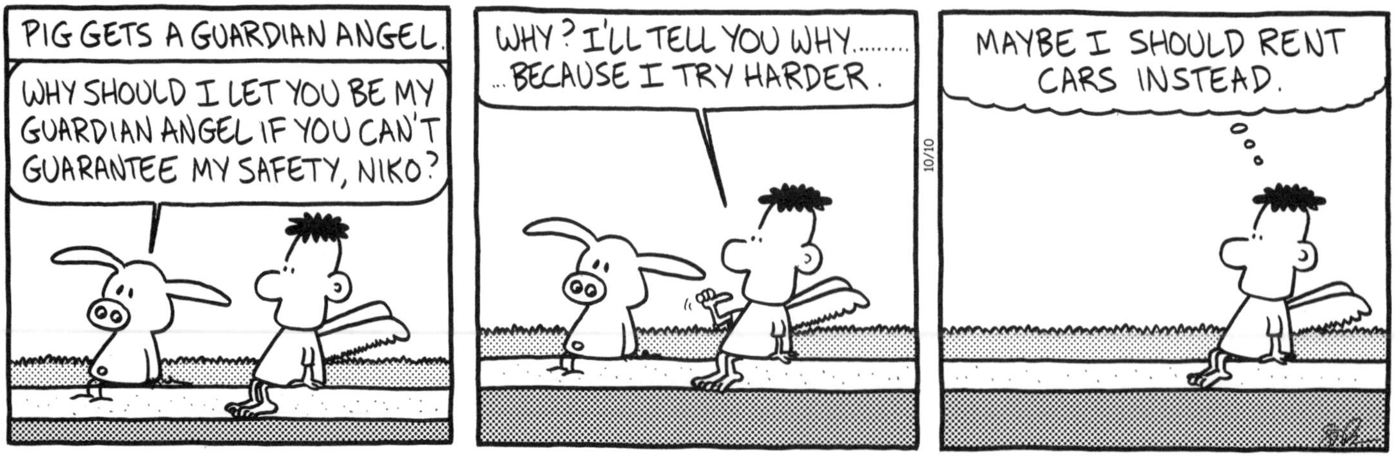
PIG GETS A GUARDIAN ANGEL.
WHY SHOULD I LET YOU BE MY GUARDIAN ANGEL IF YOU CAN'T GUARANTEE MY SAFETY, NIKO?
WHY? I'LL TELL YOU WHY.........
...BECAUSE I TRY HARDER.
10/10
MAYBE I SHOULD RENT CARS INSTEAD.

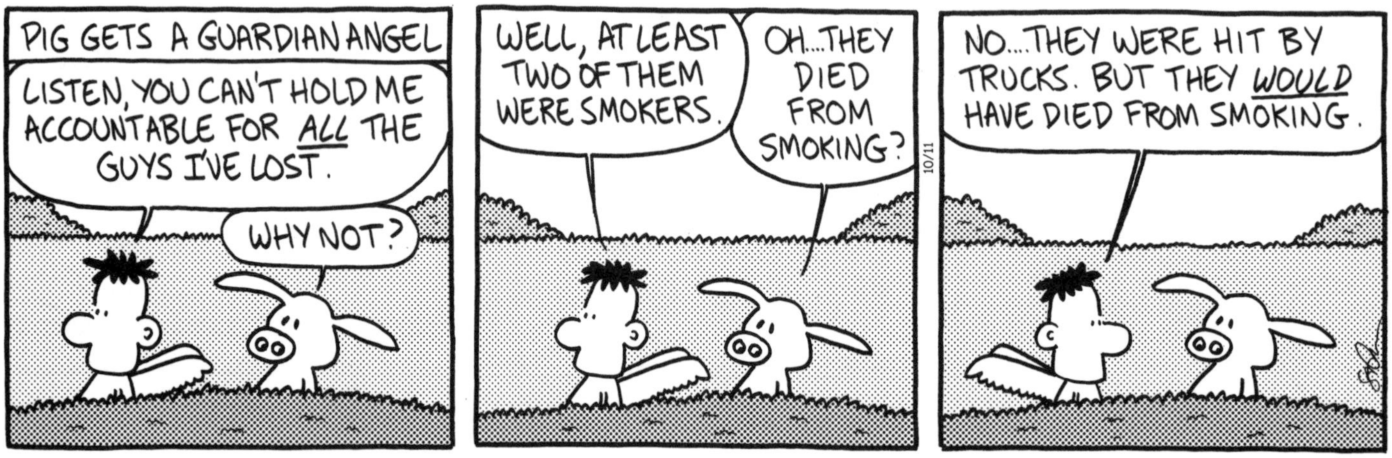
PIG GETS A GUARDIAN ANGEL
LISTEN, YOU CAN'T HOLD ME ACCOUNTABLE FOR ALL THE GUYS I'VE LOST.
WHY NOT?
WELL, AT LEAST TWO OF THEM WERE SMOKERS.
OH...THEY DIED FROM SMOKING?
10/11
NO....THEY WERE HIT BY TRUCKS. BUT THEY WOULD HAVE DIED FROM SMOKING.

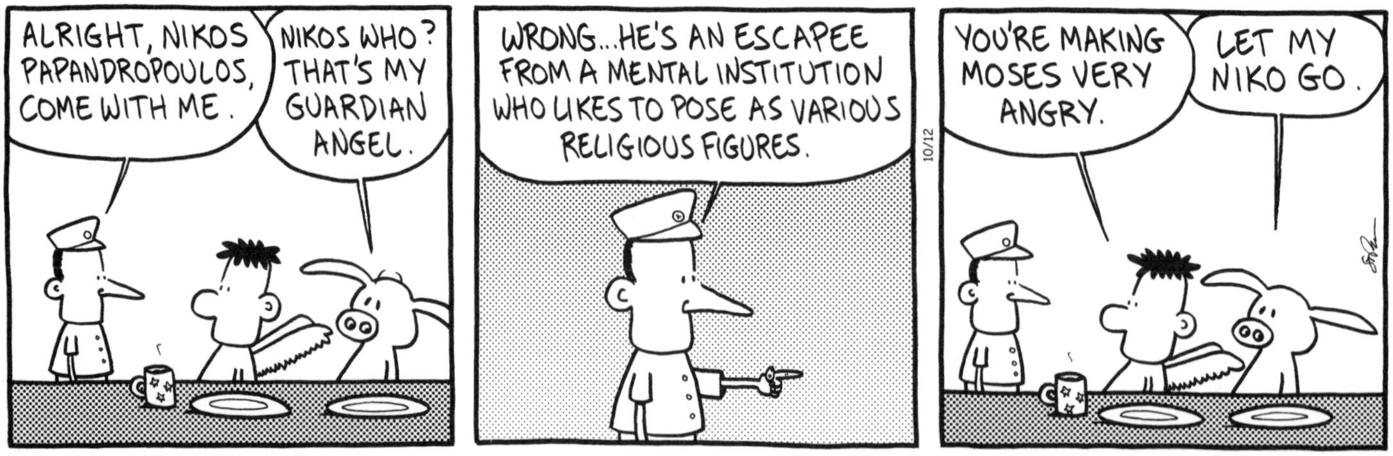
ALRIGHT, NIKOS PAPANDROPOULOS, COME WITH ME.
NIKOS WHO? THAT'S MY GUARDIAN ANGEL.
WRONG...HE'S AN ESCAPEE FROM A MENTAL INSTITUTION WHO LIKES TO POSE AS VARIOUS RELIGIOUS FIGURES.
10/12
YOU'RE MAKING MOSES VERY ANGRY.
LET MY NIKO GO.

One of the same fans who complained to newspapers about the June 19 Greek restaurant strip wrote again to newspapers after this strip ran, saying that I was now depicting all Greek people as delusional mental patients.

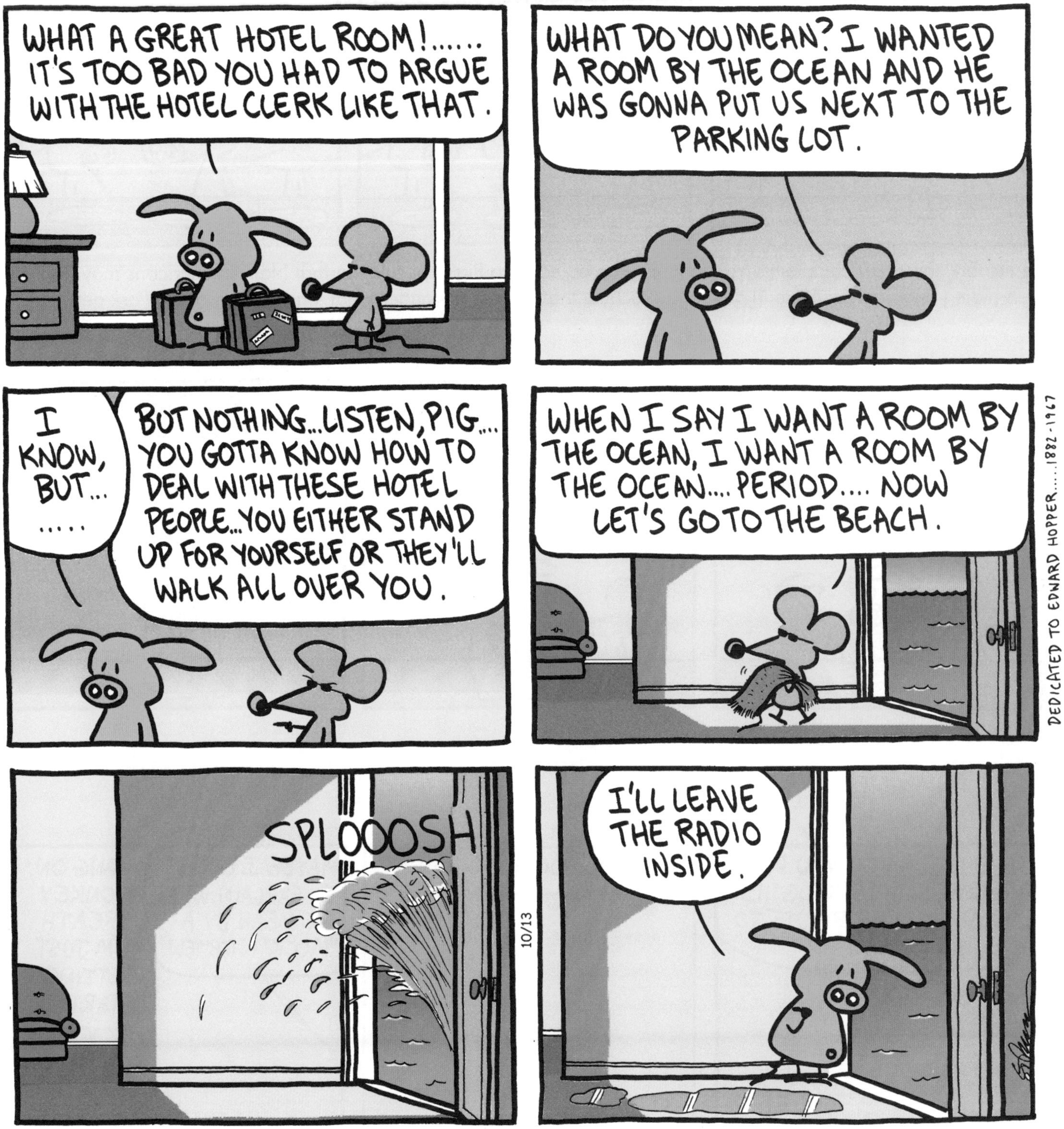
WHAT A GREAT HOTEL ROOM!...... IT'S TOO BAD YOU HAD TO ARGUE WITH THE HOTEL CLERK LIKE THAT.
WHAT DO YOU MEAN? I WANTED A ROOM BY THE OCEAN AND HE WAS GONNA PUT US NEXT TO THE PARKING LOT.
I KNOW, BUT... .....
BUT NOTHING...LISTEN, PIG.... YOU GOTTA KNOW HOW TO DEAL WITH THESE HOTEL PEOPLE...YOU EITHER STAND UP FOR YOURSELF OR THEY'LL WALK ALL OVER YOU.
WHEN I SAY I WANT A ROOM BY THE OCEAN, I WANT A ROOM BY THE OCEAN.... PERIOD.... NOW LET'S GO TO THE BEACH.
DEDICATED TO EDWARD HOPPER.....1882-1967
SPLOOOSH
10/13
I'LL LEAVE THE RADIO INSIDE.

This strip is based on the Edward Hopper painting, *Rooms by the Sea*, which I've crudely rendered in the last three panels. Hopper is one of my favorite painters.

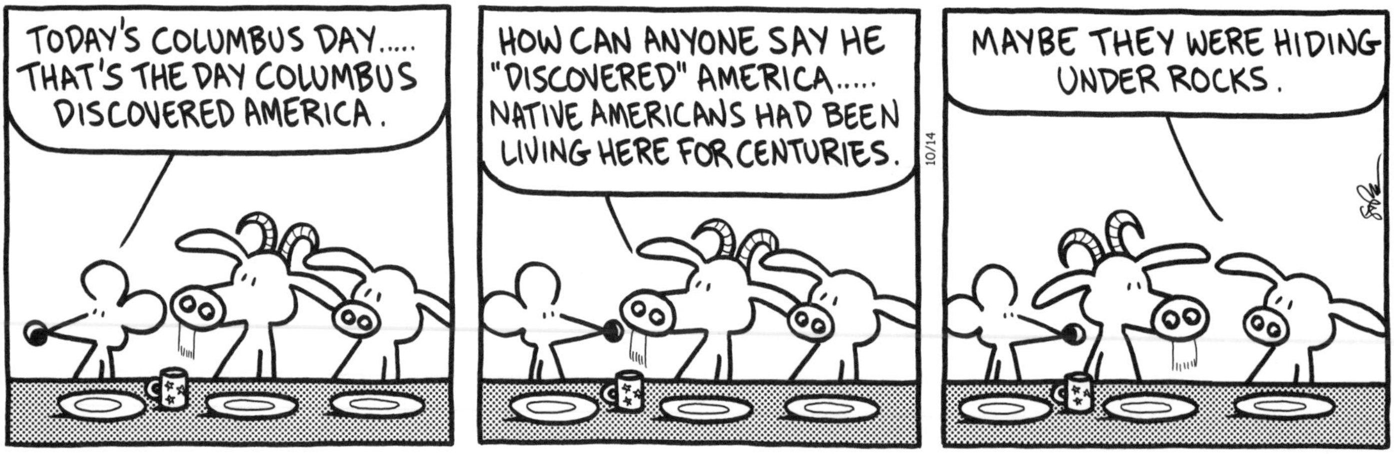
TODAY'S COLUMBUS DAY..... THAT'S THE DAY COLUMBUS DISCOVERED AMERICA.
HOW CAN ANYONE SAY HE "DISCOVERED" AMERICA..... NATIVE AMERICANS HAD BEEN LIVING HERE FOR CENTURIES.
10/14
MAYBE THEY WERE HIDING UNDER ROCKS.

Predictably, this drew complaints from people who objected to Pig's speculation that Native Americans may have been hiding under rocks. When I get e-mail such as that, I always wonder what kind of mail *South Park* gets.

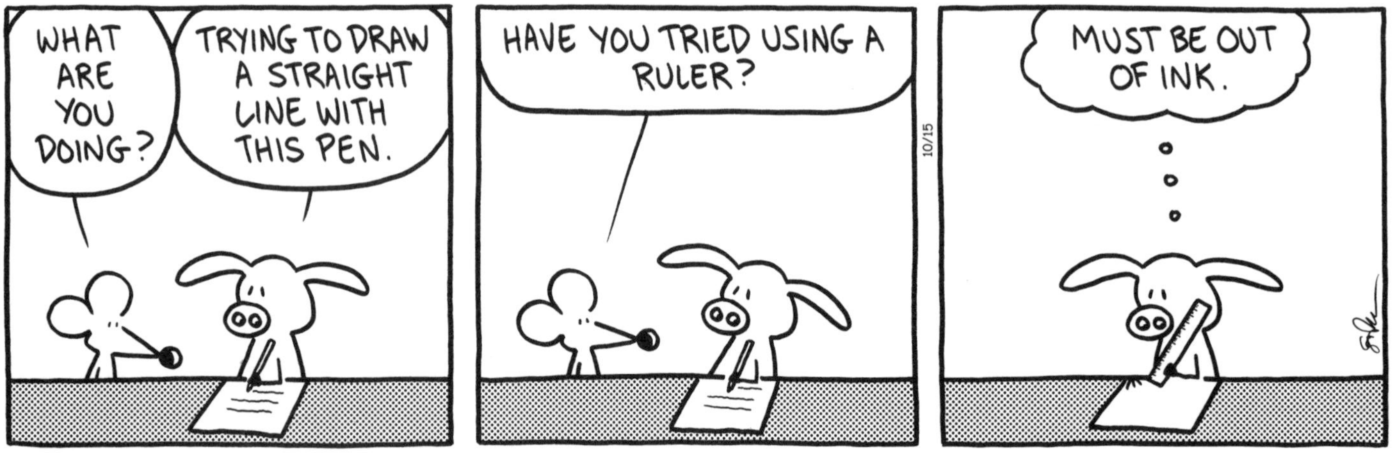
WHAT ARE YOU DOING?
TRYING TO DRAW A STRAIGHT LINE WITH THIS PEN.
HAVE YOU TRIED USING A RULER?
10/15
MUST BE OUT OF INK.

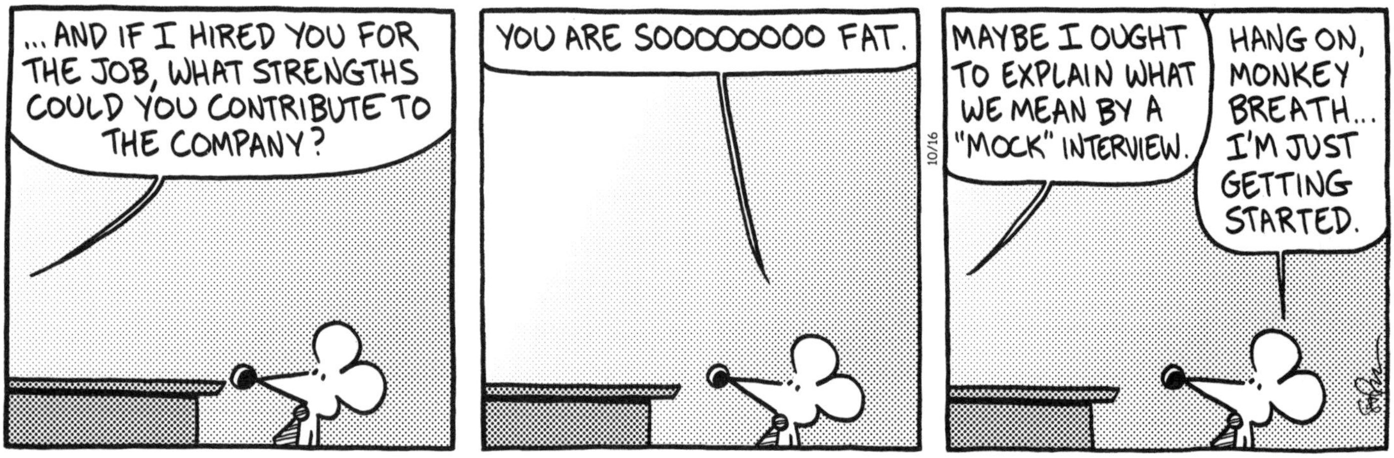
...AND IF I HIRED YOU FOR THE JOB, WHAT STRENGTHS COULD YOU CONTRIBUTE TO THE COMPANY?
YOU ARE SOOOOOOOO FAT.
10/16
MAYBE I OUGHT TO EXPLAIN WHAT WE MEAN BY A "MOCK" INTERVIEW.
HANG ON, MONKEY BREATH... I'M JUST GETTING STARTED.

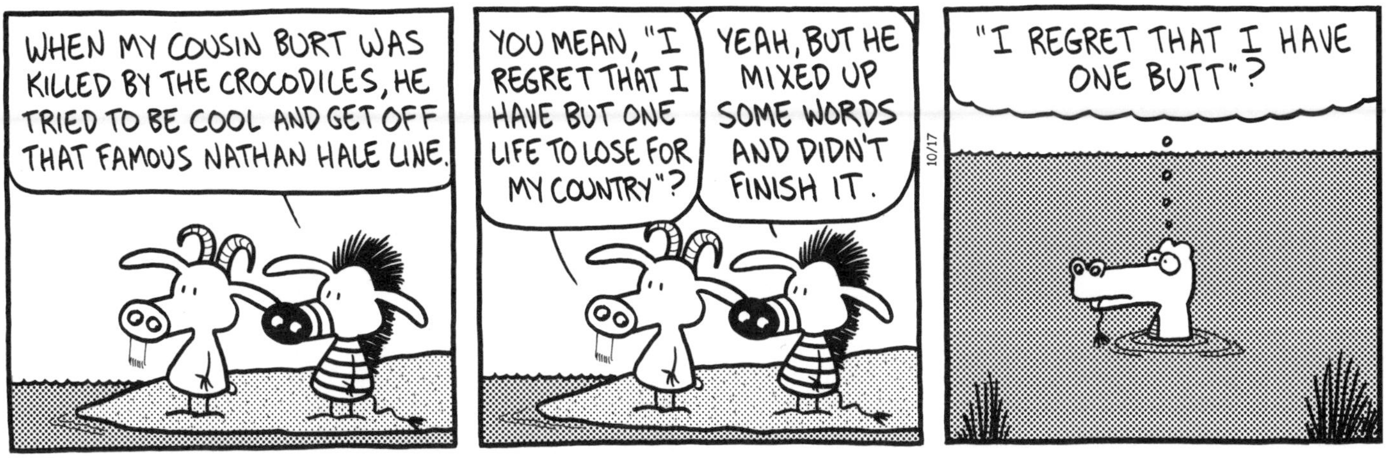
WHEN MY COUSIN BURT WAS KILLED BY THE CROCODILES, HE TRIED TO BE COOL AND GET OFF THAT FAMOUS NATHAN HALE LINE.
YOU MEAN, "I REGRET THAT I HAVE BUT ONE LIFE TO LOSE FOR MY COUNTRY"?
YEAH, BUT HE MIXED UP SOME WORDS AND DIDN'T FINISH IT.
10/17
"I REGRET THAT I HAVE ONE BUTT"?

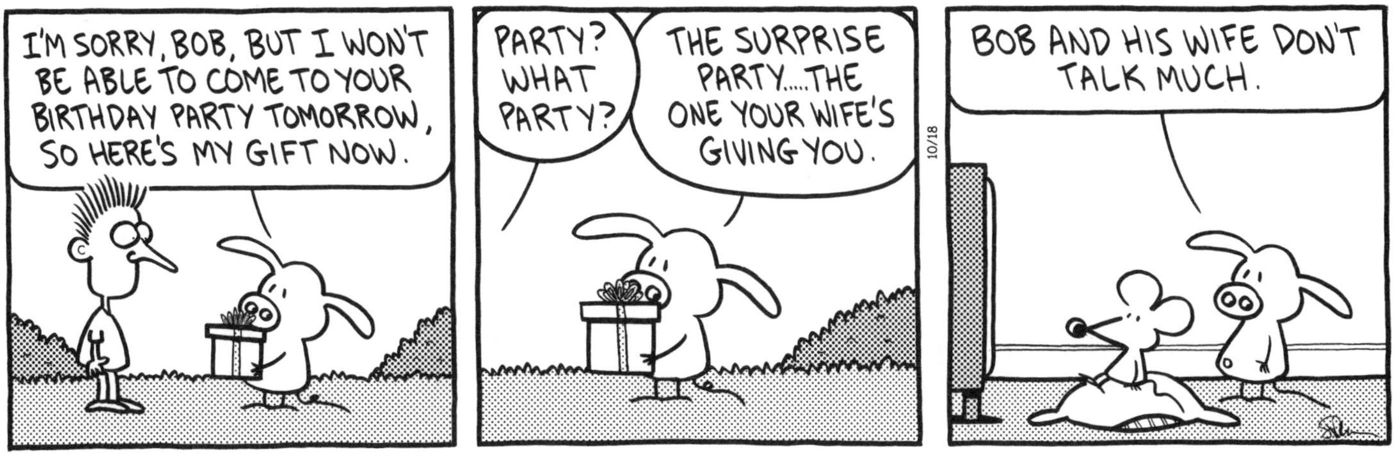
I'M SORRY, BOB, BUT I WON'T BE ABLE TO COME TO YOUR BIRTHDAY PARTY TOMORROW, SO HERE'S MY GIFT NOW.
PARTY? WHAT PARTY?
THE SURPRISE PARTY.....THE ONE YOUR WIFE'S GIVING YOU.
10/18
BOB AND HIS WIFE DON'T TALK MUCH.

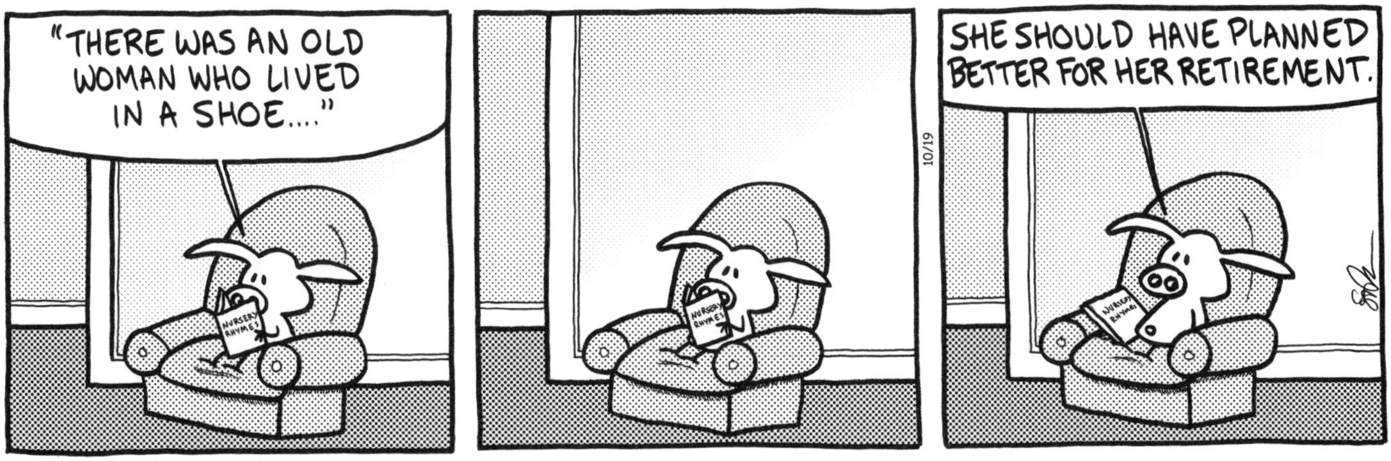
"THERE WAS AN OLD WOMAN WHO LIVED IN A SHOE...."
NURSERY RHYMES
10/19
SHE SHOULD HAVE PLANNED BETTER FOR HER RETIREMENT.

This marked the last time I would try and draw a recliner in *Pearls*. A man's gotta know his limitations.

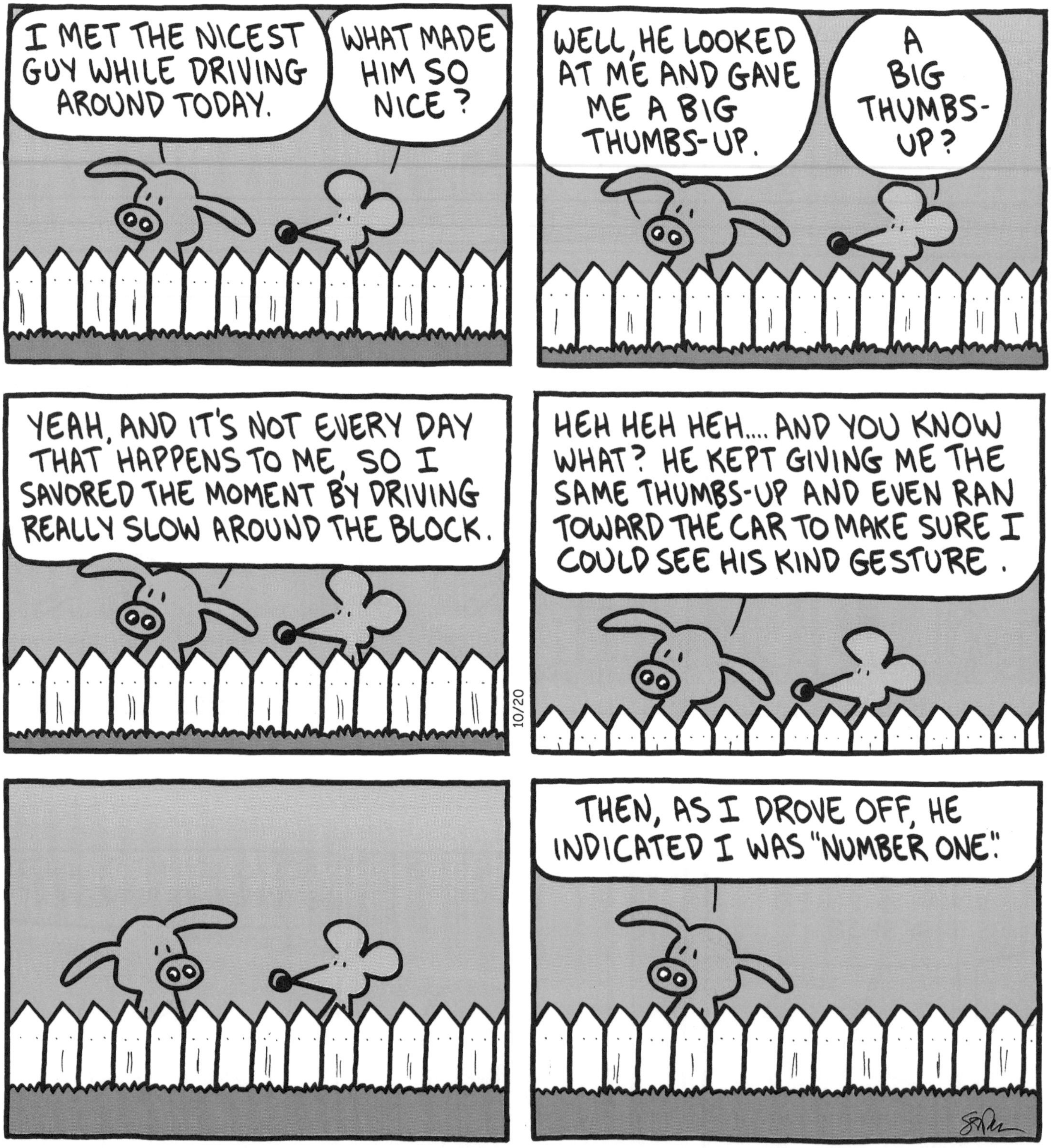
I MET THE NICEST GUY WHILE DRIVING AROUND TODAY.
WHAT MADE HIM SO NICE?
WELL, HE LOOKED AT ME AND GAVE ME A BIG THUMBS-UP.
A BIG THUMBS-UP?
YEAH, AND IT'S NOT EVERY DAY THAT HAPPENS TO ME, SO I SAVORED THE MOMENT BY DRIVING REALLY SLOW AROUND THE BLOCK.
HEH HEH HEH.... AND YOU KNOW WHAT? HE KEPT GIVING ME THE SAME THUMBS-UP AND EVEN RAN TOWARD THE CAR TO MAKE SURE I COULD SEE HIS KIND GESTURE.
THEN, AS I DROVE OFF, HE INDICATED I WAS "NUMBER ONE."
10/20

This strip drew two types of responses: 1) I don't get it; and 2) I get it and I'm mad. One mother in Florida covered both types of responses when she wrote a letter to a Florida newspaper saying it took her three readings to get the joke, but that when she finally did, it made her "hair curl."

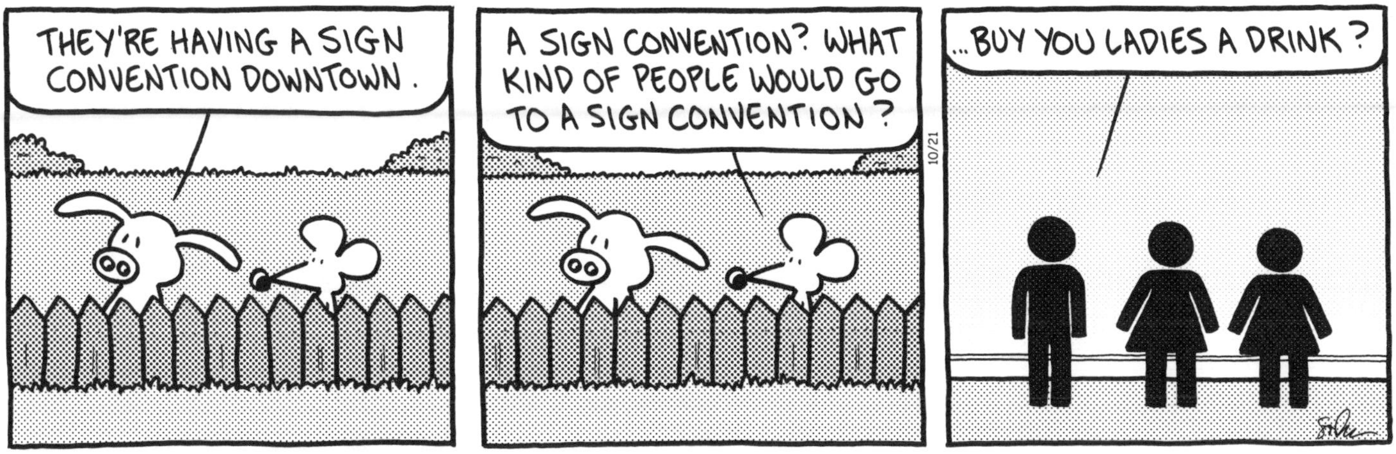
THEY'RE HAVING A SIGN CONVENTION DOWNTOWN.
A SIGN CONVENTION? WHAT KIND OF PEOPLE WOULD GO TO A SIGN CONVENTION?
10/21
...BUY YOU LADIES A DRINK?

I got the idea for this strip while attending a spring training game in Phoenix, Arizona. I'm not sure why I got the idea there, but I do know that while I was there, I thought it would be a good idea to stare at the men's and women's bathroom doors, so I could memorize what those sign guys look like. As it turned out, it was not a good idea, as just about everyone thought I was a perverted psycho.

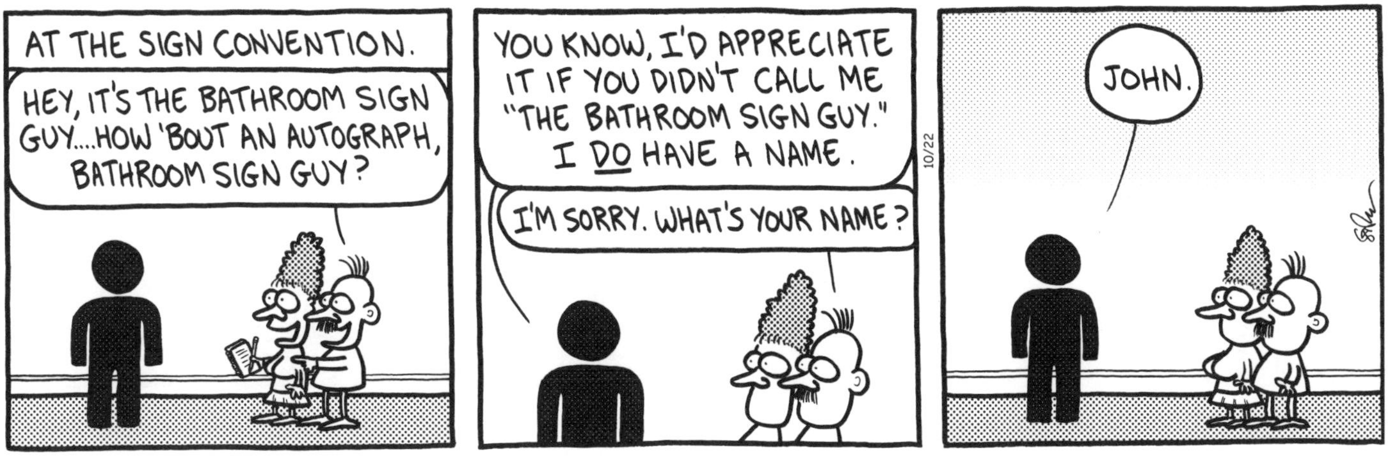
AT THE SIGN CONVENTION.
HEY, IT'S THE BATHROOM SIGN GUY....HOW 'BOUT AN AUTOGRAPH, BATHROOM SIGN GUY?
YOU KNOW, I'D APPRECIATE IT IF YOU DIDN'T CALL ME "THE BATHROOM SIGN GUY." I DO HAVE A NAME.
I'M SORRY. WHAT'S YOUR NAME?
10/22
JOHN.

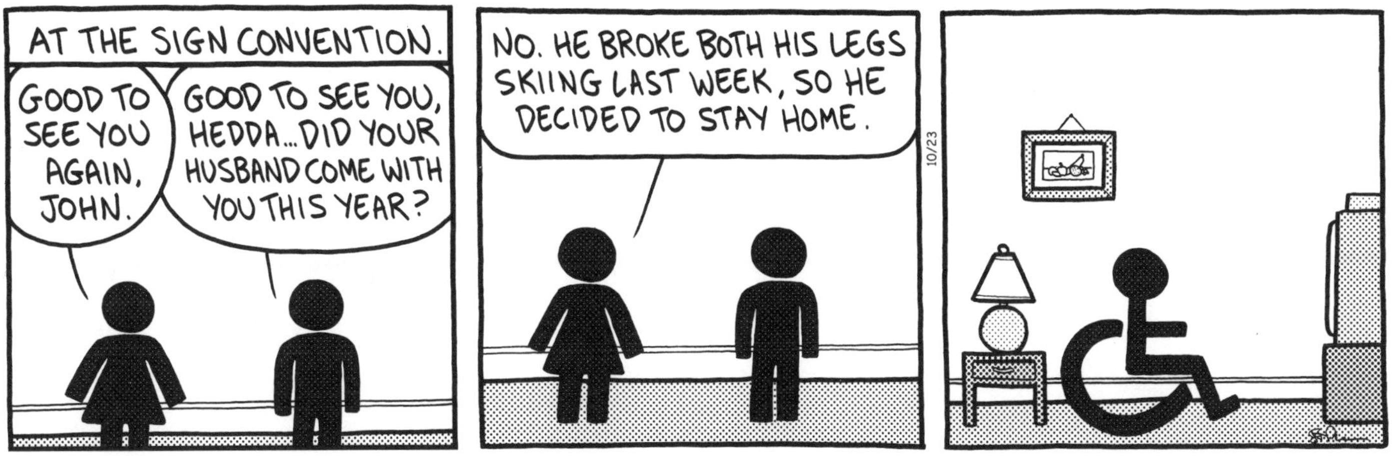
AT THE SIGN CONVENTION.
GOOD TO SEE YOU AGAIN, JOHN.
GOOD TO SEE YOU, HEDDA...DID YOUR HUSBAND COME WITH YOU THIS YEAR?
NO. HE BROKE BOTH HIS LEGS SKIING LAST WEEK, SO HE DECIDED TO STAY HOME.
10/23

The name "Hedda" was also a little joke, as it's based on another term people use for the restroom ("the head"). I was going to name another character "Lou" (the "loo"), but I thought the theme had run its course.

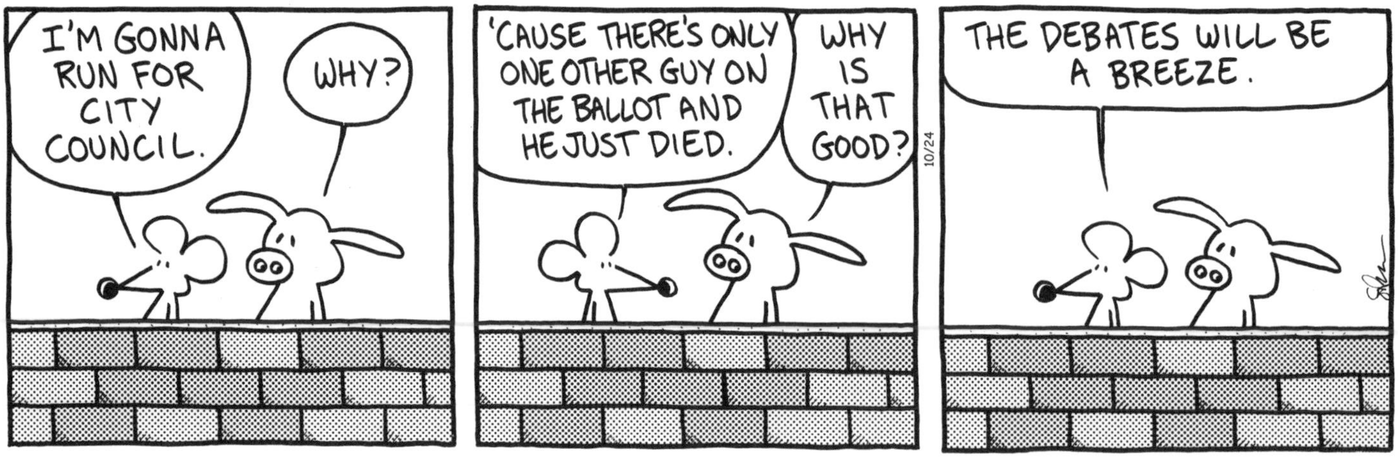
I'M GONNA RUN FOR CITY COUNCIL.
WHY?
'CAUSE THERE'S ONLY ONE OTHER GUY ON THE BALLOT AND HE JUST DIED.
WHY IS THAT GOOD?
10/24
THE DEBATES WILL BE A BREEZE.

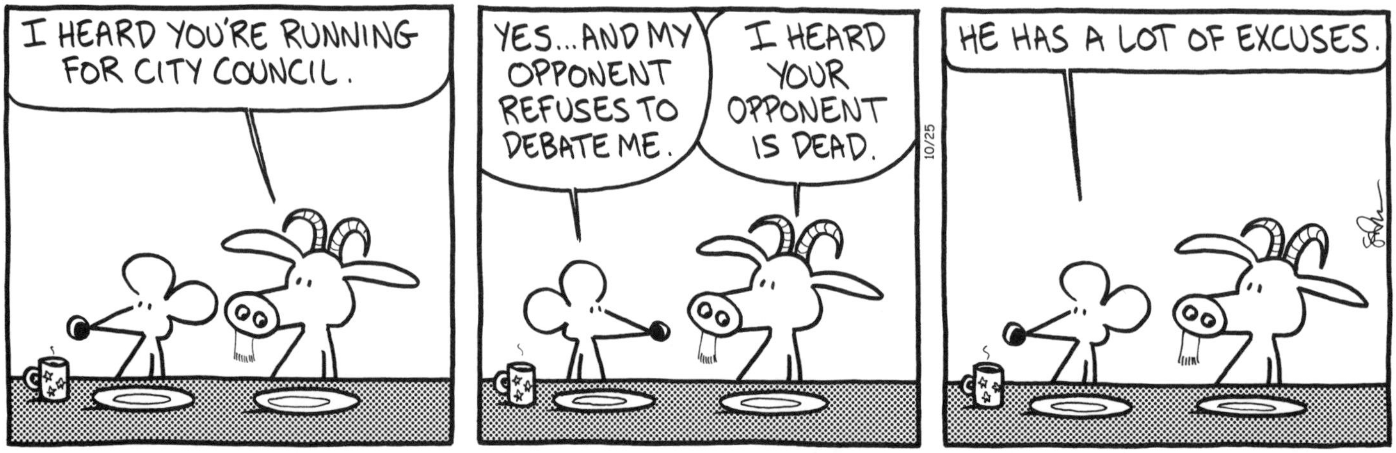
I HEARD YOU'RE RUNNING FOR CITY COUNCIL.
YES...AND MY OPPONENT REFUSES TO DEBATE ME.
I HEARD YOUR OPPONENT IS DEAD.
10/25
HE HAS A LOT OF EXCUSES.

When I originally wrote this series, I got the idea from John Ashcroft's loss to a deceased man in the 2000 Missouri Senate race. However, the series did not actually run until October 2002, and on the second day of the series, Minnesota Senator Paul Wellstone died tragically in a plane crash. As many people don't know that cartoonists work between six and eight weeks ahead of publication (for me, it's even longer, as I'm about ten months ahead of deadline), newspapers feared that readers would think the series was based on Wellstone's death. Thus, many papers nixed the entire remainder of the series.

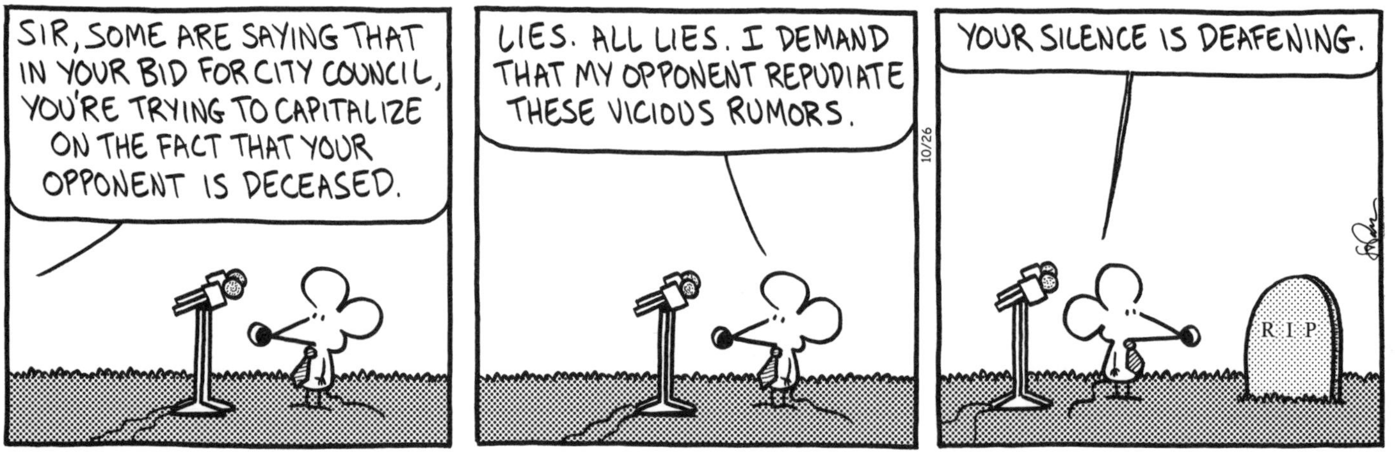
SIR, SOME ARE SAYING THAT IN YOUR BID FOR CITY COUNCIL, YOU'RE TRYING TO CAPITALIZE ON THE FACT THAT YOUR OPPONENT IS DECEASED.
LIES. ALL LIES. I DEMAND THAT MY OPPONENT REPUDIATE THESE VICIOUS RUMORS.
10/26
YOUR SILENCE IS DEAFENING.
R.I.P.

DEAR LIONS,
AS YOU KNOW, MY ZEBRA HERD HAS WRITTEN TO YOU NUMEROUS TIMES TO TRY AND IMPROVE OUR RELATIONSHIP.

GIVEN THAT THESE EFFORTS HAVE NOT BEEN SUCCESSFUL, THE TEMPTATION IS TO BLAME THE OTHER PARTY.

HOWEVER, AS SUCH ACCUSATIONS COULD ONLY BE COUNTER-PRODUCTIVE, WE ZEBRAS HAVE TAKEN IT UPON OURSELVES TO EXAMINE OUR OWN POSSIBLE FAULT IN THIS.

WHY ARE WE CONSTANTLY KILLED?..... PERHAPS WE ARE DEFEATIST... PERHAPS WE HAVE UNRESOLVED CHILDHOOD SCARS THAT CREATE A FEELING OF UNWORTHI-NESS.... PERHAPS WE'RE ENABLERS.

10/27

WE INVITE YOU TO EXAMINE YOUR OWN MOTIVES IN THIS AND REFLECT THOUGHT-FULLY UPON WHY IT IS YOU FEEL COMPELLED TO KILL... WE LOOK FORWARD TO RECEIVING YOUR THOUGHTS.

YOU TASTE GUD.

SIGH.

Another *Peanuts* influence . . . ending strips with a "Sigh."

143

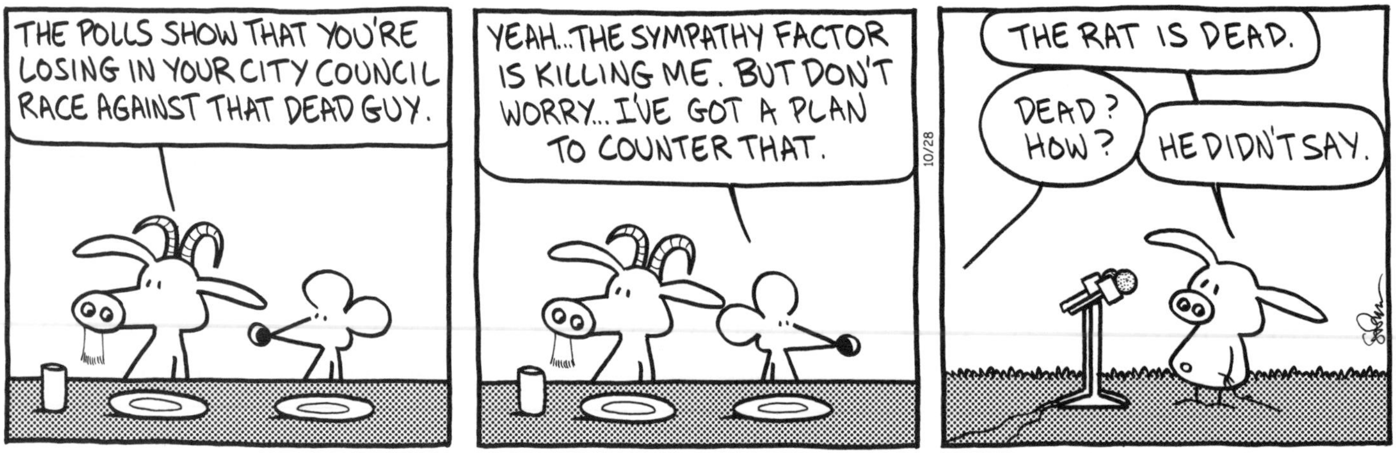
THE POLLS SHOW THAT YOU'RE LOSING IN YOUR CITY COUNCIL RACE AGAINST THAT DEAD GUY.
YEAH...THE SYMPATHY FACTOR IS KILLING ME. BUT DON'T WORRY...I'VE GOT A PLAN TO COUNTER THAT.
10/28
THE RAT IS DEAD.
DEAD? HOW?
HE DIDN'T SAY.

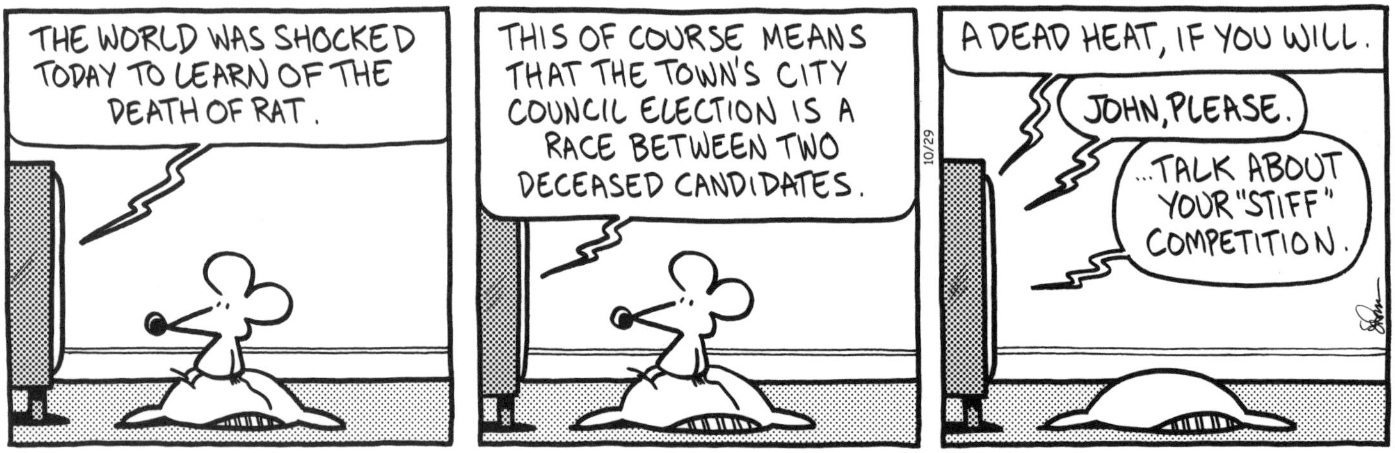
THE WORLD WAS SHOCKED TODAY TO LEARN OF THE DEATH OF RAT.
THIS OF COURSE MEANS THAT THE TOWN'S CITY COUNCIL ELECTION IS A RACE BETWEEN TWO DECEASED CANDIDATES.
10/29
A DEAD HEAT, IF YOU WILL.
JOHN, PLEASE.
...TALK ABOUT YOUR "STIFF" COMPETITION.

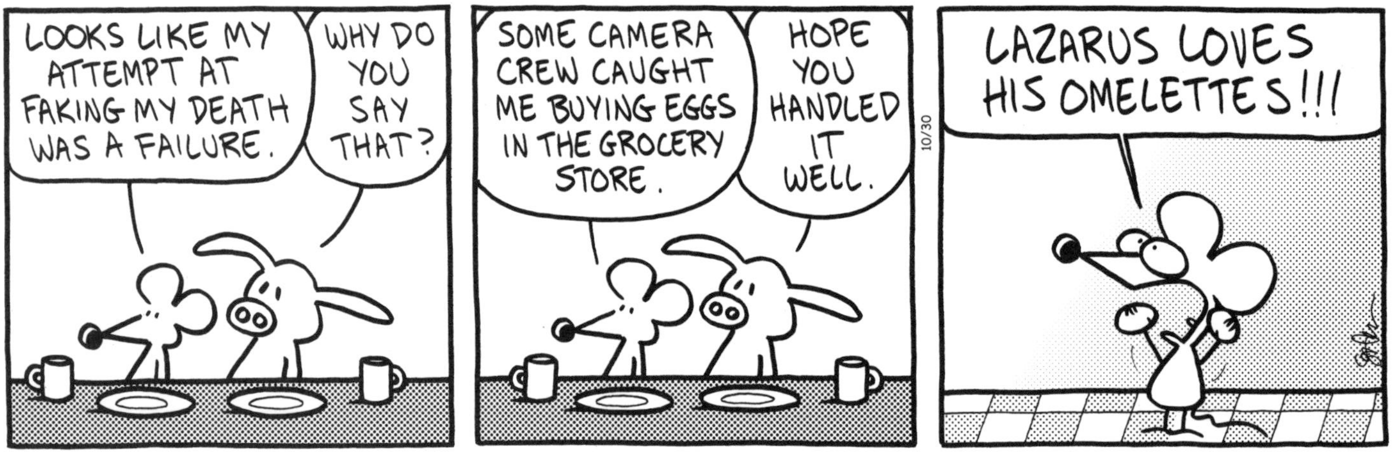
LOOKS LIKE MY ATTEMPT AT FAKING MY DEATH WAS A FAILURE.
WHY DO YOU SAY THAT?
SOME CAMERA CREW CAUGHT ME BUYING EGGS IN THE GROCERY STORE.
HOPE YOU HANDLED IT WELL.
10/30
LAZARUS LOVES HIS OMELETTES!!!

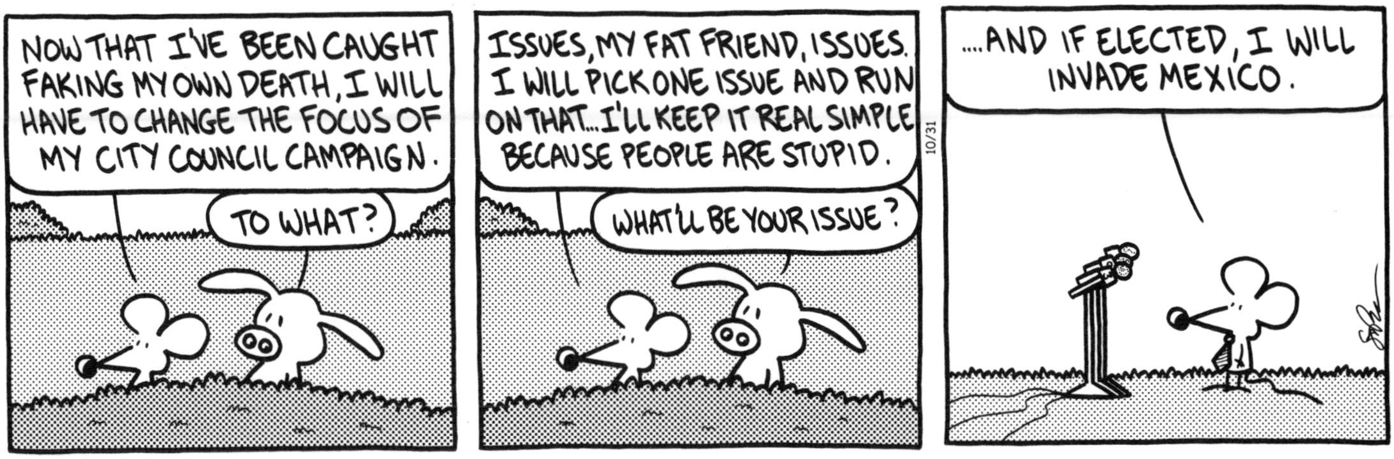
NOW THAT I'VE BEEN CAUGHT FAKING MY OWN DEATH, I WILL HAVE TO CHANGE THE FOCUS OF MY CITY COUNCIL CAMPAIGN.
TO WHAT?
ISSUES, MY FAT FRIEND, ISSUES. I WILL PICK ONE ISSUE AND RUN ON THAT...I'LL KEEP IT REAL SIMPLE BECAUSE PEOPLE ARE STUPID.
WHAT'LL BE YOUR ISSUE?
10/31
....AND IF ELECTED, I WILL INVADE MEXICO.

I like Rat's unapologetic opportunism.

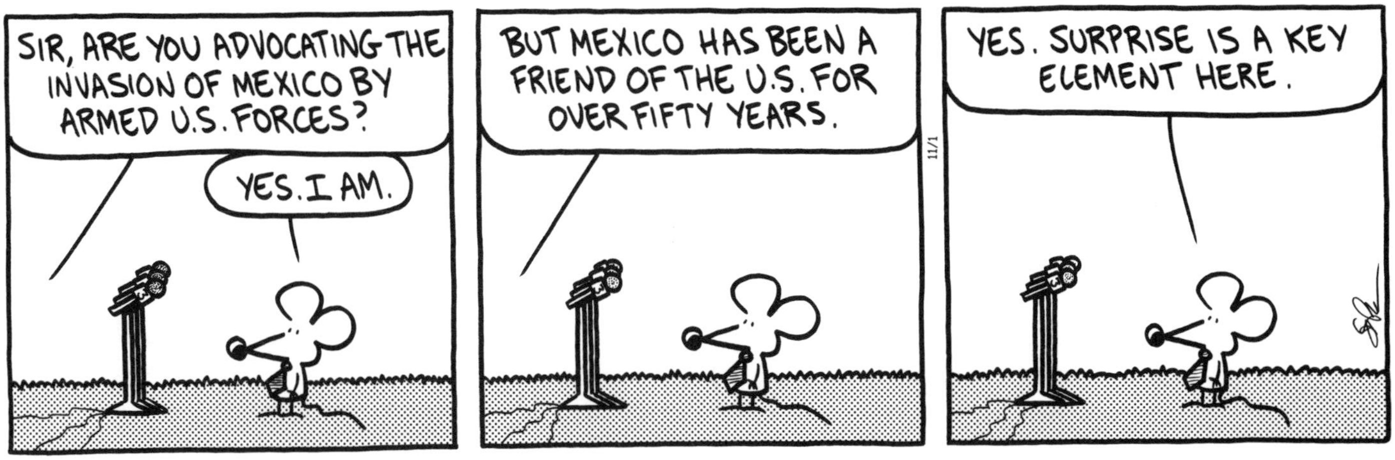
SIR, ARE YOU ADVOCATING THE INVASION OF MEXICO BY ARMED U.S. FORCES?
YES. I AM.
BUT MEXICO HAS BEEN A FRIEND OF THE U.S. FOR OVER FIFTY YEARS.
11/1
YES. SURPRISE IS A KEY ELEMENT HERE.

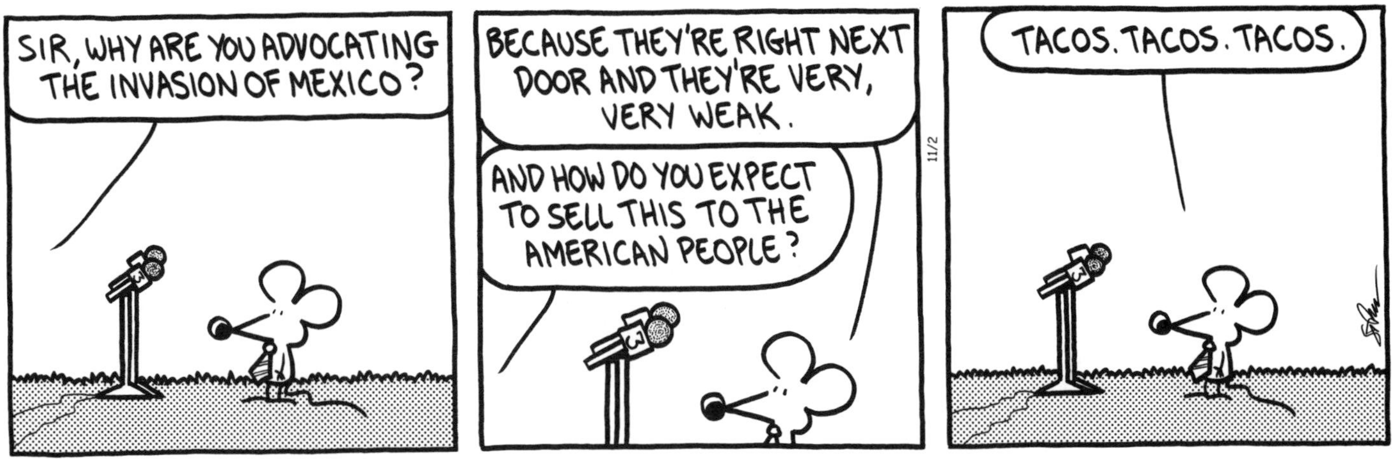
SIR, WHY ARE YOU ADVOCATING THE INVASION OF MEXICO?
BECAUSE THEY'RE RIGHT NEXT DOOR AND THEY'RE VERY, VERY WEAK.
AND HOW DO YOU EXPECT TO SELL THIS TO THE AMERICAN PEOPLE?
11/2
TACOS. TACOS. TACOS.

Change "Mexico" to "Iraq," change "they're right next door" to "they've got oil," and change "tacos" to "WMDs," and you have one very prescient little comic strip.

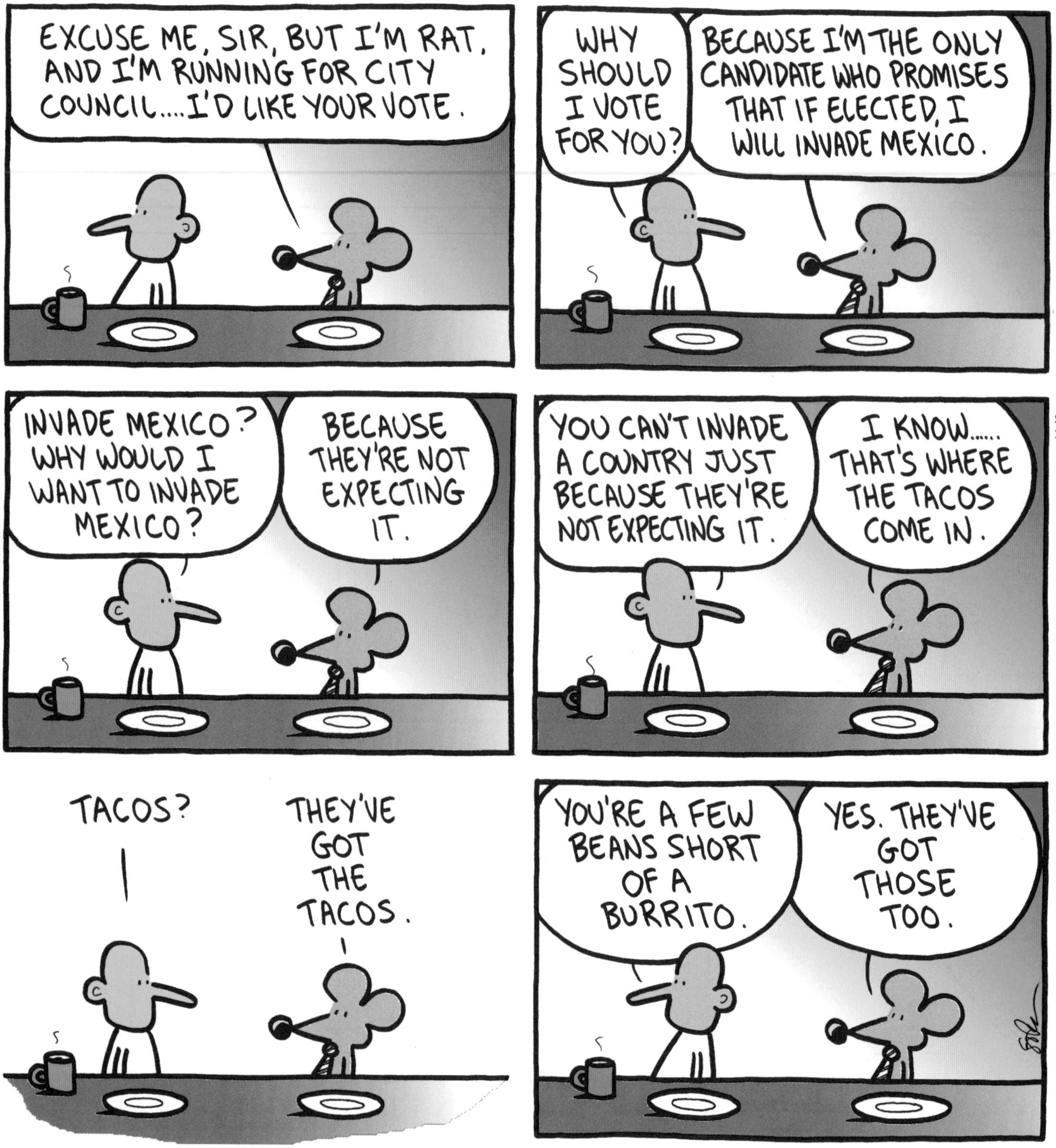
EXCUSE ME, SIR, BUT I'M RAT, AND I'M RUNNING FOR CITY COUNCIL....I'D LIKE YOUR VOTE.
WHY SHOULD I VOTE FOR YOU?
BECAUSE I'M THE ONLY CANDIDATE WHO PROMISES THAT IF ELECTED, I WILL INVADE MEXICO.
INVADE MEXICO? WHY WOULD I WANT TO INVADE MEXICO?
BECAUSE THEY'RE NOT EXPECTING IT.
YOU CAN'T INVADE A COUNTRY JUST BECAUSE THEY'RE NOT EXPECTING IT.
I KNOW...... THAT'S WHERE THE TACOS COME IN.
TACOS?
THEY'VE GOT THE TACOS.
YOU'RE A FEW BEANS SHORT OF A BURRITO.
YES. THEY'VE GOT THOSE TOO.

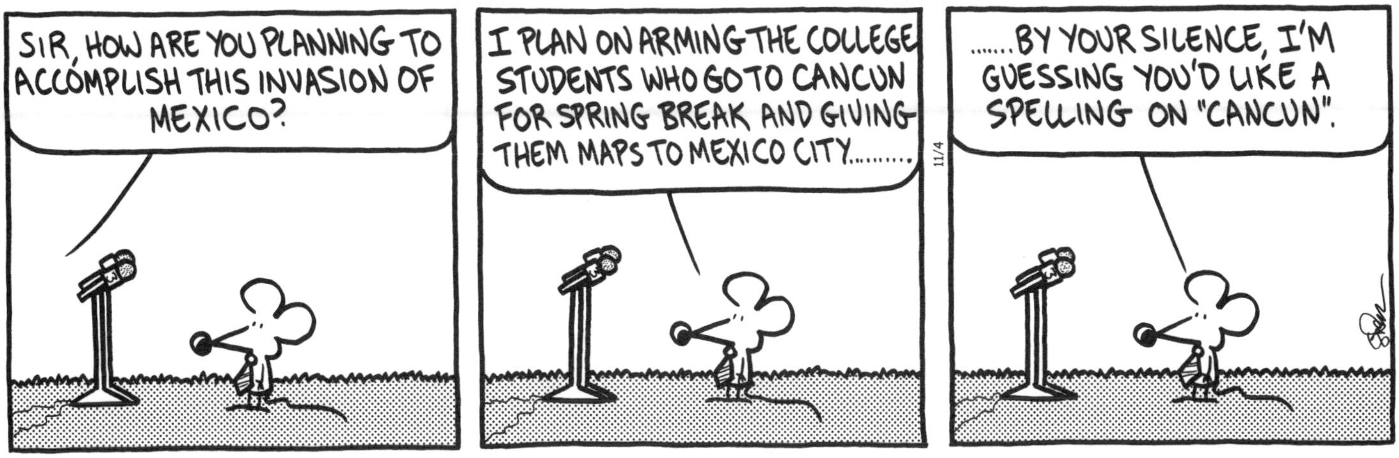
SIR, HOW ARE YOU PLANNING TO ACCOMPLISH THIS INVASION OF MEXICO?
I PLAN ON ARMING THE COLLEGE STUDENTS WHO GO TO CANCUN FOR SPRING BREAK AND GIVING THEM MAPS TO MEXICO CITY.........
11/4
.......BY YOUR SILENCE, I'M GUESSING YOU'D LIKE A SPELLING ON "CANCUN".

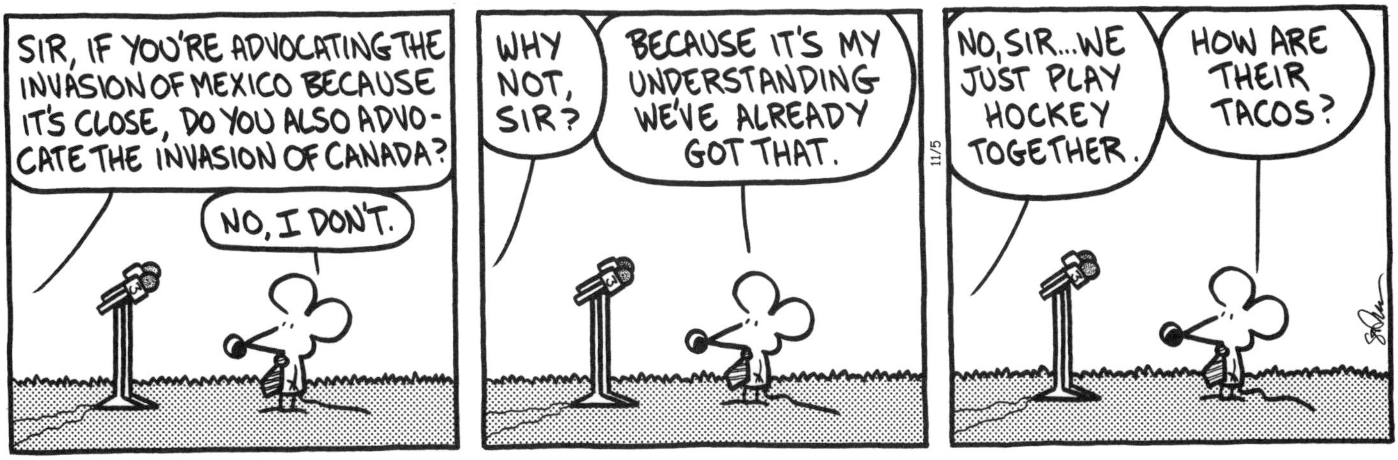
SIR, IF YOU'RE ADVOCATING THE INVASION OF MEXICO BECAUSE IT'S CLOSE, DO YOU ALSO ADVOCATE THE INVASION OF CANADA?
NO, I DON'T.
WHY NOT, SIR?
BECAUSE IT'S MY UNDERSTANDING WE'VE ALREADY GOT THAT.
11/5
NO, SIR...WE JUST PLAY HOCKEY TOGETHER.
HOW ARE THEIR TACOS?

I didn't get a single Canadian complaint on this one. What a nice people.

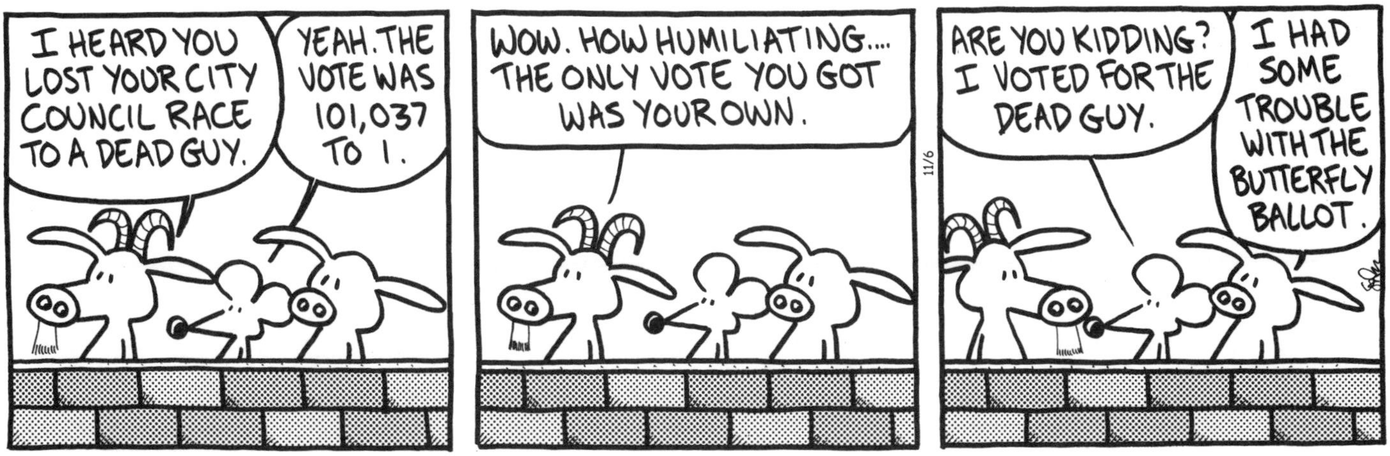
I HEARD YOU LOST YOUR CITY COUNCIL RACE TO A DEAD GUY.
YEAH. THE VOTE WAS 101,037 TO 1.
WOW. HOW HUMILIATING.... THE ONLY VOTE YOU GOT WAS YOUR OWN.
11/6
ARE YOU KIDDING? I VOTED FOR THE DEAD GUY.
I HAD SOME TROUBLE WITH THE BUTTERFLY BALLOT.

My lone reference to the 2000 U.S. presidential election.

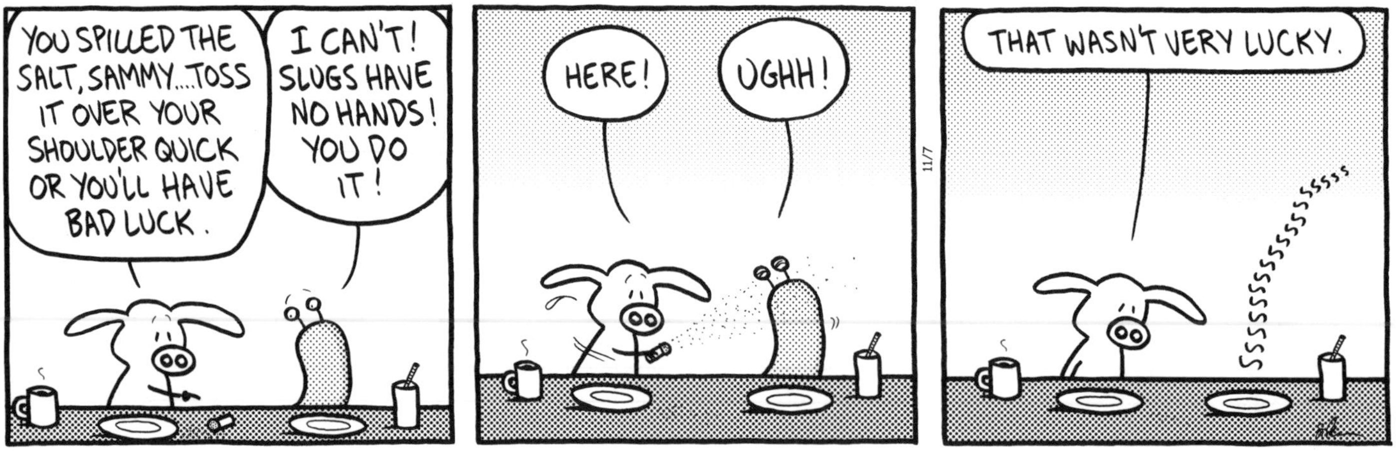
YOU SPILLED THE SALT, SAMMY...TOSS IT OVER YOUR SHOULDER QUICK OR YOU'LL HAVE BAD LUCK.
I CAN'T! SLUGS HAVE NO HANDS! YOU DO IT!
11/7
HERE!
UGHH!
THAT WASN'T VERY LUCKY.
SSSSSSSSSSSSSSSSSS

This was a very popular strip. It eventually got turned into an animated greeting card on my syndicate's Web site. I think the card said, "Better luck next time."

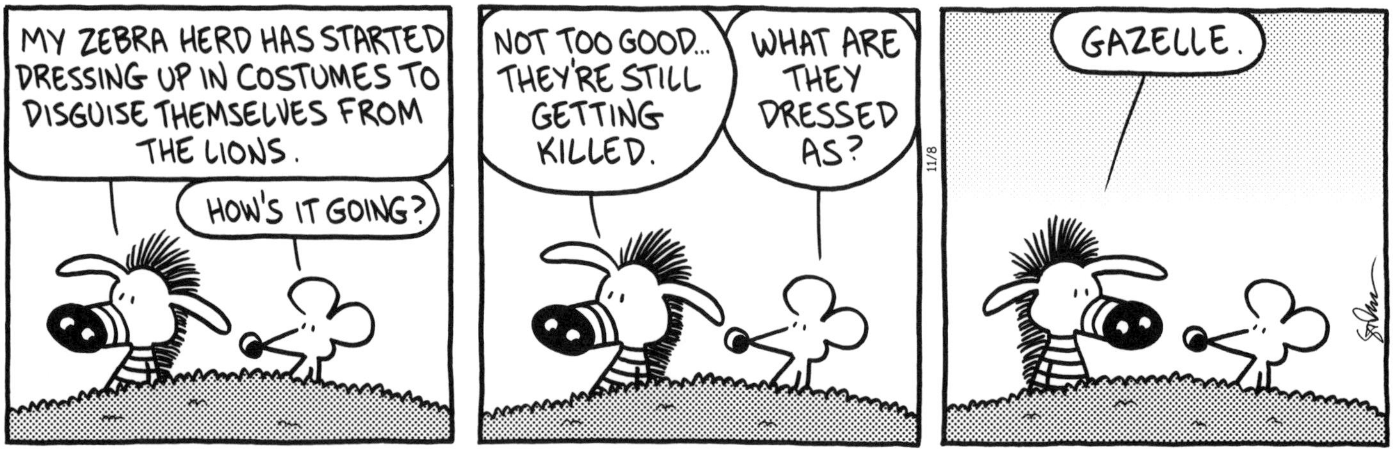
MY ZEBRA HERD HAS STARTED DRESSING UP IN COSTUMES TO DISGUISE THEMSELVES FROM THE LIONS.
HOW'S IT GOING?
11/8
NOT TOO GOOD... THEY'RE STILL GETTING KILLED.
WHAT ARE THEY DRESSED AS?
GAZELLE.

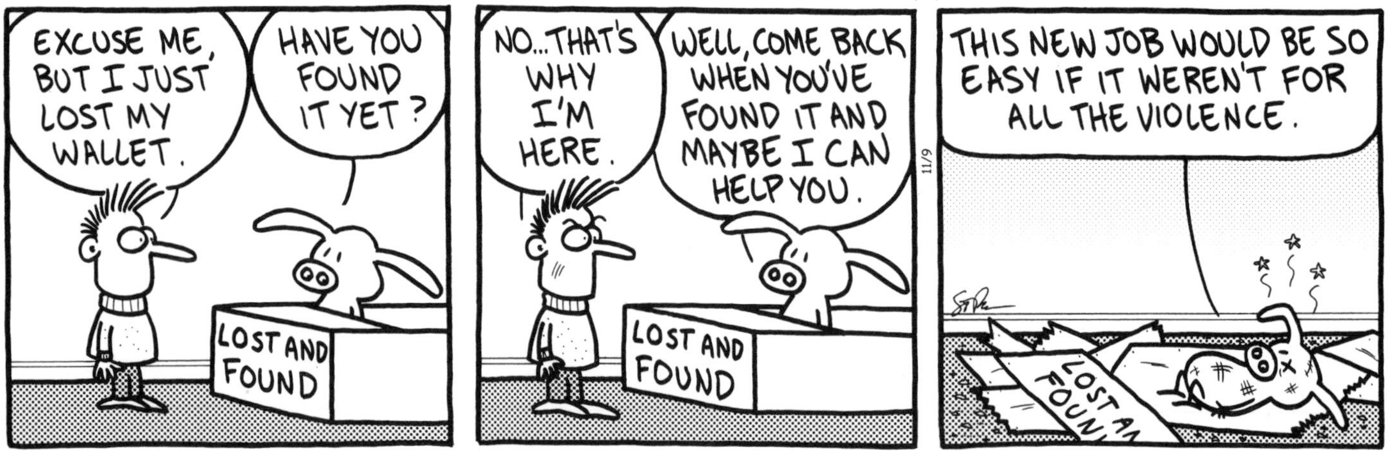
EXCUSE ME, BUT I JUST LOST MY WALLET.
HAVE YOU FOUND IT YET?
LOST AND FOUND
11/9
NO...THAT'S WHY I'M HERE.
WELL, COME BACK WHEN YOU'VE FOUND IT AND MAYBE I CAN HELP YOU.
LOST AND FOUND
THIS NEW JOB WOULD BE SO EASY IF IT WEREN'T FOR ALL THE VIOLENCE.

Take a close look at the "Lost and Found" booth, and you will see that I have again broken all laws of perspective. I'm sort of proud of that.

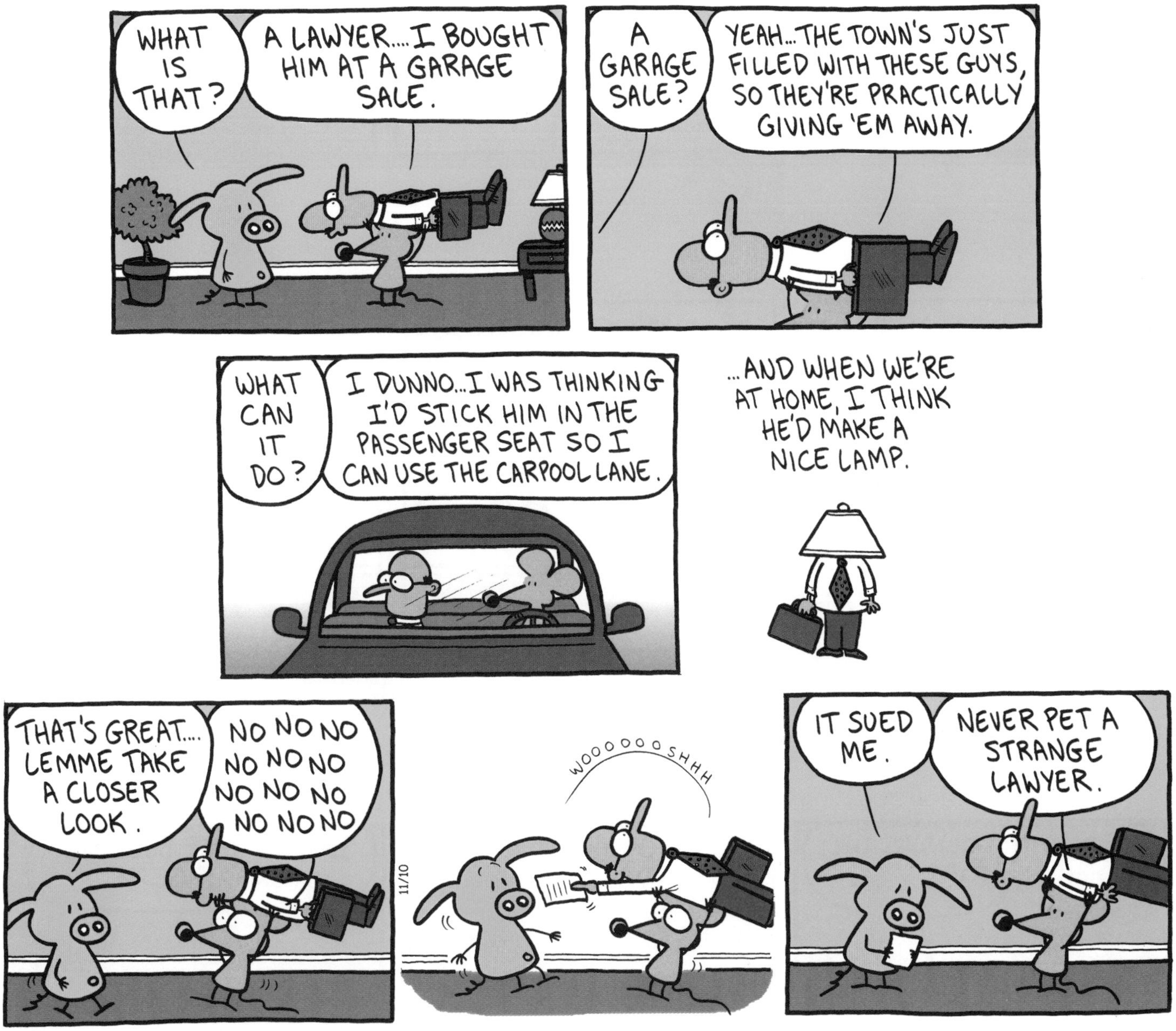
WHAT IS THAT?
A LAWYER.... I BOUGHT HIM AT A GARAGE SALE.
A GARAGE SALE?
YEAH... THE TOWN'S JUST FILLED WITH THESE GUYS, SO THEY'RE PRACTICALLY GIVING 'EM AWAY.
WHAT CAN IT DO?
I DUNNO... I WAS THINKING I'D STICK HIM IN THE PASSENGER SEAT SO I CAN USE THE CARPOOL LANE.
...AND WHEN WE'RE AT HOME, I THINK HE'D MAKE A NICE LAMP.
THAT'S GREAT.... LEMME TAKE A CLOSER LOOK.
NO NO NO NO NO NO NO NO NO NO NO NO
11/10
WOOOOOOSHHH
IT SUED ME.
NEVER PET A STRANGE LAWYER.

Sometimes I can't help taking shots at my old profession. It's fun.

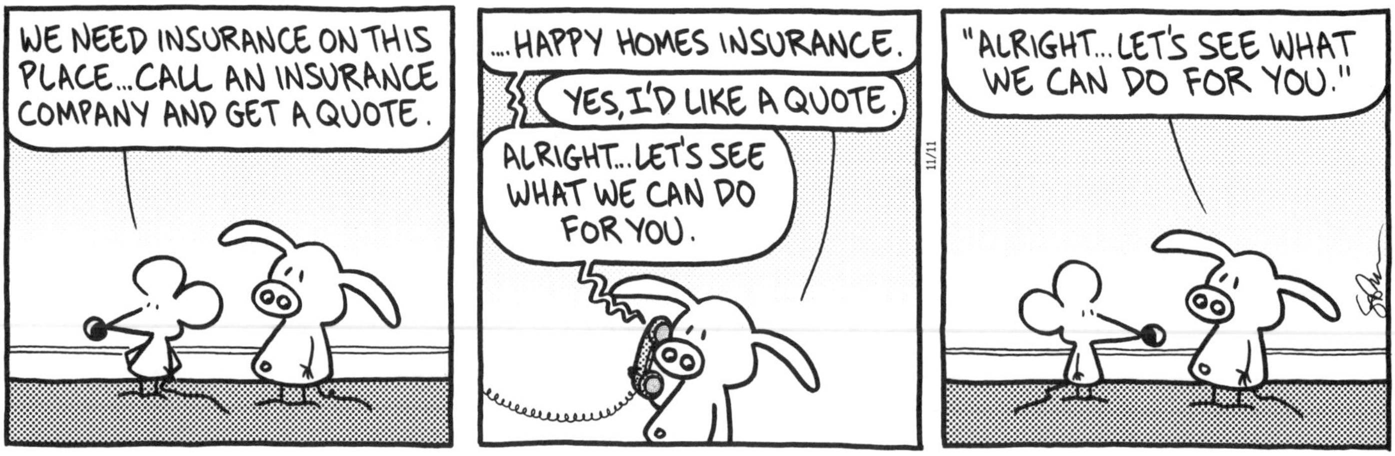
WE NEED INSURANCE ON THIS PLACE...CALL AN INSURANCE COMPANY AND GET A QUOTE.
....HAPPY HOMES INSURANCE.
YES, I'D LIKE A QUOTE.
ALRIGHT...LET'S SEE WHAT WE CAN DO FOR YOU.
11/11
"ALRIGHT... LET'S SEE WHAT WE CAN DO FOR YOU."

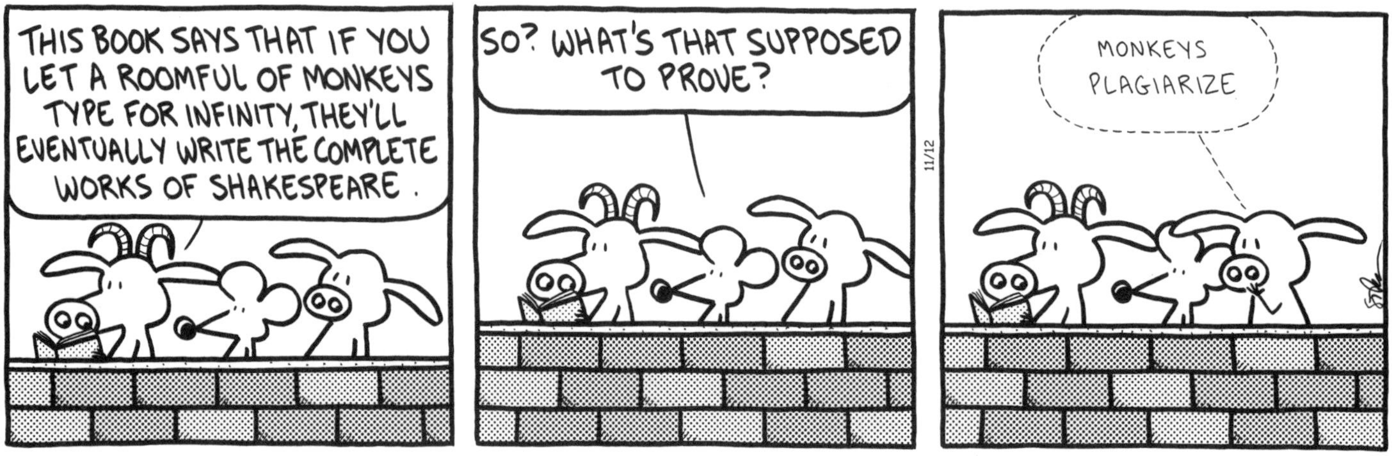
THIS BOOK SAYS THAT IF YOU LET A ROOMFUL OF MONKEYS TYPE FOR INFINITY, THEY'LL EVENTUALLY WRITE THE COMPLETE WORKS OF SHAKESPEARE.
SO? WHAT'S THAT SUPPOSED TO PROVE?
11/12
MONKEYS PLAGIARIZE

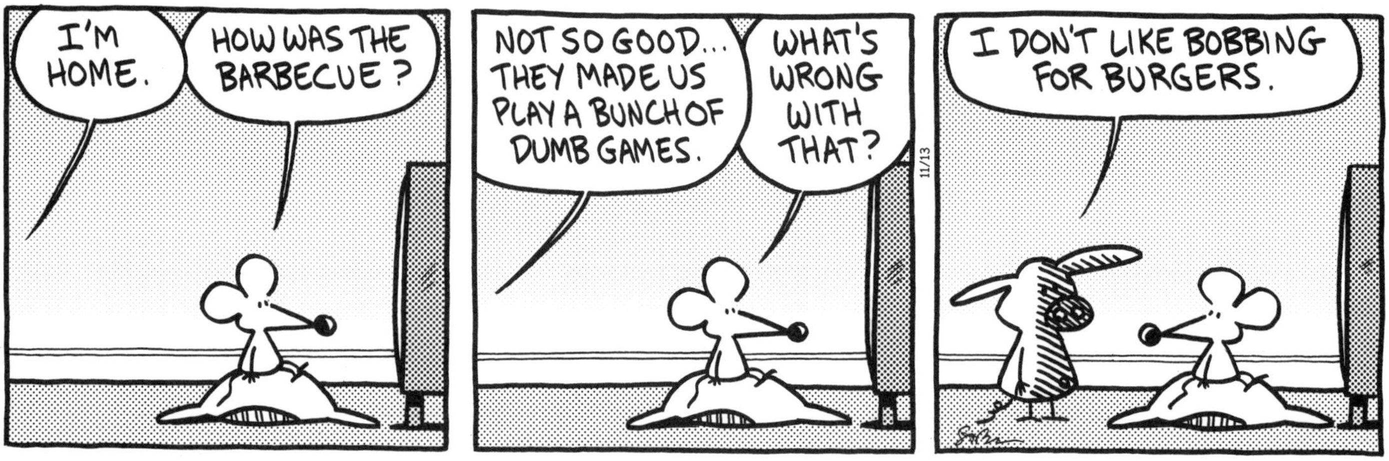
I'M HOME.
HOW WAS THE BARBECUE?
NOT SO GOOD... THEY MADE US PLAY A BUNCH OF DUMB GAMES.
WHAT'S WRONG WITH THAT?
11/13
I DON'T LIKE BOBBING FOR BURGERS.

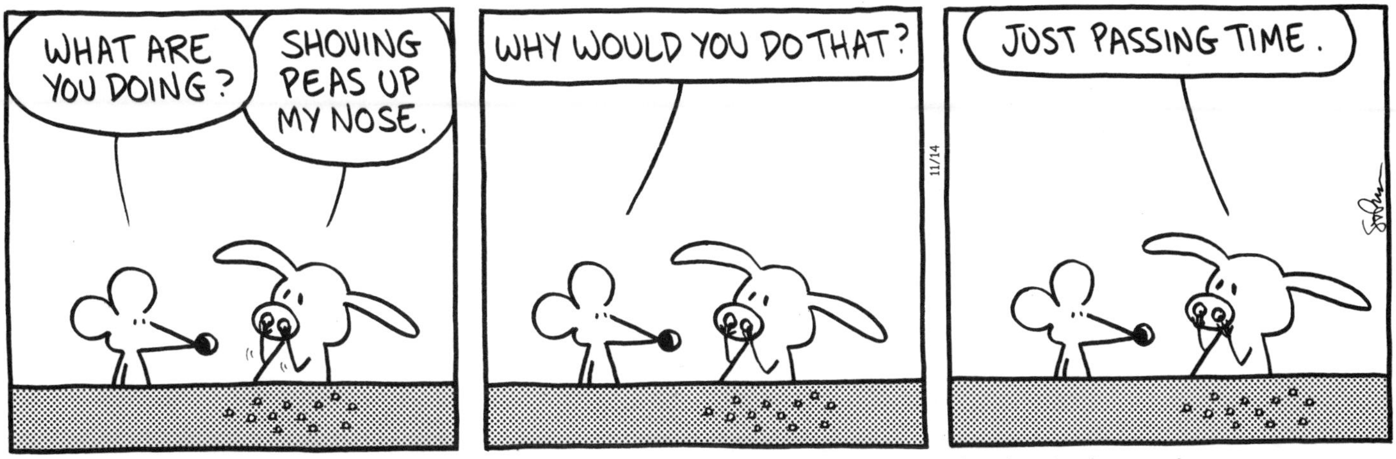
WHAT ARE YOU DOING?
SHOVING PEAS UP MY NOSE.
WHY WOULD YOU DO THAT?
11/14
JUST PASSING TIME.

This was another popular daily strip. I think it's a good example of not being afraid to look stupid in your comic strip. It seems that a lot of comic strip creators go out of their way to show you they're smart (or at least smarter than their characters). Sometimes I think it's fun to just let stupid be stupid.

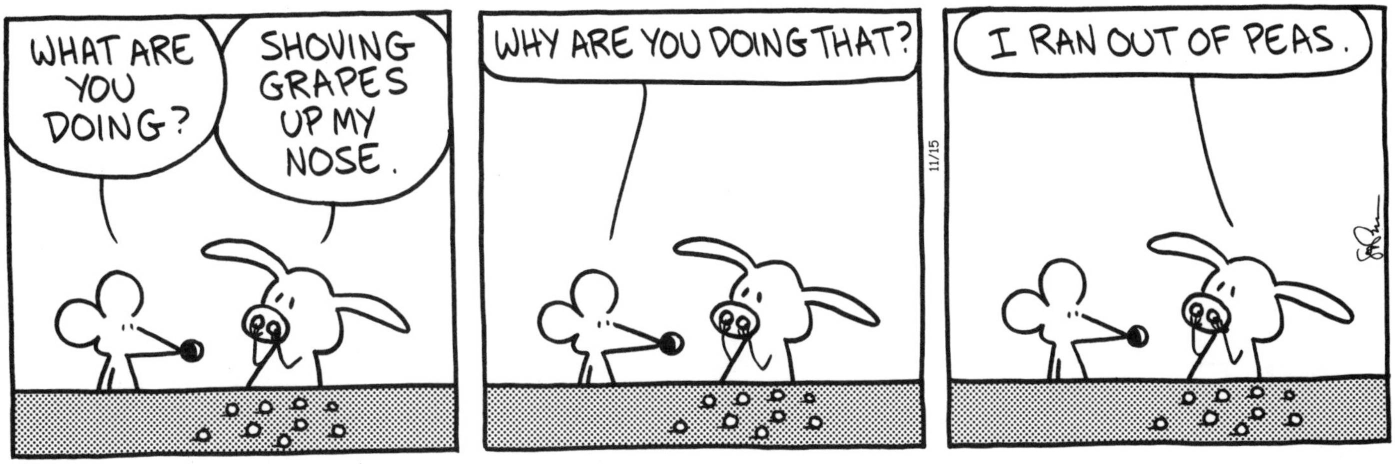
WHAT ARE YOU DOING?
SHOVING GRAPES UP MY NOSE.
WHY ARE YOU DOING THAT?
11/15
I RAN OUT OF PEAS.

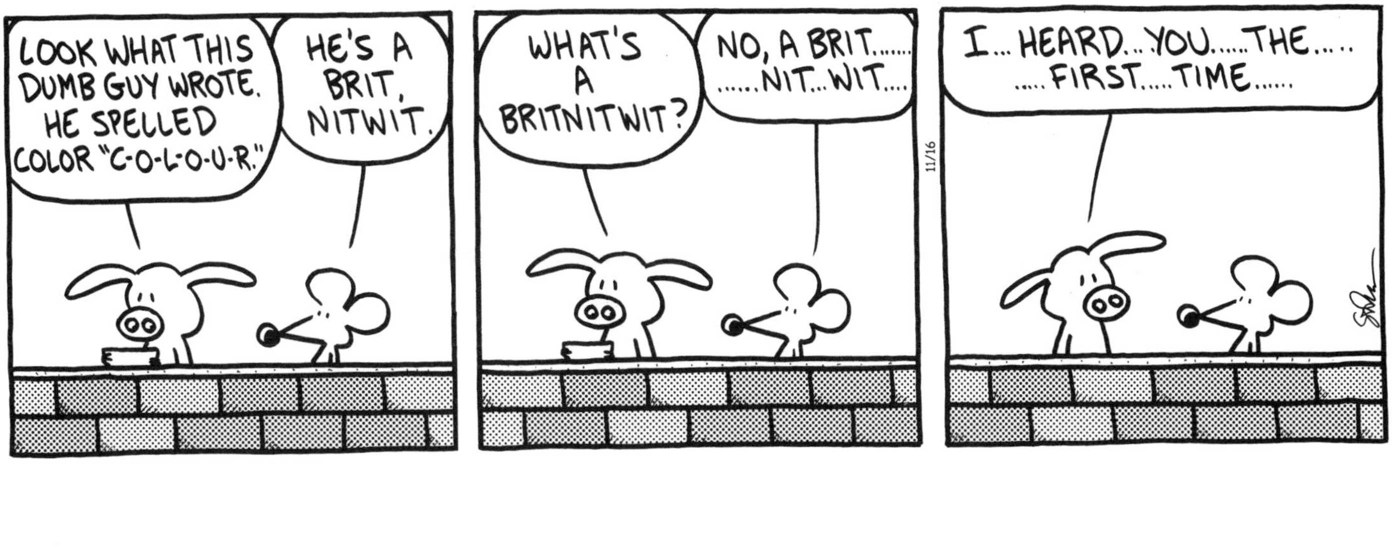
LOOK WHAT THIS DUMB GUY WROTE. HE SPELLED COLOR "C-O-L-O-U-R."
HE'S A BRIT, NITWIT.
WHAT'S A BRITNITWIT?
NO, A BRIT...... ......NIT...WIT....
11/16
I... HEARD... YOU...... THE..... ..... FIRST..... TIME......

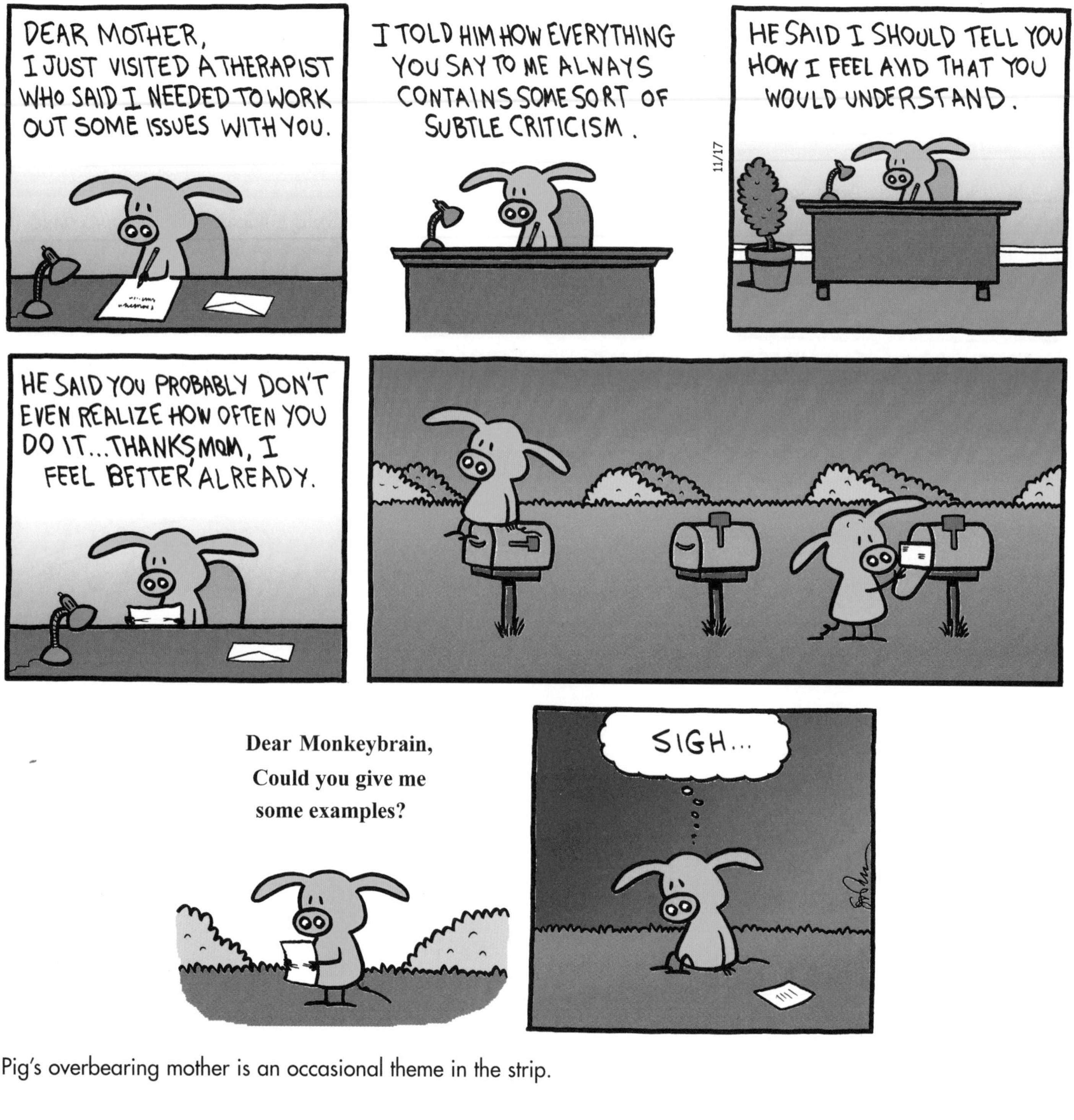
DEAR MOTHER,
I JUST VISITED A THERAPIST WHO SAID I NEEDED TO WORK OUT SOME ISSUES WITH YOU.
I TOLD HIM HOW EVERYTHING YOU SAY TO ME ALWAYS CONTAINS SOME SORT OF SUBTLE CRITICISM.
11/17
HE SAID I SHOULD TELL YOU HOW I FEEL AND THAT YOU WOULD UNDERSTAND.
HE SAID YOU PROBABLY DON'T EVEN REALIZE HOW OFTEN YOU DO IT...THANKS, MOM, I FEEL BETTER ALREADY.
Dear Monkeybrain,
Could you give me some examples?
SIGH...

Pig's overbearing mother is an occasional theme in the strip.

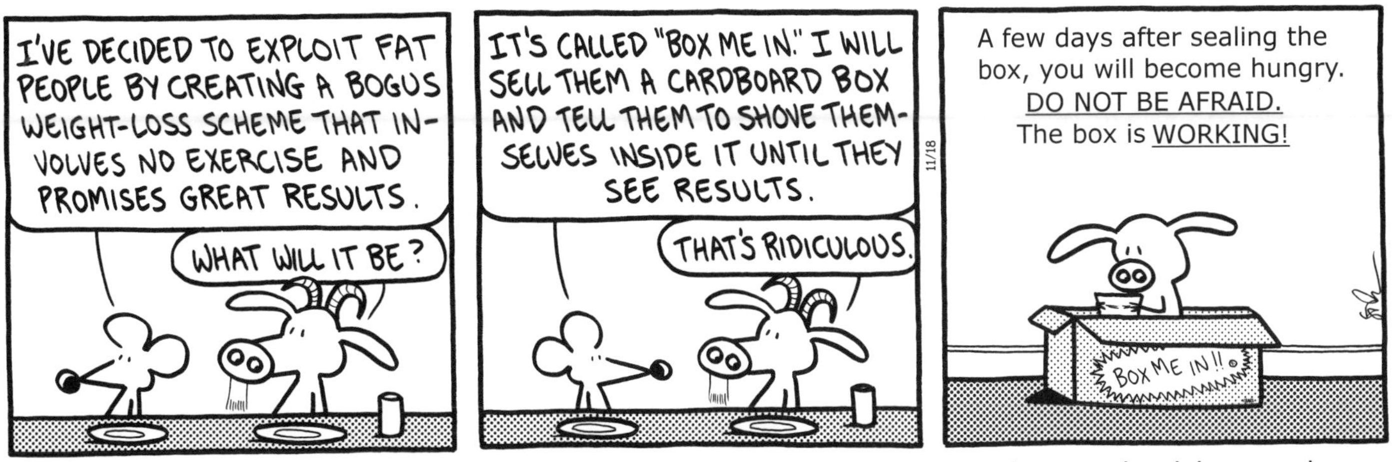
I'VE DECIDED TO EXPLOIT FAT PEOPLE BY CREATING A BOGUS WEIGHT-LOSS SCHEME THAT INVOLVES NO EXERCISE AND PROMISES GREAT RESULTS.
WHAT WILL IT BE?
IT'S CALLED "BOX ME IN." I WILL SELL THEM A CARDBOARD BOX AND TELL THEM TO SHOVE THEMSELVES INSIDE IT UNTIL THEY SEE RESULTS.
THAT'S RIDICULOUS.
11/18
A few days after sealing the box, you will become hungry.
DO NOT BE AFRAID.
The box is WORKING!
BOX ME IN!!

I wrote this series after seeing umpteen late-night ads for products that allow you to lose weight while expending virtually no effort.

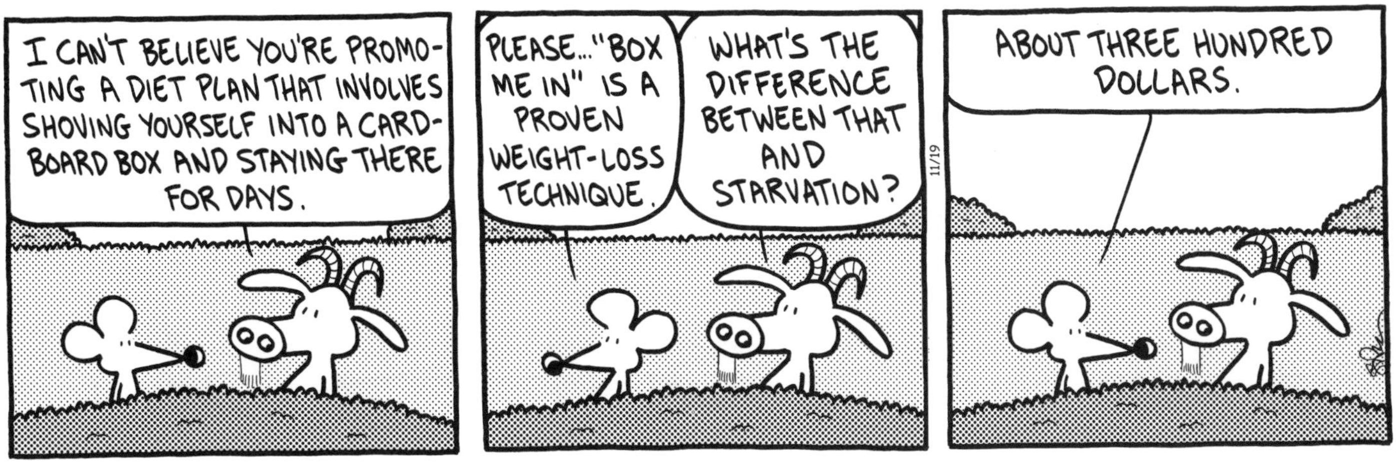
I CAN'T BELIEVE YOU'RE PROMOTING A DIET PLAN THAT INVOLVES SHOVING YOURSELF INTO A CARDBOARD BOX AND STAYING THERE FOR DAYS.
PLEASE... "BOX ME IN" IS A PROVEN WEIGHT-LOSS TECHNIQUE.
WHAT'S THE DIFFERENCE BETWEEN THAT AND STARVATION?
11/19
ABOUT THREE HUNDRED DOLLARS.

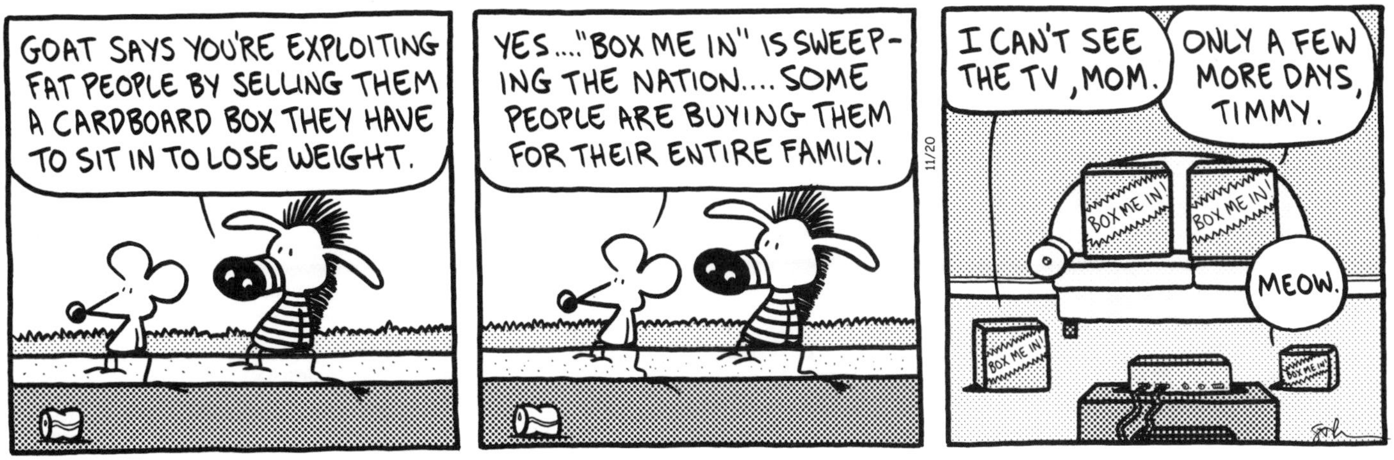
GOAT SAYS YOU'RE EXPLOITING FAT PEOPLE BY SELLING THEM A CARDBOARD BOX THEY HAVE TO SIT IN TO LOSE WEIGHT.
YES.... "BOX ME IN" IS SWEEPING THE NATION.... SOME PEOPLE ARE BUYING THEM FOR THEIR ENTIRE FAMILY.
11/20
I CAN'T SEE THE TV, MOM.
ONLY A FEW MORE DAYS, TIMMY.
BOX ME IN!
BOX ME IN!
MEOW.
BOX ME IN!
BOX ME IN!

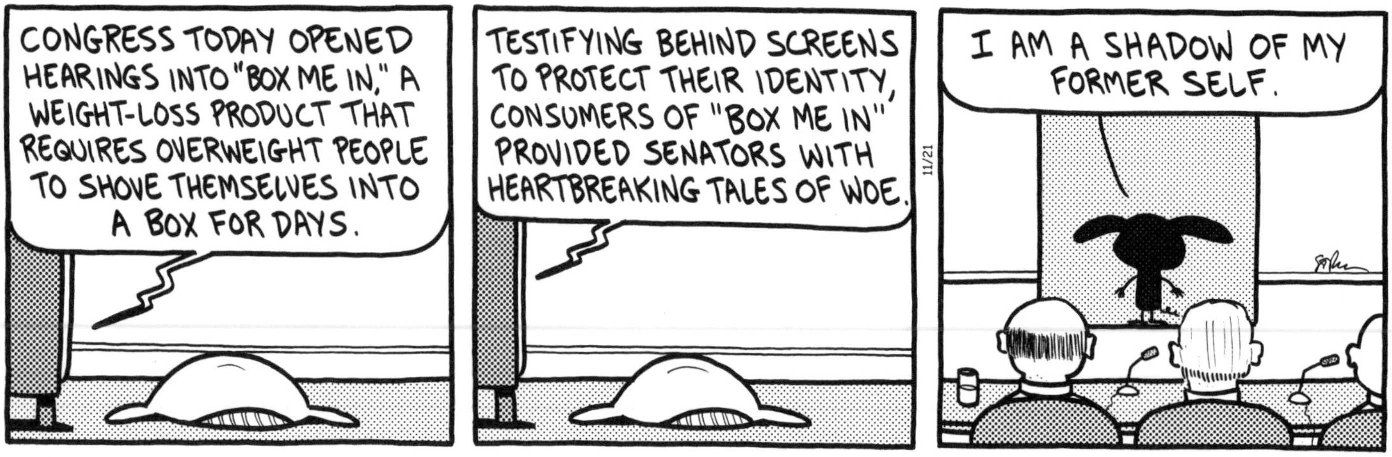
CONGRESS TODAY OPENED HEARINGS INTO "BOX ME IN," A WEIGHT-LOSS PRODUCT THAT REQUIRES OVERWEIGHT PEOPLE TO SHOVE THEMSELVES INTO A BOX FOR DAYS.
TESTIFYING BEHIND SCREENS TO PROTECT THEIR IDENTITY, CONSUMERS OF "BOX ME IN" PROVIDED SENATORS WITH HEARTBREAKING TALES OF WOE.
11/21
I AM A SHADOW OF MY FORMER SELF.

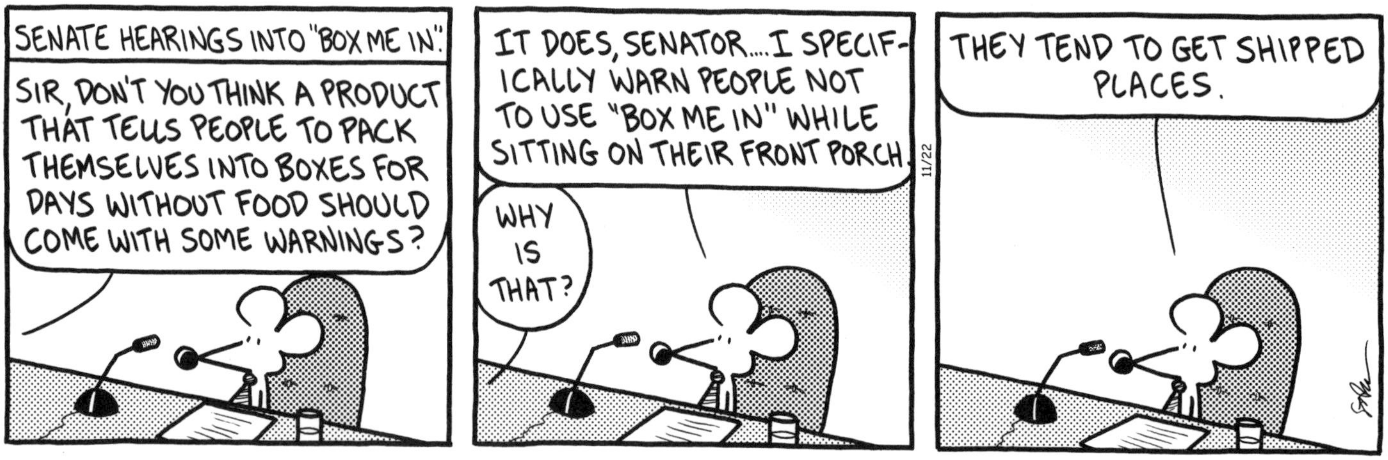
SENATE HEARINGS INTO "BOX ME IN".
SIR, DON'T YOU THINK A PRODUCT THAT TELLS PEOPLE TO PACK THEMSELVES INTO BOXES FOR DAYS WITHOUT FOOD SHOULD COME WITH SOME WARNINGS?
IT DOES, SENATOR.... I SPECIFICALLY WARN PEOPLE NOT TO USE "BOX ME IN" WHILE SITTING ON THEIR FRONT PORCH.
WHY IS THAT?
11/22
THEY TEND TO GET SHIPPED PLACES.

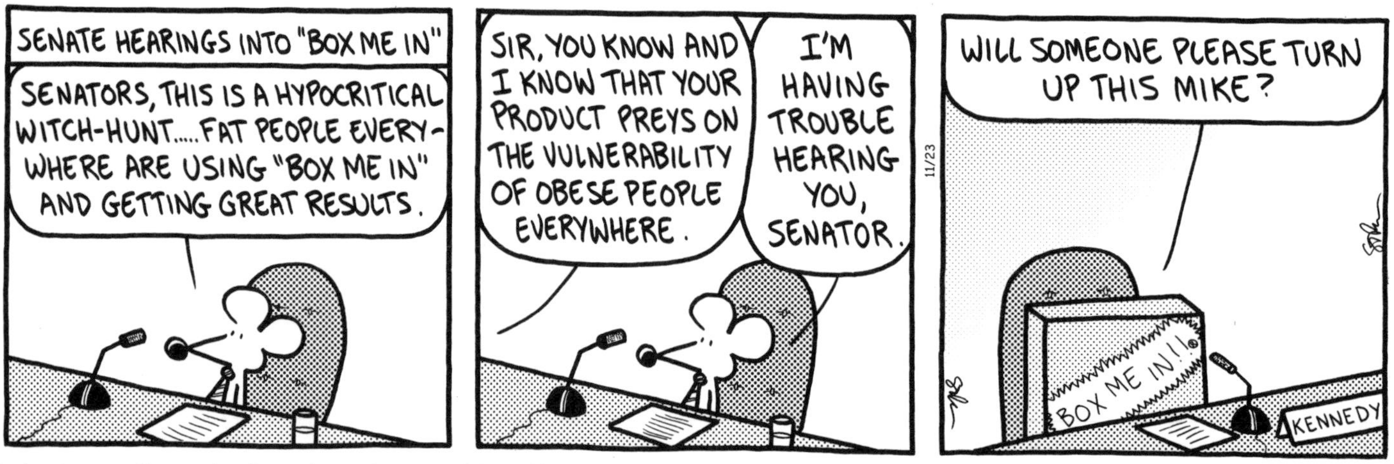
SENATE HEARINGS INTO "BOX ME IN"
SENATORS, THIS IS A HYPOCRITICAL WITCH-HUNT..... FAT PEOPLE EVERYWHERE ARE USING "BOX ME IN" AND GETTING GREAT RESULTS.
SIR, YOU KNOW AND I KNOW THAT YOUR PRODUCT PREYS ON THE VULNERABILITY OF OBESE PEOPLE EVERYWHERE.
I'M HAVING TROUBLE HEARING YOU, SENATOR.
11/23
WILL SOMEONE PLEASE TURN UP THIS MIKE?
BOX ME IN!!®
KENNEDY

I don't usually make fat jokes about public officials, but I needed a cheap and easy way to end this series.

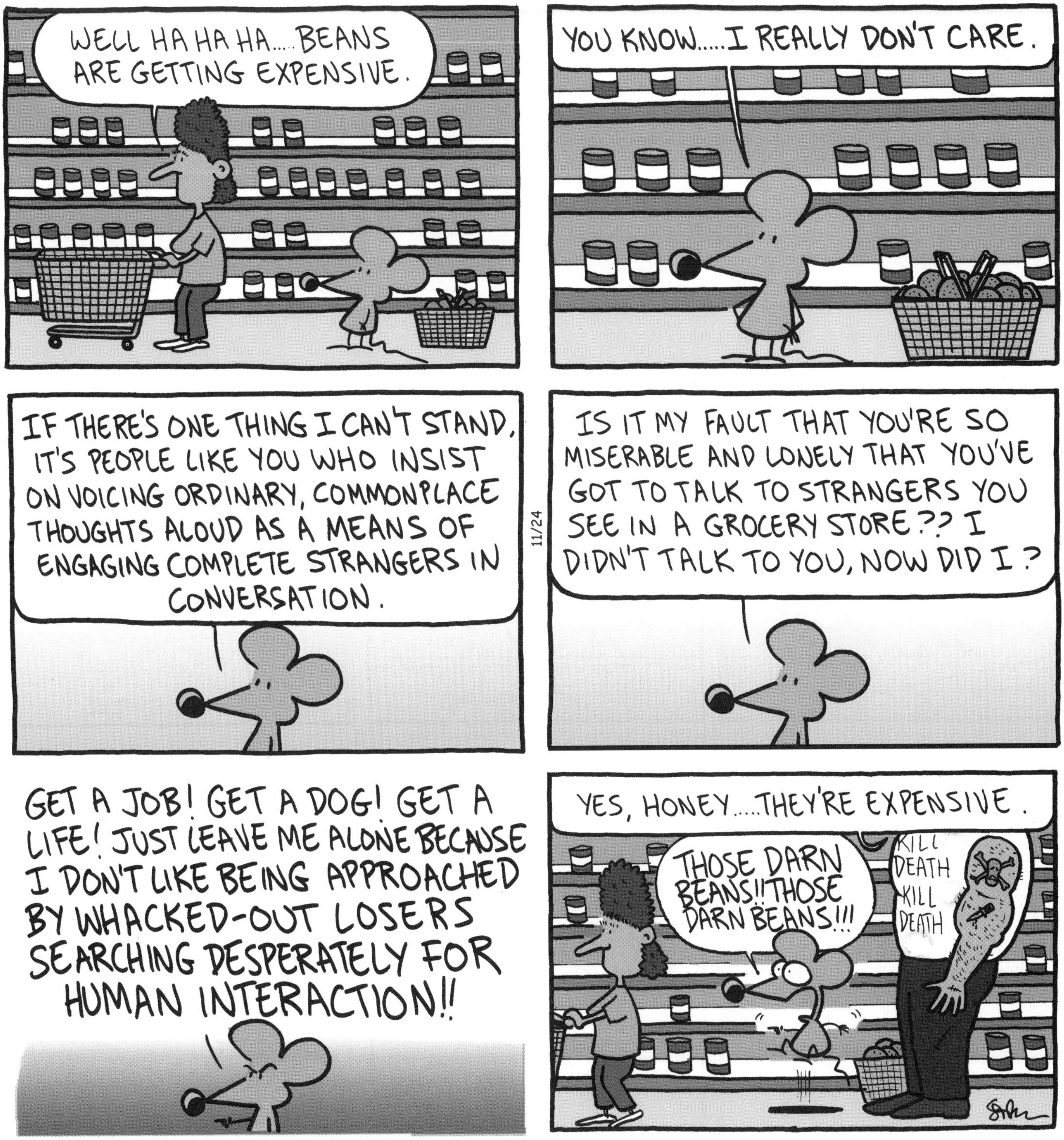
WELL HA HA HA.....BEANS ARE GETTING EXPENSIVE.
YOU KNOW.....I REALLY DON'T CARE.
IF THERE'S ONE THING I CAN'T STAND, IT'S PEOPLE LIKE YOU WHO INSIST ON VOICING ORDINARY, COMMONPLACE THOUGHTS ALOUD AS A MEANS OF ENGAGING COMPLETE STRANGERS IN CONVERSATION.
11/24
IS IT MY FAULT THAT YOU'RE SO MISERABLE AND LONELY THAT YOU'VE GOT TO TALK TO STRANGERS YOU SEE IN A GROCERY STORE?? I DIDN'T TALK TO YOU, NOW DID I?
GET A JOB! GET A DOG! GET A LIFE! JUST LEAVE ME ALONE BECAUSE I DON'T LIKE BEING APPROACHED BY WHACKED-OUT LOSERS SEARCHING DESPERATELY FOR HUMAN INTERACTION!!
YES, HONEY.....THEY'RE EXPENSIVE.
THOSE DARN BEANS!! THOSE DARN BEANS!!!
KILL DEATH KILL DEATH

All I remember about this strip is that it took me forever to draw all those @%#@%# cans.

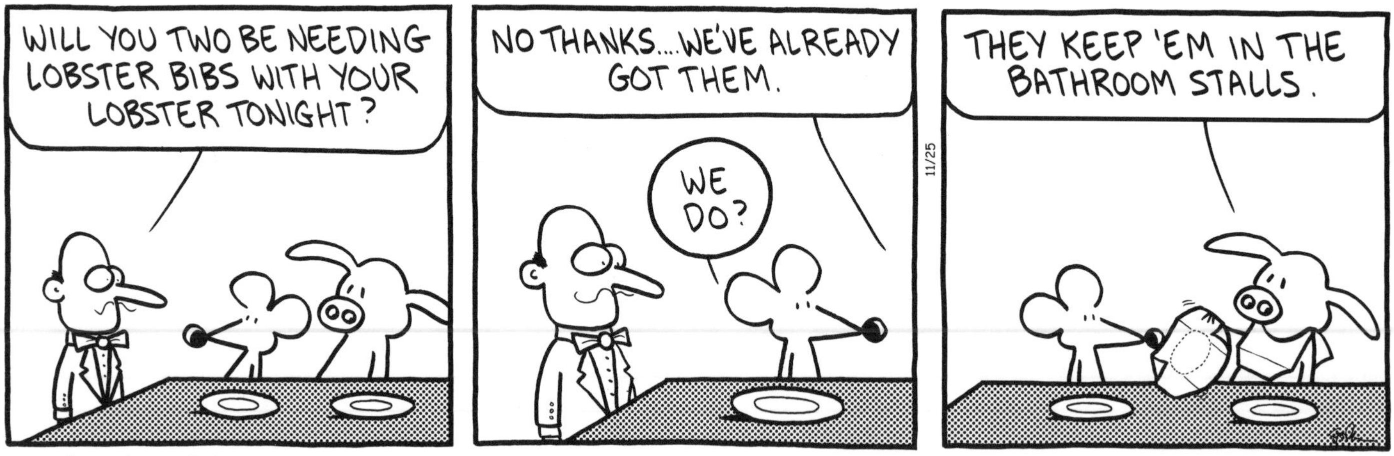
WILL YOU TWO BE NEEDING LOBSTER BIBS WITH YOUR LOBSTER TONIGHT?
NO THANKS.... WE'VE ALREADY GOT THEM.
WE DO?
11/25
THEY KEEP 'EM IN THE BATHROOM STALLS.

I got this idea while going to the bathroom during a deposition I once took in Los Angeles. I even folded up an extra toilet seat covering and put it in my suit pocket, so I would have it to draw later. That's probably more information than you wanted.

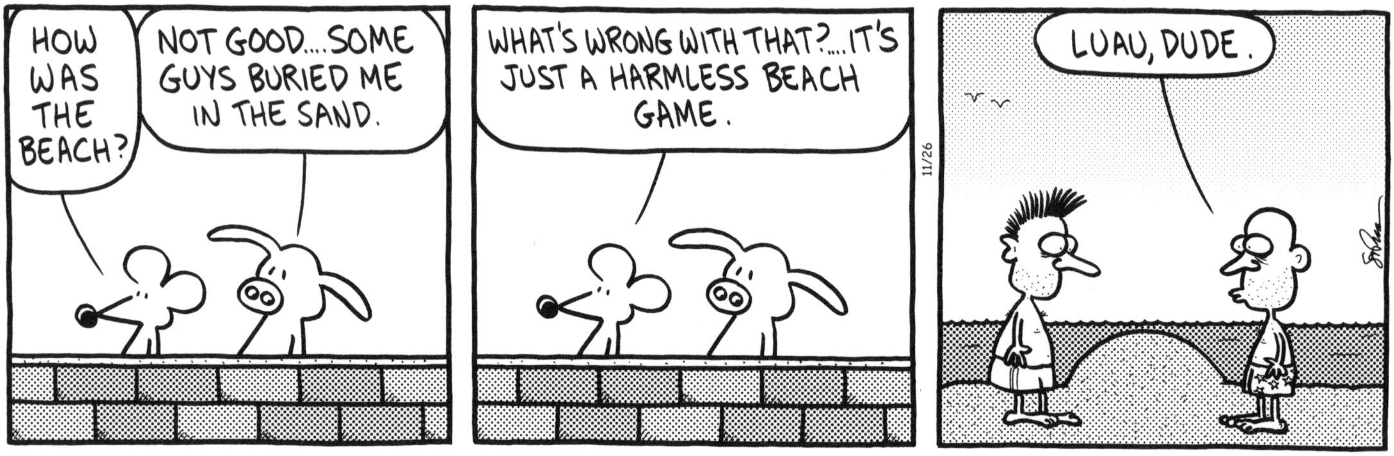
HOW WAS THE BEACH?
NOT GOOD.... SOME GUYS BURIED ME IN THE SAND.
WHAT'S WRONG WITH THAT?.... IT'S JUST A HARMLESS BEACH GAME.
11/26
LUAU, DUDE.

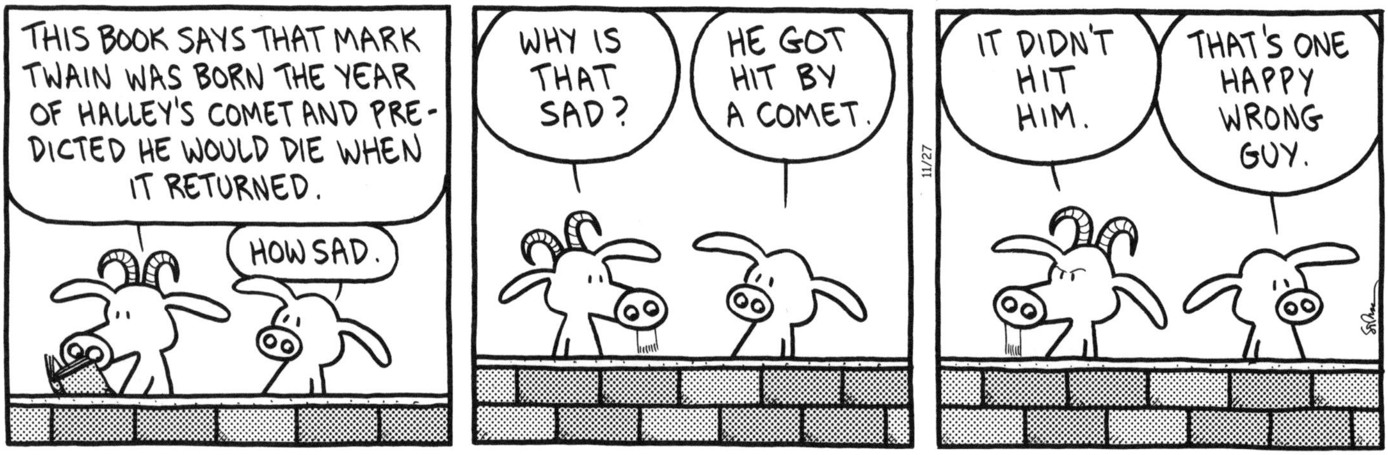
THIS BOOK SAYS THAT MARK TWAIN WAS BORN THE YEAR OF HALLEY'S COMET AND PREDICTED HE WOULD DIE WHEN IT RETURNED.
HOW SAD.
WHY IS THAT SAD?
HE GOT HIT BY A COMET.
11/27
IT DIDN'T HIT HIM.
THAT'S ONE HAPPY WRONG GUY.

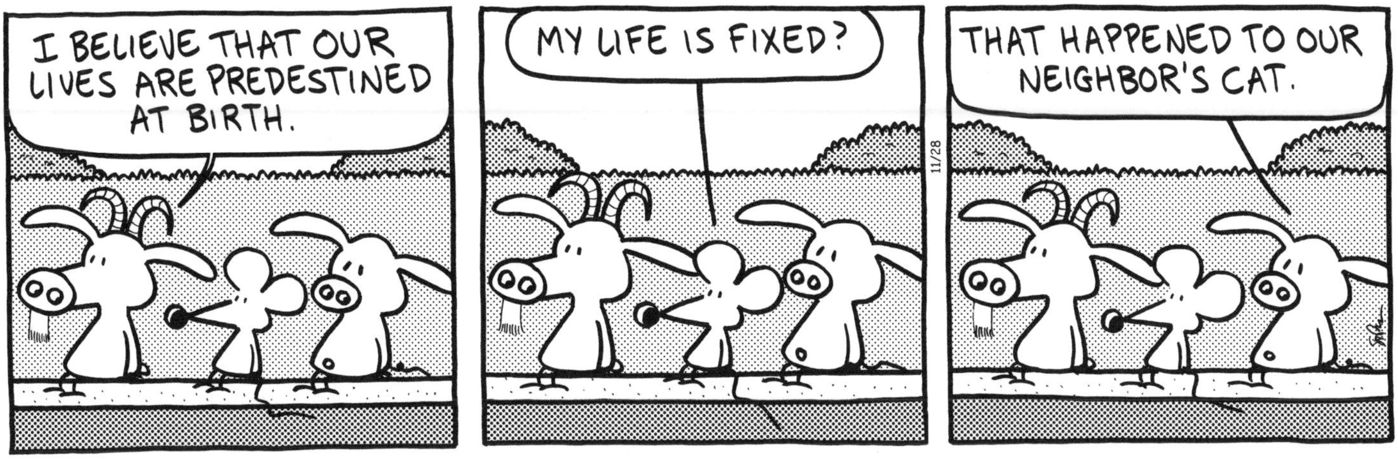
I BELIEVE THAT OUR LIVES ARE PREDESTINED AT BIRTH.
MY LIFE IS FIXED?
11/28
THAT HAPPENED TO OUR NEIGHBOR'S CAT.

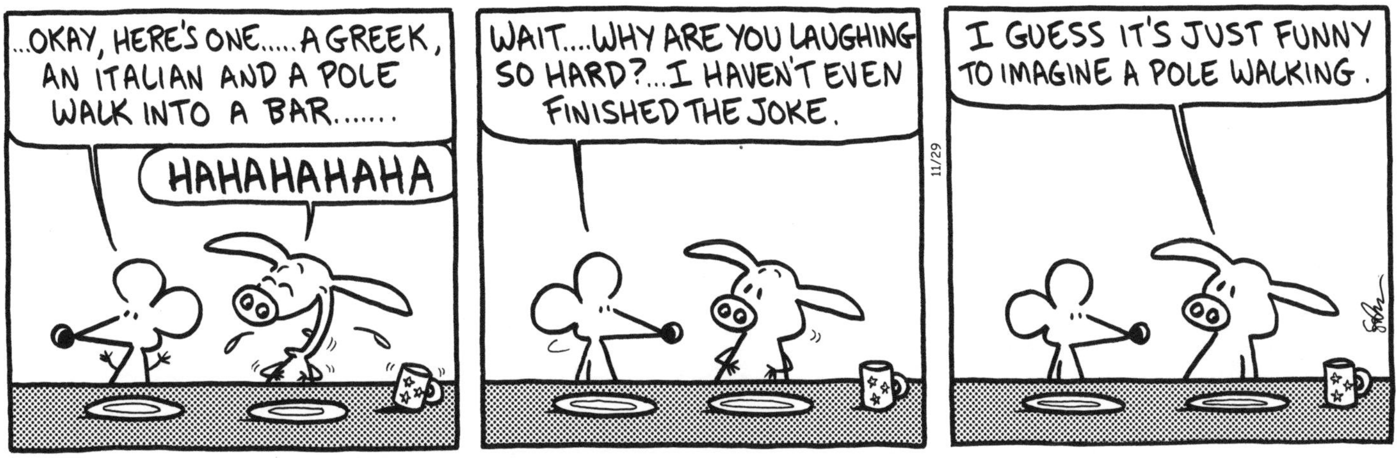
...OKAY, HERE'S ONE.....A GREEK, AN ITALIAN AND A POLE WALK INTO A BAR.......
HAHAHAHAHA
WAIT....WHY ARE YOU LAUGHING SO HARD?...I HAVEN'T EVEN FINISHED THE JOKE.
11/29
I GUESS IT'S JUST FUNNY TO IMAGINE A POLE WALKING.

I'm proud to say that not a single Pole complained about this strip

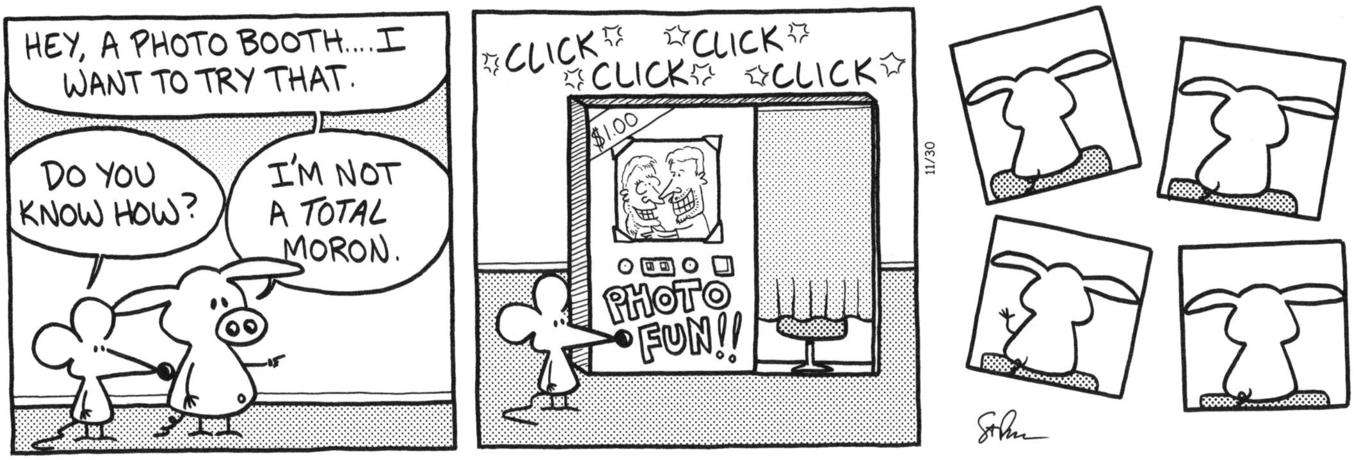
HEY, A PHOTO BOOTH....I WANT TO TRY THAT.
DO YOU KNOW HOW?
I'M NOT A *TOTAL* MORON.
CLICK CLICK CLICK CLICK
$1.00
PHOTO FUN!!
11/30

This was one of the oldest *Pearls* strips. You can tell by how much different Pig looks.

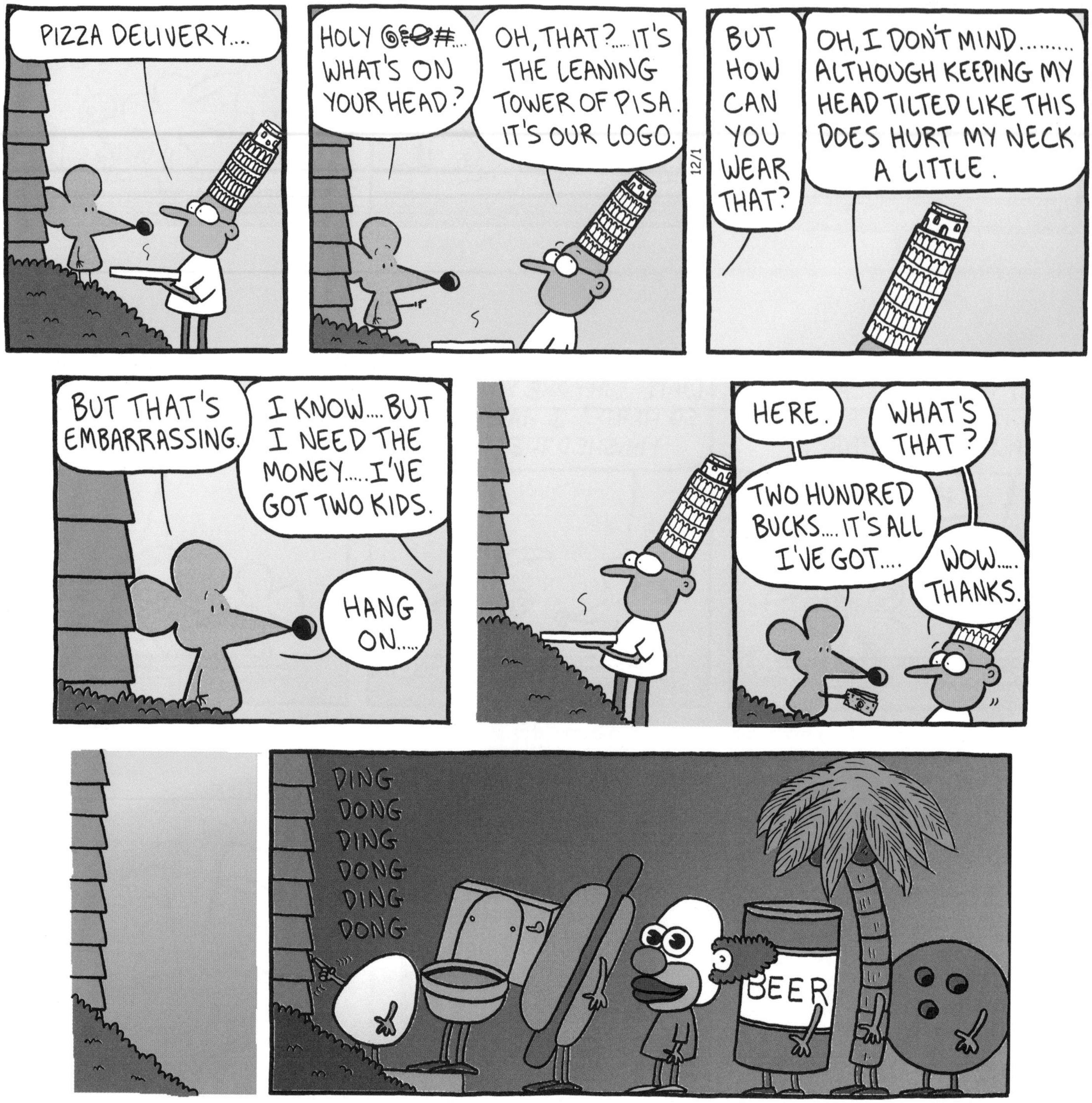
PIZZA DELIVERY....
HOLY @$@#.... WHAT'S ON YOUR HEAD?
OH, THAT?.... IT'S THE LEANING TOWER OF PISA. IT'S OUR LOGO.
12/1
BUT HOW CAN YOU WEAR THAT?
OH, I DON'T MIND......... ALTHOUGH KEEPING MY HEAD TILTED LIKE THIS DOES HURT MY NECK A LITTLE.
BUT THAT'S EMBARRASSING.
I KNOW.... BUT I NEED THE MONEY..... I'VE GOT TWO KIDS.
HANG ON.....
HERE.
WHAT'S THAT?
TWO HUNDRED BUCKS.... IT'S ALL I'VE GOT....
WOW..... THANKS.
DING
DONG
DING
DONG
DING
DONG
BEER

I sort of regret doing this strip, because it shows Rat being so kind to a stranger. While I wanted to show that Rat was not always a complete jerk, I think this showed him to be a tad too soft, and thus it was too out of character.

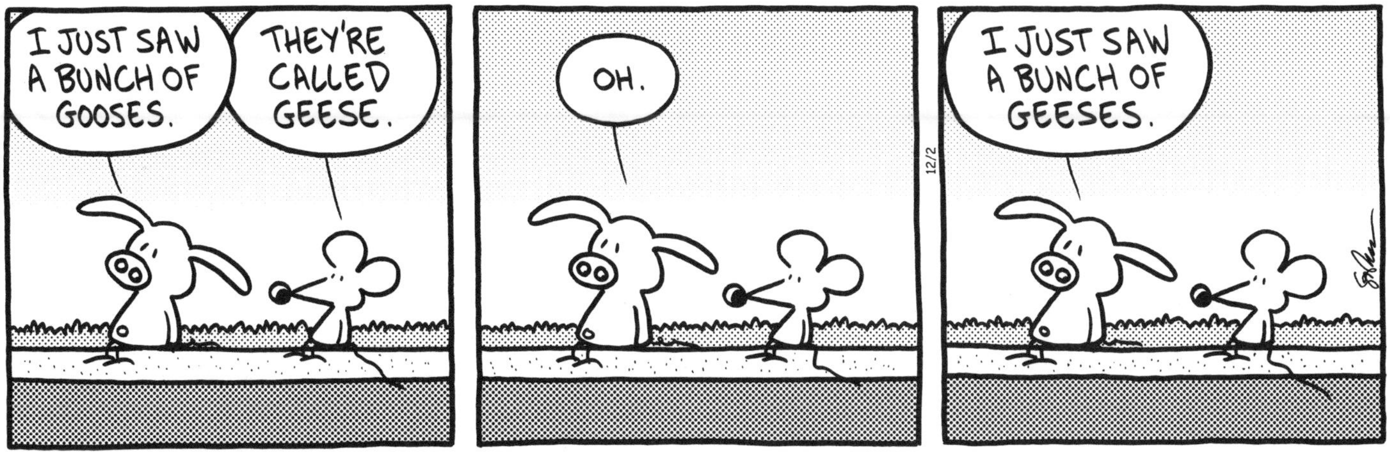
I JUST SAW A BUNCH OF GOOSES.
THEY'RE CALLED GEESE.
OH.
12/2
I JUST SAW A BUNCH OF GEESES.

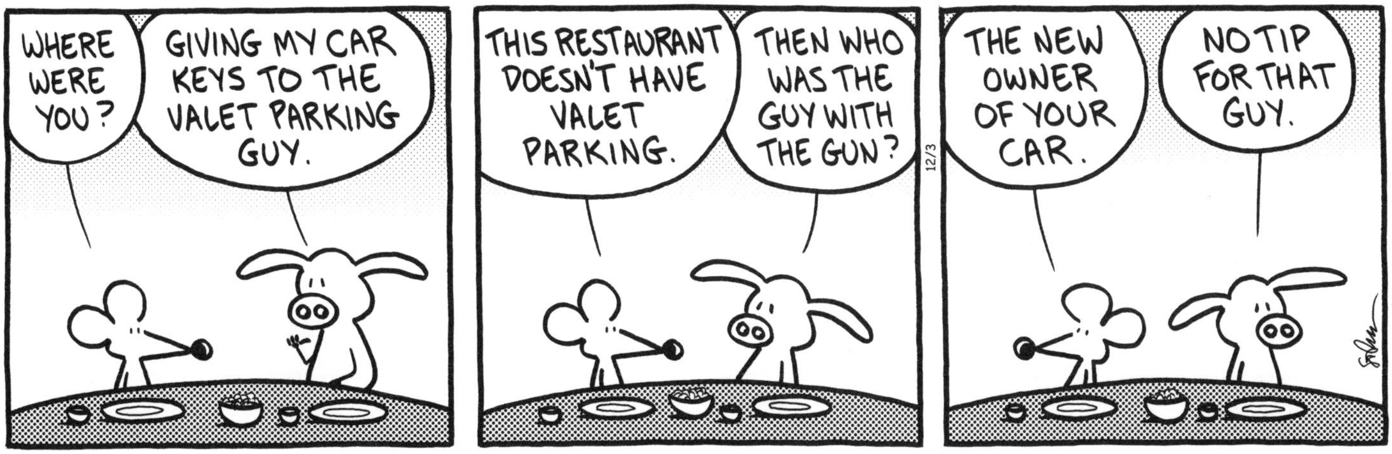
WHERE WERE YOU?
GIVING MY CAR KEYS TO THE VALET PARKING GUY.
THIS RESTAURANT DOESN'T HAVE VALET PARKING.
THEN WHO WAS THE GUY WITH THE GUN?
12/3
THE NEW OWNER OF YOUR CAR.
NO TIP FOR THAT GUY.

A reader in one city wrote me to say that her newspaper pulled this strip on the day it was supposed to run and replaced it with *Hagar the Horrible*. I'm not entirely sure why, although I assume it has something to do with the topic of carjacking.

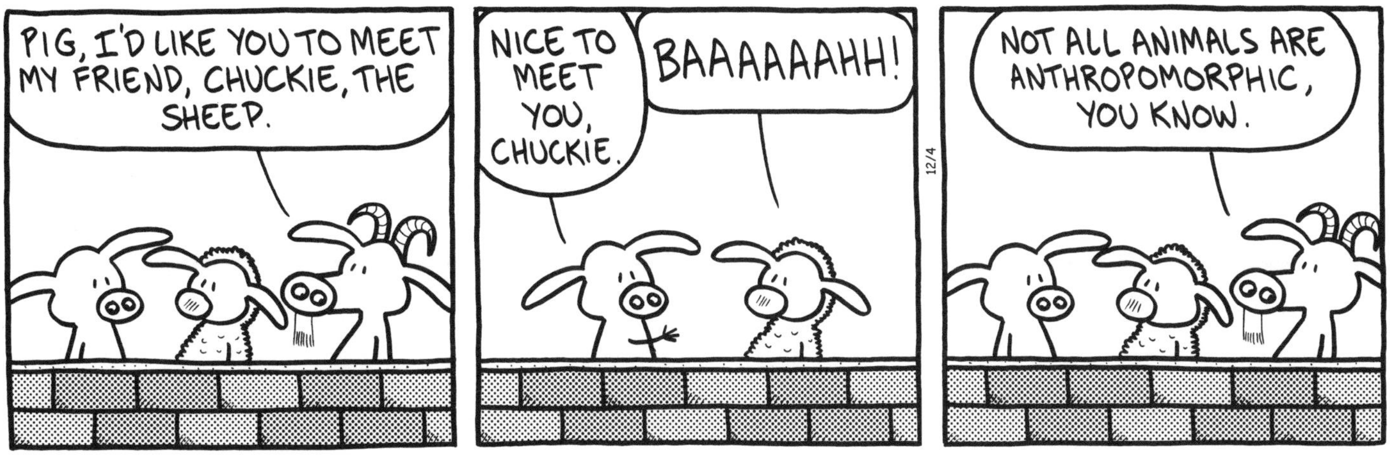
PIG, I'D LIKE YOU TO MEET MY FRIEND, CHUCKIE, THE SHEEP.
NICE TO MEET YOU, CHUCKIE.
BAAAAAAHH!
12/4
NOT ALL ANIMALS ARE ANTHROPOMORPHIC, YOU KNOW.

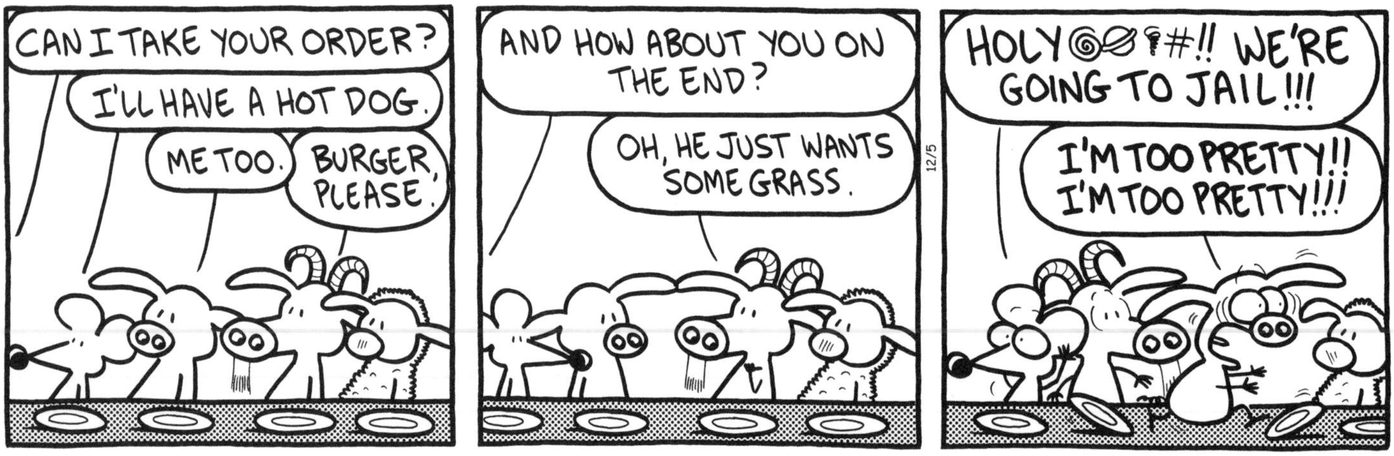
CAN I TAKE YOUR ORDER?
I'LL HAVE A HOT DOG.
ME TOO.
BURGER, PLEASE.
AND HOW ABOUT YOU ON THE END?
OH, HE JUST WANTS SOME GRASS.
12/5
HOLY @#!! WE'RE GOING TO JAIL!!!
I'M TOO PRETTY!! I'M TOO PRETTY!!!

It's not often that you can get the topics of cannibalism (pig eating the hot dog), marijuana, and the perils of prison life into one comic strip.

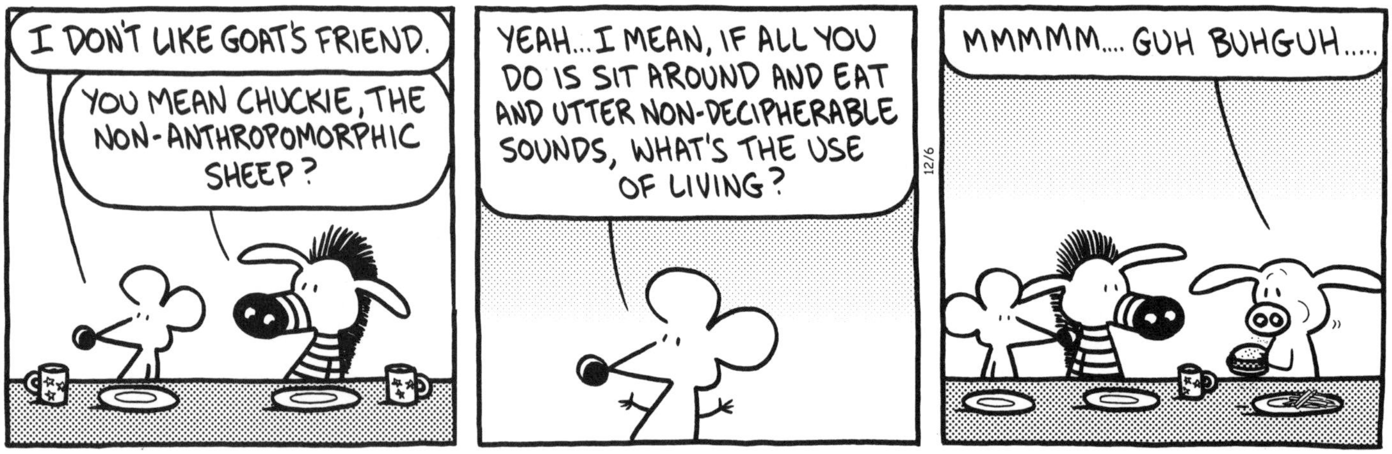
I DON'T LIKE GOAT'S FRIEND.
YOU MEAN CHUCKIE, THE NON-ANTHROPOMORPHIC SHEEP?
YEAH... I MEAN, IF ALL YOU DO IS SIT AROUND AND EAT AND UTTER NON-DECIPHERABLE SOUNDS, WHAT'S THE USE OF LIVING?
12/6
MMMMM.... GUH BUHGUH.....

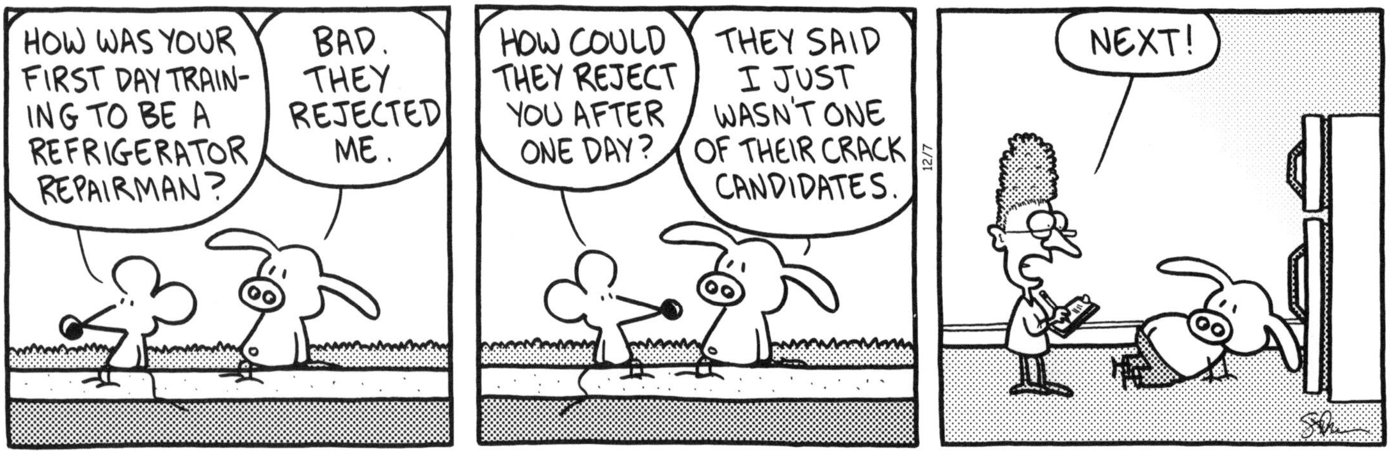
HOW WAS YOUR FIRST DAY TRAINING TO BE A REFRIGERATOR REPAIRMAN?
BAD. THEY REJECTED ME.
HOW COULD THEY REJECT YOU AFTER ONE DAY?
THEY SAID I JUST WASN'T ONE OF THEIR CRACK CANDIDATES.
12/7
NEXT!

This is one of those strips that I buried on a Saturday, so as to diminish the number of complaints.

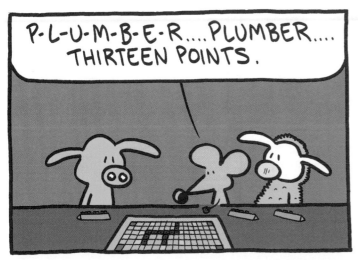

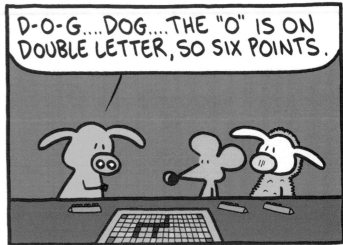

P-L-U-M-B-E-R.... PLUMBER.... THIRTEEN POINTS.
D-O-G....DOG....THE "O" IS ON DOUBLE LETTER, SO SIX POINTS.
12/8
BAAAAAAAAAHHHHHH
NOT A REAL WORD.
NO POINTS. YOU LOSE, CHUCKIE.
NON-ANTHROPOMORPHIC SHEEP HAVE NO CHANCE AT "SCRABBLE."

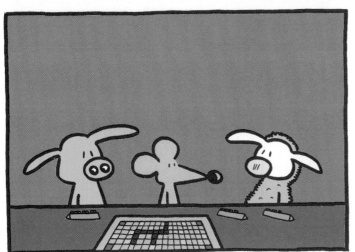

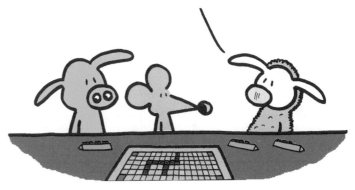

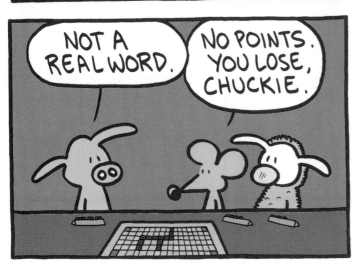

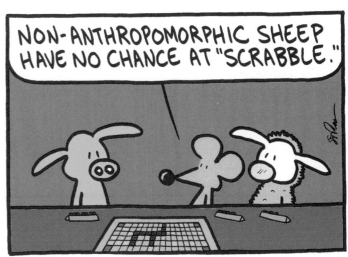

Chuckie was a fun experiment. Given that all of my animal characters are anthropomorphic (i.e., they have the qualities of a human being), I thought it would be fun to depict a sheep that was just a sheep. *Pearls* fans seemed to like it, but a couple of observant readers caught the fact that real-life sheep do not stand on their hind legs.

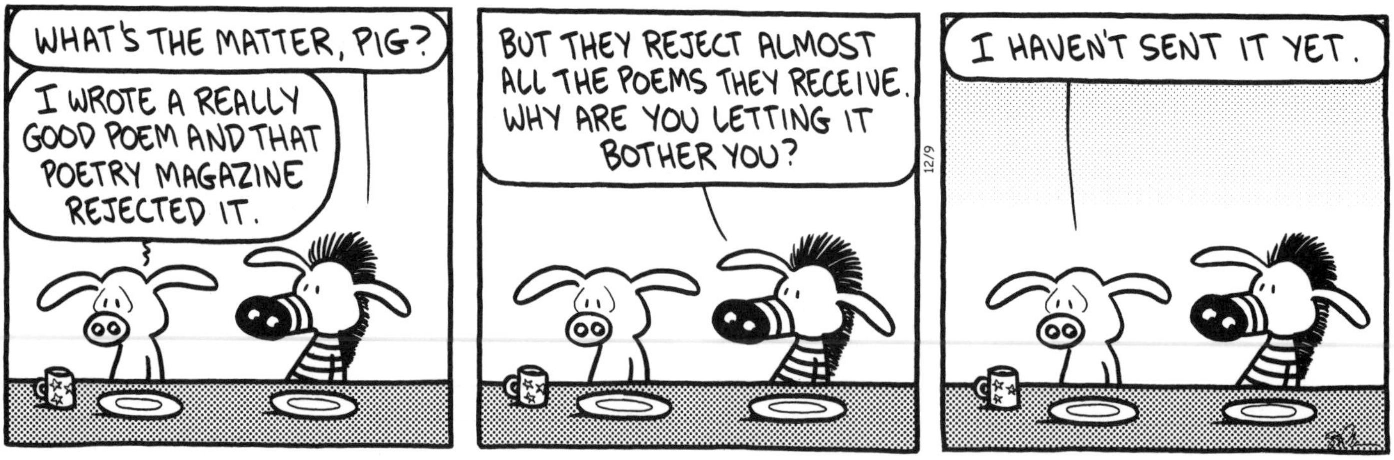
WHAT'S THE MATTER, PIG?
I WROTE A REALLY GOOD POEM AND THAT POETRY MAGAZINE REJECTED IT.
BUT THEY REJECT ALMOST ALL THE POEMS THEY RECEIVE. WHY ARE YOU LETTING IT BOTHER YOU?
12/9
I HAVEN'T SENT IT YET.

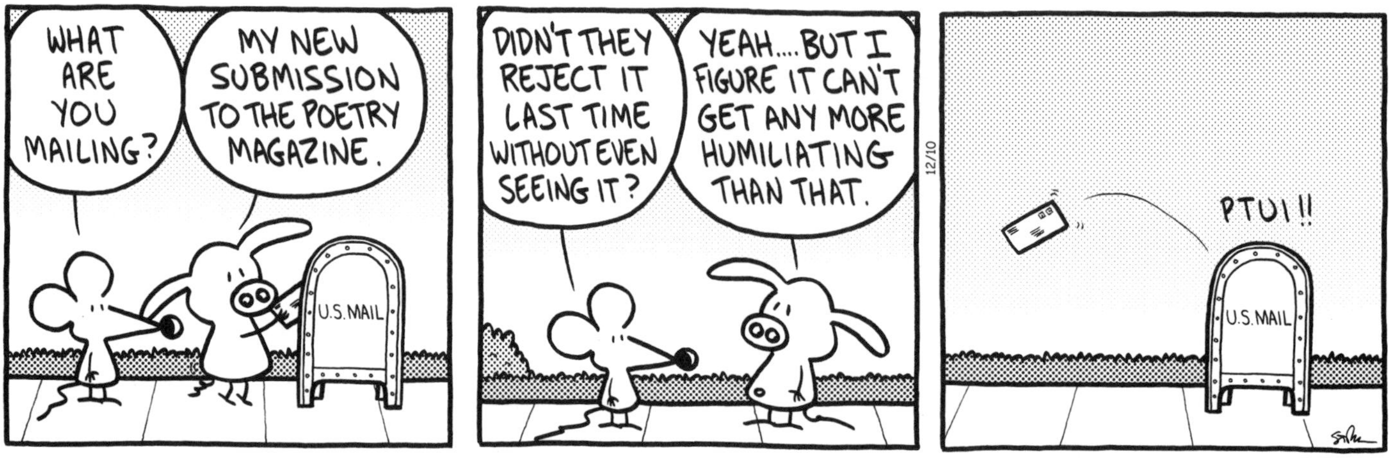
WHAT ARE YOU MAILING?
MY NEW SUBMISSION TO THE POETRY MAGAZINE.
U.S. MAIL
DIDN'T THEY REJECT IT LAST TIME WITHOUT EVEN SEEING IT?
YEAH.... BUT I FIGURE IT CAN'T GET ANY MORE HUMILIATING THAN THAT.
12/10
PTUI!!
U.S. MAIL

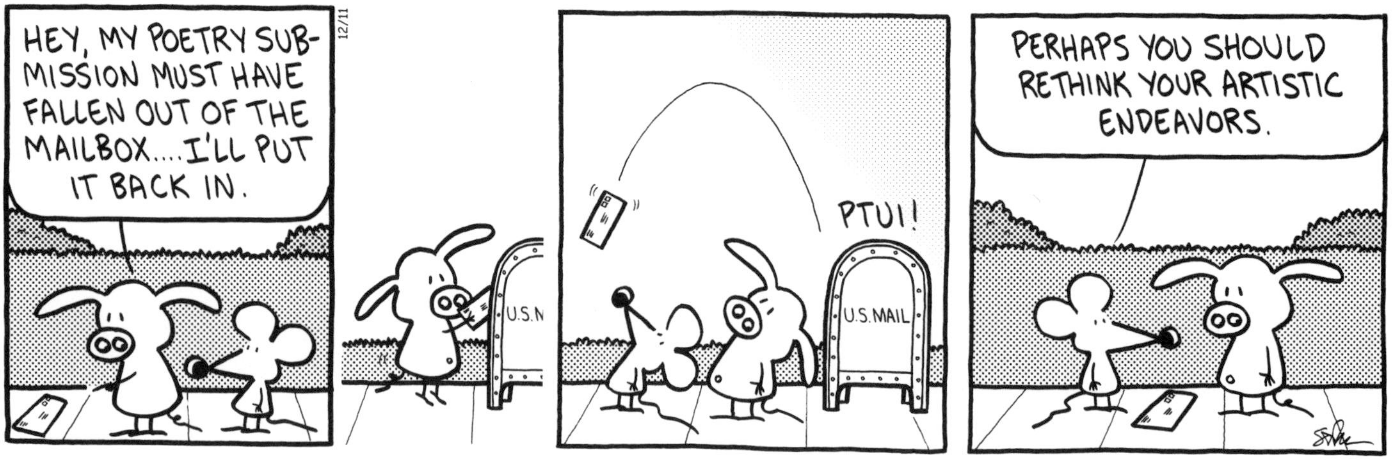
HEY, MY POETRY SUBMISSION MUST HAVE FALLEN OUT OF THE MAILBOX.... I'LL PUT IT BACK IN.
12/11
PTUI!
U.S. MAIL
PERHAPS YOU SHOULD RETHINK YOUR ARTISTIC ENDEAVORS.

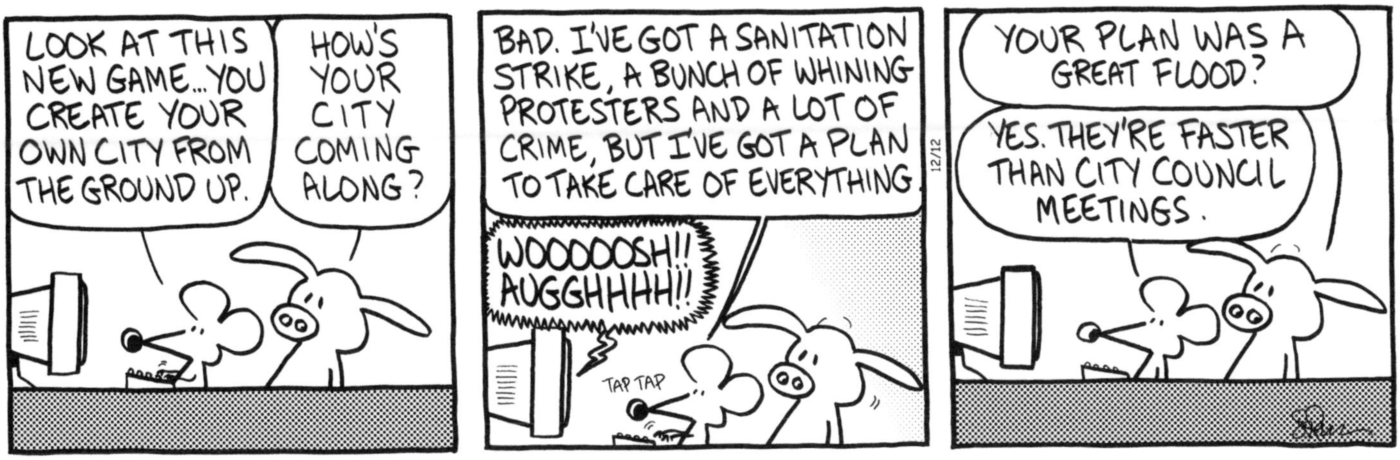
LOOK AT THIS NEW GAME...YOU CREATE YOUR OWN CITY FROM THE GROUND UP.
HOW'S YOUR CITY COMING ALONG?
BAD. I'VE GOT A SANITATION STRIKE, A BUNCH OF WHINING PROTESTERS AND A LOT OF CRIME, BUT I'VE GOT A PLAN TO TAKE CARE OF EVERYTHING.
12/12
WOOOOOSH!! AUGGHHHH!!
TAP TAP
YOUR PLAN WAS A GREAT FLOOD?
YES. THEY'RE FASTER THAN CITY COUNCIL MEETINGS.

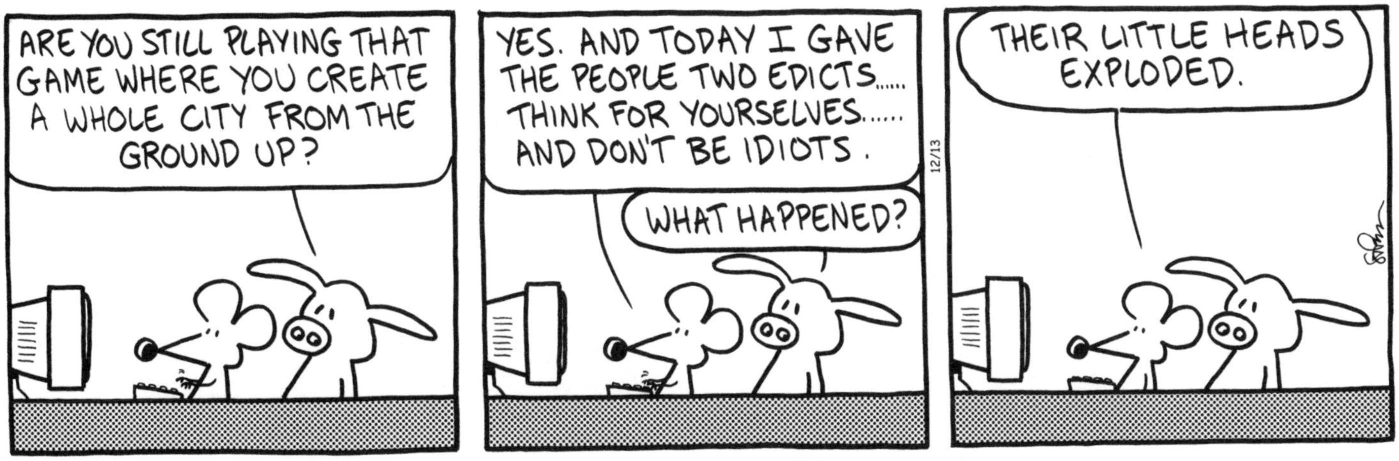
ARE YOU STILL PLAYING THAT GAME WHERE YOU CREATE A WHOLE CITY FROM THE GROUND UP?
YES. AND TODAY I GAVE THE PEOPLE TWO EDICTS...... THINK FOR YOURSELVES...... AND DON'T BE IDIOTS.
WHAT HAPPENED?
12/13
THEIR LITTLE HEADS EXPLODED.

Scary as it may be, Rat occasionally sounds like me. This is one of them.

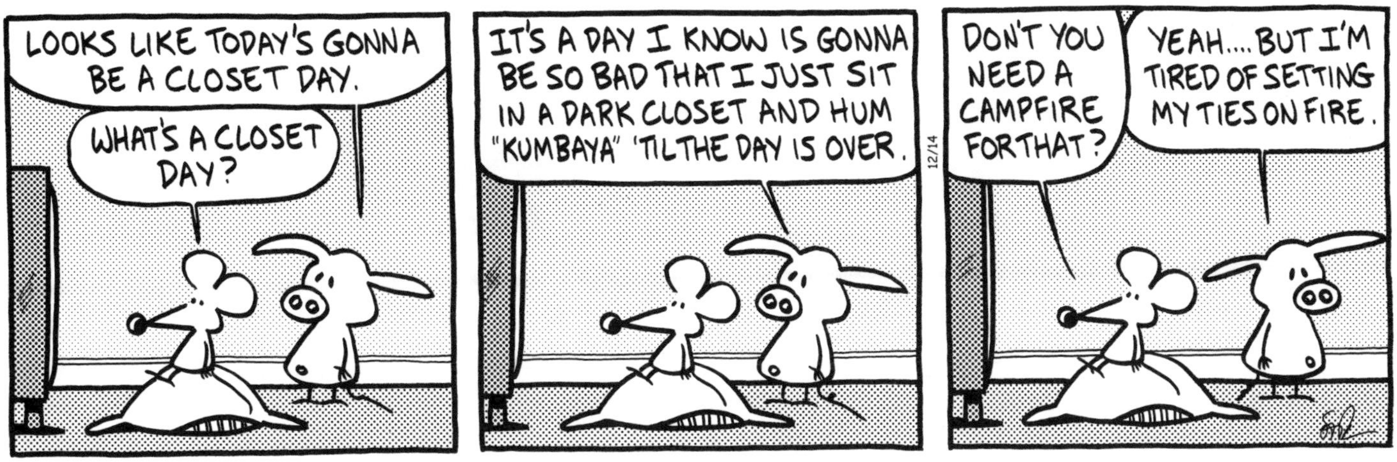
LOOKS LIKE TODAY'S GONNA BE A CLOSET DAY.
WHAT'S A CLOSET DAY?
IT'S A DAY I KNOW IS GONNA BE SO BAD THAT I JUST SIT IN A DARK CLOSET AND HUM "KUMBAYA" 'TIL THE DAY IS OVER.
12/14
DON'T YOU NEED A CAMPFIRE FOR THAT?
YEAH.... BUT I'M TIRED OF SETTING MY TIES ON FIRE.

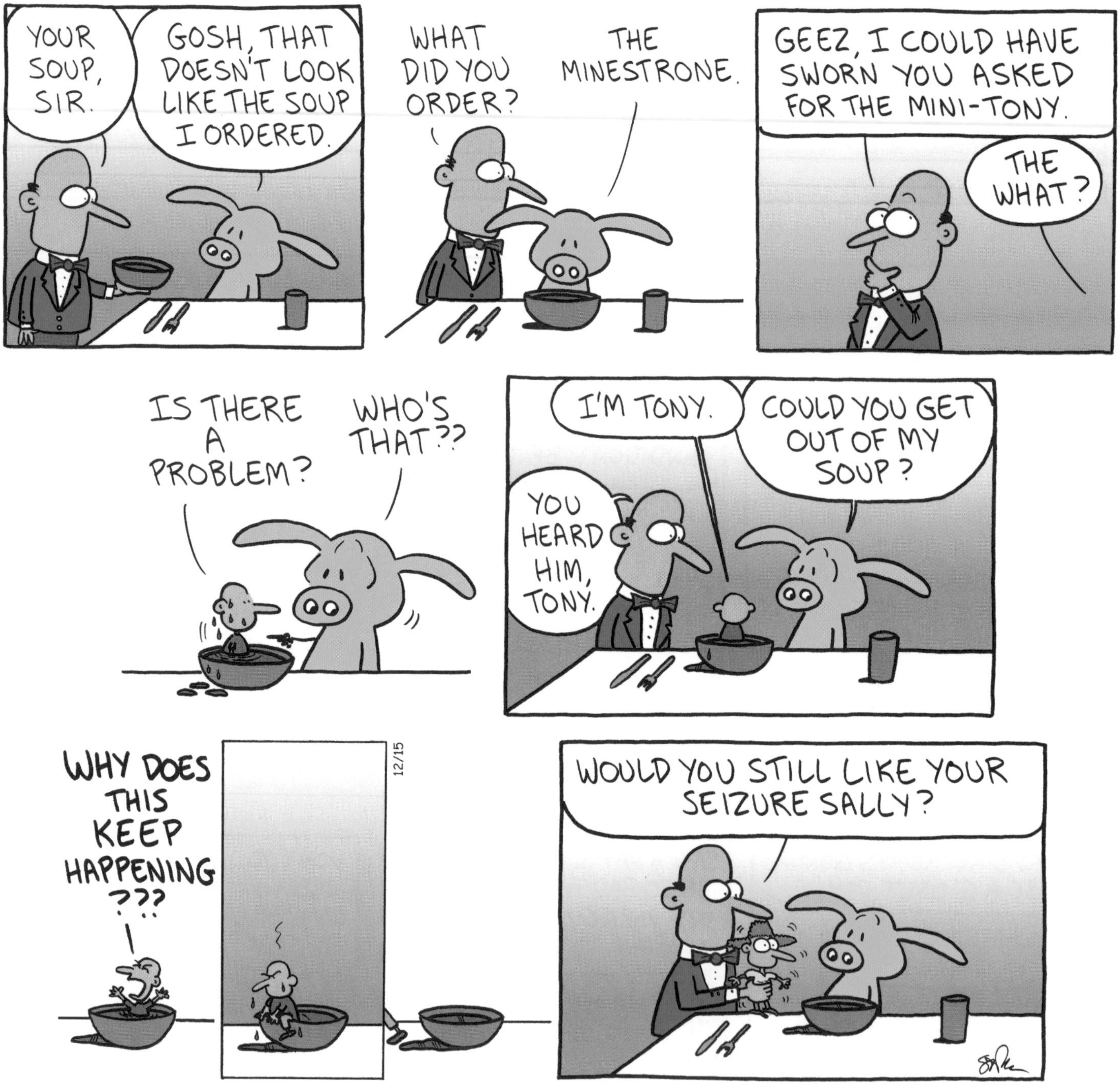
YOUR SOUP, SIR.
GOSH, THAT DOESN'T LOOK LIKE THE SOUP I ORDERED.
WHAT DID YOU ORDER?
THE MINESTRONE.
GEEZ, I COULD HAVE SWORN YOU ASKED FOR THE MINI-TONY.
THE WHAT?
IS THERE A PROBLEM?
WHO'S THAT??
I'M TONY.
COULD YOU GET OUT OF MY SOUP?
YOU HEARD HIM, TONY.
WHY DOES THIS KEEP HAPPENING???
12/15
WOULD YOU STILL LIKE YOUR SEIZURE SALLY?

This drew complaints from readers who said I was making fun of people who have seizures. On a positive note, no one wrote to complain that I was making fun of people who were six inches high.

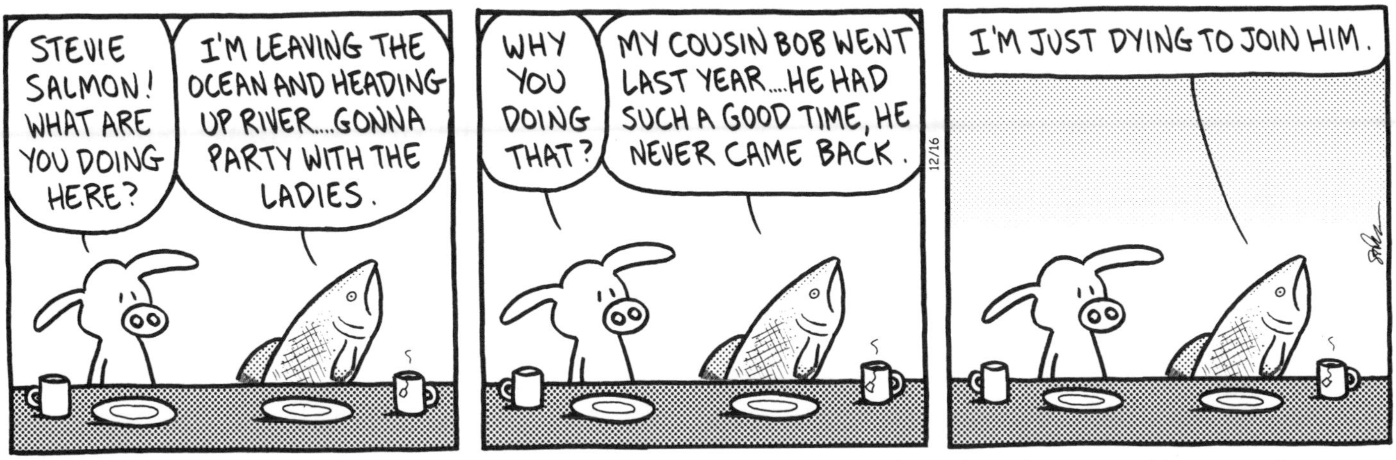
STEVIE SALMON! WHAT ARE YOU DOING HERE?
I'M LEAVING THE OCEAN AND HEADING UP RIVER....GONNA PARTY WITH THE LADIES.
WHY YOU DOING THAT?
MY COUSIN BOB WENT LAST YEAR....HE HAD SUCH A GOOD TIME, HE NEVER CAME BACK.
12/16
I'M JUST DYING TO JOIN HIM.

I like to use salmon in the strip. Somehow their futile struggle upstream (only to then die) seems like a good metaphor for the life of a human.

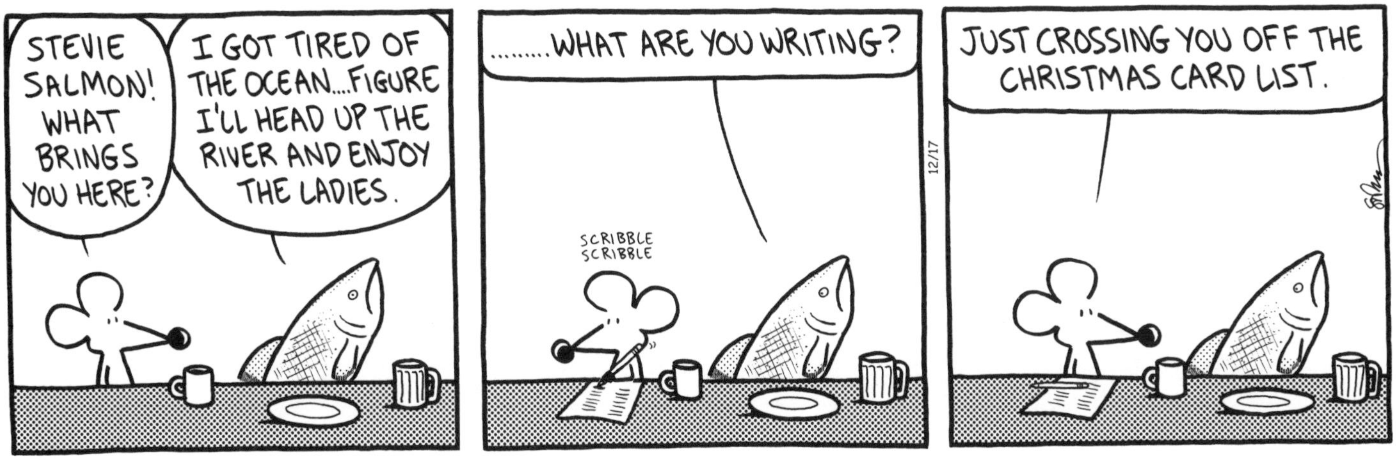
STEVIE SALMON! WHAT BRINGS YOU HERE?
I GOT TIRED OF THE OCEAN....FIGURE I'LL HEAD UP THE RIVER AND ENJOY THE LADIES.
SCRIBBLE SCRIBBLE
.........WHAT ARE YOU WRITING?
12/17
JUST CROSSING YOU OFF THE CHRISTMAS CARD LIST.

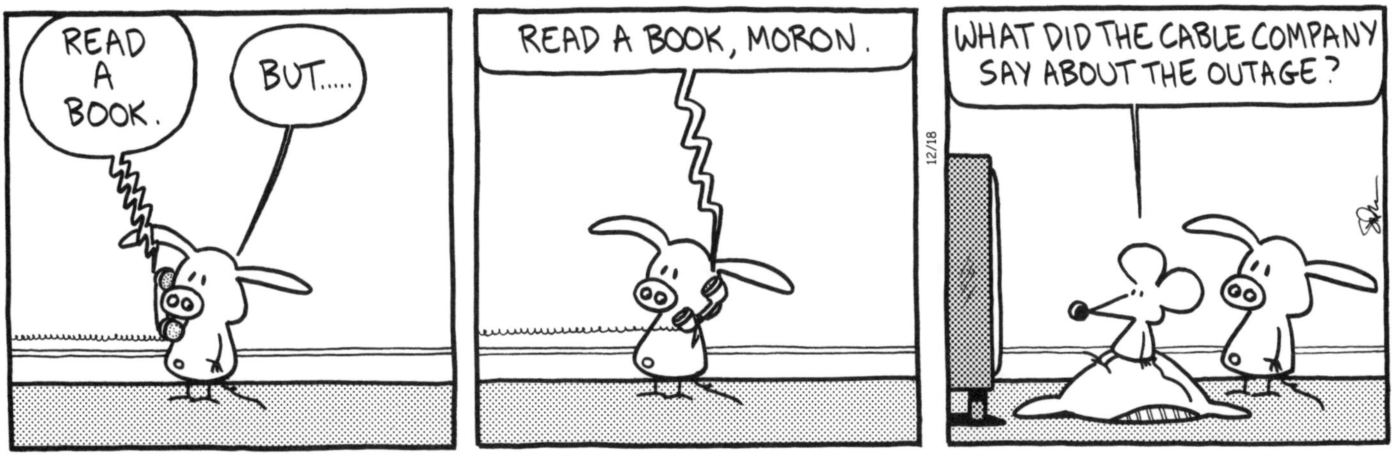
READ A BOOK.
BUT.....
READ A BOOK, MORON.
12/18
WHAT DID THE CABLE COMPANY SAY ABOUT THE OUTAGE?

A lot of people said they related to this. Apparently, I'm not the only person who has trouble getting good service from their cable company.

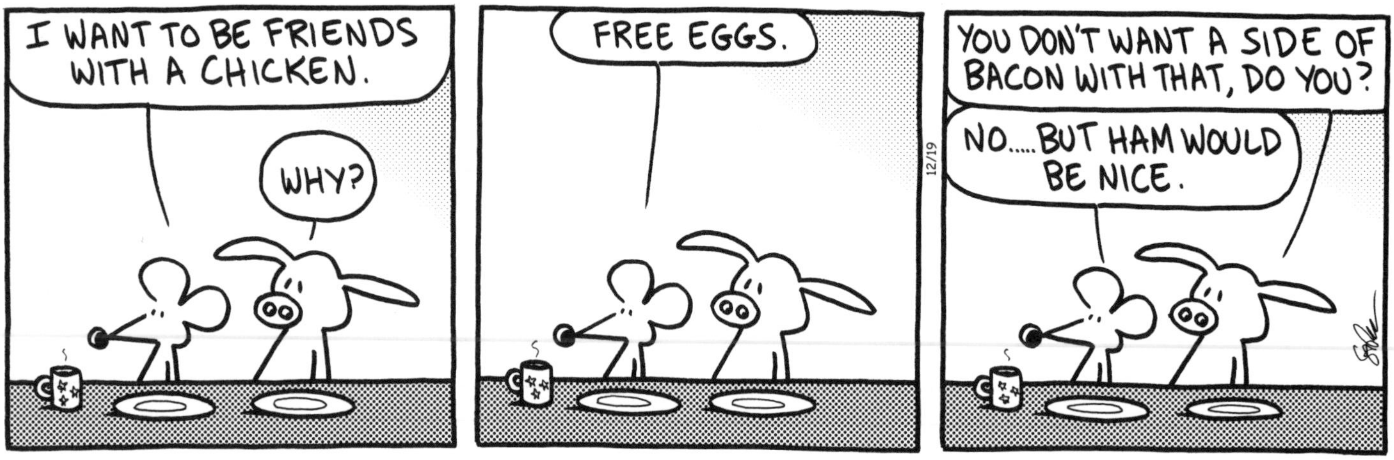
I WANT TO BE FRIENDS WITH A CHICKEN.
WHY?
FREE EGGS.
12/19
YOU DON'T WANT A SIDE OF BACON WITH THAT, DO YOU?
NO..... BUT HAM WOULD BE NICE.

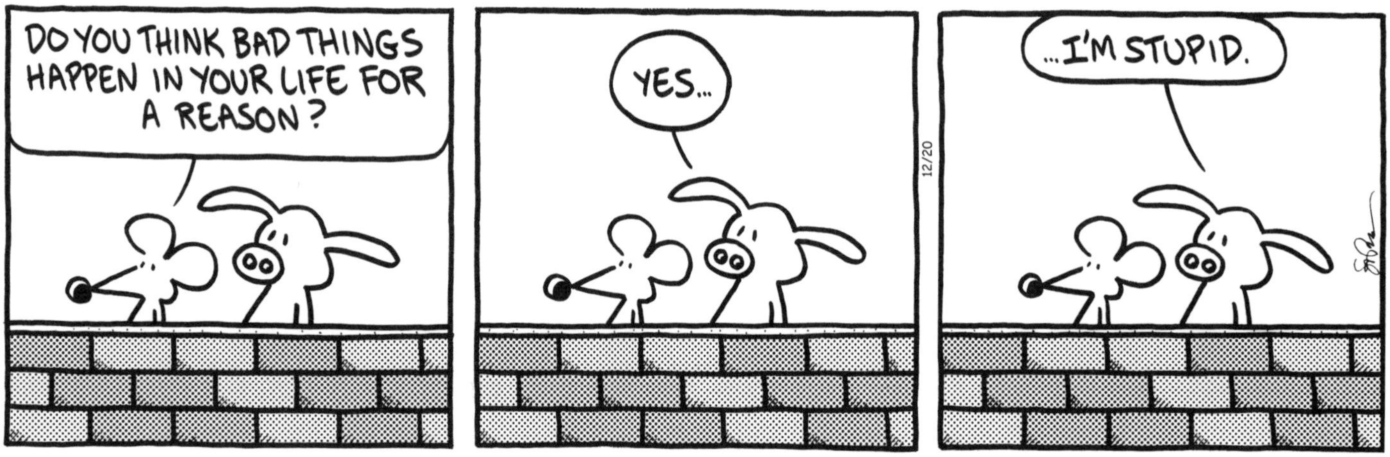
DO YOU THINK BAD THINGS HAPPEN IN YOUR LIFE FOR A REASON?
YES...
12/20
...I'M STUPID.

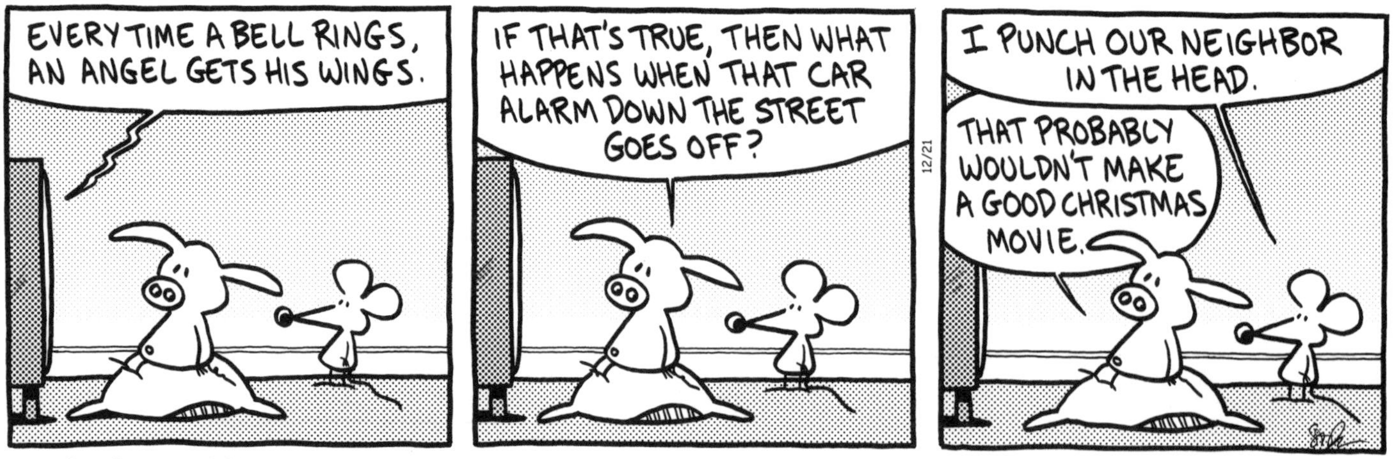
EVERY TIME A BELL RINGS, AN ANGEL GETS HIS WINGS.
IF THAT'S TRUE, THEN WHAT HAPPENS WHEN THAT CAR ALARM DOWN THE STREET GOES OFF?
12/21
I PUNCH OUR NEIGHBOR IN THE HEAD.
THAT PROBABLY WOULDN'T MAKE A GOOD CHRISTMAS MOVIE.

Actually, that would be a pretty entertaining movie.

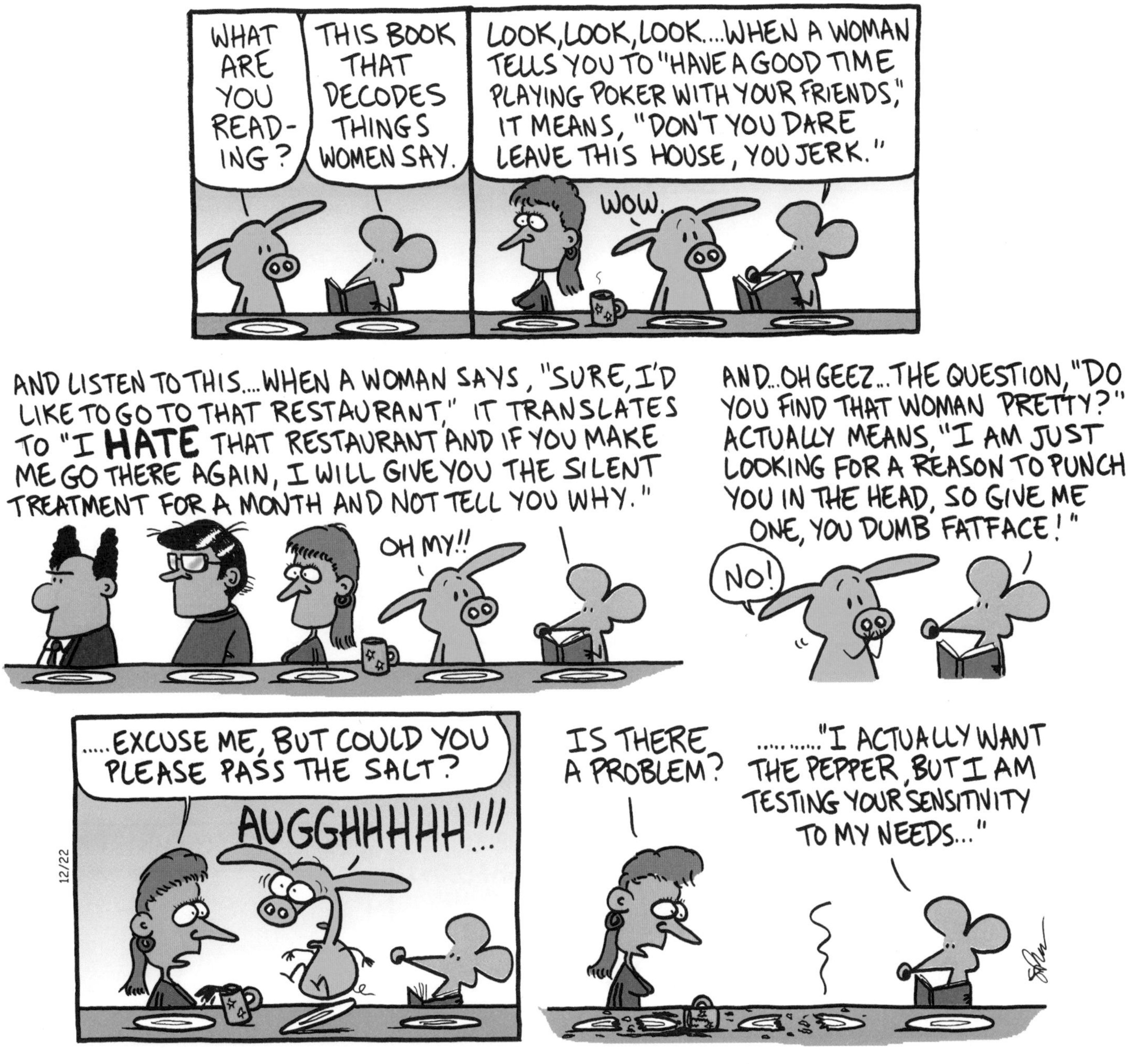
WHAT ARE YOU READING?
THIS BOOK THAT DECODES THINGS WOMEN SAY.
LOOK, LOOK, LOOK....WHEN A WOMAN TELLS YOU TO "HAVE A GOOD TIME PLAYING POKER WITH YOUR FRIENDS," IT MEANS, "DON'T YOU DARE LEAVE THIS HOUSE, YOU JERK."
WOW.
AND LISTEN TO THIS....WHEN A WOMAN SAYS, "SURE, I'D LIKE TO GO TO THAT RESTAURANT," IT TRANSLATES TO "I HATE THAT RESTAURANT AND IF YOU MAKE ME GO THERE AGAIN, I WILL GIVE YOU THE SILENT TREATMENT FOR A MONTH AND NOT TELL YOU WHY."
OH MY!!
AND...OH GEEZ...THE QUESTION, "DO YOU FIND THAT WOMAN PRETTY?" ACTUALLY MEANS, "I AM JUST LOOKING FOR A REASON TO PUNCH YOU IN THE HEAD, SO GIVE ME ONE, YOU DUMB FATFACE!"
NO!
.....EXCUSE ME, BUT COULD YOU PLEASE PASS THE SALT?
AUGGHHHHH!!!...
12/22
IS THERE A PROBLEM?
.........."I ACTUALLY WANT THE PEPPER, BUT I AM TESTING YOUR SENSITIVITY TO MY NEEDS..."

If you want to be technical, this is really the first published *Pearls* strip. The *Orlando Sentinel* bought the strip when it began and needed a Sunday strip a week early. So this ran in the *Sentinel* on December 30, 2001, one day before the *Washington Post* debuted it on December 31. But since I reran the strip on December 22, 2002, I consider this date to be its real publication date. By the way, that's *Dilbert's* boss and *Get Fuzzy*'s Rob in the third panel.

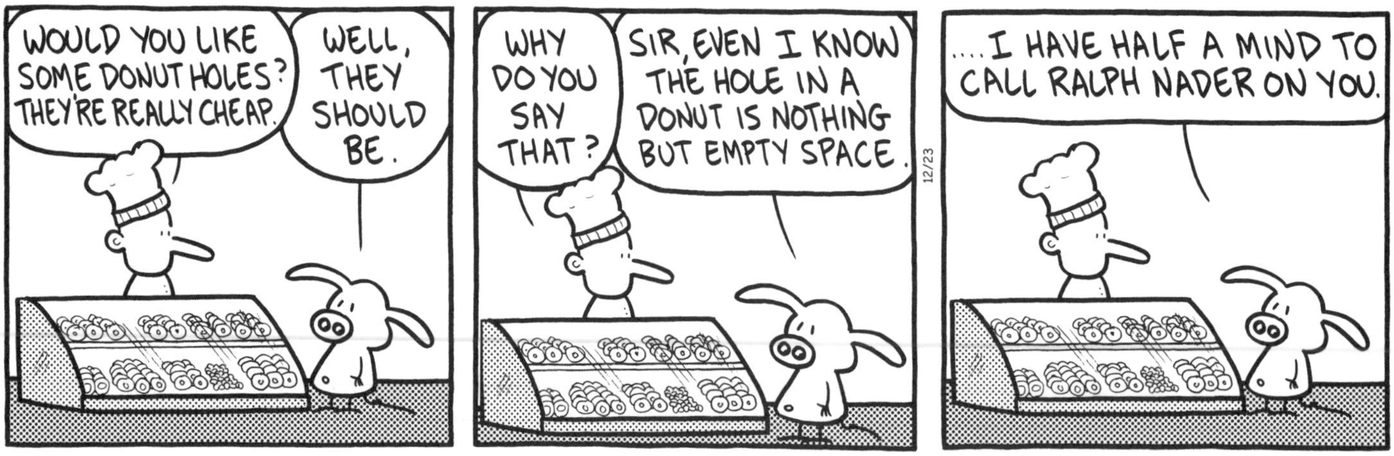
WOULD YOU LIKE SOME DONUT HOLES? THEY'RE REALLY CHEAP.
WELL, THEY SHOULD BE.
WHY DO YOU SAY THAT?
SIR, EVEN I KNOW THE HOLE IN A DONUT IS NOTHING BUT EMPTY SPACE.
12/23
....I HAVE HALF A MIND TO CALL RALPH NADER ON YOU.

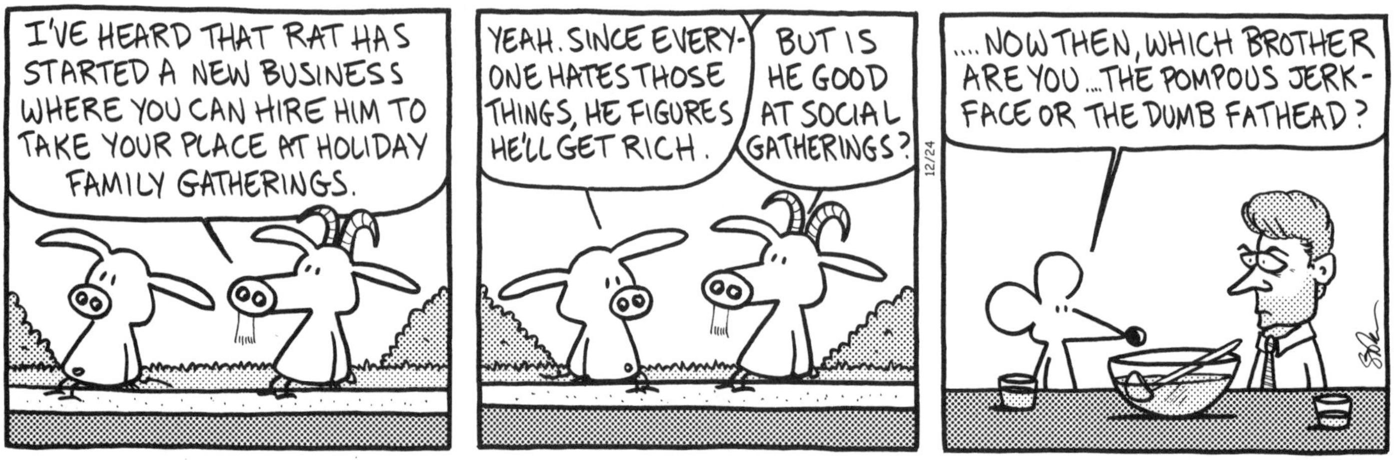
I'VE HEARD THAT RAT HAS STARTED A NEW BUSINESS WHERE YOU CAN HIRE HIM TO TAKE YOUR PLACE AT HOLIDAY FAMILY GATHERINGS.
YEAH. SINCE EVERYONE HATES THOSE THINGS, HE FIGURES HE'LL GET RICH.
BUT IS HE GOOD AT SOCIAL GATHERINGS?
12/24
....NOW THEN, WHICH BROTHER ARE YOU....THE POMPOUS JERK-FACE OR THE DUMB FATHEAD?

I'm proud of the way that punch bowl looks. Again, it's the little things.

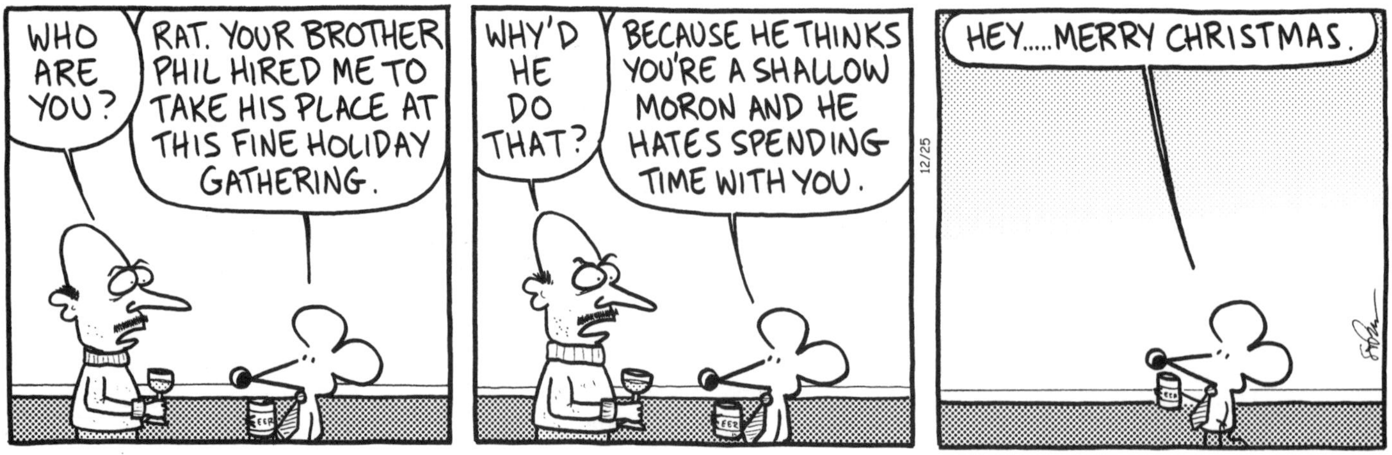
WHO ARE YOU?
RAT. YOUR BROTHER PHIL HIRED ME TO TAKE HIS PLACE AT THIS FINE HOLIDAY GATHERING.
WHY'D HE DO THAT?
BECAUSE HE THINKS YOU'RE A SHALLOW MORON AND HE HATES SPENDING TIME WITH YOU.
12/25
HEY.....MERRY CHRISTMAS.

Most cartoonists have heartwarming, feel-good Christmas strips. I have my main character swig beer and call someone a moron.

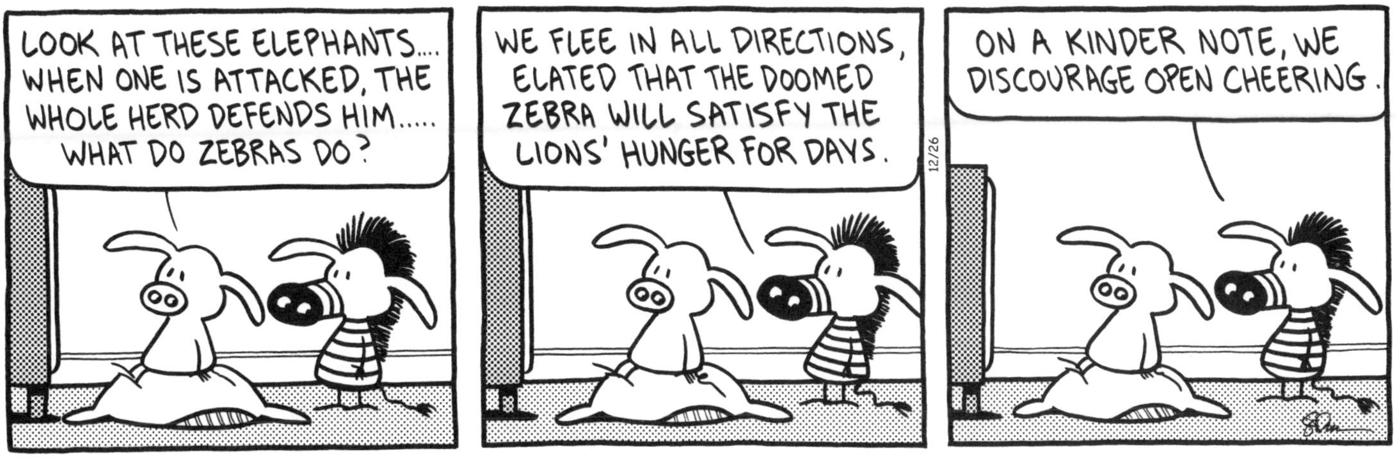
LOOK AT THESE ELEPHANTS.... WHEN ONE IS ATTACKED, THE WHOLE HERD DEFENDS HIM..... WHAT DO ZEBRAS DO?
WE FLEE IN ALL DIRECTIONS, ELATED THAT THE DOOMED ZEBRA WILL SATISFY THE LIONS' HUNGER FOR DAYS.
12/26
ON A KINDER NOTE, WE DISCOURAGE OPEN CHEERING.

Has any zebra ever defended his fellow zebra? Not in the nature shows I've been watching.

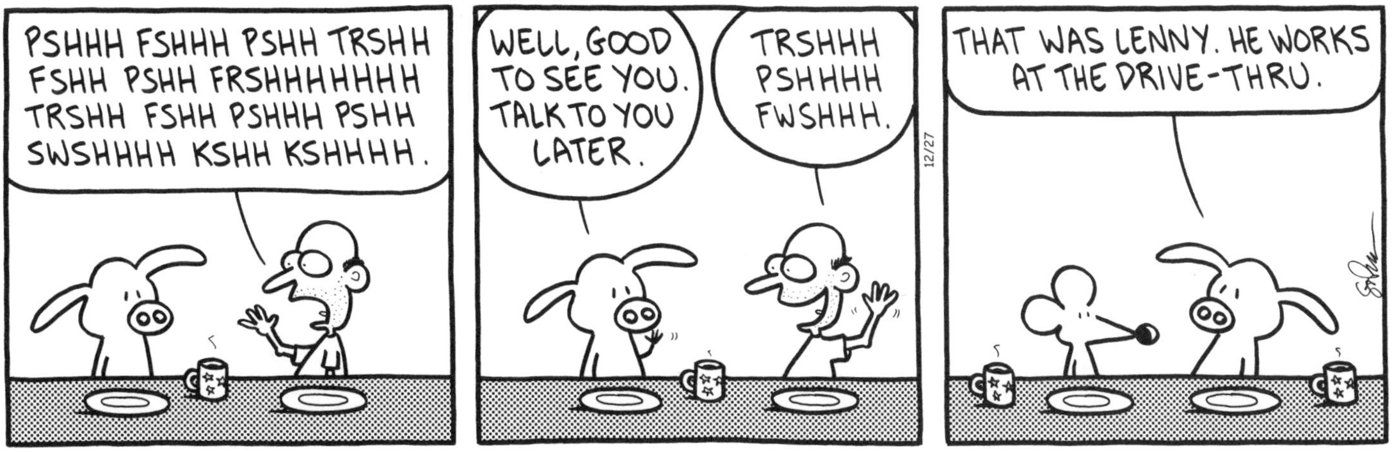
PSHHH FSHHH PSHH TRSHH FSHH PSHH FRSHHHHHHH TRSHH FSHH PSHHH PSHH SWSHHHH KSHH KSHHHH.
WELL, GOOD TO SEE YOU. TALK TO YOU LATER.
TRSHHH PSHHHH FWSHHH.
12/27
THAT WAS LENNY. HE WORKS AT THE DRIVE-THRU.

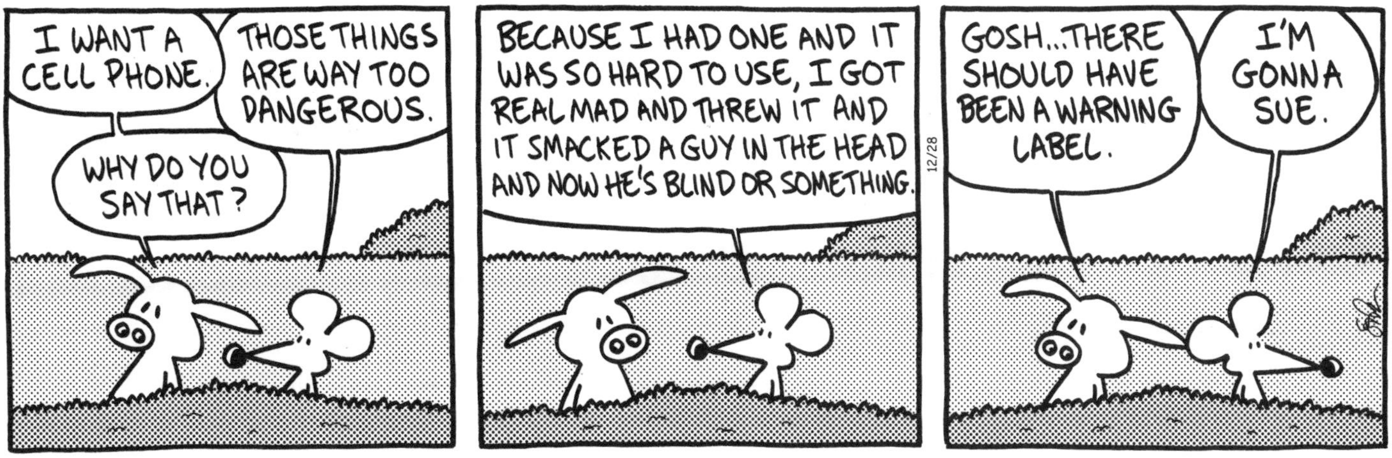
I WANT A CELL PHONE.
THOSE THINGS ARE WAY TOO DANGEROUS.
WHY DO YOU SAY THAT?
BECAUSE I HAD ONE AND IT WAS SO HARD TO USE, I GOT REAL MAD AND THREW IT AND IT SMACKED A GUY IN THE HEAD AND NOW HE'S BLIND OR SOMETHING.
12/28
GOSH...THERE SHOULD HAVE BEEN A WARNING LABEL.
I'M GONNA SUE.

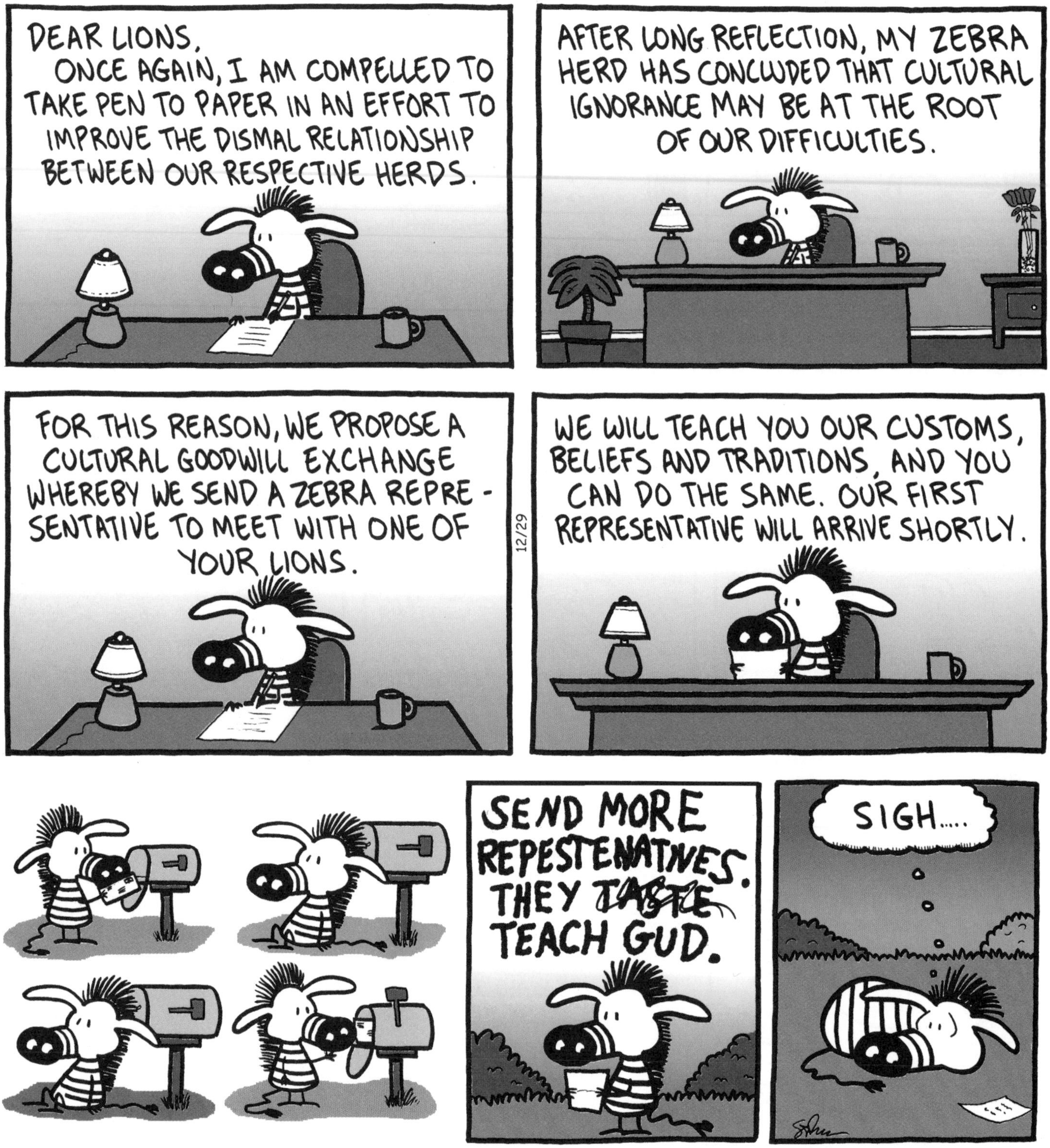
DEAR LIONS,
ONCE AGAIN, I AM COMPELLED TO TAKE PEN TO PAPER IN AN EFFORT TO IMPROVE THE DISMAL RELATIONSHIP BETWEEN OUR RESPECTIVE HERDS.
AFTER LONG REFLECTION, MY ZEBRA HERD HAS CONCLUDED THAT CULTURAL IGNORANCE MAY BE AT THE ROOT OF OUR DIFFICULTIES.
FOR THIS REASON, WE PROPOSE A CULTURAL GOODWILL EXCHANGE WHEREBY WE SEND A ZEBRA REPRE - SENTATIVE TO MEET WITH ONE OF YOUR LIONS.
12/29
WE WILL TEACH YOU OUR CUSTOMS, BELIEFS AND TRADITIONS, AND YOU CAN DO THE SAME. OUR FIRST REPRESENTATIVE WILL ARRIVE SHORTLY.
SEND MORE REPESTENATIVES.
THEY ~~TASTE~~
TEACH GUD.
SIGH.....

Sometimes my strips contain elaborate background elements, as you'll see in the second panel of this strip, where I drew a strange plant and roses in a vase. This took so much out of me that I did not repeat them in any of the other panels.

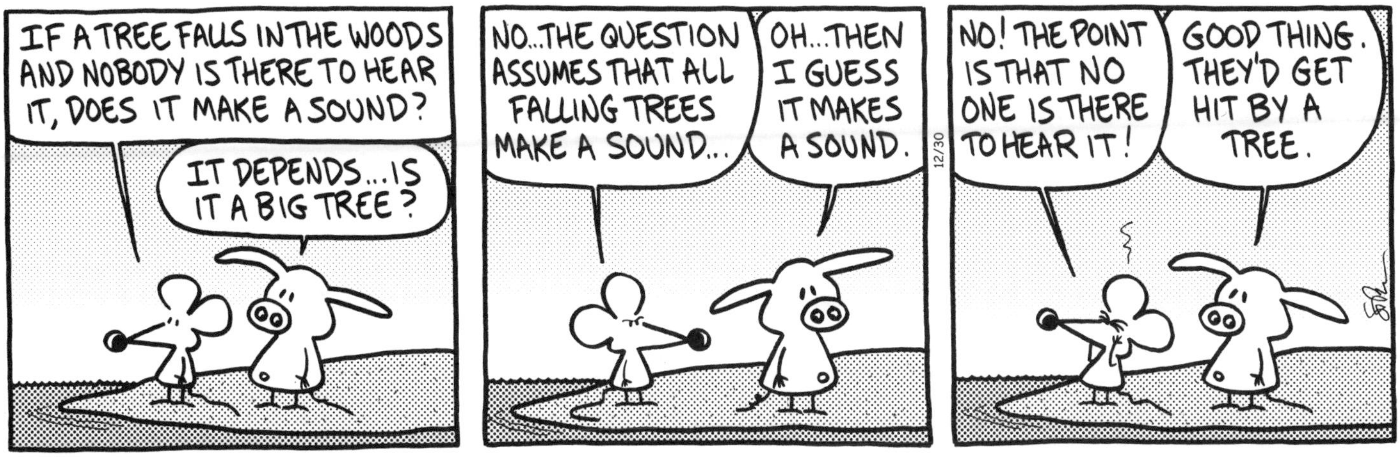
IF A TREE FALLS IN THE WOODS AND NOBODY IS THERE TO HEAR IT, DOES IT MAKE A SOUND?
IT DEPENDS...IS IT A BIG TREE?
NO...THE QUESTION ASSUMES THAT ALL FALLING TREES MAKE A SOUND...
OH...THEN I GUESS IT MAKES A SOUND.
12/30
NO! THE POINT IS THAT NO ONE IS THERE TO HEAR IT!
GOOD THING. THEY'D GET HIT BY A TREE.

Rat's facial expression in the last panel is a mistake that has always bugged me. He should have just had a blank look. To me, when a cartoonist has a character respond visually like that in the last panel, it's almost like a cheap signal to the reader that a joke has been told. The dialogue should be strong enough that the reader already knows that.

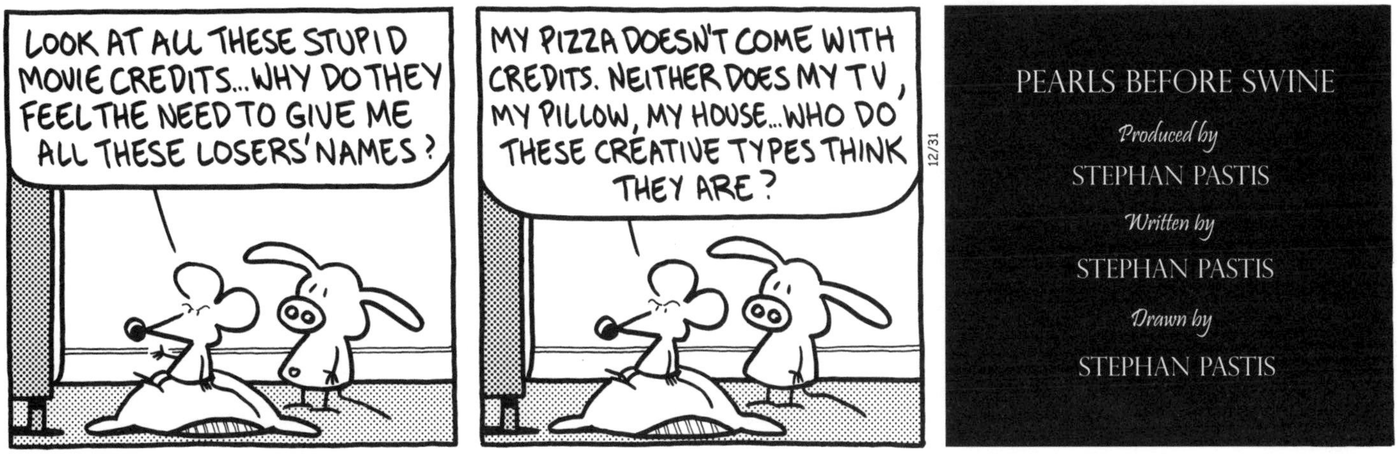
LOOK AT ALL THESE STUPID MOVIE CREDITS...WHY DO THEY FEEL THE NEED TO GIVE ME ALL THESE LOSERS' NAMES?
MY PIZZA DOESN'T COME WITH CREDITS. NEITHER DOES MY TV, MY PILLOW, MY HOUSE...WHO DO THESE CREATIVE TYPES THINK THEY ARE?
12/31
PEARLS BEFORE SWINE
Produced by
STEPHAN PASTIS
Written by
STEPHAN PASTIS
Drawn by
STEPHAN PASTIS

I've always wondered why you need to know who the "Best Grip" is.

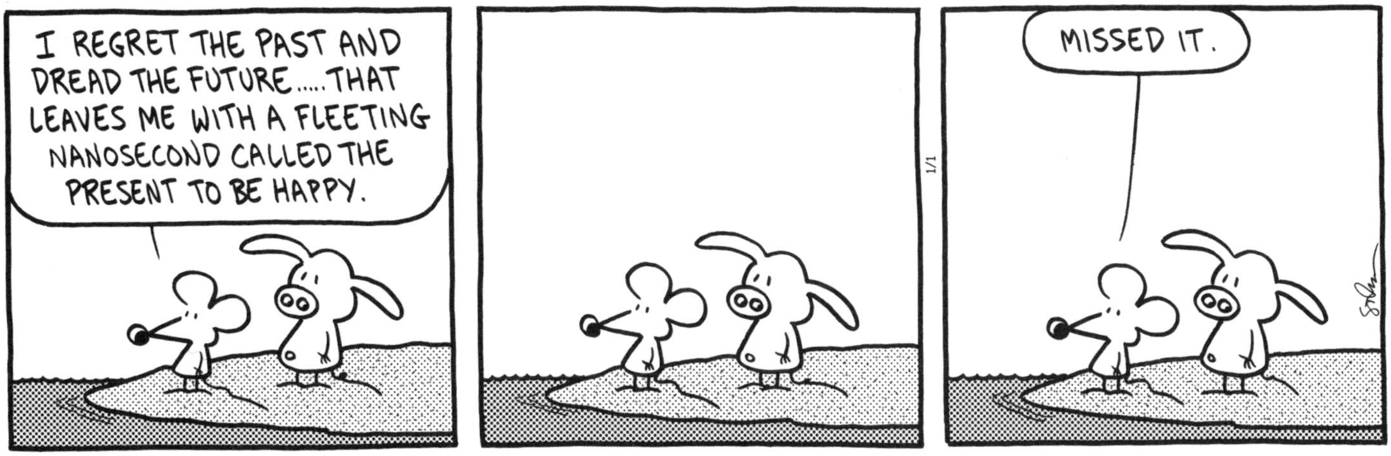
I REGRET THE PAST AND DREAD THE FUTURE.....THAT LEAVES ME WITH A FLEETING NANOSECOND CALLED THE PRESENT TO BE HAPPY.
1/1
MISSED IT.

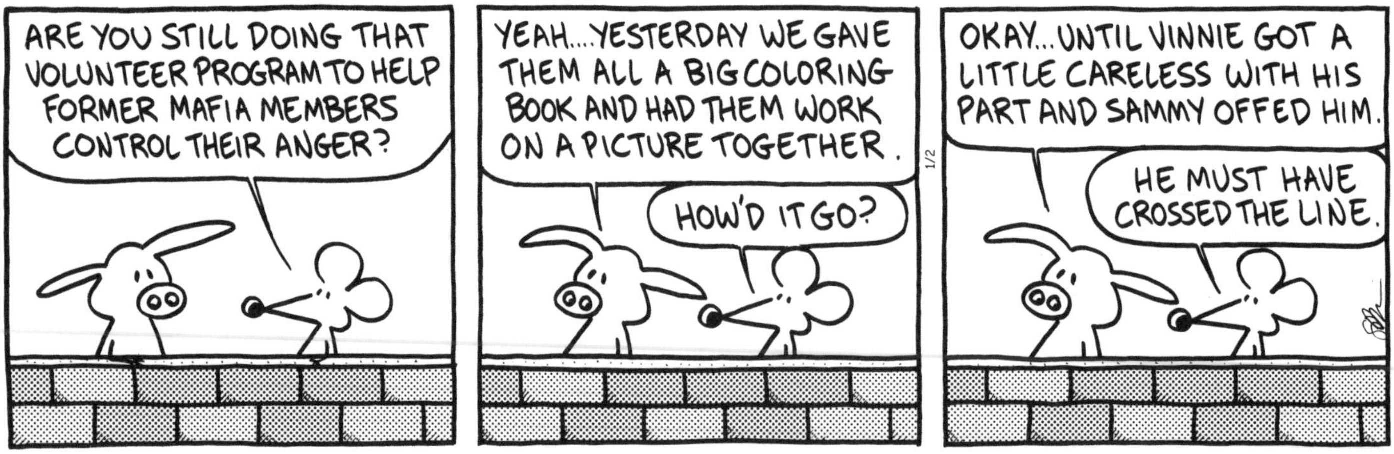
ARE YOU STILL DOING THAT VOLUNTEER PROGRAM TO HELP FORMER MAFIA MEMBERS CONTROL THEIR ANGER?
YEAH....YESTERDAY WE GAVE THEM ALL A BIG COLORING BOOK AND HAD THEM WORK ON A PICTURE TOGETHER.
HOW'D IT GO?
1/2
OKAY...UNTIL VINNIE GOT A LITTLE CARELESS WITH HIS PART AND SAMMY OFFED HIM.
HE MUST HAVE CROSSED THE LINE.

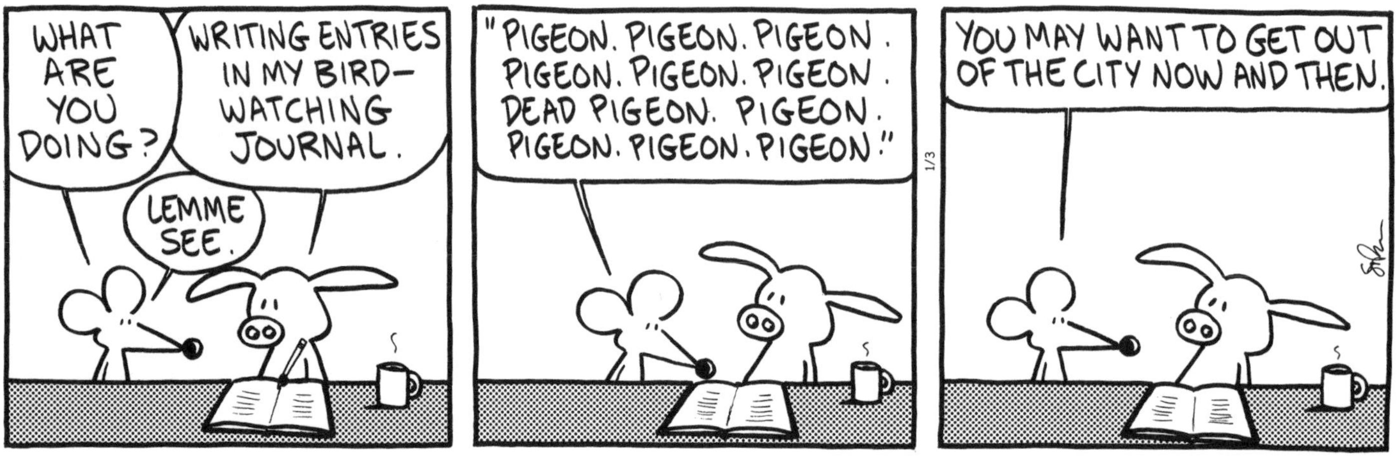
WHAT ARE YOU DOING?
WRITING ENTRIES IN MY BIRD-WATCHING JOURNAL.
LEMME SEE.
"PIGEON. PIGEON. PIGEON. PIGEON. PIGEON. PIGEON. DEAD PIGEON. PIGEON. PIGEON. PIGEON. PIGEON."
1/3
YOU MAY WANT TO GET OUT OF THE CITY NOW AND THEN.

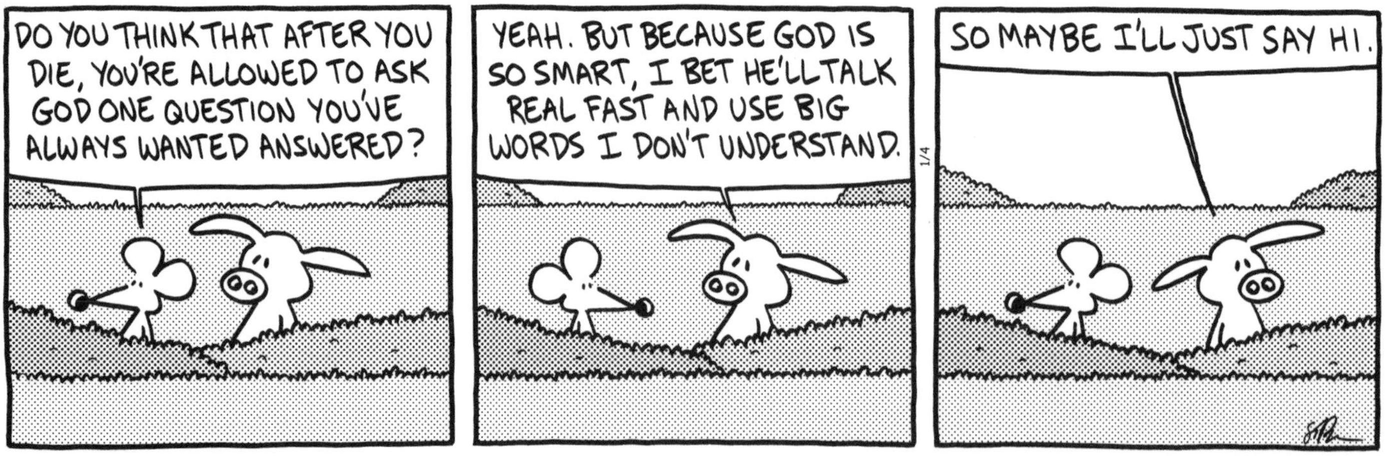
DO YOU THINK THAT AFTER YOU DIE, YOU'RE ALLOWED TO ASK GOD ONE QUESTION YOU'VE ALWAYS WANTED ANSWERED?
YEAH. BUT BECAUSE GOD IS SO SMART, I BET HE'LL TALK REAL FAST AND USE BIG WORDS I DON'T UNDERSTAND.
1/4
SO MAYBE I'LL JUST SAY HI.

On the day I drew the "one person living or dead" strip, I also did this one. I was so excited about *both* strips that I actually called my syndicate immediately after I wrote them. One strip became the fans' favorite daily, and the other (this one) turned out to be dud. This illustrates better than anything how I have virtually no ability to judge how a strip will be received (especially in the few minutes after I've written it).

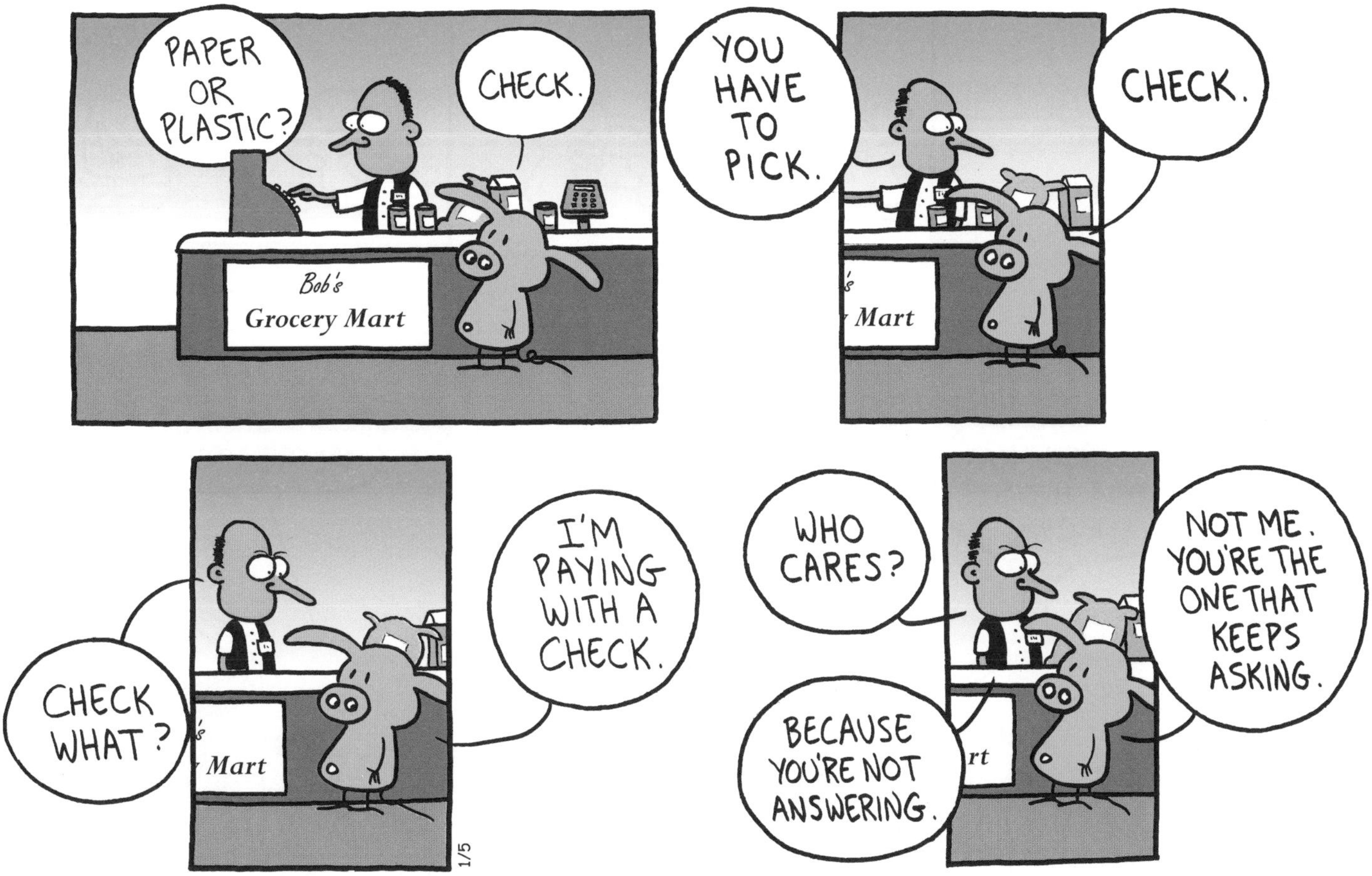
PAPER OR PLASTIC?
CHECK.
Bob's Grocery Mart
YOU HAVE TO PICK.
CHECK.
Mart
CHECK WHAT?
I'M PAYING WITH A CHECK.
Mart
WHO CARES?
NOT ME. YOU'RE THE ONE THAT KEEPS ASKING.
BECAUSE YOU'RE NOT ANSWERING.
1/5

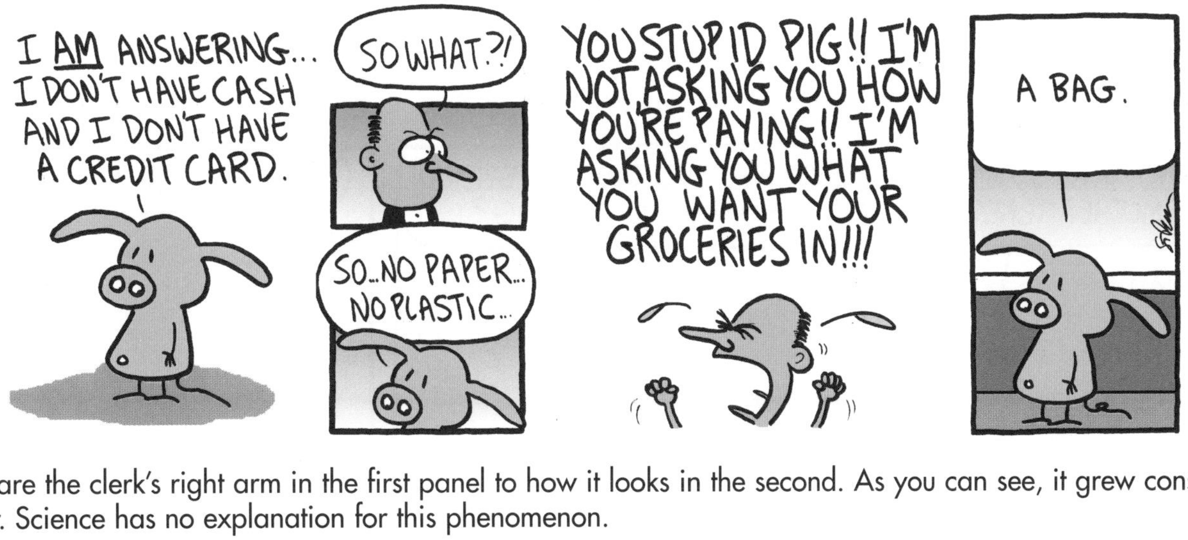
I AM ANSWERING... I DON'T HAVE CASH AND I DON'T HAVE A CREDIT CARD.
SO WHAT?!
SO...NO PAPER... NO PLASTIC...
YOU STUPID PIG!! I'M NOT ASKING YOU HOW YOU'RE PAYING!! I'M ASKING YOU WHAT YOU WANT YOUR GROCERIES IN!!!
A BAG.

Compare the clerk's right arm in the first panel to how it looks in the second. As you can see, it grew considerably longer. Science has no explanation for this phenomenon.

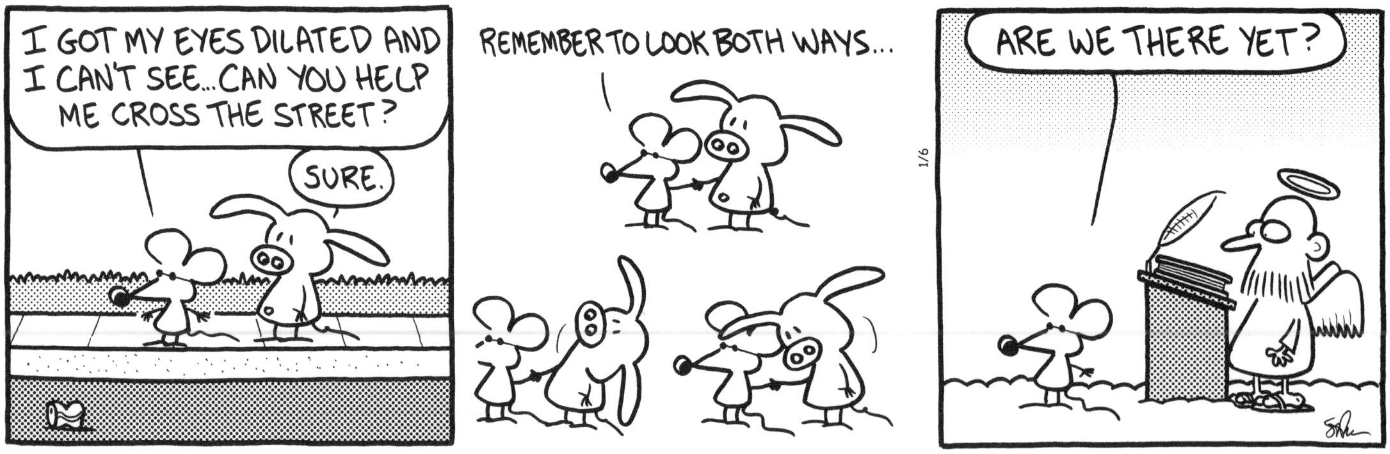
I GOT MY EYES DILATED AND I CAN'T SEE... CAN YOU HELP ME CROSS THE STREET?
SURE.
REMEMBER TO LOOK BOTH WAYS...
1/6
ARE WE THERE YET?

Actually, I think you can still see after you get your eyes dilated (everything's just a little bright). But hey, what the joke needs, the joke gets.

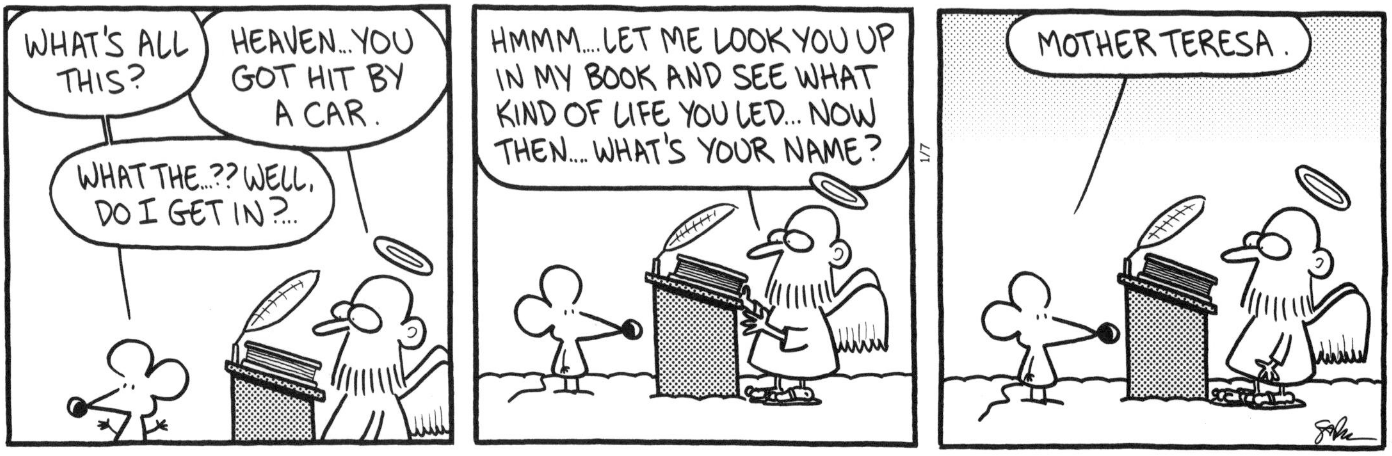
WHAT'S ALL THIS?
HEAVEN... YOU GOT HIT BY A CAR.
WHAT THE...?? WELL, DO I GET IN?...
HMMM.... LET ME LOOK YOU UP IN MY BOOK AND SEE WHAT KIND OF LIFE YOU LED... NOW THEN.... WHAT'S YOUR NAME?
1/7
MOTHER TERESA.

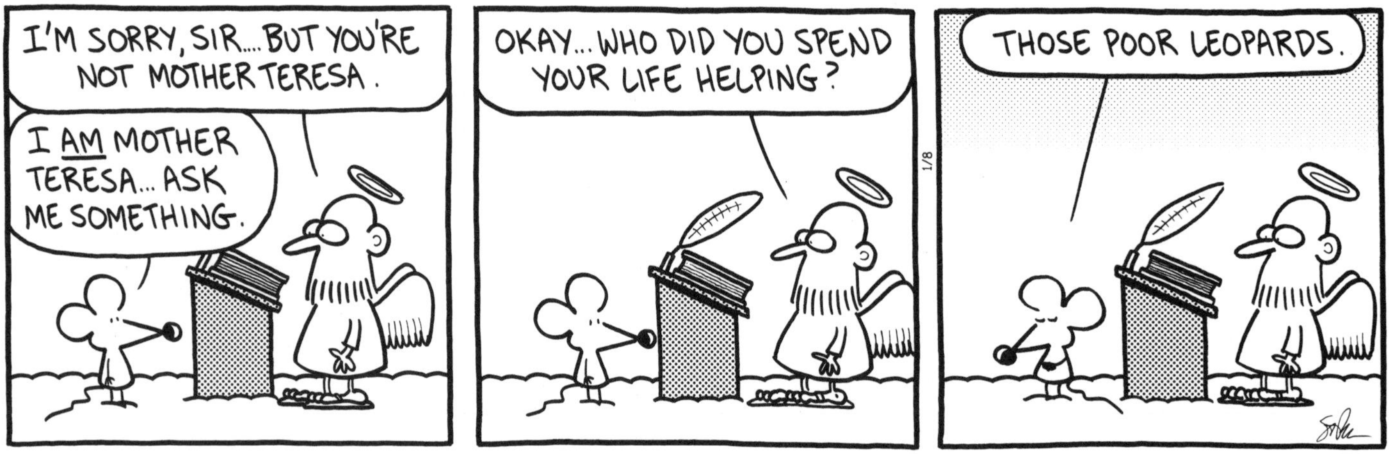
I'M SORRY, SIR.... BUT YOU'RE NOT MOTHER TERESA.
I AM MOTHER TERESA... ASK ME SOMETHING.
OKAY... WHO DID YOU SPEND YOUR LIFE HELPING?
1/8
THOSE POOR LEOPARDS.

Some people didn't get this. For those people, I provide the following explanation: Mother Teresa helped lepers. She did not help leopards. Although if a leopard was a leper, I suppose she might have done something.

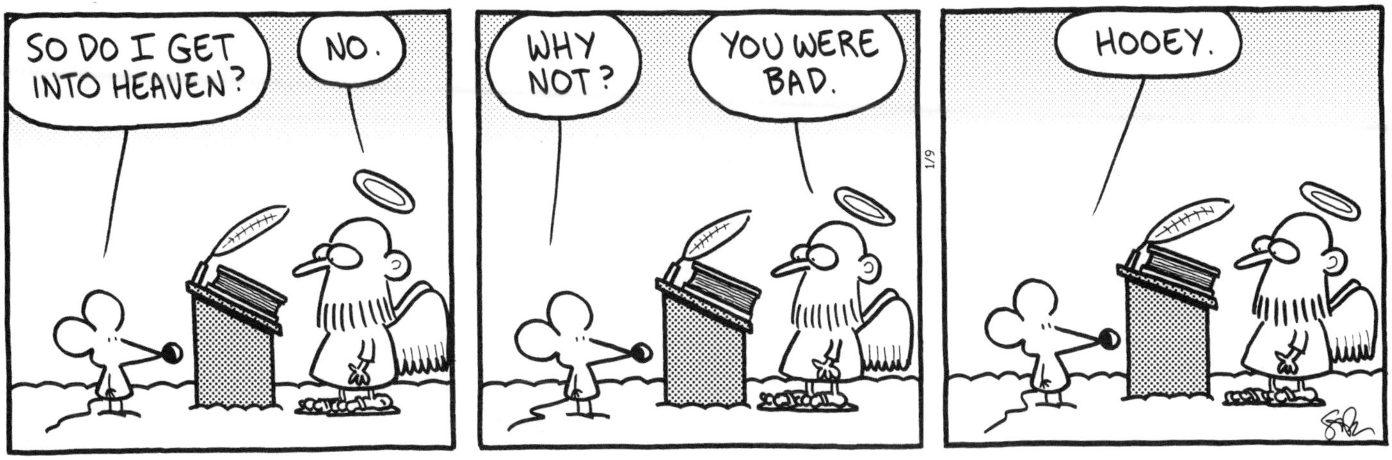
SO DO I GET INTO HEAVEN?
NO.
WHY NOT?
YOU WERE BAD.
1/9
HOOEY.

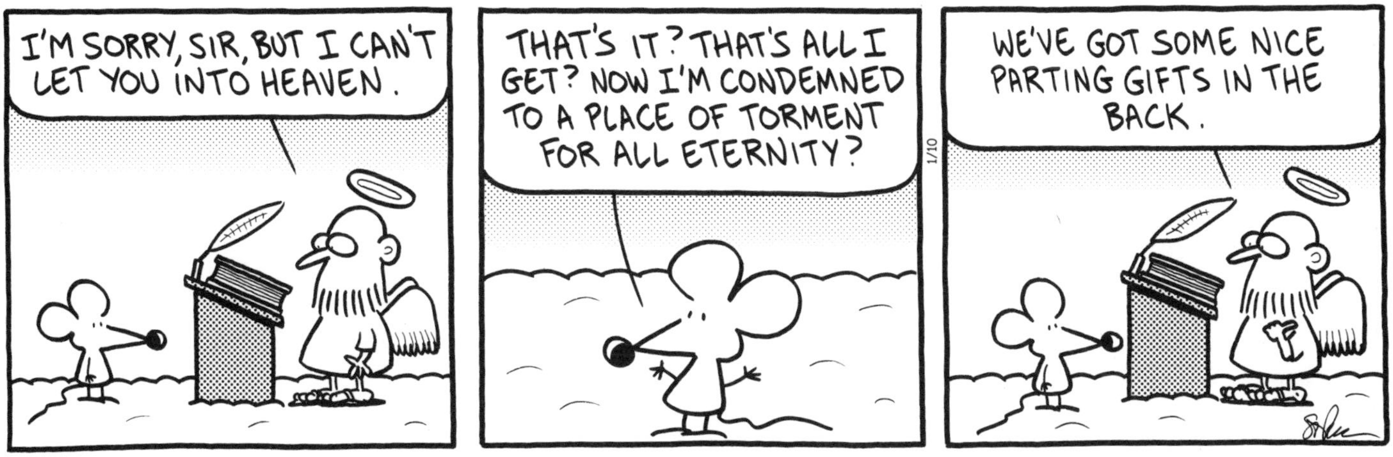
I'M SORRY, SIR, BUT I CAN'T LET YOU INTO HEAVEN.
THAT'S IT? THAT'S ALL I GET? NOW I'M CONDEMNED TO A PLACE OF TORMENT FOR ALL ETERNITY?
1/10
WE'VE GOT SOME NICE PARTING GIFTS IN THE BACK.

Round about this point, I grew very bored of drawing St. Peter's lectern, feather pen, and book of names, not to mention his wings and sandals. Good thing I didn't draw those fancy gates.

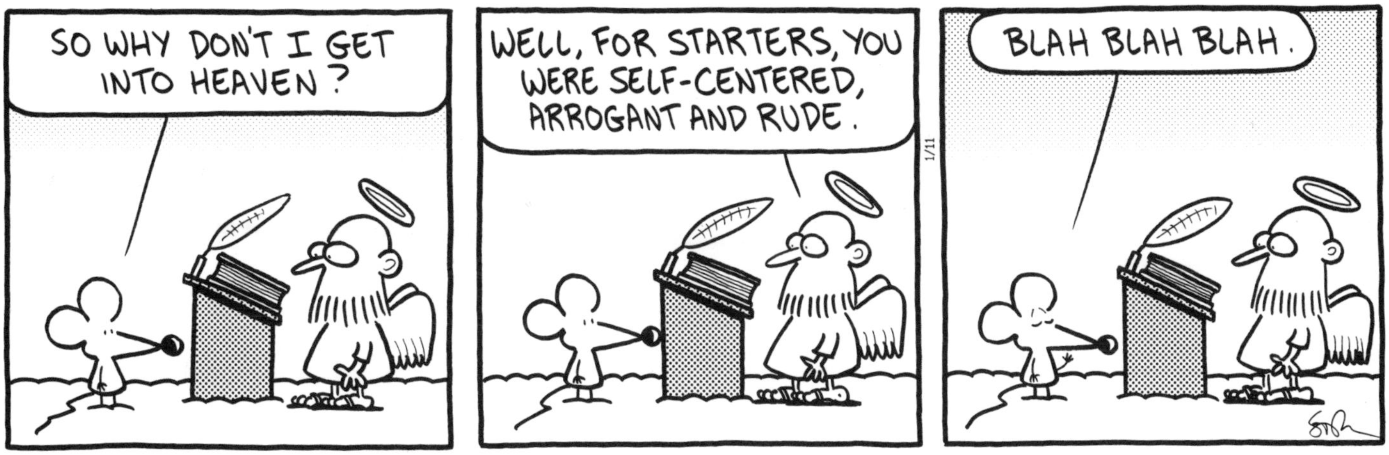
SO WHY DON'T I GET INTO HEAVEN?
WELL, FOR STARTERS, YOU WERE SELF-CENTERED, ARROGANT AND RUDE.
1/11
BLAH BLAH BLAH.

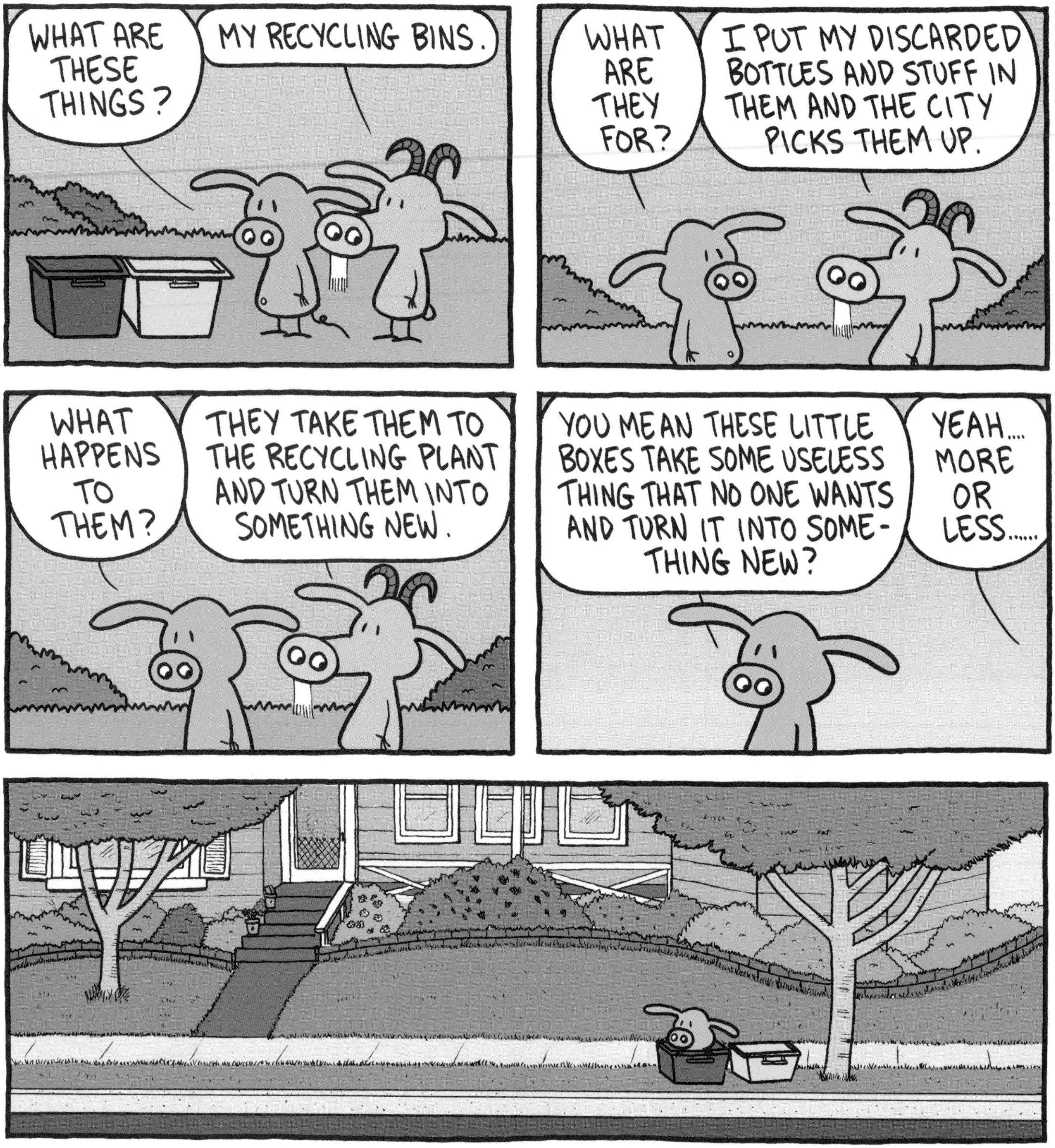
WHAT ARE THESE THINGS?
MY RECYCLING BINS.
WHAT ARE THEY FOR?
I PUT MY DISCARDED BOTTLES AND STUFF IN THEM AND THE CITY PICKS THEM UP.
WHAT HAPPENS TO THEM?
THEY TAKE THEM TO THE RECYCLING PLANT AND TURN THEM INTO SOMETHING NEW.
YOU MEAN THESE LITTLE BOXES TAKE SOME USELESS THING THAT NO ONE WANTS AND TURN IT INTO SOME-THING NEW?
YEAH.... MORE OR LESS......

At the time I drew this, we were moving out of our first house, which my wife and I really loved, but which had become too small for our growing family. With my minimal drawing skills, I did my best to draw the front of the house and put it here in the strip, which I then gave to my wife.

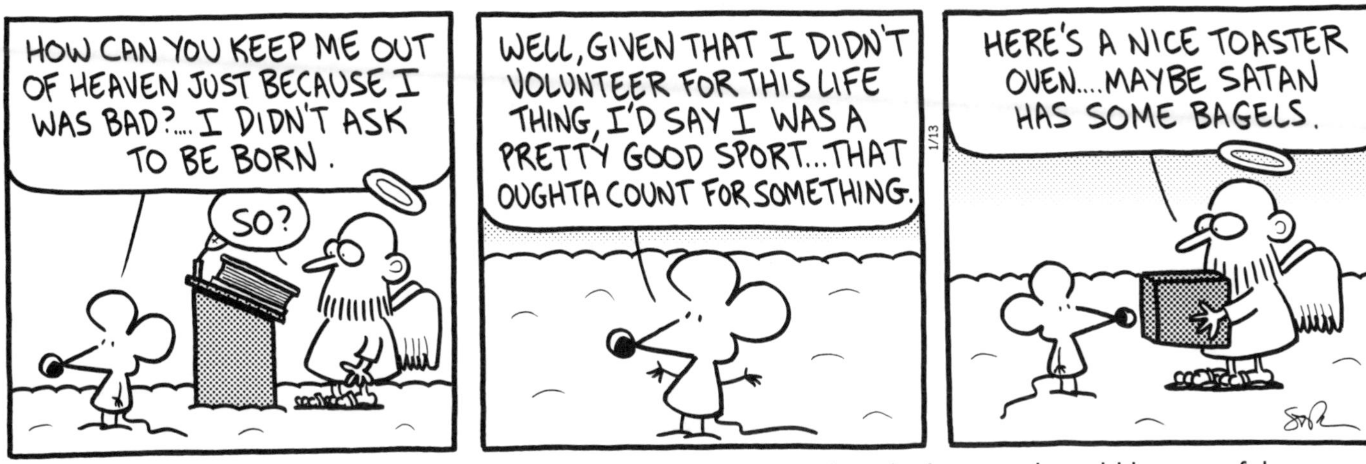
HOW CAN YOU KEEP ME OUT OF HEAVEN JUST BECAUSE I WAS BAD?.... I DIDN'T ASK TO BE BORN.
SO?
WELL, GIVEN THAT I DIDN'T VOLUNTEER FOR THIS LIFE THING, I'D SAY I WAS A PRETTY GOOD SPORT... THAT OUGHTA COUNT FOR SOMETHING.
1/13
HERE'S A NICE TOASTER OVEN.... MAYBE SATAN HAS SOME BAGELS.

If I'm allowed to have favorite lines in my own strip, St. Peter's remark in the last panel would be one of them.

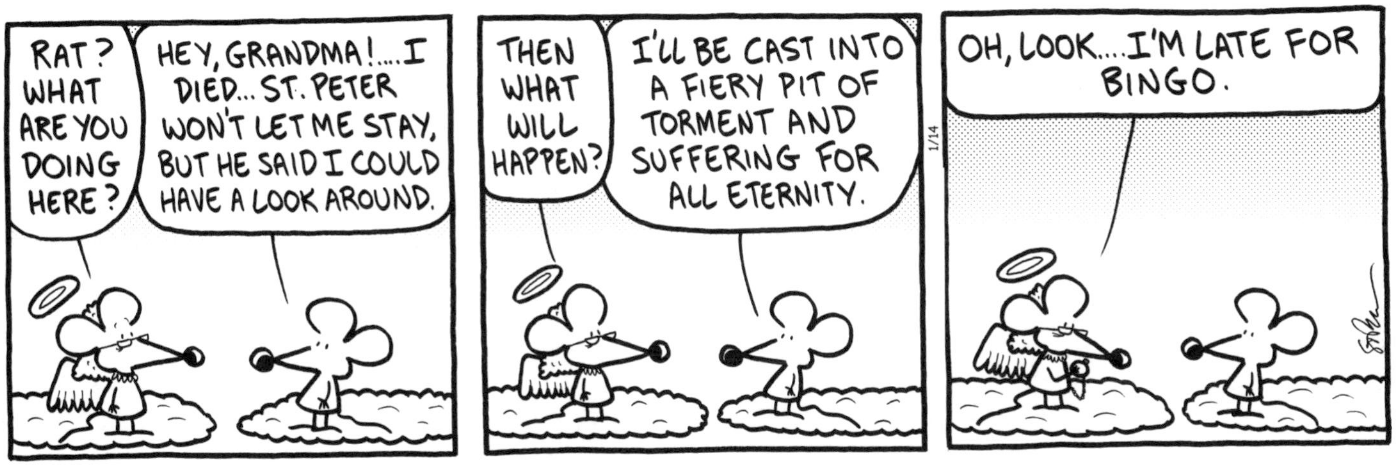
RAT? WHAT ARE YOU DOING HERE?
HEY, GRANDMA!.... I DIED... ST. PETER WON'T LET ME STAY, BUT HE SAID I COULD HAVE A LOOK AROUND.
THEN WHAT WILL HAPPEN?
I'LL BE CAST INTO A FIERY PIT OF TORMENT AND SUFFERING FOR ALL ETERNITY.
1/14
OH, LOOK.... I'M LATE FOR BINGO.

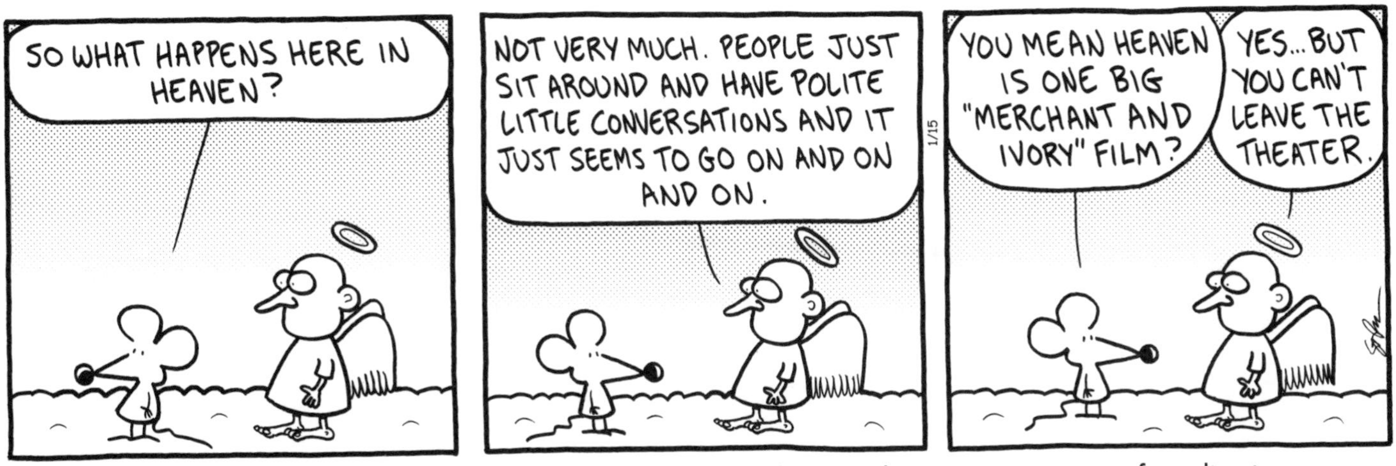
SO WHAT HAPPENS HERE IN HEAVEN?
NOT VERY MUCH. PEOPLE JUST SIT AROUND AND HAVE POLITE LITTLE CONVERSATIONS AND IT JUST SEEMS TO GO ON AND ON AND ON.
1/15
YOU MEAN HEAVEN IS ONE BIG "MERCHANT AND IVORY" FILM?
YES... BUT YOU CAN'T LEAVE THE THEATER.

For those of you keeping score at home, that's *two* Merchant and Ivory jokes in just one year of syndication.

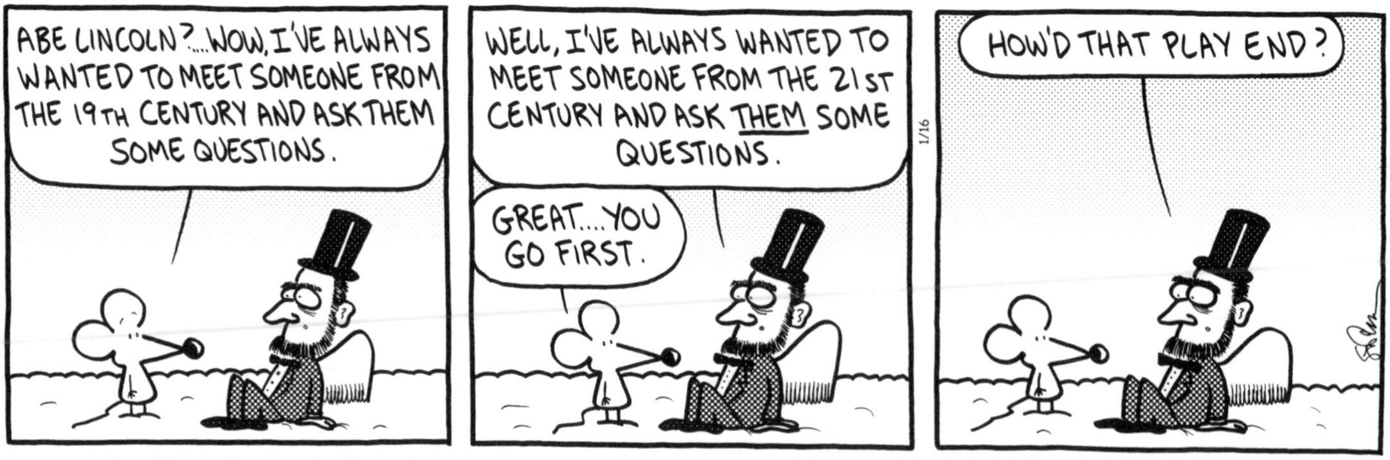
ABE LINCOLN?....WOW, I'VE ALWAYS WANTED TO MEET SOMEONE FROM THE 19TH CENTURY AND ASK THEM SOME QUESTIONS.
WELL, I'VE ALWAYS WANTED TO MEET SOMEONE FROM THE 21ST CENTURY AND ASK THEM SOME QUESTIONS.
GREAT....YOU GO FIRST.
1/16
HOW'D THAT PLAY END?

You're only allowed to make fun of a tragedy if it's 140 years old.

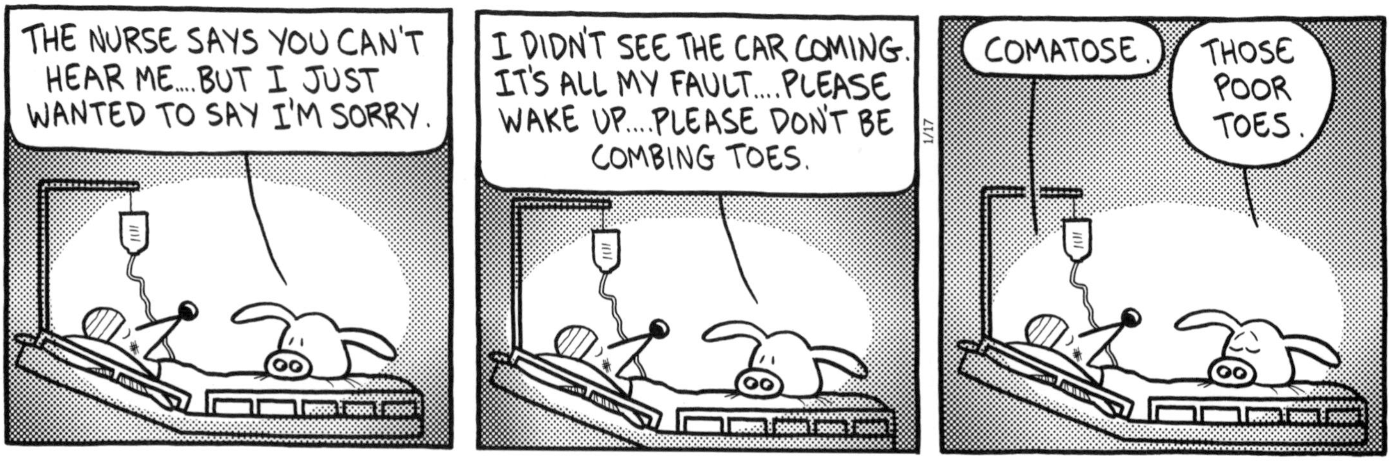
THE NURSE SAYS YOU CAN'T HEAR ME....BUT I JUST WANTED TO SAY I'M SORRY.
I DIDN'T SEE THE CAR COMING. IT'S ALL MY FAULT....PLEASE WAKE UP....PLEASE DON'T BE COMBING TOES.
1/17
COMATOSE.
THOSE POOR TOES.

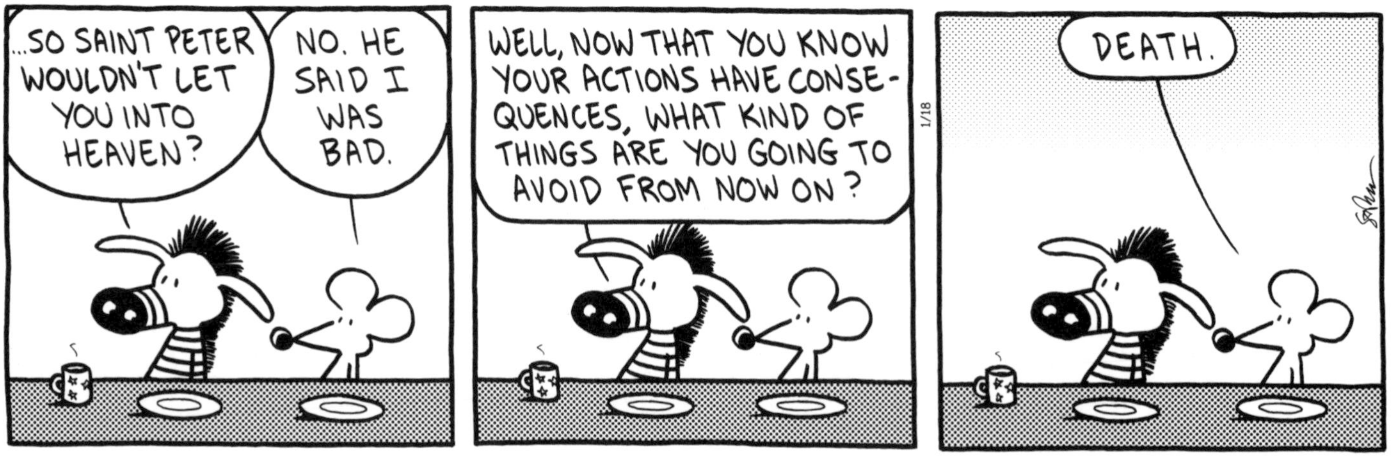
...SO SAINT PETER WOULDN'T LET YOU INTO HEAVEN?
NO. HE SAID I WAS BAD.
WELL, NOW THAT YOU KNOW YOUR ACTIONS HAVE CONSE-QUENCES, WHAT KIND OF THINGS ARE YOU GOING TO AVOID FROM NOW ON?
1/18
DEATH.

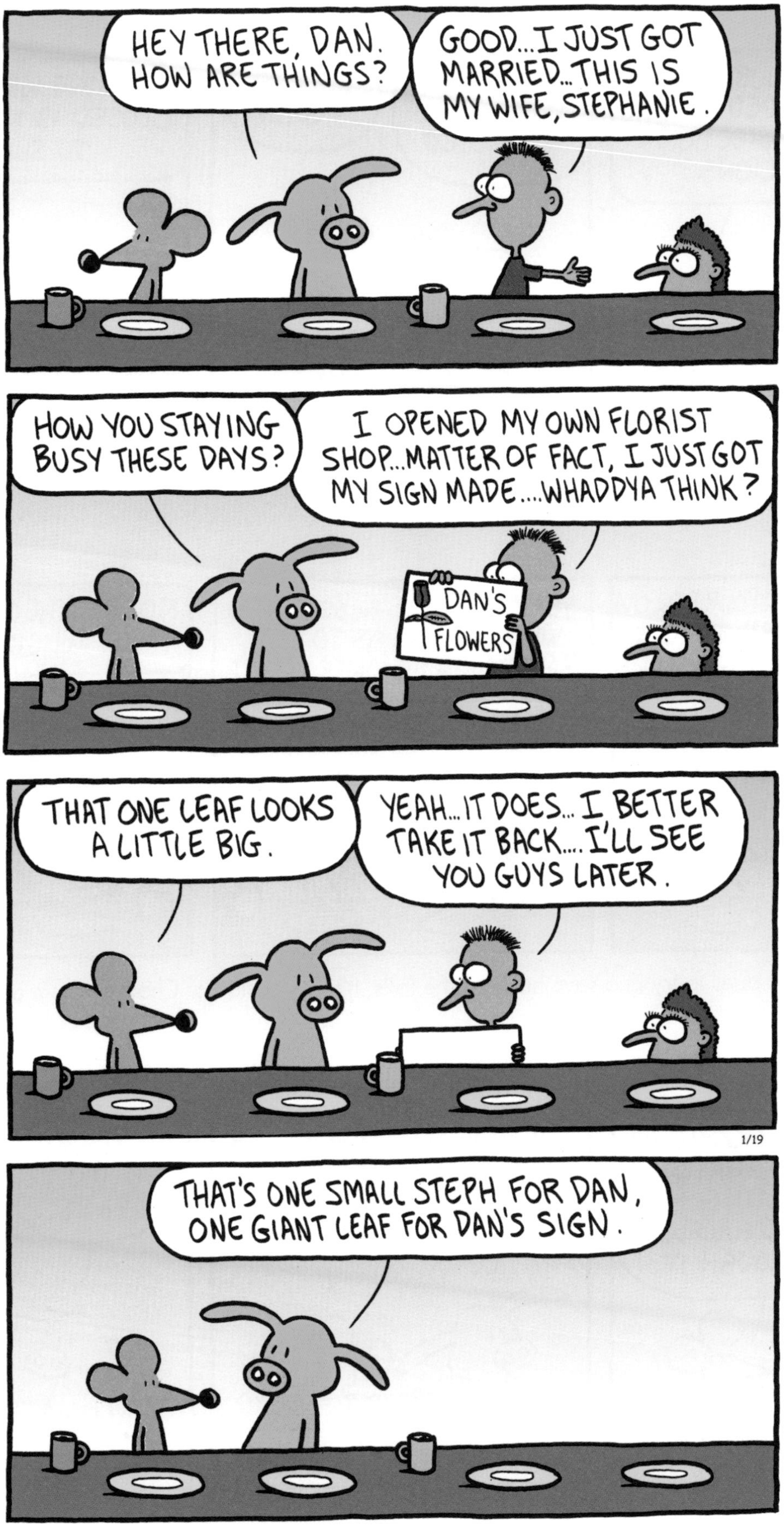
HEY THERE, DAN. HOW ARE THINGS?
GOOD...I JUST GOT MARRIED...THIS IS MY WIFE, STEPHANIE.
HOW YOU STAYING BUSY THESE DAYS?
I OPENED MY OWN FLORIST SHOP...MATTER OF FACT, I JUST GOT MY SIGN MADE....WHADDYA THINK?
DAN'S FLOWERS
THAT ONE LEAF LOOKS A LITTLE BIG.
YEAH...IT DOES... I BETTER TAKE IT BACK.... I'LL SEE YOU GUYS LATER.
1/19
THAT'S ONE SMALL STEPH FOR DAN, ONE GIANT LEAF FOR DAN'S SIGN.

I like this strip because you have no idea where it's going until you read that last panel.

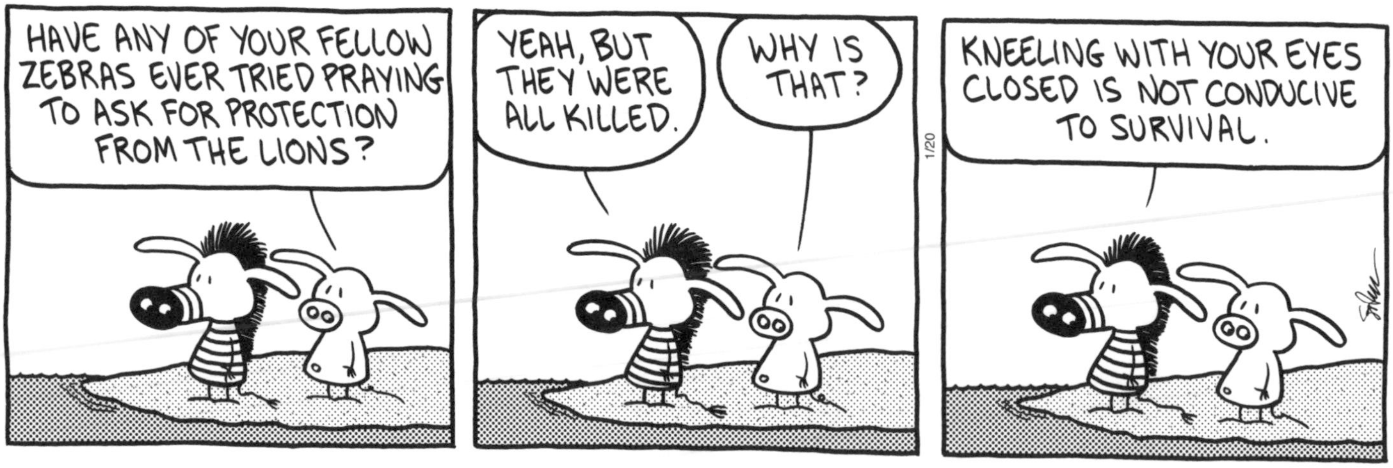
HAVE ANY OF YOUR FELLOW ZEBRAS EVER TRIED PRAYING TO ASK FOR PROTECTION FROM THE LIONS?
YEAH, BUT THEY WERE ALL KILLED.
WHY IS THAT?
KNEELING WITH YOUR EYES CLOSED IS NOT CONDUCIVE TO SURVIVAL.
1/20

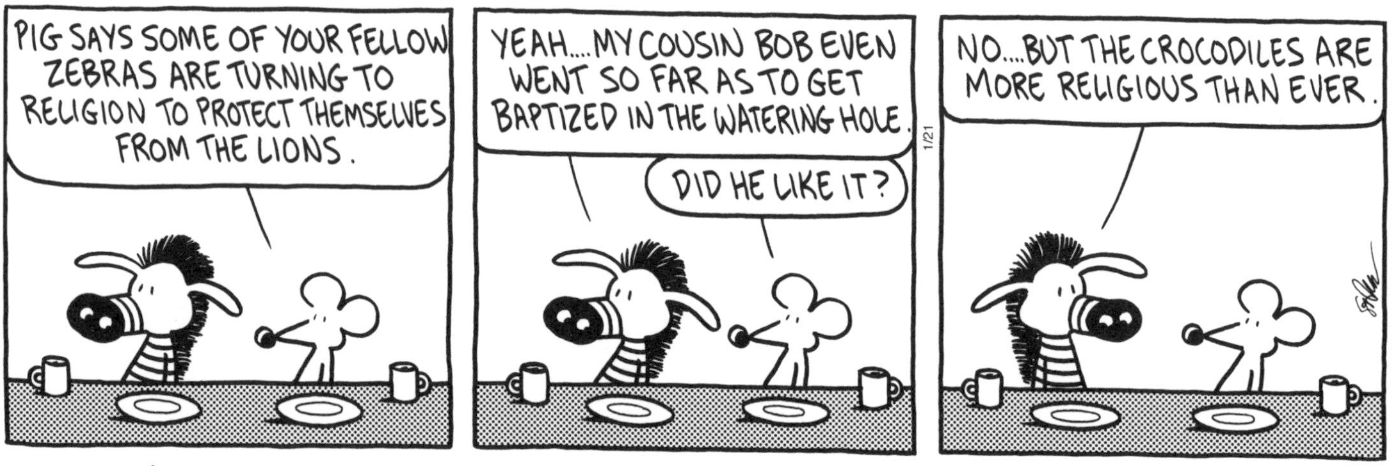
PIG SAYS SOME OF YOUR FELLOW ZEBRAS ARE TURNING TO RELIGION TO PROTECT THEMSELVES FROM THE LIONS.
YEAH.... MY COUSIN BOB EVEN WENT SO FAR AS TO GET BAPTIZED IN THE WATERING HOLE.
DID HE LIKE IT?
NO....BUT THE CROCODILES ARE MORE RELIGIOUS THAN EVER.
1/21

No matter what Zebra does to try and save his herd, he fails. It's my version of Charlie Brown and the football.

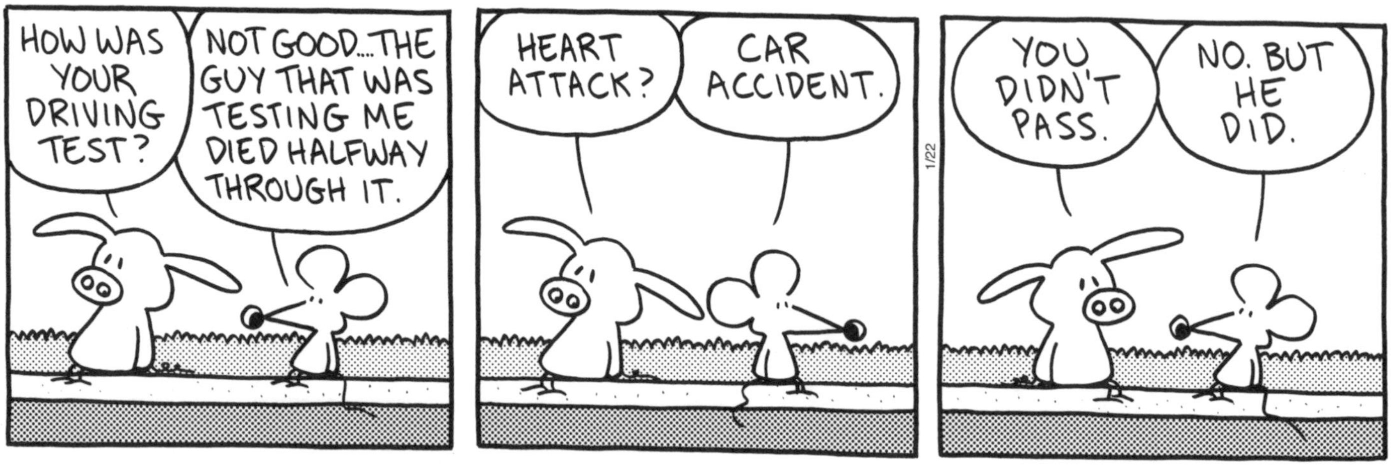
HOW WAS YOUR DRIVING TEST?
NOT GOOD....THE GUY THAT WAS TESTING ME DIED HALFWAY THROUGH IT.
HEART ATTACK?
CAR ACCIDENT.
YOU DIDN'T PASS.
NO. BUT HE DID.
1/22

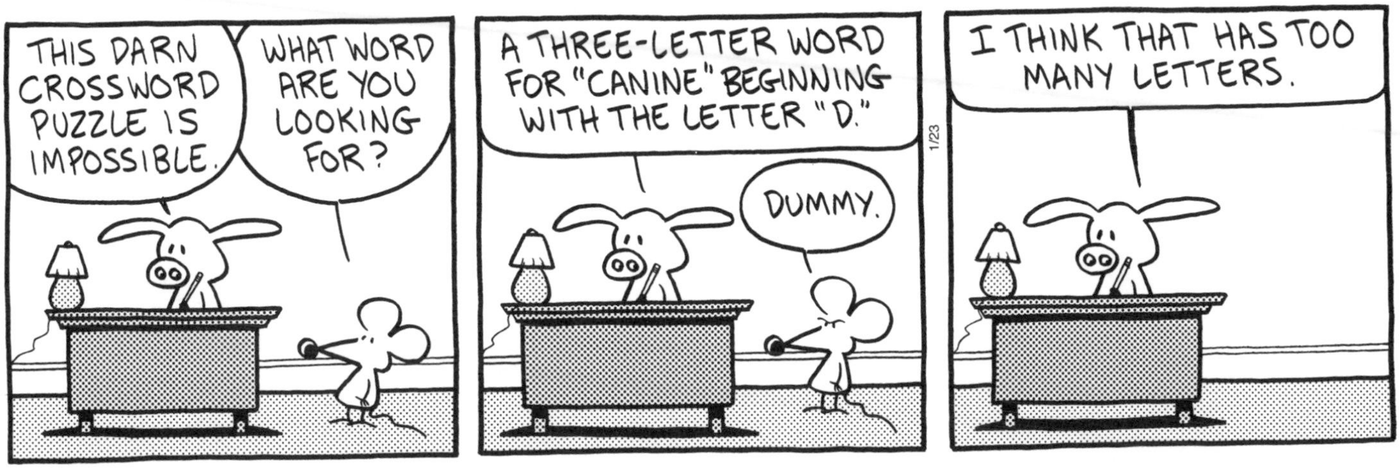
THIS DARN CROSSWORD PUZZLE IS IMPOSSIBLE.
WHAT WORD ARE YOU LOOKING FOR?
A THREE-LETTER WORD FOR "CANINE" BEGINNING WITH THE LETTER "D."
DUMMY.
1/23
I THINK THAT HAS TOO MANY LETTERS.

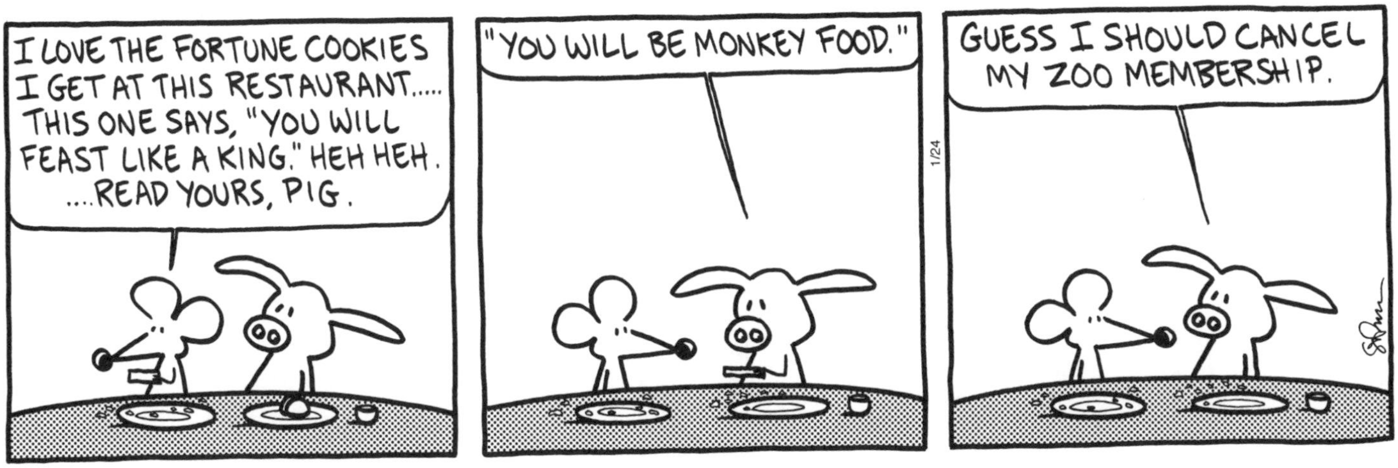
I LOVE THE FORTUNE COOKIES I GET AT THIS RESTAURANT..... THIS ONE SAYS, "YOU WILL FEAST LIKE A KING." HEH HEH. ....READ YOURS, PIG.
"YOU WILL BE MONKEY FOOD."
1/24
GUESS I SHOULD CANCEL MY ZOO MEMBERSHIP.

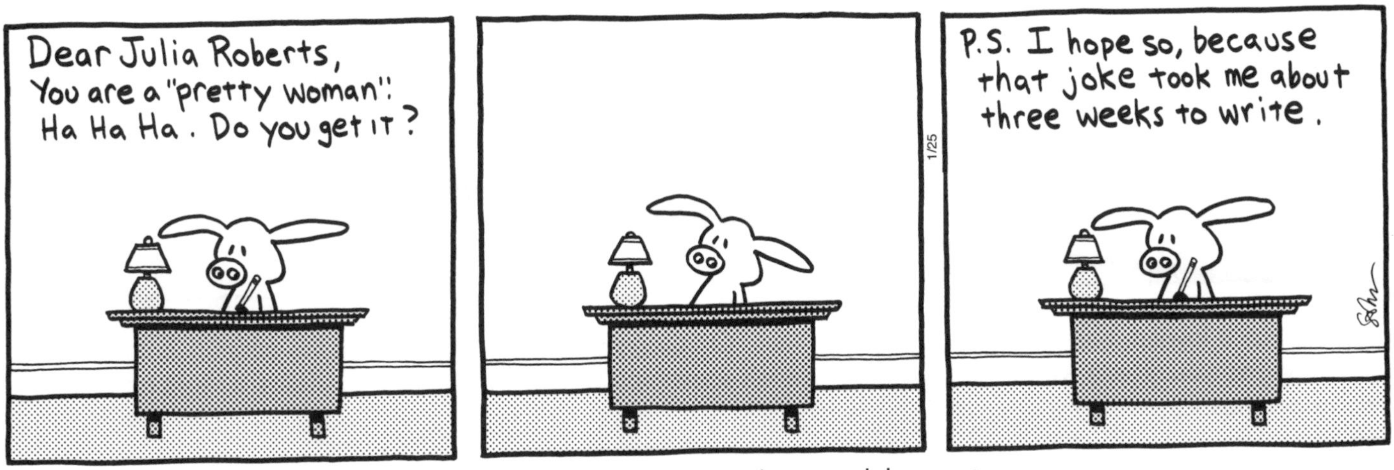
Dear Julia Roberts,
You are a "pretty woman". Ha Ha Ha. Do you get it?
1/25
P.S. I hope so, because that joke took me about three weeks to write.

This didn't get Julia Roberts's attention either. Julia Roberts needs to read the comics.

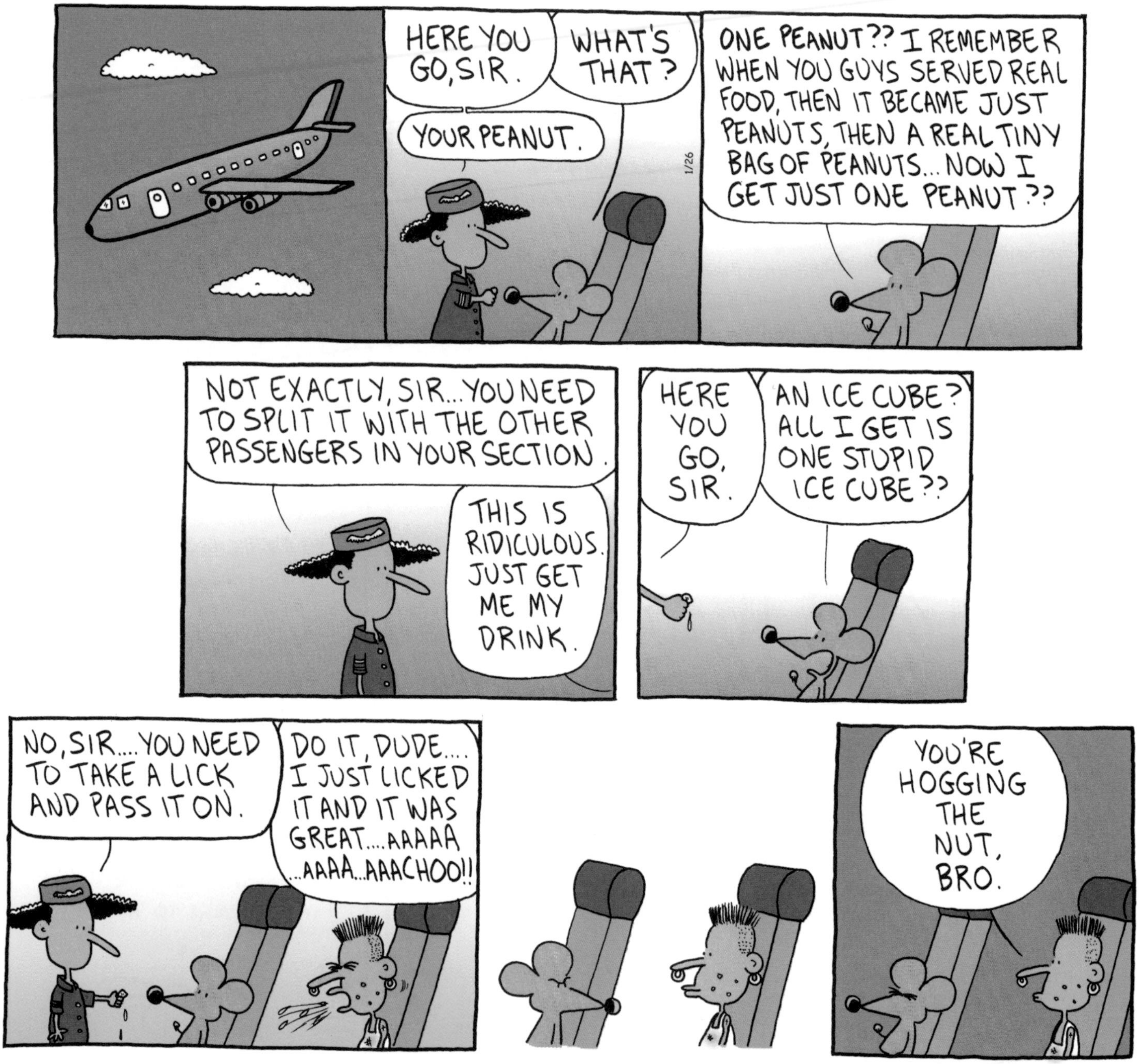
HERE YOU GO, SIR.
WHAT'S THAT?
YOUR PEANUT.
1/26
ONE PEANUT?? I REMEMBER WHEN YOU GUYS SERVED REAL FOOD, THEN IT BECAME JUST PEANUTS, THEN A REAL TINY BAG OF PEANUTS... NOW I GET JUST ONE PEANUT??
NOT EXACTLY, SIR... YOU NEED TO SPLIT IT WITH THE OTHER PASSENGERS IN YOUR SECTION.
THIS IS RIDICULOUS. JUST GET ME MY DRINK.
HERE YOU GO, SIR.
AN ICE CUBE? ALL I GET IS ONE STUPID ICE CUBE??
NO, SIR.... YOU NEED TO TAKE A LICK AND PASS IT ON.
DO IT, DUDE.... I JUST LICKED IT AND IT WAS GREAT....AAAAA ...AAAA...AAACHOO!!
YOU'RE HOGGING THE NUT, BRO.

When I was a lawyer, I used to fly to L.A. all the time. On one of those flights, I counted the peanuts in that tiny bag they give you. There were twelve peanuts. There's something wrong with paying $200 for a flight and getting twelve peanuts.

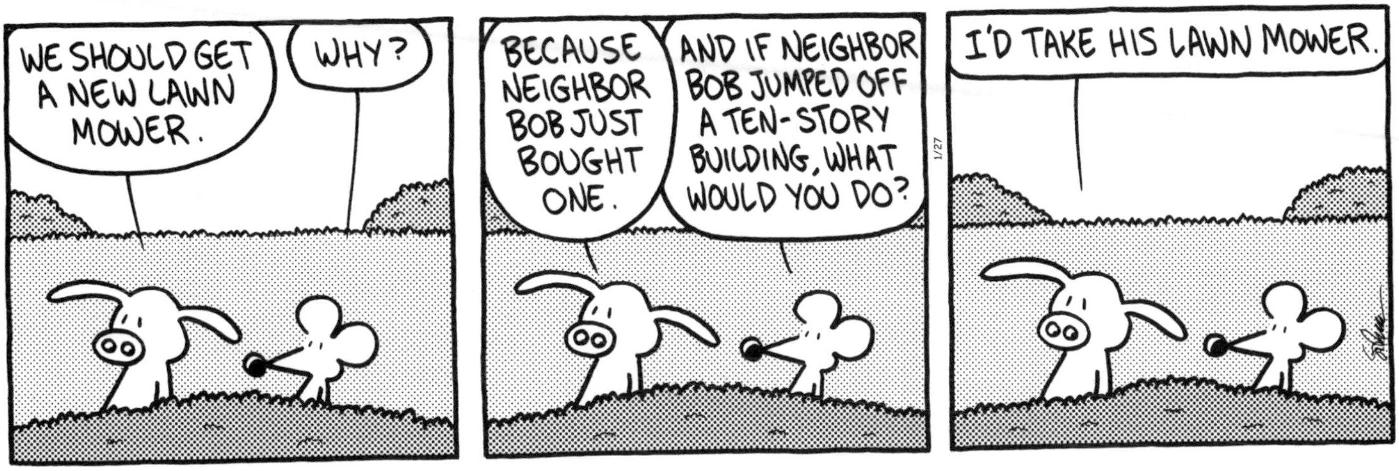
WE SHOULD GET A NEW LAWN MOWER.
WHY?
BECAUSE NEIGHBOR BOB JUST BOUGHT ONE.
AND IF NEIGHBOR BOB JUMPED OFF A TEN-STORY BUILDING, WHAT WOULD YOU DO?
1/27
I'D TAKE HIS LAWN MOWER.

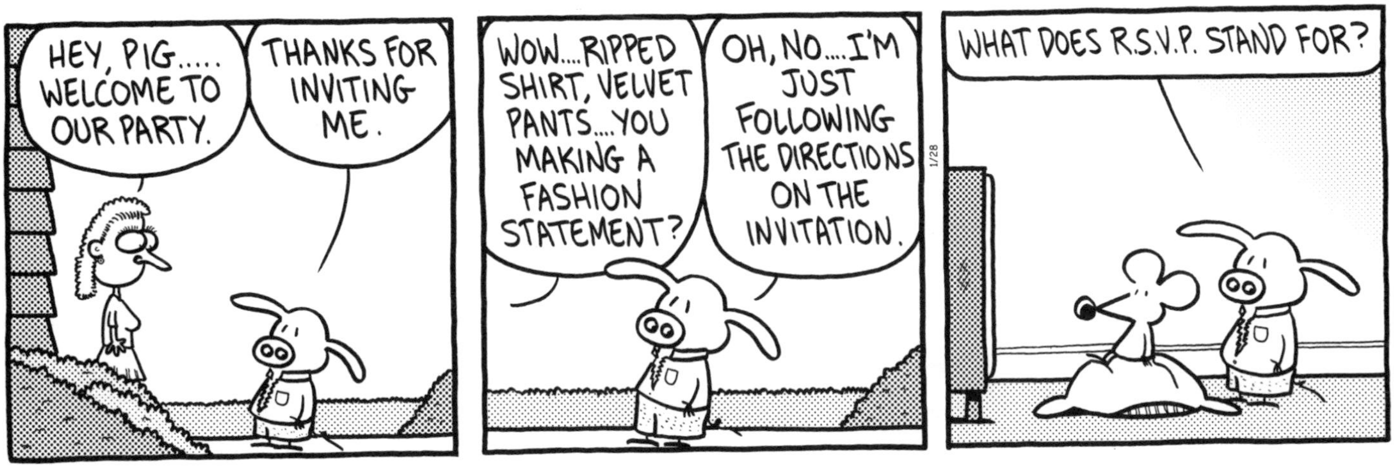
HEY, PIG..... WELCOME TO OUR PARTY.
THANKS FOR INVITING ME.
WOW....RIPPED SHIRT, VELVET PANTS....YOU MAKING A FASHION STATEMENT?
OH, NO....I'M JUST FOLLOWING THE DIRECTIONS ON THE INVITATION.
1/28
WHAT DOES R.S.V.P. STAND FOR?

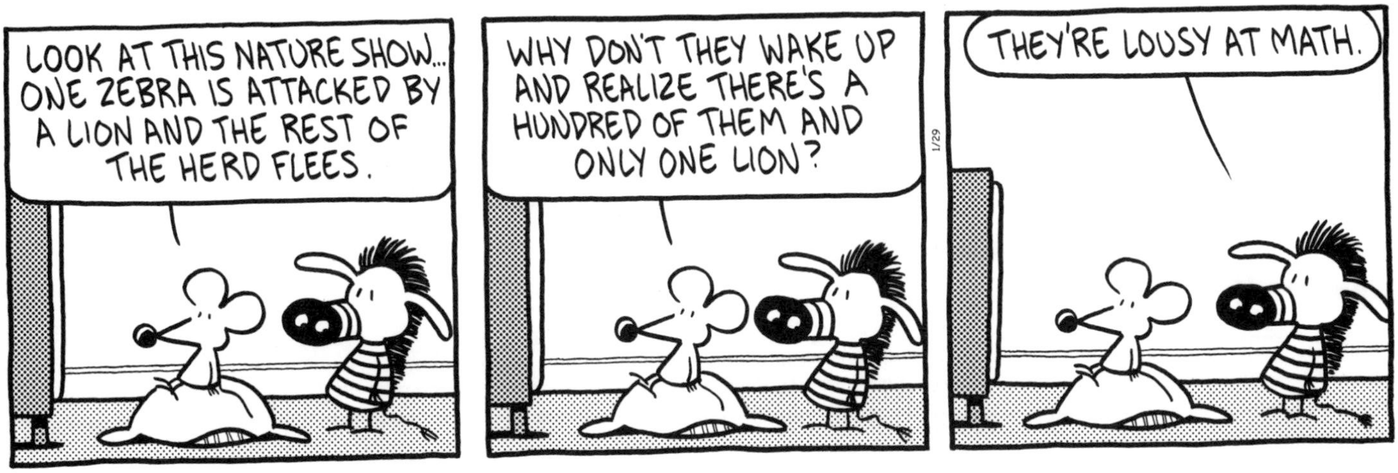
LOOK AT THIS NATURE SHOW... ONE ZEBRA IS ATTACKED BY A LION AND THE REST OF THE HERD FLEES.
WHY DON'T THEY WAKE UP AND REALIZE THERE'S A HUNDRED OF THEM AND ONLY ONE LION?
1/29
THEY'RE LOUSY AT MATH.

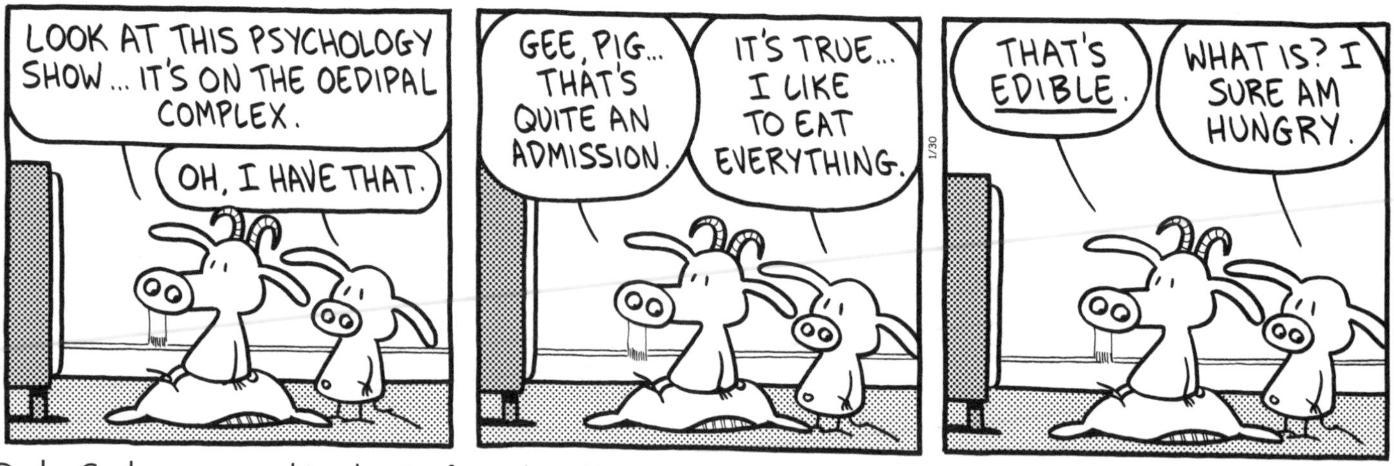
LOOK AT THIS PSYCHOLOGY SHOW... IT'S ON THE OEDIPAL COMPLEX.
OH, I HAVE THAT.
GEE, PIG... THAT'S QUITE AN ADMISSION.
IT'S TRUE... I LIKE TO EAT EVERYTHING.
1/30
THAT'S EDIBLE.
WHAT IS? I SURE AM HUNGRY.

Darby Conley gave me this joke. So if you don't like it, blame him.

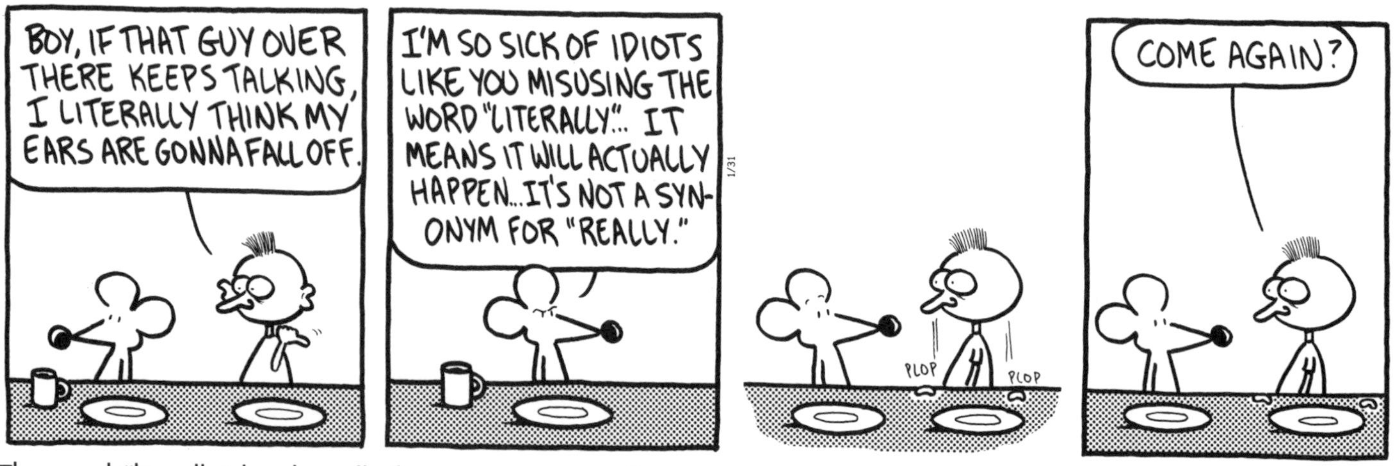
BOY, IF THAT GUY OVER THERE KEEPS TALKING, I LITERALLY THINK MY EARS ARE GONNA FALL OFF.
I'M SO SICK OF IDIOTS LIKE YOU MISUSING THE WORD "LITERALLY"... IT MEANS IT WILL ACTUALLY HAPPEN... IT'S NOT A SYNONYM FOR "REALLY."
1/31
PLOP
PLOP
COME AGAIN?

The word "literally" has lost all of its meaning. Literally.

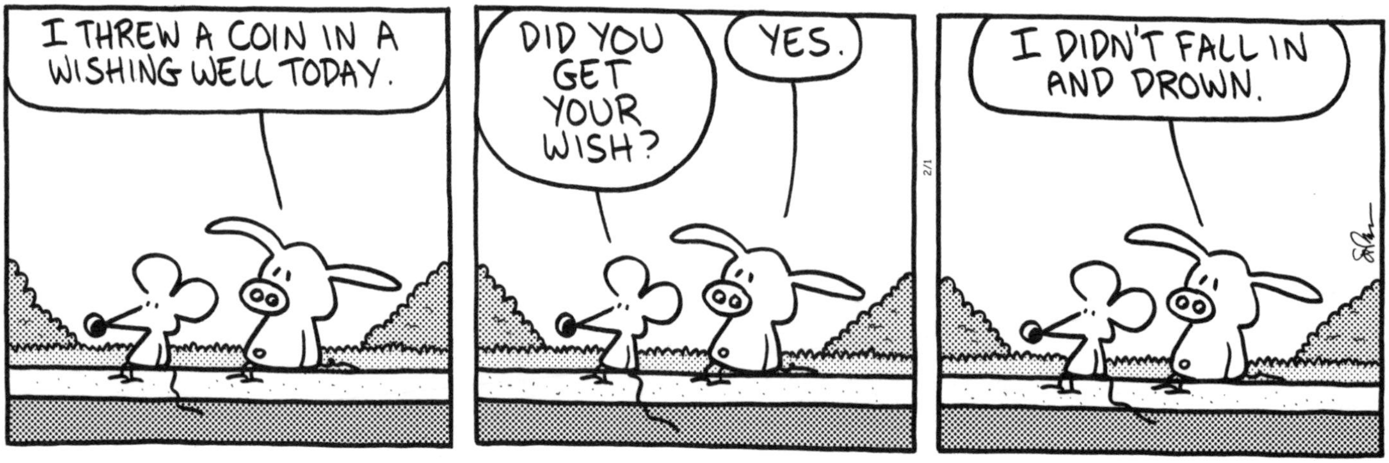
I THREW A COIN IN A WISHING WELL TODAY.
DID YOU GET YOUR WISH?
YES.
2/1
I DIDN'T FALL IN AND DROWN.

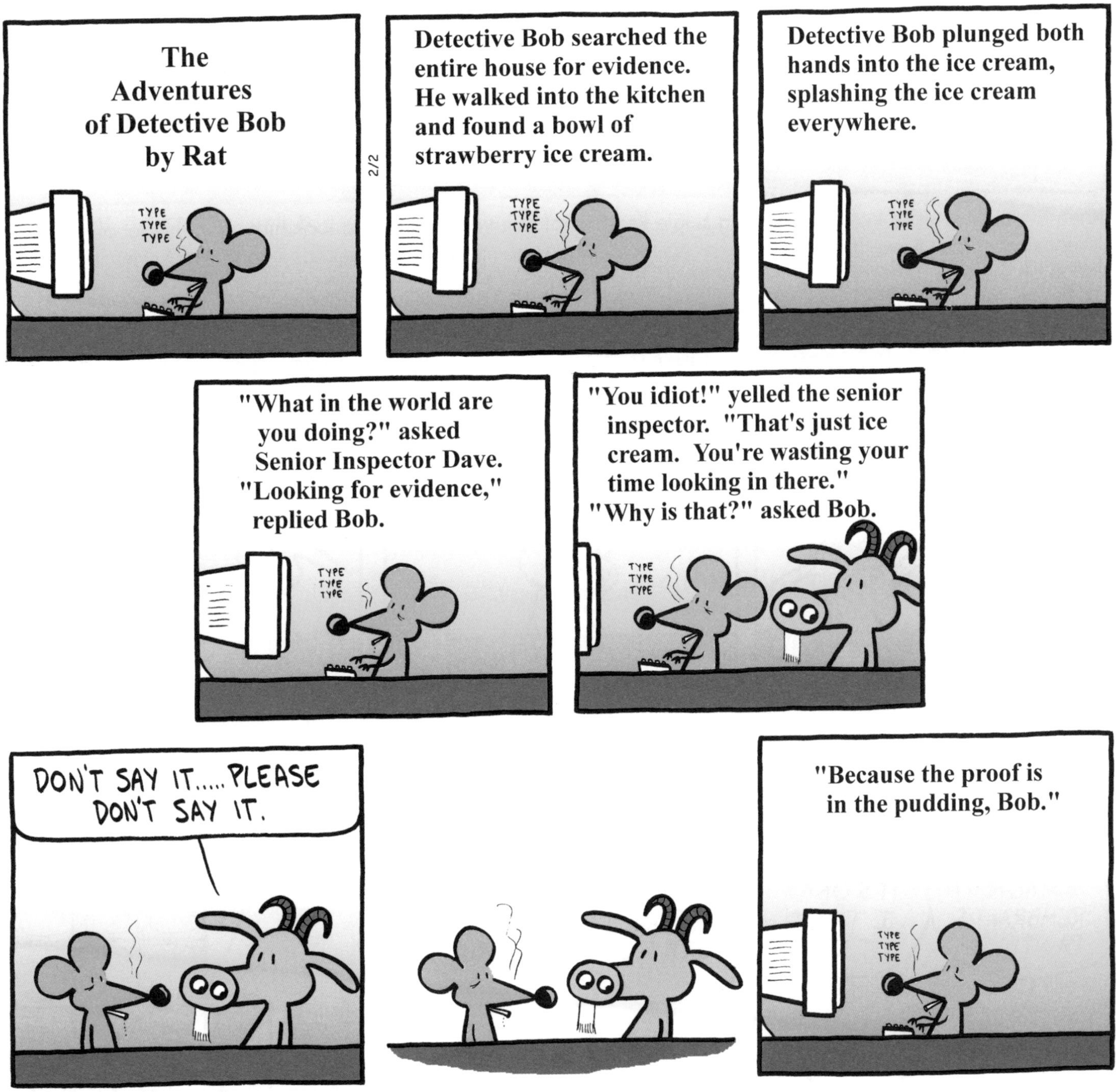
The Adventures of Detective Bob by Rat
TYPE TYPE TYPE
2/2
Detective Bob searched the entire house for evidence. He walked into the kitchen and found a bowl of strawberry ice cream.
TYPE TYPE TYPE
Detective Bob plunged both hands into the ice cream, splashing the ice cream everywhere.
TYPE TYPE TYPE
"What in the world are you doing?" asked Senior Inspector Dave. "Looking for evidence," replied Bob.
TYPE TYPE TYPE
"You idiot!" yelled the senior inspector. "That's just ice cream. You're wasting your time looking in there." "Why is that?" asked Bob.
TYPE TYPE TYPE
DON'T SAY IT..... PLEASE DON'T SAY IT.
"Because the proof is in the pudding, Bob."
TYPE TYPE TYPE

A bunch of people wrote me to say I got the "proof is in the pudding" line wrong. The actual saying is something else. But to be honest, accuracy is rarely my goal. If the phrase is commonly said in a certain way—even if wrong—I'll use it.

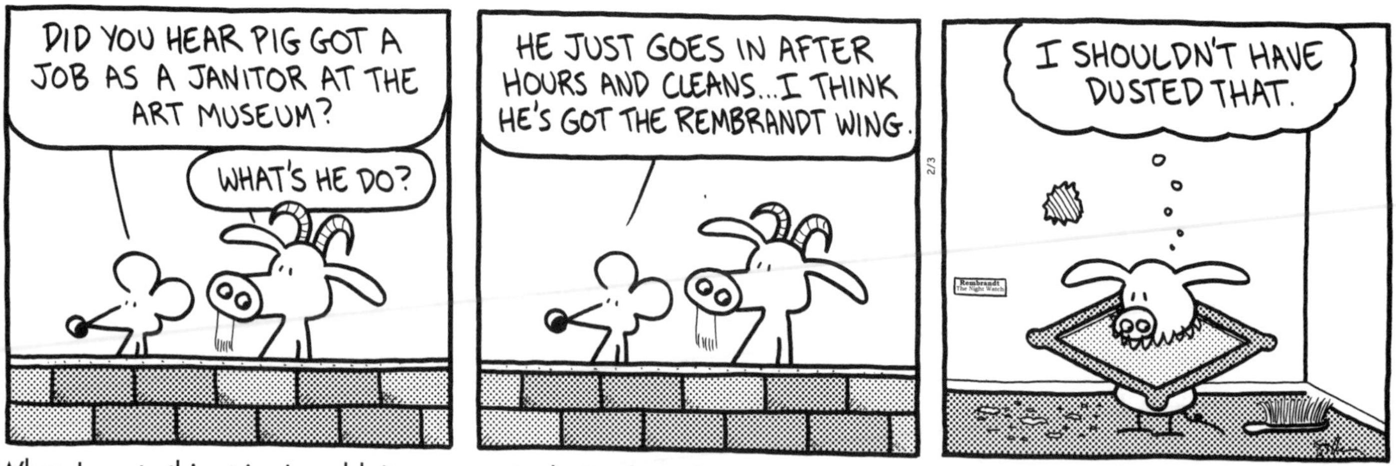
DID YOU HEAR PIG GOT A JOB AS A JANITOR AT THE ART MUSEUM?
WHAT'S HE DO?
HE JUST GOES IN AFTER HOURS AND CLEANS...I THINK HE'S GOT THE REMBRANDT WING.
2/3
Rembrandt
The Night Watch
I SHOULDN'T HAVE DUSTED THAT.

When I wrote this strip, I couldn't name a single Rembrandt painting, so I had to look him up in this set of really old encyclopedias I have. It said that one of his most famous paintings was called *The Night Watch*. Hence, the plaque on the wall.

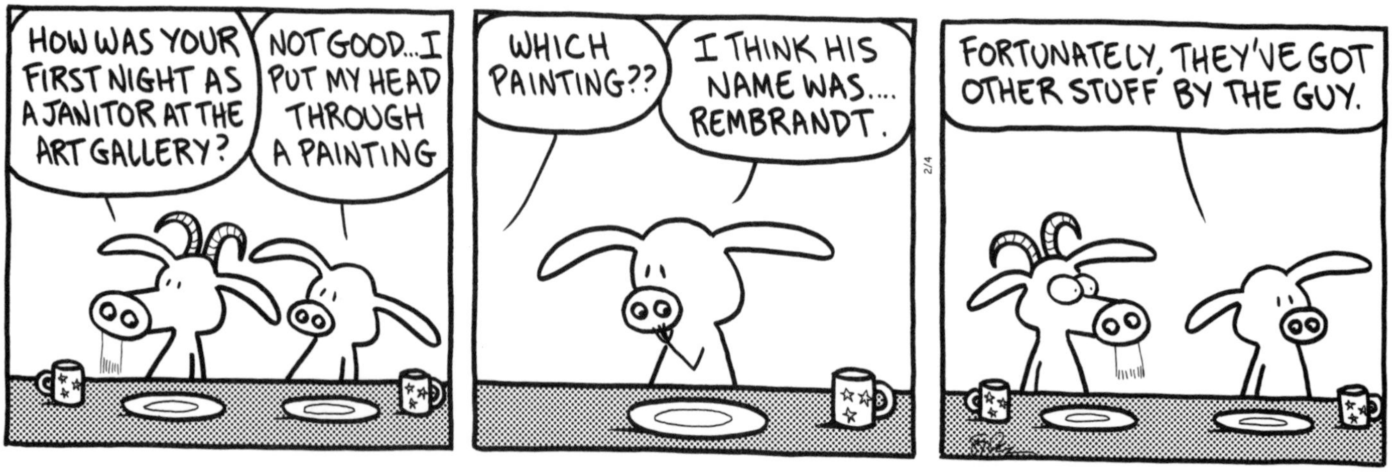
HOW WAS YOUR FIRST NIGHT AS A JANITOR AT THE ART GALLERY?
NOT GOOD...I PUT MY HEAD THROUGH A PAINTING
WHICH PAINTING??
I THINK HIS NAME WAS.... REMBRANDT.
2/4
FORTUNATELY, THEY'VE GOT OTHER STUFF BY THE GUY.

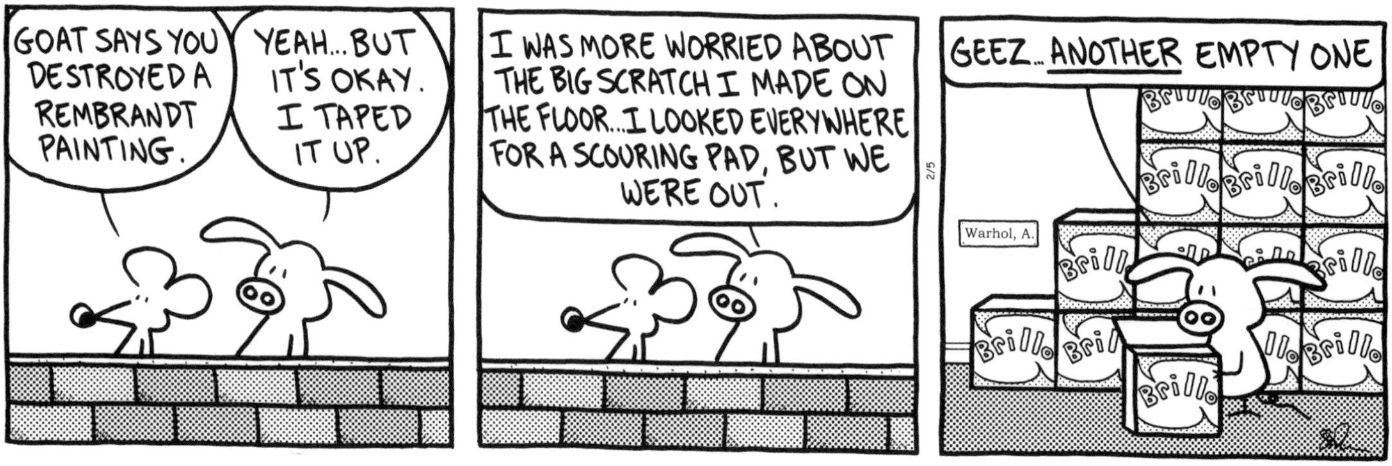
GOAT SAYS YOU DESTROYED A REMBRANDT PAINTING.
YEAH...BUT IT'S OKAY. I TAPED IT UP.
I WAS MORE WORRIED ABOUT THE BIG SCRATCH I MADE ON THE FLOOR...I LOOKED EVERYWHERE FOR A SCOURING PAD, BUT WE WERE OUT.
2/5
GEEZ...ANOTHER EMPTY ONE
Warhol, A.
Brillo

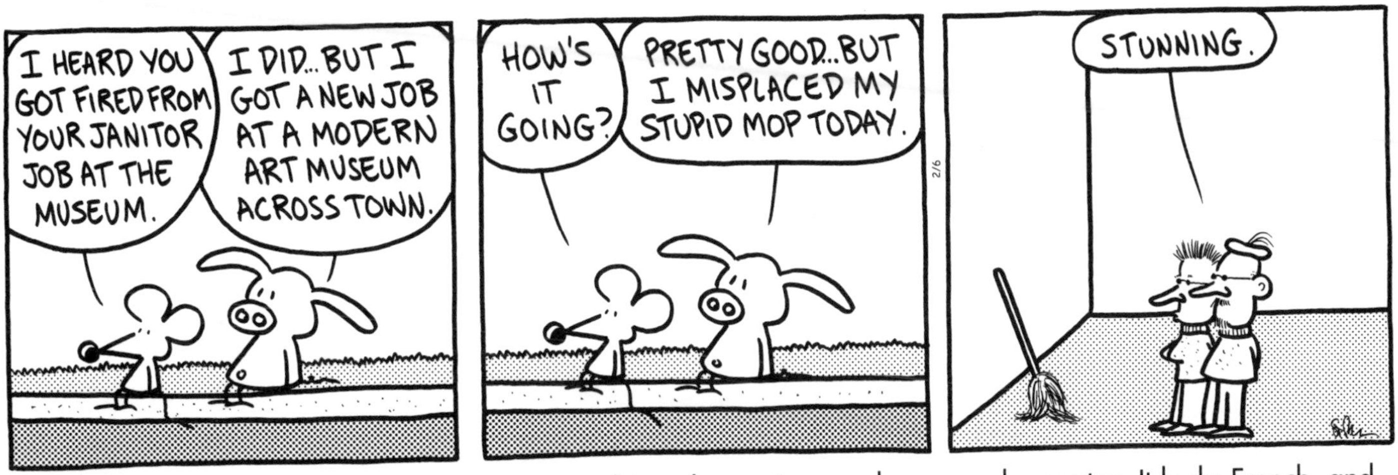
I HEARD YOU GOT FIRED FROM YOUR JANITOR JOB AT THE MUSEUM.
I DID...BUT I GOT A NEW JOB AT A MODERN ART MUSEUM ACROSS TOWN.
HOW'S IT GOING?
PRETTY GOOD...BUT I MISPLACED MY STUPID MOP TODAY.
2/6
STUNNING.

If you need to illustrate a pompous artsy guy, give him a beret, tiny sunglasses, and a goatee. It looks French, and everyone associates French people with pompous artsiness.

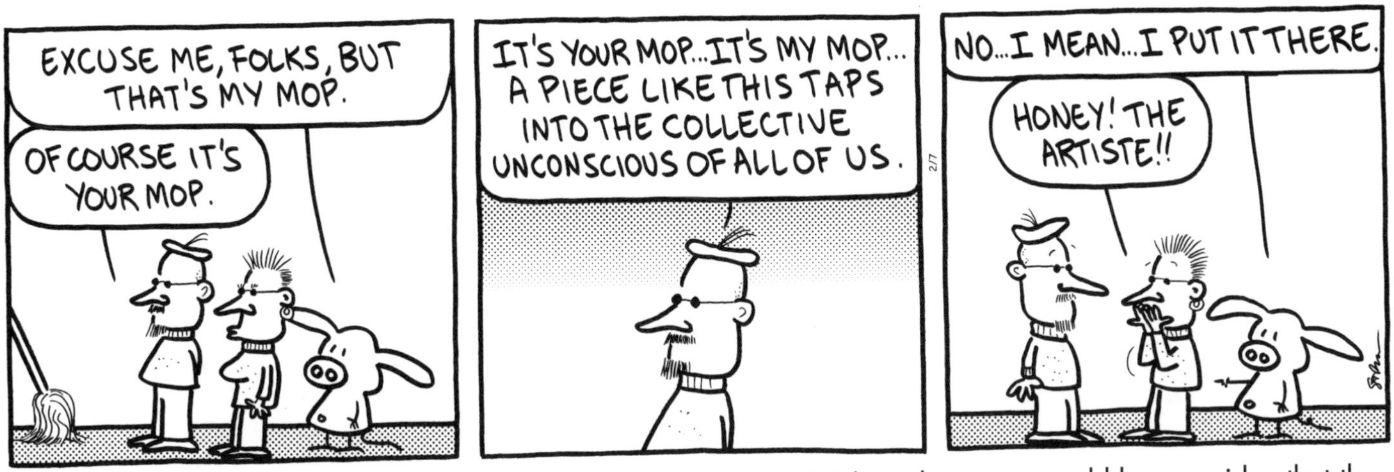
EXCUSE ME, FOLKS, BUT THAT'S MY MOP.
OF COURSE IT'S YOUR MOP.
IT'S YOUR MOP...IT'S MY MOP... A PIECE LIKE THIS TAPS INTO THE COLLECTIVE UNCONSCIOUS OF ALL OF US.
2/7
NO...I MEAN...I PUT IT THERE.
HONEY! THE ARTISTE!!

When you draw as poorly as I do, breasts can be very important. Without them, you would have no idea that the woman here is actually a woman.

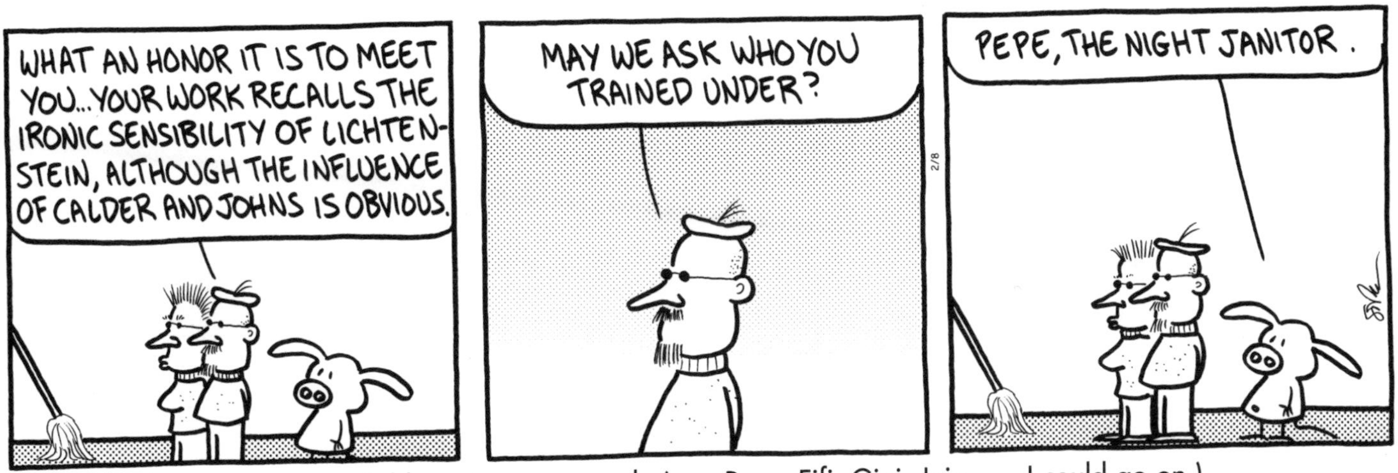
WHAT AN HONOR IT IS TO MEET YOU...YOUR WORK RECALLS THE IRONIC SENSIBILITY OF LICHTEN-STEIN, ALTHOUGH THE INFLUENCE OF CALDER AND JOHNS IS OBVIOUS.
MAY WE ASK WHO YOU TRAINED UNDER?
2/8
PEPE, THE NIGHT JANITOR.

Names that have repeating syllables = instant comedy (e.g. Pepe, Fifi, Gigi, Jojo . . . I could go on.)

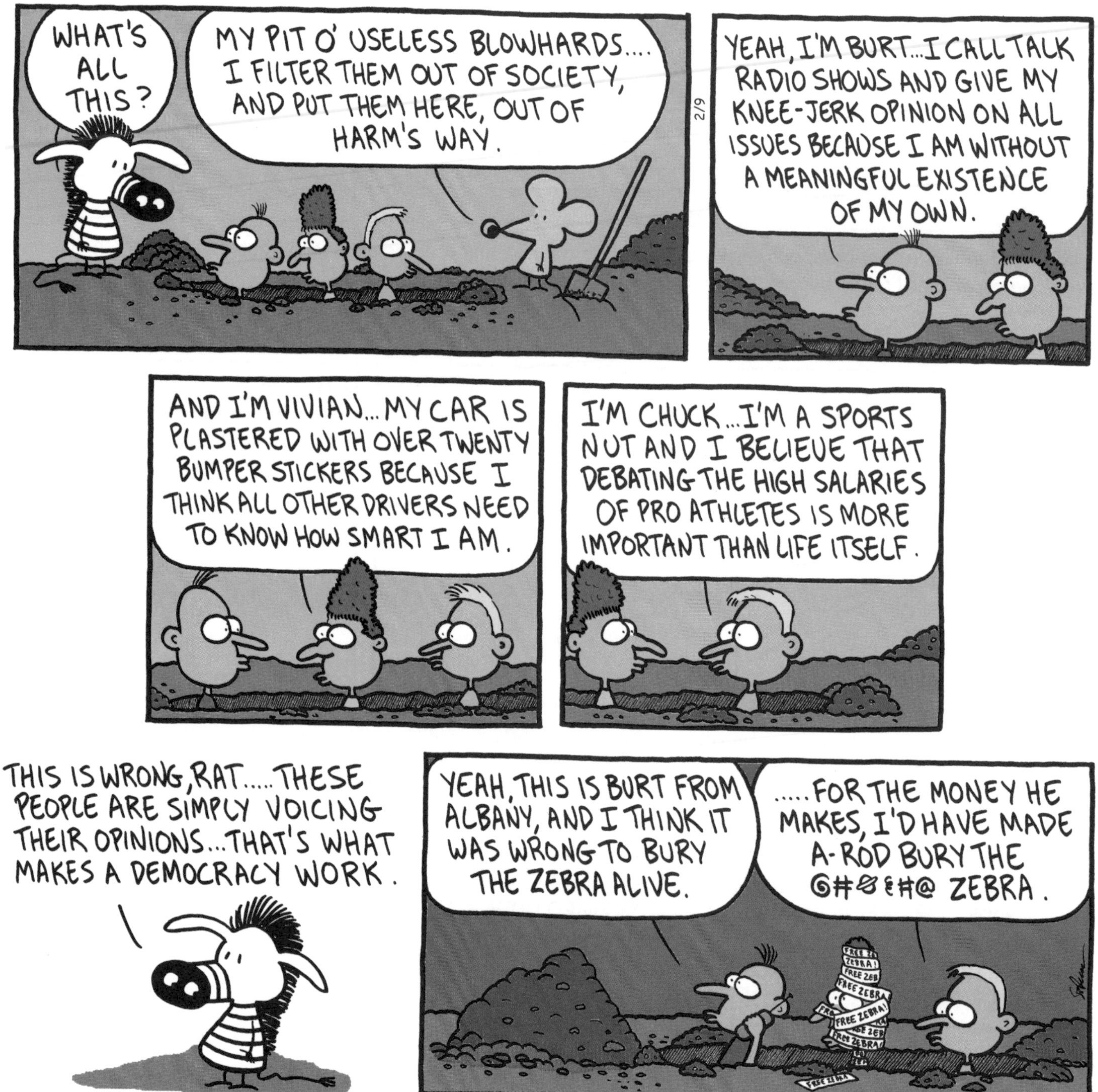
WHAT'S ALL THIS?
MY PIT O' USELESS BLOWHARDS.... I FILTER THEM OUT OF SOCIETY, AND PUT THEM HERE, OUT OF HARM'S WAY.
YEAH, I'M BURT...I CALL TALK RADIO SHOWS AND GIVE MY KNEE-JERK OPINION ON ALL ISSUES BECAUSE I AM WITHOUT A MEANINGFUL EXISTENCE OF MY OWN.
AND I'M VIVIAN... MY CAR IS PLASTERED WITH OVER TWENTY BUMPER STICKERS BECAUSE I THINK ALL OTHER DRIVERS NEED TO KNOW HOW SMART I AM.
I'M CHUCK...I'M A SPORTS NUT AND I BELIEVE THAT DEBATING THE HIGH SALARIES OF PRO ATHLETES IS MORE IMPORTANT THAN LIFE ITSELF.
THIS IS WRONG, RAT..... THESE PEOPLE ARE SIMPLY VOICING THEIR OPINIONS...THAT'S WHAT MAKES A DEMOCRACY WORK.
YEAH, THIS IS BURT FROM ALBANY, AND I THINK IT WAS WRONG TO BURY THE ZEBRA ALIVE.
.....FOR THE MONEY HE MAKES, I'D HAVE MADE A-ROD BURY THE @#$&#@ ZEBRA.

As a cartoonist, you can't help but be influenced by reader feedback. There were so many people that liked "Box O' Stupid People" that I tried to repeat it in various forms. But for some reason, you never seem to recapture what people liked the first time.

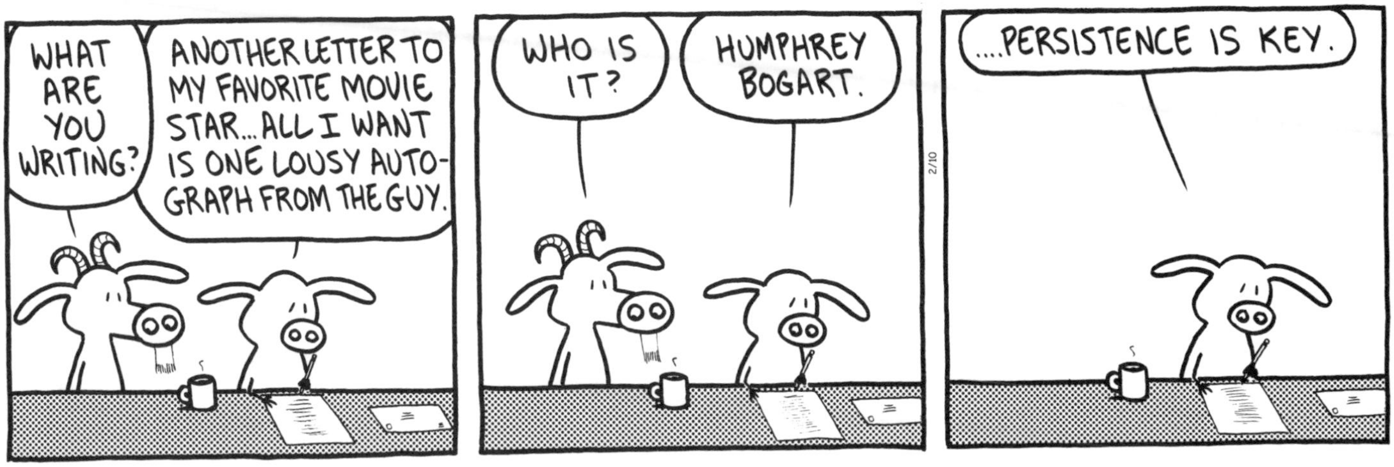
WHAT ARE YOU WRITING?
ANOTHER LETTER TO MY FAVORITE MOVIE STAR... ALL I WANT IS ONE LOUSY AUTOGRAPH FROM THE GUY.
WHO IS IT?
HUMPHREY BOGART.
2/10
....PERSISTENCE IS KEY.

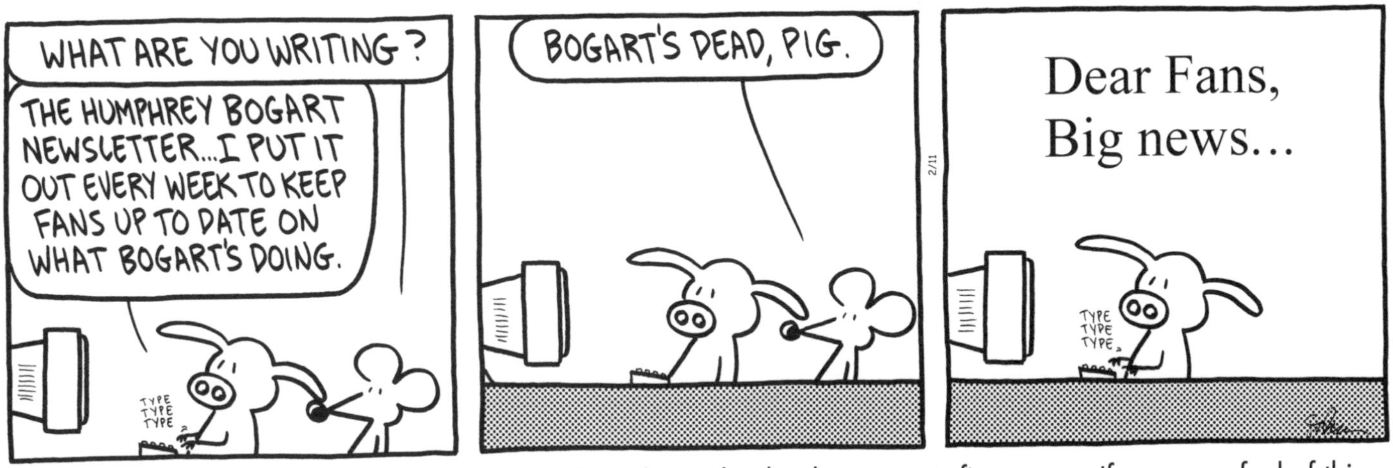
WHAT ARE YOU WRITING?
THE HUMPHREY BOGART NEWSLETTER... I PUT IT OUT EVERY WEEK TO KEEP FANS UP TO DATE ON WHAT BOGART'S DOING.
TYPE TYPE TYPE
BOGART'S DEAD, PIG.
2/11
Dear Fans,
Big news...
TYPE TYPE TYPE

Dead celebrities can be funny, but they have to have been dead at least twenty-five years. If you run afoul of this rule, you'll get mail.

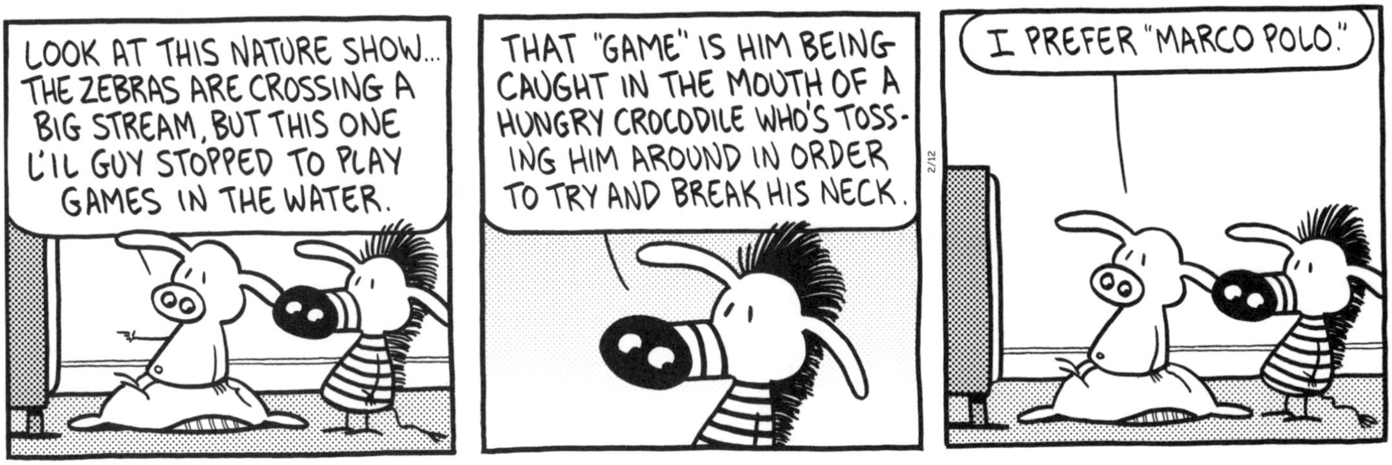
LOOK AT THIS NATURE SHOW... THE ZEBRAS ARE CROSSING A BIG STREAM, BUT THIS ONE L'IL GUY STOPPED TO PLAY GAMES IN THE WATER.
THAT "GAME" IS HIM BEING CAUGHT IN THE MOUTH OF A HUNGRY CROCODILE WHO'S TOSSING HIM AROUND IN ORDER TO TRY AND BREAK HIS NECK.
2/12
I PREFER "MARCO POLO."

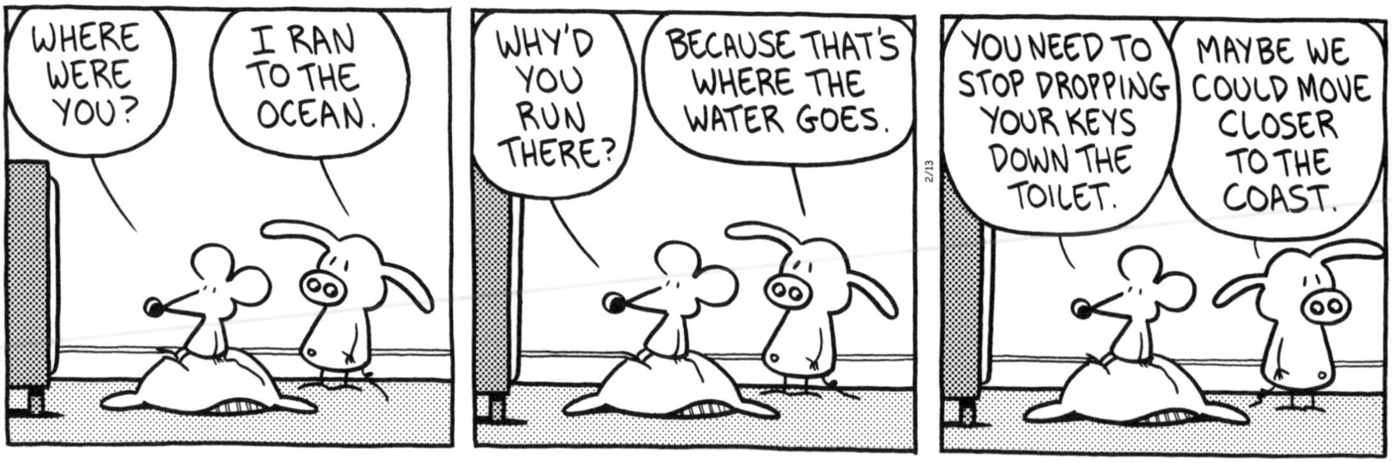
WHERE WERE YOU?
I RAN TO THE OCEAN.
WHY'D YOU RUN THERE?
BECAUSE THAT'S WHERE THE WATER GOES.
2/13
YOU NEED TO STOP DROPPING YOUR KEYS DOWN THE TOILET.
MAYBE WE COULD MOVE CLOSER TO THE COAST.

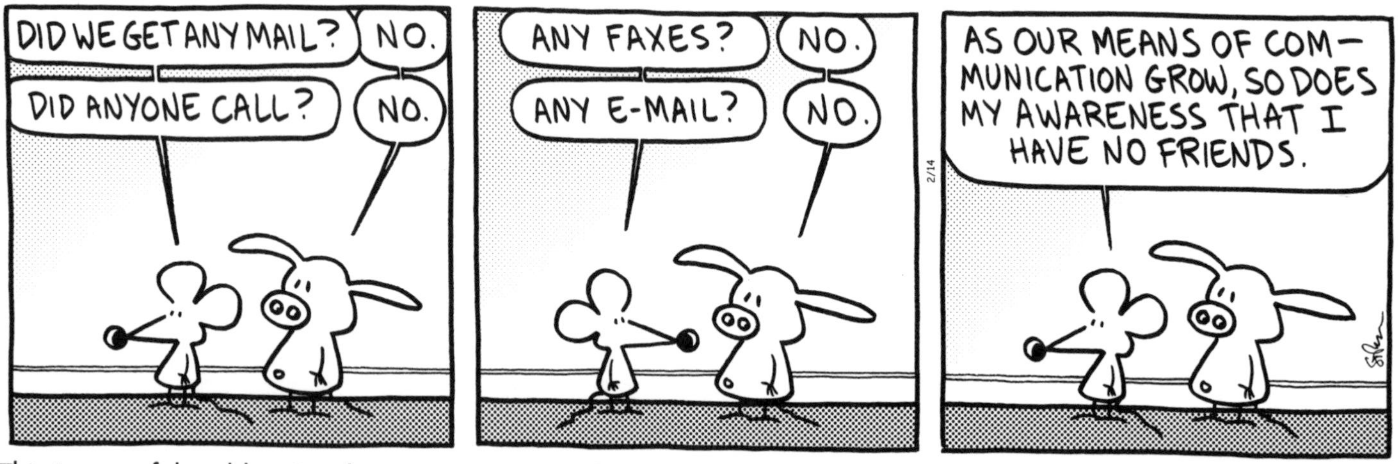
DID WE GET ANY MAIL?
NO.
DID ANYONE CALL?
NO.
ANY FAXES?
NO.
ANY E-MAIL?
NO.
2/14
AS OUR MEANS OF COM-MUNICATION GROW, SO DOES MY AWARENESS THAT I HAVE NO FRIENDS.

This is one of the oldest *Pearls* strips. It was one of the original forty or so strips I sent to the syndicates when I tried to get syndicated. For some reason, it didn't run until the second year of the strip.

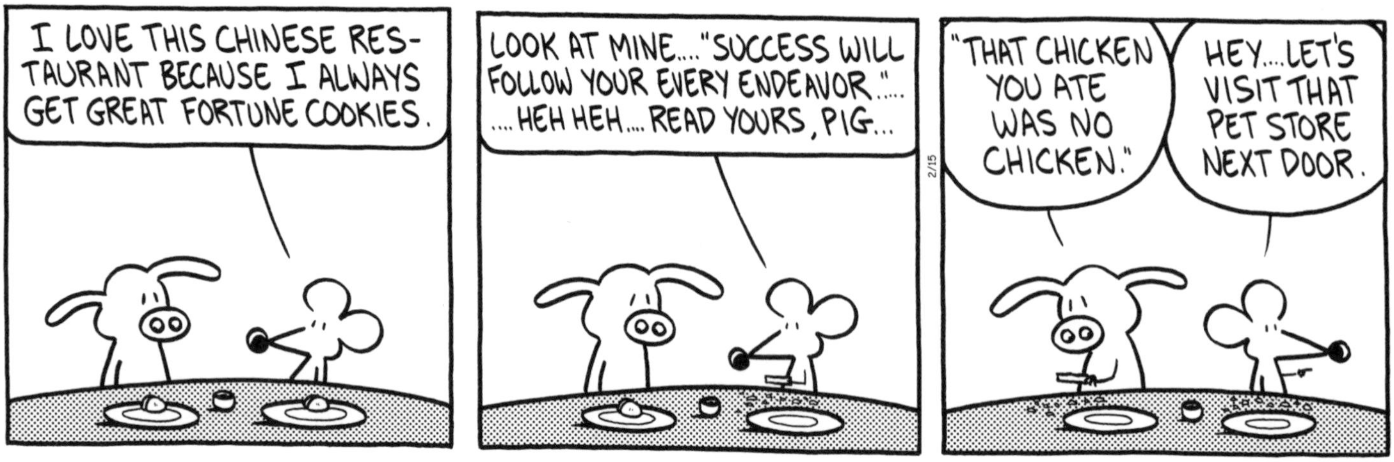
I LOVE THIS CHINESE RES-TAURANT BECAUSE I ALWAYS GET GREAT FORTUNE COOKIES.
LOOK AT MINE...."SUCCESS WILL FOLLOW YOUR EVERY ENDEAVOR."....
....HEH HEH.... READ YOURS, PIG...
2/15
"THAT CHICKEN YOU ATE WAS NO CHICKEN."
HEY....LET'S VISIT THAT PET STORE NEXT DOOR.

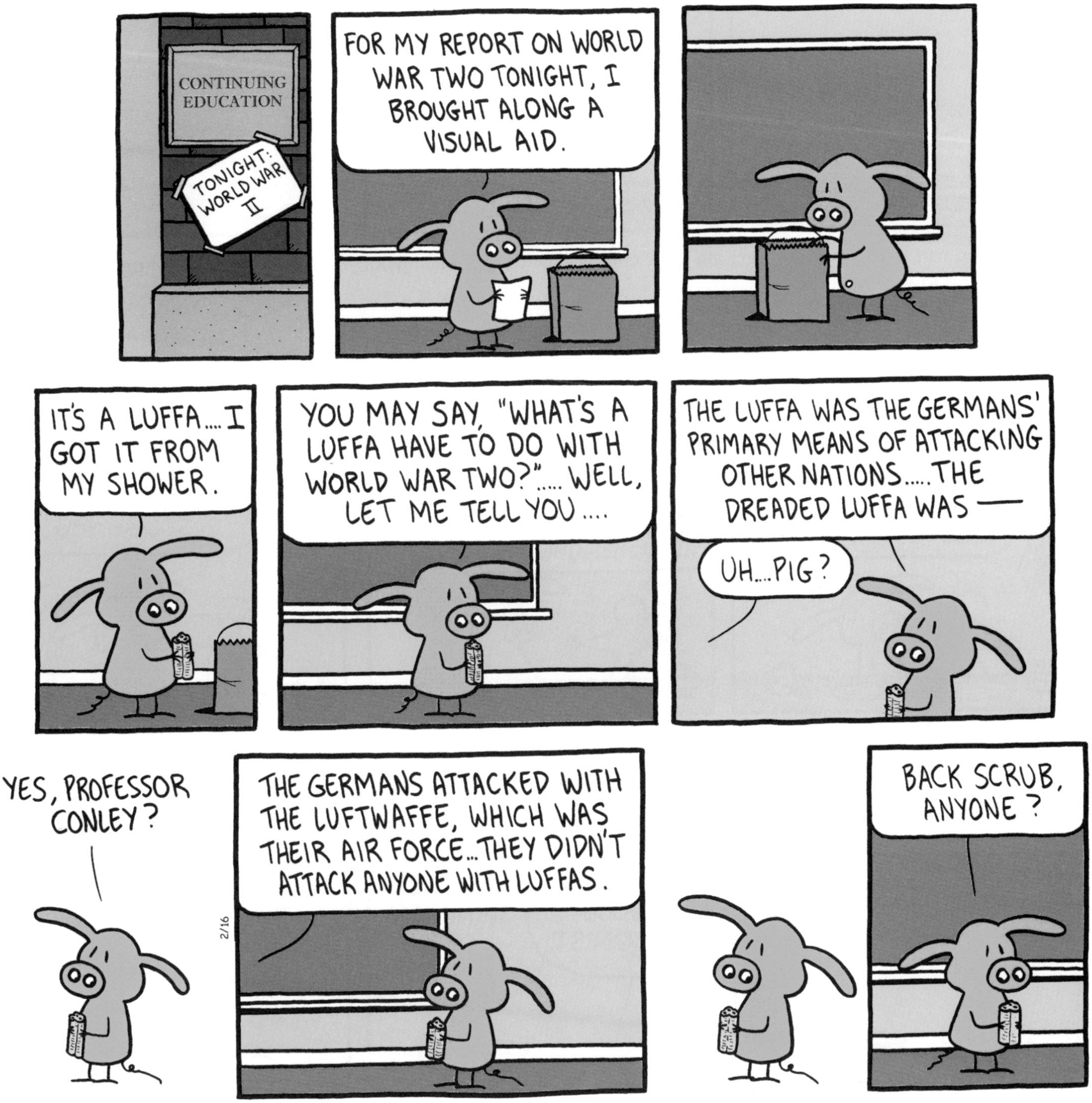
CONTINUING EDUCATION
TONIGHT: WORLD WAR II
FOR MY REPORT ON WORLD WAR TWO TONIGHT, I BROUGHT ALONG A VISUAL AID.
IT'S A LUFFA.... I GOT IT FROM MY SHOWER.
YOU MAY SAY, "WHAT'S A LUFFA HAVE TO DO WITH WORLD WAR TWO?"..... WELL, LET ME TELL YOU....
THE LUFFA WAS THE GERMANS' PRIMARY MEANS OF ATTACKING OTHER NATIONS..... THE DREADED LUFFA WAS —
UH....PIG?
YES, PROFESSOR CONLEY?
THE GERMANS ATTACKED WITH THE LUFTWAFFE, WHICH WAS THEIR AIR FORCE...THEY DIDN'T ATTACK ANYONE WITH LUFFAS.
2/16
BACK SCRUB, ANYONE?

Luffa is a funny word. The problem with this strip, though, was that there were a number of people who didn't know what a luffa was. And if you didn't know what a luffa was, you sure as heck didn't know what the Luftwaffe was. Here's a good rule of comedy: People don't laugh at jokes they don't get.

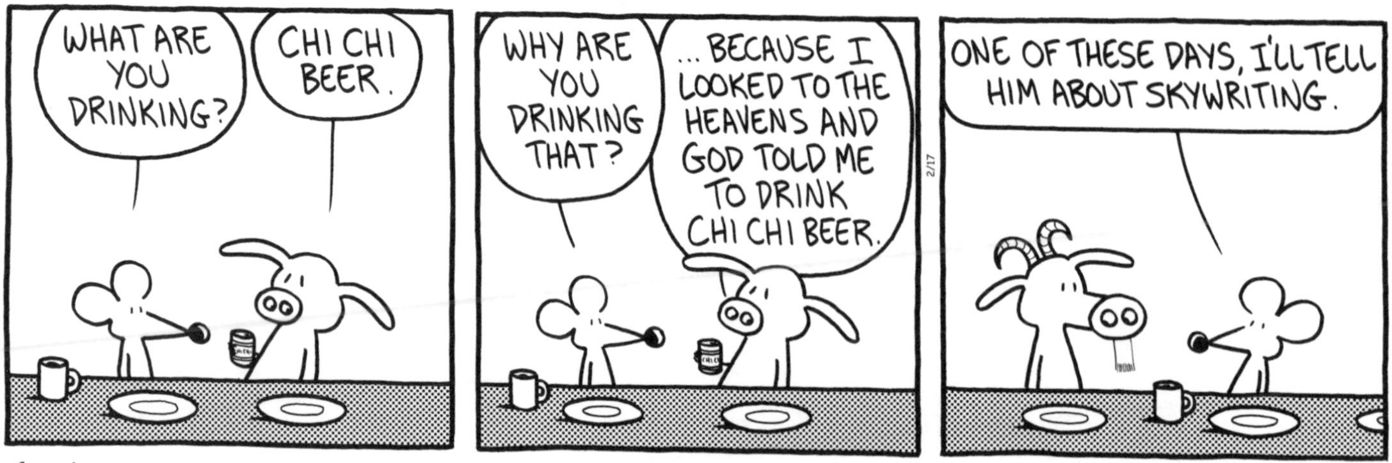
WHAT ARE YOU DRINKING?
CHI CHI BEER.
WHY ARE YOU DRINKING THAT?
... BECAUSE I LOOKED TO THE HEAVENS AND GOD TOLD ME TO DRINK CHI CHI BEER.
2/17
ONE OF THESE DAYS, I'LL TELL HIM ABOUT SKYWRITING.

After this strip ran, someone informed me that "chi chis" are a Spanish synonym for "breasts." That adds a whole new dimension to this joke.

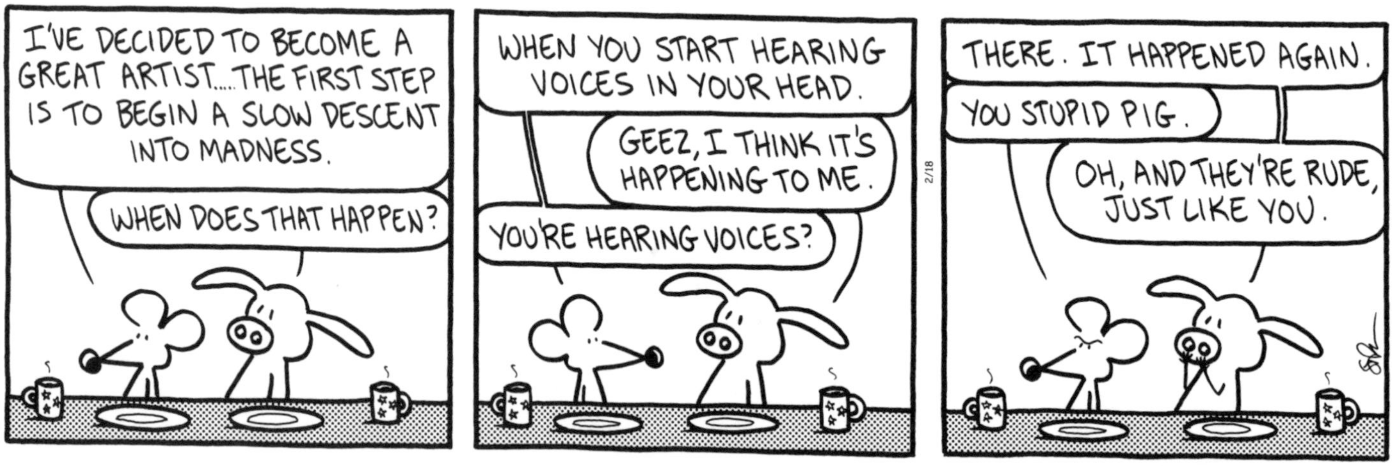
I'VE DECIDED TO BECOME A GREAT ARTIST..... THE FIRST STEP IS TO BEGIN A SLOW DESCENT INTO MADNESS.
WHEN DOES THAT HAPPEN?
WHEN YOU START HEARING VOICES IN YOUR HEAD.
GEEZ, I THINK IT'S HAPPENING TO ME.
YOU'RE HEARING VOICES?
2/18
THERE. IT HAPPENED AGAIN.
YOU STUPID PIG.
OH, AND THEY'RE RUDE, JUST LIKE YOU.

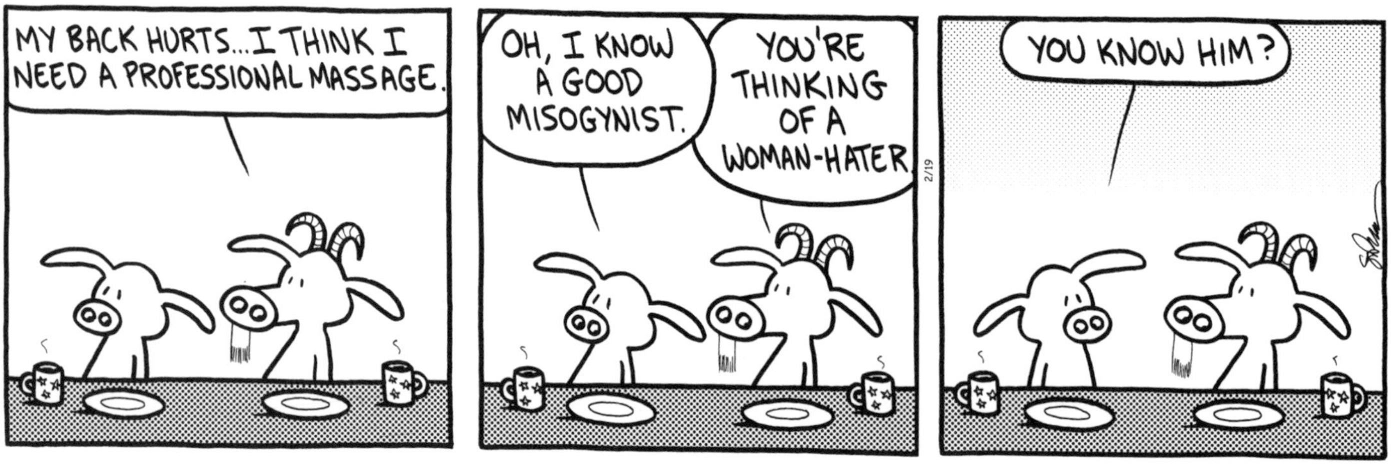
MY BACK HURTS... I THINK I NEED A PROFESSIONAL MASSAGE.
OH, I KNOW A GOOD MISOGYNIST.
YOU'RE THINKING OF A WOMAN-HATER.
2/19
YOU KNOW HIM?

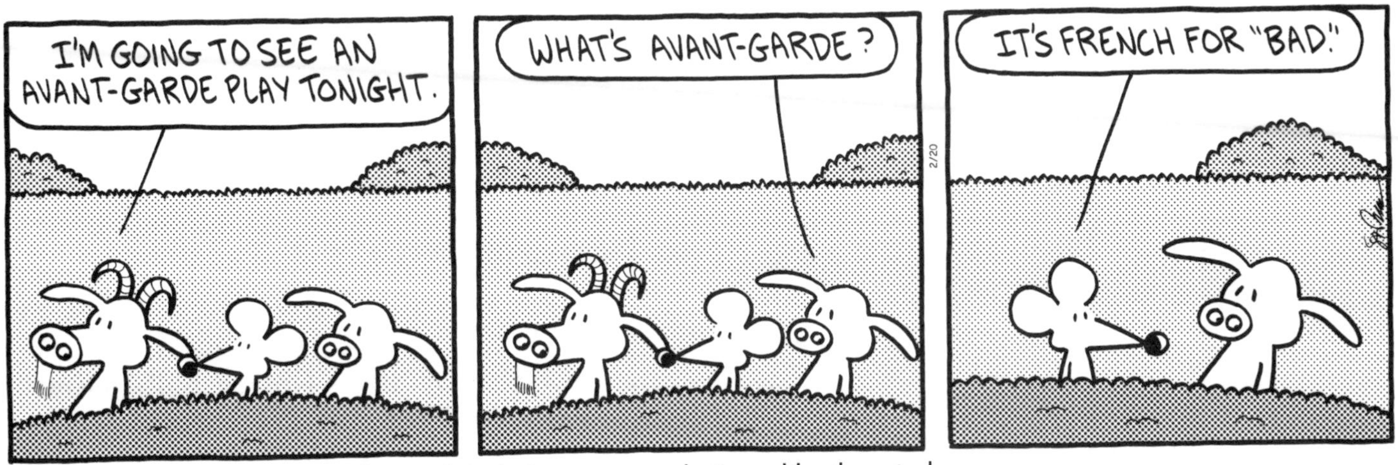
I'M GOING TO SEE AN AVANT-GARDE PLAY TONIGHT.
WHAT'S AVANT-GARDE?
2/20
IT'S FRENCH FOR "BAD."

If you ever see any artistic endeavor labeled "avant garde," run like the wind.

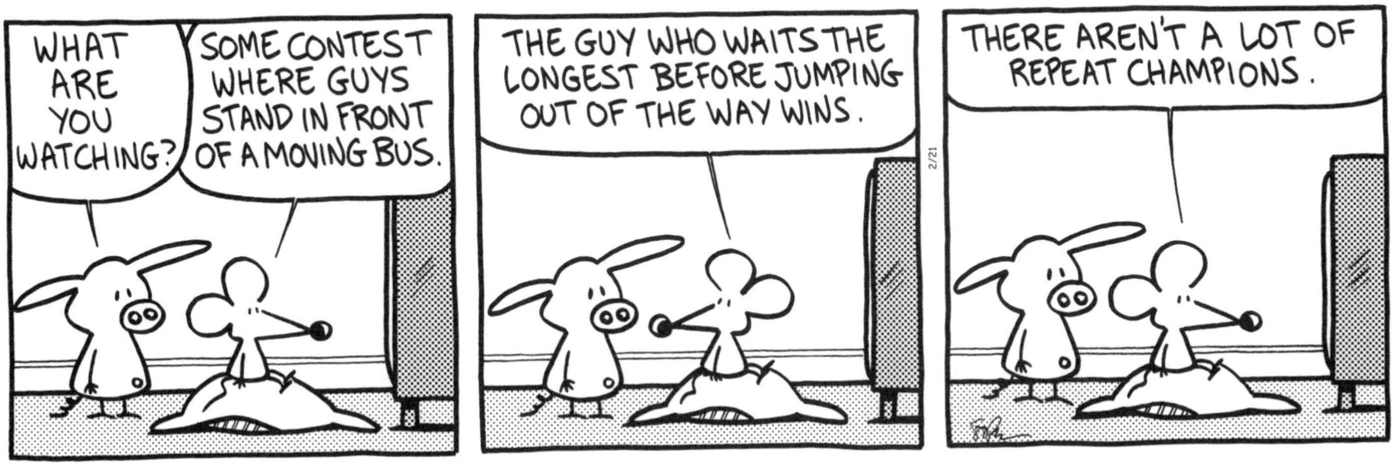
WHAT ARE YOU WATCHING?
SOME CONTEST WHERE GUYS STAND IN FRONT OF A MOVING BUS.
THE GUY WHO WAITS THE LONGEST BEFORE JUMPING OUT OF THE WAY WINS.
2/21
THERE AREN'T A LOT OF REPEAT CHAMPIONS.

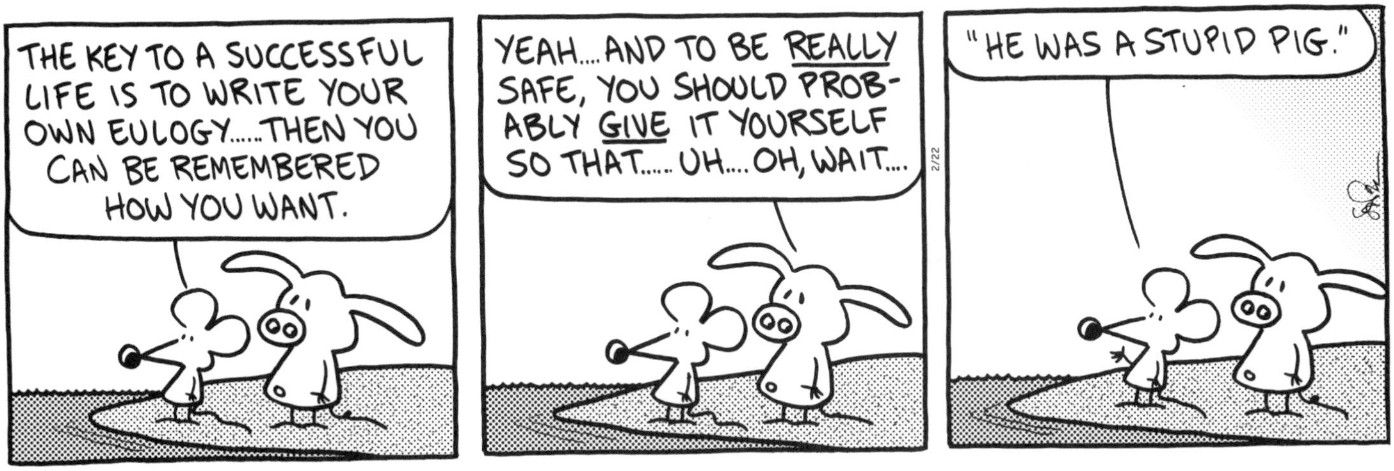
THE KEY TO A SUCCESSFUL LIFE IS TO WRITE YOUR OWN EULOGY......THEN YOU CAN BE REMEMBERED HOW YOU WANT.
YEAH....AND TO BE REALLY SAFE, YOU SHOULD PROBABLY GIVE IT YOURSELF SO THAT..... UH....OH, WAIT....
2/22
"HE WAS A STUPID PIG."

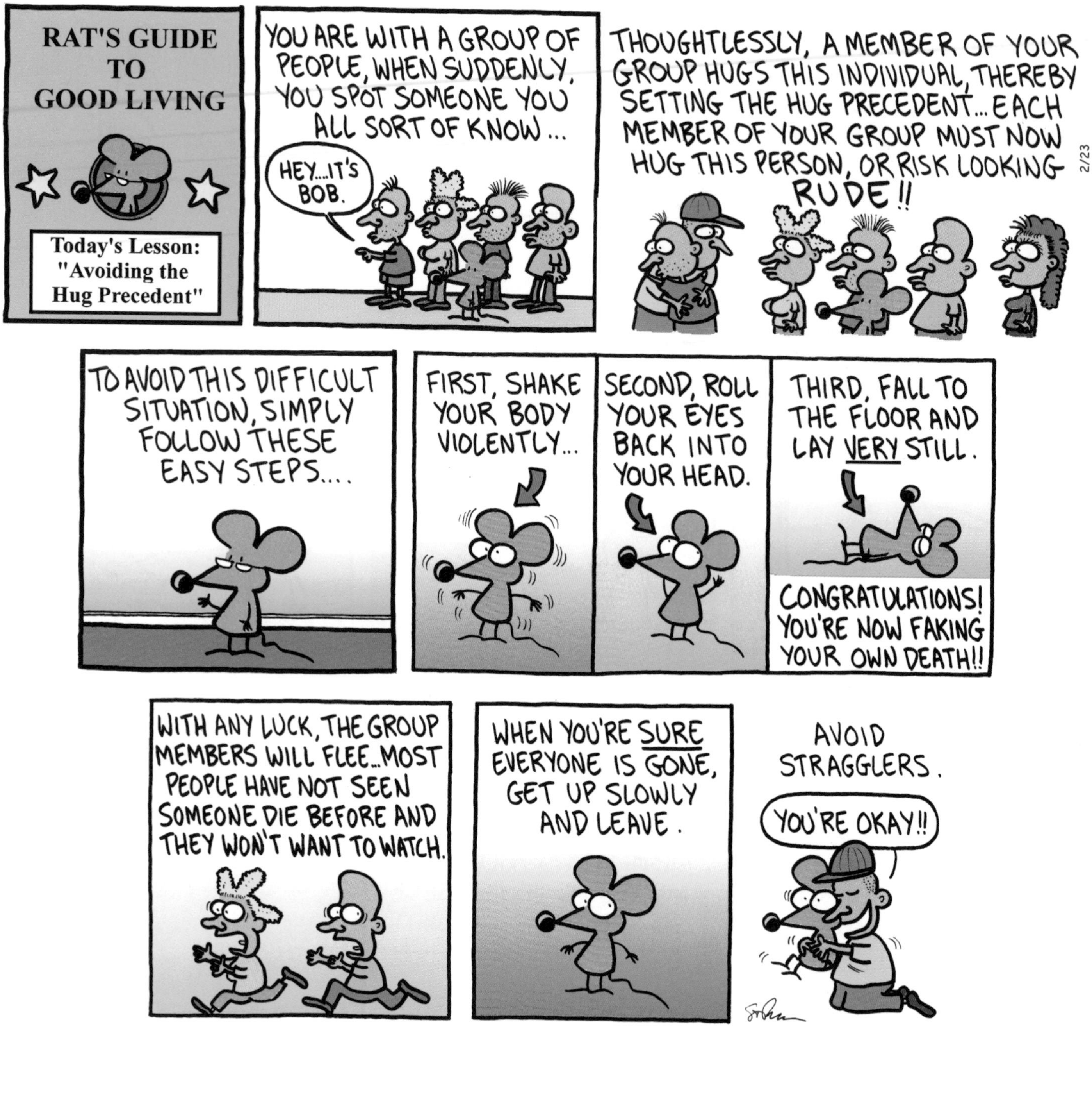
RAT'S GUIDE TO GOOD LIVING
Today's Lesson: "Avoiding the Hug Precedent"
YOU ARE WITH A GROUP OF PEOPLE, WHEN SUDDENLY, YOU SPOT SOMEONE YOU ALL SORT OF KNOW...
HEY...IT'S BOB.
THOUGHTLESSLY, A MEMBER OF YOUR GROUP HUGS THIS INDIVIDUAL, THEREBY SETTING THE HUG PRECEDENT... EACH MEMBER OF YOUR GROUP MUST NOW HUG THIS PERSON, OR RISK LOOKING RUDE!!
2/23
TO AVOID THIS DIFFICULT SITUATION, SIMPLY FOLLOW THESE EASY STEPS....
FIRST, SHAKE YOUR BODY VIOLENTLY...
SECOND, ROLL YOUR EYES BACK INTO YOUR HEAD.
THIRD, FALL TO THE FLOOR AND LAY VERY STILL.
CONGRATULATIONS! YOU'RE NOW FAKING YOUR OWN DEATH!!
WITH ANY LUCK, THE GROUP MEMBERS WILL FLEE...MOST PEOPLE HAVE NOT SEEN SOMEONE DIE BEFORE AND THEY WON'T WANT TO WATCH.
WHEN YOU'RE SURE EVERYONE IS GONE, GET UP SLOWLY AND LEAVE.
AVOID STRAGGLERS.
YOU'RE OKAY!!

My dumb people all have big puffy lips. Oddly, people now pay big money to have big puffy lips.

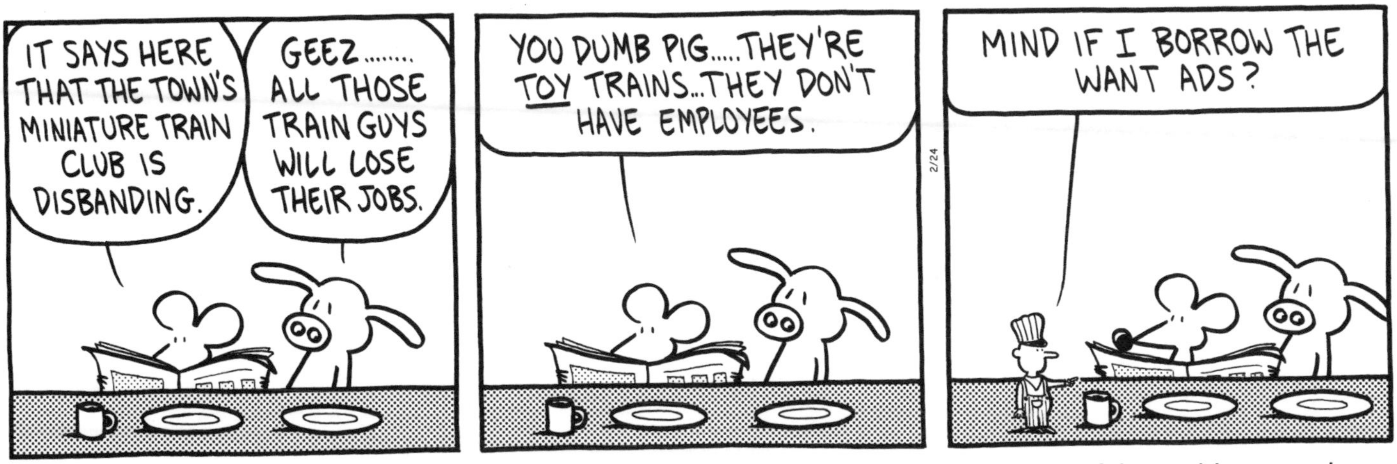
IT SAYS HERE THAT THE TOWN'S MINIATURE TRAIN CLUB IS DISBANDING.
GEEZ........ ALL THOSE TRAIN GUYS WILL LOSE THEIR JOBS.
YOU DUMB PIG.....THEY'RE TOY TRAINS...THEY DON'T HAVE EMPLOYEES.
2/24
MIND IF I BORROW THE WANT ADS?

I thought the Hobart series was my best series, but few fans seemed to agree. I think part of the problem was that they just didn't like seeing all the regular characters disappear for the week. But something about him just appeals to me, something about how he struggles valiantly and yet continues to suffer setbacks, ultimately being microwaved with the popcorn.

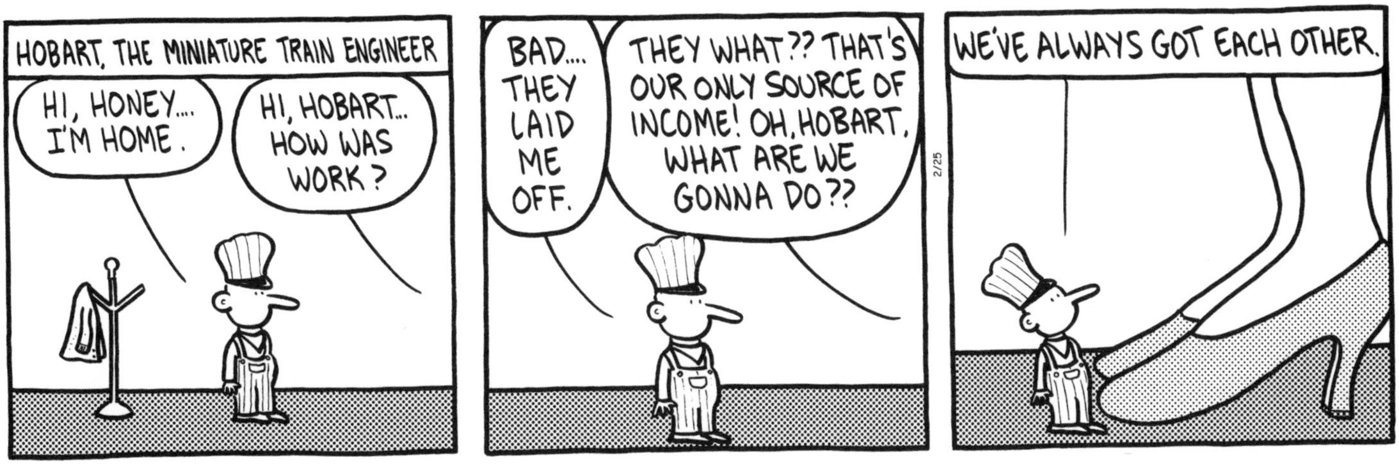
HOBART, THE MINIATURE TRAIN ENGINEER
HI, HONEY.... I'M HOME.
HI, HOBART... HOW WAS WORK?
BAD.... THEY LAID ME OFF.
THEY WHAT?? THAT'S OUR ONLY SOURCE OF INCOME! OH, HOBART, WHAT ARE WE GONNA DO??
2/25
WE'VE ALWAYS GOT EACH OTHER.

I borrowed my wife's shoe for this strip so I could see how to draw one.

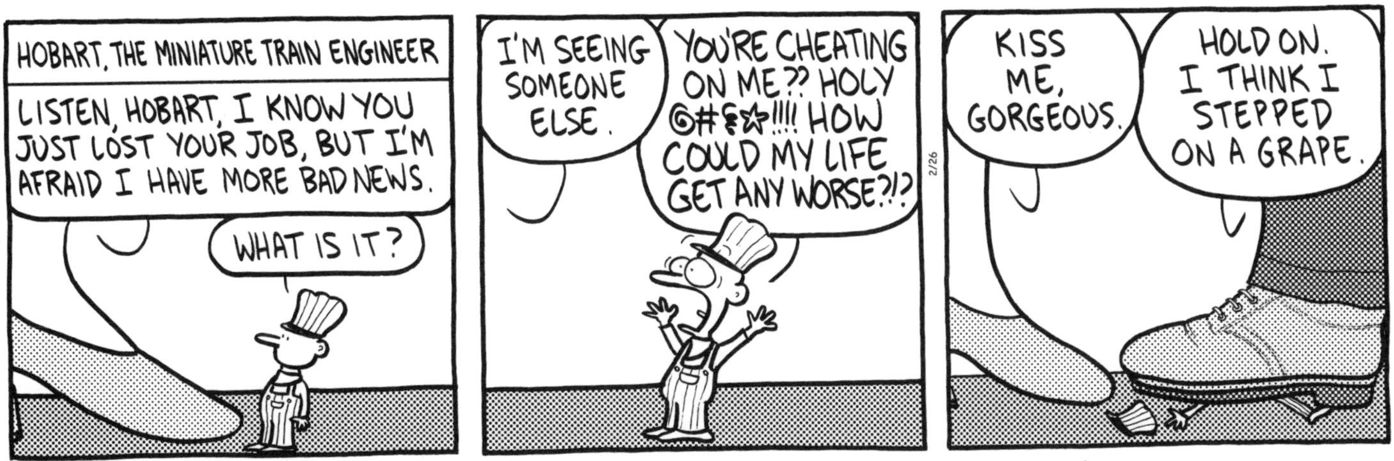
HOBART, THE MINIATURE TRAIN ENGINEER
LISTEN, HOBART, I KNOW YOU JUST LOST YOUR JOB, BUT I'M AFRAID I HAVE MORE BAD NEWS.
WHAT IS IT?
I'M SEEING SOMEONE ELSE.
YOU'RE CHEATING ON ME?? HOLY @#$☆!!!! HOW COULD MY LIFE GET ANY WORSE?!?
2/26
KISS ME, GORGEOUS.
HOLD ON. I THINK I STEPPED ON A GRAPE.

I borrowed my own shoe for this strip, and I must say, it looks pretty darn good. Please take some time to appreciate how well I drew that shoe.

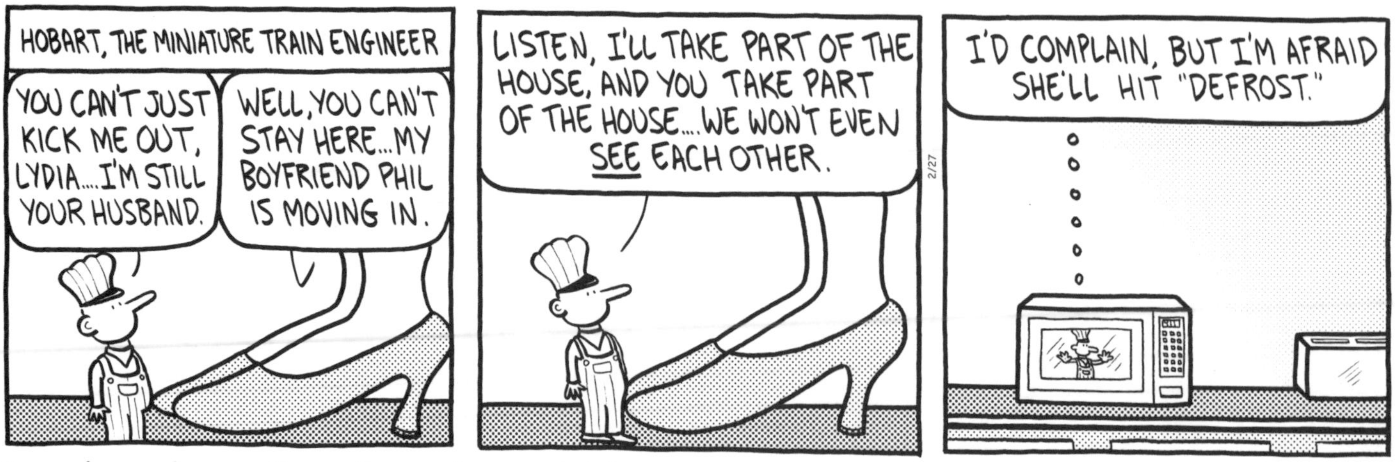
HOBART, THE MINIATURE TRAIN ENGINEER
YOU CAN'T JUST KICK ME OUT, LYDIA....I'M STILL YOUR HUSBAND.
WELL, YOU CAN'T STAY HERE...MY BOYFRIEND PHIL IS MOVING IN.
LISTEN, I'LL TAKE PART OF THE HOUSE, AND YOU TAKE PART OF THE HOUSE....WE WON'T EVEN SEE EACH OTHER.
2/27
I'D COMPLAIN, BUT I'M AFRAID SHE'LL HIT "DEFROST."

Guys who steal your wife are frequently named Phil.

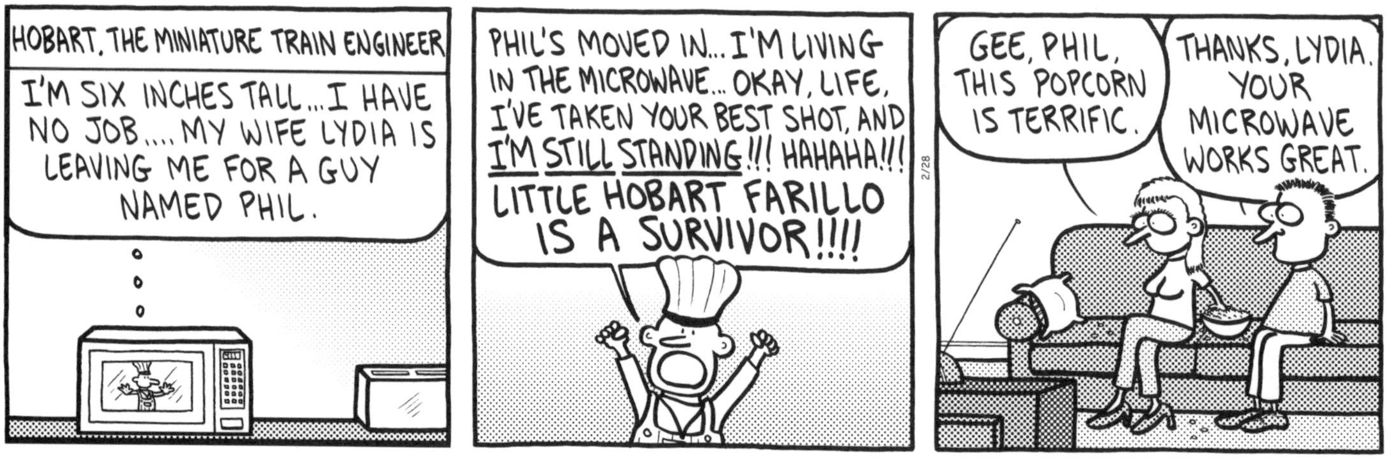
HOBART, THE MINIATURE TRAIN ENGINEER
I'M SIX INCHES TALL...I HAVE NO JOB.... MY WIFE LYDIA IS LEAVING ME FOR A GUY NAMED PHIL.
PHIL'S MOVED IN...I'M LIVING IN THE MICROWAVE... OKAY, LIFE, I'VE TAKEN YOUR BEST SHOT, AND I'M STILL STANDING!!! HAHAHA!!! LITTLE HOBART FARILLO IS A SURVIVOR!!!!
2/28
GEE, PHIL, THIS POPCORN IS TERRIFIC.
THANKS, LYDIA. YOUR MICROWAVE WORKS GREAT.

This couch scene viewed from the back of the TV is one you'd find in *Get Fuzzy*. Which I did.

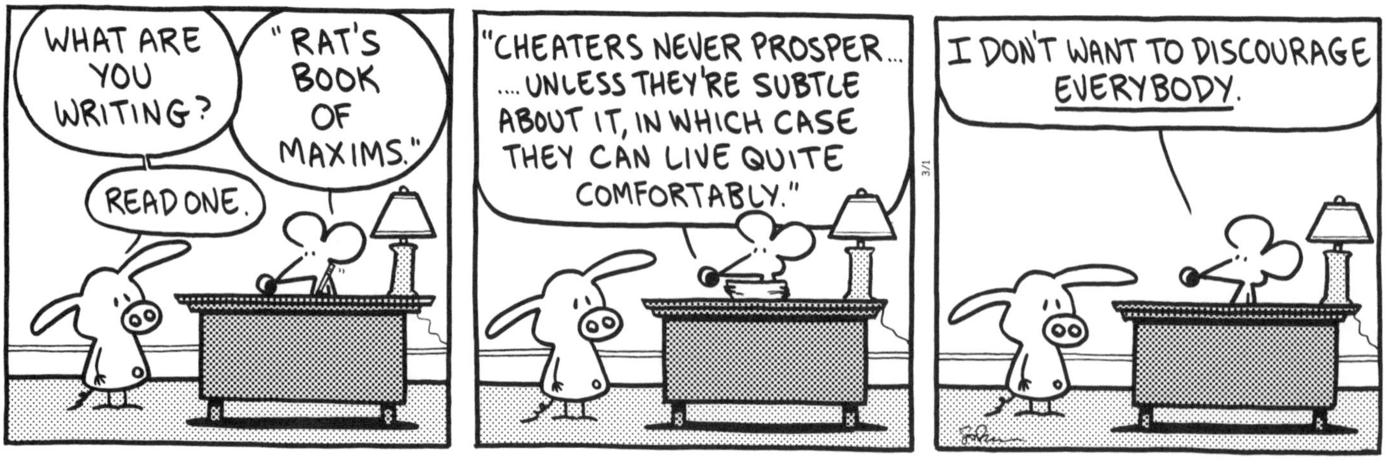
WHAT ARE YOU WRITING?
"RAT'S BOOK OF MAXIMS."
READ ONE.
"CHEATERS NEVER PROSPER... ....UNLESS THEY'RE SUBTLE ABOUT IT, IN WHICH CASE THEY CAN LIVE QUITE COMFORTABLY."
3/1
I DON'T WANT TO DISCOURAGE EVERYBODY.

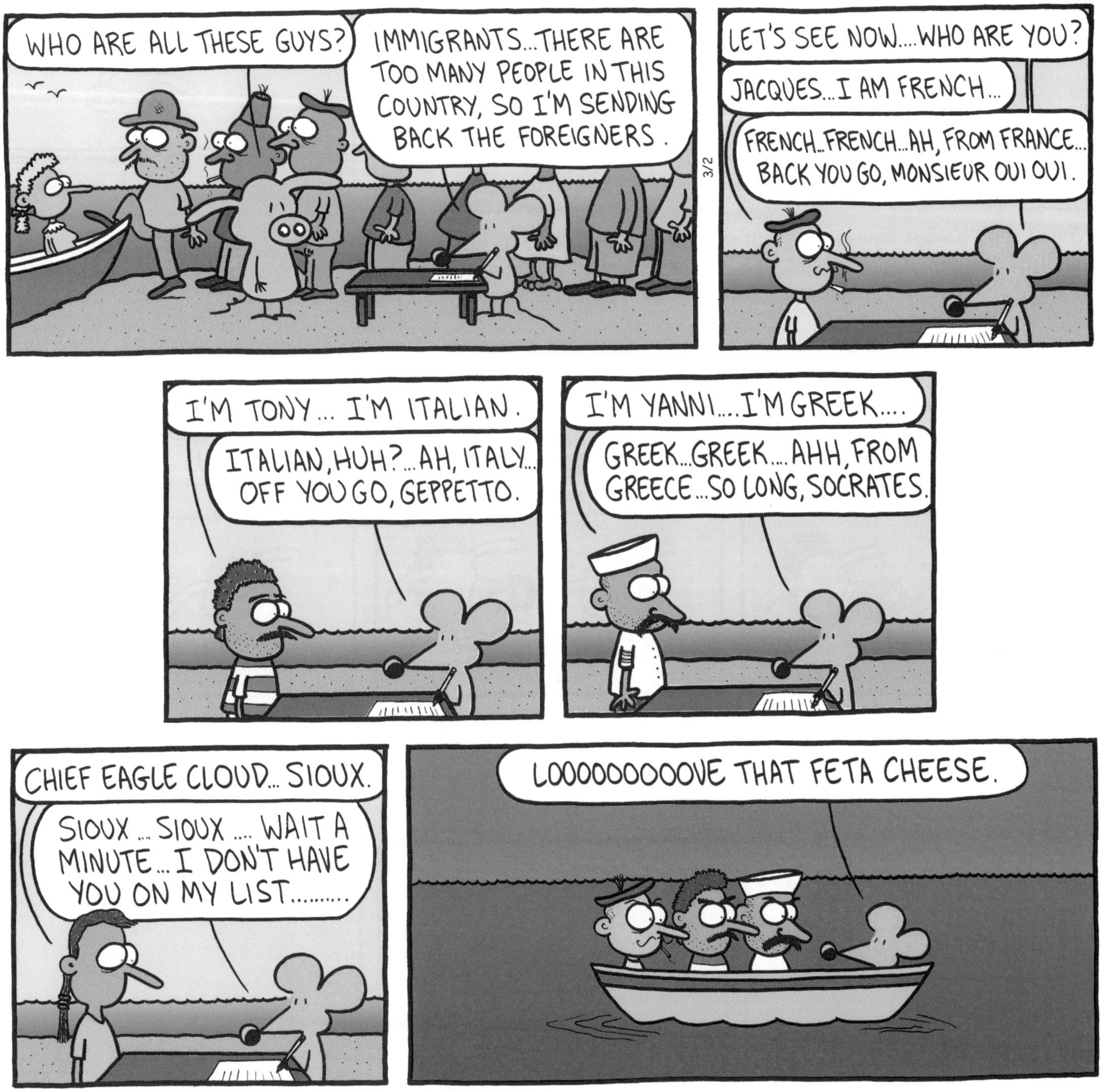
WHO ARE ALL THESE GUYS?
IMMIGRANTS...THERE ARE TOO MANY PEOPLE IN THIS COUNTRY, SO I'M SENDING BACK THE FOREIGNERS.
3/2
LET'S SEE NOW....WHO ARE YOU?
JACQUES...I AM FRENCH...
FRENCH...FRENCH...AH, FROM FRANCE... BACK YOU GO, MONSIEUR OUI OUI.
I'M TONY... I'M ITALIAN.
ITALIAN, HUH?...AH, ITALY... OFF YOU GO, GEPPETTO.
I'M YANNI....I'M GREEK....
GREEK...GREEK....AHH, FROM GREECE...SO LONG, SOCRATES.
CHIEF EAGLE CLOUD... SIOUX.
SIOUX ... SIOUX .... WAIT A MINUTE... I DON'T HAVE YOU ON MY LIST..........
LOOOOOOOOOOVE THAT FETA CHEESE.

I thought I'd get more complaints about this one, but the response was pretty subdued.

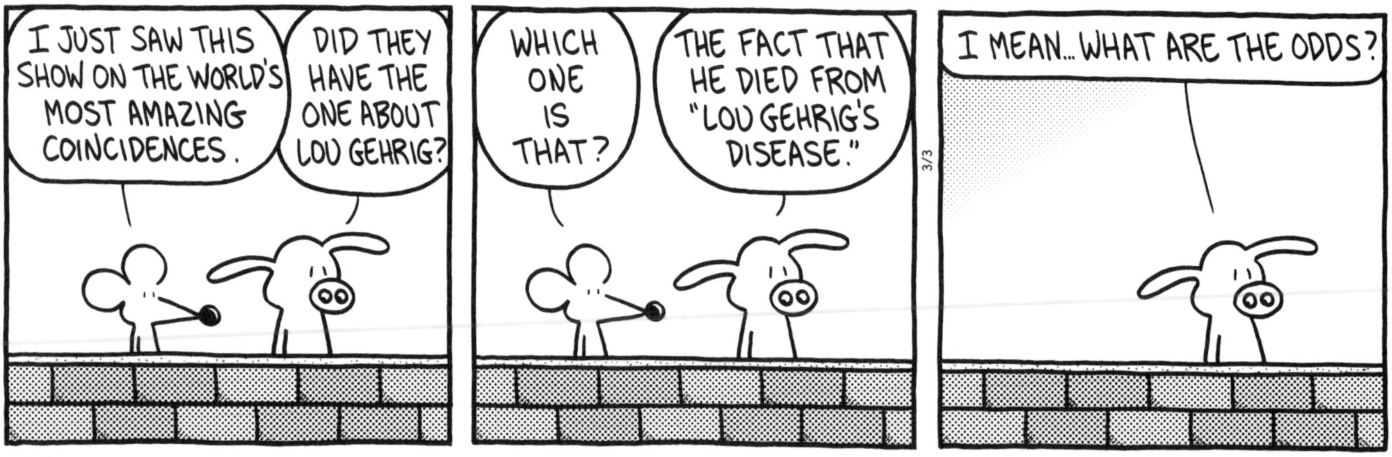
I JUST SAW THIS SHOW ON THE WORLD'S MOST AMAZING COINCIDENCES.
DID THEY HAVE THE ONE ABOUT LOU GEHRIG?
WHICH ONE IS THAT?
THE FACT THAT HE DIED FROM "LOU GEHRIG'S DISEASE."
3/3
I MEAN... WHAT ARE THE ODDS?

While I can't always anticipate which strips will be perceived as funny, I usually have a decent idea of which strips will draw complaints. But not this time. While I maintain that I was not making fun of the disease in any way, the very mention of it in a lighthearted fashion drew a great deal of very, very angry e-mail.

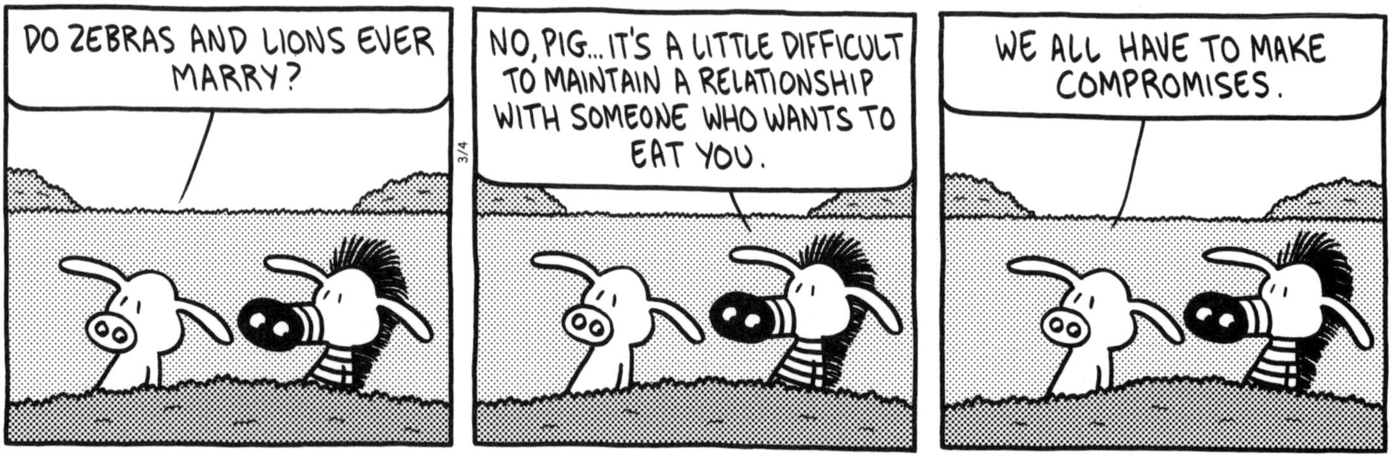
DO ZEBRAS AND LIONS EVER MARRY?
3/4
NO, PIG... IT'S A LITTLE DIFFICULT TO MAINTAIN A RELATIONSHIP WITH SOMEONE WHO WANTS TO EAT YOU.
WE ALL HAVE TO MAKE COMPROMISES.

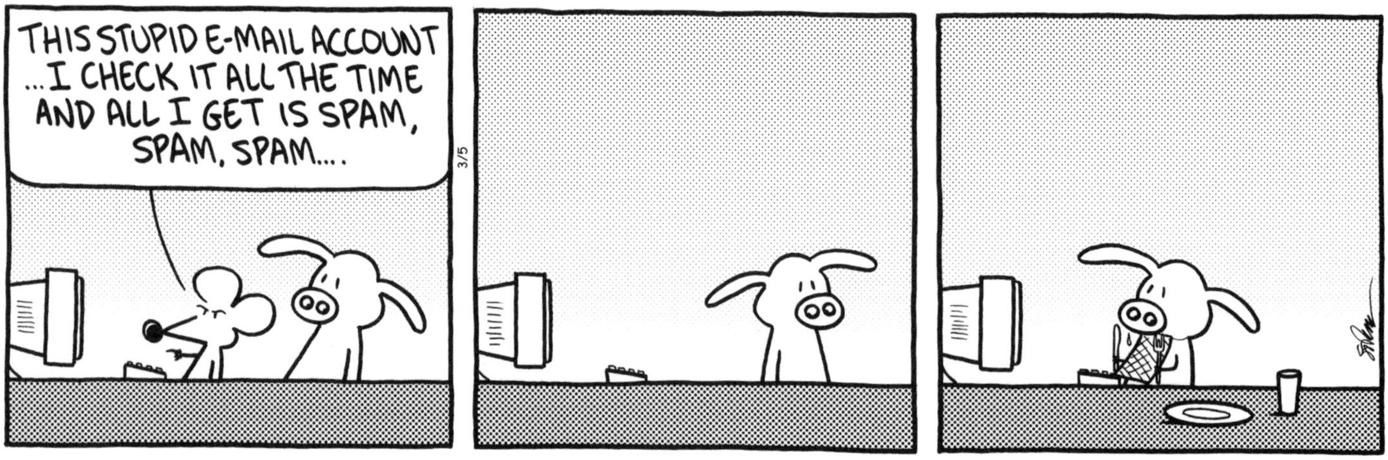
THIS STUPID E-MAIL ACCOUNT ...I CHECK IT ALL THE TIME AND ALL I GET IS SPAM, SPAM, SPAM....
3/5

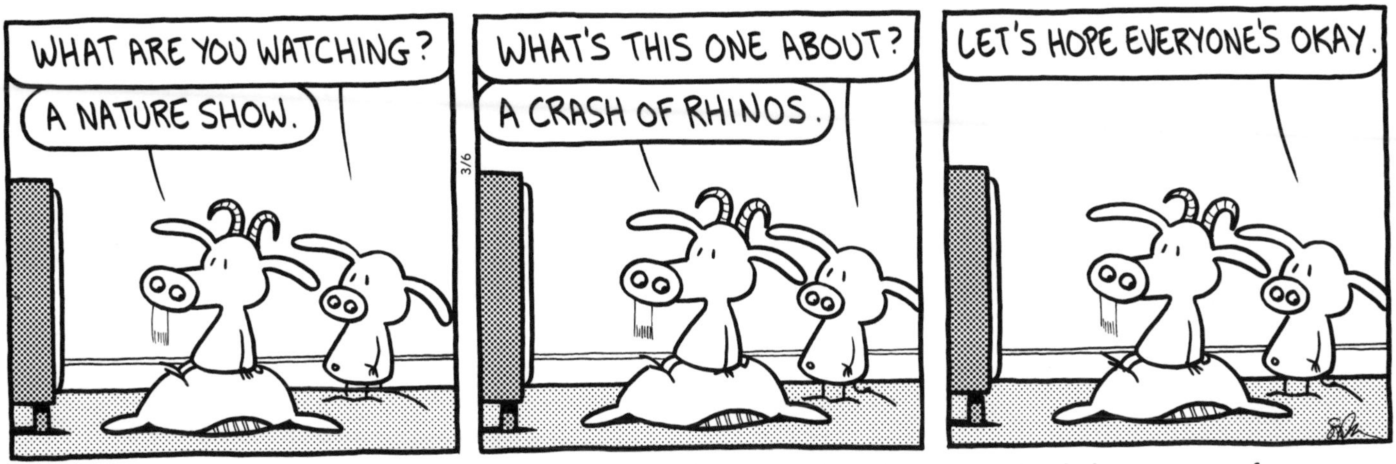
WHAT ARE YOU WATCHING?
A NATURE SHOW.
3/6
WHAT'S THIS ONE ABOUT?
A CRASH OF RHINOS.
LET'S HOPE EVERYONE'S OKAY.

A lot of people didn't realize that a group of rhinos is called a "crash." That's topped only by a group of crows, which is called a "murder." Hang on, I just thought of a strip.

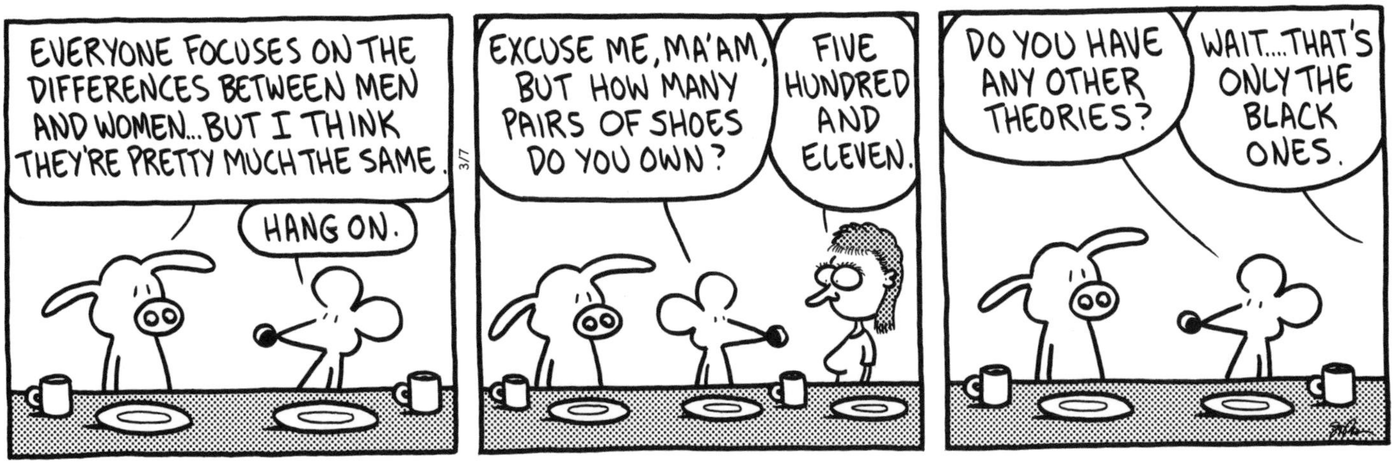
EVERYONE FOCUSES ON THE DIFFERENCES BETWEEN MEN AND WOMEN...BUT I THINK THEY'RE PRETTY MUCH THE SAME.
HANG ON.
3/7
EXCUSE ME, MA'AM, BUT HOW MANY PAIRS OF SHOES DO YOU OWN?
FIVE HUNDRED AND ELEVEN.
DO YOU HAVE ANY OTHER THEORIES?
WAIT....THAT'S ONLY THE BLACK ONES.

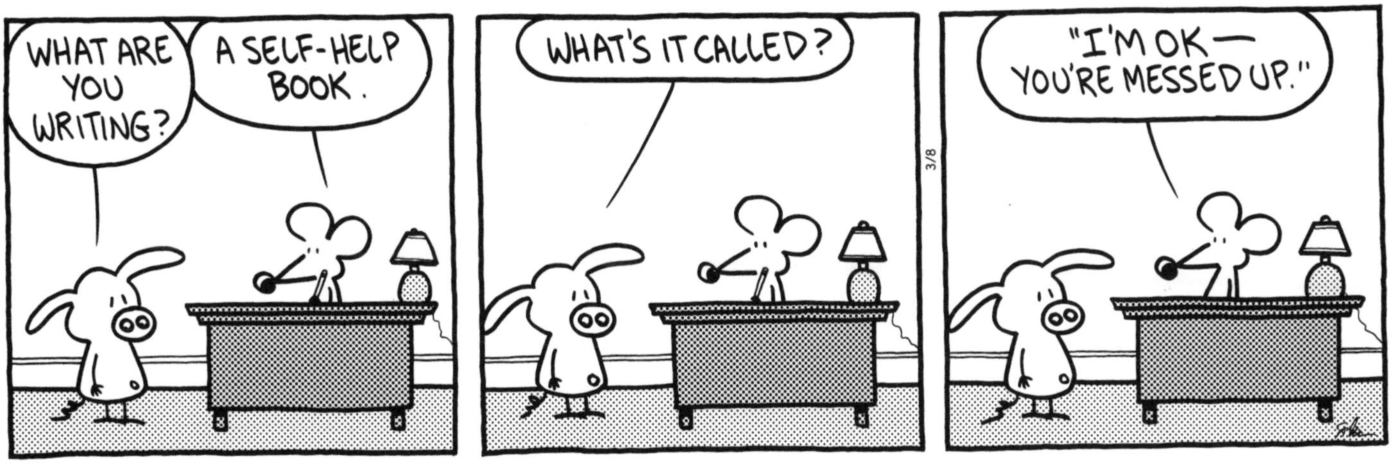
WHAT ARE YOU WRITING?
A SELF-HELP BOOK.
WHAT'S IT CALLED?
3/8
"I'M OK — YOU'RE MESSED UP."

This was a play on the popular, self-help book titled *I'm OK, You're OK.*

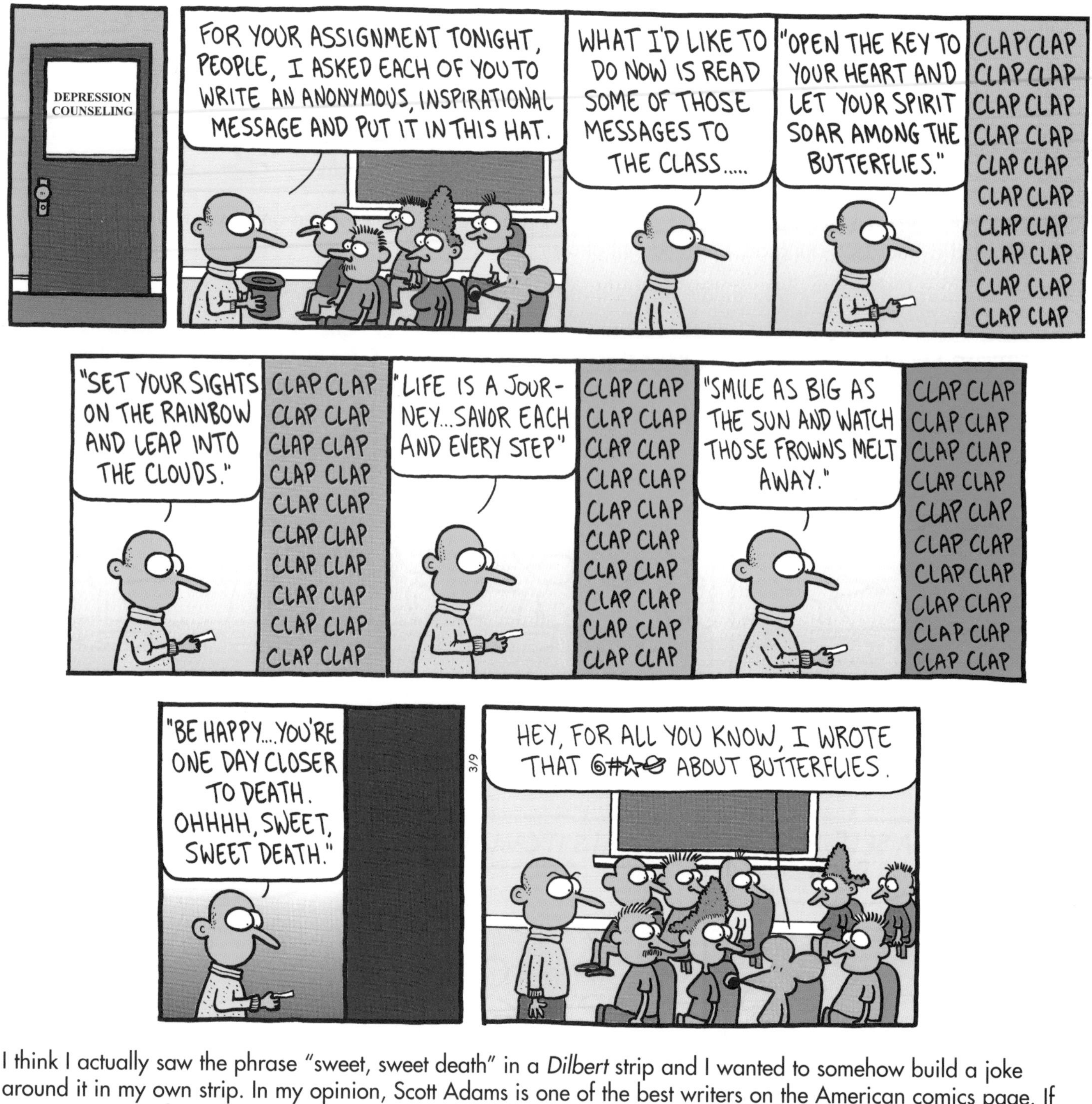
DEPRESSION COUNSELING
FOR YOUR ASSIGNMENT TONIGHT, PEOPLE, I ASKED EACH OF YOU TO WRITE AN ANONYMOUS, INSPIRATIONAL MESSAGE AND PUT IT IN THIS HAT.
WHAT I'D LIKE TO DO NOW IS READ SOME OF THOSE MESSAGES TO THE CLASS.....
"OPEN THE KEY TO YOUR HEART AND LET YOUR SPIRIT SOAR AMONG THE BUTTERFLIES."
CLAP CLAP CLAP CLAP CLAP CLAP CLAP CLAP CLAP CLAP CLAP CLAP CLAP CLAP CLAP CLAP CLAP CLAP CLAP CLAP
"SET YOUR SIGHTS ON THE RAINBOW AND LEAP INTO THE CLOUDS."
CLAP CLAP CLAP CLAP CLAP CLAP CLAP CLAP CLAP CLAP CLAP CLAP CLAP CLAP CLAP CLAP CLAP CLAP CLAP CLAP
"LIFE IS A JOURNEY...SAVOR EACH AND EVERY STEP"
CLAP CLAP CLAP CLAP CLAP CLAP CLAP CLAP CLAP CLAP CLAP CLAP CLAP CLAP CLAP CLAP CLAP CLAP CLAP CLAP
"SMILE AS BIG AS THE SUN AND WATCH THOSE FROWNS MELT AWAY."
CLAP CLAP CLAP CLAP CLAP CLAP CLAP CLAP CLAP CLAP CLAP CLAP CLAP CLAP CLAP CLAP CLAP CLAP CLAP CLAP
"BE HAPPY....YOU'RE ONE DAY CLOSER TO DEATH. OHHHH, SWEET, SWEET DEATH."
3/9
HEY, FOR ALL YOU KNOW, I WROTE THAT @#☆@ ABOUT BUTTERFLIES.

I think I actually saw the phrase "sweet, sweet death" in a *Dilbert* strip and I wanted to somehow build a joke around it in my own strip. In my opinion, Scott Adams is one of the best writers on the American comics page. If you ever want to learn how to write a comic strip, study *Dilbert.*

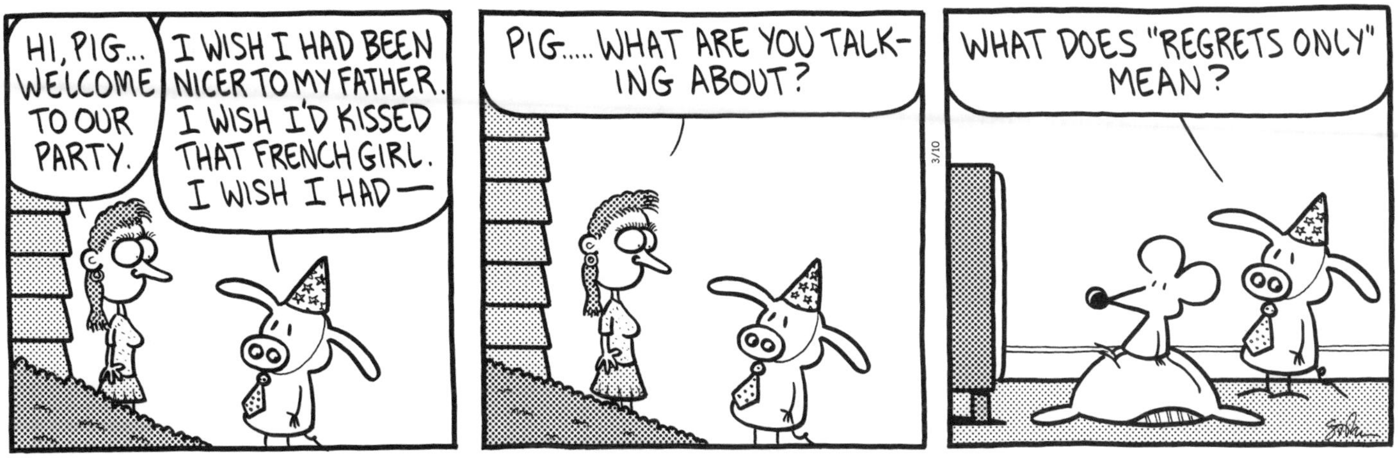
HI, PIG... WELCOME TO OUR PARTY.
I WISH I HAD BEEN NICER TO MY FATHER. I WISH I'D KISSED THAT FRENCH GIRL. I WISH I HAD—
PIG..... WHAT ARE YOU TALKING ABOUT?
WHAT DOES "REGRETS ONLY" MEAN?
3/10

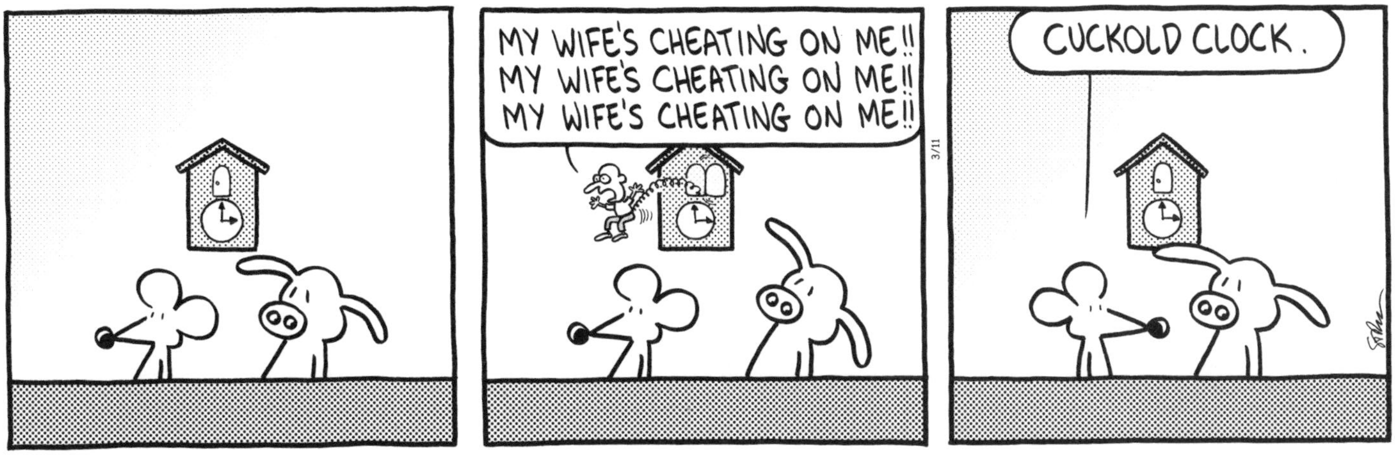
MY WIFE'S CHEATING ON ME!! MY WIFE'S CHEATING ON ME!! MY WIFE'S CHEATING ON ME!!
CUCKOLD CLOCK.
3/11

This is another one that sailed over some heads because of the use of the word "cuckold." A "cuckold" is a man whose wife cheats on him.

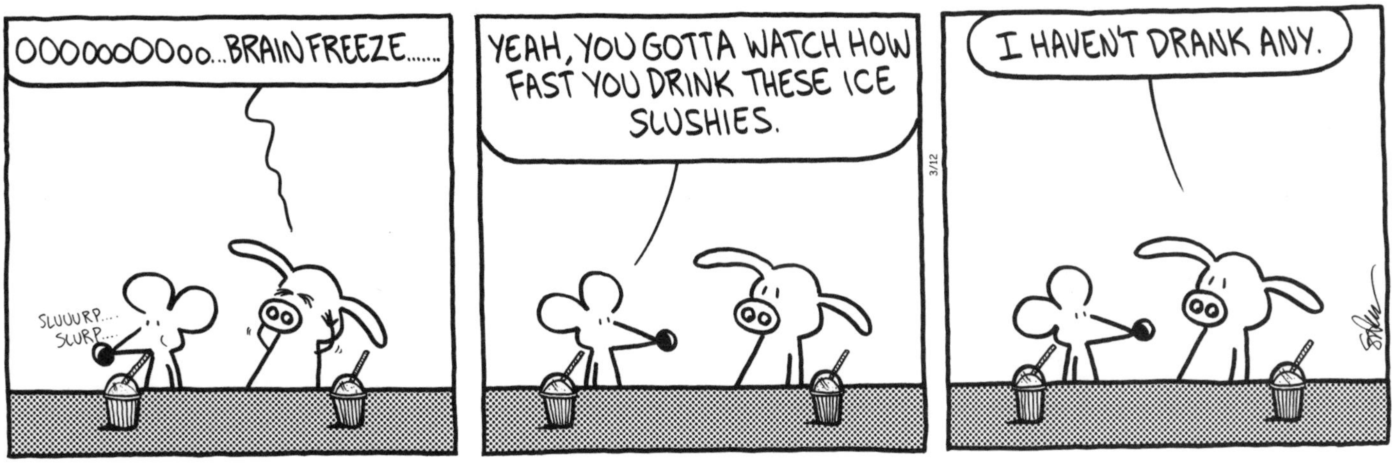
OOOOOOOOOo...BRAIN FREEZE.......
SLUUURP.... SLURP....
YEAH, YOU GOTTA WATCH HOW FAST YOU DRINK THESE ICE SLUSHIES.
I HAVEN'T DRANK ANY.
3/12

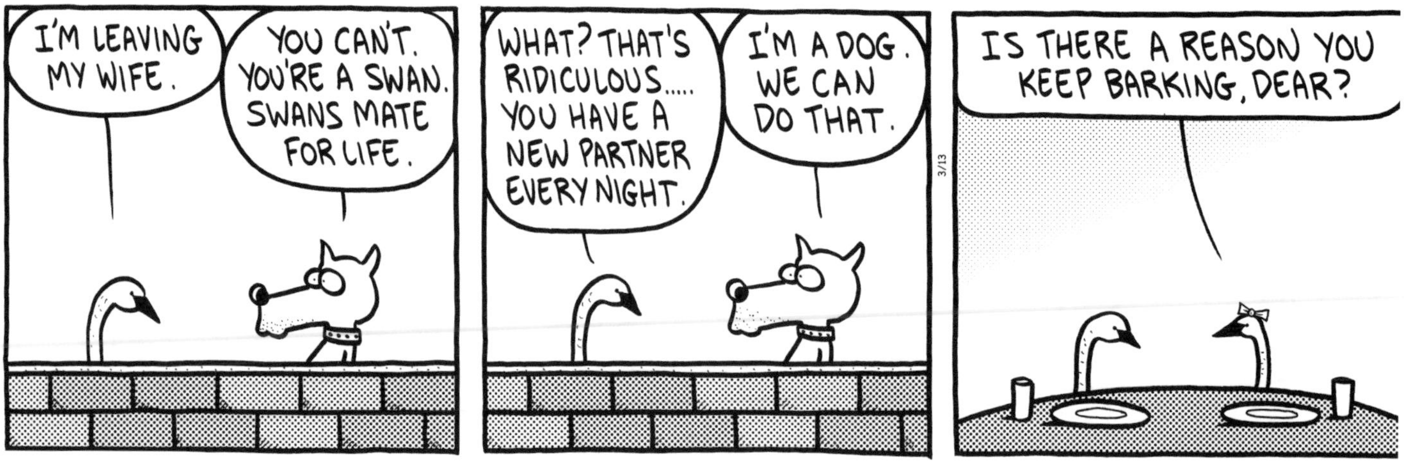
I'M LEAVING MY WIFE.
YOU CAN'T. YOU'RE A SWAN. SWANS MATE FOR LIFE.
WHAT? THAT'S RIDICULOUS..... YOU HAVE A NEW PARTNER EVERY NIGHT.
I'M A DOG. WE CAN DO THAT.
3/13
IS THERE A REASON YOU KEEP BARKING, DEAR?

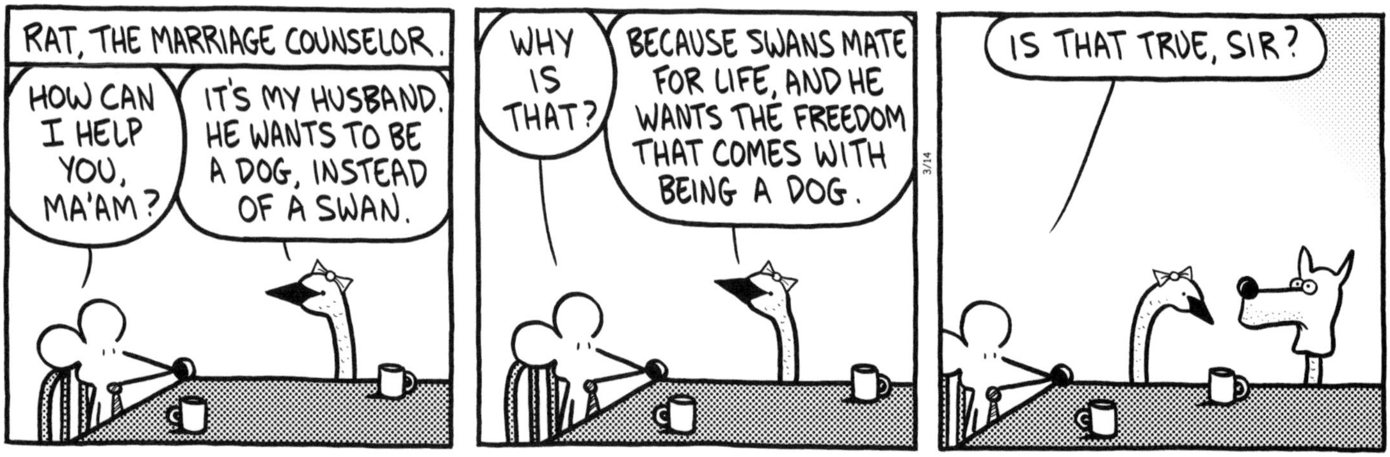
RAT, THE MARRIAGE COUNSELOR.
HOW CAN I HELP YOU, MA'AM?
IT'S MY HUSBAND. HE WANTS TO BE A DOG, INSTEAD OF A SWAN.
WHY IS THAT?
BECAUSE SWANS MATE FOR LIFE, AND HE WANTS THE FREEDOM THAT COMES WITH BEING A DOG.
3/14
IS THAT TRUE, SIR?

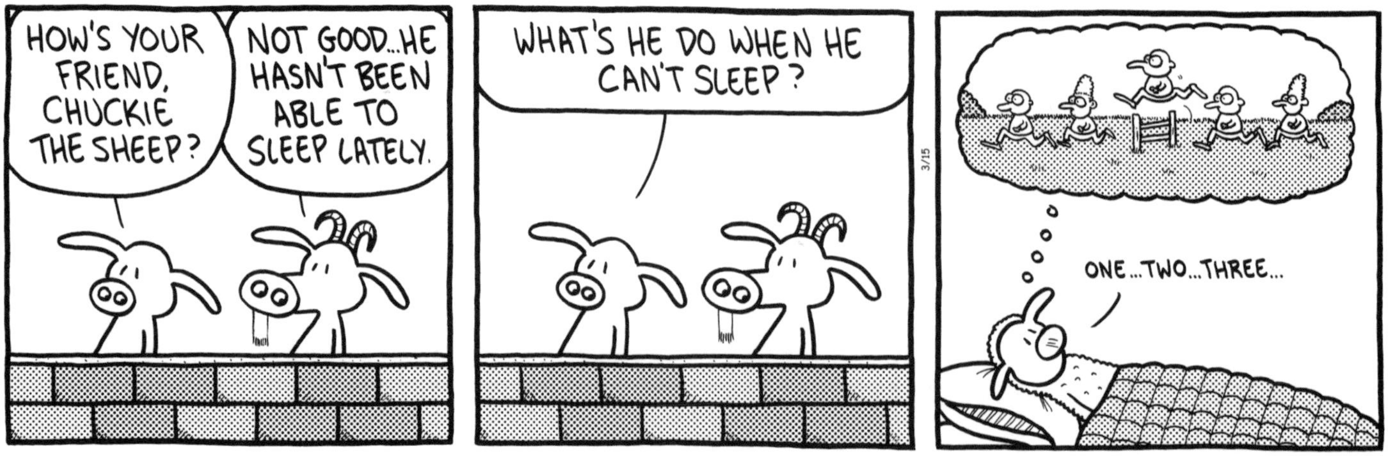
HOW'S YOUR FRIEND, CHUCKIE THE SHEEP?
NOT GOOD...HE HASN'T BEEN ABLE TO SLEEP LATELY.
WHAT'S HE DO WHEN HE CAN'T SLEEP?
3/15
ONE...TWO...THREE...

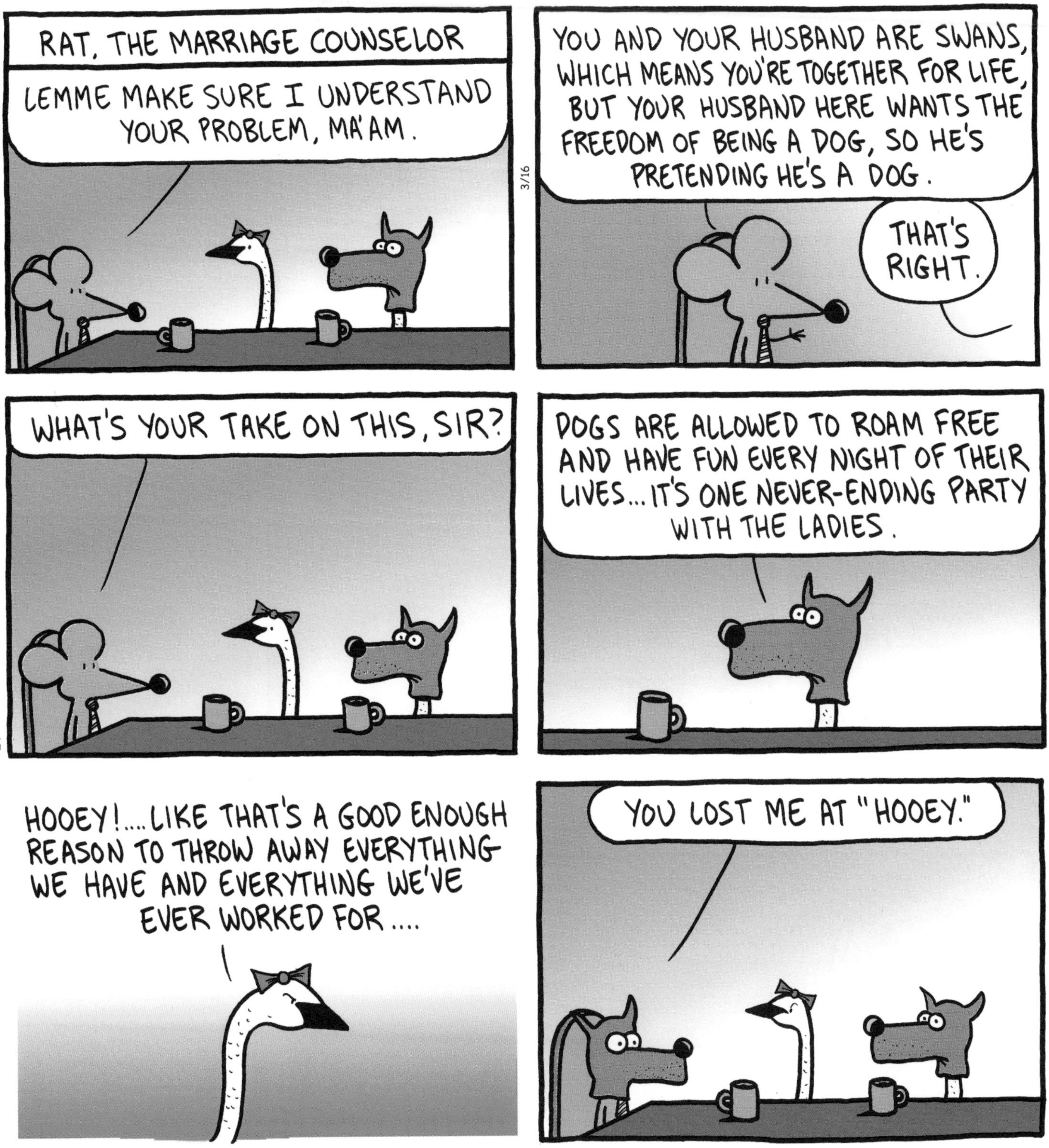
RAT, THE MARRIAGE COUNSELOR
LEMME MAKE SURE I UNDERSTAND YOUR PROBLEM, MA'AM.
3/16
YOU AND YOUR HUSBAND ARE SWANS, WHICH MEANS YOU'RE TOGETHER FOR LIFE, BUT YOUR HUSBAND HERE WANTS THE FREEDOM OF BEING A DOG, SO HE'S PRETENDING HE'S A DOG.
THAT'S RIGHT.
WHAT'S YOUR TAKE ON THIS, SIR?
DOGS ARE ALLOWED TO ROAM FREE AND HAVE FUN EVERY NIGHT OF THEIR LIVES... IT'S ONE NEVER-ENDING PARTY WITH THE LADIES.
HOOEY!.... LIKE THAT'S A GOOD ENOUGH REASON TO THROW AWAY EVERYTHING WE HAVE AND EVERYTHING WE'VE EVER WORKED FOR....
YOU LOST ME AT "HOOEY."

That last line was a loose parody of the famous *Jerry Maguire* line, "You had me at 'hello.'"

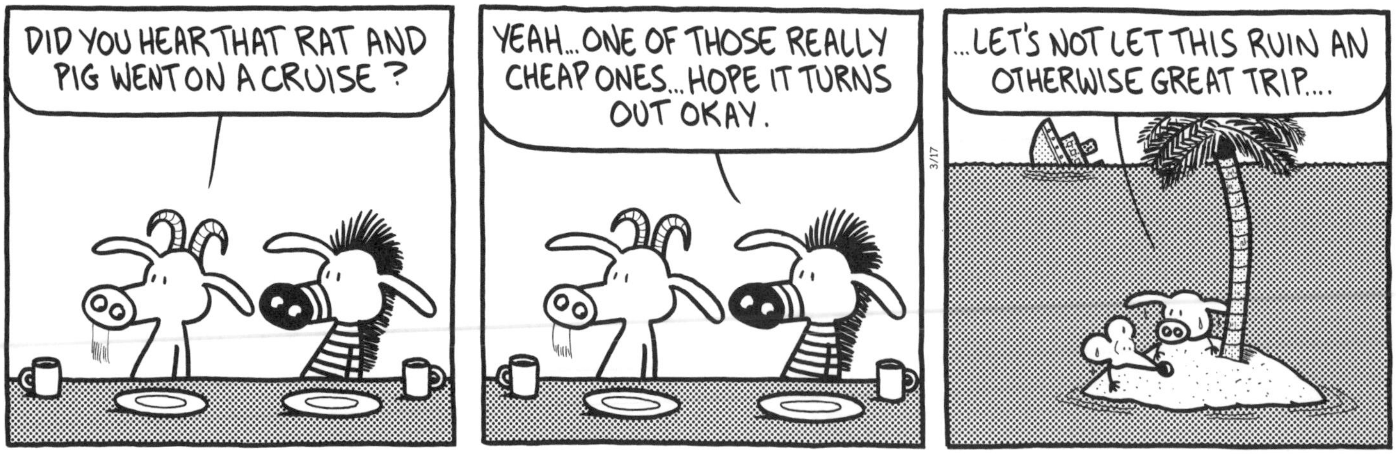
DID YOU HEAR THAT RAT AND PIG WENT ON A CRUISE?
YEAH... ONE OF THOSE REALLY CHEAP ONES... HOPE IT TURNS OUT OKAY.
3/17
...LET'S NOT LET THIS RUIN AN OTHERWISE GREAT TRIP....

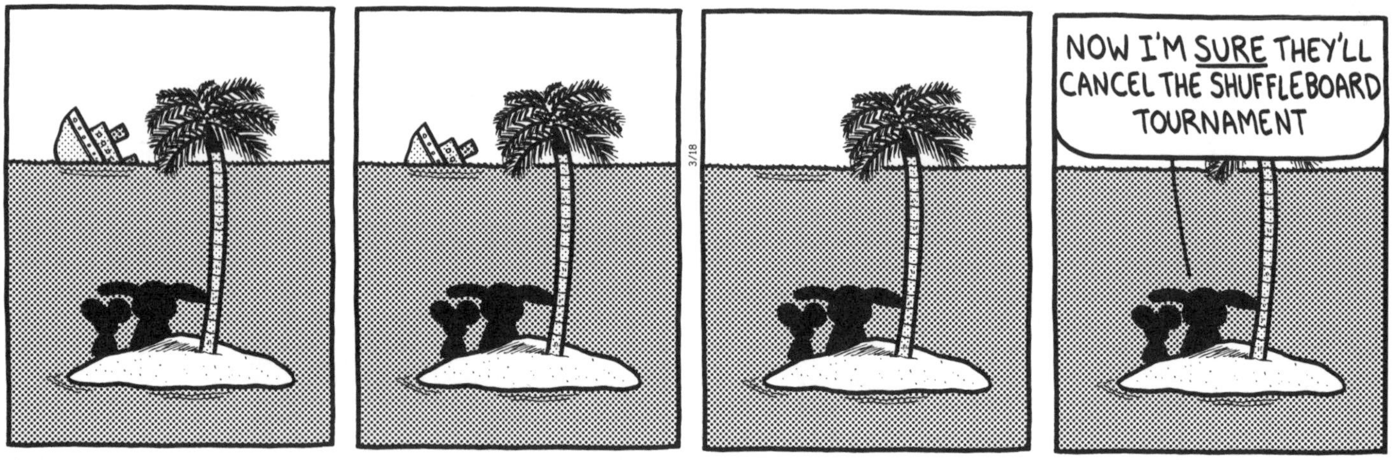
3/18
NOW I'M SURE THEY'LL CANCEL THE SHUFFLEBOARD TOURNAMENT

Ships are hard to draw, so I just draw snippets of them and then sink them. If I ever have to do a week of strips where Rat and Pig actually sail on a cruise ship that does *not* sink, I'll have a big problem on my hands.

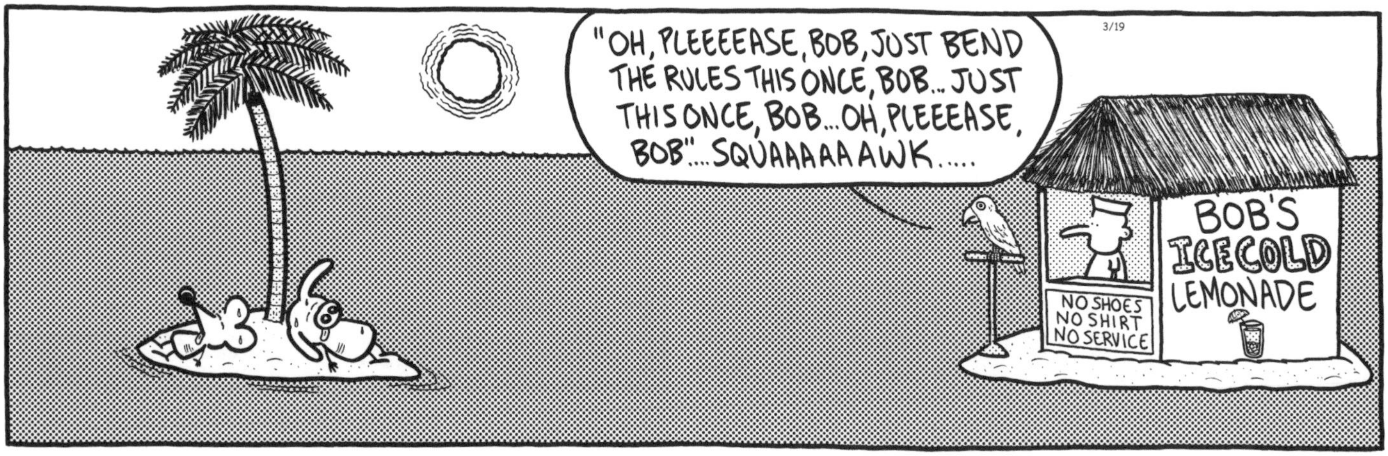
3/19
"OH, PLEEEEASE, BOB, JUST BEND THE RULES THIS ONCE, BOB... JUST THIS ONCE, BOB... OH, PLEEEASE, BOB"... SQUAAAAAAWK.....
BOB'S ICE COLD LEMONADE
NO SHOES NO SHIRT NO SERVICE

Clearly, I was influenced by *The Far Side* here. To me, *The Far Side* is the funniest comic ever created and Larson is the biggest genius the field has yet produced. I've always thought that Larson was to comics what Jimi Hendrix was to rock: Both seemed to have come from another planet, both performed at a level no one else could perform at, and both changed the art form forever.

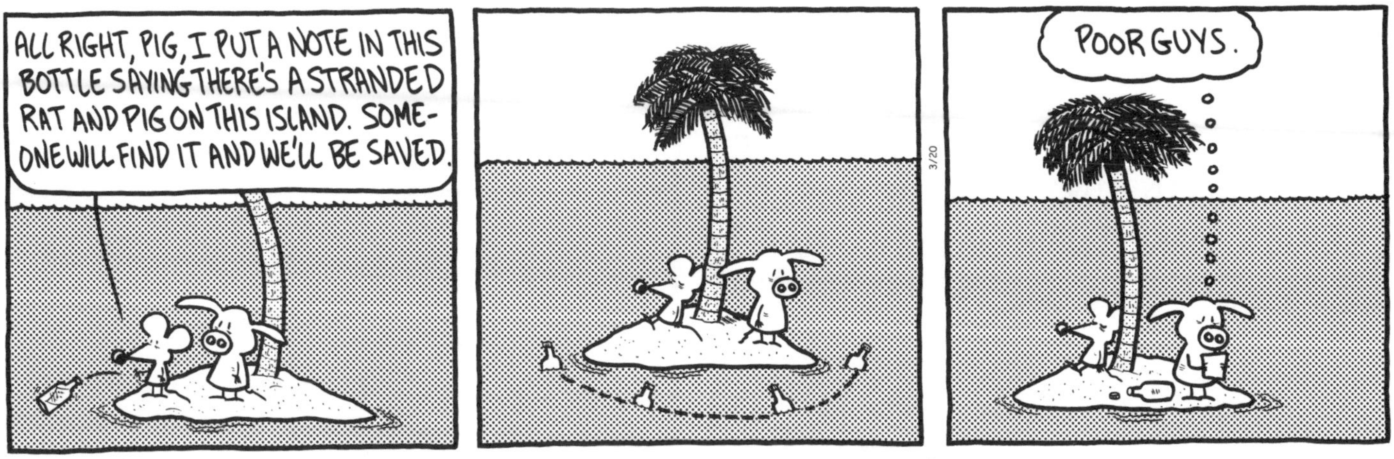
ALL RIGHT, PIG, I PUT A NOTE IN THIS BOTTLE SAYING THERE'S A STRANDED RAT AND PIG ON THIS ISLAND. SOMEONE WILL FIND IT AND WE'LL BE SAVED.
3/20
POOR GUYS.

This strip was animated and turned into a screen saver. I currently have it as the screen saver on my computer. When you have an ego as out-of-control as mine, you do things like that.

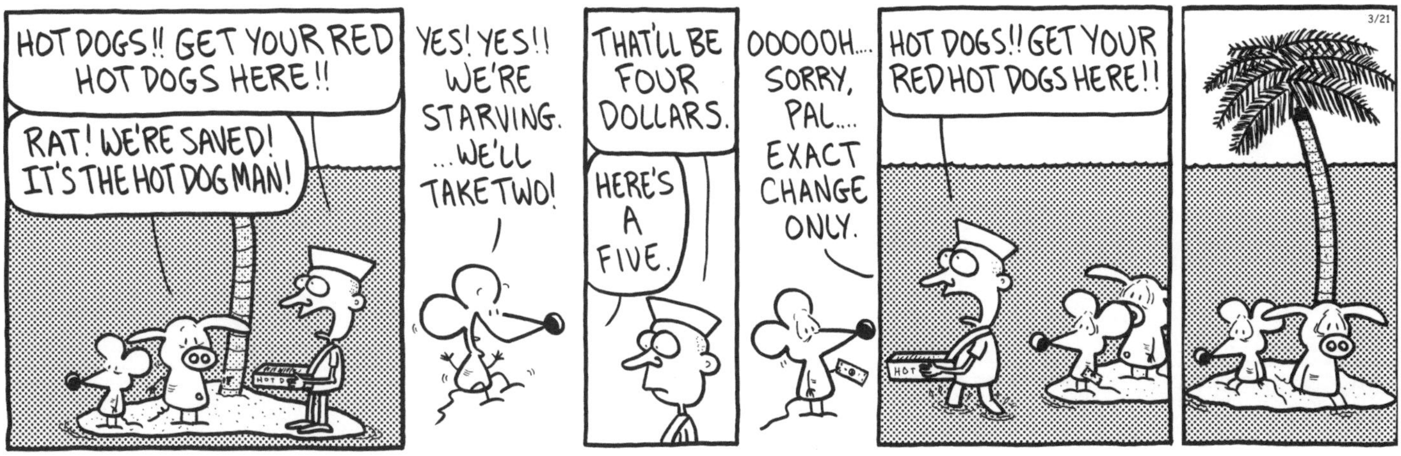
HOT DOGS!! GET YOUR RED HOT DOGS HERE!!
RAT! WE'RE SAVED! IT'S THE HOT DOG MAN!
YES! YES!! WE'RE STARVING. ...WE'LL TAKE TWO!
THAT'LL BE FOUR DOLLARS.
HERE'S A FIVE.
OOOOOH.... SORRY, PAL.... EXACT CHANGE ONLY.
HOT DOGS!! GET YOUR RED HOT DOGS HERE!!
3/21

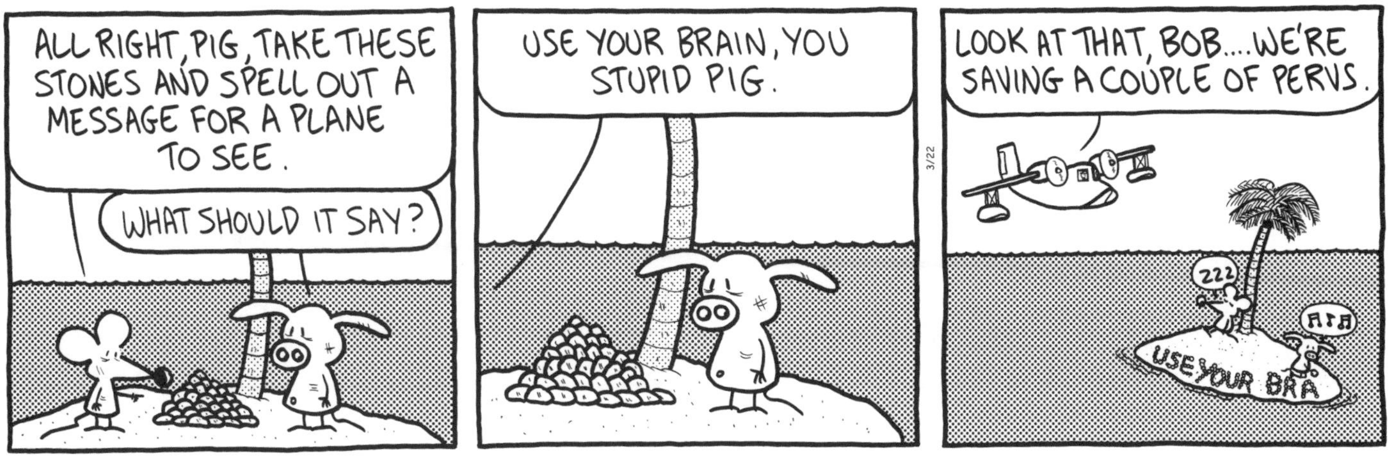
ALL RIGHT, PIG, TAKE THESE STONES AND SPELL OUT A MESSAGE FOR A PLANE TO SEE.
WHAT SHOULD IT SAY?
USE YOUR BRAIN, YOU STUPID PIG.
3/22
LOOK AT THAT, BOB....WE'RE SAVING A COUPLE OF PERVS.
ZZZ
USE YOUR BRA

For those wondering, that's a plane in the sky.

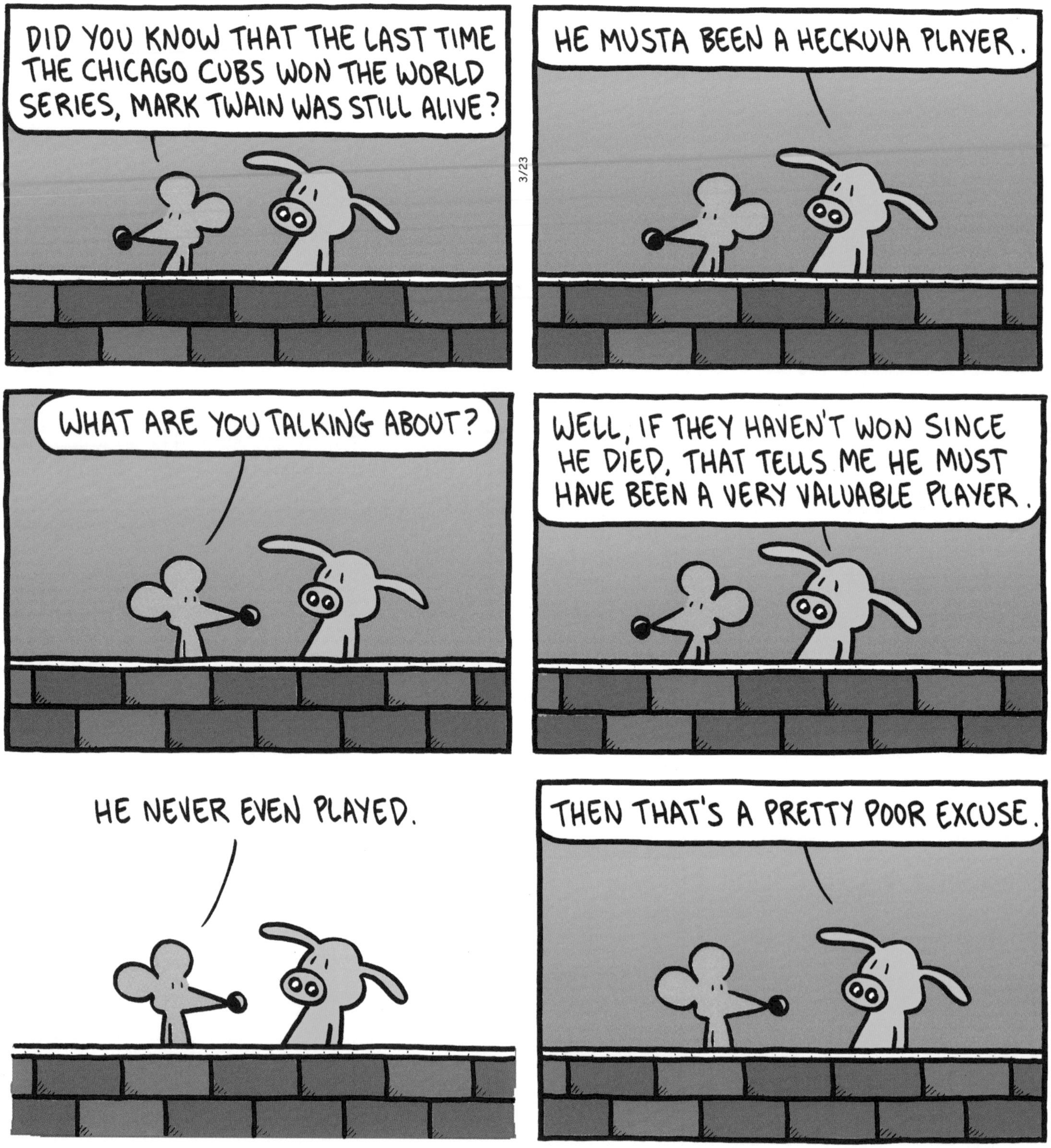
DID YOU KNOW THAT THE LAST TIME THE CHICAGO CUBS WON THE WORLD SERIES, MARK TWAIN WAS STILL ALIVE?
3/23
HE MUSTA BEEN A HECKUVA PLAYER.
WHAT ARE YOU TALKING ABOUT?
WELL, IF THEY HAVEN'T WON SINCE HE DIED, THAT TELLS ME HE MUST HAVE BEEN A VERY VALUABLE PLAYER.
HE NEVER EVEN PLAYED.
THEN THAT'S A PRETTY POOR EXCUSE.

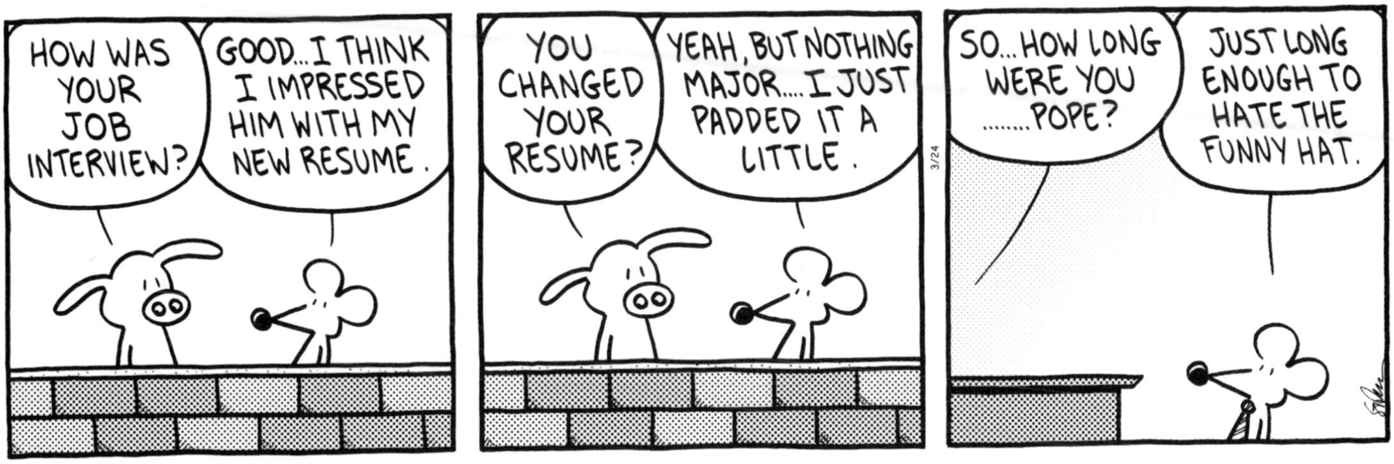
HOW WAS YOUR JOB INTERVIEW?
GOOD...I THINK I IMPRESSED HIM WITH MY NEW RESUME.
YOU CHANGED YOUR RESUME?
YEAH, BUT NOTHING MAJOR.... I JUST PADDED IT A LITTLE.
3/24
SO...HOW LONG WERE YOU ....POPE?
JUST LONG ENOUGH TO HATE THE FUNNY HAT.

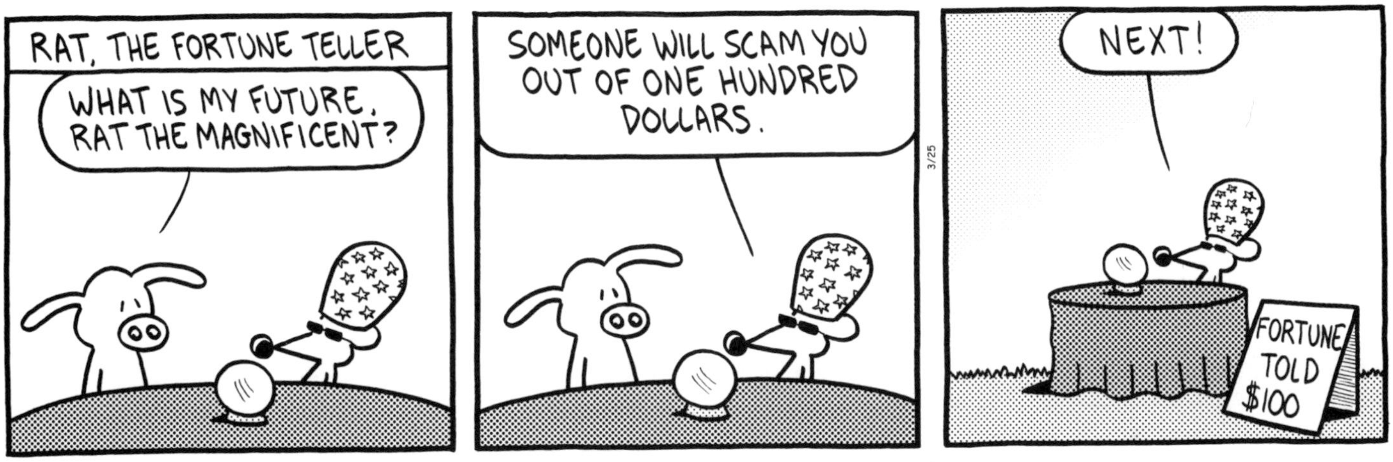
RAT, THE FORTUNE TELLER
WHAT IS MY FUTURE, RAT THE MAGNIFICENT?
SOMEONE WILL SCAM YOU OUT OF ONE HUNDRED DOLLARS.
3/25
NEXT!
FORTUNE TOLD $100

Look at the elaborate use of shadows in that third panel. Dan Piraro's got nothing on me.

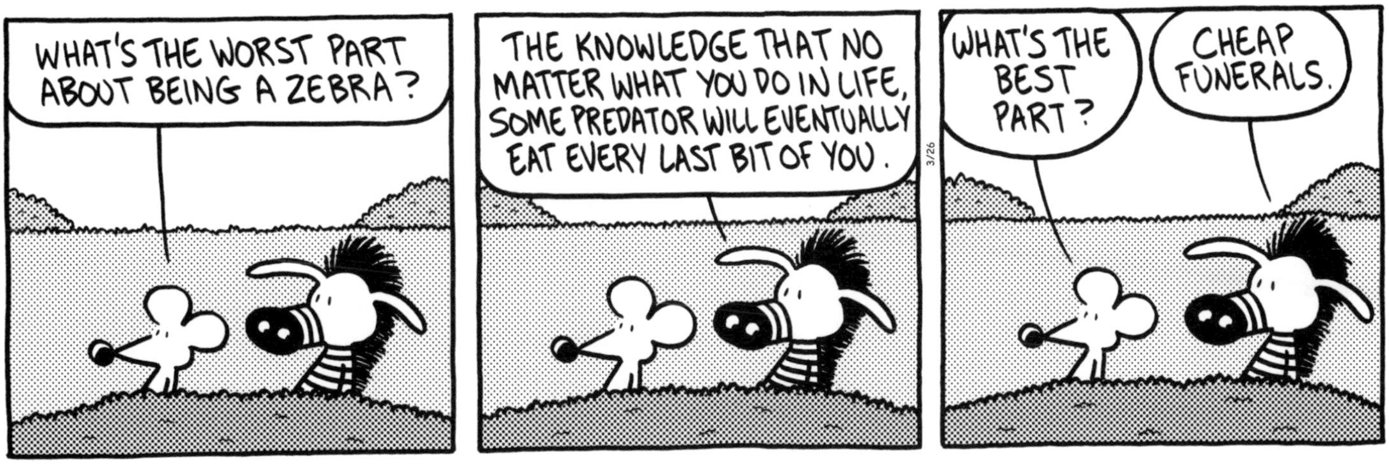
WHAT'S THE WORST PART ABOUT BEING A ZEBRA?
THE KNOWLEDGE THAT NO MATTER WHAT YOU DO IN LIFE, SOME PREDATOR WILL EVENTUALLY EAT EVERY LAST BIT OF YOU.
3/26
WHAT'S THE BEST PART?
CHEAP FUNERALS.

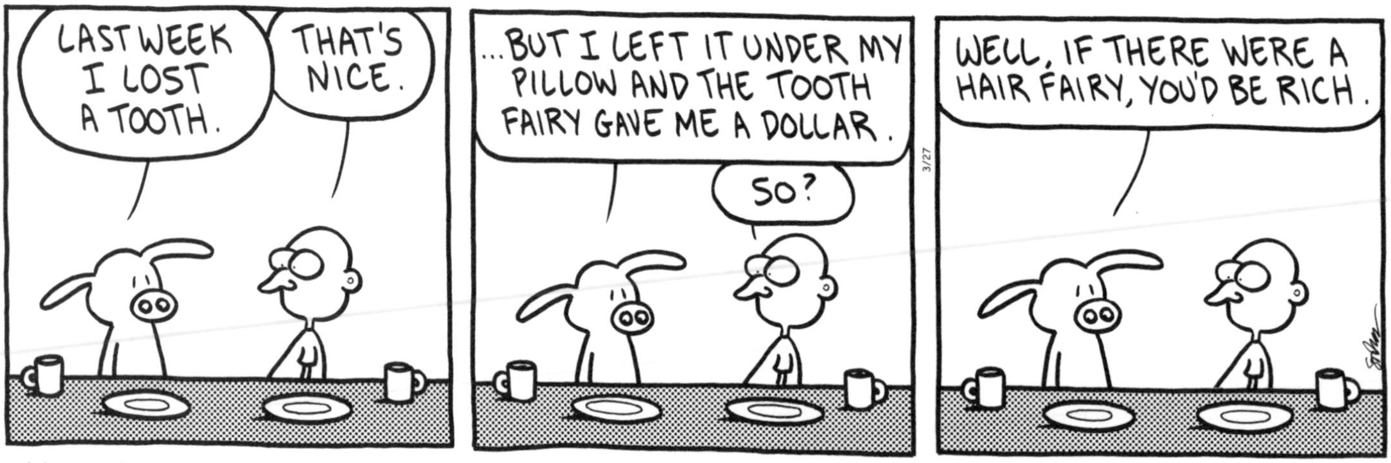
LAST WEEK I LOST A TOOTH.
THAT'S NICE.
...BUT I LEFT IT UNDER MY PILLOW AND THE TOOTH FAIRY GAVE ME A DOLLAR.
SO?
WELL, IF THERE WERE A HAIR FAIRY, YOU'D BE RICH.
3/27

Bald people are one of the last groups of human beings you can still make fun of.

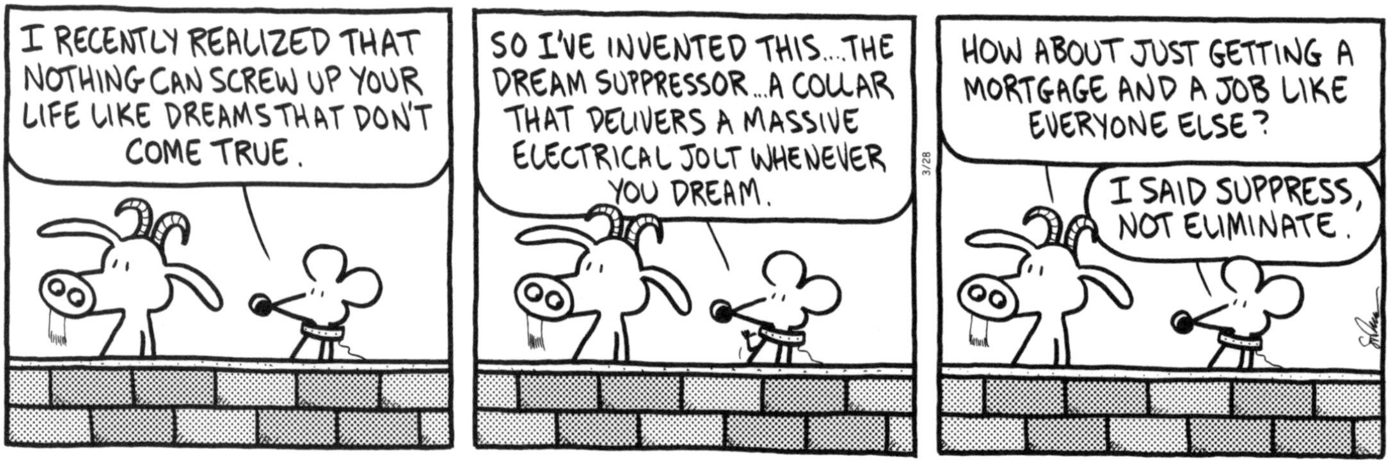
I RECENTLY REALIZED THAT NOTHING CAN SCREW UP YOUR LIFE LIKE DREAMS THAT DON'T COME TRUE.
SO I'VE INVENTED THIS....THE DREAM SUPPRESSOR...A COLLAR THAT DELIVERS A MASSIVE ELECTRICAL JOLT WHENEVER YOU DREAM.
HOW ABOUT JUST GETTING A MORTGAGE AND A JOB LIKE EVERYONE ELSE?
I SAID SUPPRESS, NOT ELIMINATE.
3/28

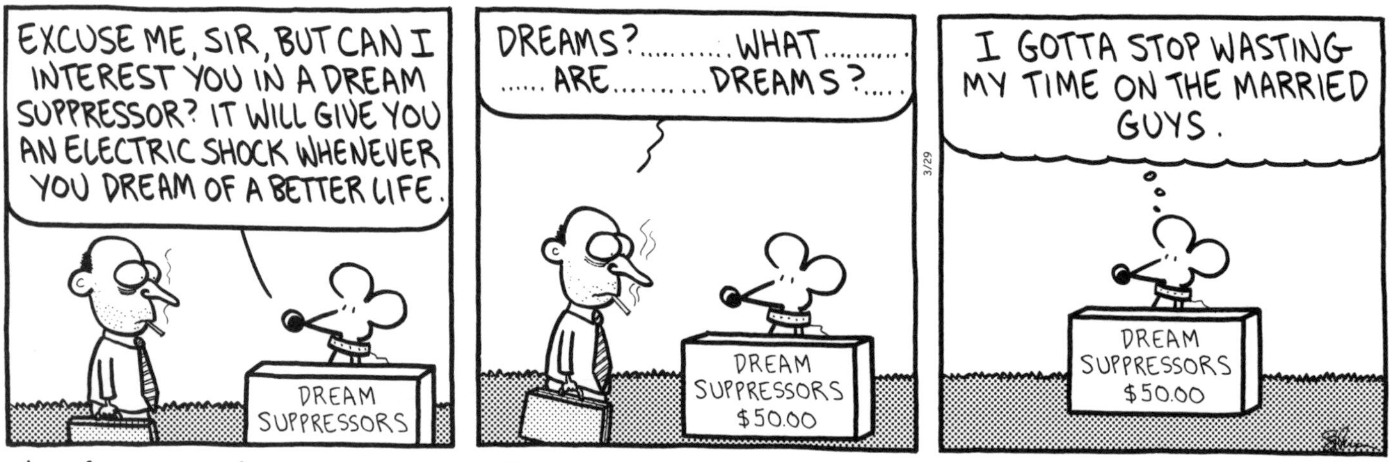
EXCUSE ME, SIR, BUT CAN I INTEREST YOU IN A DREAM SUPPRESSOR? IT WILL GIVE YOU AN ELECTRIC SHOCK WHENEVER YOU DREAM OF A BETTER LIFE.
DREAM SUPPRESSORS
DREAMS?..........WHAT..........
......ARE..........DREAMS?.....
DREAM SUPPRESSORS $50.00
I GOTTA STOP WASTING MY TIME ON THE MARRIED GUYS.
DREAM SUPPRESSORS $50.00
3/29

Okay, fine . . . maybe *Pearls* is *occasionally* cynical.

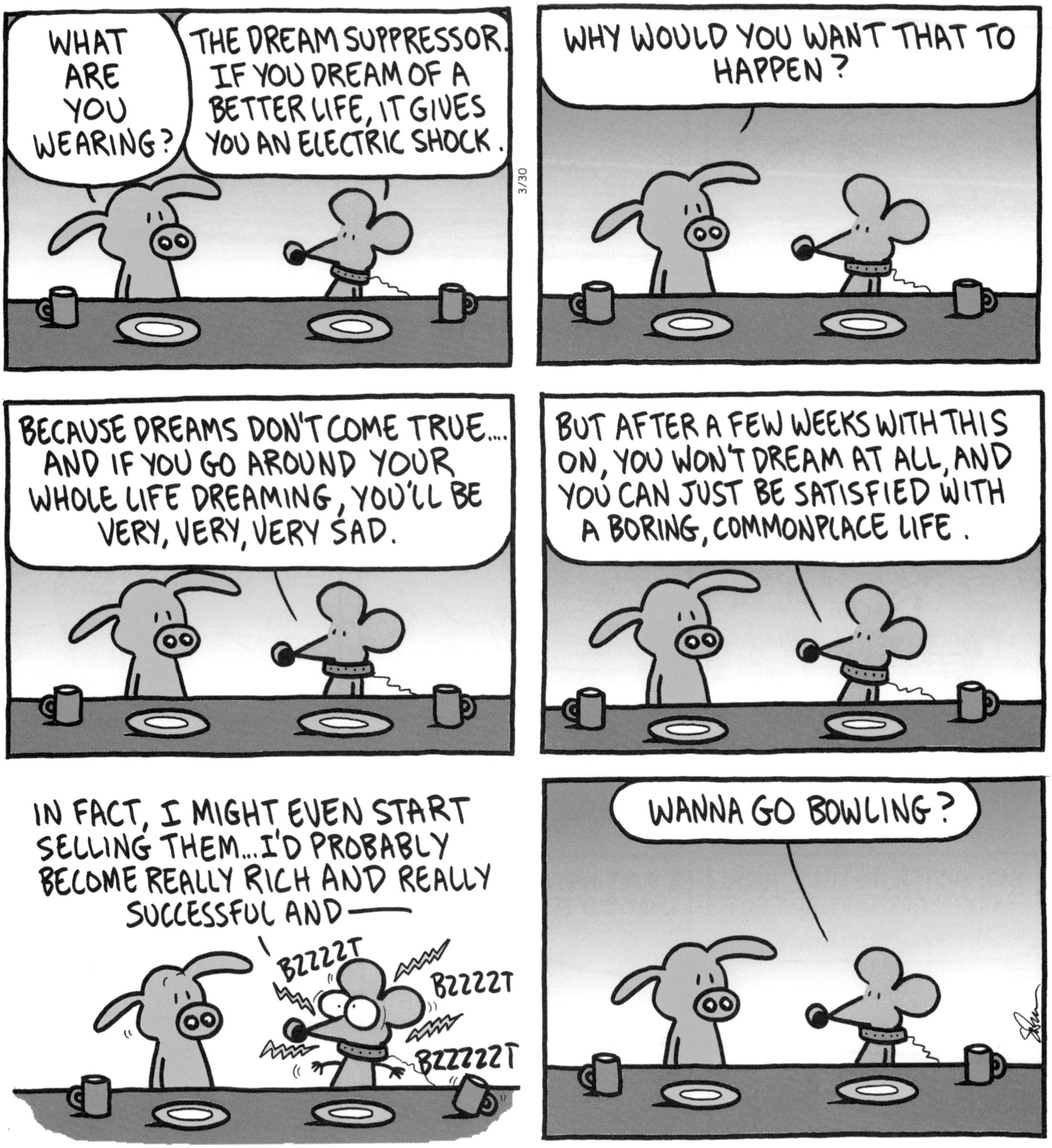
WHAT ARE YOU WEARING?
THE DREAM SUPPRESSOR. IF YOU DREAM OF A BETTER LIFE, IT GIVES YOU AN ELECTRIC SHOCK.
3/30
WHY WOULD YOU WANT THAT TO HAPPEN?
BECAUSE DREAMS DON'T COME TRUE.... AND IF YOU GO AROUND YOUR WHOLE LIFE DREAMING, YOU'LL BE VERY, VERY, VERY SAD.
BUT AFTER A FEW WEEKS WITH THIS ON, YOU WON'T DREAM AT ALL, AND YOU CAN JUST BE SATISFIED WITH A BORING, COMMONPLACE LIFE.
IN FACT, I MIGHT EVEN START SELLING THEM...I'D PROBABLY BECOME REALLY RICH AND REALLY SUCCESSFUL AND—
BZZZZT
BZZZZT
BZZZZZT
WANNA GO BOWLING?

No bowlers complained.

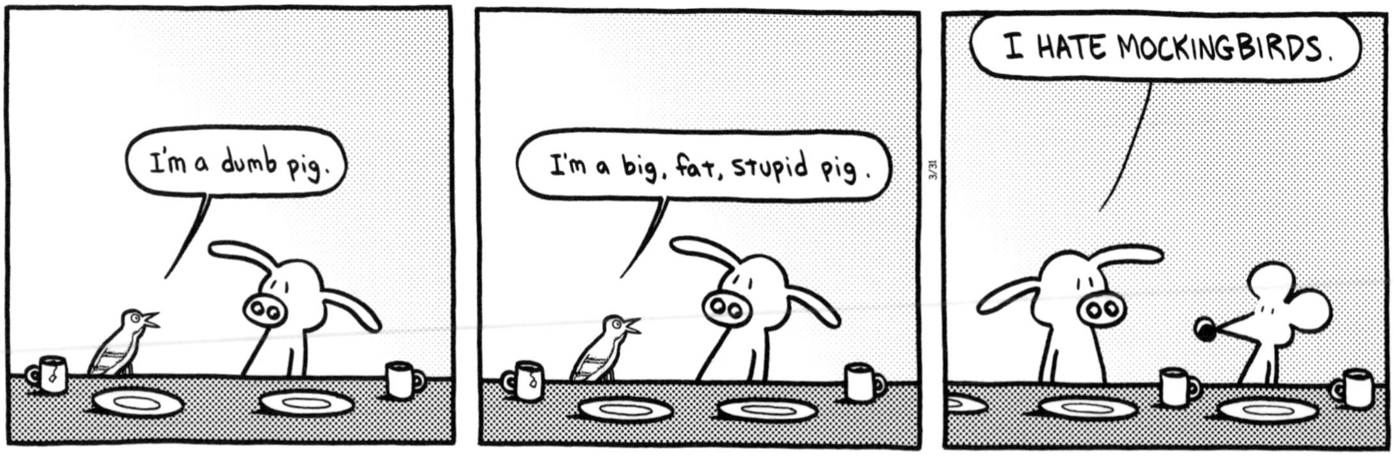
I'm a dumb pig.
I'm a big, fat, stupid pig.
3/31
I HATE MOCKINGBIRDS.

Note the tea bag hanging from the bird's cup. It has no significance to the strip, but it shows that when I draw beverages, I have *range*.

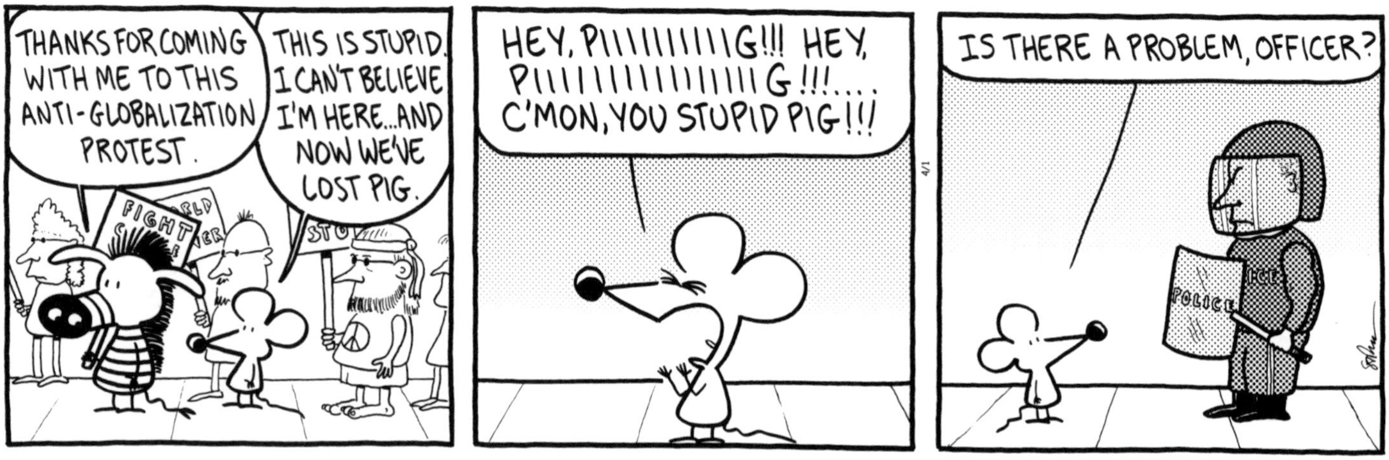
THANKS FOR COMING WITH ME TO THIS ANTI-GLOBALIZATION PROTEST.
THIS IS STUPID. I CAN'T BELIEVE I'M HERE...AND NOW WE'VE LOST PIG.
FIGHT
HEY, PIIIIIIIIIIG!!! HEY, PIIIIIIIIIIIIIIIIG!!!....
C'MON, YOU STUPID PIG!!!
4/1
IS THERE A PROBLEM, OFFICER?
POLICE

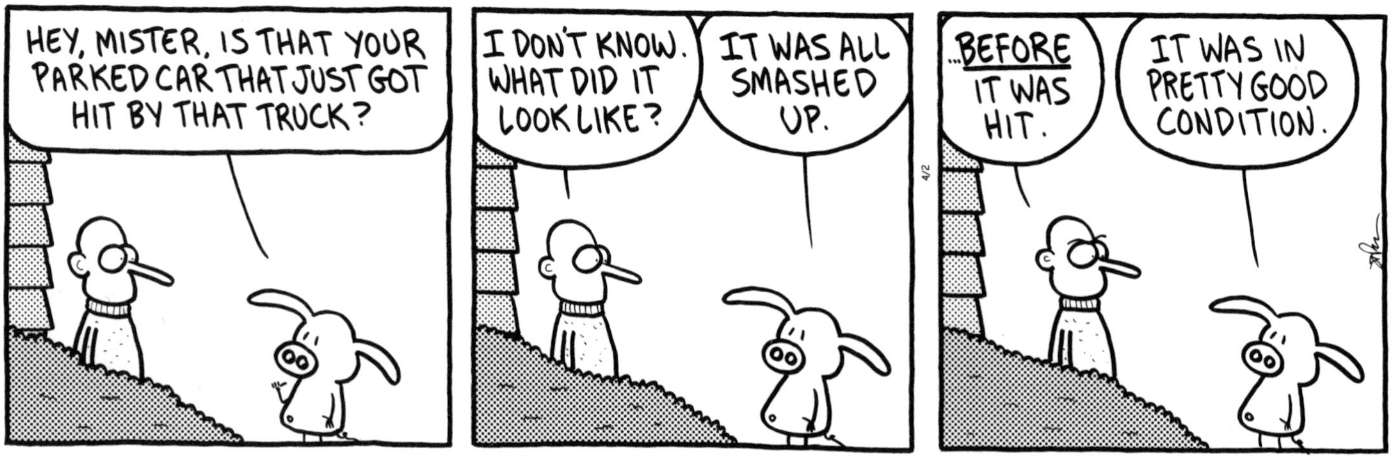
HEY, MISTER, IS THAT YOUR PARKED CAR THAT JUST GOT HIT BY THAT TRUCK?
I DON'T KNOW. WHAT DID IT LOOK LIKE?
IT WAS ALL SMASHED UP.
4/2
...BEFORE IT WAS HIT.
IT WAS IN PRETTY GOOD CONDITION.

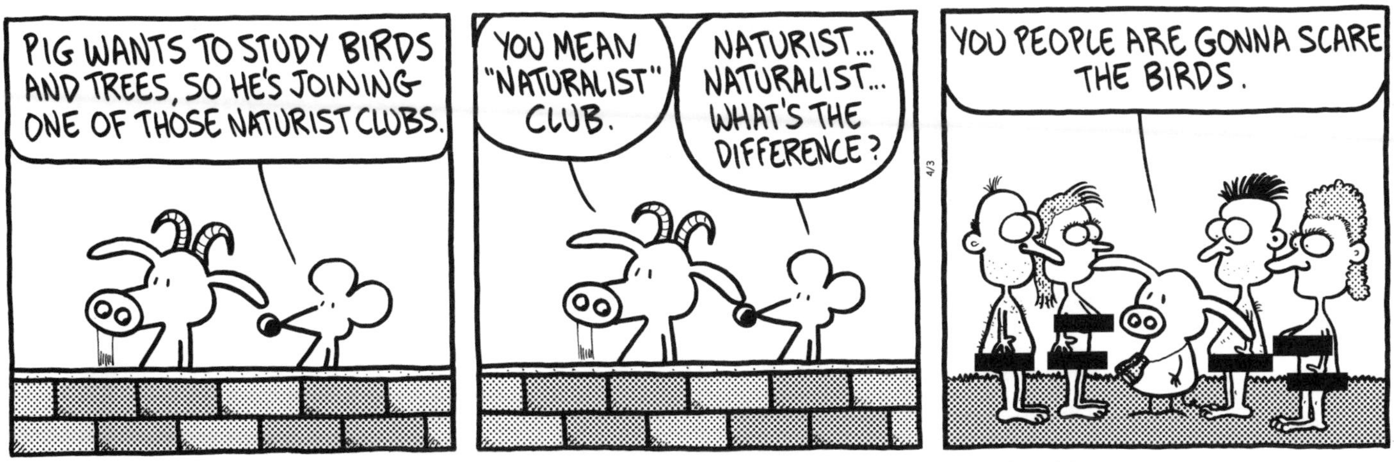
PIG WANTS TO STUDY BIRDS AND TREES, SO HE'S JOINING ONE OF THOSE NATURIST CLUBS.
YOU MEAN "NATURALIST" CLUB.
NATURIST... NATURALIST... WHAT'S THE DIFFERENCE?
4/3
YOU PEOPLE ARE GONNA SCARE THE BIRDS.

On the original, I actually drew the body parts. If you think I draw noses bad, you should see my ————.

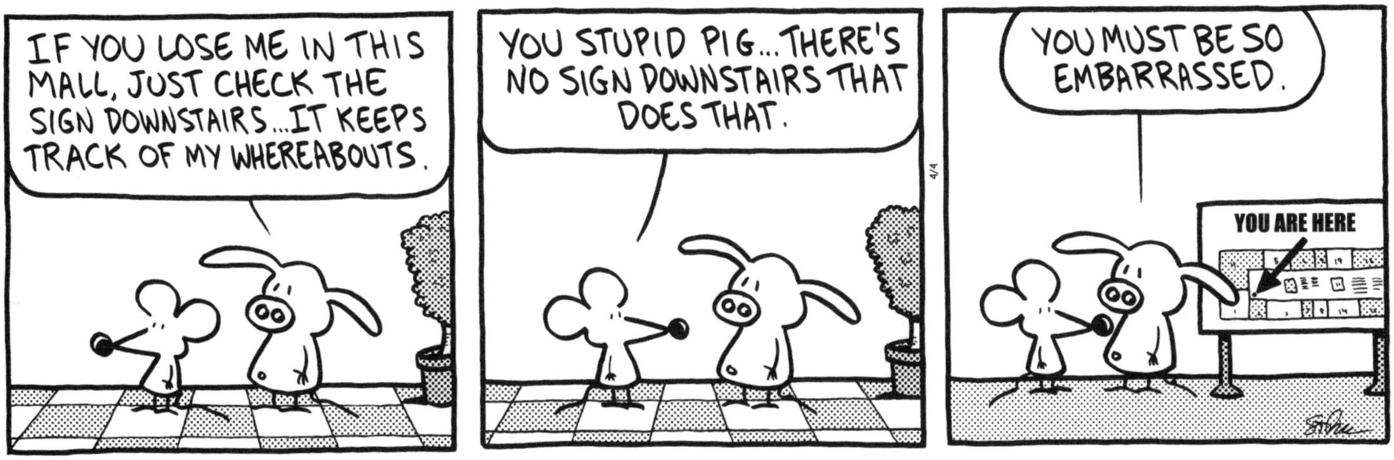
IF YOU LOSE ME IN THIS MALL, JUST CHECK THE SIGN DOWNSTAIRS...IT KEEPS TRACK OF MY WHEREABOUTS.
YOU STUPID PIG...THERE'S NO SIGN DOWNSTAIRS THAT DOES THAT.
4/4
YOU MUST BE SO EMBARRASSED.
YOU ARE HERE

Pig's endless well of stupidity makes for some easy jokes.

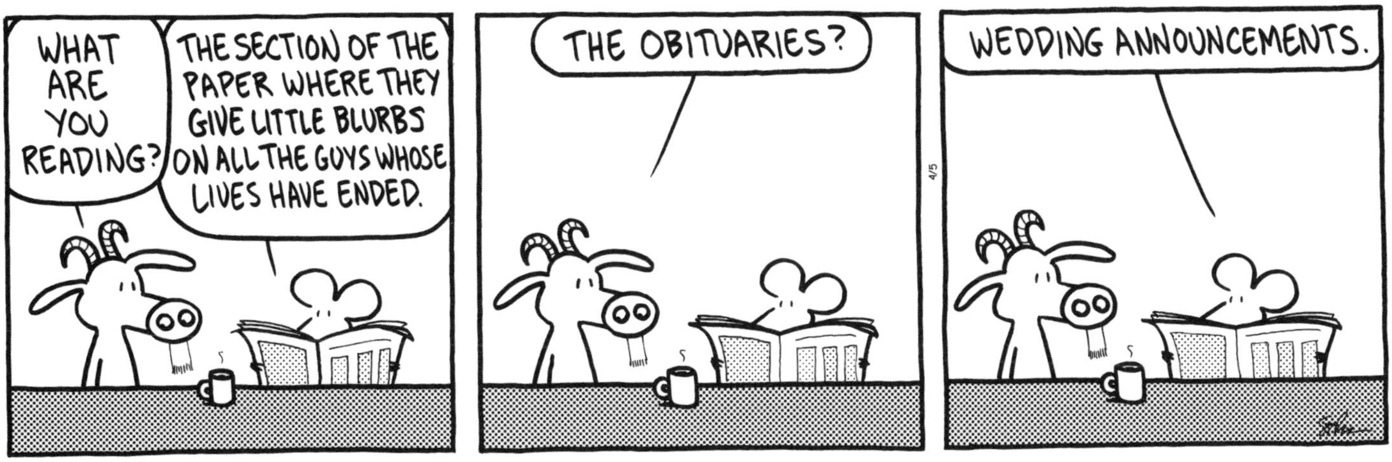
WHAT ARE YOU READING?
THE SECTION OF THE PAPER WHERE THEY GIVE LITTLE BLURBS ON ALL THE GUYS WHOSE LIVES HAVE ENDED.
THE OBITUARIES?
4/5
WEDDING ANNOUNCEMENTS.

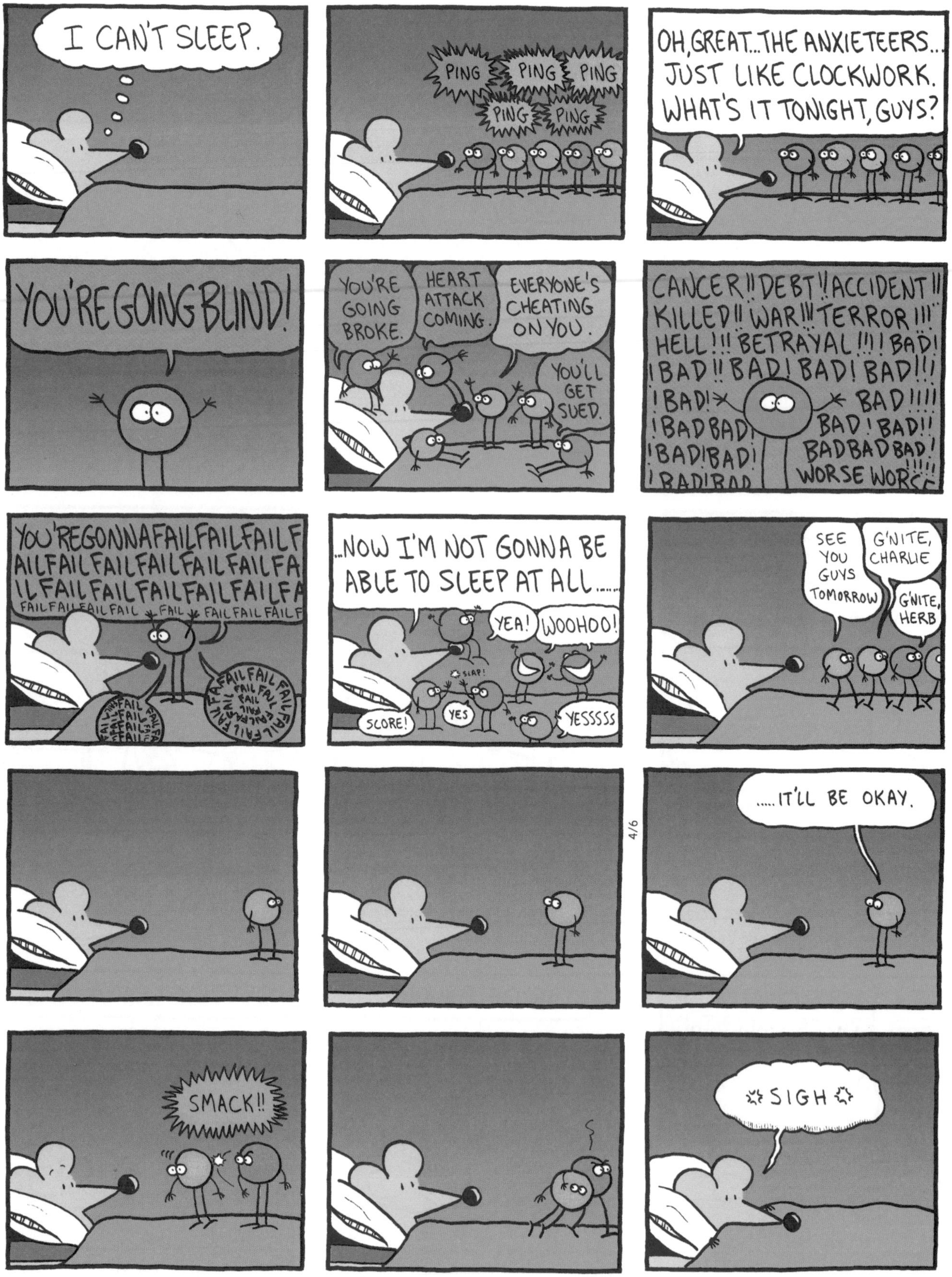
I CAN'T SLEEP.
PING PING PING PING PING
OH, GREAT... THE ANXIETEERS... JUST LIKE CLOCKWORK. WHAT'S IT TONIGHT, GUYS?
YOU'RE GOING BLIND!
YOU'RE GOING BROKE.
HEART ATTACK COMING.
EVERYONE'S CHEATING ON YOU.
YOU'LL GET SUED.
CANCER!! DEBT!! ACCIDENT!! KILLED!! WAR!!! TERROR!!! HELL!!! BETRAYAL!!!! BAD! BAD!! BAD! BAD! BAD! BAD!!! BAD! BAD!!!! BADBAD! BAD! BAD!! BAD! BAD! BADBADBAD! WORSE
YOU'REGONNAFAILFAILFAILFAILFAILFAILFAILFAILFAILFAILFAILFAILFAILFAILFAILFAIL FAIL FAILFAILFAIL
...NOW I'M NOT GONNA BE ABLE TO SLEEP AT ALL......
YEA!
WOOHOO!
SLAP!
SCORE!
YES
YESSSSS
SEE YOU GUYS TOMORROW
G'NITE, CHARLIE
G'NITE, HERB
4/6
.....IT'LL BE OKAY.
SMACK!!
SIGH

This one surprised me. I thought it was sort of a cute, harmless strip, but it was very popular with readers, probably due to the fact that so many people relate to late-night worries. In my short time being syndicated, I've learned that a decent joke that relates *directly* to people's lives will beat a great, surreal joke every time.

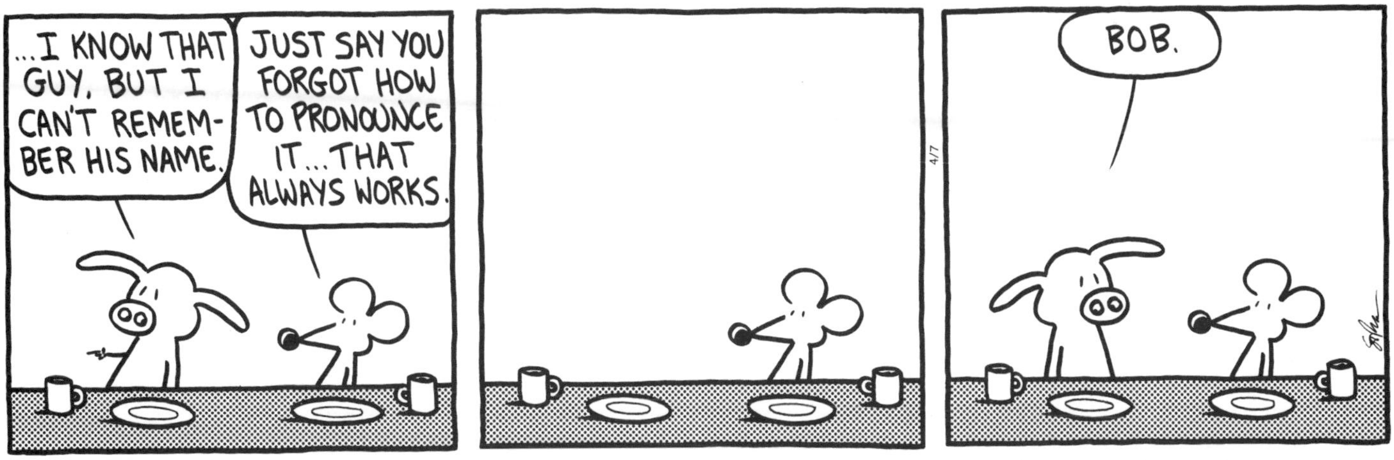
...I KNOW THAT GUY, BUT I CAN'T REMEMBER HIS NAME.
JUST SAY YOU FORGOT HOW TO PRONOUNCE IT...THAT ALWAYS WORKS.
4/7
BOB.

The name "Bob" has it all. It has two B's ("B" is a funny sounding letter), it's a palindrome, and it's a funny verb.

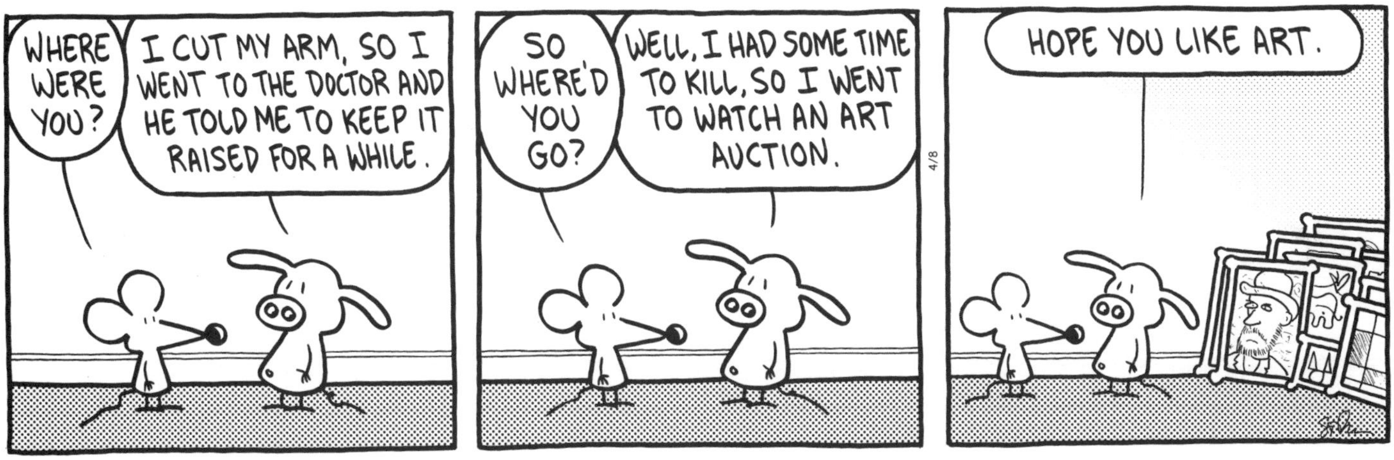
WHERE WERE YOU?
I CUT MY ARM, SO I WENT TO THE DOCTOR AND HE TOLD ME TO KEEP IT RAISED FOR A WHILE.
SO WHERE'D YOU GO?
WELL, I HAD SOME TIME TO KILL, SO I WENT TO WATCH AN ART AUCTION.
4/8
HOPE YOU LIKE ART.

Those are all extremely crude sketches of actual paintings. There's a Van Gogh, a Miró, and a Mondrian. I don't even know who those last two guys are, but I found the paintings in a book and included them in the strip to show readers how smart I am.

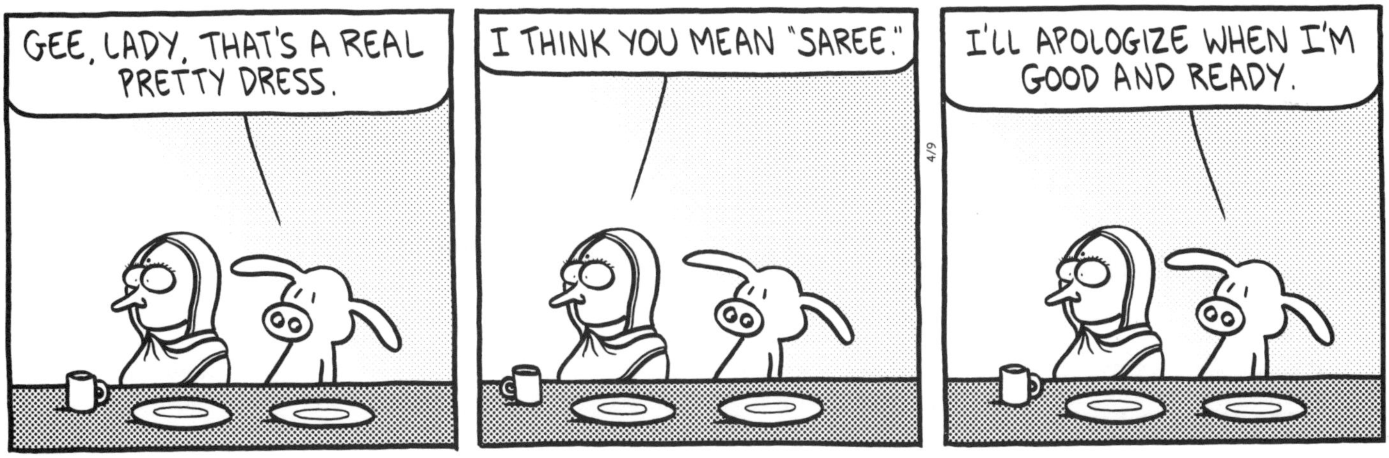
GEE, LADY, THAT'S A REAL PRETTY DRESS.
I THINK YOU MEAN "SAREE."
4/9
I'LL APOLOGIZE WHEN I'M GOOD AND READY.

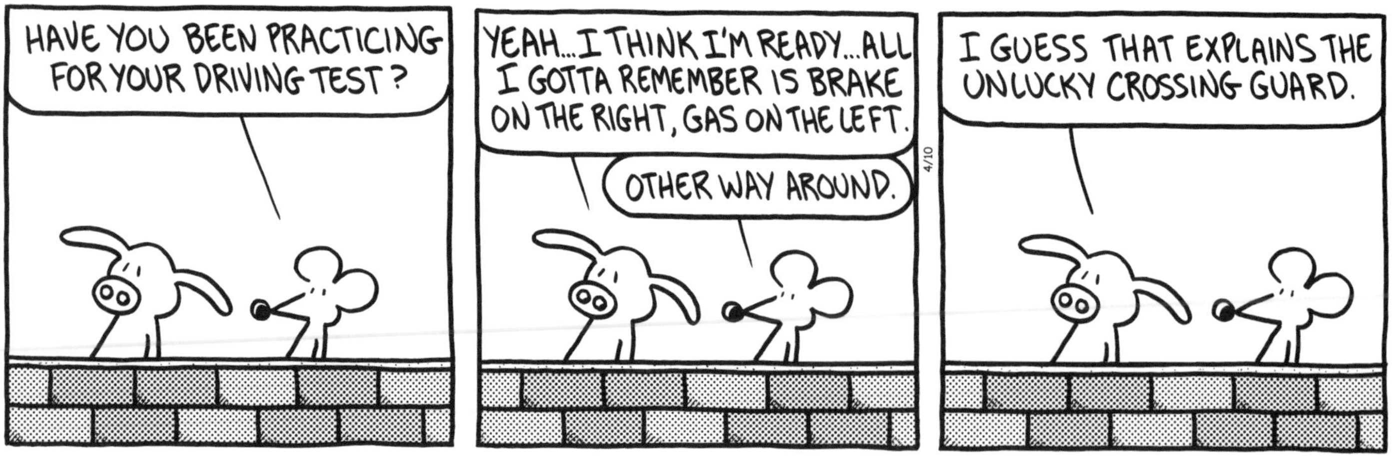
HAVE YOU BEEN PRACTICING FOR YOUR DRIVING TEST?
YEAH...I THINK I'M READY...ALL I GOTTA REMEMBER IS BRAKE ON THE RIGHT, GAS ON THE LEFT.
OTHER WAY AROUND.
4/10
I GUESS THAT EXPLAINS THE UNLUCKY CROSSING GUARD.

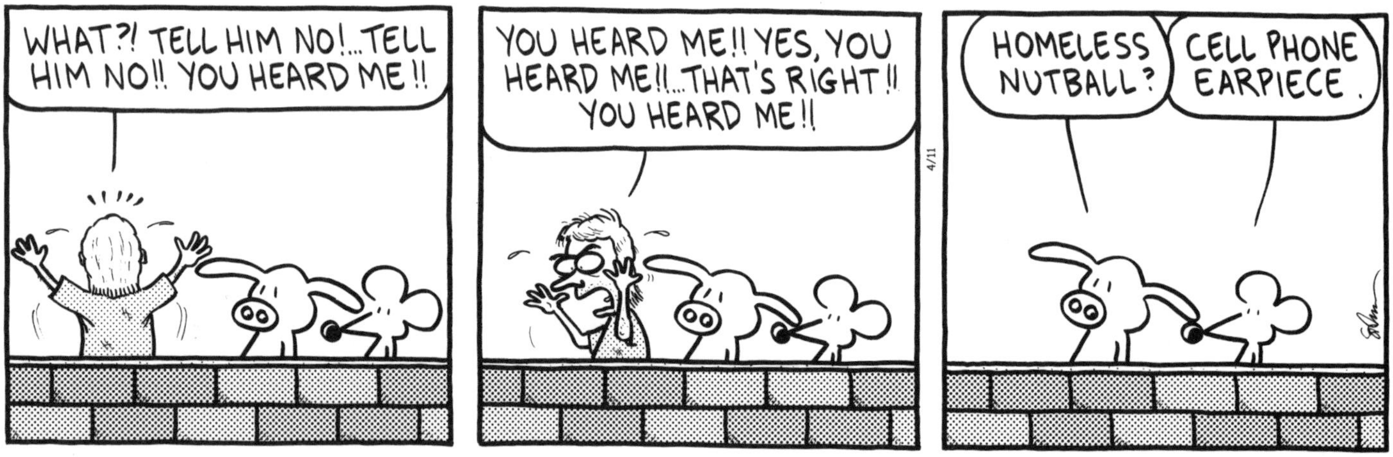
WHAT?! TELL HIM NO!...TELL HIM NO!! YOU HEARD ME!!
YOU HEARD ME!! YES, YOU HEARD ME!!...THAT'S RIGHT!! YOU HEARD ME!!
4/11
HOMELESS NUTBALL?
CELL PHONE EARPIECE.

When I see people with these barely discernable earpieces talking to someone on the phone, I stare at them. I do this to give them the impression that I really do think they're psychotic nutballs talking to themselves.

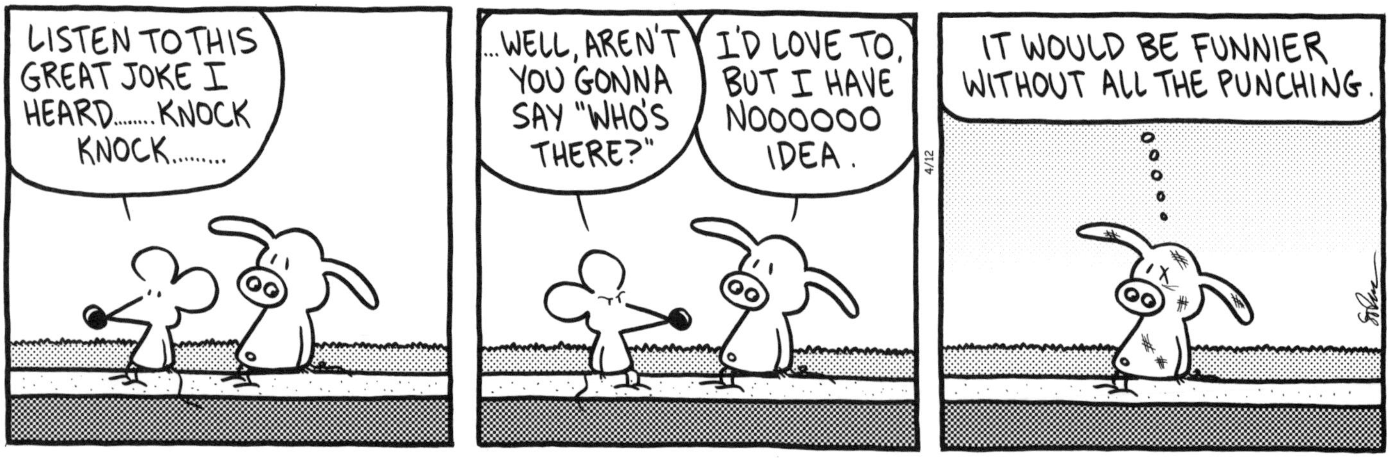
LISTEN TO THIS GREAT JOKE I HEARD....... KNOCK KNOCK.........
...WELL, AREN'T YOU GONNA SAY "WHO'S THERE?"
I'D LOVE TO, BUT I HAVE NOOOOOO IDEA.
4/12
IT WOULD BE FUNNIER WITHOUT ALL THE PUNCHING.

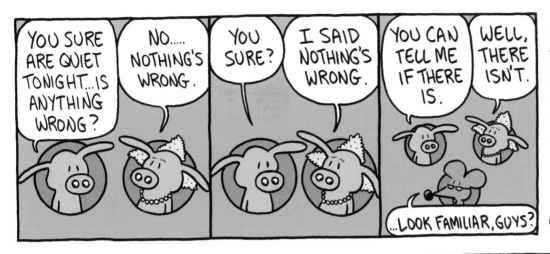

YOU SURE ARE QUIET TONIGHT...IS ANYTHING WRONG?
NO..... NOTHING'S WRONG.
YOU SURE?
I SAID NOTHING'S WRONG.
YOU CAN TELL ME IF THERE IS.
WELL, THERE ISN'T.
...LOOK FAMILIAR, GUYS?
HI, I'M DR. RAT, WORLD-RENOWNED RELATIONSHIP COUNSELOR AND AUTHOR OF "MEN ARE FROM MARS, WOMEN ARE METEORS CRASHING INTO MARS."
MEN, WE'VE ALL FACED THE "WHAT'S WRONG-NOTHING'S WRONG" CONUNDRUM...THE PROBLEM? THE PROBLEM IS YOU, FELLAS.
YOU HAVE MADE THE ASSUMPTION THAT YOUR WIFE OR GIRLFRIEND CONTINUES TO SPEAK ENGLISH...
....OH, YOU POOR, LOST SOULS....
RECENT STUDIES SHOW THAT THE FEMALE SEX INTERMITTENTLY CROSSES OVER TO THE "FEMINESE" DIALECT, A BAFFLING CODE THAT MAKES THE NAVAJO LANGUAGE LOOK LIKE A "DICK AND JANE" PRIMER.
WHAT'S A POOR FELLOW TO DO?...NOT TO WORRY... FOR JUST $79.95, THE DR. RAT INSTITUTE WILL SEND YOU A SERIES OF TEN AUDIOTAPES THAT WILL TEACH YOU THE WARNING SIGNS OF A "FEMINESE" CROSSOVER AND DECIPHER KEY PHRASES...JUST WATCH.......
WHAT'S WRONG, DEAR?
NOTHING, PIG, NOTHING.
OH, HONEY, I'M SO SORRY THAT LAST TUESDAY, I USED THE LAST PAPER TOWEL WITHOUT REPLACING THE WHOLE ROLL.
OHHH, PIG..... I LOVE YOU SO MUCH!
ORDER YOURS TODAY!
4/13

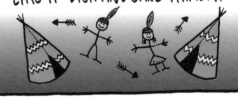

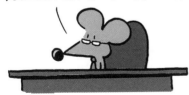

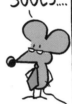

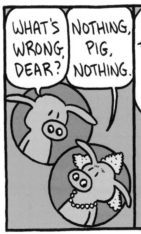

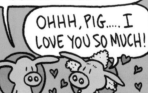

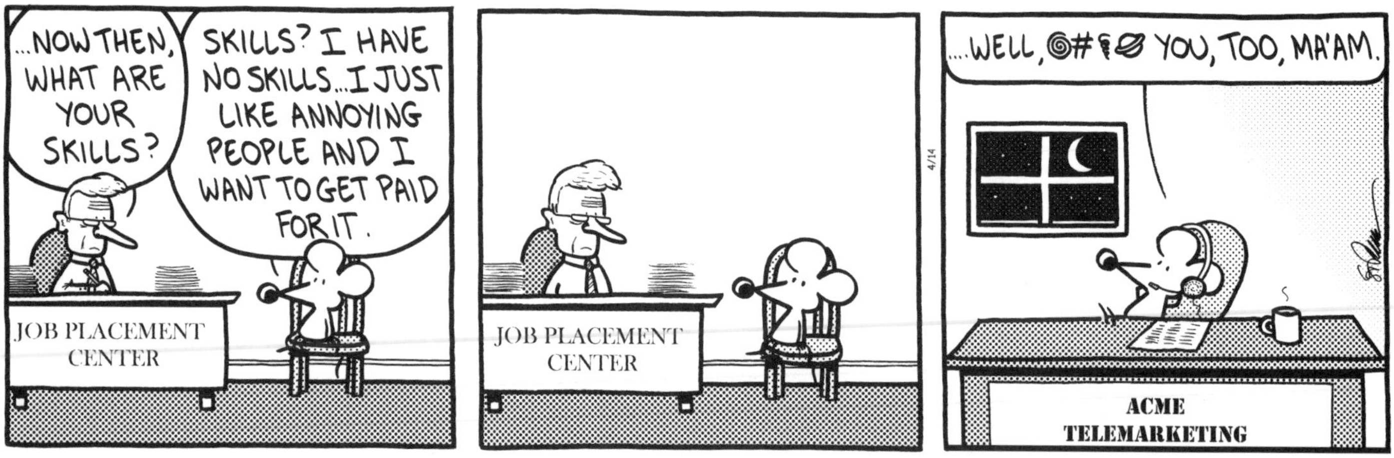
...NOW THEN, WHAT ARE YOUR SKILLS?
SKILLS? I HAVE NO SKILLS...I JUST LIKE ANNOYING PEOPLE AND I WANT TO GET PAID FOR IT.
JOB PLACEMENT CENTER
JOB PLACEMENT CENTER
4/14
....WELL, # YOU, TOO, MA'AM.
ACME TELEMARKETING

When one of these telemarketers called my house once offering me a credit card, I told them that I was wanted for credit card fraud and was actually in hiding from law enforcement. They paused for a moment, and then offered me the credit card anyway.

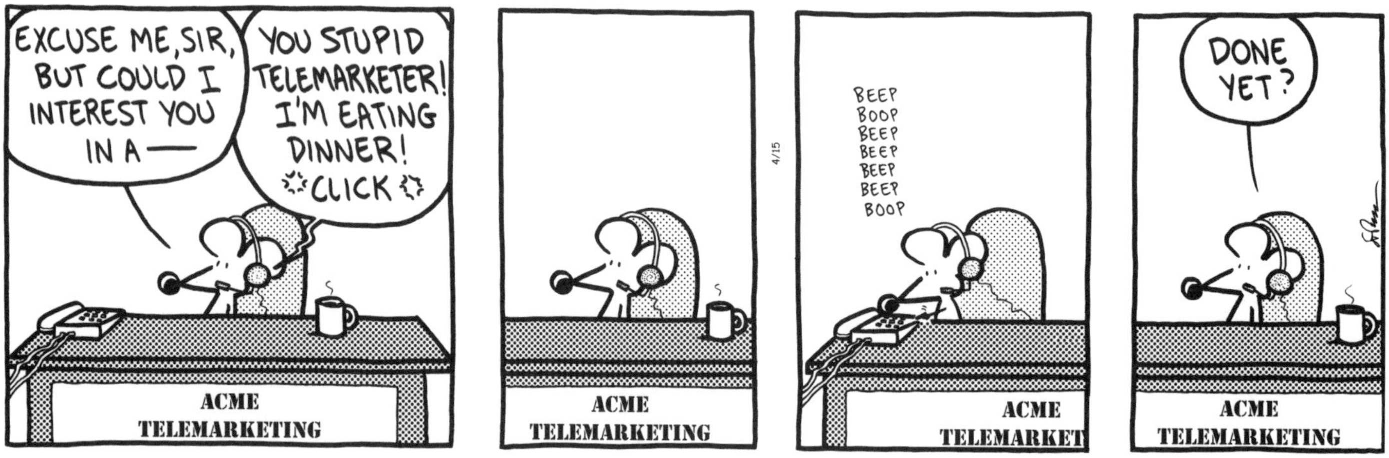
EXCUSE ME, SIR, BUT COULD I INTEREST YOU IN A—
YOU STUPID TELEMARKETER! I'M EATING DINNER! CLICK
ACME TELEMARKETING
4/15
ACME TELEMARKETING
BEEP BOOP BEEP BEEP BEEP BEEP BOOP
ACME TELEMARKET
DONE YET?
ACME TELEMARKETING

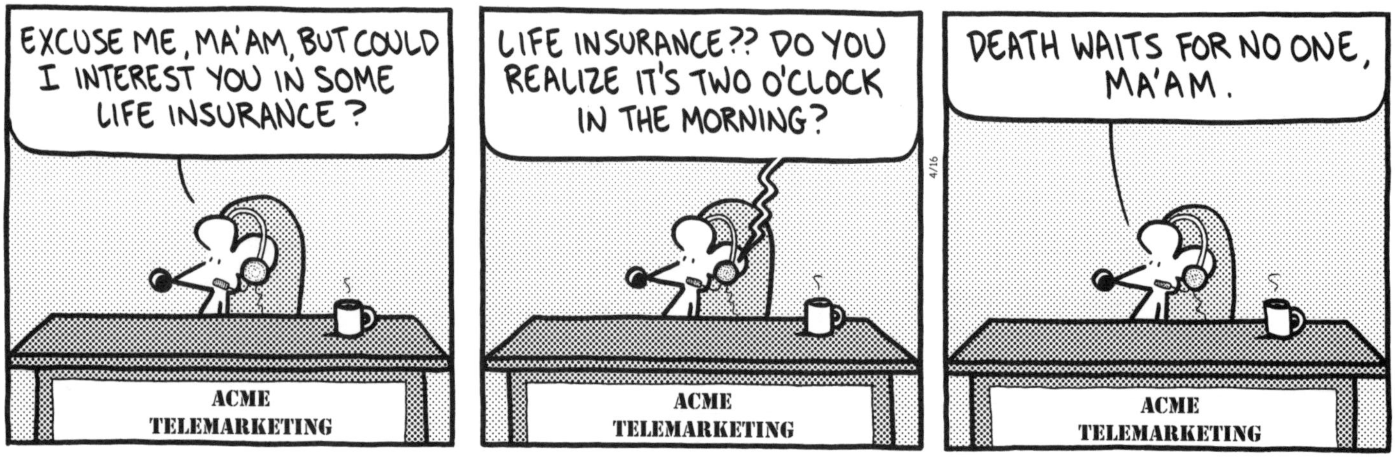
EXCUSE ME, MA'AM, BUT COULD I INTEREST YOU IN SOME LIFE INSURANCE?
ACME TELEMARKETING
LIFE INSURANCE?? DO YOU REALIZE IT'S TWO O'CLOCK IN THE MORNING?
ACME TELEMARKETING
4/16
DEATH WAITS FOR NO ONE, MA'AM.
ACME TELEMARKETING

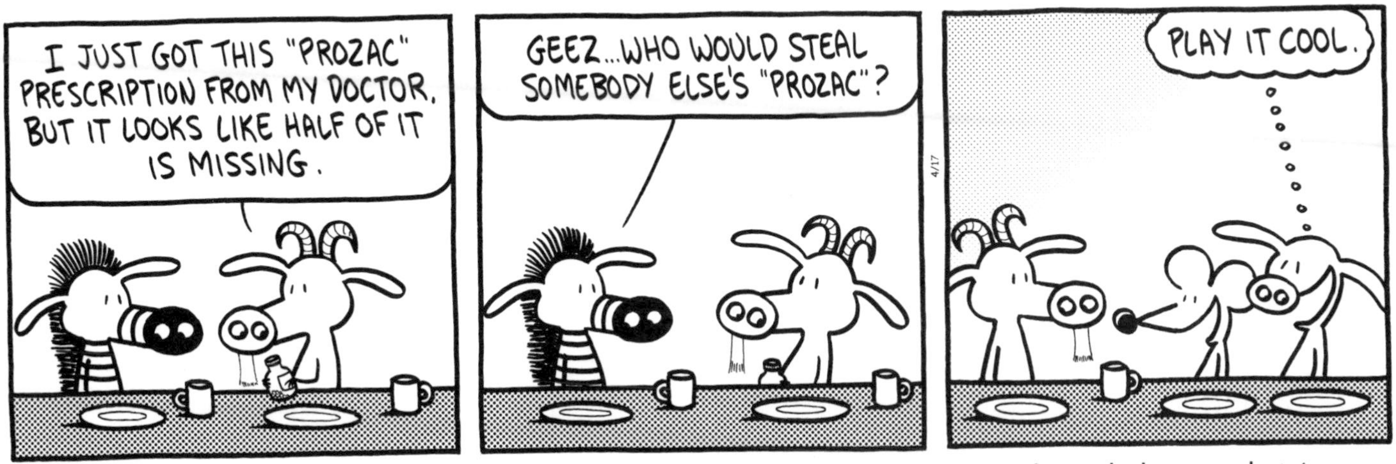
I JUST GOT THIS "PROZAC" PRESCRIPTION FROM MY DOCTOR, BUT IT LOOKS LIKE HALF OF IT IS MISSING.
GEEZ...WHO WOULD STEAL SOMEBODY ELSE'S "PROZAC"?
4/17
PLAY IT COOL.

One of a small handful of *Pearls* strips where the characters are actually smiling. (And it took drugs to do it.)

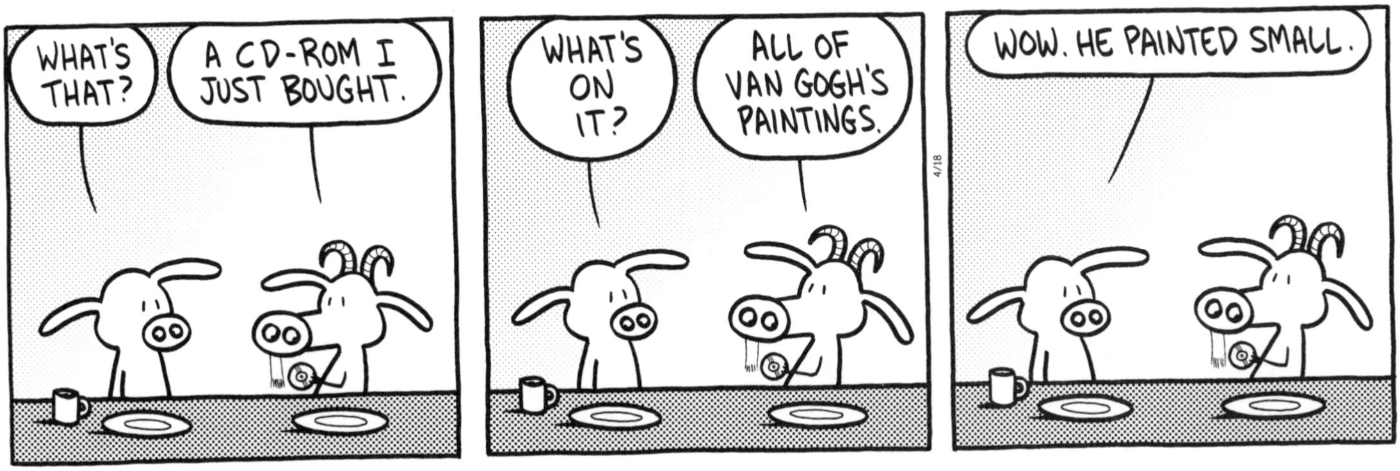
WHAT'S THAT?
A CD-ROM I JUST BOUGHT.
WHAT'S ON IT?
ALL OF VAN GOGH'S PAINTINGS.
4/18
WOW. HE PAINTED SMALL.

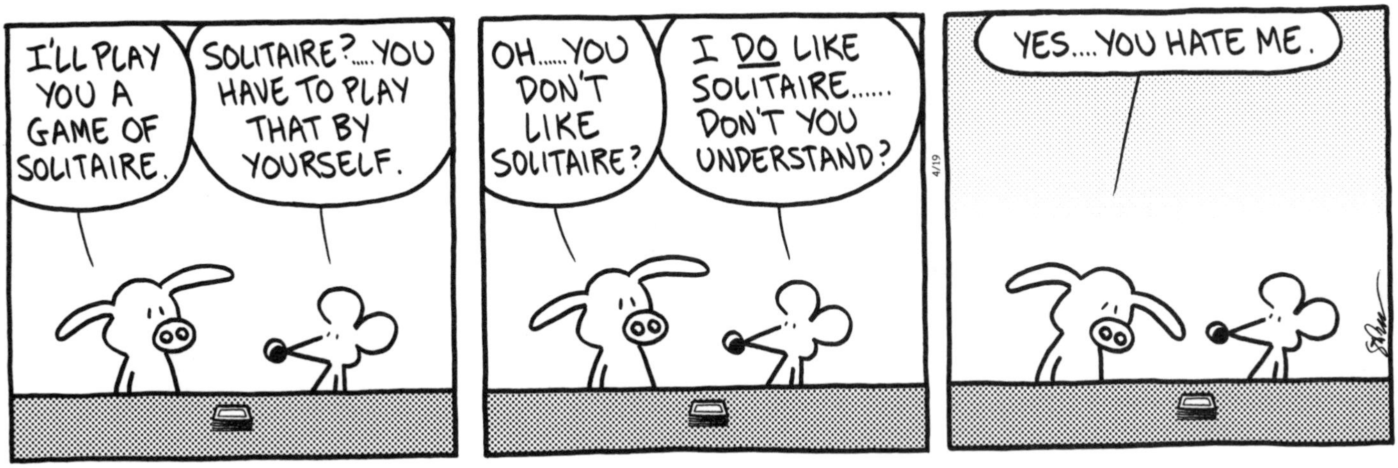
I'LL PLAY YOU A GAME OF SOLITAIRE.
SOLITAIRE?.....YOU HAVE TO PLAY THAT BY YOURSELF.
OH......YOU DON'T LIKE SOLITAIRE?
I DO LIKE SOLITAIRE...... DON'T YOU UNDERSTAND?
4/19
YES....YOU HATE ME.

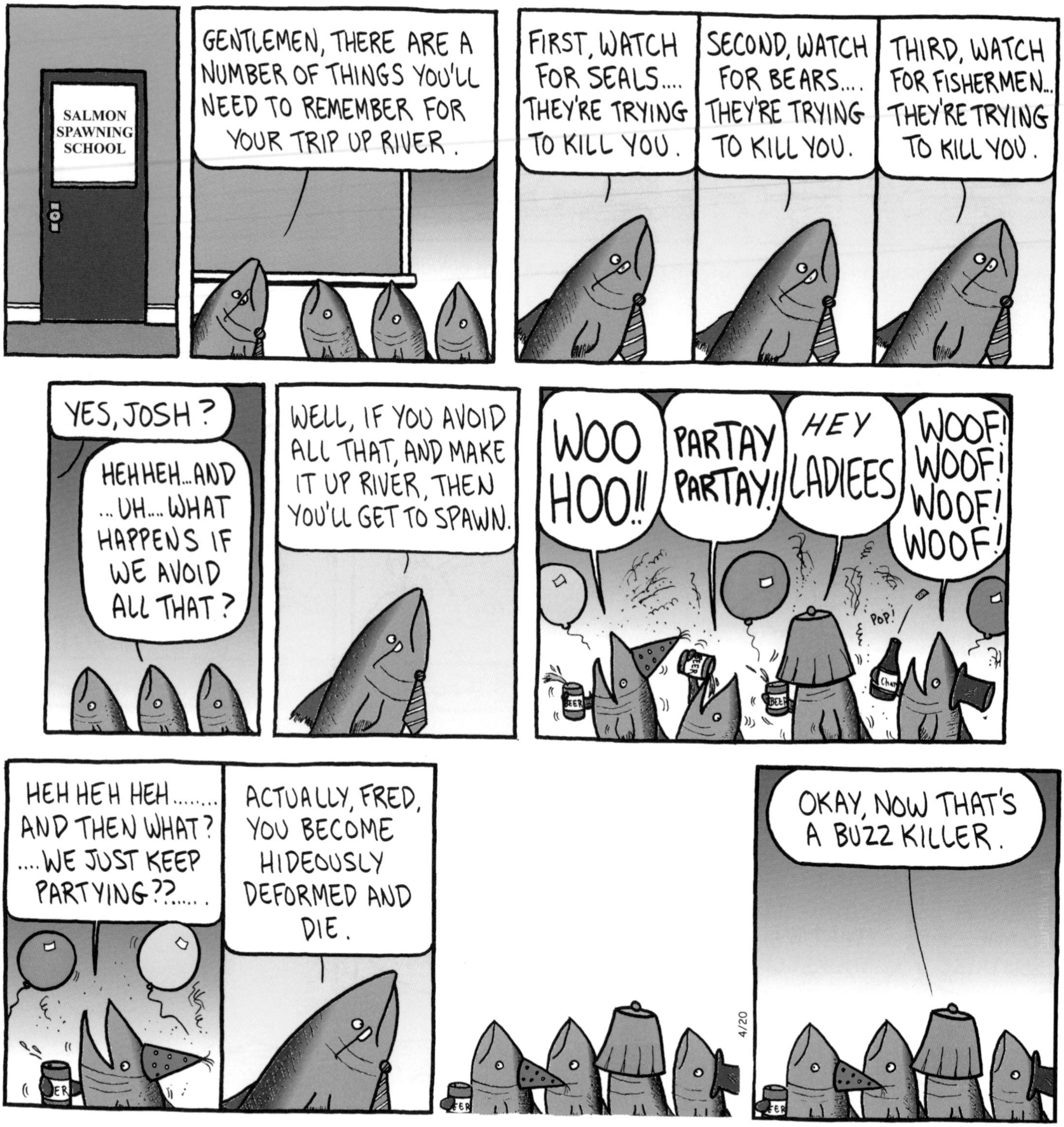
SALMON SPAWNING SCHOOL
GENTLEMEN, THERE ARE A NUMBER OF THINGS YOU'LL NEED TO REMEMBER FOR YOUR TRIP UP RIVER.
FIRST, WATCH FOR SEALS.... THEY'RE TRYING TO KILL YOU.
SECOND, WATCH FOR BEARS.... THEY'RE TRYING TO KILL YOU.
THIRD, WATCH FOR FISHERMEN... THEY'RE TRYING TO KILL YOU.
YES, JOSH?
HEHHEH...AND ...UH.... WHAT HAPPENS IF WE AVOID ALL THAT?
WELL, IF YOU AVOID ALL THAT, AND MAKE IT UP RIVER, THEN YOU'LL GET TO SPAWN.
WOO HOO!!
PARTAY PARTAY!
HEY LADIEES
WOOF! WOOF! WOOF! WOOF!
POP!
HEH HEH HEH....... AND THEN WHAT? ....WE JUST KEEP PARTYING??.....
ACTUALLY, FRED, YOU BECOME HIDEOUSLY DEFORMED AND DIE.
4/20
OKAY, NOW THAT'S A BUZZ KILLER.

Doomed salmon = instant comedy.

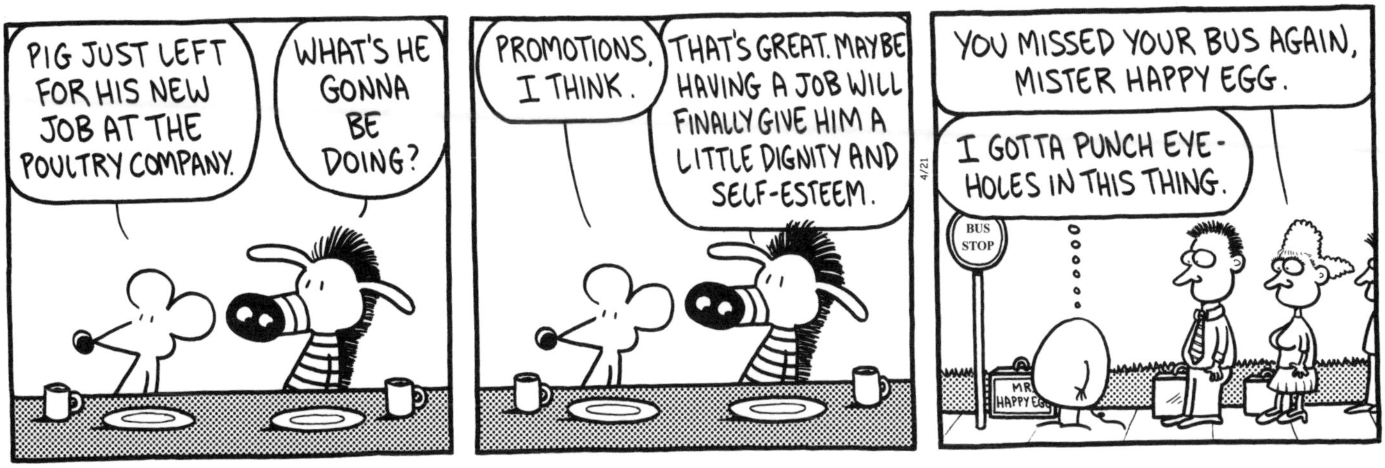
PIG JUST LEFT FOR HIS NEW JOB AT THE POULTRY COMPANY.
WHAT'S HE GONNA BE DOING?
PROMOTIONS, I THINK.
THAT'S GREAT. MAYBE HAVING A JOB WILL FINALLY GIVE HIM A LITTLE DIGNITY AND SELF-ESTEEM.
4/21
YOU MISSED YOUR BUS AGAIN, MISTER HAPPY EGG.
I GOTTA PUNCH EYE-HOLES IN THIS THING.
BUS STOP
MR HAPPY EGG

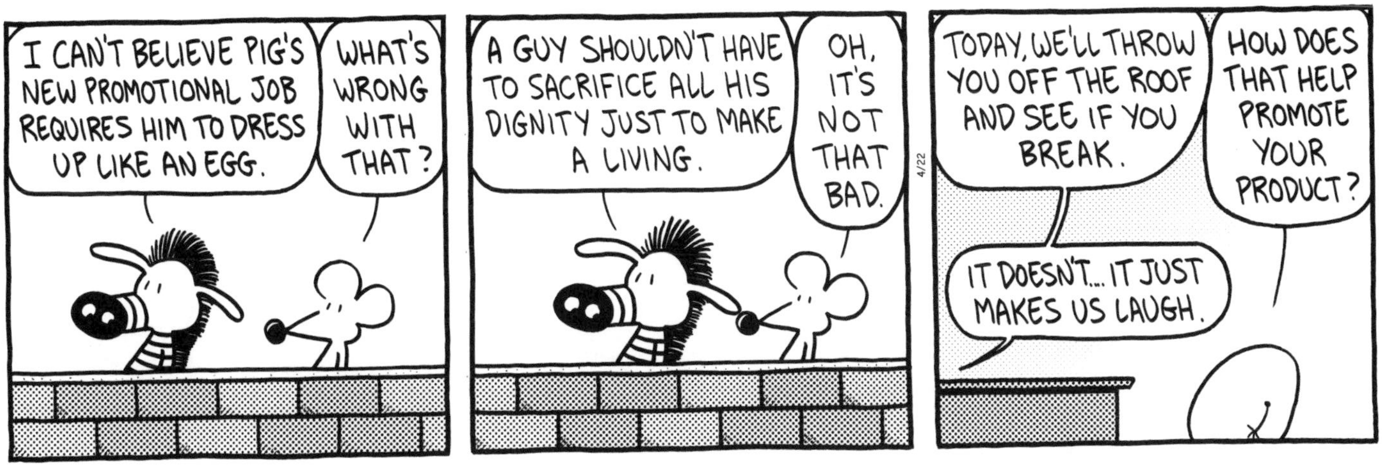
I CAN'T BELIEVE PIG'S NEW PROMOTIONAL JOB REQUIRES HIM TO DRESS UP LIKE AN EGG.
WHAT'S WRONG WITH THAT?
A GUY SHOULDN'T HAVE TO SACRIFICE ALL HIS DIGNITY JUST TO MAKE A LIVING.
OH, IT'S NOT THAT BAD.
4/22
TODAY, WE'LL THROW YOU OFF THE ROOF AND SEE IF YOU BREAK.
HOW DOES THAT HELP PROMOTE YOUR PRODUCT?
IT DOESN'T... IT JUST MAKES US LAUGH.

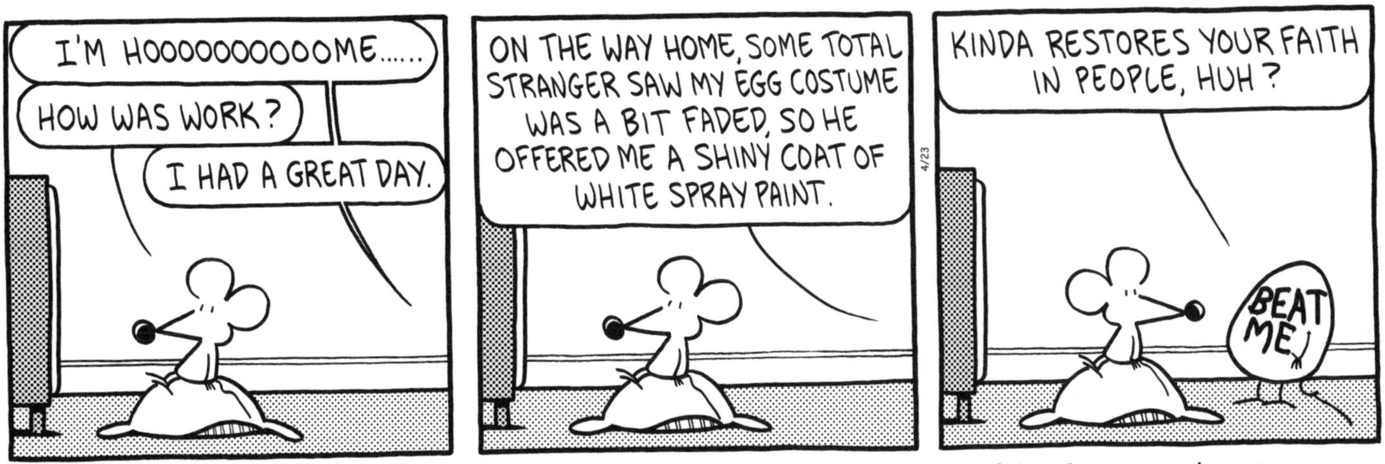
I'M HOOOOOOOOOOME......
HOW WAS WORK?
I HAD A GREAT DAY.
ON THE WAY HOME, SOME TOTAL STRANGER SAW MY EGG COSTUME WAS A BIT FADED, SO HE OFFERED ME A SHINY COAT OF WHITE SPRAY PAINT.
4/23
KINDA RESTORES YOUR FAITH IN PEOPLE, HUH?
BEAT ME

I think that strips work well when the reader knows or can see something that one of the characters doesn't.

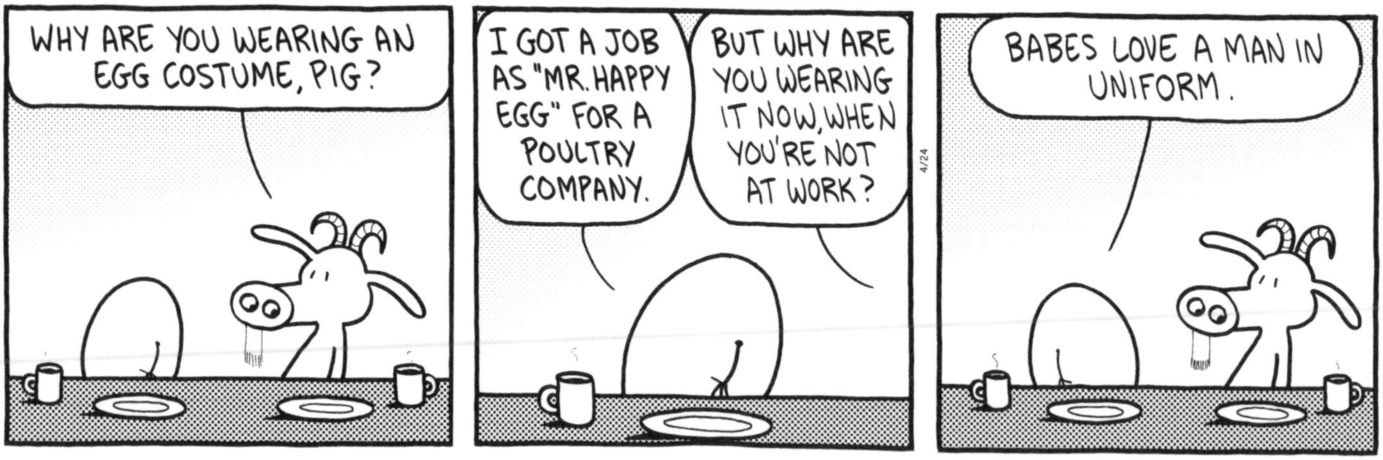
WHY ARE YOU WEARING AN EGG COSTUME, PIG?
I GOT A JOB AS "MR. HAPPY EGG" FOR A POULTRY COMPANY.
BUT WHY ARE YOU WEARING IT NOW, WHEN YOU'RE NOT AT WORK?
4/24
BABES LOVE A MAN IN UNIFORM.

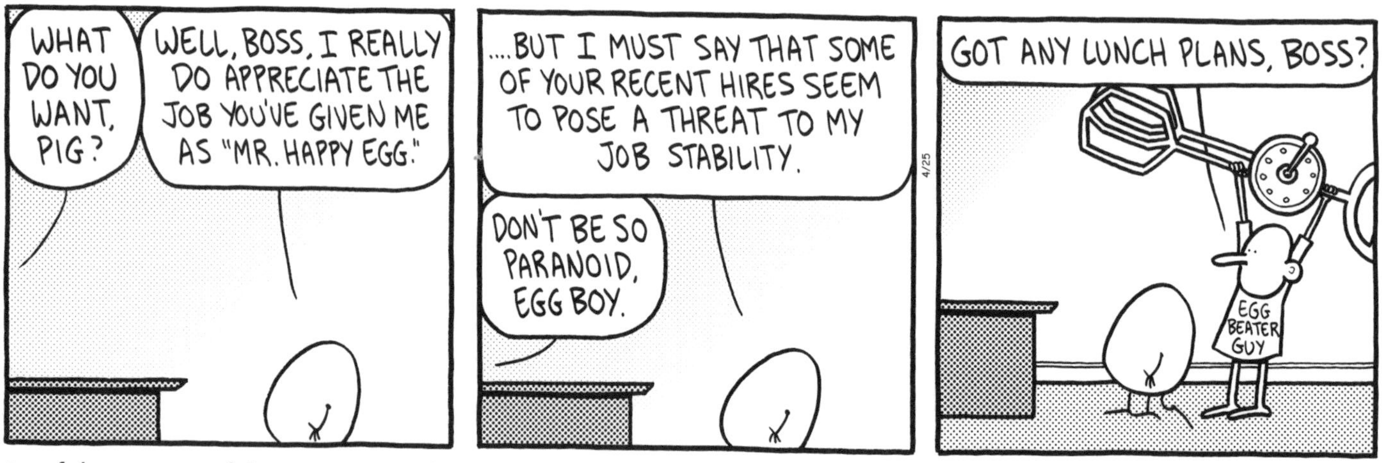
WHAT DO YOU WANT, PIG?
WELL, BOSS, I REALLY DO APPRECIATE THE JOB YOU'VE GIVEN ME AS "MR. HAPPY EGG."
....BUT I MUST SAY THAT SOME OF YOUR RECENT HIRES SEEM TO POSE A THREAT TO MY JOB STABILITY.
DON'T BE SO PARANOID, EGG BOY.
4/25
GOT ANY LUNCH PLANS, BOSS?
EGG BEATER GUY

As of the writing of this comment, I have already finished the cover for this treasury. And I'm regretting not putting the "Egg Beater Guy" on it. I should have stuck him in the back between that moose and the voodoo lady. Curses.

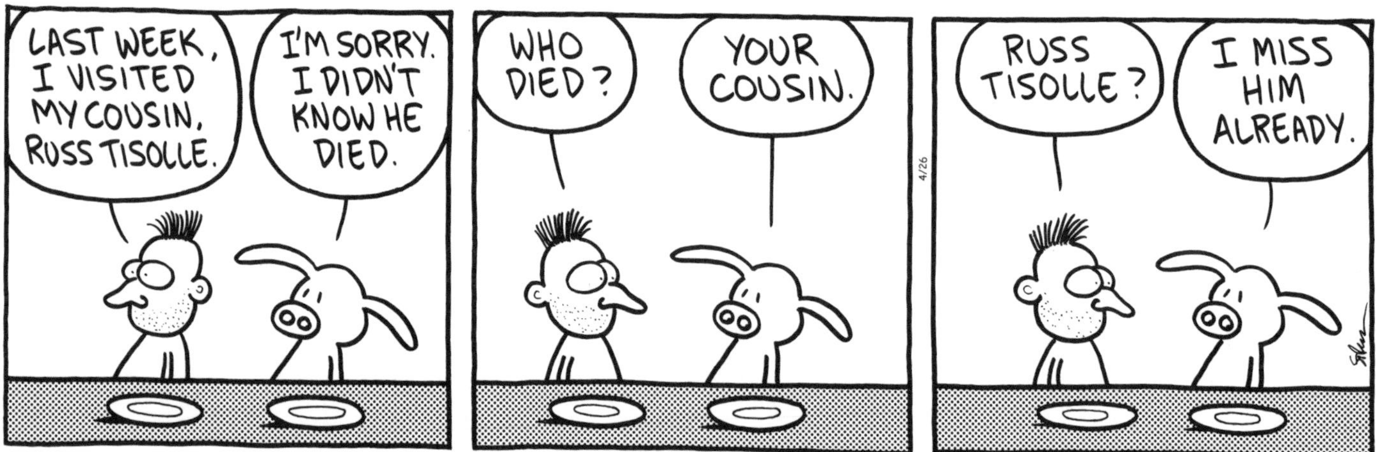
LAST WEEK, I VISITED MY COUSIN, RUSS TISOLLE.
I'M SORRY. I DIDN'T KNOW HE DIED.
WHO DIED?
YOUR COUSIN.
4/26
RUSS TISOLLE?
I MISS HIM ALREADY.

This was clearly one of the hardest strips for many *Pearls* readers to understand. Say the man's name a few times and you'll get it. (Hint: It's something you say after you hear the name of someone who's passed away.)

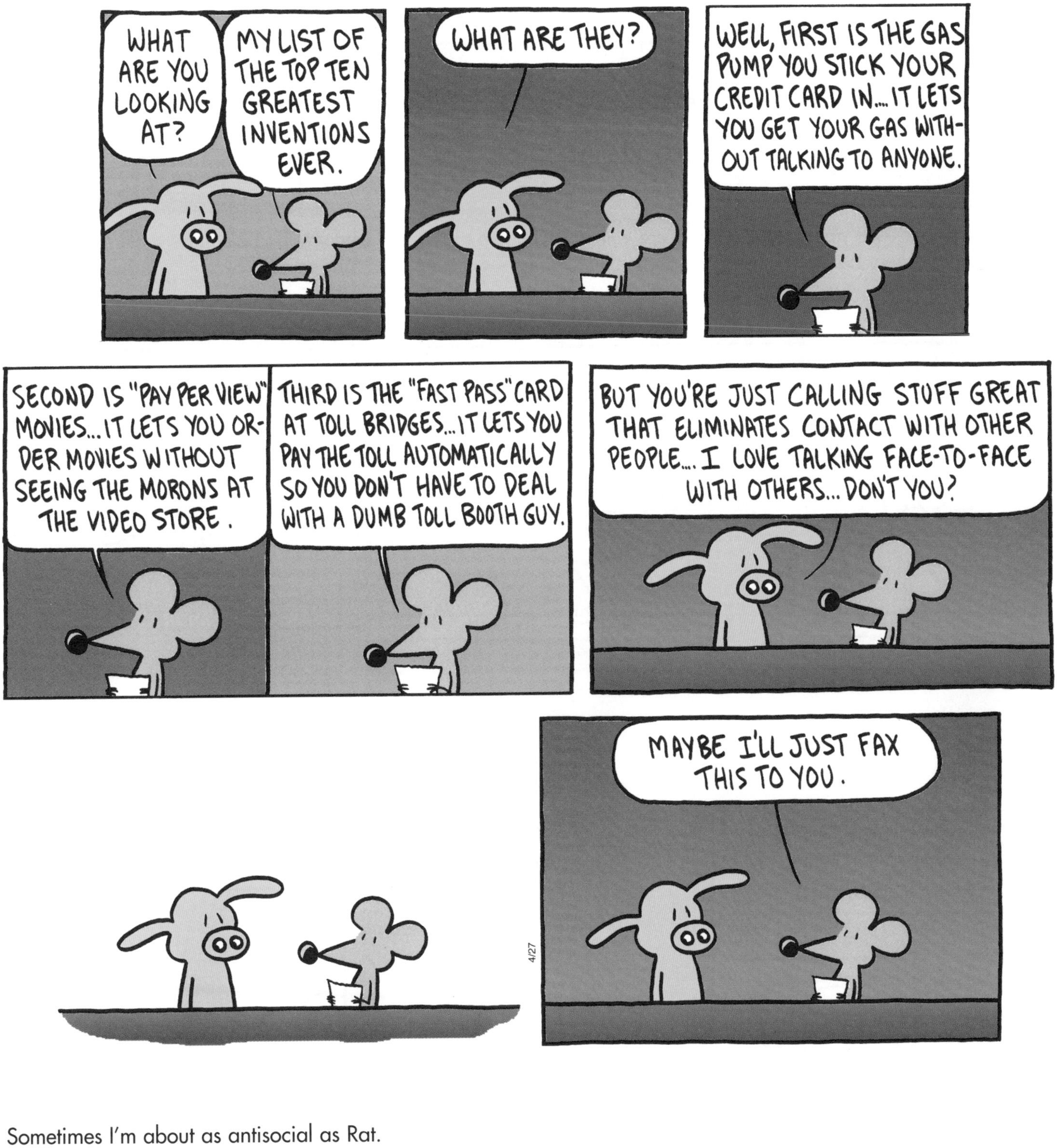
WHAT ARE YOU LOOKING AT?
MY LIST OF THE TOP TEN GREATEST INVENTIONS EVER.
WHAT ARE THEY?
WELL, FIRST IS THE GAS PUMP YOU STICK YOUR CREDIT CARD IN.... IT LETS YOU GET YOUR GAS WITHOUT TALKING TO ANYONE.
SECOND IS "PAY PER VIEW" MOVIES... IT LETS YOU ORDER MOVIES WITHOUT SEEING THE MORONS AT THE VIDEO STORE.
THIRD IS THE "FAST PASS" CARD AT TOLL BRIDGES... IT LETS YOU PAY THE TOLL AUTOMATICALLY SO YOU DON'T HAVE TO DEAL WITH A DUMB TOLL BOOTH GUY.
BUT YOU'RE JUST CALLING STUFF GREAT THAT ELIMINATES CONTACT WITH OTHER PEOPLE.... I LOVE TALKING FACE-TO-FACE WITH OTHERS... DON'T YOU?
MAYBE I'LL JUST FAX THIS TO YOU.
4/27

Sometimes I'm about as antisocial as Rat.

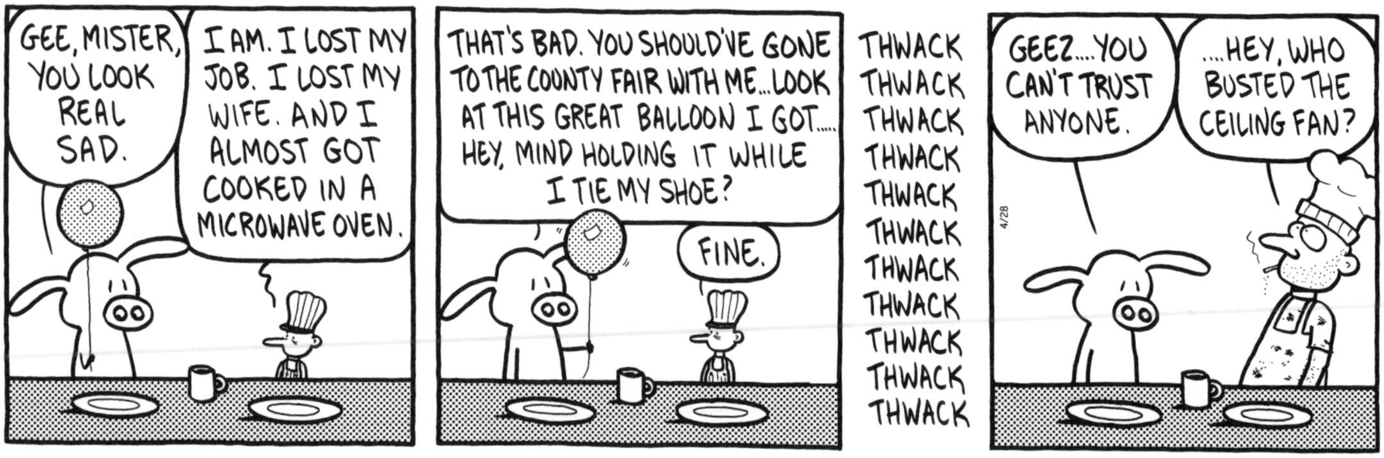
GEE, MISTER, YOU LOOK REAL SAD.
I AM. I LOST MY JOB. I LOST MY WIFE. AND I ALMOST GOT COOKED IN A MICROWAVE OVEN.
THAT'S BAD. YOU SHOULD'VE GONE TO THE COUNTY FAIR WITH ME...LOOK AT THIS GREAT BALLOON I GOT..... HEY, MIND HOLDING IT WHILE I TIE MY SHOE?
FINE.
THWACK THWACK THWACK THWACK THWACK THWACK THWACK THWACK THWACK THWACK THWACK
4/28
GEEZ....YOU CAN'T TRUST ANYONE.
....HEY, WHO BUSTED THE CEILING FAN?

Although Hobart was not popular, there were actually a couple of readers who wrote to ask if he really died in the microwave, adding that if he did not die, they'd like him brought back. I wrote and said I would bring him back. I left out the fact that he would die again.

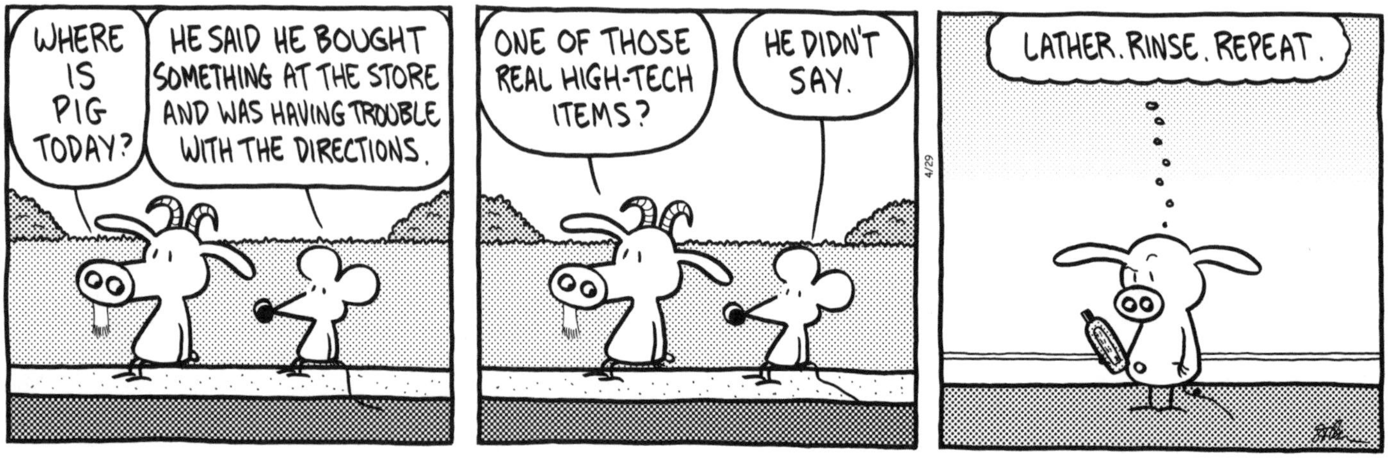
WHERE IS PIG TODAY?
HE SAID HE BOUGHT SOMETHING AT THE STORE AND WAS HAVING TROUBLE WITH THE DIRECTIONS.
ONE OF THOSE REAL HIGH-TECH ITEMS?
HE DIDN'T SAY.
4/29
LATHER. RINSE. REPEAT.

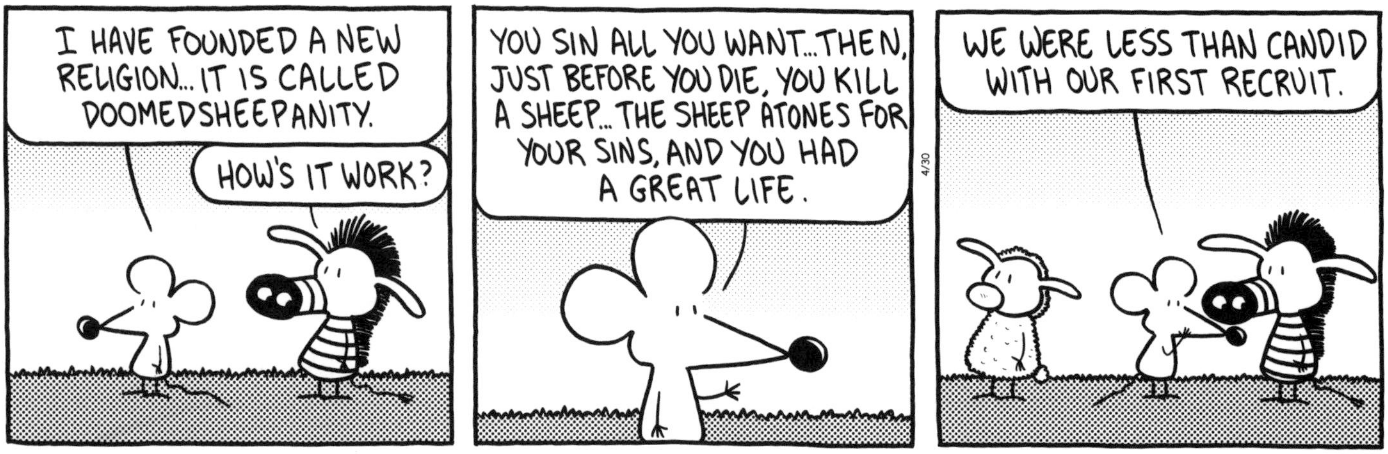
I HAVE FOUNDED A NEW RELIGION...IT IS CALLED DOOMEDSHEEPANITY.
HOW'S IT WORK?
YOU SIN ALL YOU WANT...THEN, JUST BEFORE YOU DIE, YOU KILL A SHEEP... THE SHEEP ATONES FOR YOUR SINS, AND YOU HAD A GREAT LIFE.
4/30
WE WERE LESS THAN CANDID WITH OUR FIRST RECRUIT.

Mentioning religion is almost a guaranteed way to draw complaints.

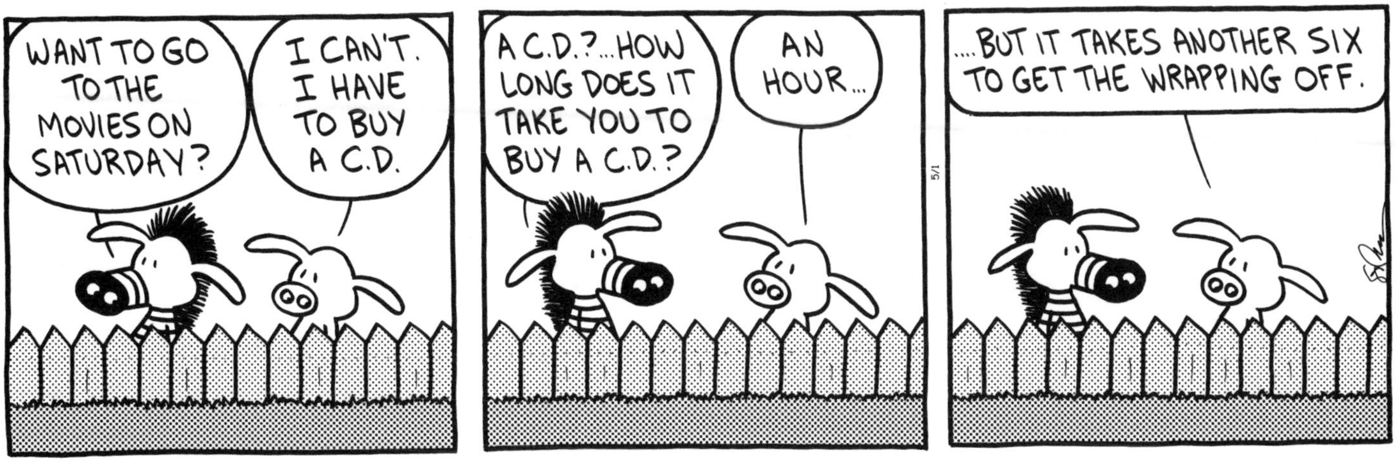
WANT TO GO TO THE MOVIES ON SATURDAY?
I CAN'T. I HAVE TO BUY A C.D.
A C.D.?...HOW LONG DOES IT TAKE YOU TO BUY A C.D.?
AN HOUR...
....BUT IT TAKES ANOTHER SIX TO GET THE WRAPPING OFF.

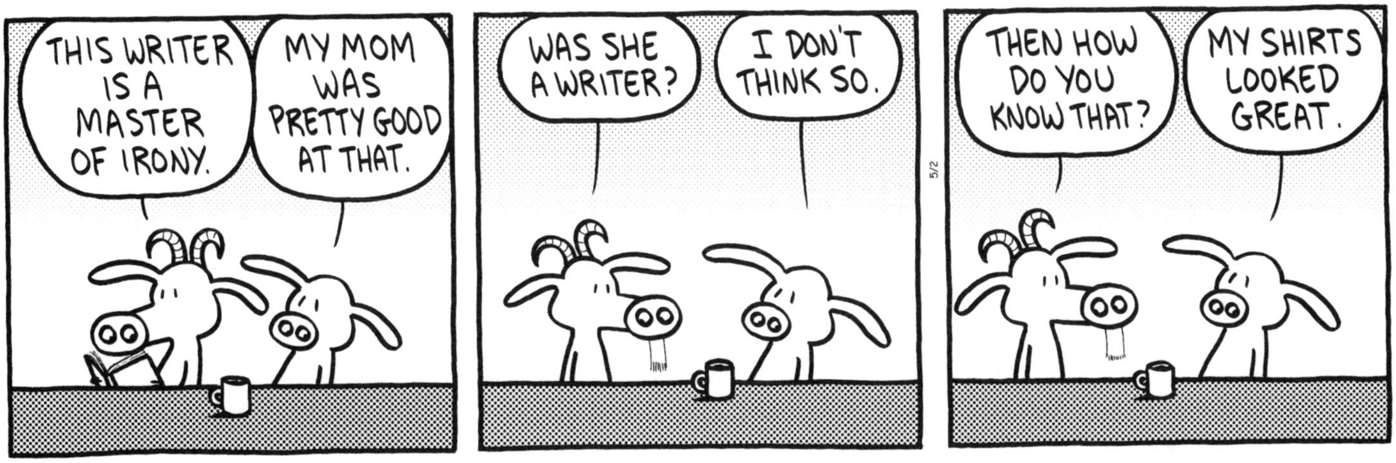
THIS WRITER IS A MASTER OF IRONY.
MY MOM WAS PRETTY GOOD AT THAT.
WAS SHE A WRITER?
I DON'T THINK SO.
THEN HOW DO YOU KNOW THAT?
MY SHIRTS LOOKED GREAT.

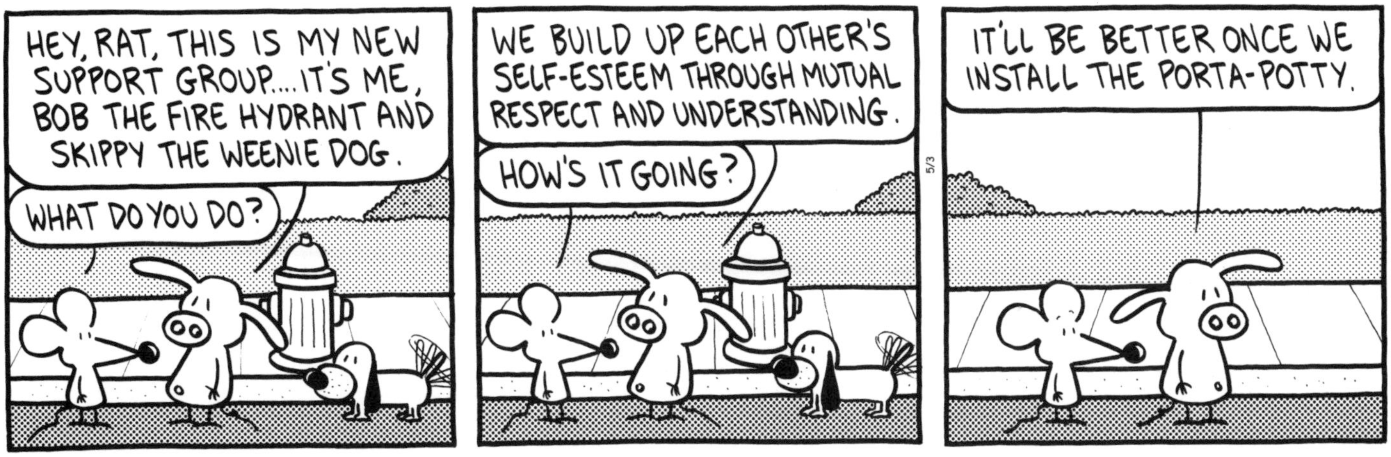
HEY, RAT, THIS IS MY NEW SUPPORT GROUP.... IT'S ME, BOB THE FIRE HYDRANT AND SKIPPY THE WEENIE DOG.
WHAT DO YOU DO?
WE BUILD UP EACH OTHER'S SELF-ESTEEM THROUGH MUTUAL RESPECT AND UNDERSTANDING.
HOW'S IT GOING?
IT'LL BE BETTER ONCE WE INSTALL THE PORTA-POTTY.

I'm surprised I got away with this one.

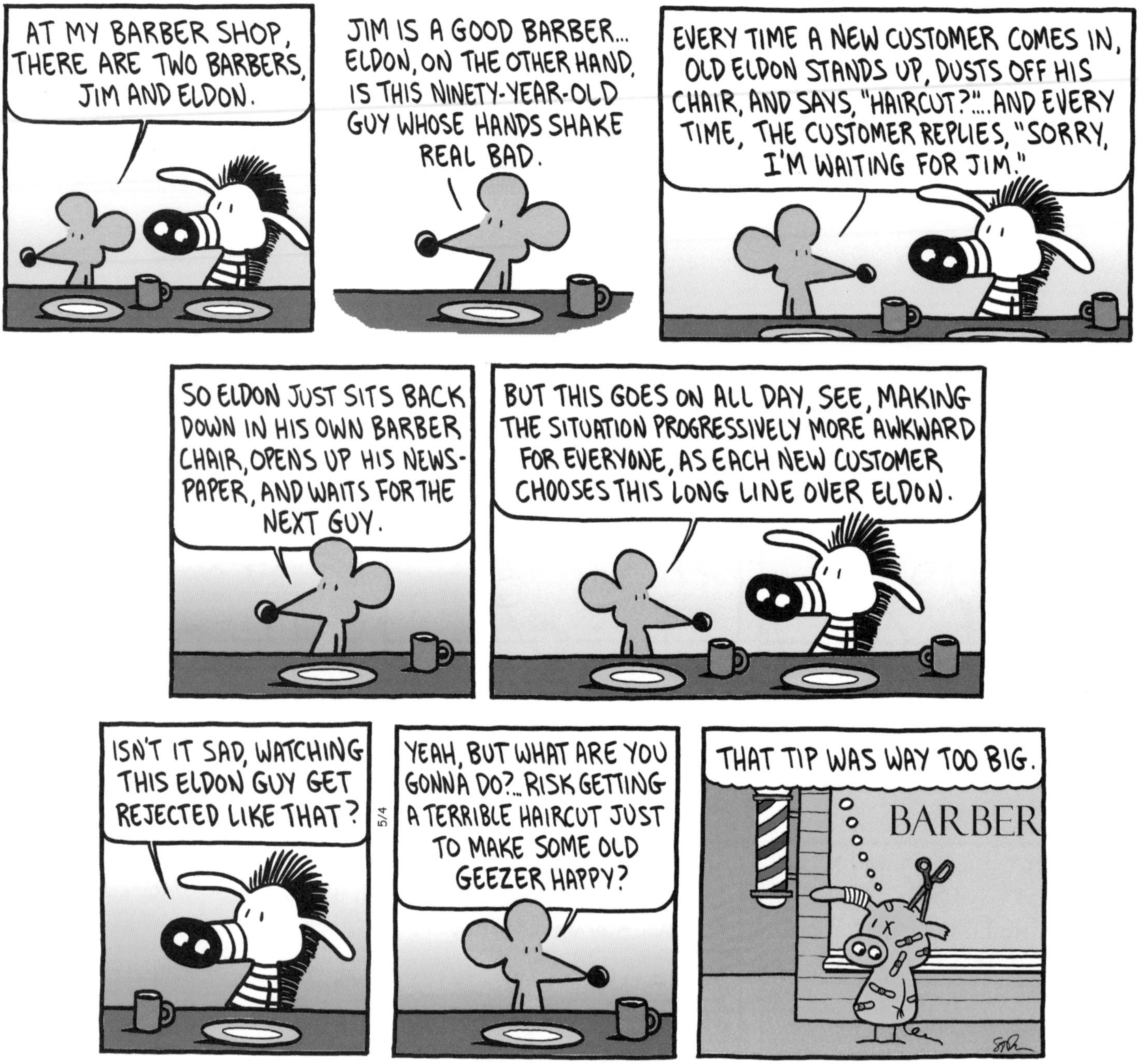
AT MY BARBER SHOP, THERE ARE TWO BARBERS, JIM AND ELDON.
JIM IS A GOOD BARBER... ELDON, ON THE OTHER HAND, IS THIS NINETY-YEAR-OLD GUY WHOSE HANDS SHAKE REAL BAD.
EVERY TIME A NEW CUSTOMER COMES IN, OLD ELDON STANDS UP, DUSTS OFF HIS CHAIR, AND SAYS, "HAIRCUT?"... AND EVERY TIME, THE CUSTOMER REPLIES, "SORRY, I'M WAITING FOR JIM."
SO ELDON JUST SITS BACK DOWN IN HIS OWN BARBER CHAIR, OPENS UP HIS NEWS-PAPER, AND WAITS FOR THE NEXT GUY.
BUT THIS GOES ON ALL DAY, SEE, MAKING THE SITUATION PROGRESSIVELY MORE AWKWARD FOR EVERYONE, AS EACH NEW CUSTOMER CHOOSES THIS LONG LINE OVER ELDON.
ISN'T IT SAD, WATCHING THIS ELDON GUY GET REJECTED LIKE THAT?
5/4
YEAH, BUT WHAT ARE YOU GONNA DO?... RISK GETTING A TERRIBLE HAIRCUT JUST TO MAKE SOME OLD GEEZER HAPPY?
THAT TIP WAS WAY TOO BIG.
BARBER

This Eldon story was the scene every time I got a haircut at the corner barber shop when I was growing up. It's one of the few strips that comes directly from my own life.

Panel 1:

I HEARD YOU STARTED AN ONLINE ADVICE COLUMN TO HELP YOUR FELLOW ZEBRAS ON THE PLAINS.

YEAH, AND I ALREADY GOT MY FIRST E-MAIL FROM A ZEBRA.

Panel 2:

LET'S HEAR IT.

fasde45dt56d4
%^tfy;TFR%
%GHUYjhkj
UGYT&*KL
78=oiuoiuoh

Panel 3:

...IT'S HARD TO TYPE WITH HOOVES.

Panel 4:

ZEBRA, THE ONLINE ADVICE COLUMNIST

To: Ask Zebra
From: Concerned Zebra
Subj: Problem

Althow Ime a zebra, I lives in an allygator swampe. I am stuk at the bottum...Pleeze send sumwon to jump in and sayve mee.

Panel 5:

Dear Concerned Zebra,
    Hang on, my friend!! I will contact all the zebras I know and they will rush to the swamp to save you!

TYPE TYPE
TYPE TYPE
TYPE

Panel 6:

THAT WAS EASY.

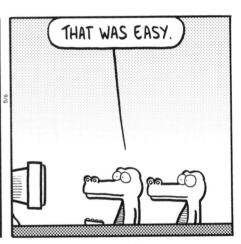

While I frequently make fun of my own art, I will say that I like the look of the crocodiles. Their smile suggests a sort of malicious glee.

Panel 7:

ZEBRA, THE ONLINE ADVICE COLUMNIST

To: Ask Zebra
From: Worried Zebra
Subj: Fears

Lions are staring at me. I think I'm going to die.

Panel 8:

Dear Worried,
    There really is no need for such gloom. You just need to smile more. Remember, smile and the world smiles with you...

TYPE TYPE
TYPE

Panel 9:

...Are you smiling? :)

Holy $%#@, this is *dark*. I must have been having a bad day.

225

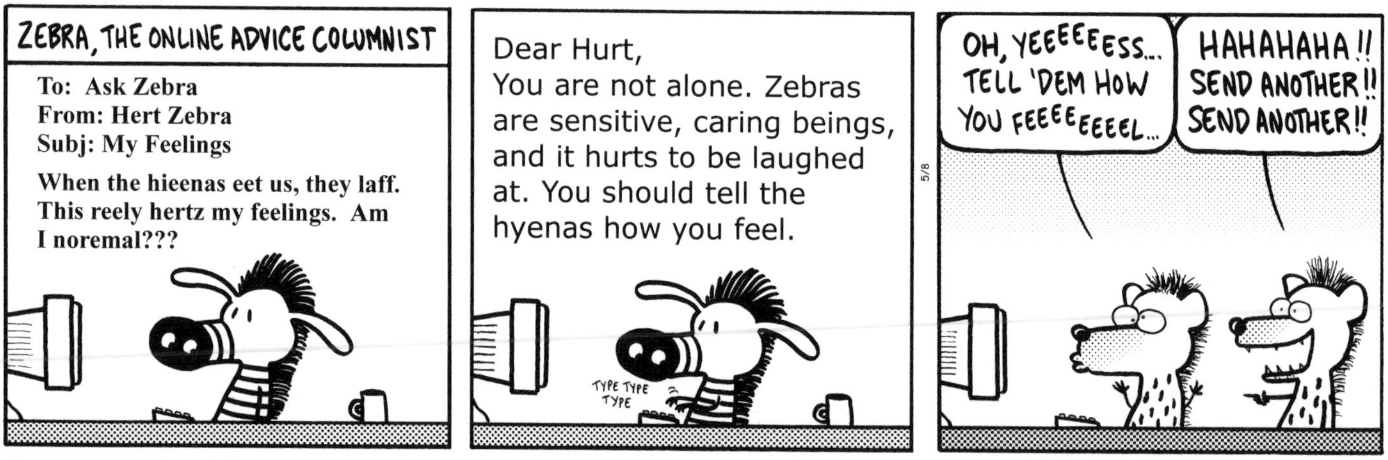
ZEBRA, THE ONLINE ADVICE COLUMNIST
To: Ask Zebra
From: Hert Zebra
Subj: My Feelings
When the hieenas eet us, they laff. This reely hertz my feelings. Am I noremal???
Dear Hurt,
You are not alone. Zebras are sensitive, caring beings, and it hurts to be laughed at. You should tell the hyenas how you feel.
TYPE TYPE TYPE
5/8
OH, YEEEEEESS... TELL 'DEM HOW YOU FEEEEEEEL...
HAHAHAHA!! SEND ANOTHER!! SEND ANOTHER!!

I have a couple of friends, who, when they make fun of me, do it in this high-pitched whiny voice, which is the voice I hear in my head for the "oh, yeeeees" hyena. I'm telling you, there is no way to overcome that "high-pitched" mockery. You just have to take it, or else get new friends.

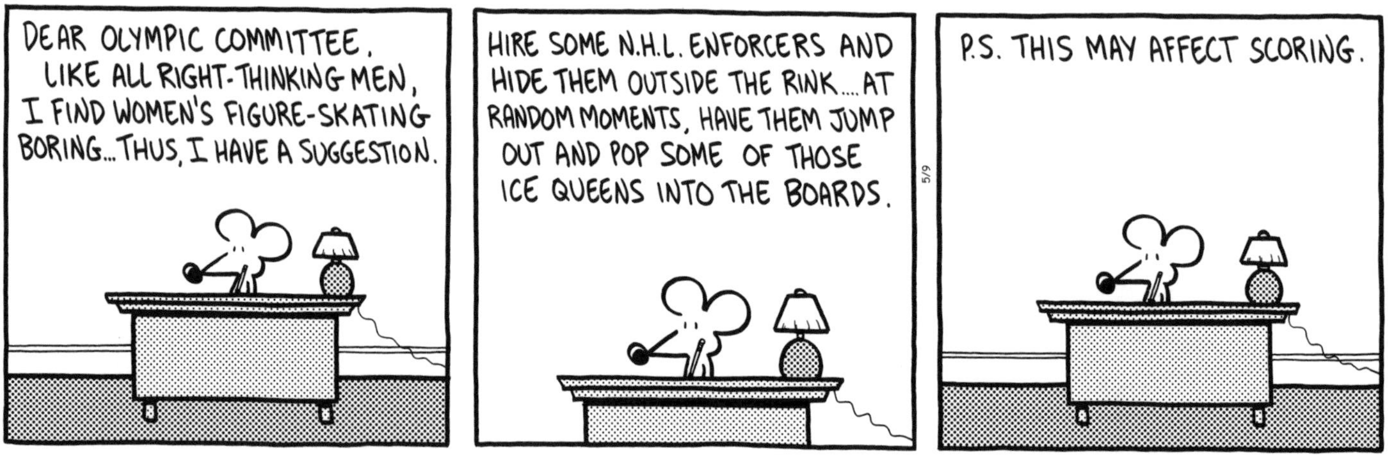
DEAR OLYMPIC COMMITTEE, LIKE ALL RIGHT-THINKING MEN, I FIND WOMEN'S FIGURE-SKATING BORING... THUS, I HAVE A SUGGESTION.
HIRE SOME N.H.L. ENFORCERS AND HIDE THEM OUTSIDE THE RINK.... AT RANDOM MOMENTS, HAVE THEM JUMP OUT AND POP SOME OF THOSE ICE QUEENS INTO THE BOARDS.
5/9
P.S. THIS MAY AFFECT SCORING.

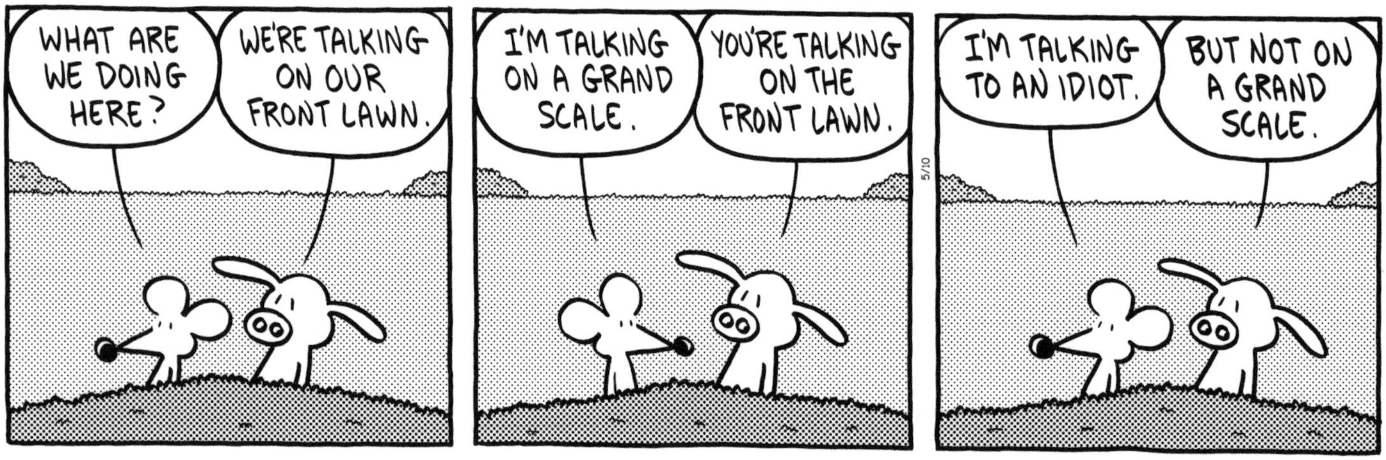
WHAT ARE WE DOING HERE?
WE'RE TALKING ON OUR FRONT LAWN.
I'M TALKING ON A GRAND SCALE.
YOU'RE TALKING ON THE FRONT LAWN.
5/10
I'M TALKING TO AN IDIOT.
BUT NOT ON A GRAND SCALE.

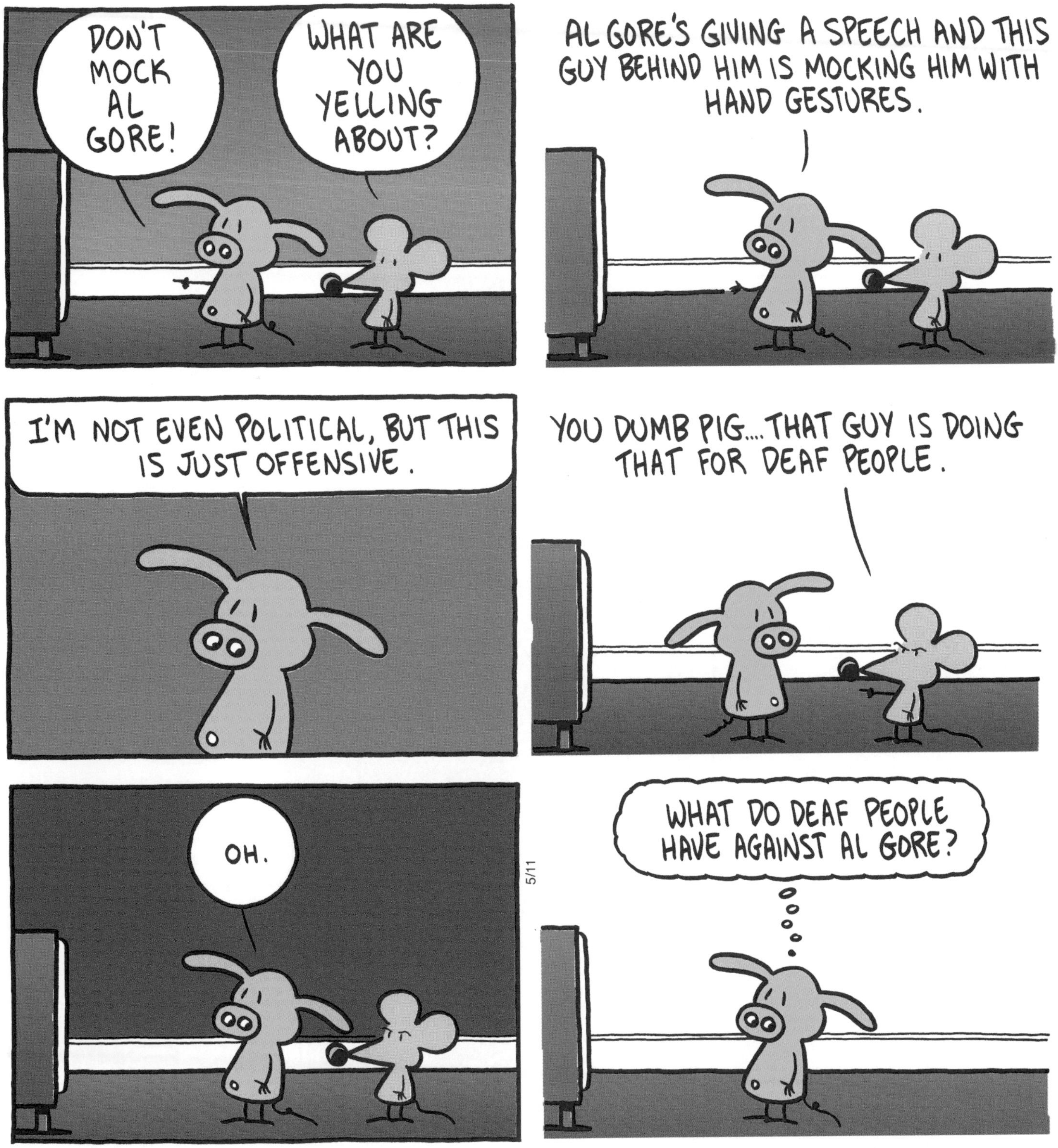
DON'T MOCK AL GORE!
WHAT ARE YOU YELLING ABOUT?
AL GORE'S GIVING A SPEECH AND THIS GUY BEHIND HIM IS MOCKING HIM WITH HAND GESTURES.
I'M NOT EVEN POLITICAL, BUT THIS IS JUST OFFENSIVE.
YOU DUMB PIG.... THAT GUY IS DOING THAT FOR DEAF PEOPLE.
OH.
WHAT DO DEAF PEOPLE HAVE AGAINST AL GORE?
5/11

No deaf people complained. And neither did Al Gore.

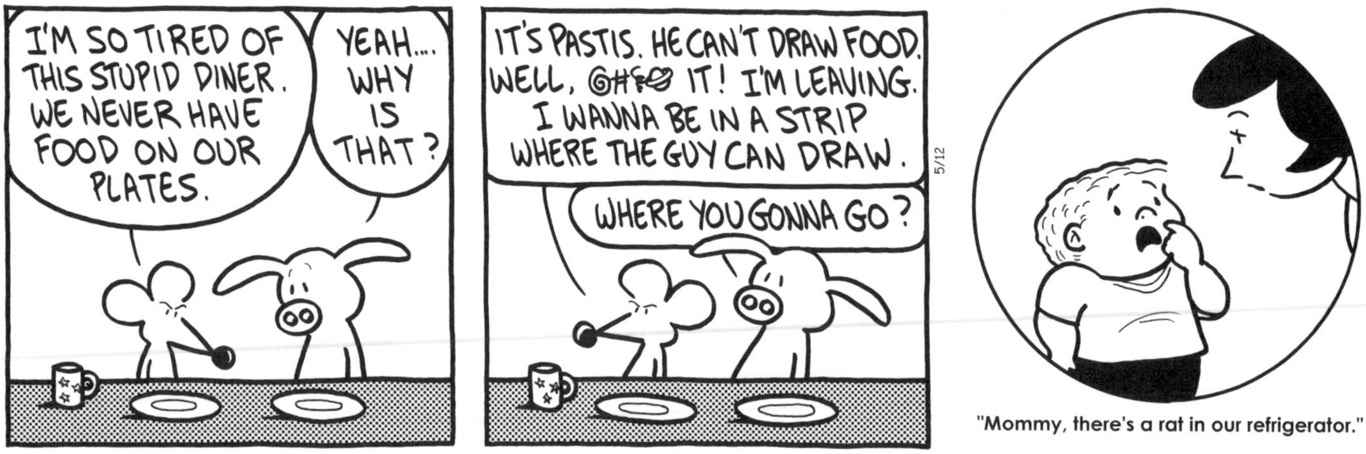
I'M SO TIRED OF THIS STUPID DINER. WE NEVER HAVE FOOD ON OUR PLATES.
YEAH.... WHY IS THAT?
IT'S PASTIS. HE CAN'T DRAW FOOD. WELL, @#$@ IT! I'M LEAVING. I WANNA BE IN A STRIP WHERE THE GUY CAN DRAW.
WHERE YOU GONNA GO?
5/12
"Mommy, there's a rat in our refrigerator."

When these first two *Family Circus* strips ran, I got an e-mail from Bil Keane's son, Jeff, who I believe currently works on the strip. He was extremely nice and asked if he could have the originals. I said yes, and told him that I if I could in turn get an original *Family Circus*, I would throw in the "dead grandpa" strip that would appear later in the week (a strip he hadn't yet seen). For whatever reason, this ended the transaction. I've never been sure if I offended him with the "dead grandpa" reference, or if he just didn't want to give me a *Family Circus*, or if he just forgot.

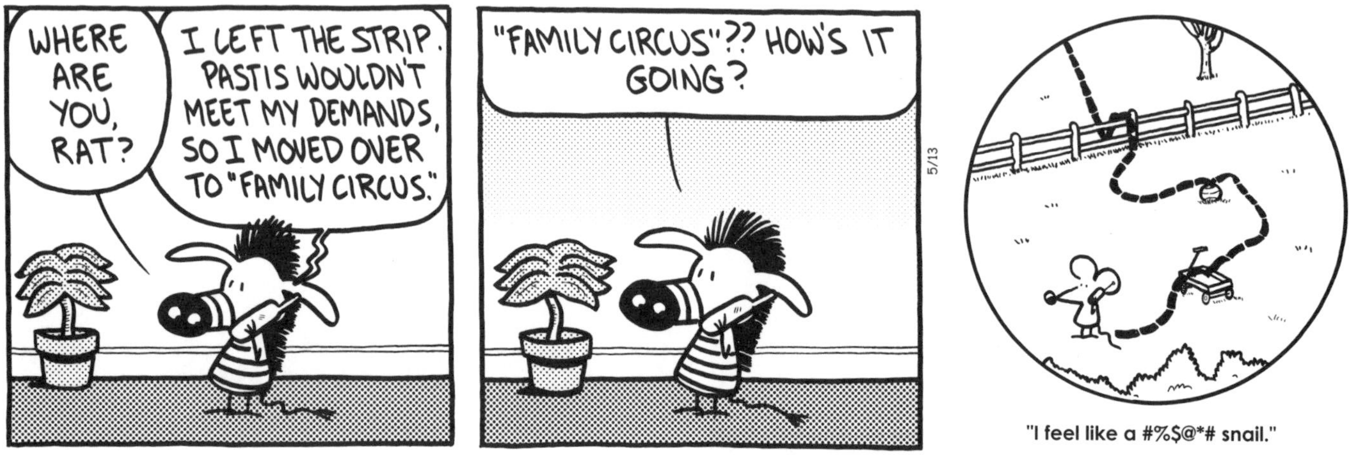
WHERE ARE YOU, RAT?
I LEFT THE STRIP. PASTIS WOULDN'T MEET MY DEMANDS, SO I MOVED OVER TO "FAMILY CIRCUS."
"FAMILY CIRCUS"?? HOW'S IT GOING?
5/13
"I feel like a #%$@*# snail."

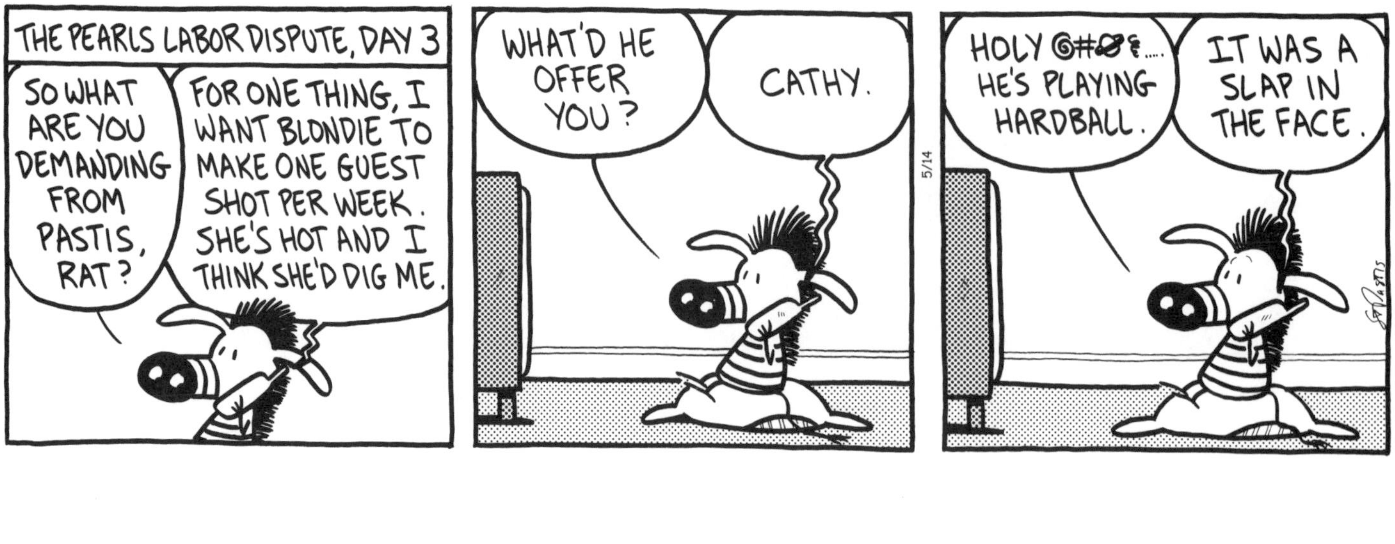
THE PEARLS LABOR DISPUTE, DAY 3
SO WHAT ARE YOU DEMANDING FROM PASTIS, RAT?
FOR ONE THING, I WANT BLONDIE TO MAKE ONE GUEST SHOT PER WEEK. SHE'S HOT AND I THINK SHE'D DIG ME.
WHAT'D HE OFFER YOU?
CATHY.
HOLY @#$@.....HE'S PLAYING HARDBALL.
IT WAS A SLAP IN THE FACE.
5/14

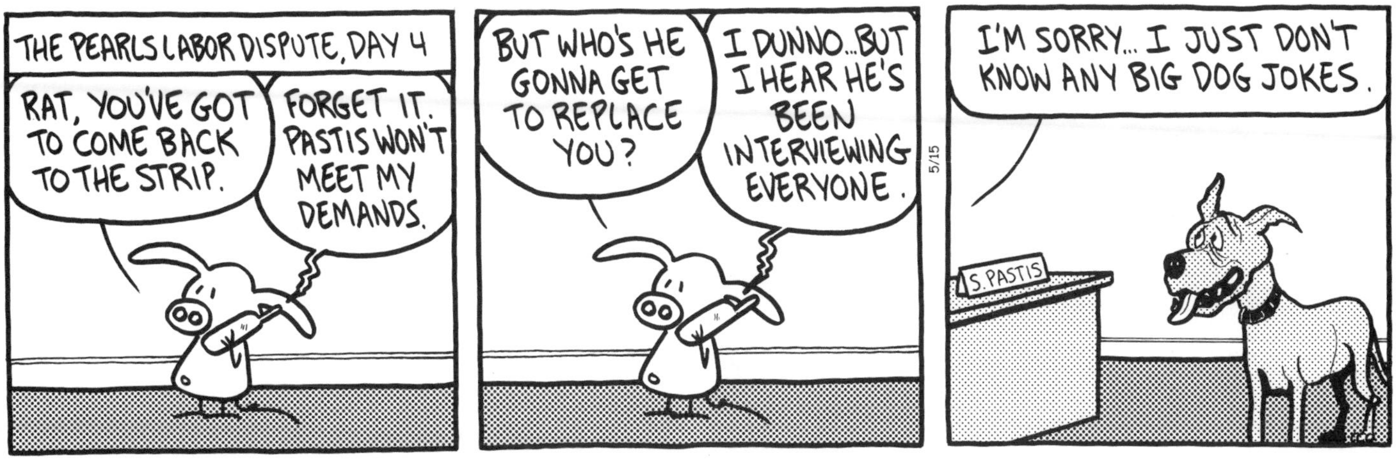
THE PEARLS LABOR DISPUTE, DAY 4
RAT, YOU'VE GOT TO COME BACK TO THE STRIP.
FORGET IT. PASTIS WON'T MEET MY DEMANDS.
BUT WHO'S HE GONNA GET TO REPLACE YOU?
I DUNNO...BUT I HEAR HE'S BEEN INTERVIEWING EVERYONE.
5/15
I'M SORRY... I JUST DON'T KNOW ANY BIG DOG JOKES.
S. PASTIS

I found Marmaduke incredibly hard to draw.

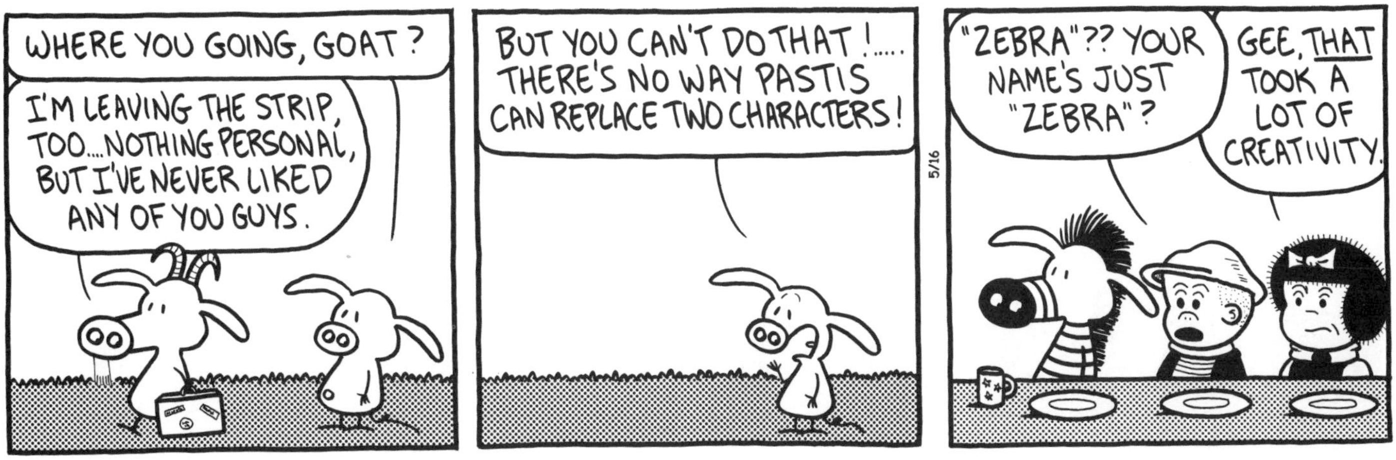
WHERE YOU GOING, GOAT?
I'M LEAVING THE STRIP, TOO....NOTHING PERSONAL, BUT I'VE NEVER LIKED ANY OF YOU GUYS.
BUT YOU CAN'T DO THAT!..... THERE'S NO WAY PASTIS CAN REPLACE TWO CHARACTERS!
5/16
"ZEBRA"?? YOUR NAME'S JUST "ZEBRA"?
GEE, THAT TOOK A LOT OF CREATIVITY.

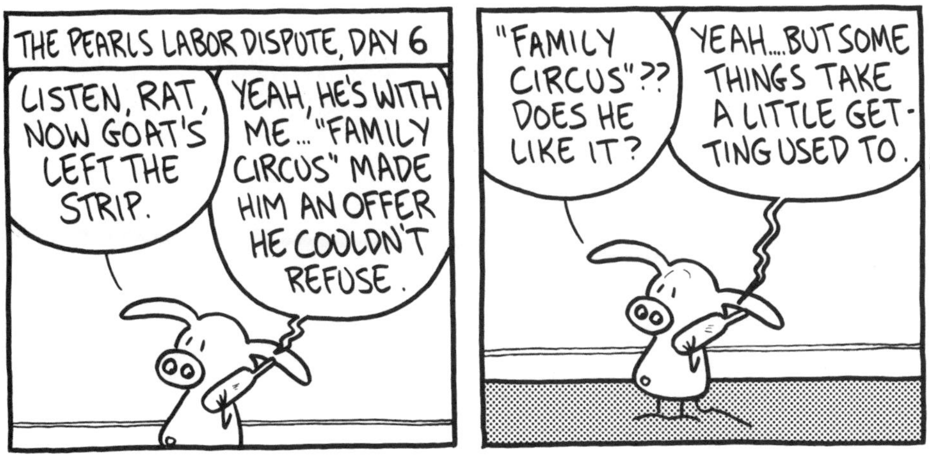
THE PEARLS LABOR DISPUTE, DAY 6
LISTEN, RAT, NOW GOAT'S LEFT THE STRIP.
YEAH, HE'S WITH ME... "FAMILY CIRCUS" MADE HIM AN OFFER HE COULDN'T REFUSE.
"FAMILY CIRCUS"?? DOES HE LIKE IT?
YEAH....BUT SOME THINGS TAKE A LITTLE GETTING USED TO.
5/17

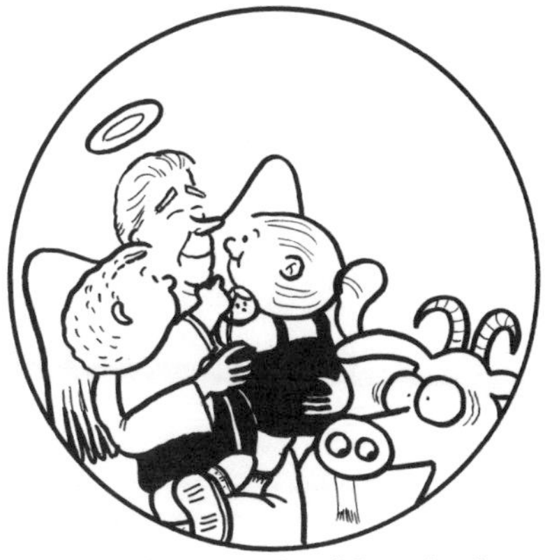

"We love you, dead Grandpa."

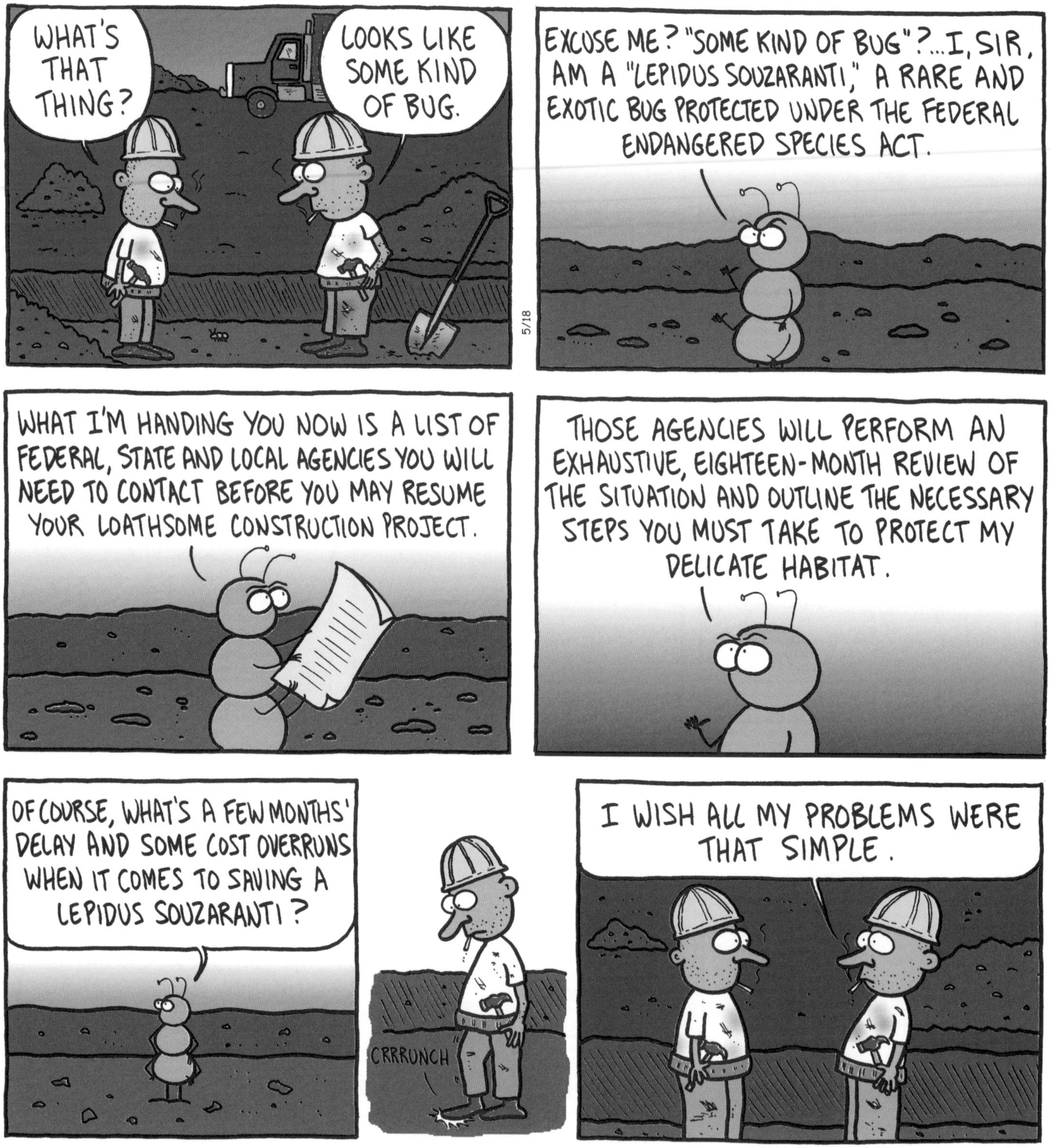
WHAT'S THAT THING?
LOOKS LIKE SOME KIND OF BUG.
5/18
EXCUSE ME? "SOME KIND OF BUG"?...I, SIR, AM A "LEPIDUS SOUZARANTI," A RARE AND EXOTIC BUG PROTECTED UNDER THE FEDERAL ENDANGERED SPECIES ACT.
WHAT I'M HANDING YOU NOW IS A LIST OF FEDERAL, STATE AND LOCAL AGENCIES YOU WILL NEED TO CONTACT BEFORE YOU MAY RESUME YOUR LOATHSOME CONSTRUCTION PROJECT.
THOSE AGENCIES WILL PERFORM AN EXHAUSTIVE, EIGHTEEN-MONTH REVIEW OF THE SITUATION AND OUTLINE THE NECESSARY STEPS YOU MUST TAKE TO PROTECT MY DELICATE HABITAT.
OF COURSE, WHAT'S A FEW MONTHS' DELAY AND SOME COST OVERRUNS WHEN IT COMES TO SAVING A LEPIDUS SOUZARANTI?
CRRRUNCH
I WISH ALL MY PROBLEMS WERE THAT SIMPLE.

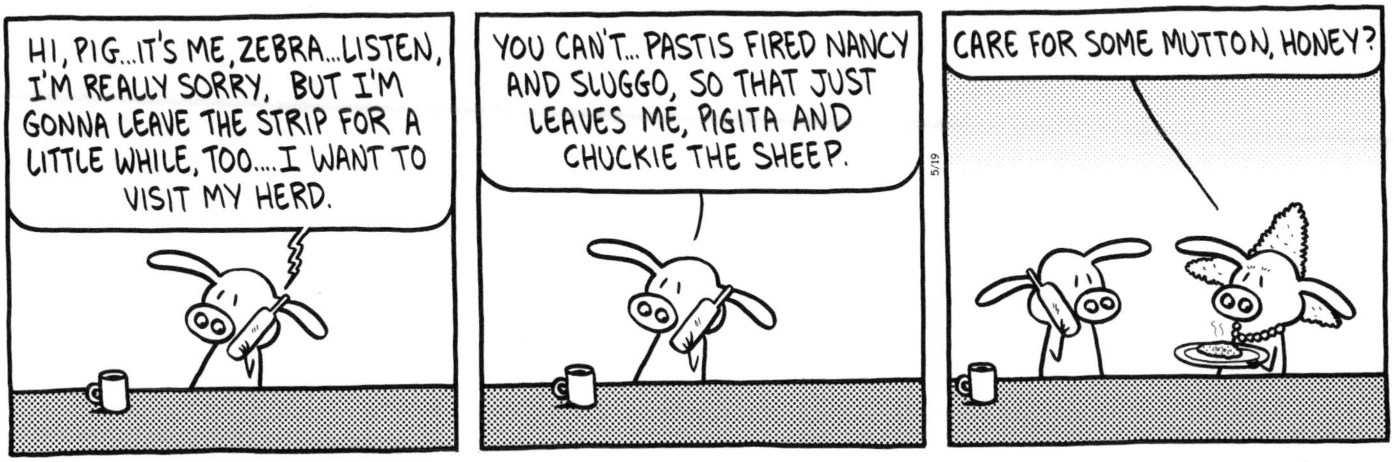
HI, PIG...IT'S ME, ZEBRA...LISTEN, I'M REALLY SORRY, BUT I'M GONNA LEAVE THE STRIP FOR A LITTLE WHILE, TOO....I WANT TO VISIT MY HERD.
YOU CAN'T...PASTIS FIRED NANCY AND SLUGGO, SO THAT JUST LEAVES ME, PIGITA AND CHUCKIE THE SHEEP.
5/19
CARE FOR SOME MUTTON, HONEY?

If I'm not mistaken, I think Chuckie the Sheep later returns. I think I kill and unkill more characters than just about any other cartoonist.

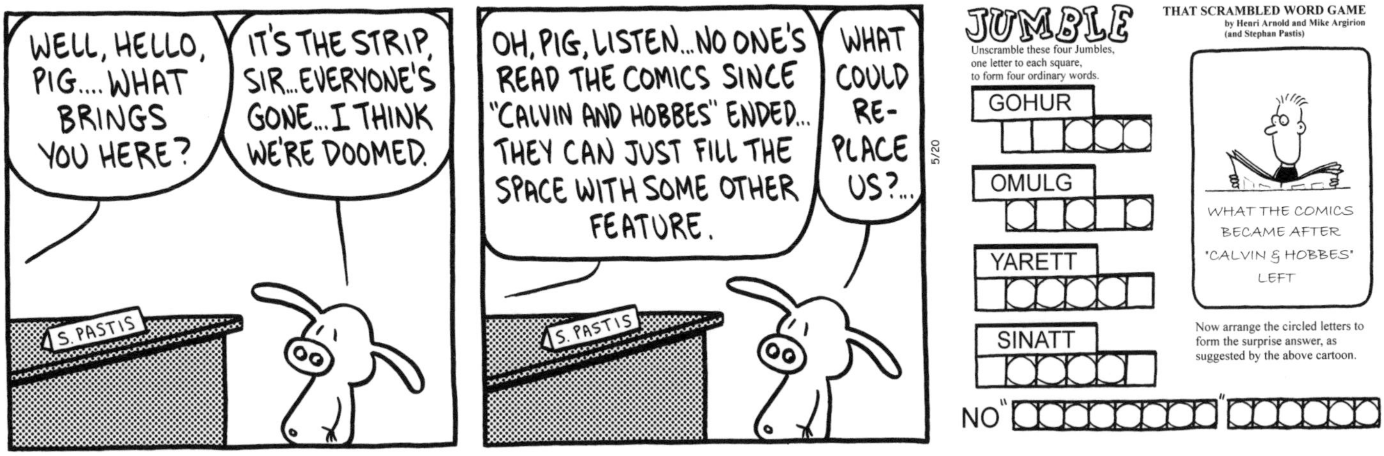
WELL, HELLO, PIG.... WHAT BRINGS YOU HERE?
IT'S THE STRIP, SIR...EVERYONE'S GONE...I THINK WE'RE DOOMED.
S. PASTIS
OH, PIG, LISTEN...NO ONE'S READ THE COMICS SINCE "CALVIN AND HOBBES" ENDED... THEY CAN JUST FILL THE SPACE WITH SOME OTHER FEATURE.
WHAT COULD RE-PLACE US?...
S. PASTIS
5/20
JUMBLE
THAT SCRAMBLED WORD GAME
by Henri Arnold and Mike Argirion (and Stephan Pastis)
Unscramble these four Jumbles, one letter to each square, to form four ordinary words.
GOHUR
OMULG
YARETT
SINATT
WHAT THE COMICS BECAME AFTER "CALVIN & HOBBES" LEFT
Now arrange the circled letters to form the surprise answer, as suggested by the above cartoon.
NO " "

Man, I love those Jumbles. I can usually get the five-letter words in a snap, but the six-letter ones are much harder. And just so I never have to answer another e-mail on this again, the answers are: "rough," "mogul," "treaty," and "taints." The final answer is "no laughing matter."

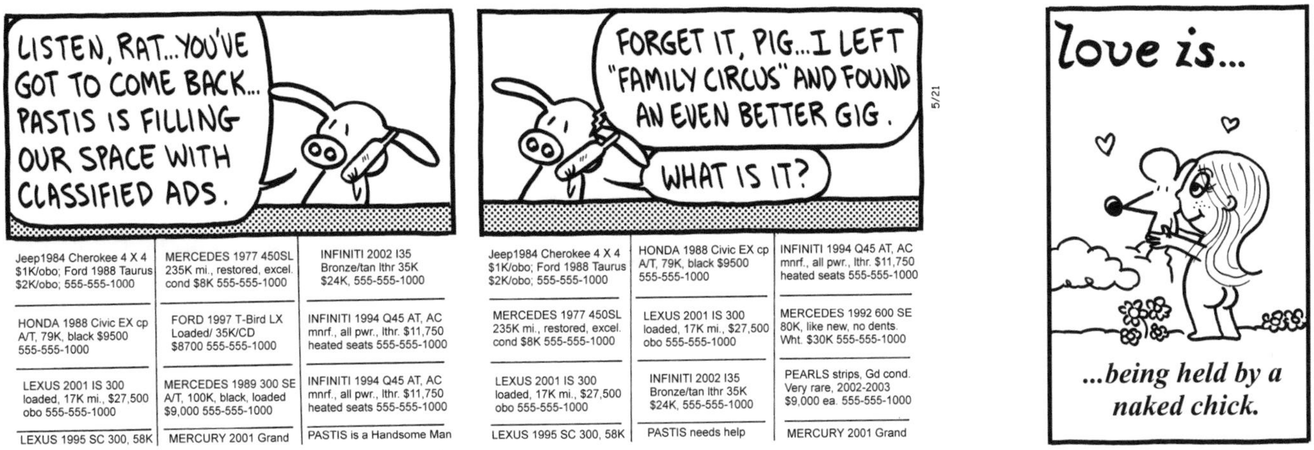
LISTEN, RAT...YOU'VE GOT TO COME BACK... PASTIS IS FILLING OUR SPACE WITH CLASSIFIED ADS.
Jeep1984 Cherokee 4 X 4 $1K/obo; Ford 1988 Taurus $2K/obo; 555-555-1000
HONDA 1988 Civic EX cp A/T, 79K, black $9500 555-555-1000
LEXUS 2001 IS 300 loaded, 17K mi., $27,500 obo 555-555-1000
LEXUS 1995 SC 300, 58K
MERCEDES 1977 450SL 235K mi., restored, excel. cond $8K 555-555-1000
FORD 1997 T-Bird LX Loaded/ 35K/CD $8700 555-555-1000
MERCEDES 1989 300 SE A/T, 100K, black, loaded $9,000 555-555-1000
MERCURY 2001 Grand
INFINITI 2002 I35 Bronze/tan lthr 35K $24K, 555-555-1000
INFINITI 1994 Q45 AT, AC mnrf., all pwr., lthr. $11,750 heated seats 555-555-1000
INFINITI 1994 Q45 AT, AC mnrf., all pwr., lthr. $11,750 heated seats 555-555-1000
PASTIS is a Handsome Man
FORGET IT, PIG...I LEFT "FAMILY CIRCUS" AND FOUND AN EVEN BETTER GIG.
WHAT IS IT?
5/21
Jeep1984 Cherokee 4 X 4 $1K/obo; Ford 1988 Taurus $2K/obo; 555-555-1000
MERCEDES 1977 450SL 235K mi., restored, excel. cond $8K 555-555-1000
LEXUS 2001 IS 300 loaded, 17K mi., $27,500 obo 555-555-1000
LEXUS 1995 SC 300, 58K
HONDA 1988 Civic EX cp A/T, 79K, black $9500 555-555-1000
LEXUS 2001 IS 300 loaded, 17K mi., $27,500 obo 555-555-1000
INFINITI 2002 I35 Bronze/tan lthr 35K $24K, 555-555-1000
PASTIS needs help
INFINITI 1994 Q45 AT, AC mnrf., all pwr., lthr. $11,750 heated seats 555-555-1000
MERCEDES 1992 600 SE 80K, like new, no dents. Wht. $30K 555-555-1000
PEARLS strips, Gd cond. Very rare, 2002-2003 $9,000 ea. 555-555-1000
MERCURY 2001 Grand
love is...
...being held by a naked chick.

Read the classifieds carefully and you'll find I am a handsome man in need of help.

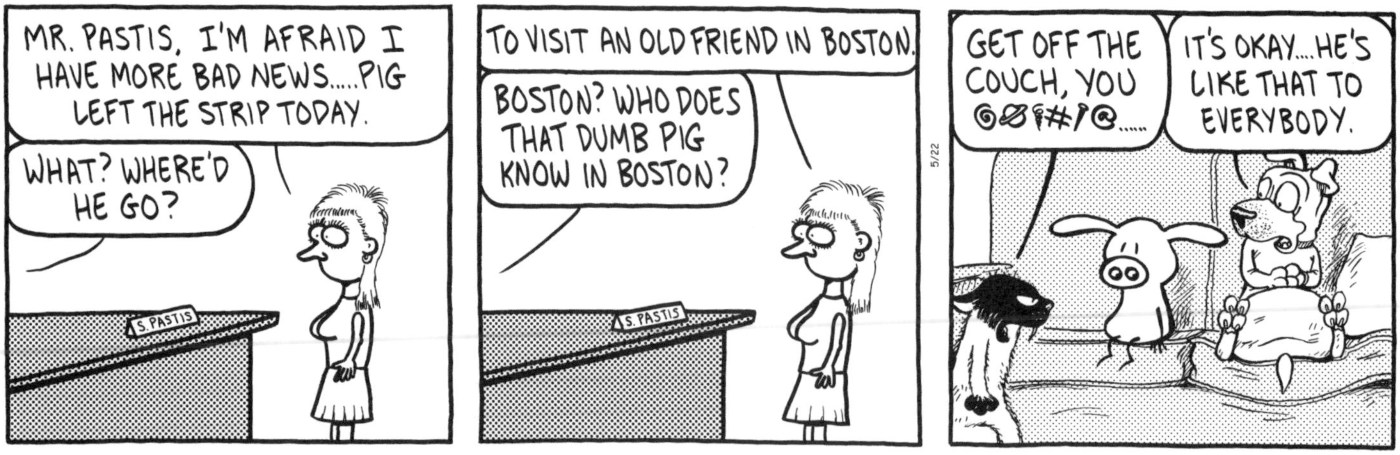
MR. PASTIS, I'M AFRAID I HAVE MORE BAD NEWS.....PIG LEFT THE STRIP TODAY.
WHAT? WHERE'D HE GO?
S. PASTIS
TO VISIT AN OLD FRIEND IN BOSTON.
BOSTON? WHO DOES THAT DUMB PIG KNOW IN BOSTON?
S. PASTIS
5/22
GET OFF THE COUCH, YOU
IT'S OKAY....HE'S LIKE THAT TO EVERYBODY.

I absolutely could not draw the *Get Fuzzy* characters, so I enlisted the help of my friend, Paige Braddock, who draws *Jane's World*. Other than the speech balloons and text, she drew the entire last panel.

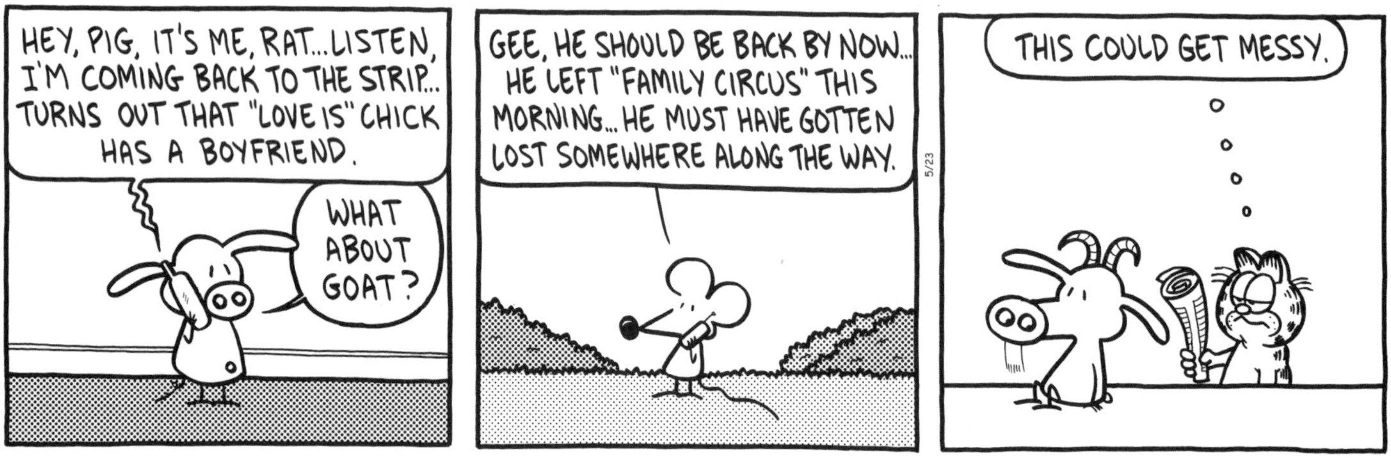
HEY, PIG, IT'S ME, RAT...LISTEN, I'M COMING BACK TO THE STRIP... TURNS OUT THAT "LOVE IS" CHICK HAS A BOYFRIEND.
WHAT ABOUT GOAT?
GEE, HE SHOULD BE BACK BY NOW... HE LEFT "FAMILY CIRCUS" THIS MORNING... HE MUST HAVE GOTTEN LOST SOMEWHERE ALONG THE WAY.
5/23
THIS COULD GET MESSY.

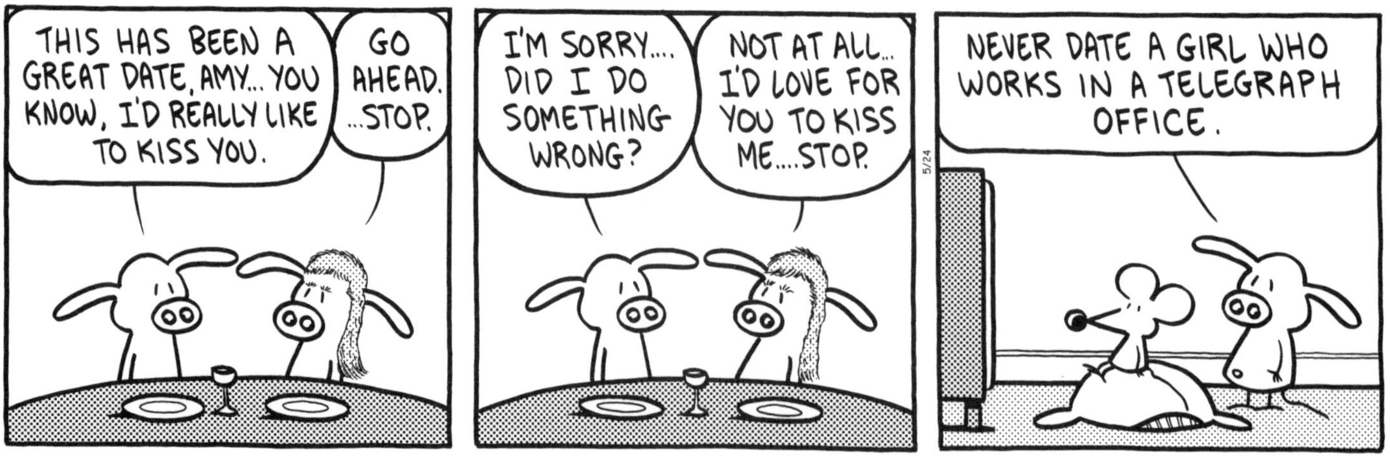
THIS HAS BEEN A GREAT DATE, AMY... YOU KNOW, I'D REALLY LIKE TO KISS YOU.
GO AHEAD. ...STOP.
I'M SORRY.... DID I DO SOMETHING WRONG?
NOT AT ALL... I'D LOVE FOR YOU TO KISS ME....STOP.
5/24
NEVER DATE A GIRL WHO WORKS IN A TELEGRAPH OFFICE.

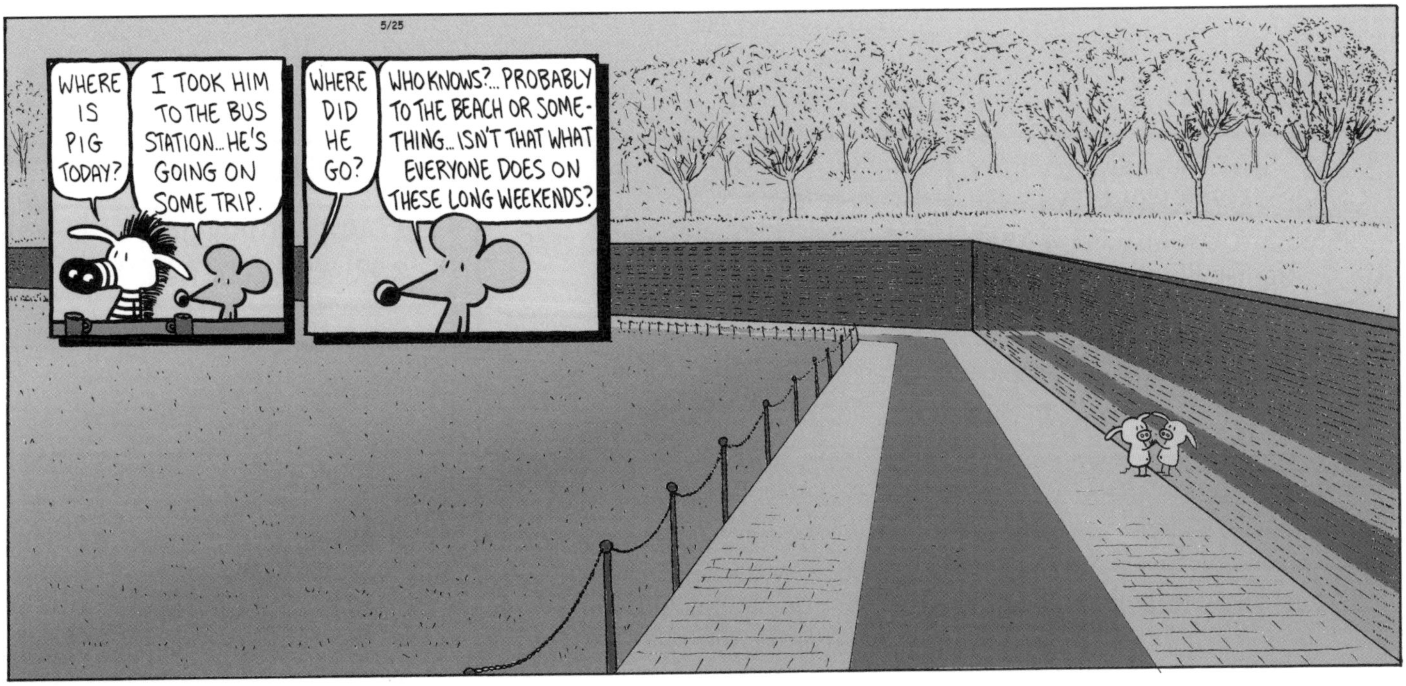
5/25
WHERE IS PIG TODAY?
I TOOK HIM TO THE BUS STATION... HE'S GOING ON SOME TRIP.
WHERE DID HE GO?
WHO KNOWS?... PROBABLY TO THE BEACH OR SOMETHING... ISN'T THAT WHAT EVERYONE DOES ON THESE LONG WEEKENDS?

I received more e-mail in response to this strip than for any other strip I had done to date. And many of the e-mails were among the most positive and touching I had ever received. Many were from veterans and the family of veterans. One woman just thanked me, saying simply, "My son's name is on the wall."

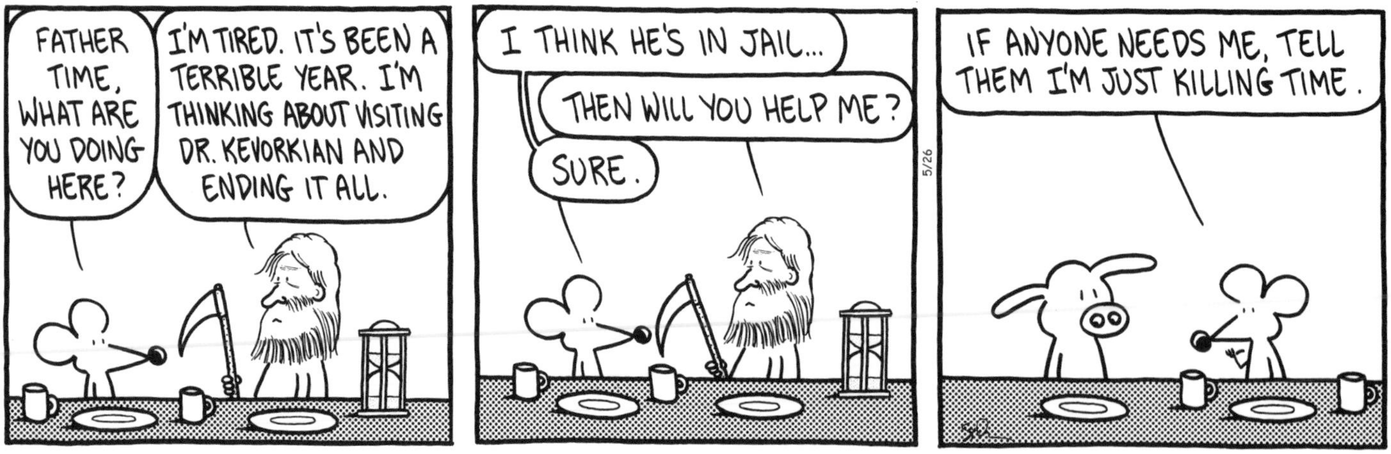
FATHER TIME, WHAT ARE YOU DOING HERE?
I'M TIRED. IT'S BEEN A TERRIBLE YEAR. I'M THINKING ABOUT VISITING DR. KEVORKIAN AND ENDING IT ALL.
I THINK HE'S IN JAIL...
THEN WILL YOU HELP ME?
SURE.
5/26
IF ANYONE NEEDS ME, TELL THEM I'M JUST KILLING TIME.

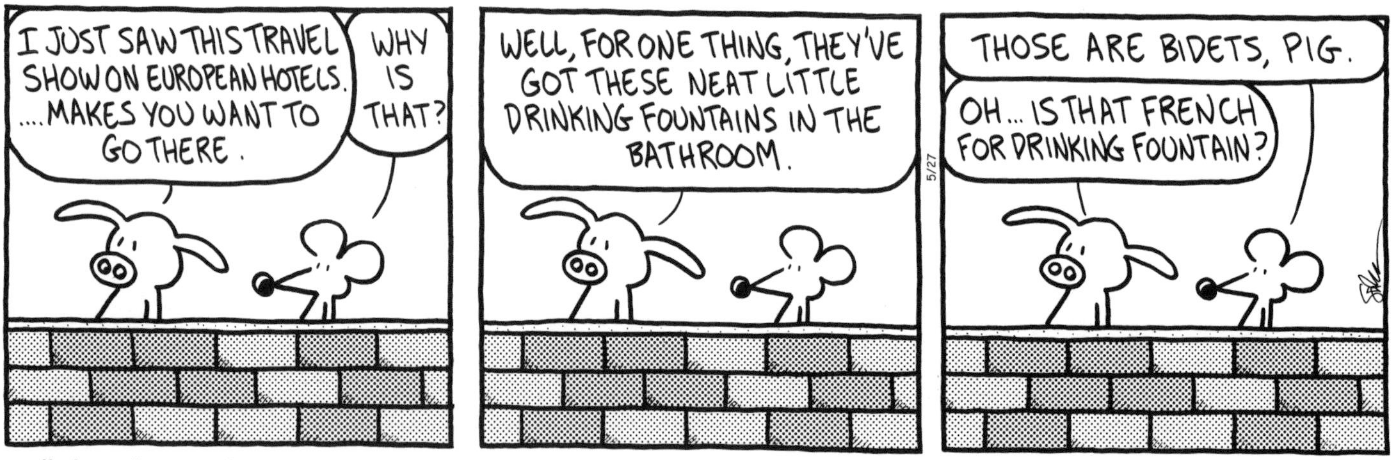
I JUST SAW THIS TRAVEL SHOW ON EUROPEAN HOTELS. ....MAKES YOU WANT TO GO THERE.
WHY IS THAT?
WELL, FOR ONE THING, THEY'VE GOT THESE NEAT LITTLE DRINKING FOUNTAINS IN THE BATHROOM.
5/27
THOSE ARE BIDETS, PIG.
OH... IS THAT FRENCH FOR DRINKING FOUNTAIN?

I still don't know what those things are for, and I don't want to know. So please don't write and tell me.

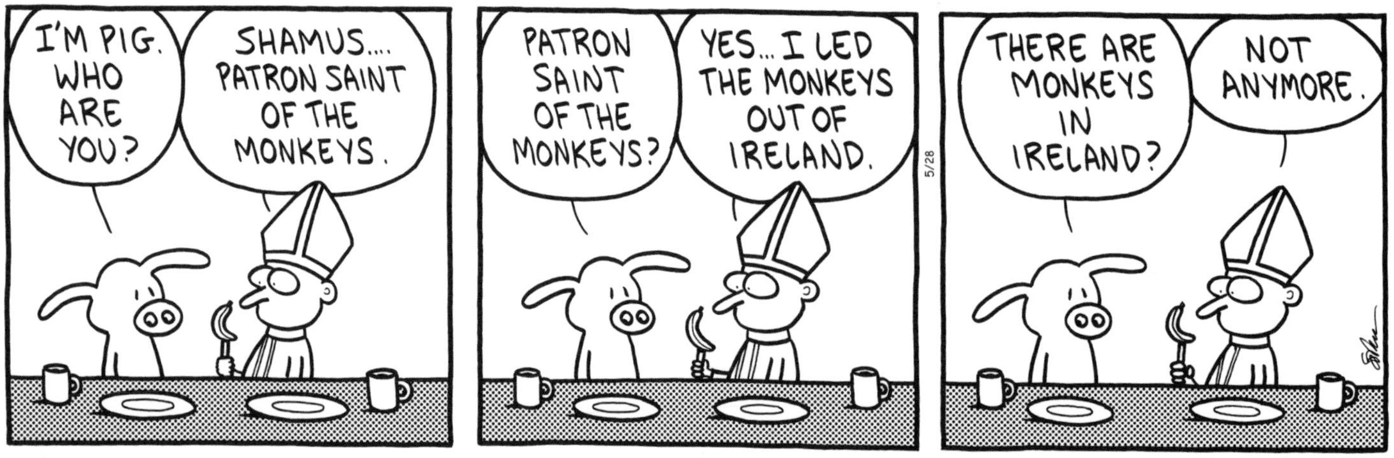
I'M PIG. WHO ARE YOU?
SHAMUS.... PATRON SAINT OF THE MONKEYS.
PATRON SAINT OF THE MONKEYS?
YES... I LED THE MONKEYS OUT OF IRELAND.
5/28
THERE ARE MONKEYS IN IRELAND?
NOT ANYMORE.

Darby Conley gave me this idea because he thought I should introduce a character who was the "Patron Saint of the Monkies." The strip then infuriated one reader who termed it "an unnecessary debasing" of Catholicism.

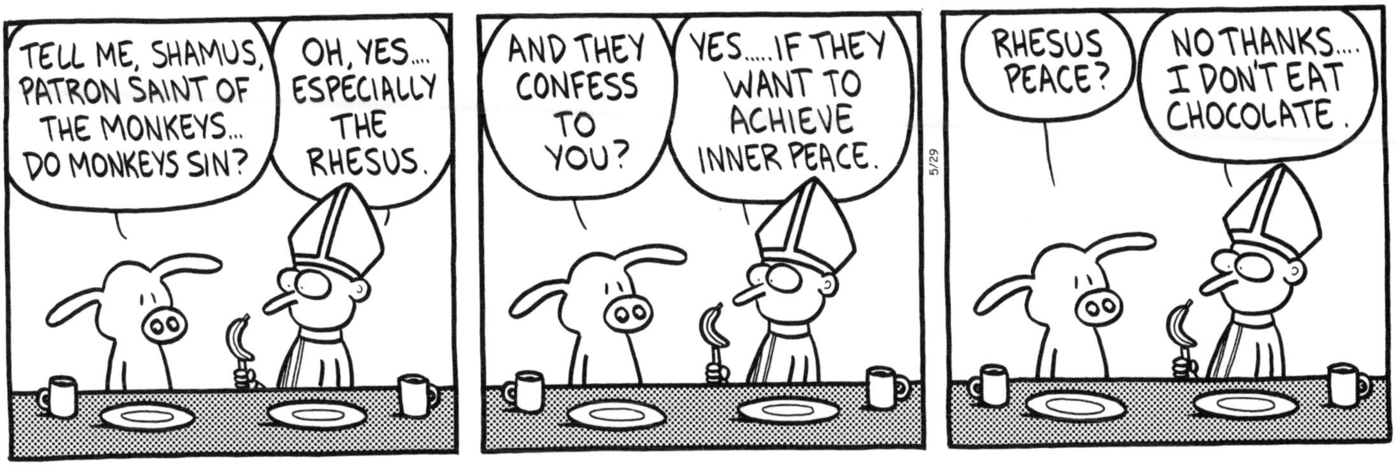
TELL ME, SHAMUS, PATRON SAINT OF THE MONKEYS... DO MONKEYS SIN?
OH, YES.... ESPECIALLY THE RHESUS.
AND THEY CONFESS TO YOU?
YES.....IF THEY WANT TO ACHIEVE INNER PEACE.
5/29
RHESUS PEACE?
NO THANKS.... I DON'T EAT CHOCOLATE.

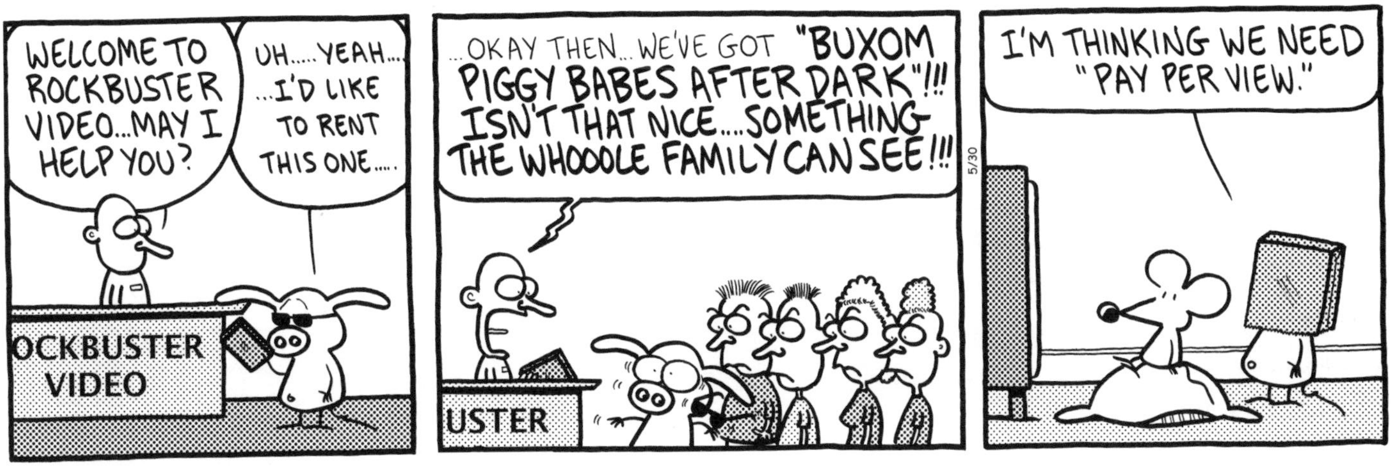
WELCOME TO ROCKBUSTER VIDEO...MAY I HELP YOU?
UH.....YEAH... ...I'D LIKE TO RENT THIS ONE.....
OCKBUSTER VIDEO
...OKAY THEN...WE'VE GOT "BUXOM PIGGY BABES AFTER DARK"!!! ISN'T THAT NICE....SOMETHING THE WHOOOLE FAMILY CAN SEE!!!
USTER
5/30
I'M THINKING WE NEED "PAY PER VIEW."

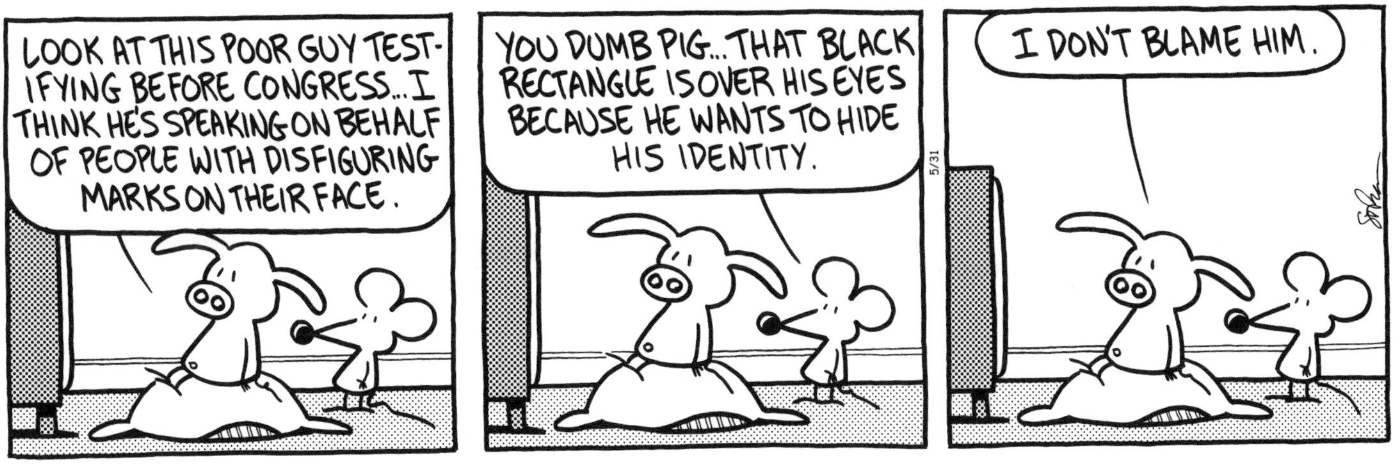
LOOK AT THIS POOR GUY TEST-IFYING BEFORE CONGRESS...I THINK HE'S SPEAKING ON BEHALF OF PEOPLE WITH DISFIGURING MARKS ON THEIR FACE.
YOU DUMB PIG...THAT BLACK RECTANGLE IS OVER HIS EYES BECAUSE HE WANTS TO HIDE HIS IDENTITY.
5/31
I DON'T BLAME HIM.

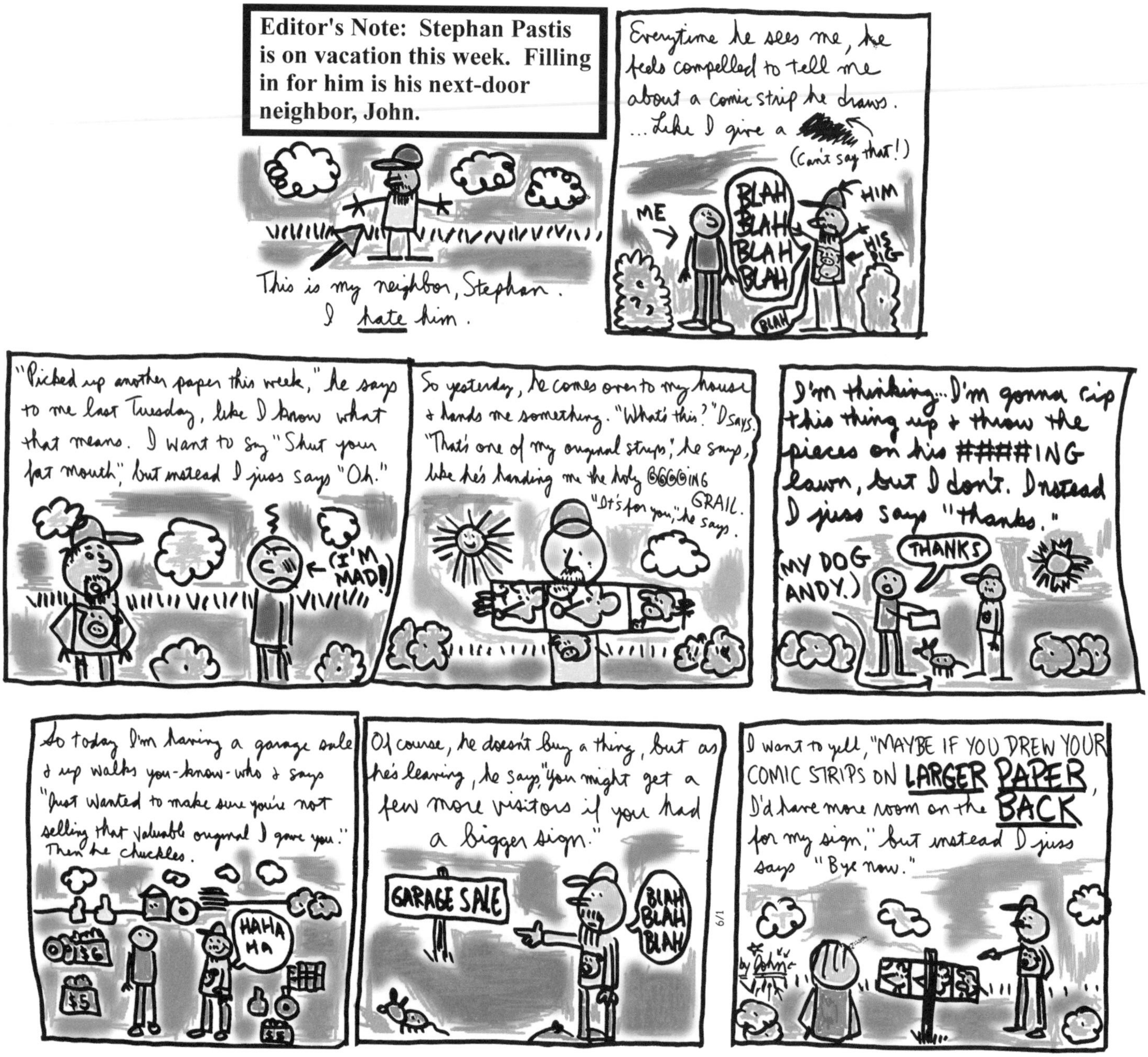

Editor's Note: Stephan Pastis is on vacation this week. Filling in for him is his next-door neighbor, John.
This is my neighbor, Stephan. I hate him.
Everytime he sees me, he feels compelled to tell me about a comic strip he draws. ...Like I give a [redacted]
(Can't say that!)
ME
BLAH BLAH BLAH BLAH
HIM
HIS PIG
BLAH
"Picked up another paper this week," he says to me last Tuesday, like I know what that means. I want to say "Shut your fat mouth," but instead I juss says "Oh."
(I'M MAD!)
So yesterday, he comes over to my house & hands me something. "What's this?" I says. "That's one of my original strips," he says, like he's handing me the holy @@@@ING GRAIL.
"It's for you," he says.
I'm thinking... I'm gonna rip this thing up + throw the pieces on his ####ING lawn, but I don't. Instead I juss says "thanks."
(MY DOG ANDY.)
THANKS
So today I'm having a garage sale & up walks you-know-who & says "Just wanted to make sure you're not selling that valuable original I gave you." Then he chuckles.
HAHA HA
$5
Of course, he doesn't buy a thing, but as he's leaving, he says "You might get a few more visitors if you had a bigger sign."
GARAGE SALE
BLAH BLAH BLAH
6/1
I want to yell, "MAYBE IF YOU DREW YOUR COMIC STRIPS ON LARGER PAPER, I'd have more room on the BACK for my sign," but instead I juss says "Bye now."
by John

An editor of a large newspaper cut this strip out of his paper and mailed it to me, saying that some readers had found it offensive. I wasn't sure which part of it was offensive until I noticed his highlighting of the words "@@@@ing" and "####ing." He thought they too closely telegraphed a certain swear word. I actually agreed, and have tried not to do it again.

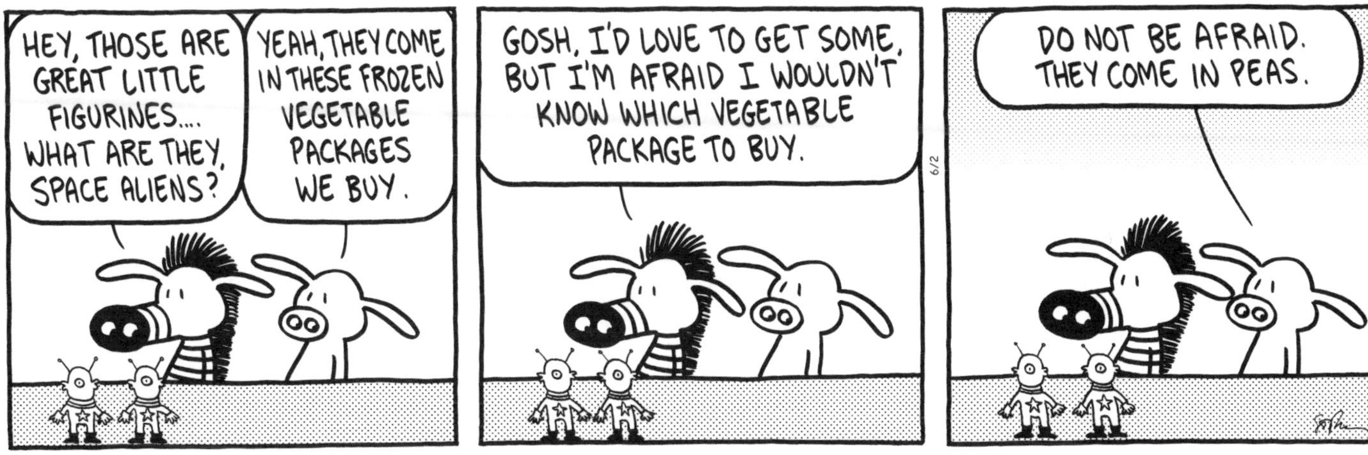
HEY, THOSE ARE GREAT LITTLE FIGURINES.... WHAT ARE THEY, SPACE ALIENS?
YEAH, THEY COME IN THESE FROZEN VEGETABLE PACKAGES WE BUY.
GOSH, I'D LOVE TO GET SOME, BUT I'M AFRAID I WOULDN'T KNOW WHICH VEGETABLE PACKAGE TO BUY.
6/2
DO NOT BE AFRAID. THEY COME IN PEAS.

This strip turned out to be one of the more popular dailies. I will go to great lengths for a bad pun.

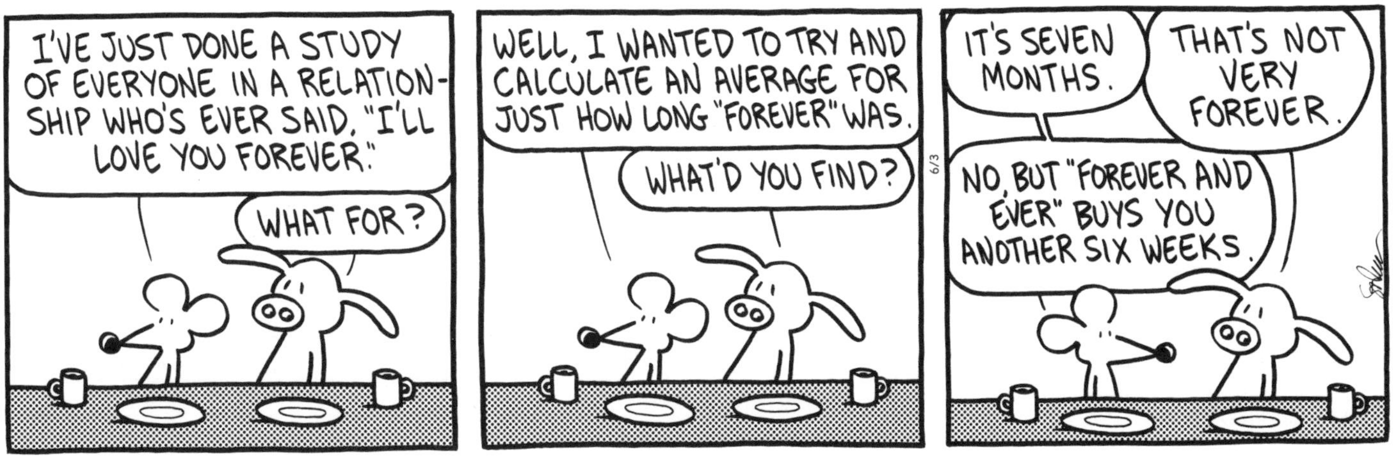
I'VE JUST DONE A STUDY OF EVERYONE IN A RELATIONSHIP WHO'S EVER SAID, "I'LL LOVE YOU FOREVER."
WHAT FOR?
WELL, I WANTED TO TRY AND CALCULATE AN AVERAGE FOR JUST HOW LONG "FOREVER" WAS.
WHAT'D YOU FIND?
6/3
IT'S SEVEN MONTHS.
THAT'S NOT VERY FOREVER.
NO, BUT "FOREVER AND EVER" BUYS YOU ANOTHER SIX WEEKS.

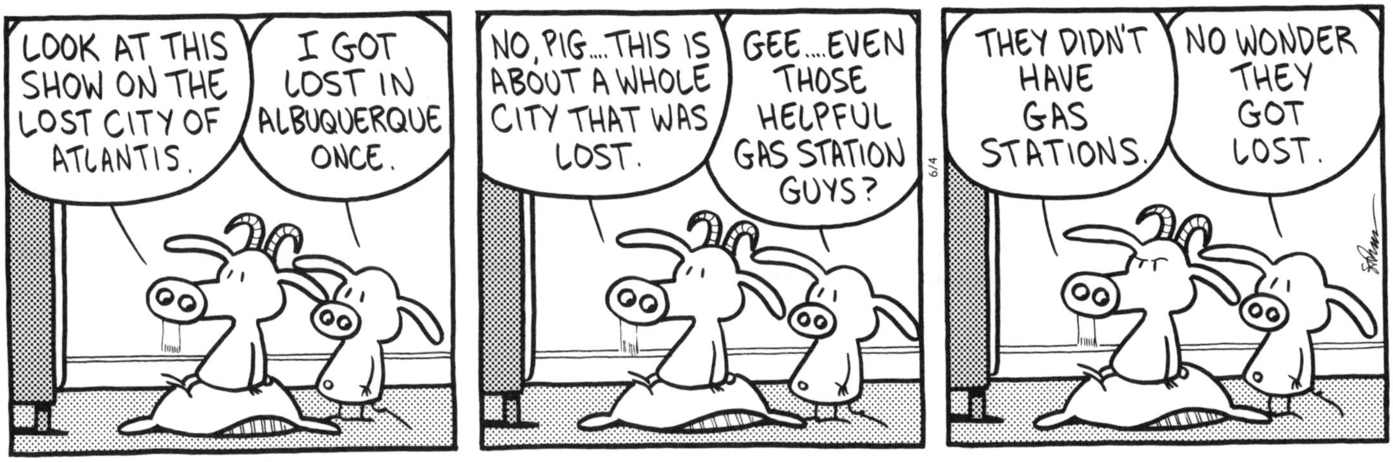
LOOK AT THIS SHOW ON THE LOST CITY OF ATLANTIS.
I GOT LOST IN ALBUQUERQUE ONCE.
NO, PIG....THIS IS ABOUT A WHOLE CITY THAT WAS LOST.
GEE....EVEN THOSE HELPFUL GAS STATION GUYS?
6/4
THEY DIDN'T HAVE GAS STATIONS.
NO WONDER THEY GOT LOST.

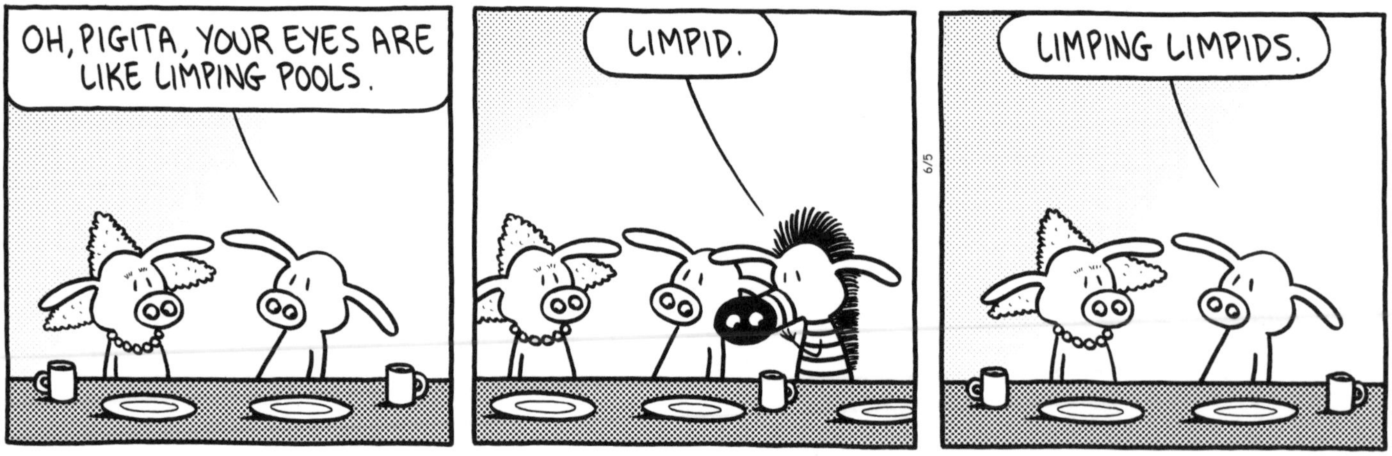
OH, PIGITA, YOUR EYES ARE LIKE LIMPING POOLS.
LIMPID.
6/5
LIMPING LIMPIDS.

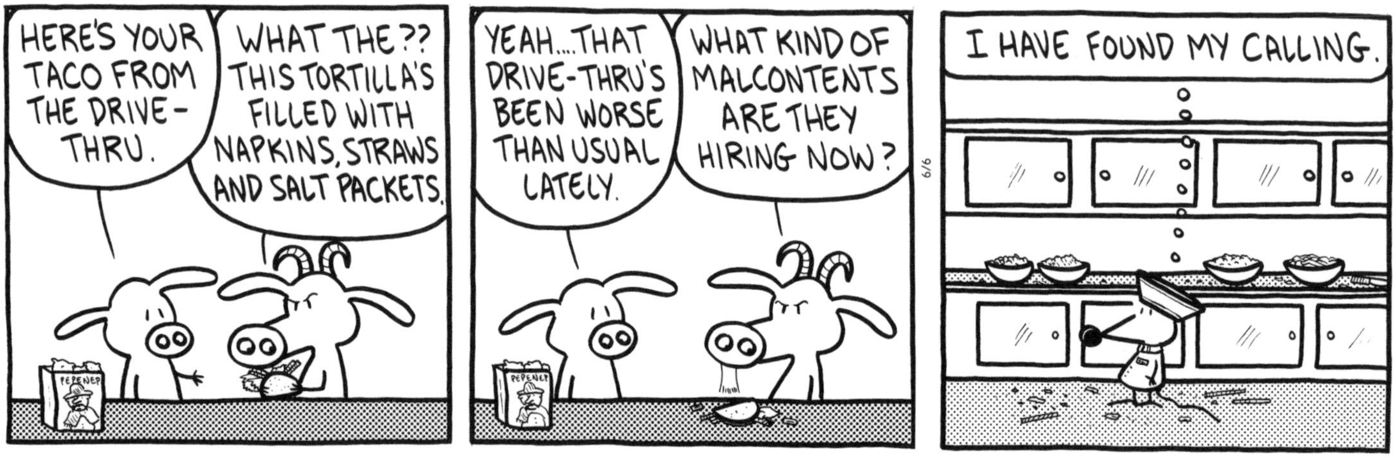
HERE'S YOUR TACO FROM THE DRIVE-THRU.
WHAT THE?? THIS TORTILLA'S FILLED WITH NAPKINS, STRAWS AND SALT PACKETS.
YEAH....THAT DRIVE-THRU'S BEEN WORSE THAN USUAL LATELY.
WHAT KIND OF MALCONTENTS ARE THEY HIRING NOW?
6/6
I HAVE FOUND MY CALLING.

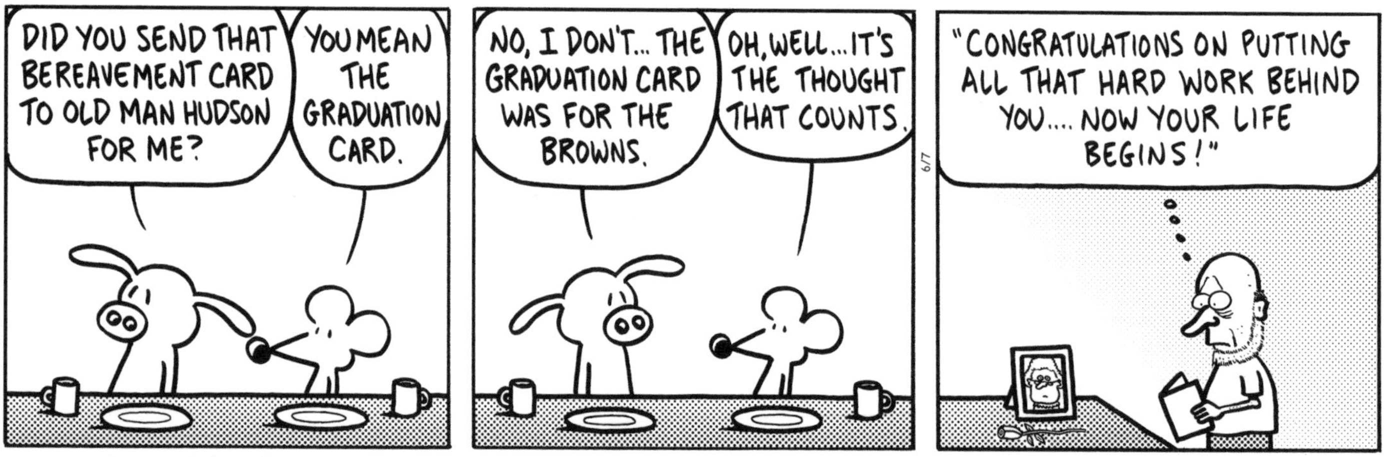
DID YOU SEND THAT BEREAVEMENT CARD TO OLD MAN HUDSON FOR ME?
YOU MEAN THE GRADUATION CARD.
NO, I DON'T... THE GRADUATION CARD WAS FOR THE BROWNS.
OH, WELL...IT'S THE THOUGHT THAT COUNTS.
6/7
"CONGRATULATIONS ON PUTTING ALL THAT HARD WORK BEHIND YOU.... NOW YOUR LIFE BEGINS!"

One reader said that this strip was unfunny and mean. Mean, fine. But unfunny? How dare you.

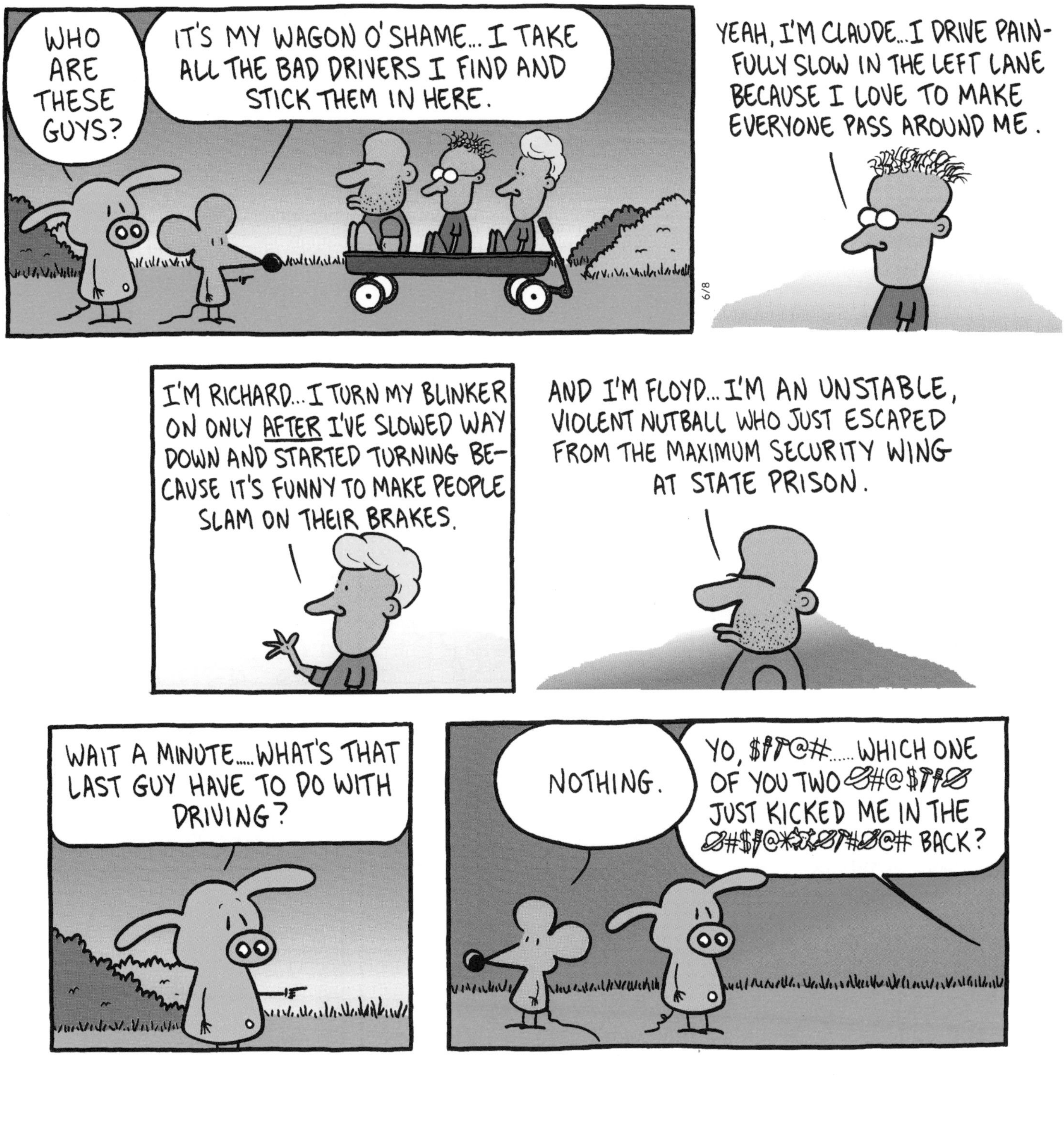
WHO ARE THESE GUYS?
IT'S MY WAGON O'SHAME... I TAKE ALL THE BAD DRIVERS I FIND AND STICK THEM IN HERE.
6/8
YEAH, I'M CLAUDE... I DRIVE PAIN-FULLY SLOW IN THE LEFT LANE BECAUSE I LOVE TO MAKE EVERYONE PASS AROUND ME.
I'M RICHARD... I TURN MY BLINKER ON ONLY AFTER I'VE SLOWED WAY DOWN AND STARTED TURNING BE-CAUSE IT'S FUNNY TO MAKE PEOPLE SLAM ON THEIR BRAKES.
AND I'M FLOYD... I'M AN UNSTABLE, VIOLENT NUTBALL WHO JUST ESCAPED FROM THE MAXIMUM SECURITY WING AT STATE PRISON.
WAIT A MINUTE..... WHAT'S THAT LAST GUY HAVE TO DO WITH DRIVING?
NOTHING.
YO, $!!@#...... WHICH ONE OF YOU TWO @#@$!!@ JUST KICKED ME IN THE @#$!@*!@!#@@# BACK?

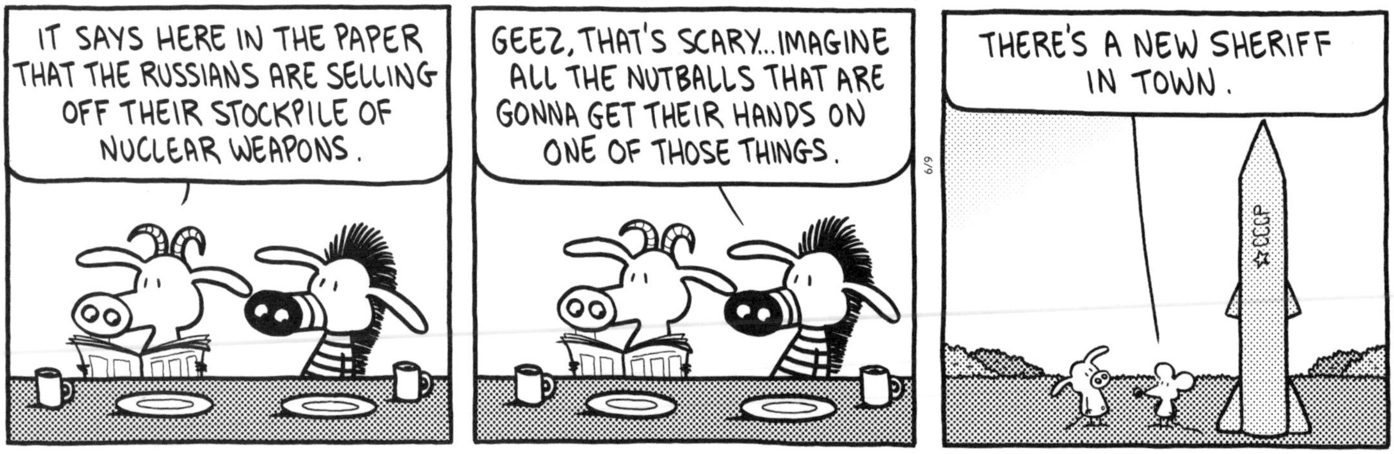
IT SAYS HERE IN THE PAPER THAT THE RUSSIANS ARE SELLING OFF THEIR STOCKPILE OF NUCLEAR WEAPONS.
GEEZ, THAT'S SCARY...IMAGINE ALL THE NUTBALLS THAT ARE GONNA GET THEIR HANDS ON ONE OF THOSE THINGS.
6/9
THERE'S A NEW SHERIFF IN TOWN.
CCCP

This series turned out to be pretty popular with readers. Please note how dramatically the size of the missile changes between strips.

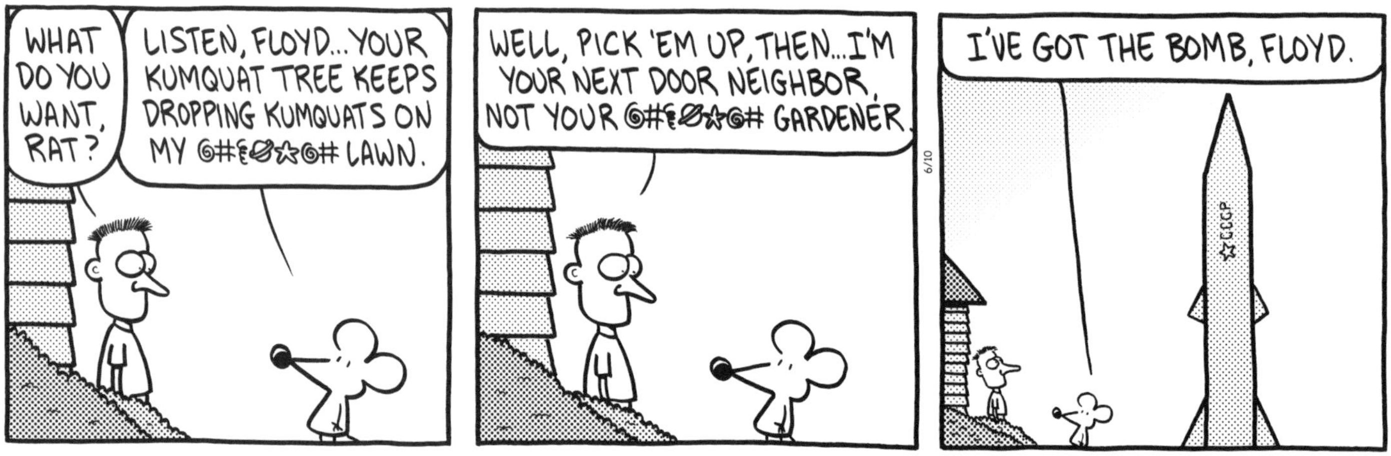
WHAT DO YOU WANT, RAT?
LISTEN, FLOYD...YOUR KUMQUAT TREE KEEPS DROPPING KUMQUATS ON MY @#€@☆@# LAWN.
WELL, PICK 'EM UP, THEN...I'M YOUR NEXT DOOR NEIGHBOR, NOT YOUR @#€@☆@# GARDENER.
6/10
I'VE GOT THE BOMB, FLOYD.
CCCP

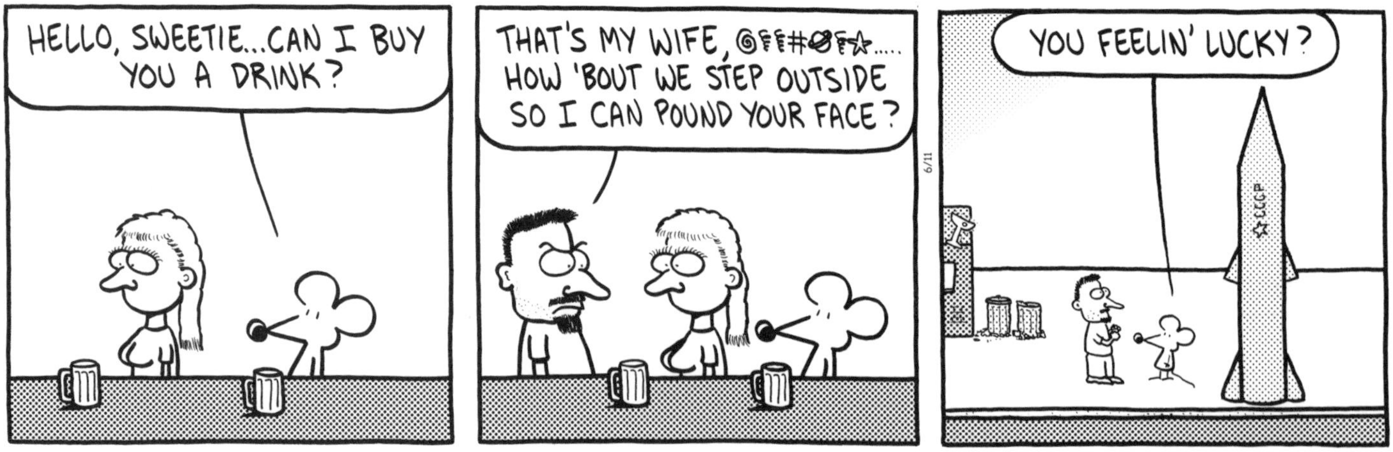
HELLO, SWEETIE...CAN I BUY YOU A DRINK?
THAT'S MY WIFE, @€€#@€☆.....HOW 'BOUT WE STEP OUTSIDE SO I CAN POUND YOUR FACE?
6/11
YOU FEELIN' LUCKY?
CCCP

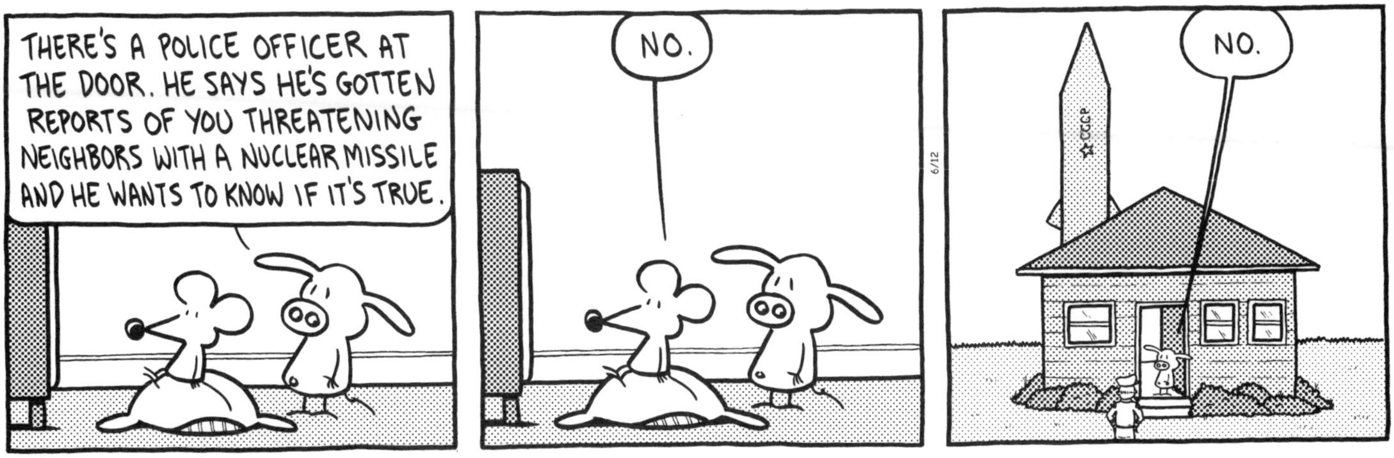
THERE'S A POLICE OFFICER AT THE DOOR. HE SAYS HE'S GOTTEN REPORTS OF YOU THREATENING NEIGHBORS WITH A NUCLEAR MISSILE AND HE WANTS TO KNOW IF IT'S TRUE.
NO.
6/12
NO.
CCCP

That house in the third panel took much too long to draw. I won't do that again.

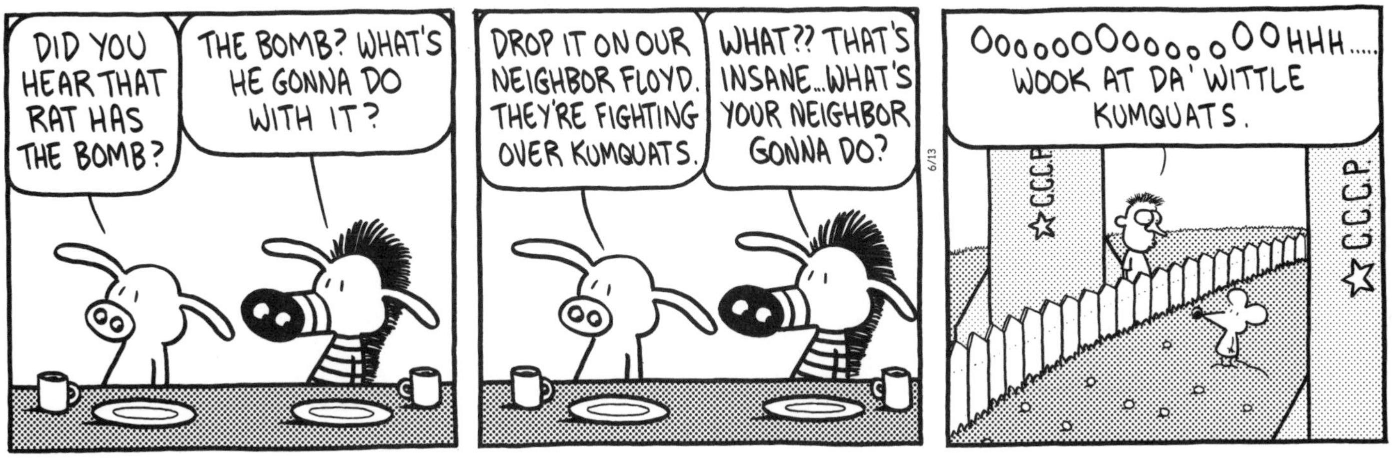
DID YOU HEAR THAT RAT HAS THE BOMB?
THE BOMB? WHAT'S HE GONNA DO WITH IT?
DROP IT ON OUR NEIGHBOR FLOYD. THEY'RE FIGHTING OVER KUMQUATS.
WHAT?? THAT'S INSANE...WHAT'S YOUR NEIGHBOR GONNA DO?
6/13
OooooOOoooooOOHHH.....
WOOK AT DA' WITTLE KUMQUATS.
C.C.C.P.
C.C.C.P.

Kumquats + nuclear war = instant comedy.

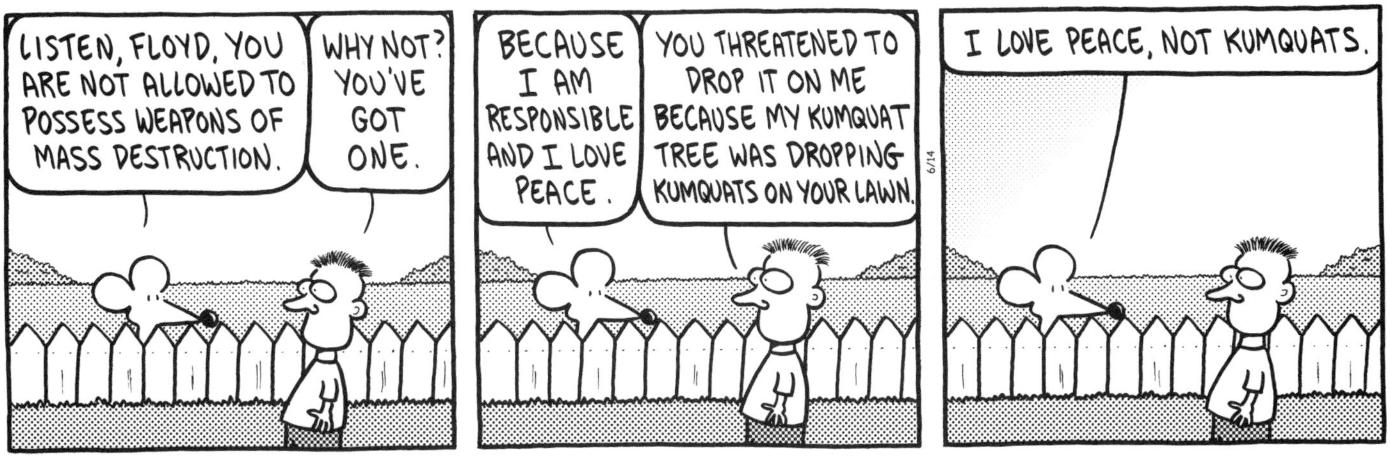
LISTEN, FLOYD, YOU ARE NOT ALLOWED TO POSSESS WEAPONS OF MASS DESTRUCTION.
WHY NOT? YOU'VE GOT ONE.
BECAUSE I AM RESPONSIBLE AND I LOVE PEACE.
YOU THREATENED TO DROP IT ON ME BECAUSE MY KUMQUAT TREE WAS DROPPING KUMQUATS ON YOUR LAWN.
6/14
I LOVE PEACE, NOT KUMQUATS.

Sometimes the real world creeps into *Pearls*.

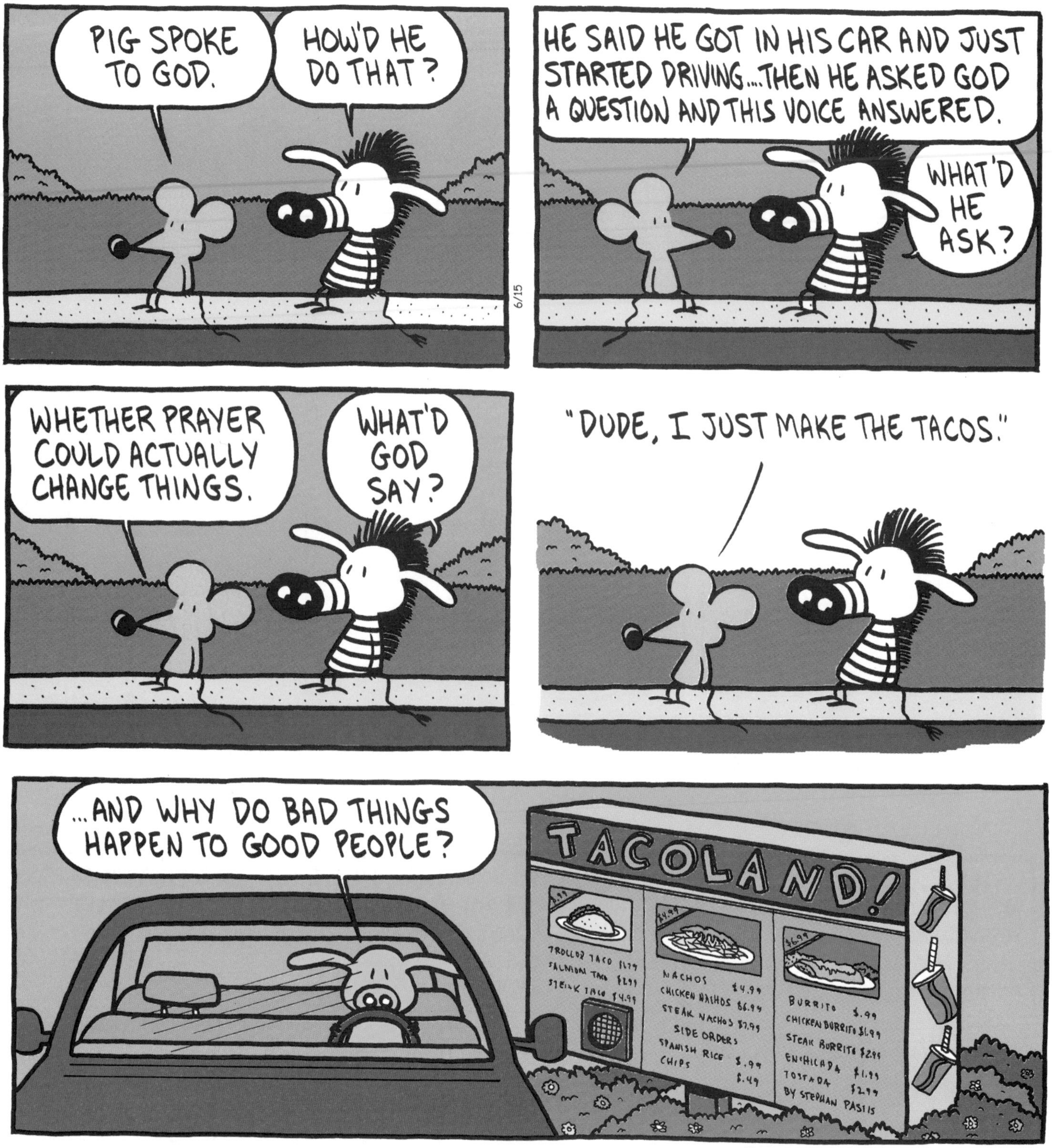
PIG SPOKE TO GOD.
HOW'D HE DO THAT?
6/15
HE SAID HE GOT IN HIS CAR AND JUST STARTED DRIVING....THEN HE ASKED GOD A QUESTION AND THIS VOICE ANSWERED.
WHAT'D HE ASK?
WHETHER PRAYER COULD ACTUALLY CHANGE THINGS.
WHAT'D GOD SAY?
"DUDE, I JUST MAKE THE TACOS."
...AND WHY DO BAD THINGS HAPPEN TO GOOD PEOPLE?
TACOLAND!
BY STEPHAN PASTIS

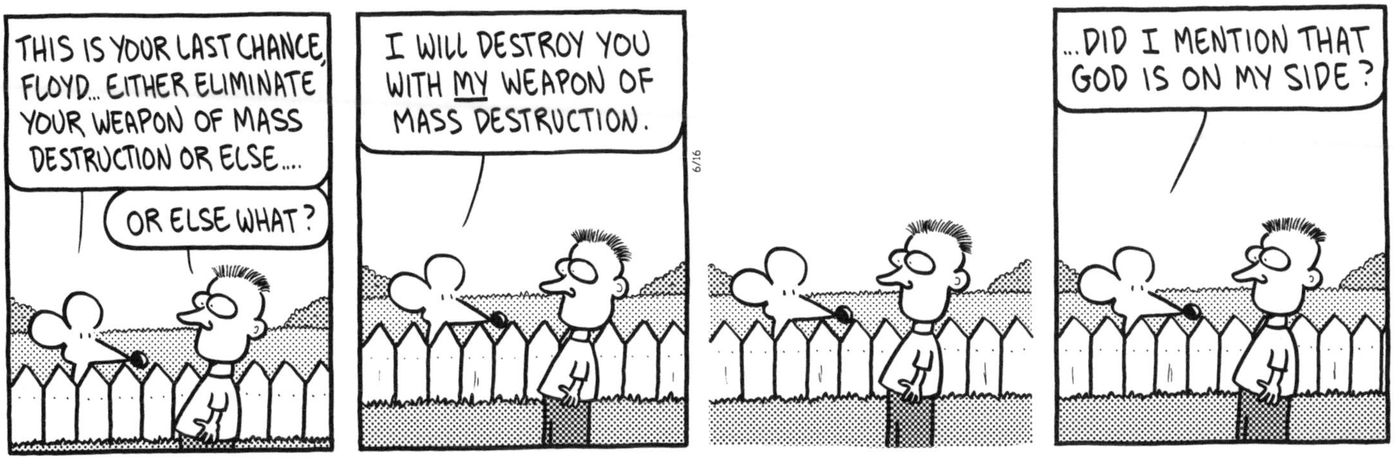
THIS IS YOUR LAST CHANCE, FLOYD... EITHER ELIMINATE YOUR WEAPON OF MASS DESTRUCTION OR ELSE....
OR ELSE WHAT?
I WILL DESTROY YOU WITH MY WEAPON OF MASS DESTRUCTION.
6/16
...DID I MENTION THAT GOD IS ON MY SIDE?

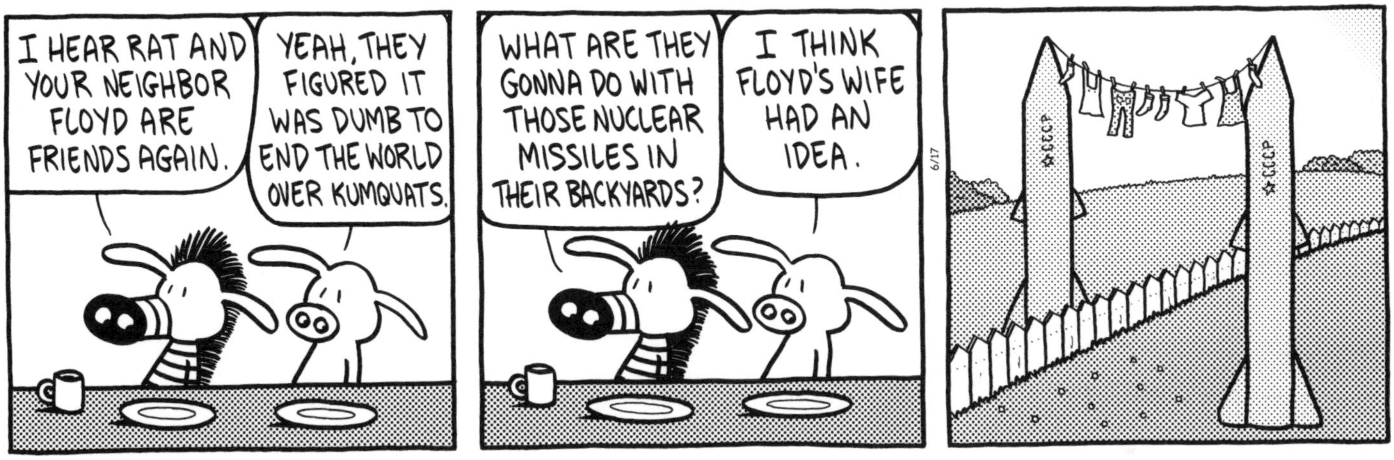
I HEAR RAT AND YOUR NEIGHBOR FLOYD ARE FRIENDS AGAIN.
YEAH, THEY FIGURED IT WAS DUMB TO END THE WORLD OVER KUMQUATS.
WHAT ARE THEY GONNA DO WITH THOSE NUCLEAR MISSILES IN THEIR BACKYARDS?
I THINK FLOYD'S WIFE HAD AN IDEA.
6/17
CCCP
CCCP

I think there's a little bit of *Dr. Strangelove* here.

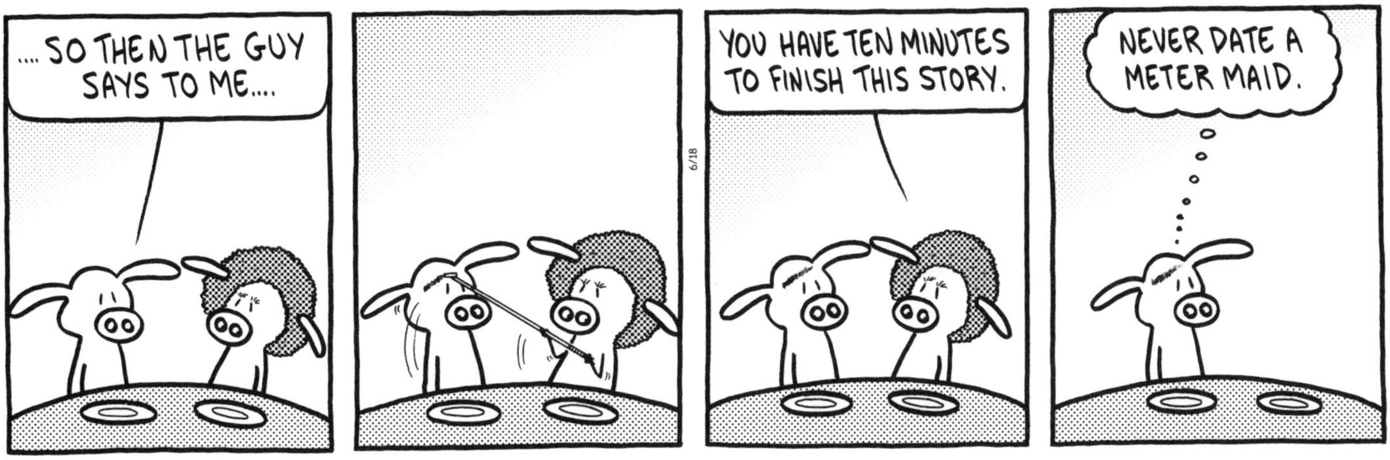
.... SO THEN THE GUY SAYS TO ME....
6/18
YOU HAVE TEN MINUTES TO FINISH THIS STORY.
NEVER DATE A METER MAID.

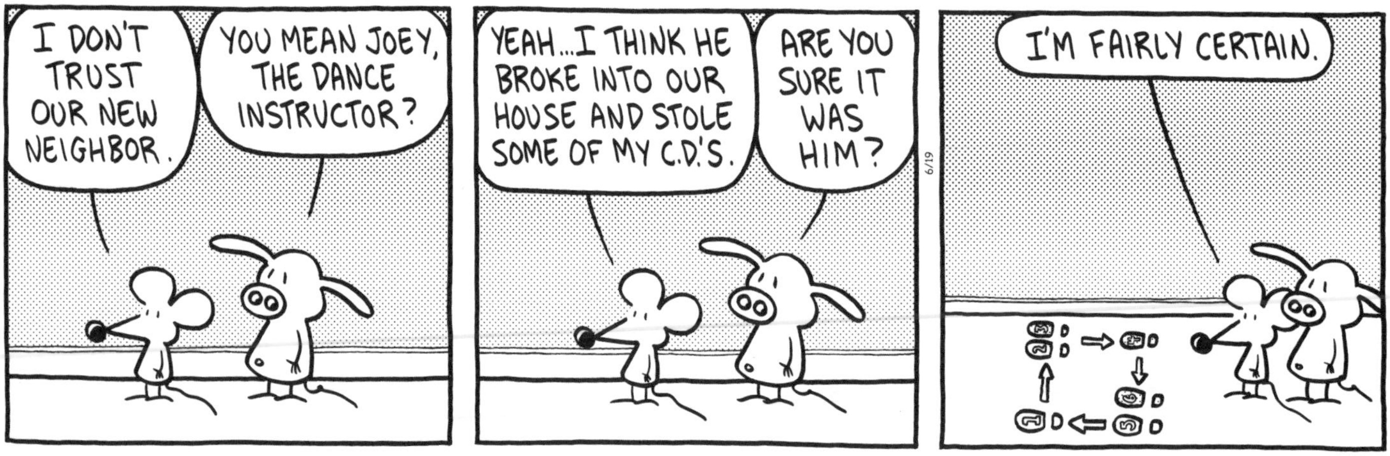
I DON'T TRUST OUR NEW NEIGHBOR.
YOU MEAN JOEY, THE DANCE INSTRUCTOR?
YEAH...I THINK HE BROKE INTO OUR HOUSE AND STOLE SOME OF MY C.D.'S.
ARE YOU SURE IT WAS HIM?
6/19
I'M FAIRLY CERTAIN.

Talk about your perspective debacles. The angle of the floor in that last panel is a tour de force.

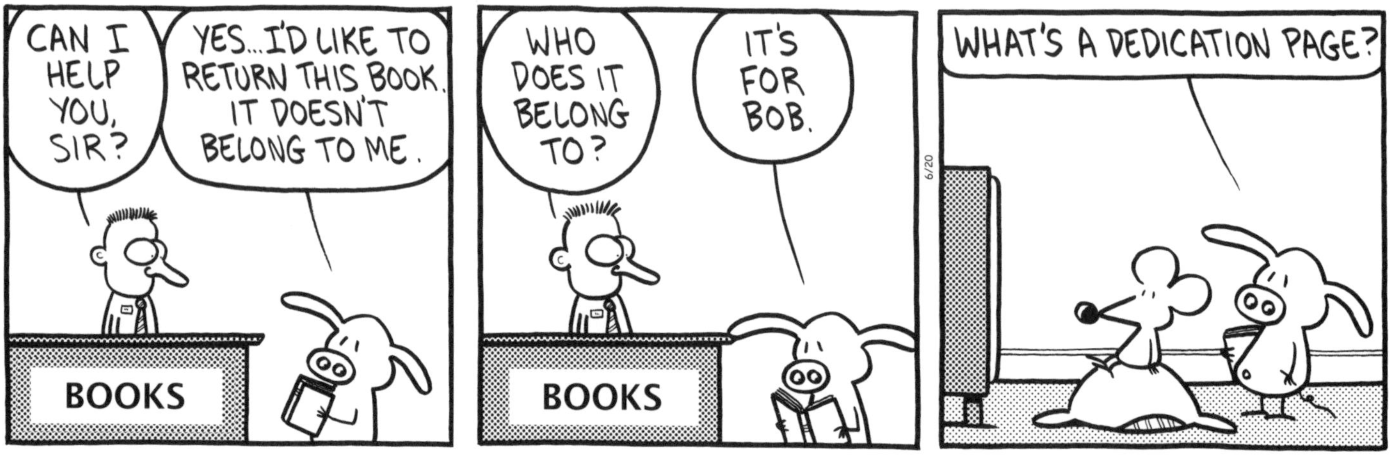
CAN I HELP YOU, SIR?
YES...I'D LIKE TO RETURN THIS BOOK. IT DOESN'T BELONG TO ME.
BOOKS
WHO DOES IT BELONG TO?
IT'S FOR BOB.
BOOKS
6/20
WHAT'S A DEDICATION PAGE?

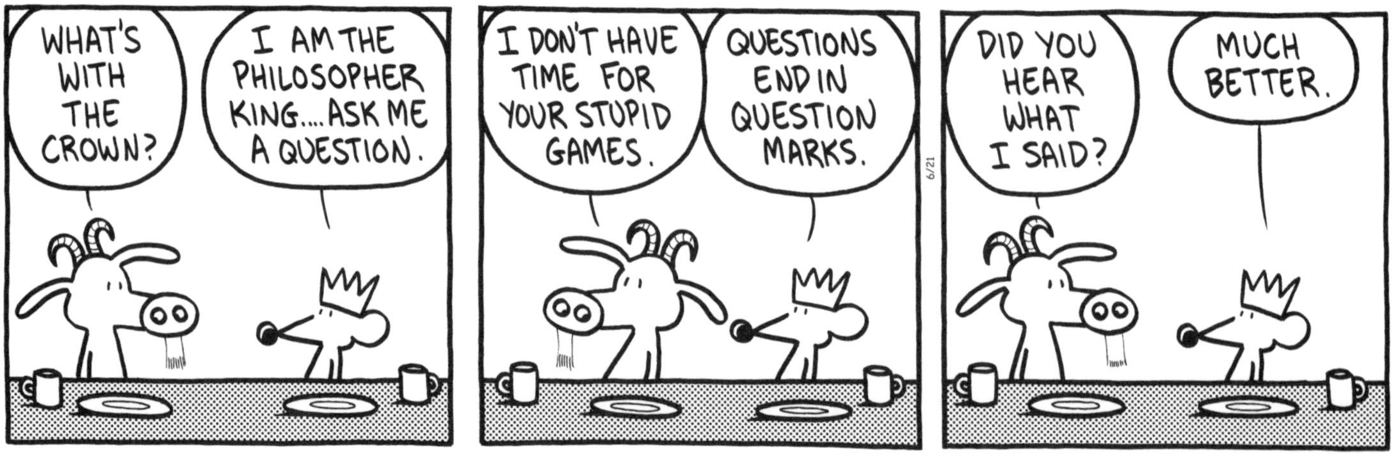
WHAT'S WITH THE CROWN?
I AM THE PHILOSOPHER KING....ASK ME A QUESTION.
I DON'T HAVE TIME FOR YOUR STUPID GAMES.
QUESTIONS END IN QUESTION MARKS.
6/21
DID YOU HEAR WHAT I SAID?
MUCH BETTER.

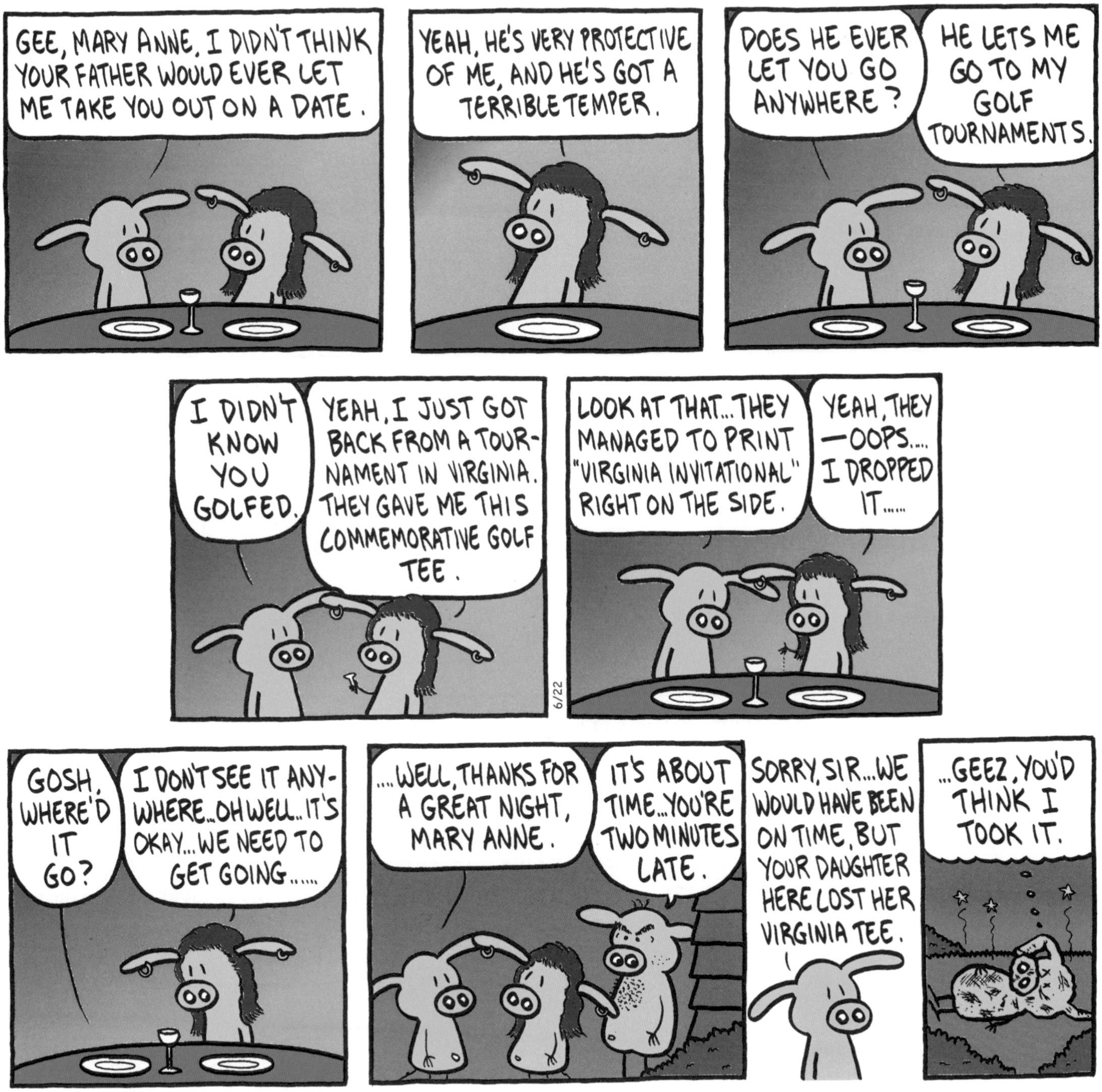
GEE, MARY ANNE, I DIDN'T THINK YOUR FATHER WOULD EVER LET ME TAKE YOU OUT ON A DATE.
YEAH, HE'S VERY PROTECTIVE OF ME, AND HE'S GOT A TERRIBLE TEMPER.
DOES HE EVER LET YOU GO ANYWHERE?
HE LETS ME GO TO MY GOLF TOURNAMENTS.
I DIDN'T KNOW YOU GOLFED.
YEAH, I JUST GOT BACK FROM A TOURNAMENT IN VIRGINIA. THEY GAVE ME THIS COMMEMORATIVE GOLF TEE.
6/22
LOOK AT THAT... THEY MANAGED TO PRINT "VIRGINIA INVITATIONAL" RIGHT ON THE SIDE.
YEAH, THEY —OOPS.... I DROPPED IT......
GOSH, WHERE'D IT GO?
I DON'T SEE IT ANYWHERE... OH WELL... IT'S OKAY... WE NEED TO GET GOING......
....WELL, THANKS FOR A GREAT NIGHT, MARY ANNE.
IT'S ABOUT TIME... YOU'RE TWO MINUTES LATE.
SORRY, SIR... WE WOULD HAVE BEEN ON TIME, BUT YOUR DAUGHTER HERE LOST HER VIRGINIA TEE.
...GEEZ, YOU'D THINK I TOOK IT.

This was one of the most popular Sundays.

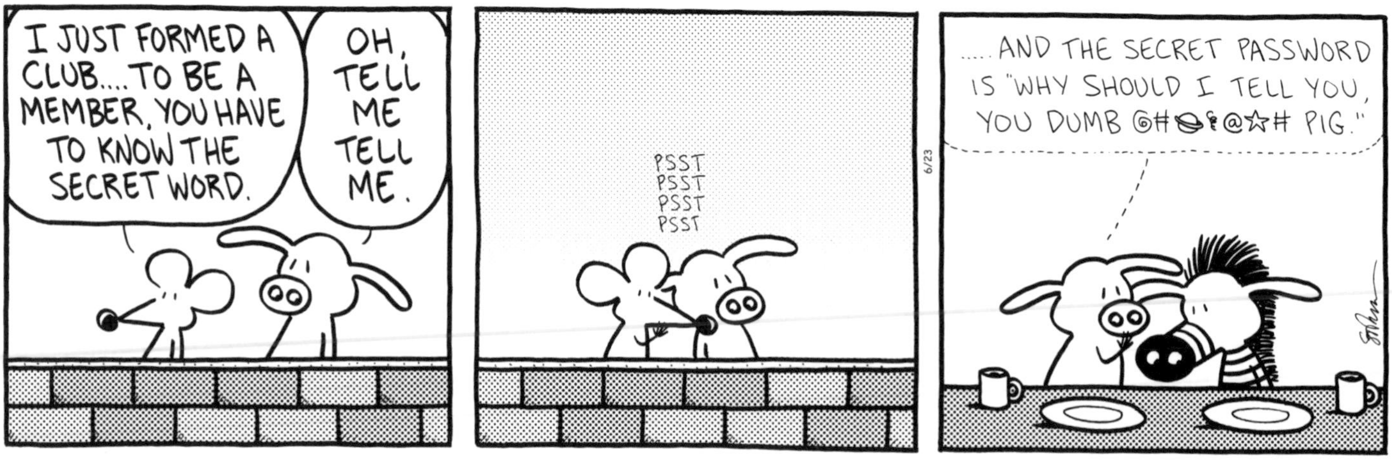
I JUST FORMED A CLUB.... TO BE A MEMBER, YOU HAVE TO KNOW THE SECRET WORD.
OH, TELL ME TELL ME.
PSST PSST PSST PSST
6/23
..... AND THE SECRET PASSWORD IS "WHY SHOULD I TELL YOU, YOU DUMB @#☆!@☆# PIG."

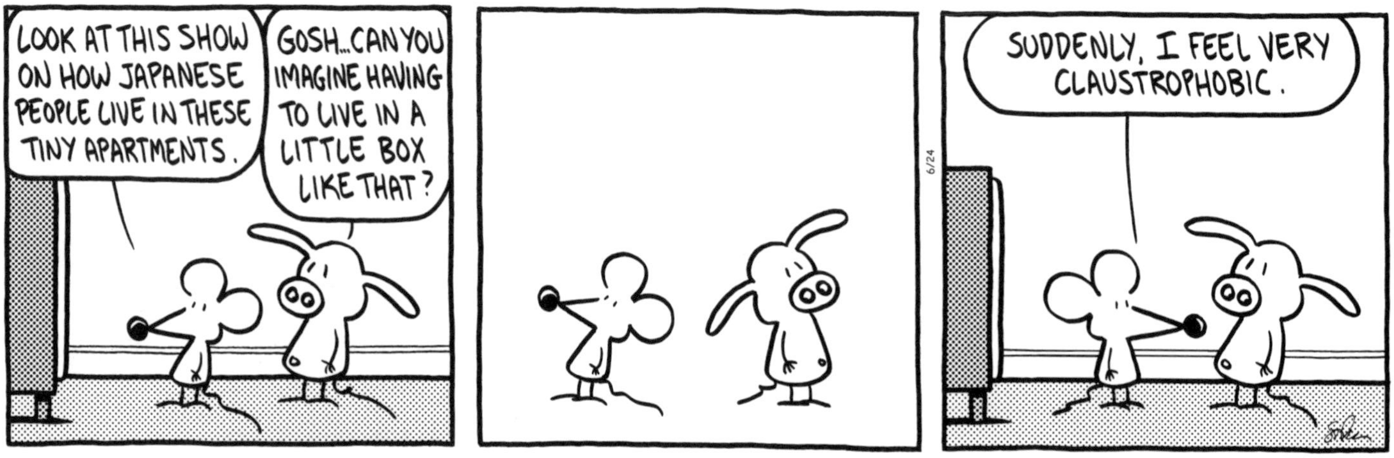
LOOK AT THIS SHOW ON HOW JAPANESE PEOPLE LIVE IN THESE TINY APARTMENTS.
GOSH... CAN YOU IMAGINE HAVING TO LIVE IN A LITTLE BOX LIKE THAT?
6/24
SUDDENLY, I FEEL VERY CLAUSTROPHOBIC.

I like occasionally playing around with the notion that the characters live in a printed, three-panel comic strip.

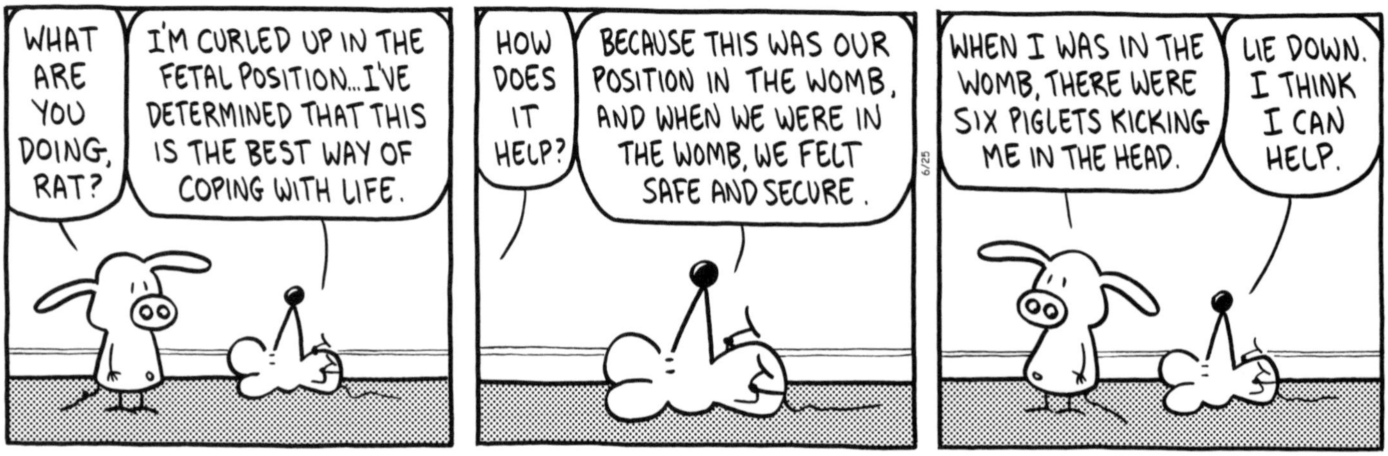
WHAT ARE YOU DOING, RAT?
I'M CURLED UP IN THE FETAL POSITION... I'VE DETERMINED THAT THIS IS THE BEST WAY OF COPING WITH LIFE.
HOW DOES IT HELP?
BECAUSE THIS WAS OUR POSITION IN THE WOMB, AND WHEN WE WERE IN THE WOMB, WE FELT SAFE AND SECURE.
6/25
WHEN I WAS IN THE WOMB, THERE WERE SIX PIGLETS KICKING ME IN THE HEAD.
LIE DOWN. I THINK I CAN HELP.

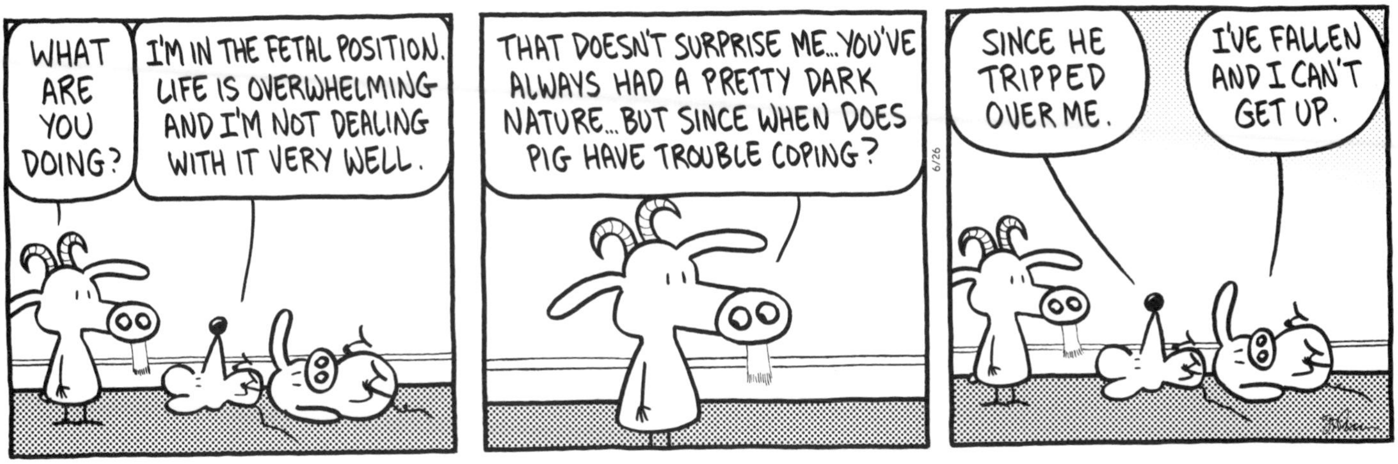
WHAT ARE YOU DOING?
I'M IN THE FETAL POSITION. LIFE IS OVERWHELMING AND I'M NOT DEALING WITH IT VERY WELL.
THAT DOESN'T SURPRISE ME... YOU'VE ALWAYS HAD A PRETTY DARK NATURE... BUT SINCE WHEN DOES PIG HAVE TROUBLE COPING?
6/26
SINCE HE TRIPPED OVER ME.
I'VE FALLEN AND I CAN'T GET UP.

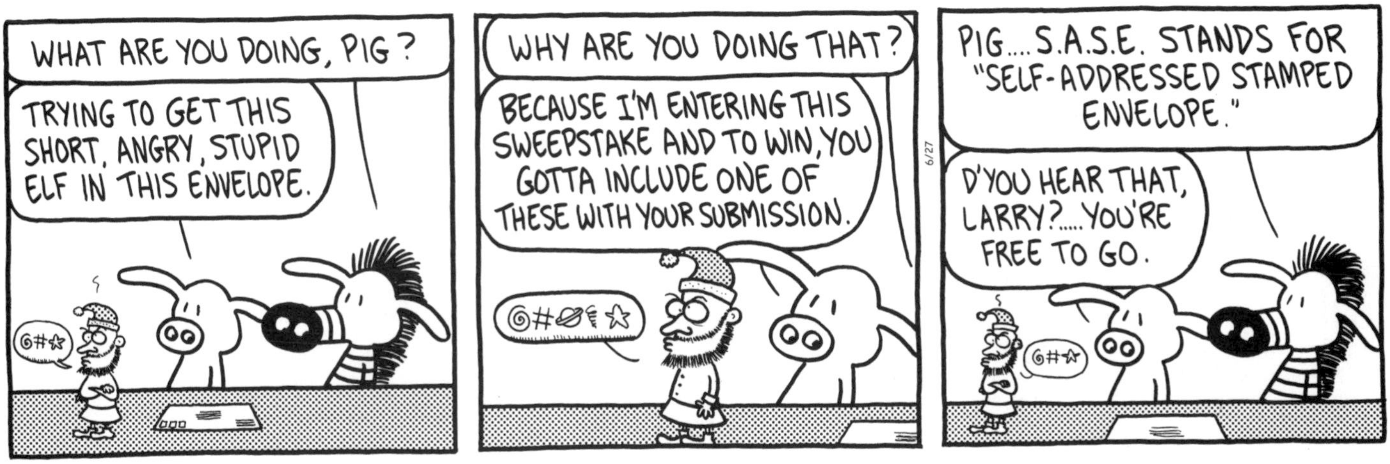
WHAT ARE YOU DOING, PIG?
TRYING TO GET THIS SHORT, ANGRY, STUPID ELF IN THIS ENVELOPE.
WHY ARE YOU DOING THAT?
BECAUSE I'M ENTERING THIS SWEEPSTAKE AND TO WIN, YOU GOTTA INCLUDE ONE OF THESE WITH YOUR SUBMISSION.
6/27
PIG.... S.A.S.E. STANDS FOR "SELF-ADDRESSED STAMPED ENVELOPE."
D'YOU HEAR THAT, LARRY?..... YOU'RE FREE TO GO.

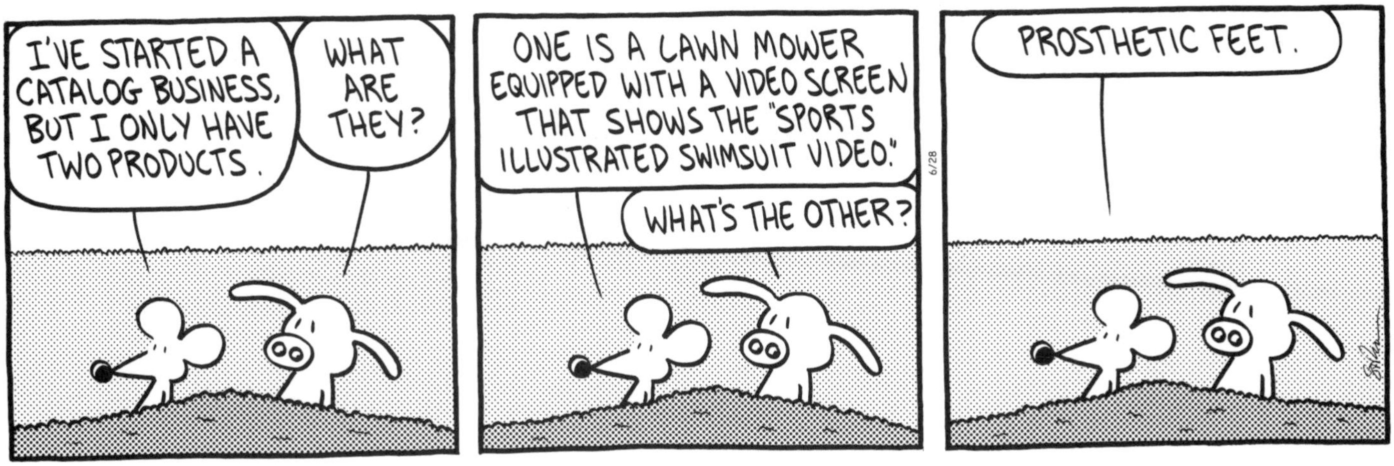
I'VE STARTED A CATALOG BUSINESS, BUT I ONLY HAVE TWO PRODUCTS.
WHAT ARE THEY?
ONE IS A LAWN MOWER EQUIPPED WITH A VIDEO SCREEN THAT SHOWS THE "SPORTS ILLUSTRATED SWIMSUIT VIDEO."
WHAT'S THE OTHER?
6/28
PROSTHETIC FEET.

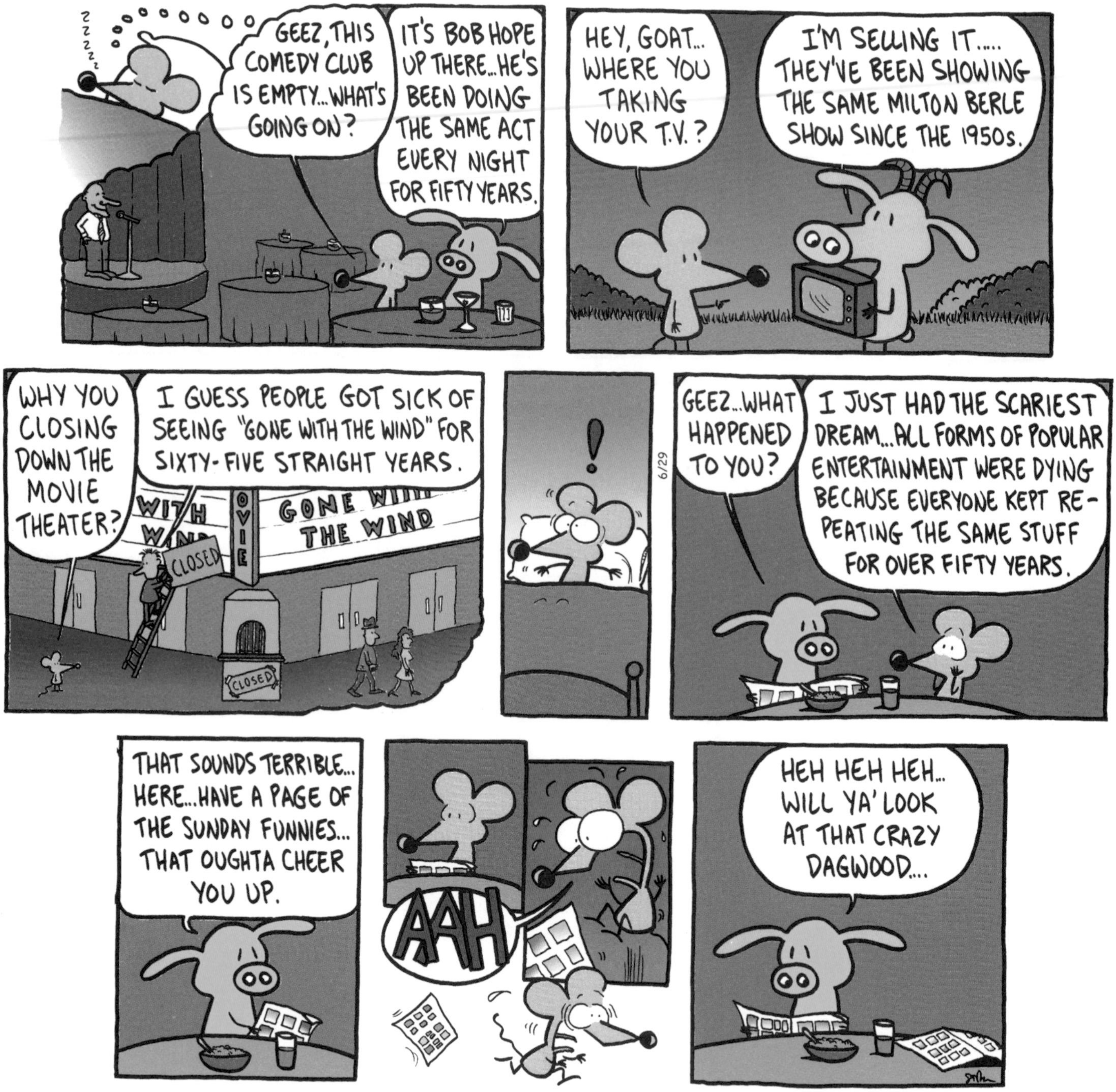
GEEZ, THIS COMEDY CLUB IS EMPTY...WHAT'S GOING ON?
IT'S BOB HOPE UP THERE...HE'S BEEN DOING THE SAME ACT EVERY NIGHT FOR FIFTY YEARS.
HEY, GOAT... WHERE YOU TAKING YOUR T.V.?
I'M SELLING IT..... THEY'VE BEEN SHOWING THE SAME MILTON BERLE SHOW SINCE THE 1950s.
WHY YOU CLOSING DOWN THE MOVIE THEATER?
I GUESS PEOPLE GOT SICK OF SEEING "GONE WITH THE WIND" FOR SIXTY-FIVE STRAIGHT YEARS.
GONE WITH THE WIND
CLOSED
CLOSED
!
6/29
GEEZ...WHAT HAPPENED TO YOU?
I JUST HAD THE SCARIEST DREAM...ALL FORMS OF POPULAR ENTERTAINMENT WERE DYING BECAUSE EVERYONE KEPT REPEATING THE SAME STUFF FOR OVER FIFTY YEARS.
THAT SOUNDS TERRIBLE... HERE...HAVE A PAGE OF THE SUNDAY FUNNIES... THAT OUGHTA CHEER YOU UP.
AAH
HEH HEH HEH... WILL YA' LOOK AT THAT CRAZY DAGWOOD....

This generated favorable e-mail from cartoonists whose features were relatively new. It did not generate favorable e-mail from cartoonists whose features were over fifty years old. Please note how wonderfully I captured Bob Hope in that first panel.

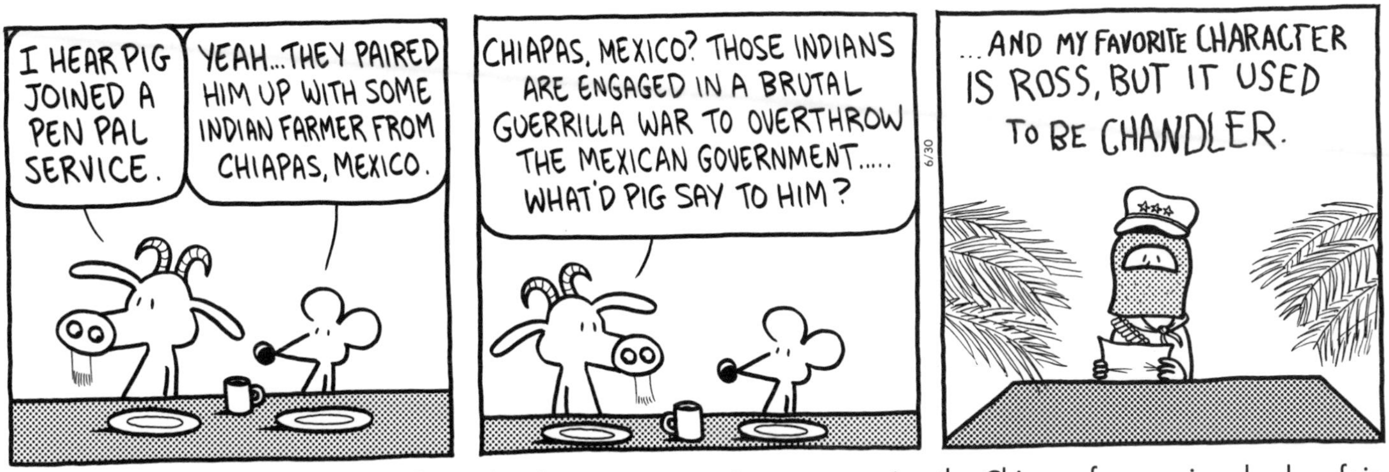
I HEAR PIG JOINED A PEN PAL SERVICE.
YEAH...THEY PAIRED HIM UP WITH SOME INDIAN FARMER FROM CHIAPAS, MEXICO.
CHIAPAS, MEXICO? THOSE INDIANS ARE ENGAGED IN A BRUTAL GUERRILLA WAR TO OVERTHROW THE MEXICAN GOVERNMENT..... WHAT'D PIG SAY TO HIM?
6/30
...AND MY FAVORITE CHARACTER IS ROSS, BUT IT USED TO BE CHANDLER.

You wouldn't believe the number of people who wrote to say I was portraying the Chiapas farmers in a bad, unfair light. At times, I feel like absolutely everyone has lost their sense of humor.

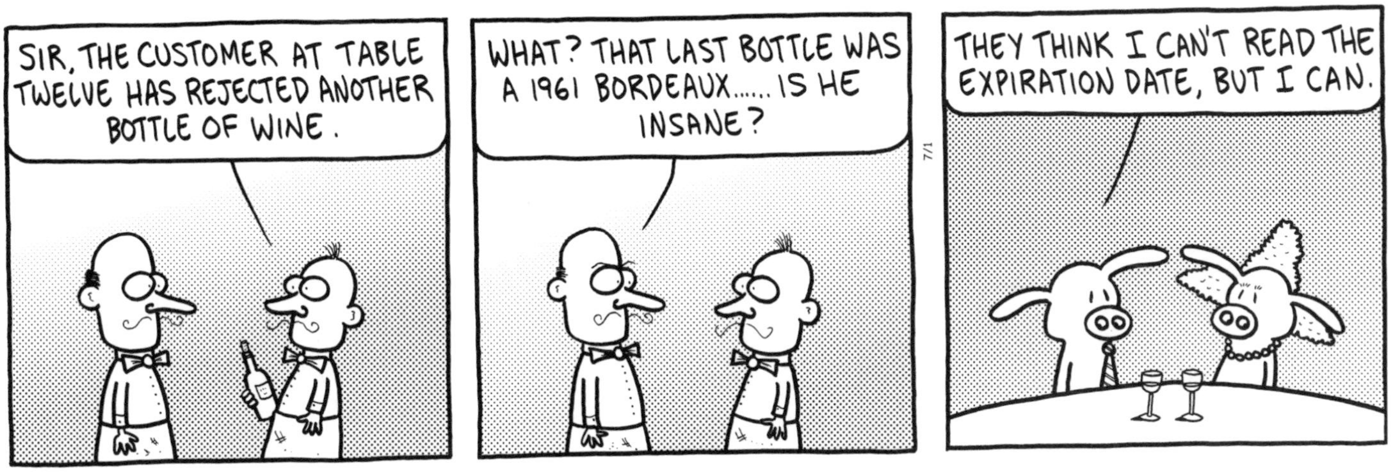
SIR, THE CUSTOMER AT TABLE TWELVE HAS REJECTED ANOTHER BOTTLE OF WINE.
WHAT? THAT LAST BOTTLE WAS A 1961 BORDEAUX...... IS HE INSANE?
7/1
THEY THINK I CAN'T READ THE EXPIRATION DATE, BUT I CAN.

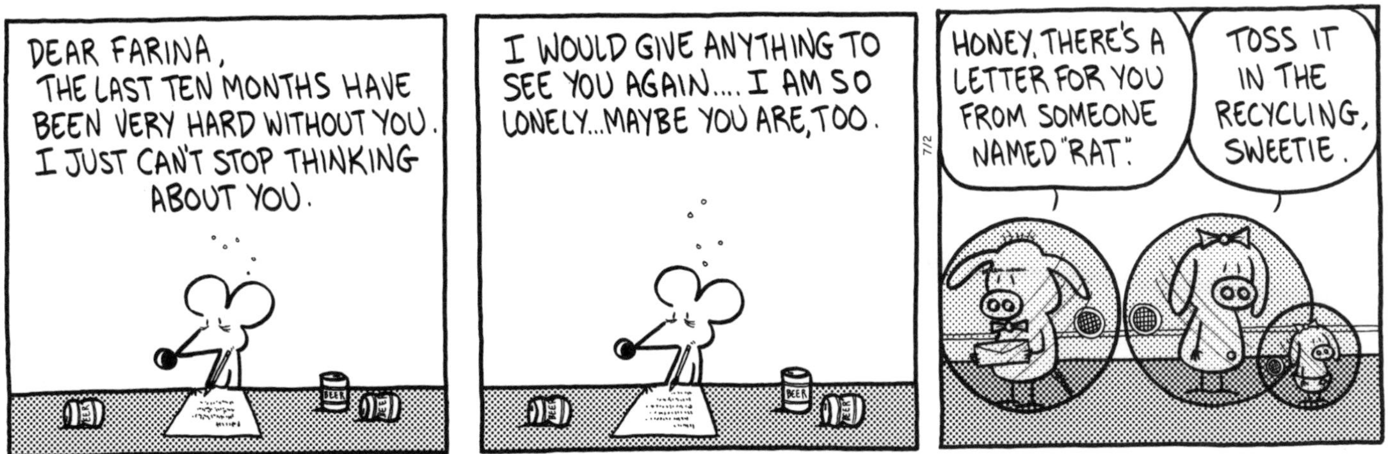
DEAR FARINA, THE LAST TEN MONTHS HAVE BEEN VERY HARD WITHOUT YOU. I JUST CAN'T STOP THINKING ABOUT YOU.
I WOULD GIVE ANYTHING TO SEE YOU AGAIN.... I AM SO LONELY...MAYBE YOU ARE, TOO.
7/2
HONEY, THERE'S A LETTER FOR YOU FROM SOMEONE NAMED "RAT".
TOSS IT IN THE RECYCLING, SWEETIE.

I brought Farina back, only to show that she was now married with kids. I think it's good to have someone who gets the better of Rat.

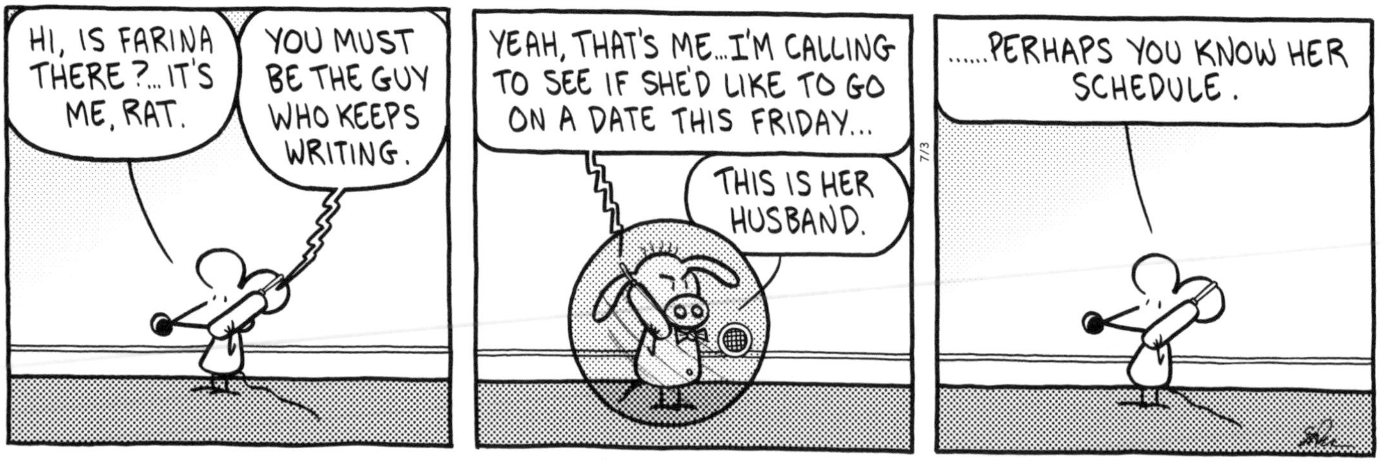
HI, IS FARINA THERE?... IT'S ME, RAT.
YOU MUST BE THE GUY WHO KEEPS WRITING.
YEAH, THAT'S ME... I'M CALLING TO SEE IF SHE'D LIKE TO GO ON A DATE THIS FRIDAY...
THIS IS HER HUSBAND.
7/3
......PERHAPS YOU KNOW HER SCHEDULE.

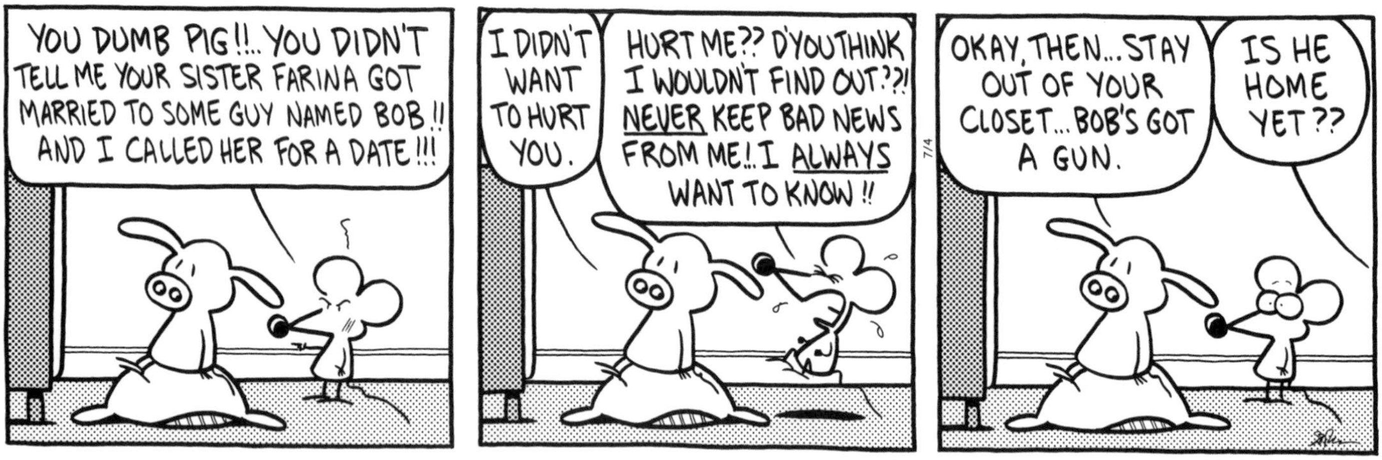
YOU DUMB PIG!!.. YOU DIDN'T TELL ME YOUR SISTER FARINA GOT MARRIED TO SOME GUY NAMED BOB!! AND I CALLED HER FOR A DATE!!!
I DIDN'T WANT TO HURT YOU.
HURT ME?? D'YOUTHINK I WOULDN'T FIND OUT??! NEVER KEEP BAD NEWS FROM ME!.. I ALWAYS WANT TO KNOW!!
7/4
OKAY, THEN... STAY OUT OF YOUR CLOSET... BOB'S GOT A GUN.
IS HE HOME YET??

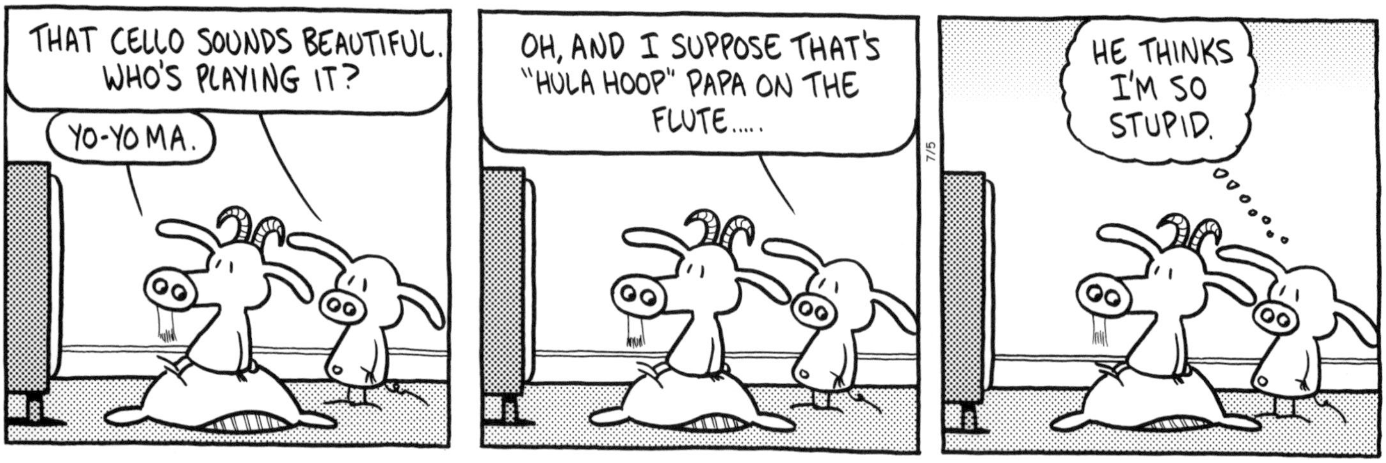
THAT CELLO SOUNDS BEAUTIFUL. WHO'S PLAYING IT?
YO-YO MA.
OH, AND I SUPPOSE THAT'S "HULA HOOP" PAPA ON THE FLUTE.....
7/5
HE THINKS I'M SO STUPID.

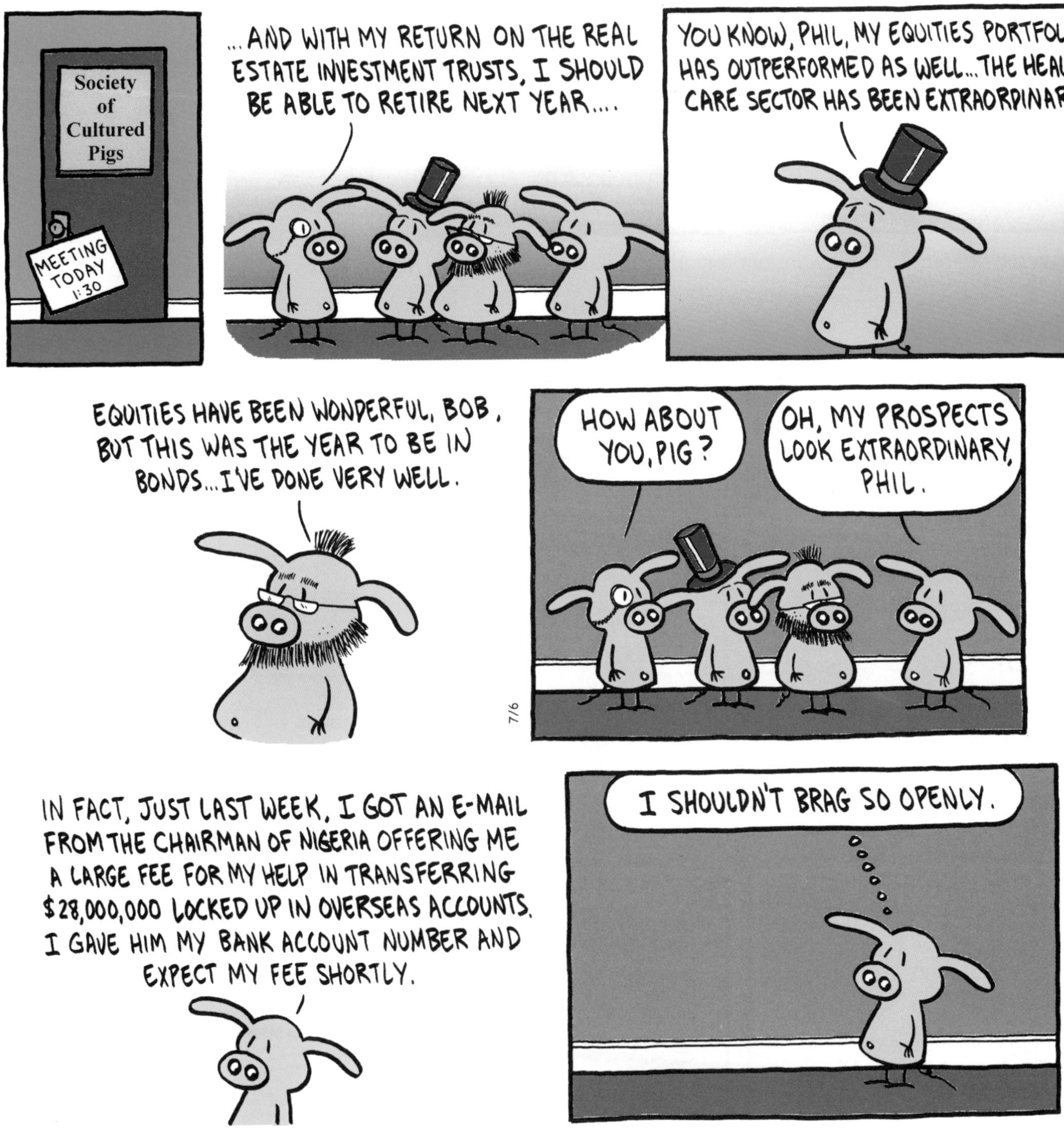
Society of Cultured Pigs
MEETING TODAY 1:30
...AND WITH MY RETURN ON THE REAL ESTATE INVESTMENT TRUSTS, I SHOULD BE ABLE TO RETIRE NEXT YEAR....
YOU KNOW, PHIL, MY EQUITIES PORTFOLIO HAS OUTPERFORMED AS WELL...THE HEALTH CARE SECTOR HAS BEEN EXTRAORDINARY.
EQUITIES HAVE BEEN WONDERFUL, BOB, BUT THIS WAS THE YEAR TO BE IN BONDS...I'VE DONE VERY WELL.
HOW ABOUT YOU, PIG?
OH, MY PROSPECTS LOOK EXTRAORDINARY, PHIL.
7/6
IN FACT, JUST LAST WEEK, I GOT AN E-MAIL FROM THE CHAIRMAN OF NIGERIA OFFERING ME A LARGE FEE FOR MY HELP IN TRANSFERRING $28,000,000 LOCKED UP IN OVERSEAS ACCOUNTS. I GAVE HIM MY BANK ACCOUNT NUMBER AND EXPECT MY FEE SHORTLY.
I SHOULDN'T BRAG SO OPENLY.

Like everyone, I get my fair share of these Nigerian fund e-mails.

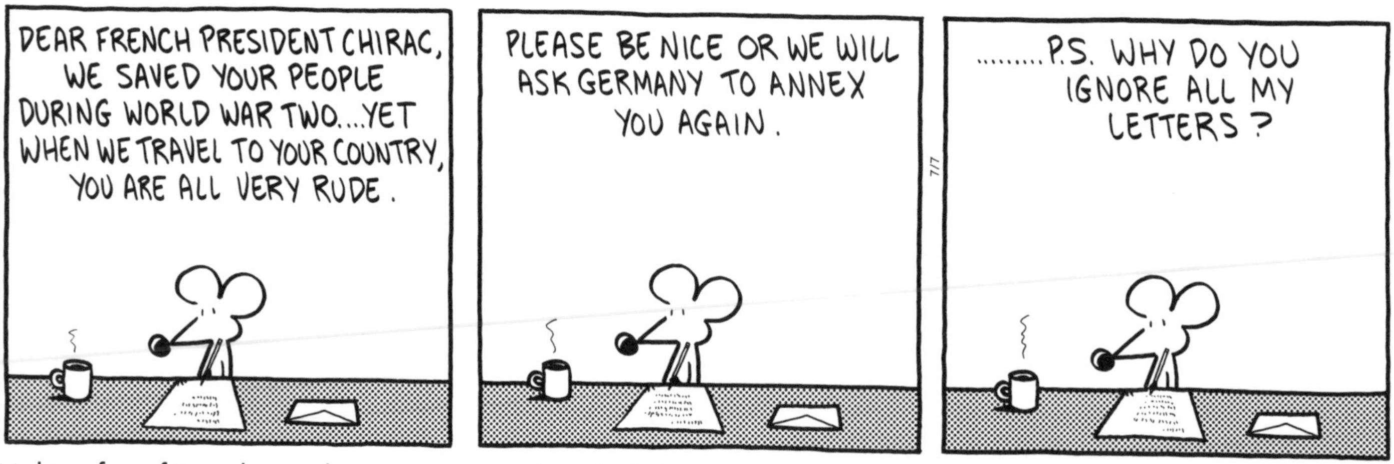
DEAR FRENCH PRESIDENT CHIRAC, WE SAVED YOUR PEOPLE DURING WORLD WAR TWO....YET WHEN WE TRAVEL TO YOUR COUNTRY, YOU ARE ALL VERY RUDE.
PLEASE BE NICE OR WE WILL ASK GERMANY TO ANNEX YOU AGAIN.
7/7
.........P.S. WHY DO YOU IGNORE ALL MY LETTERS?

Making fun of French people = instant comedy. I think that even French people make fun of French people.

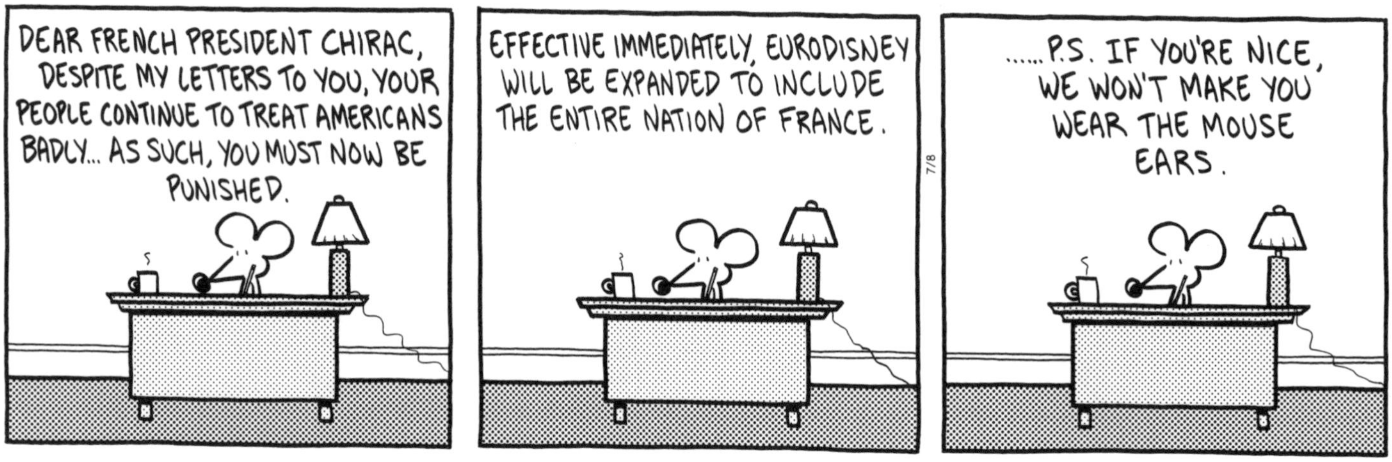
DEAR FRENCH PRESIDENT CHIRAC, DESPITE MY LETTERS TO YOU, YOUR PEOPLE CONTINUE TO TREAT AMERICANS BADLY... AS SUCH, YOU MUST NOW BE PUNISHED.
EFFECTIVE IMMEDIATELY, EURODISNEY WILL BE EXPANDED TO INCLUDE THE ENTIRE NATION OF FRANCE.
7/8
......P.S. IF YOU'RE NICE, WE WON'T MAKE YOU WEAR THE MOUSE EARS.

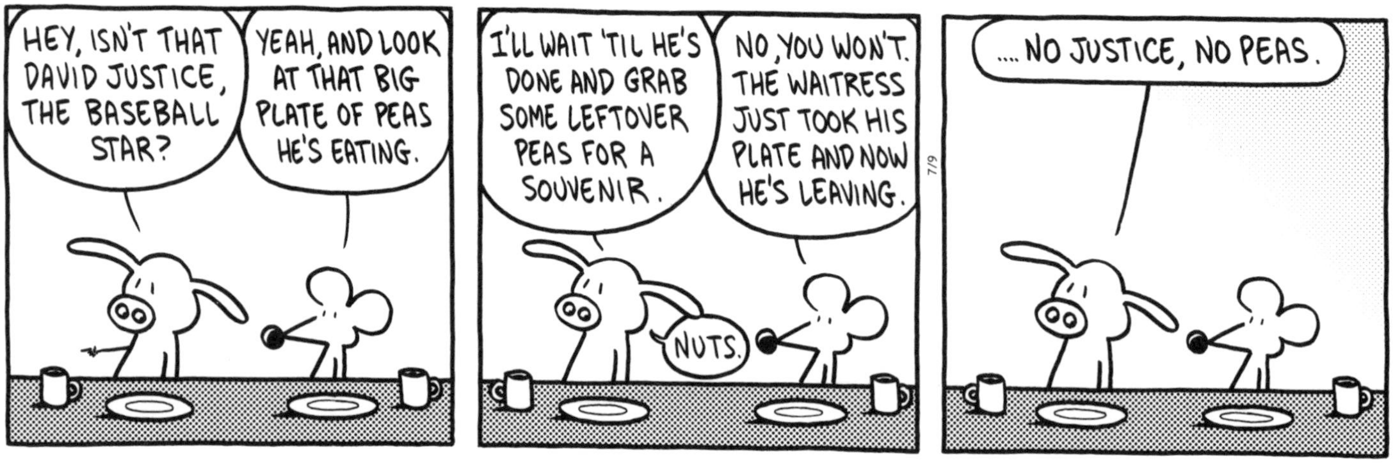
HEY, ISN'T THAT DAVID JUSTICE, THE BASEBALL STAR?
YEAH, AND LOOK AT THAT BIG PLATE OF PEAS HE'S EATING.
I'LL WAIT 'TIL HE'S DONE AND GRAB SOME LEFTOVER PEAS FOR A SOUVENIR.
NO, YOU WON'T. THE WAITRESS JUST TOOK HIS PLATE AND NOW HE'S LEAVING.
NUTS.
7/9
.... NO JUSTICE, NO PEAS.

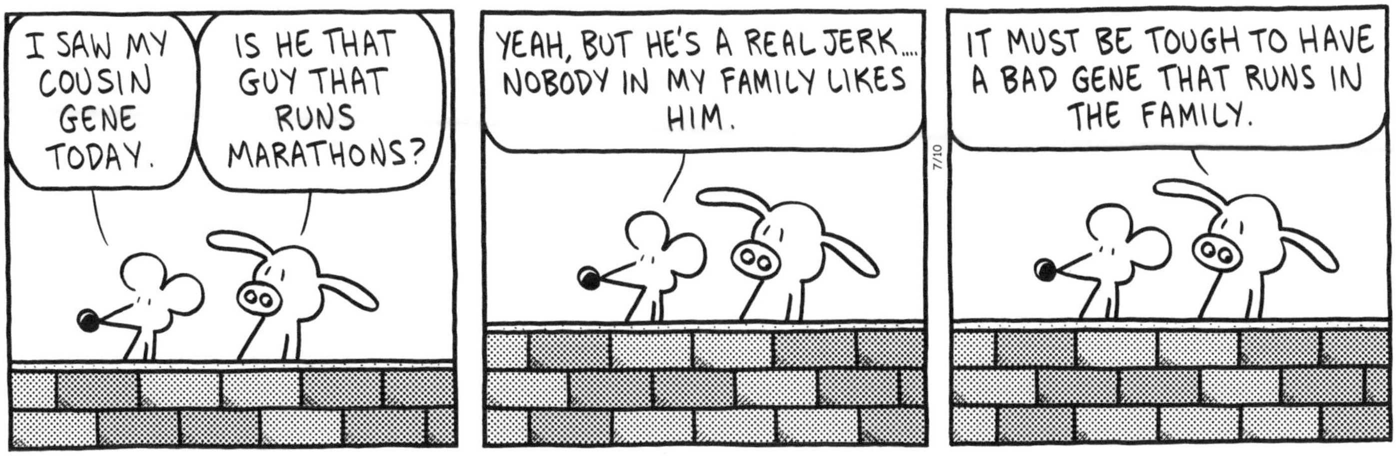
I SAW MY COUSIN GENE TODAY.
IS HE THAT GUY THAT RUNS MARATHONS?
YEAH, BUT HE'S A REAL JERK.... NOBODY IN MY FAMILY LIKES HIM.
7/10
IT MUST BE TOUGH TO HAVE A BAD GENE THAT RUNS IN THE FAMILY.

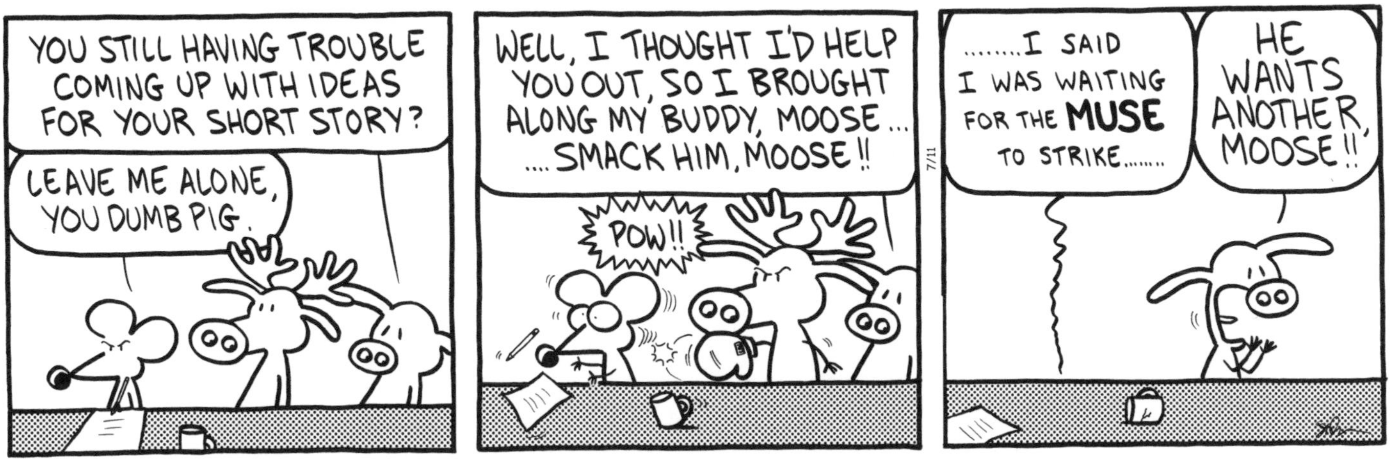
YOU STILL HAVING TROUBLE COMING UP WITH IDEAS FOR YOUR SHORT STORY?
LEAVE ME ALONE, YOU DUMB PIG.
WELL, I THOUGHT I'D HELP YOU OUT, SO I BROUGHT ALONG MY BUDDY, MOOSE... ....SMACK HIM, MOOSE!!
POW!!
7/11
........I SAID I WAS WAITING FOR THE **MUSE** TO STRIKE........
HE WANTS ANOTHER MOOSE!!

A rare action shot in *Pearls*. Perhaps I have a career in DC Comics.

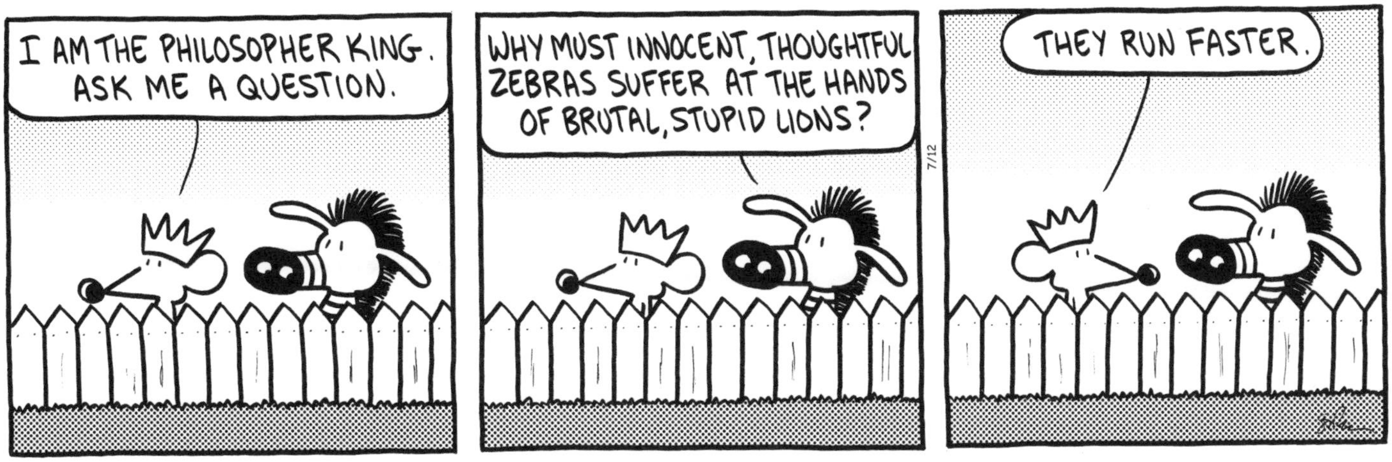
I AM THE PHILOSOPHER KING. ASK ME A QUESTION.
WHY MUST INNOCENT, THOUGHTFUL ZEBRAS SUFFER AT THE HANDS OF BRUTAL, STUPID LIONS?
7/12
THEY RUN FASTER.

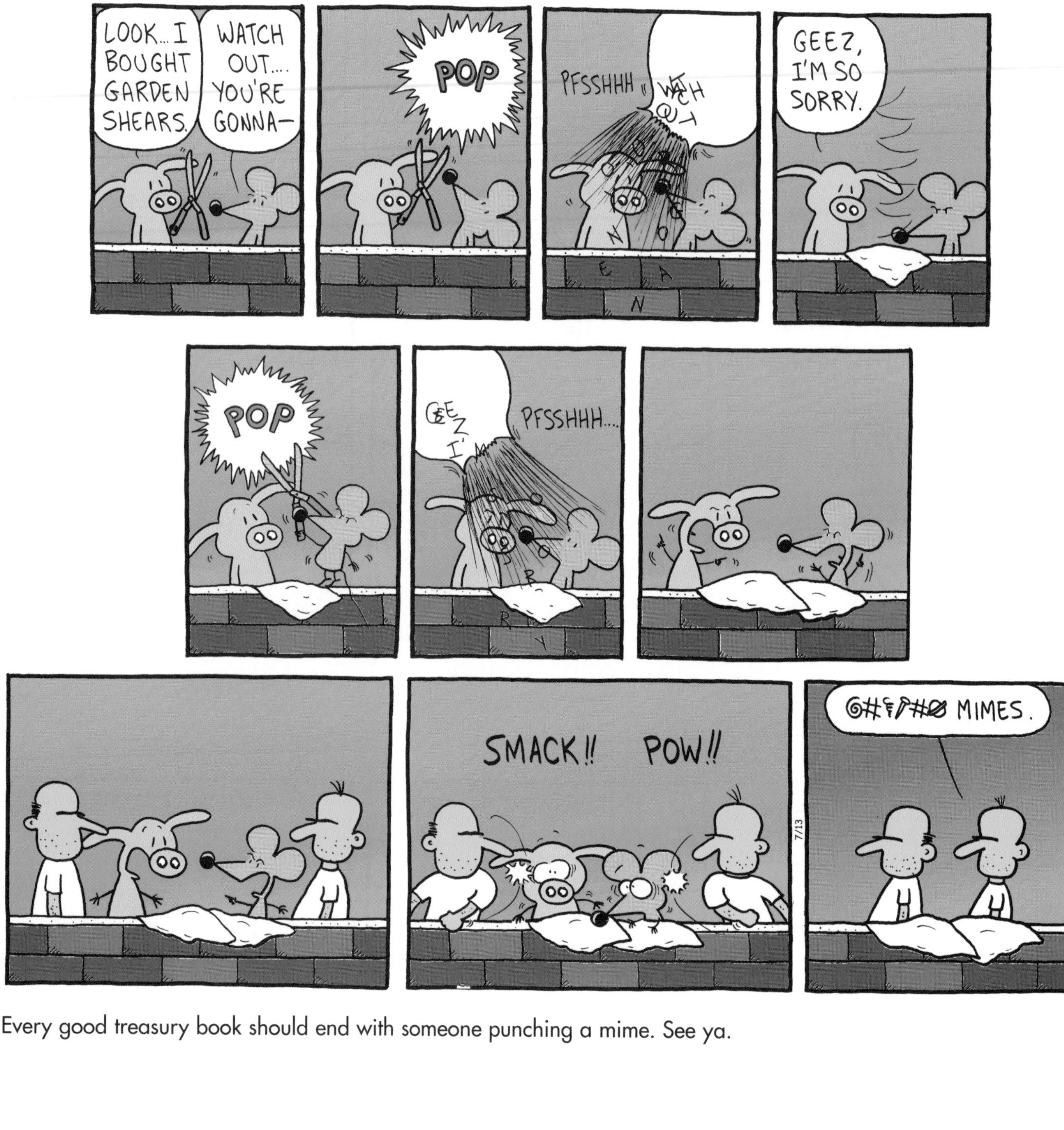
LOOK... I BOUGHT GARDEN SHEARS.
WATCH OUT.... YOU'RE GONNA—
POP
PFSSHHH
GEEZ, I'M SO SORRY.
POP
PFSSHHH....
SMACK!!
POW!!
7/13
MIMES.

Every good treasury book should end with someone punching a mime. See ya.

How well do you think you know *Pearls Before Swine*?
Take the *Pearls Before Swine* test and find out!

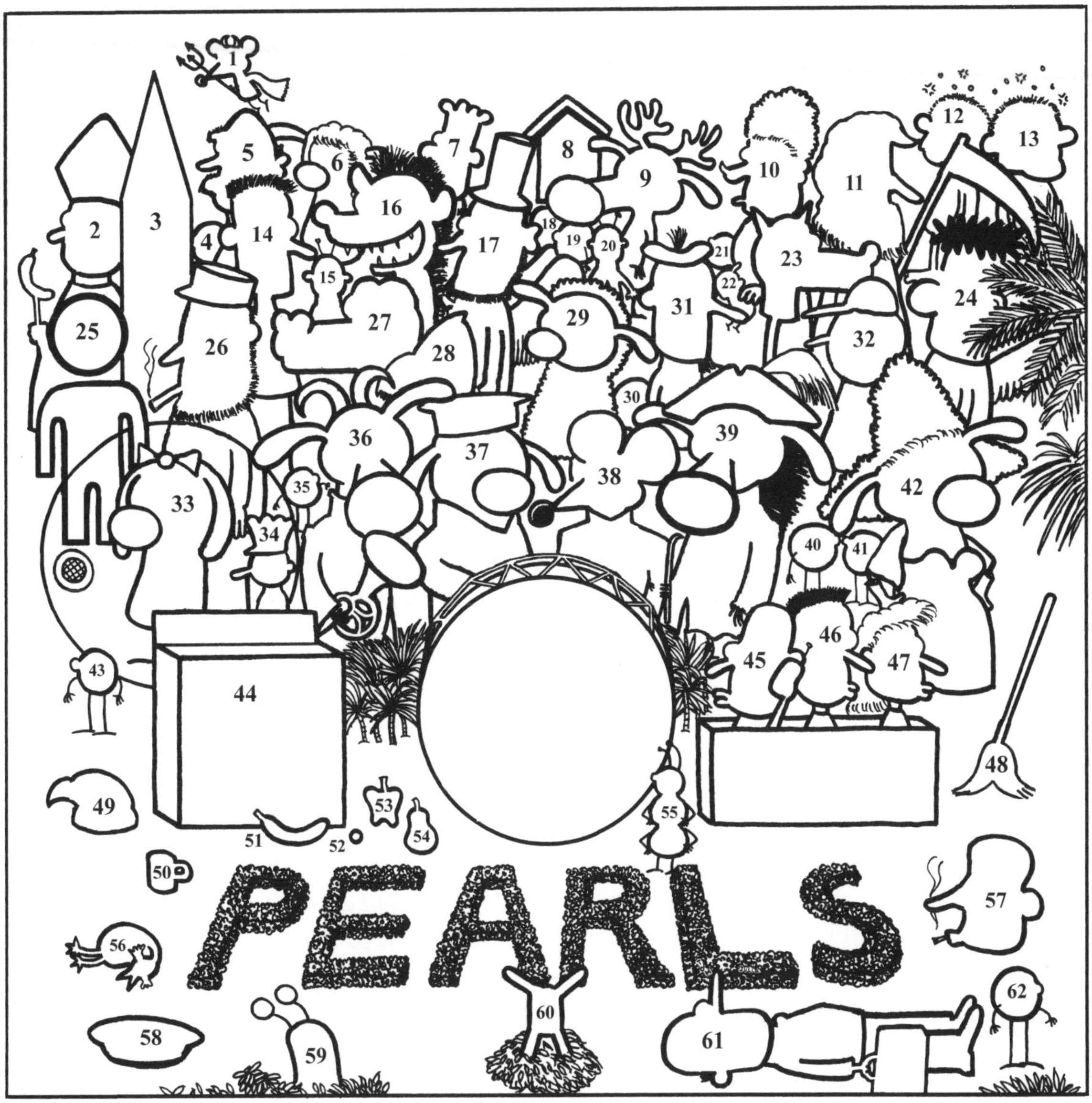
PEARLS
1 2 3 4 5 6 7 8 9 10 11 12 13 14 15 16 17 18 19 20 21 22 23 24 25 26 27 28 29 30 31 32 33 34 35 36 37 38 39 40 41 42 43 44 45 46 47 48 49 50 51 52 53 54 55 56 57 58 59 60 61 62

All of the numbered characters/objects on the front cover drawing have appeared in at least one of the *Pearls* strips in this book. How many of them do you recognize? The answers appear on the following page. Scoring is as follows:

Answers Right	**Pearls Classification**
All 62	*Pearls* freak. You apparently know the strip better than I do
51-61	*Pearls* expert. You have learned the strip very well. Kudos to you.
40 to 50	*Pearls* pro. You know the strip but could use some tutoring. Seek assistance from a *Pearls* freak.
29 to 39	*Pearls* novice. You have spent far too much time reading other comic strips.
28 or Under	"Box O' Stupid People" Candidate. You make me sad.

1	Rat's guardian devil	32	Stephan Pastis, as drawn by his neighbor John
2	Shamus, Patron Saint of the Monkeys	33	Farina, the Bubble Girl
3	Rat's nuclear missile	34	Hobart the Miniature Train Engineer
4	Anxieteer	35	Anxieteer
5	Owner of Greek restaurant	36	Goat
6	Mary Anne, the "Virginia Tee" girl	37	Pig
7	Bildert (subtract 5 points if you said Dilbert)	38	Rat
8	Cuckold clock	39	Zebra
9	Moose	40	Anxieteer
10	Voodoo lady	41	Anxieteer
11	Father Time	42	Pigita
12	Drunk stock-picking monkey	43	Anxieteer
13	Drunk stock-picking monkey	44	Bob the Dryer
14	Floyd, Rat's nuclear-missile-bearing neighbor	45	Fred (from "Box O' Stupid People")
15	Space-alien figurine	46	Dirk (from "Box O' Stupid People")
16	Hyena	47	Myrna (from "Box O' Stupid People")
17	Abraham Lincoln in heaven	48	Pig's mop at the museum
18	Anxieteer	49	Rat's Cap O' Immortality
19	Anxieteer	50	Diner mug
20	Space-alien figurine	51	Secretary Banana (one of the "Fruit Buddies")
21	Anxieteer	52	Georgie Grape (one of the "Fruit Buddies")
22	Pig voodoo doll	53	Annie Apple (one of the "Fruit Buddies")
23	Swan who wants to be a dog	54	Brother Pear (one of the "Fruit Buddies")
24	Niko, Pig's guardian angel	55	Lepidus Souzaranti bug
25	John, the Bathroom Sign Guy	56	Mikey the Rubber Chicken
26	Fidel Castro	57	The "Bob the Angry Smoker Football"
27	Crocodile	58	Diner plate
28	Stevie Salmon	59	Sammy the Slug
29	Chuckie, the Non-Anthropomorphic sheep	60	Tooty the Gingerbread Man
30	Anxieteer	61	Lawyer that Rat bought at garage sale
31	Guy at the modern art museum who loves Pig's mop	62	Anxieteer